lege
Library

D1082887

A HISTORY OF
CHRISTIAN-LATIN POETRY

A HISTORY OF
CHRISTIAN-LATIN POETRY

FROM THE BEGINNINGS TO THE CLOSE OF

THE MIDDLE AGES

BY

F. J. E. RABY

SECOND EDITION

OXFORD
AT THE CLARENDON PRESS

Oxford University Press, Ely House, London W. 1

GLASGOW NEW YORK TORONTO MELBOURNE WELLINGTON
CAPE TOWN SALISBURY IBADAN NAIROBI LUSAKA ADDIS ABABA
BOMBAY CALCUTTA MADRAS KARACHI LAHORE DACCA
KUALA LUMPUR HONG KONG

FIRST EDITION 1927
SECOND EDITION 1953
REPRINTED LITHOGRAPHICALLY IN GREAT BRITAIN
AT THE UNIVERSITY PRESS, OXFORD
1966

871.109
R114

PREFACE TO THE SECOND EDITION

IN preparing a second edition of this work, which was published as long ago as 1927, I have been compelled, for several
reasons, to confine myself very largely to the correction of
misprints and of minor errors, and, for the rest, to give the results
of recent research in a form which would not necessitate the re-
casting of the book as a whole. The greater part of the new
material concerns the history of the origins of the Sequence and
an account of the poetry of John of Howden. I wish that it had
been possible to give a longer and more adequate summary, in
the section on the Sequence, of the work of Professor W. von
den Steinen, who was so good as to send me a copy of his articles
on the subject; but considerations of space made this impossible.

I was well aware that much of the book would not be able to
stand the test of a fundamental criticism, but it seemed better
to re-issue it as soon as possible, in the hope that it might be of
use to students, than to attempt to rewrite it or to recast it in
what might seem to be a more satisfactory manner.

The bibliography has been brought reasonably up to date by
the inclusion of references to the more important books and
articles that have appeared since 1927, but I have not always
thought it necessary to include material that has already appeared
in the bibliography to my *History of Secular Latin Poetry in
the Middle Ages*.

I cannot conclude this preface without referring to the loss
which medieval studies sustained in the death in 1941 of Dom
André Wilmart, a loss to the extent of which so many additions
to my bibliography bear witness; a loss also of a more personal
kind to those who, like myself, were privileged to share his
friendship.

F. J. E. R.

JESUS COLLEGE, CAMBRIDGE

108108

PREFACE TO THE FIRST EDITION

I HAVE attempted this sketch in outline of the development of Christian-Latin poetry from its beginnings to the fourteenth century in the hope that it may be of use not only to students of medieval literature, but also to students of the general history of the Middle Ages, who are now being encouraged to devote more attention to the 'cultural' achievements of a period so rich in its artistic and literary monuments, and in its social, legal, and speculative activity.

The literary history of the Middle Ages remains and will long remain to be written. An account of the history of medieval Latin poetry has this advantage—it moves along the broad lines of intellectual and social growth, and of religious development. It will be found to contain the names of many of the great men within the Church, who helped to build up the fabric of the new Christian civilization out of the apparent wreck of the ancient world.

In quality the Latin verse of the Middle Ages exhibits an immense variety; for medieval literature, unlike the literature of antiquity, has come down to us in a vast bulk, in which good and bad are mingled, the tentative along with the complete achievement. My aim has been by means of ample quotation to enable the reader to follow the process of formal development or change, and at the same time to appreciate the quality of the poetical attainment.

I am greatly indebted to the Delegates of the Clarendon Press for their kindness in undertaking the publication of this book, and, in particular, I wish to thank Mr. Kenneth Sisam, the Assistant Secretary, for advice and encouragement, and Mr. Frederick Page, of the Oxford Press, for reading the manuscript and proofs, and for many suggestions which have been of great value. To the Reverend Dom André Wilmart, O.S.B., whose learning has illuminated many aspects of medieval history and literature, I owe a debt of special gratitude. He has not only been so kind as to read part of the manuscript and the whole of the proofs, but he has allowed me to draw without limit upon his learning and experience, and has patiently instructed me on many points where I should otherwise have gone seriously astray. He has directed my attention to many important monographs which I could not have discovered alone, and he has often saved me from those conclusions which are so easily formed at second-hand. The interest which he has taken in what is, after all, the mere outline of a great and difficult subject, has been an unfailing encouragement to one who had begun with too much confidence and too little experience a voyage of discovery in what was, for him, an almost unknown country.

F. J. E. R.

CONTENTS

THE BEGINNINGS OF CHRISTIAN-LATIN POETRY

§ 1. *Christianity and Hellenistic-Roman Civilization.*

THE earliest Christian community began as a Jewish sect. The Apostles at Jerusalem after the death of Jesus continued to worship in the Temple and to observe the ordinances of the Jewish religion. For the Christians at Jerusalem, Jesus was still, above everything, the Jewish Messiah; they still acknowledged the Law, and the Old Testament was their only sacred book. Christianity became in the true sense a universal religion only when it had spread beyond the Palestinian communities into the wider world of Hellenism. There it underwent the transformation necessary to its survival; it assumed the external appearance of a mystery-cult and drew upon the common fund of religious conceptions and practices which the Hellenistic world had acquired as a result of the mingling of east and west in the Empire of Alexander and in the kingdoms of his successors. This transformation of the new religion must have begun very soon in the original Hellenistic-Christian communities which lie between the Jewish-Palestinian Church and the advent of Paul. For Paul cannot be regarded as the inventor of this new type of Christianity, however greatly he may have influenced it in the direction of a higher spirituality and in the restraint of unhealthy and too obviously pagan practices. Yet he accepted it broadly as it stood, with its cult, not of the Palestinian Messiah, but of the Kyrios Christos,[1] Son of God and Saviour. Christianity was now launched into world-history, and became one of the many forces which issued from the 'Oriental fringe' of the

---

[1] This is Bousset's view (that the Kyrios cult sprang up in Syria) in his *Kyrios Christos*; but Ed. Meyer (*Ursprung und Anfänge des Christentums*, iii. 218, Berlin 1923) would find its roots in Judaism, and Deissmann (*Paulus*, Tübingen 1925, p. 100) agrees. In any case, the full development must surely be Hellenistic.

B

Roman Empire and were the main agents of those vast changes which produced the Catholic civilization of the Middle Ages.[1]

Yet the Church still showed unmistakable signs of its Jewish parentage. Paul might substitute grace for the law, but for him always the Old Testament was the inspired and sacred book of the Church, possessing a weight and authority which could never be set aside. The Church learned at once to see in all its pages no other figure than that of Jesus, who was foretold by all the prophets, and was typified by king and priest and patriarch of the old dispensation. The Psalms of David became the hymn-book of the Church. Allegorically and symbolically interpreted, they were made to adapt themselves to Christian uses. Thus the Hebrew Scriptures (in the Greek translation of the Seventy) were the most potent literary influence which made itself felt among the Christians of the first century. The worship of Christian communities was modelled on the service of the Jewish Synagogue, which consisted of lessons, psalms, prayers, and homily. The only new institution was the order of the Lord's Supper, but even there the service was composed of similar elements, and was closely related to the Jewish Passover. Judaic influences, therefore, determined the form of the early Christian service. The spiritual influence of the Psalter remained throughout the whole development of the new religion, and the Jewish psalm was the model of the earliest Christian hymns.

But another influence was making itself felt by the side of the tradition which Christianity inherited from its Jewish origin. This influence was the Hellenistic ·culture which had become the common heritage of all the different races gathered together under the Empire of Rome. In the course of a century, and especially after the destruction of Jerusalem in A.D. 70, Asia Minor, Syria, Egypt, Greece, and Italy had become the main seats of the Christian religion. Christianity there underwent a thorough process of Hellenization, a process which, as we have seen, was reflected in the new conception of Jesus as Saviour, Lord, and

---

[1] An important observation by Kornemann (*Die römische Kaiserzeit, Einleitung in die Altertumswissenschaft*, Leipzig 1912, iii. 296) is worth quoting in this connexion : ' Wer die schwierigste aller Probleme, dasjenige vom " Untergang der antiken Welt ", wirklich in der Tiefe fassen will, darf nicht im Westen, sondern muss im Osten des Mittelmeergebietes seinen Standort wählen und muss die frühislamische Welt mit in den Bereich seiner Betrachtung ziehen. Der Weg zum Verständnis des Mittelalters geht über den Orient.' See also Ed. Meyer, *Blüte und Niedergang des Hellenismus in Asien*, Berlin 1925, pp. 75 sqq.

Son of God, and was continued by Justin, and later by Clement of Alexandria and Origen, who were deeply influenced by the tendencies of later Greek philosophy.

The first Christian literature in the West was written wholly in Greek. For a long time the majority of the Church at Rome was composed of Greek-speaking Christians, many of them Jewish in origin, and in Africa too (or at any rate in Carthage) the Greek element was important.[1] Greek was indeed the first language of the Church in Italy, in Gaul, and in Africa, and as late as the third century it was the language of the Christian liturgy at Rome; but worship must have been conducted in Latin as well, and the first Latin versions of the Bible had begun to be made before the time of Tertullian. After the middle of the third century, and especially after the division of the Empire, Greek speech began to die out in the West. During the first two centuries, the cultured world of the Empire had been bi-lingual, the educated Roman spoke Greek as well as Latin, and men of letters like Suetonius, Fronto, Apuleius, and even Tertullian, wrote with equal ease in either language.[2] But the fourth century saw the decay of the knowledge of Greek in Italy, Gaul, Spain, and Africa. In the course of that century, Rome became once more a Latin-speaking city, but the process was naturally slower in the South of Gaul and the South of Italy.[3] Augustine did not read Plato in the original, and in Gaul Ausonius could make his knowledge of Greek an occasion for boasting. Late in the second century, Latin Christian literature began in Africa with Tertullian, whose 'burning tracts burst upon the world with the suddenness of a tropical sunrise'.[4] Africa is thus the 'Motherland of Latin Christian literature';[5] but it was not long before Italy, Gaul, and Spain had followed the example. Latin, therefore, became in the West the sole liturgical and literary language of the Church.

Before the middle of the third century, there is no definite

[1] Cf. Harnack, *Die Chronologie der alt-christlichen Litteratur*, ii. 297 (Leipzig 1904).
[2] Cf. E. Norden, *Die lateinische Literatur im Übergang vom Altertum zum Mittelalter*, in *Die Kultur der Gegenwart*, i. viii, p. 485 sq.; also Norden, *Antike Kunstprosa*, ii. 574, 608.
[3] Harnack, *Mission*, i. 19; ii. 241-2, on the growth of the Latin element in the Church at Rome; but in the fourth century Photinus of Sirmium wrote in both languages. See Vincent of Lérins, *Commonitorium*, xi, p. 42, Cambridge 1915.
[4] Garfield, *Africa and Christian Latin Literature* (*American Journal of Theology*, Jan. 1907), p. 101; cf. the striking estimate of Tertullian by Vincent of Lérins, *Commonitorium*, xviii, p. 75.
[5] Harnack, *Mission*, ii. 279-80.

trace of Latin Christian poetry, and the earliest extant Latin hymns belong to the fourth century. What Latin hymns existed in earlier days were doubtless modelled on those which are known to have been used in the Eastern Churches and went back to Hebrew rather than to classical originals. Such was the *Gloria in Excelsis*, and there were many hymns or 'private psalms' which have not survived. As in the Eastern Greek-speaking communities, so in the West, the Psalms were the hymn-book of the Church; but when Latin Christian poetry really began in the West, the main literary influence could hardly fail to be that of the Latin classical poets, the only possible models for men who had received their education in the public schools.

The public schools were the last stronghold of pagan culture. They were supported by endowments and immunities at the expense both of the central government and of the municipalities. The instruction given was inherited from the scholastic system of the older Greek world, and the main constituents were grammar and rhetoric. The education thus afforded, if judged by modern standards, was doubtless very incomplete. It possessed all the defects of an education which was purely literary in character, emphasizing form at the expense of solid intellectual content, and it tended to produce a lettered class able to write or declaim trivialities in an artificial language which only those who knew the rules could easily understand. This education, in its better days, had a meaning and an object. While political life still existed, in the age of Greek democracy or in the days of the Gracchi, the mastery of rhetoric was a means to political power, and the style and manner of the orator were adapted carefully to the particular end in view.[1] But this special education, in the end, overshadowed all others; so that grammar and rhetoric became the recognized constituents of a general education. With the decline of political life and the establishment of the Empire, the training in rhetoric ceased to have the same relevance to the world of political affairs. It became a means to the mastery of an art which did not cease to be admired for all its apparent uselessness. Private declamations on trivial subjects drew large and enthusiastic audiences, and it was possible to win fame and honours by a public *panegyric* on a phantom emperor. The *panegyric* remained

[1] Cf. Seeck, *Geschichte des Untergangs der antiken Welt*, iv. 169.

the only real exercise of the rhetorician's art, though he might sometimes practise at the bar; and apart from an occasional show of public importance, the learned classes were confined to the practice of an elaborate *dilettantism* concentrated in private circles.[1] The acquisition of style was the one thing to be aimed at, and to that end the schools of grammar and rhetoric put forth all their efforts. The professors of rhetoric often made large fortunes and could boast of a crowd of rich and noble pupils.

The study of grammar included the study of literature as a whole. After reading and writing had been mastered, the grammarian, whose position was comparatively humble, taught his pupil the elements of grammar, pronunciation and accent, and the correct use of words. Along with these purely grammatical studies, the poets were read and explained, and enough isolated facts of history, geometry, astronomy, music, &c., were added to make the author's allusions intelligible to the student. There was no systematic study of natural science or of mathematics; the grammarian's business was simply to impart the minimum of the subsidiary knowledge requisite for the understanding of the author's text. The poets were the first and the main object of study. The student was taught to understand the text, to explain the various mythological and historical allusions, and to detect unusual grammatical uses. At the same time, he committed passages to memory.

The school of grammar provided therefore a basis for the study of literature and especially of the poets. In the school of rhetoric, the pupil read the historians and orators, and the reading was accompanied by the study of the technicalities of style as exhibited in the works of the masters of oratory and written prose. The whole aim of the rhetorician was to teach his pupil the art of composition and declamation according to the accepted models. Artificiality and a servile imitation which did not altogether exclude new fashions, tended therefore to flourish. That scholar was near perfection who could compose in verse or prose according to the recognized rules; provided that the form was acceptable, the content was more or less indifferent.

At the time when Christianity came into decisive contact with the Roman civilization, the public schools still provided the only

---

[1] We shall see how later on, especially in Gaul, serious men with rhetorical gifts found a career in the episcopate.

available approach to a liberal education, and the Church soon realized that it was impossible to stand aloof. With admixtures indeed of other influences and cultures, she adopted the language and style of Graeco-Roman culture as her own. By the end of the fourth century, as we have seen, the Western part of the Roman Empire had been completely latinized. Greek influences had declined, both in Rome, and, if we except the southern parts of Gaul and of Italy, throughout the entire West. Latin was the language of law, administration, and commerce, at the time when the Church had reached its full territorial expansion within the boundaries of the Empire.

In accepting the Latin language, the Church had also to accept the system of education by which it was conveyed. But that education was rooted and grounded in paganism, with its associations of polytheism and immorality, its dangerous philosophy and its sensual love of beauty. At the same time, if Christianity were to meet paganism on a common intellectual level, the Christians must avail themselves of the schools. This was the dilemma, and the answer of the Church was of a practical kind. In theory, the Latin fathers sternly reprobated paganism and all its works. Tertullian formally condemned secular letters as ' foolishness in the eyes of God ',[1] but, although he took the view that a Christian master might not teach in a heathen school, he saw that it was folly to deprive a Christian of all possibility of general culture. Hence he agreed that it was lawful for a Christian scholar to attend the schools, admitting the force of the argument: 'Quomodo repudiamus saecularia studia, sine quibus divina non possunt ? '[2] Jerome knew and loved the classical writers and had been a pupil of the great grammarian Donatus. But, as a Christian, he was constrained to condemn ' poetry, the wisdom of the world, the pompous eloquence of the orators, this food of devils '.[3] Too much stress need not be laid on his famous dream in which, he says, he was brought before the seat of judgement, and when, to the question put concerning his faith, he replied, ' I am a Christian ', he received the terrible answer, ' Thou art a Ciceronian, not a Christian; where thy treasure is, there is thy heart also '.[4] Jerome's formal conclusion is this. Liberal studies are a necessary preliminary to a Christian education;

[1] *De Spect.* xviii.
[2] *De Idol.* x, but he adds, ' Diversa est enim ratio discendi et docendi '.
[3] *Epist.* xxi. 13.
[4] ib. xxii. 30.

but, once mastered, they can be laid aside, for their use is over. But in practice, for Jerome himself, the old charm could never be laid aside, and it was only in his moods of self-accusation that he began to doubt whether he were a Ciceronian or truly a Christian.

A similar contradiction appears even in the firmer spirit of Augustine. Virgil remained always for him the prince of poets, and in his *Confessions* he relates how as a boy he had shed tears for Dido, and how deeply the *Hortensius* of Cicero had moved him in his early manhood. But the devices of the rhetorician appeared to him, in his severer moments, as merely meretricious ornaments and the business of rhetoric as akin to falsehood. So in the *Confessions*,[1] he cries, 'Truly over the door of the grammar school there hangs a curtain, yet is that curtain the shroud of falsehood, not the veil of mysteries'. But in his sermons Augustine used every device of rhetoric, and he recognized the value of a good style in the defence of the Christian faith, where a too simple and vulgar presentation would hinder its acceptance.[2] He was led to justify the establishment of a Christian culture on the basis of secular letters by an appeal to the example of the Hebrews, who, with the divine permission, 'spoiled the Egyptians'.[3] Similarly, Jerome appeals to the ordinance in Deut. xxii. 12, which allows a Jew to take to wife a gentile woman, if 'she shall shave her head and pare her nails'.[4]

So the Christians had come to terms with the public schools, and in the brief revival of paganism under Julian, they bitterly resented the contemptuous edict by which the Emperor forbade them to do violence to their conscience by teaching pagan letters in the schools.[5] The influence of the schools of grammar and rhetoric is apparent in every page of Tertullian, of Jerome, and of Augustine, and until we arrive at the sixth and seventh centuries, we shall hardly find a Christian poet who does not owe his training entirely to the grammarians and rhetoricians.

The age which saw the beginnings of Christian literature saw also the beginnings of Christian art.[6] That art in its first developments shows the same mixture of Judaic and Hellenistic

---

[1] i. 13 ; cf. Prudentius, Prologue to the *Cathemerinon*.

[2] *De Doct. Christ.* iv. 2.

[3] ib. ii. 40.

[4] *Epist.* lxx. 2.

[5] Duchesne, *Hist. de l'Église*, ii. 330.

[6] The reader may conveniently consult Kaufmann, *Handbuch der christlichen Archäologie*, Paderborn 1905 ; Kraus, *Geschichte der christlichen Kunst*, i, Freiburg-im-Breisgau 1896 ; Bréhier, *L'Art chrétien*, Paris 1918.

influences which was manifested in the theology and the ceremonial of the Church. It began, not with the sanction, but rather with the disapproval, of the Church, among the 'burial societies', which the Christians formed on the model of similar societies existing among the pagan population. The motives of many of the inscriptions and monuments resemble those of their heathen models. Thus, in the cemetery of Domitilla, Orpheus appears as a type of Christ, and Amor and Psyche are represented with a reference to the Christian redemption. But the symbolical character of this early art is best seen in the representation of more purely Christian figures, such as those borrowed from the Old Testament or from the life of Christ. For the most part, and naturally, they bear reference to the destiny of the dead, for whose sake they were created; setting forth symbolically, under the figures of Noah, of Moses, of Isaac, of Jonah, or of Daniel, the deliverance of the soul by Jesus, who appears himself as an ideal Shepherd, the good Shepherd who gave his life for the sheep. Such symbolical figures, drawn largely from the Old Testament, the only considerable storehouse from which a Christian 'mythology' could be collected, show that Christian art, like Christian poetry, was bound to go for much of its content to Jewish sources. But, as with Christian poetry, it was compelled to seek its form in Hellenistic-Roman models. Thus the figure of the Christ, once it began to be more freely represented, is based on the conventional classical figure of the ideal orator or philosopher.[1] Christian art, says M. Bréhier,[2] is in its last analysis, only the final flowering of Hellenistic art, but in adopting the style of a decadent culture, it gave it a new charm and freshness, and, finally, breaking free from its earlier trammels and receiving the sanction and encouragement of the Church, became the Catholic art of the Middle Ages. Similarly, from the dying literary culture of the ancient world proceeded the vigorous shoot of Christian literature, which was to issue in the Latin of the Vulgate, and, at a later date, in the poetry of the *Stabat Mater* and the *Dies Irae*.

The death of the ancient world was hastened by the enormous

[1] Bréhier, *L'Art chrétien*, p. 53.
[2] ib., p. 55. I do not, however, wish to minimize or exclude, by using the word 'Hellenistic', those influences vaguely called 'Eastern' which showed themselves conspicuously in the Oriental fringe of the Graeco-Roman world, and, as Prof. Strzygowski has proved, are, at the lowest estimate, of very great importance.

changes produced by the inroads and settlements of the northern barbarians within the boundaries of the Roman Empire. Out of the social and political wreck in which the western part of that Empire was involved, there emerged slowly and painfully a new order, strangely different from the old, but even more clearly a Christian order, dominated by a Church which had survived all shocks and changes, and was intellectually and morally superior to the new society which it was called upon to educate, admonish, and, if possible, to control. The unity of Rome lived on in the Catholic Church, which became the religious and political schoolmaster of the young kingdoms. The Franks, whose rise to supremacy in Gaul was all the more important as they became converts to Catholicism instead of to Arianism, lent their support to the Papacy, and helped it to make good its assertion of supremacy over the Western world. Thus side by side with the growing importance of the new kingdoms went the increasing power and more solid organization of the Church. Paganism was now almost extinct. The barbarian rulers, though Christian, were unlettered, ignorant, and uncivilized. Almost the only spark of intellectual life which remained was nourished by the Church. War and religion shared the whole life of the most important part of the population—the ruling classes and the clergy. The new nobility had little interest in letters; they were too much occupied with continual wars and the problems of governing a society which had to be organized primarily for defence. It was inevitable therefore that an almost complete monopoly of learning and literature should fall to the only part of the population which possessed the leisure necessary even for a mediocre culture. The cause of civilization was thus entrusted to the Catholic Church. The language of this civilization continued to be Latin, but it was no longer the Latin of Cicero, of Quintilian, or even of Prudentius. It was a Latin transformed to meet the needs of a new civilization. The literary language of Rome was already in the time of Ennius becoming distinct from the spoken language alike of the upper classes (*sermo cotidianus*) and of the masses (the *sermo·plebeius* or *lingua rustica*). Caesar and Cicero put the finishing touches to a process of polish and refinement, which aimed at making the language of letters and of oratory a reflection of the great achievement of Greece. This literary language was within the compass only of the educated few, while the vulgar Latin remained the property of the lower classes, and served the practical ends of trade and of ordinary intercourse. But the great social changes which struck a fatal blow at the old aristocracy and the old middle class, produced a new arrangement of society which was favourable to the revival of the vulgar speech. The new rich, the new official class, the swarms of provincials who invaded Rome, had more use for the practical speech of every day than for a literary language which had to be painfully learned in the school of the grammarian. Shut up in the schools, and a prey to a dwindling class of *littérateurs*, the learned language in the age of Marcus Aurelius dragged on an artificial life. Burdened with self-conscious archaisms and preciosities, and spiced with vulgarisms which were introduced to give piquancy and effect, it lost its vitality, while the vulgar Latin gained ground at the bar, in technical works, and in the romantic novels which were now being produced. In poetry, however, it held out with more success, since imitation was of the very essence of composition in verse. When Christianity had won a number of gentile converts in the West, it was compelled to use the vulgar tongue, not indeed in its polemical and theological literature, but in its sermons and in its versions of the Bible. If the great Latin fathers maintained the learned tradition, and Prudentius and Paulinus of Nola took Horace and Virgil as their models, the vulgar Latin yet made a permanent contribution to the language of the Church. The first translations of the Bible, and the liturgy itself, bear witness to this fact. The language of the Vulgate gathers up the various influences which had been at work in creating the appropriate medium for the expression of Christian thought in the West. Jerome indeed owed much to his unknown predecessors who had based their versions on the Septuagint and had introduced along with Hellenic elements the flavour of the vulgar tongue.[1] He combined with these elements others derived from the Hebrew; so a part of the Hebraic spirit passed into his version. New rhythms appeared, a new and more romantic imagery. The mystical fervour of the prophets, the melancholy of the penitential psalms or of the *Lamentations* could not be rendered in Latin without giving that severe and logical language a strange flexibility, an emotional and

---

[1] On the first Latin versions and the Vulgate see Labriolle, pp. 63 sqq.; Schanz, iv. i. 451 sqq.; Harnack, *Mission*, ii. 242.

symbolical quality which had been foreign to its nature.[1] The whole literary imagination of the West was to be fed on the sonorous sentences of the Latin Bible, and Christian poetry, though true so long to its learned traditions, could not escape the spell or fail to learn the new language, when it spoke in the poetical prose of lines like these:

> iuxta est dies domini magnus,
> iuxta est et velox nimis:
> vox diei domini amara,
> tribulabitur ibi fortis.
> dies irae, dies illa,
> dies tribulationis et angustiae,
> dies calamitatis et miseriae,
> dies tenebrarum et caliginis,
> dies nebulae et turbinis,
> dies tubae et clangoris
> super civitates munitas, et super angulos excelsos.[2]

Out of this music was to issue the poetry of the future, the poetry in which the Catholic emotion was to discover its final expression. It is the music of a new world, for out of it appeared at last, when its religious mission had been fulfilled, the romantic poetry of the modern world.

§ 2. *The Earliest Christian-Latin Poetry; from Commodian to Damasus.*

Although the earliest Christian writers in the West, who made use of the Latin language, owed their education to the pagan schools and used well the art of rhetoric which they had learned by continuous imitation of classical models, yet the first extant Latin verses composed by a Christian poet are mainly of interest because they show a departure from the methods of classical Latin poetry. The *Instructiones* and *Carmen Apologeticum* of Commodian,[3] who lived about the middle of the third century,[4]

[1] Cf. Ozanam, *La Civilisation au V*[e] *siècle*, ii. 135.
[2] Zephaniah i. 14–16; Tischendorf's text.
[3] *Commodiani Carmina*, ed. Dombart, *C. S. E. L.* xv.
[4] The date of Commodian has been hotly debated (for literature see *Bibliography*). F. X. Kraus puts him at the beginning of the fourth century.

Ramundo argues for the time of Julian the Apostate, when the conditions suggested by the poems (hesitation between description of imminent persecution and a persecution already begun) may be regarded as fulfilled. He also makes Commodian a native of Gaza and a Palestinian bishop. Brewer made an elaborate attempt to prove that Commodian wrote under Christian emperors, e.g. (1) the poet refers to a are composed in a rude and unadorned measure, which, although based on the classical hexameter, shows but the smallest observation of quantity and neglects the stricter rules of syntax. It was once supposed that Commodian was a native of Gaza in Palestine, but it is certain that he belonged to Africa. He lived through one phase of persecution, and therefore he must be assigned to an age when martyrdom was more than a mere tradition invested with wonder and miracle. So he addresses one of his acrostic poems to 'one who would be a martyr'.[1]

Martyrium volenti

Martyrium, fili, quoniam desideras, audi.
Abel qualis erat, esto, aut qualis ipse magister.
Rectamque delegit Stephanus sibi viam in iter.
Tu quidem quod optas, res est felicibus apta.
Vince prius malum benefactis recte vivendo.
Rex illa tuus cum viderit, esto securus.
Ipsius est tempus et nos in utrumque gerentes;
Ut si bellum adest, in pace martyres ibunt?
Multi quidem errant dicentes : Sanguine nostro

Vincimus Iniquum ; quem manentem vincere nolunt.
Obsidiando perit et ideo sentit Iniquus,
Legitimus autem non sentit poenas ad actus;
Eiula euoque zelando pectus pugnis pertunde.
Nunc si benefactis vinces, eris martyr in illo ;
Tu ergo qui quaeris martyrium tollere verbo,
In pace te vesti bonis et esto securus.

To which admirable exhortation we may join the grave words of Cyprian with which Commodian was doubtless familiar; 'nec enim sanguinem Deus nostrum sed fidem quaerit'.[2]

Syrian god who was robbed of his treasures by the Emperor ; (2) he refers to the capture of Rome by Alaric and to the events of A.D. 458. Brewer concludes that the poet lived in S. Gaul, c. 458-66, that he was neither bishop nor priest, but an 'ascetic'. F. X. Zeller demolishes these ingenious arguments. If Commodian had lived in S. Gaul at the time suggested, he would have had to take notice of semi-Pelagianism ; he knows nothing of Arianism, of the Council of Nicaea or of the victory of the Church. He constantly refers to martyrdom, is very familiar with Cyprian, mentions the schism over the *Lapsi*, and is hostile to the (obviously heathen) government. The conclusion is that he was a contemporary of Cyprian. Dombart agrees with this view and argues further that as Commodian in his *Carmen Apolog.* uses only the first two books of Cyprian's *Testimonia*, which appeared in 248, he completed that poem before book iii appeared (249).

It is surprising to find Ed. Meyer (*Ursprung und. Anfänge des Christentums*, iii. 508) accepting Brewer's conclusions.

[1] *Carmina*, p. 89.
[2] *De mortalitate*, c. 17; ed. Hartel, *Opera*, p. 308, C.S.E.L. iii.

The eighty poems which made up the two books of the *Instructiones* are all in acrostic or alphabetical form, and this fact, together with their didactic content, makes it likely that they were intended to be committed to memory by converts who required to be grounded in the faith. The verses consist partly of polemic against the gods of the heathen, and partly of censure of the Jews, while the later poems are admonitions to Christians who, in spite of their profession, do not always pursue the way of life. The terrors and wonders of the last day, a subject to which Commodian loves to recur, are described in verses which, when we have become accustomed to their strange form, are not without a show of impressiveness.[1]

> Dat tuba caelo signum sublato leone [2]
> Et fiunt desubito tenebrae cum caeli fragore.
>
> Summittit oculos dominus, ut terra tremescat,
> Adclamat et iam, ut audiant omnes, in orbem :
> Ecce diu tacui sufferens tanto tempore vestra!
> Conclamant pariter plangentes sero gementes,
> Ululatur, ploratur, nec spatium datur iniquis.
> Lactanti quid faciat mater, cum ipsa crematur ?
> In flamma ignis dominus iudicabit iniquos.

The long *Carmen Apologeticum*, to give it the title invented somewhat unhappily by its first editor, is a kind of exposition of Christian doctrine, describing the creation, God's revelation of Himself to man, the coming of Antichrist, and the end of the world. The aim of the poem is instruction, and it is useless to look for beauty of form or poetical ideas in a composition consciously directed to men of little learning.

The poems of Commodian, then, are the earliest example of Latin verse which was intended for and, we must assume, appreciated by uncultured members of the Church. It is for this reason that their language and prosody are worthy of detailed study. For our present purpose we need note only a few of the characteristics of his verse, which have a bearing on the later developments of medieval rhythmical poetry. In the first place, it should be observed that Commodian, although

---

[1] *Carmina*, p. 61.
[2] Should this be Nerone, as Dombart suggests? Cf. *Carmen Apologeticum*, 891, p. 172. Nero is used to represent the forerunner of Antichrist; see Bousset, *The Antichrist Legend*, p. 79 sq., London 1896 ; but Antichrist is a lion, p. 25, and like Dan his prototype, a lion's whelp, p. 137.

his language and syntax are corrupt and often barbarous, had some acquaintance with the rules of quantitative verse, and his neglect of quantity may perhaps be conscious and studied. Thus Meyer maintains that where a line ends on a two-syllabled word, the poet rarely neglects the correct quantity. Similarly, in the last syllable but one before the *caesura*, he carefully observes the quantity. Such verses, as Meyer says,[1] would not have been possible if Commodian had had before his eyes specimens of verses in which word-accent was substituted for quantity. Hence the early rhythmical poetry of the Latin Church was not due to the mere substitution of word-accent for quantity, making the accent fall where the *ictus* had been. The verses of Commodian are evidently not to be read on any such rhythmical scheme; indeed, they cannot, in the accepted sense, be said to have any definite rhythm at all; they are only rhythmical in the sense that they were meant to be read according to their word-accent, as though they were prose.[2] Meyer has pointed out further that Commodian has learned to construct strophes or groups of lines, and to join them together with acrostics or, more remarkable still, with a form of rime which consists of ending his lines each with the same vowel.

> Paenitens es factus: noctibus diebusque precare,
> Attamen a matre noli discedere longe,
> Et tibi misericors poterit altissimus esse,
> Non fiet in vacuum confusio culpae proinde,
> In reatu tuo sorde manifesta deflere,
> Tu si vulnus habes altum, medicumque require,
> Et tamen in poenis poteris tua damna lenire,[3] &c.

We find then in Commodian some of the principal characteristics of rhythmical poetry, at any rate in the germ, but the essential feature of equality in the number of syllables is absent. If we are to seek a true parallel to his scheme of versification, we must not seek it in the later rhythmical poetry of the Church, but in the metrical inscriptions both pagan and Christian which have come to light in the Roman province of Africa.[4] A whole group of these inscriptions exhibits the same misuse or ignorance of quantity, the same fixed *caesura*, with a well-marked rhythm

---

[1] Meyer, *Rythmik*, ii. 6; Monceaux, iii. 486, contests this and says that it is simpler to suppose that Commodian wished to compose correct hexameters, but failed through ignorance of prosody.

[2] Meyer, *Rythmik*, ii. 35.

[3] *Carmina*, p. 69 sq.

[4] Monceaux, iii. 432 sqq.

only in the end syllables, and, in addition, rime and assonance, and, more rarely, the acrostic construction. Commodian, therefore, whether consciously or not, wrote the rude verses of the half-educated classes, and his poetry belongs rather to a barbarized classicism than to the new Christian rhythm. In a few of the Christian inscriptions there is a hint of the future principle of rhythmical verse—the fixity of the number of syllables,[1] but that principle did not really emerge until Augustine composed his famous psalm.

Meanwhile the classical tradition held sway, for the Christian-Latin poets of the third and fourth centuries, whose works have been preserved, learned their art in the schools of rhetoric; their verses are the compositions of cultured men, and could be understood only by readers of the same class. Such is the beautiful poem on the *Phoenix*, which has been ascribed to the African Lactantius, one of the ablest writers of the Latin Church. It is in elegiacs and tells the well-known fable of the Phoenix with what has been regarded, in spite of the apparatus of classical allusion, as a Christian reference to the resurrection.[2] Similarly, the two short hexameter poems, *De Sodoma* and *De Iona*, ascribed without warrant to Tertullian or to Cyprian, are fair specimens of Christian versification on classical lines, though there is a tendency to leonine and other rimes.[3] The first poem describes the doom of Sodom, the escape of Lot, and the fate of his wife, who in her strange transformation, still stands for the curious traveller to see:

> in fragilem mutata salem stetit ipsa sepulchrum,
> ipsa et imago sibi, formam sine corpore servans.
> durat enim adhuc nuda statione sub aethra,
> nec pluviis dilapsa situ nec diruta ventis.

The second poem is a fragment, by the same author, telling the story of Jonah up to the time when he was swallowed by the great fish. The reference is especially to the resurrection of Christ. The theme is a favourite one with the early Church,

[1] Monceaux, p. 448.
[2] Text in Baehrens, *Poetae Latini Minores*, iii. 253 sqq. Claudian, who was perhaps a Christian in name, did not disdain to imitate this poem. Both Harnack, *Altchristliche Litteratur*, ii. 425, and Monceaux iii. 507, are disposed to ascribe it to Lactantius; Riese (*Rhein. Mus.* xxxi, p. 446 sq.) detected Christian and chiliastic references which point to Lactantius as the author. Brandt (*Rhein. Mus.*, xlvii, pp. 390 sqq.) and Pichon, *Lactance*, pp. 464 sqq., are against the Christian character of the poem, and say that if Lactantius wrote it, it was before his conversion. I am much inclined to accept their view.
[3] Text in *C. S. E. L.* xxiii, pp. 212 sqq.

and it appears in the art of the catacombs and of Christian sarcophagi.

The work of a Christian rhetorician appears very clearly in the poem on the Maccabees,[1] ascribed to Marius Victorinus who is probably identical with Victorinus (b. *circa* A.D. 300), the African rhetorician, whose conversion is related by Augustine in his *Confessions*.[2]   It is written in hexameters and is full of speeches which are composed according to the rules of the schools.   Victorinus is also the reputed author of verses *De Pascha*,[3] an allegory on the Cross, the tree of life under whose branches the nations of the world find life and food, and the way to overcome death.   These not unpleasing verses are almost a Virgilian cento, but they do not follow Virgil so closely as the curious cento composed by Proba, the Christian daughter of a Roman Consul.[4]   The fashion of the cento had been set by Hosidius Geta, whose tragedy on the subject of Medea, composed in Africa in the second century, is one of the curiosities of later classical literature.   The most amusing Christian cento is in the form of a Virgilian *Eclogue*[5] in which Tityrus,

patulae recubans sub tegmine fagi,

initiates Meliboeus into the mysteries of the Catholic faith. Another cento has for its subject the *Incarnation*, while a third, on the *Church*, ends with a cento which is said to have been actually improvised by the author when his delighted audience hailed him as 'Maro iunior'.[6]

> ne, quaeso, ne me ad tales inpellite pugnas!
> namque erit ille mihi semper deus, ille magister.
> nam memini—neque enim ignari sumus ante malorum—
> formosum pastor Phoebum superare canendo
> dum cupit et cantu vocat in certamina divos,
> membra deo victus ramo frondente pependit.

---

[1] *C.S.E.L.* xxiii, pp. 255 sqq.; Monceaux iii. 519–20, refuses to admit the authorship of Victorinus the African; cf. Teuffel-Schwabe, ii. 337.

[2] viii. 2.

[3] *C.S.E.L.* iii, Part III, Appendix, pp. 305 sqq.

[4] Text in *C.S.E.L.* xvi. 511 sqq. The subjects are taken from the Old and New Testaments; on Proba see Glover, *Life and Letters in the Fourth Century*, pp. 144 sqq.

[5] *C.S.E.L.* xvi. 609 sqq., for this and the centos on the *Incarnation* and the *Church*.

[6] See Comparetti, *Virgil in the Middle Ages*, p. 55, London 1908. The author's name was probably Mavortius. He also composed a cento on the Judgement of Paris.

The first important names in the history of the earlier Christian-Latin poetry are those of two Spanish poets whose compositions exercised a considerable influence over their successors. Juvencus,[1] or to give him his full name, Caius Vettius Aquilinus Juvencus, was a noble Spaniard, and a priest, who composed a Christian epic on the Gospels, in the reign of Constantine. He was educated in the schools of grammar and rhetoric, he knew his Virgil, Lucretius, and Statius well, and had acquired a facility in composition which he turned to account for didactic purposes. He was, so far as we know, the first of the Latins to attempt to provide for educated Christian readers a substitute for the perilous beauties of the classical poets.[2] In his verse-preface he says that nothing in the world is everlasting, neither the earth, nor human kingdoms, not 'golden Rome', nor sea, nor earth, nor the stars of heaven,

> nam statuit genitor rerum irrevocabile tempus,
> quo cunctum torrens rapiat flamma ultima mundum.

But poets have striven to keep alive the memory and deeds of men. Homer and Virgil have celebrated such men in song, and themselves have won high fame. But if these poems, compact of falsehood, have earned such lasting fame, how much more worthy is the verse which sings the deeds of Christ,

> divinum populis falsi sine crimine donum.

There is no fear, the Christian poet boasts; that his song will be consumed when the world is burned by fire.

> hoc etenim forsan me subtrahet igni
> tunc, cum flammivoma discendet nube coruscans
> iudex, altithroni genitoris gloria, Christus.
> ergo age! sanctificus adsit mihi carminis auctor
> spiritus, et puro mentem riget amne canentis
> dulcis Iordanis, ut Christo digna loquamur.

Of the poem itself we need only say that it is a faithful and simple narrative of the Gospel story, clear and unadorned, but thoroughly Virgilian even to the imitation of the great poet's characteristic archaisms. Its interest lies in the attempt to

[1] Texts of *Evangeliorum Libri IV*, &c., ed. Hümer, *C.S.E.L.* xxiv; see Boissier, *La Fin du paganisme*, ii. 43 sqq.

[2] Socrates, *H.E.* iii. 16, refers to certain Greek attempts; Labriolle, pp. 416–17.

provide a Christian literature which might counteract the influence of the pagan poets by showing that the Church had her own heroic story, her own epic of the incarnation, the wonderful life, death, and resurrection of the Saviour. It is true that the Old Testament offered a better field for the Christian effort, and this was seen by later poets like Cyprian and Avitus. For the richness of incident and of material capable of lively treatment in the epic manner was wellnigh inexhaustible, and out of it could be created a Christian 'mythology' which, fascinating as it was for its own sake, could be referred always to its allegorical and dogmatic meaning. The history of the Christian epic will be continued when we reach the poets of the fifth century.

The second name among the Spanish poets of the fourth century is that of Damasus, who under troubled circumstances became Bishop of Rome in A.D. 366.[1] His epigrams and inscriptions are of considerable historical interest. They were composed to preserve the memory of his numerous restorations of the monuments of the early Church, and some of them are still to be read in all the beauty of their original lettering, while others owe their preservation to copies made before the originals perished. These short poems, which are mainly in hexameters,[2] contain many sins against pure prosody and show little or no poetical feeling. But it is interesting to note that, before Prudentius, Damasus had led the way in celebrating the sufferings of the martyrs, although the limits of the epigram did not allow of more than a very summary treatment of such a theme. The following epigram is dedicated to S. Agnes,[3] and can still be read in splendid lettering at S. Agnese fuori le mura.

> fama refert sanctos dudum retulisse parentes
> Agnen, cum lugubres cantus tuba concrepuisset,
> nutricis gremium subito liquisse puellam,
> sponte trucis calcasse minas rabiemque tyranni.
> urere cum flammis voluisset nobile corpus,
> viribus immensum parvis superasse timorem,

---

[1] On Damasus see Duchesne, *Hist. de l'Église*, ii. 456 sqq.; text Ihm, *Anthol. Latina*, Suppl. I, Leipzig 1895.

[2] Nos. 70 and 71 (Ihm, 73 sqq.) on S. Andrew and S. Agatha, in lyric measure, with frequent rime, must belong to a later date and are not the work of Damasus. As regards the genuine verses, Duchesne (op. cit., ii. 483) remarks, 'Jamais plus mauvais vers n'ont été transcrits avec un tel luxe'. Duchesne takes an unfavourable view of the Bishop's whole career.

[3] Ihm, p. 43.

nudaque profusum crinem per membra dedisse,
ne domini templum facies peritura videret.
o veneranda mihi, sanctum decus, alma, pudoris,
ut Damasi precibus faveas precor, inclyta martyr.

The Pope's own epitaph, which he himself composed, was
inscribed on his tomb in the basilica of the Apostles, afterwards
called S. Sebastian, which he had built *ad Catacumbas* on the
Appian Way, and although the tomb perished when the body
was removed at a later date to S. Lorenzo in Damaso, within
the city, the verses have survived.

qui gradiens pelagi fluctus compressit amaros,
vivere qui praestat morientia semina terrae,
solvere qui potuit letalia vincula mortis,
post tenebras fratrem, post tertia lumina solis
ad superos iterum Marthae donare sorori,
post cineres Damasum faciet quia surgere credo.[1]

This brief account of Christian-Latin verse in the third and
fourth centuries has shown that the main tradition followed
by the Christian poets was that of the declining classical world.
The strength of this tradition lay in the public schools and
it was to continue with diminishing force for several centuries.
In following the further history of Christian verse in the West
we have to consider at every step the fate of this tradition
in the great transition from the ancient to the medieval world.
It was not until the Roman civilization had been entirely
transformed in the long and wonderful process by which the
Empire of the Caesars became the Catholic Europe of feudal
times, that the lyrical genius of the Christian religion found
the true medium for its expression in a verse based no longer
on elaborate rules of quantity but on a new system which was
to give birth to the great national poetry of modern Europe.
The origins of rhythm and rime are still obscure, and an
adequate discussion of the various efforts which have been
made to trace the beginnings and development of rhythmical
poetry cannot be attempted here. But an account, in outline,
of the main characteristics of the new verse-forms, is an essential
preliminary to the study of the Christian poetry of the centuries
which followed the break-up of the old civilization. This

---

[1] Ihm, p. 13; text also in Scaglia, *Manuel d'archéologie chrétienne*, Turin
1916, p. 110.

account may well be linked to the consideration of Augustine's remarkable *Psalmus contra partem Donati*, which, although composed towards the end of the fourth century, already exhibits the true characteristics of the earlier rhythmical verse of the Middle Ages.

§ 3. *Augustine's Psalm and the Origins of Latin Rhythmical and Rimed Poetry.*

Augustine, who stands between the ancient world and the Middle Ages as the first great constructive thinker of the Western Church, and the father of medieval Catholicism, possessed to the full the mastery of those qualities which ally the rhetorician so closely to the poet. It is of the glowing periods of his rhetorical prose that Norden was thinking when he called him 'the greatest poet of the early Church',[1] but, by a lucky chance we possess a religious poem, the authorship of which can be assigned to Augustine without a shadow of doubt, for he refers to it unmistakably in his *Retractationes*.[2] Of this *Psalm against the Donatists*, he says, 'Volens etiam causam Donatistarum ad ipsius humillimi vulgi et omnino imperitorum atque idiotarum notitiam pervenire et eorum quantum fieri posset per nos inhaerere memoriae, psalmum qui eis cantaretur, per latinas litteras feci, sed usque ad v litteram. Tales autem *abecedarios* appellant.' Augustine therefore intended this hymn or psalm to be sung by the congregation for the purposes of dogmatical instruction, so that they might not be led astray by the heresy of the Donatists.[3] It was, in fact, a counterblast to the popular 'psalms' with which the Donatists had conducted their own propaganda. The poem is constructed in long strophes each of which begins with a letter of the alphabet; each line ends on the vowel *e* or *ae*, and there is a refrain which besides being linked to the strophe by its end-rime possesses also an internal rime.

omnes qui gaudetis de pace, modo verum iudicate.

---

[1] 'Augustinus war der grösste Dichter der alten Kirche, mag er auch in Versen so weniges geschrieben haben wie Platon'; *Die lateinische Lit. im Übergang vom Altertum zum Mittelalter*, in *Die Kultur der Gegenwart*, I. viii. 501.

[2] i. 19.

[3] Text, M. Petschenig, *Augustini Scripta contra Donatistas*, i, *C.S.E.L.*, li, pp. 3 sqq.; for criticism of text see Meyer, *Rythmik*, ii. 18; see also Monceaux, iii. 491 sqq.; vii. 81 sqq.

But what is of particular interest is the fact that these verses are not constructed after the manner of the classical poetry which Augustine had loved so dearly in his youth. If we examine their structure, we see that if elision is observed as a general but not invariable rule, and if in certain cases two adjoining vowels are allowed to run together, the lines are composed of sixteen syllables, divided equally by the *caesura*, and that the only law observed beyond that of a rough syllabic equality is that of a regular accent which falls in each half-line on the penultimate syllable.[1] The beginning of the first strophe will serve to explain the structure.

> Abundantia peccatorum solet fratres conturbare.
> propter hoc dominus noster voluit nos praemonere
> comparans regnum caelorum reticulo misso in mare
> congreganti multos pisces omne genus hinc et inde.
> quos quum traxissent ad litus, tunc coeperunt separare,
> bonos in vasa miserunt, reliquos malos in mare.
> quisquis novit evangelium, recognoscat cum timore.

In this hymn we see more distinctly than in Commodian the appearance of a new kind of poetical construction. For there is no clear evidence that the popular verse of the Romans was other than quantitative ;[2] rhythmical verse in the West was entirely a Christian possession and it was never employed by pagan writers. Its principle is the strophic grouping of lines which contain an equal number of syllables, and are divided by a fixed *caesura*, and frequently there is the constant or sporadic ornament of a more or less developed rime. The basic characteristic of this early rhythmical verse is the *numbering of syllables*, which decisively differentiates it from classical verse, but relates it, in Meyer's opinion, to Semitic poetry, and in particular to Syriac hymns like those of Ephrem Syrus.[3] Meyer therefore holds firmly to an ultimately Semitic origin of rhythmical verse, but it can hardly be said that his theory has won general acceptance.[4] Once the principles of quantitative verse

---

[1] Engelbrecht (*Zeitsch. f. d. österreich. Gymnas.*, lix, p. 588) would prefer to speak of the rhythm as trochaic, falling at the end of each 'half-line' with the word-accent, but in other places emancipating itself.

[2] Meyer, *Rythmik*, ii. 3 sqq. ; the examples given by Suetonius (cf. e.g. *Caesar* 51 and 80) support this view ; Dreves (*Gött. Gelehrt. Anzeig.*, 1886, pp. 285 sqq.)

dissents, and holds for the survival of an accented popular poetry (from the old Saturnian).

[3] Meyer, *Rythmik*, ii. 104 sqq. ; 114 sqq.

[4] See R. Duval, *La Littérature syriaque*, Paris 1899, p. 17. It is true that Syriac versification is based on the numbering of syllables, and acrostic and alphabetical verses were popular. Rime

were abandoned, it was essential, if the new rhythmical verse were to have any principle at all, that some such basis as the numbering of syllables should be adopted. Equality of syllables replaced equality of feet; but the new measures were not, from the first, based on the old by the mere substitution of word-accent for the ancient *ictus*. The earlier rhythmical verse was a kind of prose, with no fixed accentual rhythm carried throughout the line, although, as in Augustine's *Psalm*, there might be a regular cadence in the middle and at the end of a line. The nearest parallel to this rhythmical system is to be found in the rhetorical prose of classical times which followed elaborate rules, based on quantity, for the ending of clauses. Not only Symmachus in later times, but Christian writers like Cyprian turned this occasional ornament into a general rule, and the tendency was, as in the Greek prose of the Byzantine centuries, for accent to triumph over quantity.[1]

Progress towards verse of definitely rhythmical structure was slow, but it was naturally aided by the possibility of imitating trochaic and iambic schemes. Yet it was not until the eleventh century that the principles of accentual verse were fully developed and fully mastered, so that a regular cadence was produced when the words were read according to their grammatical accent. The rule, observed more strictly by the better poets, was that, while there was no elision, hiatus should be avoided. Rime or assonance, used frequently as an occasional ornament, was seldom, until the eleventh century, applied to the whole of a poem.

The origin of the use of rime for the adornment of verse still remains somewhat obscure. Meyer is anxious again to prove a Semitic origin. He argues that rime was known to the Arabs (at any rate about the beginning of the sixth century) and is used occasionally in Hebrew and in Syriac religious poetry;[2] but it is not possible to trace with any clearness a direct influence on Greek or Latin religious verse. In any case, the use of rime was perfectly well known to the writers of antiquity. Parallelism of form was the most marked feature of both Greek and Latin rhetorical prose.[3] To this parallelism of form is

appears in the later poetry, borrowed, it seems, from the Arabs ; but the Syriac poetry can hardly have been a decisive influence in Greek and Latin lands.

[1] Meyer, *Rythmik*, i. 12 sqq.

[2] ib., i. 117.

[3] See Norden, *Die antike Kunstprosa*, ii. 810 sqq., *Anhang I, Über die Geschichte des Reims*.

joined the rhetorical device of ὁμοιοτέλευτον ('similar ending', assonance or rime) which had the effect of prominently marking the end of the clause. The use of the rhetorical rime in rhythmical prose shows itself in Apuleius in lines like these:

> aut ara floribus redimita,
> aut quercus cornibus onerata,
> aut fagus pellibus coronata.[1]

and in Tertullian with:

> tot pernicies quot et species,
> tot dolores quot et colores.[2]

Cyprian's *De Mortalitate* is full of this rimed prose:

> si avaritia prostrata est,
> exsurgit libido:
> si libido compressa est,
> succedit ambitio:
> si ambitio contempta est, ira exasperat,
> inflat superbia, vinolentia invitat:
> invidia concordiam rumpit
> amicitiam zelus abscidit.[3]

Augustine, too, employed such rimes to lend effect to passages of high feeling or pathos:

> eo nascente superi novo honore claruerunt,
> quo moriente inferi novo timore tremuerunt,
> quo resurgente discipuli novo amore exarserunt,
> quo ascendente caeli novo obsequio patuerunt.[4]

And, again:

> vigilat iste, ut laudet medicum liberatus,
> vigilat ille, ut blasphemet iudicem condemnatus.
> vigilat iste mentibus piis fervens et lucescens,
> vigilat ille dentibus suis frendens et tabescens,
> denique istum caritas
>> illum iniquitas,
>> istum christianus vigor
>> illum diabolicus livor
> nequaquam dormire in hac celebritate permittit.[5]

---

[1] Quoted by Prof. Garfield, *Africa and the beginnings of Christian-Latin Literature*, *American Journal of Theology*, Jan. 1907, p. 104; see the *Golden Ass*, xi. 25, for a rimed litany to Isis, which has a parallel in later litanies of the Virgin; de Jong, *Das antike Mysterienwesen*, p. 73, note 1, Leiden 1909.

[2] Garfield, p. 104; *Scorp.* i.
[3] *De Mortalitate*, 5.
[4] *Sermo* 199, 2 (Migne, xxxviii, col. 1028); Norden, ii. 622; see for further examples, Sister Inviolata Barry, *St. Augustine, the Orator*, pp. 85 sqq.; pp. 169 sqq.
[5] *Sermo* 219 (Migne, xxxviii, col. 1088); Norden, ii. 622.

Hence, it appears reasonable to assume that the use of the rhetorical rime in rhythmical prose, after passing into the popular sermons of the Greek and Latin Church, found its way into Christian poetry at a time when the feeling for quantity was dying out and a new verse-form was being constructed. Rhetorical rime had indeed appeared in classical poetry, where it was used, on rare occasions, as a device consciously borrowed from the rhetorical prose. The verses of Ennius quoted by Cicero[1] are well known:

> caelum mitescere, arbores frondescere,
> vites laetificae pampinis pubescere,
> rami bacarum ubertate incurvescere.

and,

> haec omnia vidi inflammari,
> Priamo vi vitam evitari,
> Iovis aram sanguine turpari.

Cicero himself used the rhetorical device of the ὁμοιοτέλευτον in the poem on his consulship, but it was avoided by the best classical poets and it remained an ornament of rhetorical prose.

In the early hymn-writers rime is merely occasional and sporadic. We have seen how Commodian and Augustine employed a rudimentary form by ending a series of lines on the same vowel. A similar device appears in the long poem *Ad Flavium Felicem de resurrectione mortuorum*,[2] where there are numerous end- and internal-rimes in -*as*, e.g.:

> qui mihi ruricolas optavi carmine musas
> et vernis roseas titulavi floribus auras
> aestivasque graves maturavi messis aristas, &c.

This poem is probably to be assigned to the beginning of the sixth century. Rime is to be found in the genuine hymns of Ambrose, but its presence can largely be explained by the accident of construction, as in the first two stanzas of the *Veni redemptor gentium*:

> veni redemptor gentium,
> ostende partum virginis,
> miretur omne saeculum,
> talis decet partus deum.

---

[1] *Tusc. Disp.* i. 69, 85.
[2] Cyprian, ed. Von Hartel, *C.S.E.L.* iii,   Appendix, pp. 308 sqq.; see also Meyer, *Rythmik*, ii. 122.

non ex virili semine,
sed mystico spiramine
verbum dei factum est caro,
fructusque ventris floruit.

Again, in Prudentius, a stanza appears like the following: [1]

peccator, intueberis
celsum coruscis nubibus,
deiectus ipse et irritis
plangens reatum fletibus.

Sedulius, in the fifth century, is the first hymn-writer to make any considerable use of rime, for it appears in nearly every stanza of the *A solis ortus cardine.* Fortunatus in the next century uses it with well-designed effect in the *Vexilla regis prodeunt* :

arbor decora et fulgida
ornata regis purpura,
electa digno stipite
tam sancta membra tangere,

and it is used likewise in the *Quem terra pontus aethera* :

o gloriosa domina
excelsa super sidera,
qui te creavit provide
lactasti sacro ubere.

Until the eleventh century rime continued to appear in liturgical verse, but it rarely persisted through all the lines of a hymn. The one-syllabled rime is used almost without exception, because the favourite hymn-metres, such as the iambic dimeter, did not lend themselves to a rime of two syllables. But the pure two-syllabled rime was not unknown, as it had been used so often in the rhetorical prose of the fathers. An example of its liturgical use occurs in a *responsorium* used at Rome in the office for the festival of the Virgin :

gaude, Maria Virgo ! cunctas haereses sola interemisti,
qui Gabrielis archangeli dictis credidisti,
dum virgo deum et hominem genuisti,
et post partum virgo inviolata permansisti.
Gabrielem archangelum credimus divinitus te esse affatum,
uterum tuum de spiritu sancto credimus impregnatum.
erubescat Iudaeus infelix, qui dicit Christum ex Ioseph semine
esse natum ! [2]

---

[1] *Cath.* xi. 101–4.
[2] See Batiffol (*Histoire du bréviaire romain*, p. 171), who would assign it to the seventh century.

There are early examples, too, of the use of two-syllabled rimes, in the grammarian Virgilius Maro (*circ.* A. D. 600),[1] and in the seventh-century Bangor Antiphonary. From the Irish, the use of rime passed to Æthelwald and Boniface, and through Irish and Anglo-Saxon poets it established itself on the Continent, suffering only a temporary eclipse during the classical renaissance of Charles the Great. Gottschalk (d. 869) and Wipo (d. 1050) used two-syllabled rimes freely, but it is in Hildebert and Marbod, in the later eleventh century, that this rime approaches its perfection. Hildebert's couplets contain an equal number of syllables, stressed alternately and ending with a two-syllabled rime. The development of rhythmical poetry was then nearly complete. It only remained for Hildebert's successors to invent new varieties of structure, new combinations of accent and rime, and the secrets of rhythmical verse were revealed to prepare the way for the marvellous achievements of modern poetry.

But rhythmical poetry never succeeded in entirely replacing the ancient quantitative verse, which still maintained a considerable prestige The hexameter and elegiac, and, to some extent, the Sapphic measures, were persistently imitated throughout the whole of the Middle Ages, and generations of scholars who passed through the secular, the monastic, and the cathedral schools found a delight in those forms of composition in which, they proudly felt, they were the followers of a great tradition. But at the same time they loved to adorn their hexameters and pentameters with various kinds of rime. Such rimes had indeed appeared occasionally in the classical poets, in rare instances by design, more often by reason of the similar ending of noun and corresponding adjective.[2] Thus leonine rimes like the following appear in Lucretius :

> tuto res teneras effert in luminis oras [3]

and

> saepe salutantum tactu praeterque meantum.[4]

Similar instances, though the two-syllabled rime is rarer, might be cited from Virgil ;[5] but rime was, on the whole, avoided, and the leonine and other rimes did not come thoroughly

[1] Meyer, *Rythmik*, i. 119 sqq., 202–3.
[2] See Traube, *Einleitung in die lateinische Philologie des Mittelalters*, pp. 110 sqq. ; W. Grimm, *Zur Geschichte des* *Reims*, in *Kleinere Schriften*, pp. 125 sqq.
[3] i. 179.
[4] i. 318.
[5] e.g. *Bucol.* vi. 86 ; vi. 24.

into fashion until the tenth and eleventh centuries.   Examples
of conscious leonine rimes have been found in the seventh
and eighth centuries,[1] but it is not until the tenth century that
we see the full use of the one-syllabled leonine rime, in the verses
of Hrothswitha, and the *Ecbasis captivi*.   The two-syllabled
leonine rime is seen at its best in the eleventh century in
Marbod of Rennes.   The large and varied nomenclature
attached to the different kinds of rimes employed in metrical
hexameters bears witness to the extreme popularity of this form
of composition.[2]   In the eleventh century, rimed hexameters are
at least as numerous as those of the classical kind.

In the following chapters we shall trace the development
of Christian Latin poetry, not merely from the point of view
of form and technical structure, but also in relation to the
religious and intellectual conditions under which it was produced.

The poetry of the Church was such a characteristic achievement of Western Christianity, and bore such fruit late in the
vernacular literature of the modern world,[3] that it has seemed
worth while to show in what different countries, under what
various cultural traditions, and in relation to what changing
religious outlooks, the vast body of Catholic poetry was built
up by the labour of more than a thousand years.   This Christian
poetry, beginning under the influence of antique traditions, to
which it returned again in times of classical revival, was
able in the end to create for itself its own appropriate form,
which alone was capable of expressing the meaning and the
emotion of Western Christianity.   In the course of this survey
it will be seen how the needs of the Catholic office influenced
both the form and the subject-matter of the hymn, restricting
it at first to simple forms and to doctrinal themes ; how monastic
hymnody reflected its origin faithfully by dwelling on the
wickedness of this world, on the pains of hell and the joys of
heaven ; how the symbolism and allegory which appear in the
earliest Christian literature, art, and poetry, and continue all

---

[1] Meyer, *Rythmik*, i. 193, note 1 ;
Ronca, *Cultura medievale e poesia latina
in Italia*, i. 347.

[2] Meyer, *Rythmik*, i. 79 sqq.

[3] Cf. Meyer, *Der Gelegenheitsdichter
Fortunatus*, p. 5 ; also Dreves-Blume,
*Ein Jahrtausend lateinischer Hymnen-
dichtung*, ii, p. iii : ' Wir dürfen nämlich

nicht übersehen, dass im christlichen
Altertume und insbesondere im Mittelalter die geistliche Lyrik oder Hymnodie
mit dem ganzen kulturellen Leben, in
dem das religiöse die Hauptrolle spielt,
aufs innigste, und in einer bislang kaum ge-
ahnten Weise, verbunden, ja verschmol-
zen war.'

through the Middle Ages, find their completest expression in the sequences of Adam, the poet of the Abbey of S. Victor, where symbolical and allegorical methods were most cherished in the twelfth century. Finally, it will be seen how the Franciscan religious revival breathed a new spirit into the old doctrinal hymnology, and, using the perfected verse forms of the twelfth century, filled them with an emotion hitherto unknown, an emotion of personal pathos and pity which was destined profoundly to influence the lyrical poetry of the modern world.[1]

§ 4. *The Use of Hymns in the Latin Church;* Ambrose, A.D. 340-397

The divine office or the daily round of prayer and praise (apart from the Eucharist) consists of elements—prayers, psalms, and lessons—which were the constituents of the service of the Jewish Synagogue.[2] In seeking the origins of the daily canonical hours, we naturally begin with Jewish practice in the Apostolic age. The morning and evening sacrifices at the Temple in Jerusalem were reflected in the morning and evening prayers in the Synagogue, and the Apostolic Church may have

---

[1] The following recent German expression of the 'inner principle' governing the transition from the old to the new verse-form is worth quotation. It is taken from Karl Borinski, *Die antike in Poetik und Kunsttheorie vom Ausgang des klassischen Altertums*, Leipzig 1914, i. 48: ' Es sind vielleicht innere Wandlungen im Empfindungsleben der historischen Menschheit, und keine bloss von aussen kommenden Einflüsse, die die antike rein metrisch taktierende, den Wortton nur melodisch berücksichtigende, Versübung beim Beginn der neuen Ära verdrängt haben. Denn alle Versuche, sie wiederherzustellen, die mit Methode und enthusiastisch die Renaissance anstellte, indem sie sie sogar auf die modernen Sprachen aufpropfen wollte, sind misslungen. Die Tendenz, den beherrschenden, für alle massgebenden Wortton, an Stelle des von ihm unabhängigen nur gebildeten Ohren fühlbaren Silbenmasses, den Verstakt bestimmen zu lassen, trifft nur allzu deutlich zusammen mit der Unterwerfung aller—auch der geistigen Elite, die das

klassische Altertum trug—unter das allgemeine soziale Prinzip, wie sie das Christentum fordert.'

Since writing this chapter I have read an interesting article by W. B. Sedgwick, *The Origin of Rhyme* (*Revue Bénédictine*, 1924, pp. 330 sqq.) in which it is argued that 'the interaction of 'music and verse produced rime . The author's argument is difficult to follow, but the article contains a great deal of instructive matter. It is clear, in any case, that music must have given an irresistible impulse to the use of rime.

[2] I have deemed it prudent to follow somewhat closely (though I have softened the sharpness of his contours) Dom Suitbert Bäumer's *Histoire du bréviaire* (Fr. trans. by Dom R. Biron), Paris 1905, 2 vols.; see also Duchesne, *Origines du culte chrétien*, last chapter; P. Batiffol, *Histoire du bréviaire romain*, Paris 1911. As regards Duchesne, the reader should not fail to see the remarks of Edmund Bishop, *Liturgica Historica*, p. 60.

followed this custom.   If this is the case, it may be said that
Lauds and Vespers belong, in germ, to the time of the Apostles.
It has been suggested that the origin of Vigils or the nocturnal
office is to be found either in the meetings at night on the eve
of Sunday, which were rendered necessary by the persecutions,
or in the great Easter vigil which in the days of Clement of
Alexandria was celebrated by each community, while daily
vigils were still no more than the private duty of the faithful.
From Clement, as from Tertullian, we learn that beside the
canonically established morning and evening prayers, the private
hours of Tierce, Sext, and None (tertia, sexta, and nona; *sc.*
hora) were kept, though not of obligation and remaining private
in character.   Only on Wednesdays and Fridays (the fast days)
was it customary, for those who were able, to attend in Church
until None.   Psalms and hymns were sung, according to Tertullian ; but hymns were merely psalm-like pieces outside the
psalter, and not metrical compositions like the hymns of later
date.   Cyprian in the third century confirms the witness of
Tertullian.

Such, in brief, is the history of the office up to the end of
the third century.   The fourth century saw great developments
in the Church, where monasticism, from Palestine and Egypt,
became a growing force.   The office was naturally a main
occupation of the monks, but as yet there was no organization
of it in the direction of a celebration of all the recognized
hours in common and in church.   Basil, in his rule for monks,
which was destined to spread over the greater part of the
Eastern Church, prescribes prayer in the morning, and at the
hours of Tierce, Sext, and None, at the end of the day, at
the beginning of night, and according to the example of Paul
and Silas, at midnight.   He enjoins prayer also at dawn, quoting
the Psalmist : *I prevented the morning light.*[1]   But only the
prayers of morning, evening, and night took place in church ;
the remaining hours, though obligatory, were private.   Lauds
and Vespers had always occupied a special place in the services
of the Church, but the monks began to attach a similar importance to the nocturnal prayer.   The manner in which they
gave this emphasis varied in Egypt and in Syria.   The Egyptian
monks withdrew their morning office to the night time, making
of Lauds an office which we should recognize as Matins, while

[1] Ps. cxix. 147.

in Palestine and in the East generally, the morning prayer remained in its place and the night office became what we know as Matins. Meanwhile, the secular clergy began to add the regular practice of vigils to the morning and evening offices, which were daily celebrated in the West in the time of Hilary. For the West followed in the wake of the more rapid development of the East, and Cassian (d. 435), abbot of a monastery at Marseilles, who had learned much from his stay among the monks of Bethlehem and of the Thebaïd, hastened the process by adapting the practice of oriental monasticism to the requirements of the Western Church.

An office to which Benedict later gives the name of Prime was added as a second morning office towards the end of the fourth century. Introduced in a monastery at Bethlehem, it spread with considerable rapidity, though only in the monasteries, in East and West. So the seven canonical hours were created—Vigils (Matins), Lauds, Prime, Tierce, Sext, None, and Vespers—conforming to the declaration of the Psalmist: *seven times a day do I praise Thee.* One further office was added, but at what date is not very clear. Compline, in Benedict's Rule, is a full canonical office, but it is not improbable that it occupied that position in the East before his time.[1] Benedict made Vespers a day office, and Compline thus became the office ' lucis ante terminum '.

What hymns were sung or said in the offices during the early centuries of the Church it is impossible to determine in detail. Paul speaks of 'hymns and spiritual odes', which were either taken from the Old Testament or were free compositions, improvised ἐν πνεύματι or of an exalted nature. Attempts have been made to discover fragments of apostolic hymnody in the New Testament. But passages like:

$$\text{ὃς ἐφανερώθη ἐν σαρκί,}$$
$$\text{ἐδικαιώθη ἐν πνεύματι,}$$
$$\text{ὤφθη ἀγγέλοις,}$$
$$\text{ἐκηρύχθη ἐν ἔθνεσιν,}$$
$$\text{ἐπιστεύθη ἐν κόσμῳ,}$$
$$\text{ἀνελήμφθη ἐν δόξῃ.}[2]$$

are more probably liturgical or confessional in character.[3] Basil (d. 379) gives the text of a Vesper chant, the φῶς ἱλαρόν, a hymn

---

[1] Bäumer, i. 255 (note by the French translator).
[2] 1 Tim. iii. 16; cf. 2 Tim. ii. 11–13.
[3] E. Norden, *Agnostos Theos*, Leipzig 1913, pp. 250 sqq.

of free composition, which has been ascribed to various authors and may go back beyond the third century.[1] The *Gloria in Excelsis* was at an early date a morning hymn, and in the fifth century the *Te Deum* was sung at Lauds on Sundays. Numerous canticles were taken from the Old and New Testaments.[2] The *Odes of Solomon*, which were discovered by Dr. Rendel Harris, show what hymns were sung by Catechumens in the Syriac-speaking Church of the second or third century.[3]

The oriental cults employed elaborate hymns or psalms which were imitated by the 'Christian' Gnostics in their effort to capture the inheritance of the Church. How powerfully their sweet and sensuous appeal must have worked upon those numerous seekers after religion to whom beauty and mystery, especially mystery, never called in vain, we can imagine when we read the *Hymn of the Soul*, embedded in the Syriac *Acts of Thomas*.[4] Bardaisan, too, in the second century, a heretic and a man of original power, composed in Syriac hymns of a similar character, distilling the same sweet poison, and the Neoplatonists, in days when philosophy was more than tinged with Hellenistic-oriental religious ideas, wrote odes and hymns which left their mark on the Platonizing compositions of Synesius.[5] Greek hymnody never wholly escaped the influence of this mystical and sensuous poetry which finds its fitting culmination in the cadences of the *Akathistos Hymn*;[6] but in the West the beginnings of Latin hymnody are associated with the sober sense of a Hilary and an Ambrose. After the Gnostics, Paul of Samosata and the Arians made use of hymns to spread their heretical doctrines. Voices were, therefore, raised in the Church against those who ventured to introduce other chants than the psalms or similar biblical compositions. The Council of Laodicea (*circ.* A.D. 361) placed its ban upon such innovations, and as late as 637, the fourth Council of Toledo found it necessary to deal with those who

[1] Text in W. Christ and H. Paranikas, *Anthologia graeca carminum christianorum*, Leipzig 1871, p. 40.
[2] J. Mearns, *The Canticles of the Church in Early and Medieval Times*, Cambridge 1914; article *Cantiques* in Cabrol's *Dictionary*.
[3] J. H. Bernard, *The Odes of Solomon, Texts and Studies*, viii, iii, Cambridge 1912. Bernard's views are not, however, generally accepted, especially in Germany, where the tendency is to minimize the 'speci-

fically Christian' element in the Odes to the benefit of Gnosticism or a 'Judaizing Gnosis'.
[4] F. C. Burkitt, *Early Eastern Christianity*, London 1904, pp. 193 sqq.; translation of the *Hymn*, pp. 218 sqq.
[5] Cf. E. Norden, *Agnostos Theos*, p. 79; J. Geffcken, *Der Ausgang des griechisch-römischen Heidentums*, pp. 219 sq.
[6] Text in Christ and Paranikas, pp. 140 sqq.

rejected all non-biblical hymns. In 563 the Council of Braga in Spain had adopted the view of Laodicea, while in 567 the second Council of Tours had taken a middle course, allowing beside 'Ambrosian hymns' others which went under the guarantee of a known authorship. The fathers of Toledo in 637 pointed out that the rejection of all but biblical chants ruled out all the non-canonical hymns composed 'humano studio in laudem dei atque apostolorum et martyrum triumphos', and meant logically the rejection of the *Gloria in Excelsis*, since the angels sang only the first part, the remainder being the composition of doctors of the Church. Therefore, 'excommunicatione plectendi qui hymnos reiicere fuerint ausi'.

The real history of hymns in the West begins with Ambrose, the bishop of Milan. In a well-known passage of the *Confessions*, Augustine describes under what circumstances the singing of hymns was introduced. 'It was about a year from the time when Justina, mother of the boy-emperor Valentinian, entered upon her persecution of Thy holy man Ambrose, because he resisted the heresy into which she had been seduced by the Arians. The people of God were keeping ward in the Church ready to die with Thy servant, their bishop. Among them was my mother, living unto prayer, and bearing a chief part in that anxious watch. Even I myself, though as yet untouched by the fire of Thy Spirit, shared in the general alarm and distraction. Then it was that the custom arose of singing hymns and psalms, after the use of the Eastern provinces, to save the people from being utterly worn out by their long and sorrowful vigils. From that day to this it has been retained, and many, I might say all Thy flocks, throughout the rest of the world now follow our example.'[1] The Basilica at Milan, beset by the Gothic soldiery of Valentinian, heard the first strains of Catholic hymnody, in which with simplicity and beauty, Ambrose set forth the doctrines of the orthodox faith. The hymns of Ambrose became popular in the truest sense, for they made way into the experience of the Christian Church and were treasured in most of the Western hymnaries until they found a permanent place in the Roman office. How deeply the appeal of their music could reach is shown in the confession

---

[1] *Conf.* ix. 7 'Tunc hymni et psalmi ut canerentur, secundum morem orientalium partium, ne populus moeroris taedio contabesceret, institutum est'; I have used Dr. Bigg's translation; cf. Isidore of Sevile, *De Off. Eccles.* i. 7 (Migne, lxxxiii, col. 743); see Hodgkin, *Italy and her Invaders*, i. 437.

of Augustine, to whose memory they recurred in times of trouble and anxiety. 'What tears', he says, 'did I shed over the hymns and canticles, when the sweet sound of the music of Thy Church thrilled my soul! As the music flowed into my ears, and Thy truth trickled into my heart, the tide of devotion swelled high within me, and the tears ran down, and there was gladness in those tears.'[1] Sorrowing in secret for his mother's death—'for the bitterness of my sorrow could not be washed away from my heart'—he remembered, as he lay upon his bed, the verses of Ambrose :

> deus creator omnium
> polique rector, vestiens
> diem decoro lumine,
> noctem soporis gratia.
>
> artus solutos ut quies
> reddat laboris usui,
> mentesque fessas allevet,
> luctusque solvat anxios.[2]

The hymns of Ambrose were written definitely for congregational purposes and they soon found their way into the Milanese and other liturgies. Their immense popularity encouraged imitation. A crowd of hymns in the same metre —the familiar classical *iambic dimeter*[3]—gained the common title of *hymni Ambrosiani*, and the *iambic dimeter* was known as the 'Ambrosian' metre. The fact that these later hymns were admitted into the Liturgy by the side of the genuine hymns of Ambrose led, in the course of time, to the greatest uncertainty as to which were really the work of the Bishop of Milan. The problem cannot now be regarded as completely solved, but it seems probable that out of the mass of early hymns in the Ambrosian metre, about eighteen can be regarded, with great though varying degrees of certainty, as genuinely the work of Ambrose.[4] Augustine vouches directly for four of the finest hymns, 'Deus creator omnium ; Aeterne rerum conditor ; Iam surgit hora tertia ; Intende qui regis Israel (better known

---

[1] *Confessions*, ix. 6. [2] ib., ix. 12.
[3] On Ambrose's careful regard for quantity see Ebert, i. 181 ; there is no effort to make *ictus* and accent fall together.
[4] One of the best modern discussions of the subject is the excellent monograph of Father Dreves, *Aurelius Ambrosius, der*

Vater des Kirchengesanges, Freiburg im Breisgau 1893. He supports the conclusions of Biraghi, *Inni sinceri e carmi di Sant' Ambrogio* (Milan 1862), a work to which scant justice had been done by Dreves' predecessors ; see also Schanz, iv. i. 228 sqq. ; Bardenhewer, iii. 543 sqq.

as Veni redemptor gentium)'.[1] For ten others there is very good evidence that Ambrose is the author, while for the remaining four it can be said that if Ambrose did not compose them, they are the work of a poet of equal genius.

Composed with the practical aim of expounding the doctrines of the Catholic faith in a manner sufficiently simple to capture the imagination of the unlearned, these hymns possess at the same time the admirable qualities of dignity, directness, and evangelical fervour. The two examples which follow give a true idea of the poetical quality of the first Latin Christian hymns which succeeded in establishing for themselves a permanent position in the worship of the Catholic Church.

Aeterne rerum conditor.

aeterne rerum conditor,
noctem diemque qui regis
et temporum das tempora,
ut alleves fastidium ;

praeco diei iam sonat,
noctis profundae pervigil,
nocturna lux viantibus,
a nocte noctem segregans.

hoc excitatus lucifer
solvit polum caligine,
hoc omnis erronum chorus
vias nocendi deserit.

hoc nauta vires colligit
pontique mitescunt freta,
hoc ipse, petra ecclesiae,
canente culpam diluit.

surgamus ergo strenue,
gallus iacentes excitat
et somnolentos increpat,
gallus negantes arguit.

gallo canente spes redit,
aegris salus refunditur,
mucro latronis conditur,
lapsis fides revertitur.

Iesu, labantes respice
et nos videndo corrige ;
si respicis, lapsus cadunt,
fletuque culpa solvitur.

tu lux refulge sensibus
mentisque somnum discute,
te nostra vox primum sonet
et ora solvamus tibi.

[1] As regards the rest of the eighteen, Dreves bases his arguments on (1) ancient attribution, e.g. probable mention of *Splendor paternae gloriae*, by Ambrose himself, and certainly by Fulgentius, (2) use in the Milanese Liturgy, (3) stylistic and metrical evidence, based on the hymns which are known to be genuine, (4) evidence of similarity of phrase, &c., drawn from Ambrose's prose works. The evidence is less convincing for four of the hymns, *Iesu corona virginum ; Nunc sancte nobis spiritus ; Rector potens verax Deus ; Rerum Deus tenax vigor*, though all of them were used in the Milanese rite. The titles of the other hymns which Dreves regards as genuine are, besides the four vouched for by Augustine, *Splendor paternae gloriae ; Amore Christi nobilis ; Illuminans altissimus ; Agnes, beatae virginis ; Hic est dies verus Dei ; Victor, Nabor, Felix pii ; Grates, tibi, Iesu, novas ; Apostolorum passio ; Apostolorum supparem ; Aeterna Christi munera*. Steier, *Untersuchungen über die Echtheit der Hymnen des Ambrosius*, recognizes fourteen hymns as genuine.

Splendor paternae gloriae.

splendor paternae gloriae,
de luce lucem proferens,
lux lucis et fons luminis,
diem dies inluminans.

verusque sol, inlabere
micans nitore perpeti,
iubarque sancti spiritus
infunde nostris sensibus.

votis vocemus et Patrem,
Patrem perennis gloriae,
Patrem potentis gratiae:
culpam releget lubricam.

informet actus strenuos,
dentem retundat invidi,
casus secundet asperos,
donet gerendi gratiam.

mentem gubernet et regat
casto fideli corpore,
fides calore ferveat,
fraudis venena nesciat.

Christusque nobis sit cibus,
potusque noster sit fides,
laeti bibamus sobriam
ebrietatem spiritus.

laetus dies hic transeat,
pudor sit ut diluculum,
fides velut meridies,
crepusculum mens nesciat.

aurora cursus provehit,
aurora totus prodeat,
in Patre totus Filius,
et totus in Verbo Pater.

The hymns of Ambrose reflect the mind of the great teacher of the Latin Church. Bred as a lawyer and man of affairs, with all the practical genius of the Roman and that leaning to the ethical outlook which characterized the Roman mind,[1] Ambrose cared little for the speculations which exercised such a fascination over the Greek fathers. He naturally accepted the orthodox Trinitarian position and he spent his life in building up his flock in this faith, inculcating those practical virtues and that simple piety which were always for him the true and characteristic fruit of the Gospel. For Ambrose is always the teacher rather than the theologian. His homilies, full as they are of allegory and the most curious and strained interpretations which he borrowed from the Greek fathers, have always the single aim of moral and spiritual edification. None of the great Latin bishops, before or after, so thoroughly won the hearts of his people by his eloquence, his devoted service, and his own example.

In speaking of the importance of the hymns of Ambrose in literary history, Ebert remarks that they are the beginning not merely of the Christian lyric, but also of true Christian poetry in

---

[1] In laying the foundations of Catholic ethics in his *De Officiis Ministrorum*, Ambrose based his work on the famous treatise of Cicero; on this subject and on Ambrose generally see Labriolle, *Saint Ambroise*; Duchesne, *Hist. de l'Église*, ii. 523 sqq.

general in the West. 'The hymns appear', he says, 'as the ripest fruit of the process of the assimilation on the part of Christianity of the formal education of the ancient world.' If, as regards form, the hymns of Ambrose follow the heathen models, they are a true effort of original creation, in which the Christian spirit controls the artistic form, and not a series of imitations in which the form controls the content of the verse.[1] The poetry of Juvencus and later of Sedulius was, on the other hand, an attempt to clothe the story of the Gospels in the guise of a Virgilian epic. There is no trace of the creative faculty, and the result is tasteless and artificial.

In one further respect, the hymns of Ambrose bear a Christian character. Wilhelm Meyer [2] has pointed out that although the verses are strictly quantitative, their structure follows the rules of the new rhythmical poetry. After the second line in each strophe there is usually a 'sense pause', and, indeed, in the manuscripts the strophes are written as though composed of two long lines. There is, of course, a more emphatic pause at the end of each strophe, but, most important of all, after each two strophes there is a sense pause which can only be explained by the fact that the hymns were composed to be sung by alternate choirs.

The hymns of Ambrose formed the nucleus round which was collected the hymnary of the Church of Milan, or, as we are accustomed to call it, the Ambrosian hymnary. They were, indeed, an important element in the Western hymnaries as a whole. Benedict of Nursia, in his Rule, gave hymns a prominent place in the divine office by ordaining that at each canonical hour a certain hymn should be sung. But he merely says, 'Sequatur Ambrosianum' or 'hymnus eiusdem horae', leaving for us unsolved the problem of what hymns were actually in use. The question is one of unusual interest in view of the remarkable attempt of Father Blume to reconstruct the early Benedictine hymnal from the scanty sources now available.[3] He begins with the witness of Caesarius, Bishop of Arles, 503–43, who in his Rule for nuns, based for the most part (so he tells us) on the custom of Lérins, ordains the use of

---

[1] Ebert, i. 172; cf. i. 184: 'So antik diese Dichtung in ihren Anfängen in Bezug auf die Dichtungsform ist, so echt christlich ist sie sogleich in Bezug auf ihre Darstellung, die allein durch die neue Weltanschauung bedingt ist'.

[2] *Rythmik*, ii. 119, note 1.

[3] C. Blume, *Der Cursus S. Benedicti Nursini und die liturgischen Hymnen des 6-9 Jahrhunderts*, Leipzig 1908.

hymns and gives us the opening words of a substantial number. Aurelian, likewise, his second successor, gives a list of hymns in his Rules for the use of monks and nuns, confirming the list of Caesarius, and adding two other hymns. Now the group of hymns thus obtained, when compared with the hymns contained in five manuscript hymnaries, which, although written at a later date than the Rules of Caesarius and Aurelian, are among the oldest hymnaries before the tenth century (excluding those of Irish provenance), enables Father Blume to construct a list of some thirty-three hymns which may be taken, with some degree of accuracy, as forming a more or less complete hymnary such as we may imagine was used, at Arles and elsewhere, in the days of Benedict. Blume concludes almost at once that we have here in essence the original Benedictine hymnary; but a glance at the list shows that, apart from the hymns of Ambrose and one or two others, this group of hymns is entirely different in composition from the oldest hymnaries of Irish provenance, and from all the hymnaries written after the end of the ninth century. These latter form a group which grew into the Roman hymnal, as we know it to-day. So there are two lists, essentially different, the older and the later hymnal as they have been called,[1] or A and B, and Blume asks us for the following reasons to accept his thesis that the 'older' group represents the Benedictine hymnal:—

(i) Benedict, as is known, based his Rule, not on his free fancy, but with sound conservative instinct, on what had been tried before and found good. The manner in which he prescribes his hymns (e.g. *hymnus eiusdem horae*) shows that he was ordaining for his *Cursus* the hymns which were ordinarily in liturgical use.

(ii) With the aid of Caesarius and of Aurelian, combined with the witness of the earliest hymnaries before the end of the ninth century, we can construct a group of hymns which, in whole or in part, was definitely in use about the time of Benedict.

(iii) This list of hymns fits in well with the directions given in the Rule, if, as we are entitled to do, we translate 'Ambrosianum' as a 'hymn by S. Ambrose'.

(iv) If Caesarius transplanted the hymnary of Lérins to Arles, the same must, in all probability, have been done by other

---

[1] A. S. Walpole, *Early Latin Hymns*, Cambridge 1922, p. xi. Walpole accepts Blume's views.

bishops and abbots who left Lérins for Gaul and Northern Italy. Hence it is reasonable to assume that the hymnary of Arles gives us a picture of the use of other churches, and that within this list are to be found the hymns which Benedict prescribed in his *Cursus*.

(v) The hymns of this group are demonstrably older than those in the competing group, not only because the sources themselves are older, better, and more numerous, but because the hymnal of Group B in providing a hymn for each day of the week, not only for Lauds but also for Nocturns and Vespers, indicates a time when the canonical hours were more completely developed. Group B also displays the existence of a *Commune Sanctorum* entirely lacking in A.

For these and other reasons, we are to assume that Group A contains the Benedictine hymnary and that from Carolingian times onward it lost ground before the later group of northern origin, which under the influence of that liturgical movement associated with Alcuin, Amalar, and Helisachar, made its way with increasing success even at Rome itself, until it had completely ousted the older hymnal.[1]

The story is strange, and, as Blume presents it, it may appear convincing. But can the traditional and opposite theory be supported on the same facts? Dom Wilmart, a Benedictine, thinks that it can, and he has given a hint of the way in which the thesis can be defended, that the Roman and the Benedictine hymnary are and have been essentially one.[2] For him the community of content shown by the lists of Caesarius and Aurelian with the manuscripts of Group A points merely to one result. Group A represents a Gallican hymnary and nothing else, for its manuscripts have all a 'Gallican' origin, whether from Northern France or Belgium (Vatican. Reginensis 11), from Corbie (Paris 14068; saec. IX), from Murbach (Bodl.

---

[1] Blume attempted to explain further the success of hymnal B by endeavouring to associate it with Gregory the Great. He suggested that Gregory composed the Vesper hymns and arranged the hymnal for Irish and Anglo-Saxon use. Associated with his name, it returned eastwards during the period of Irish and Anglo-Saxon influence, and met with complete success. The question is discussed below, p. 124. Alcuin, Amalar, and Helisachar were liturgical reformers (of the missal and antiphonary), but they certainly had nothing to do with the introduction of a new hymnary. On Amalar, a pupil of Alcuin and *Chorepiscopus* of Metz, see article in Hauck, *Realencykl.*; on Helisachar, arch-chancellor of Louis the Pious, a Goth of Septimania, an abbot but not a monk, see Edmund Bishop, *Abbat Helisachar*, in *Liturgica Historica*, Oxford 1918, pp. 333 sqq.

[2] D. A. Wilmart, *Le Psautier de la Reine, N. xi, sa provenance et sa date*, in *Revue Bénédictine*, July–Oct. 1911, pp. 341 sqq.

Junius, 25, saec. IX), or Rheinau (Zurich, Bibl. Cantonale, n. 34, saec. IX). 'Le P. Blume a seulement reconnu et reconstitué le groupe des témoins de l'ancien usage gallican',[1] and he is not entitled to conclude that he has done anything more. In Italy we already know the Ambrosian hymnal, and in Spain the Mozarabic. Benedict used, it is admitted, an existent hymnal, one in monastic use; for the secular clergy, at any rate in Rome, do not appear to have accorded the hymn a permanent and effective place in their office.[2] When Benedict speaks of the 'Ambrosian' hymns, he no more than the fathers of Tours in 567 [3] can have really known which were the genuine hymns of Ambrose, and we cannot argue that he is prescribing, in any case, one of the hymns which we now know to be genuinely the work of the Bishop of Milan. So we have Group B, or rather its nucleus, the true Benedictine hymnary; alterations and addition it suffered, enriching itself in times of change in order to meet new needs, making its way in the very age of Benedictine expansion, until apart from Spain and Milan it had no rival. The Carolingian period saw at the same time the definite triumph of the Roman rite, although the Roman missal in Frankish hands 'assumed a form and embodied rites which Pope Hadrian, who sent it to Charles the Great, would not have recognized as his own'.[4] But this was not the case with the hymnary and for good reasons. It was not edited by Alcuin, Amalar, or Helisachar. Hymns were not a part of the office of the Roman secular clergy, and when the Roman office was introduced into the Carolingian empire, it would almost seem that they disappeared from the office of the secular clergy.[5] But the monks at any rate can hardly have abandoned them, and they soon returned to general use. The Benedictines must have been, as from the first, the chief influence in the maintenance of hymns as an integral part of the divine service. Is it not therefore, on the whole, simpler to suppose, even on the facts presented by Blume, that the original Benedictine hymnal persisted and triumphed, rather than that another hymnal, obscure in its origin and equally obscure in its progress, came

---

[1] ib., p. 362.
[2] Bäumer, i. 368; ii. 35.
[3] 'Licet hymnos Ambrosianos habeamus in canone, tamen quoniam reliquorum sunt aliqui, qui digni sunt forma cantari, volumus libenter amplecti eos praeterea, quorum auctorum nomina fuerint in limine praenotata' (Bäumer, ii. 34).
[4] E. Bishop, *The Genius of the Roman Rite, Liturgica Historica*, p. 15.
[5] So Bäumer, ii. 35, but his *ex silentio* argument refers only to Metz and Lyons.

'from the north', and won the Benedictines to abandon a hymnal associated so intimately and continuously with the *opus dei*? The expansion of Benedictinism, not merely by means of new foundations but by the gradual acceptance of the Rule by existing monasteries,[1] may explain, at any rate in part, the success of the Benedictine hymnary. But it is not safe to assume with too much confidence that Rule and hymnary went together. The Rule might be observed at Murbach in the ninth century,[2] but we may still find the scribes there copying the 'Gallican' hymnary. But the tide of observance was doubtless followed by the hymnary, as in England and Germany. About the middle of the seventh century the Rule was imposed at Lérins,[3] and in the seventh and eighth centuries the custom of Columbanus was yielding on every hand to Benedict's rule. The tendency to uniformity inherent in the reforms of Benedict of Aniane worked in the same direction, and, all things considered, it is not strange that the Gallican hymnary maintained itself with difficulty and finally disappeared.[4]

We have already seen that besides the genuine hymns of Ambrose, a number of other hymns composed in the same metre but of very unequal merit found their way into the hymnaries of various Churches in the West, especially in Italy, Gaul, and Spain. It was inevitable that these compositions should ultimately find a place in the office by the side of the older hymns. Although a few Churches resisted the innovation, the use of hymns rapidly made its way in the West; the Roman Church remaining, at first, an exception in its adhesion to the old tradition. Meanwhile, the development of the hymnary proceeded. Prudentius, Sedulius, Fortunatus, and the poets of the Carolingian renaissance were admitted, and the Irish Churches had flourishing native hymnaries of their own.

One of the best known and most beautiful of 'Ambrosian'

---

[1] M. Heimbucher, *Die Orden und Kongregationen der katholischen Kirche*, 2nd edit., Paderborn 1907, i. 190.

[2] ib., i. 227.

[3] ib., i. 174, 232. It is worth noting that Charles the Great obtained from Monte Cassino a true copy of Benedict's autograph of the Rule, and that other copies were made by his order for circulation: cf. *Chron. Benedictburanum, M. G. H.*, Ss. VII, p. 216, 'regulamque S. Benedicti patris de ipso codice, quem ipse suis sanctis manibus exaravit, transcriptum direxit'.

[4] Blume, p. 77, makes the point that the Vesper hymns of Group A regard Vespers as a *night*-office, thus pointing to an earlier date than those of B, which are composed for a *day*-office. This may be so; but as Benedict made Vespers a day-office (Bäumer, ii. 254), the Benedictine hymnal should reflect this fact, whereas the hymnal of Arles would not necessarily do so.

hymns is the *Te lucis ante terminum*, sung daily at Compline in the Roman Office:

te lucis ante terminum,
rerum creator, poscimus,
ut solita clementia
sis praesul ad custodiam.

procul recedant somnia
et noctium phantasmata,
hostemque nostrum comprime
ne polluantur corpora.[1]

Another famous 'Ambrosian' hymn is the *Ad coenam agni providi*, still sung, in sadly mutilated form, at Vespers from Easter to the Vigil of the Ascension:

ad coenam agni providi,
stolis albis candidi,
post transitum maris rubri
Christo canamus principi.

cuius sacrum corpusculum
in ara crucis torridum,
cruore eius roseo
gustando vivimus deo,

protecti paschae vespero
a devastante angelo,
erepti de durissimo
Pharaonis imperio.

iam pascha nostrum Christus est,
qui immolatus agnus est,
sinceritatis azyma
caro eius oblata est.

o vere digna hostia,
per quem fracta sunt tartara,
redempta plebs captivata,
reddita vitae praemia.

cum surgit Christus tumulo,
victor redit de barathro,
tyrannum trudens vinculo
et reserans paradisum.

quaesumus, auctor omnium,
in hoc paschali gaudio:
ab omni mortis impetu
tuum defendas populum.[2]

In this hymn the weakening of the old prosody, accompanied by frequent rime, shows the beginnings of the change from the quantitive poetry of Ambrose to the typical verse form of the Middle Ages.

§ 5. *Hilary of Poitiers; circa* A.D. 310–66.

If Ambrose of Milan is rightly regarded as the father of Catholic hymnody, because he created a school and a tradition which found a permanent place in the liturgy of the Church,

---

[1] *Anal. Hymn.* li, p. 42. [2] *Anal. Hymn.* li, p. 87.

yet Hilary of Poitiers before him had made a serious attempt at writing original hymns in the Latin tongue. The attempt was a failure, as none of Hilary's compositions achieved the popularity of those of Ambrose or found its way into the Breviaries of later times. Indeed, the 'liber hymnorum', which, on the evidence of Jerome,[1] was composed by Hilary, has been lost, and not until 1884 were fragments of it brought to light by Gamurrini.[2] Hilary was one of the most important fathers of the fourth century. Born of heathen parents, he was converted to Christianity and became bishop of his native city of Poitiers. Pagan philosophy had been his schoolmaster to bring him to Christ, and he was above all a teacher and a theologian. The work of his life was directed to the defence of the orthodox Trinitarian doctrine against the Arians, and his zeal brought him into conflict with the Arian Emperor Constantius, who banished him to Asia Minor. His stay in the East brought him into intimate relation with the richer culture and learning of the Greek Churches, and there he must have conceived the idea of introducing a Latin hymnody into the West. In 360 he returned from exile and devoted himself with success to the purging of Gaul from the heresy of Arius.

The three surviving fragments of the hymns of Hilary do not convey an impression of poetical genius, but they are of considerable interest to the student of the beginnings of Christian-Latin verse. They are metrical in character, allowing a not infrequent *hiatus*; further they are obscurely phrased and therefore ill-adapted to congregational purposes. The first is an alphabetical hymn on Hilary's favourite subject of the Trinitarian faith. It begins:

> ante saecula qui manes
> semperque nate, semper ut est pater!—
> namque te sine quomodo
> dici, ni pater est, quod pater sit, potest?—
> bis nobis genite deus,
> Christe! dum innato nasceris a deo
> vel dum corporeum et deum
> mundo te genuit virgo puerpera:

---

[1] *De viris illustr.* 100, Migne, xxiii, col. 701; cf. Isidore, *De eccles. officiis,* i. 6; Migne, lxxxiii, col. 743.
[2] Text in Feder, *C. S. E. L.,* lxv, pp. 209 sqq.; *Anal. Hymn.* l, pp. 1 sqq. The *Lucis largitor splendide,* and the *Ad caeli clara non sum dignus sidera,* often ascribed to Hilary, are not his work. But in the *Bangor Antiphonary,* a further hymn, *Hymnum dicat turba fratrum,* is attributed to Hilary, and it may indeed be his; see A. J. Mason, *J. T. S.,* v. 413 sqq.; Walpole, *J. T. S.,* vi. 599 sqq.

> credens te populus rogat,
> hymnorum resonas mitis ut audias
> voces, quas tibi concinit
> aetas omnigena, sancte, gregis tui.
>
> dum te fida rogat, sibi
> clemens ut maneas, plebs tui nominis
> in te, innascibilem deum
> orat, quod maneat alter in altero.[1]

The third and fourth stanzas show that the hymn was intended for liturgical purposes. The second hymn, also alphabetical, is, perhaps, the confession of the newly baptized soul which has been freed from the dominion of sin—

> renata sum, o vitae laeta exordia!
> novisque vivo christiana legibus.

—but Ebert has argued, somewhat inconclusively, that the speaker is a woman, and that the hymn cannot therefore be ascribed to Hilary.[2] The last hymn, in trochaic tetrameters, celebrates the victory of the second Adam over the power of evil.

> Adae carnis gloriosa et caduci corporis [3]
> in caelesti rursum Adam concinamus proelia,
> per quae primum satanas est Adam victus in novo.
>
> hostis fallax saeculorum et dirae mortis artifex
> iam consiliis toto in orbe viperinis consitis
> ad salutem nil restare spei humanae existimat.
>
> gaudet aris, gaudet templis, gaudet sanie victimae;
> gaudet falsis, gaudet stupris, gaudet belli sanguine;
> gaudet caeli conditorem ignorari gentibus.

So the hymn drags on, tedious and prosaic to the end of the fragment. Enough has been quoted to show why the hymns of Hilary failed to survive beside the simple and vigorous compositions of Ambrose. But his theological writings more than held their own throughout the whole of the Middle Ages, and his prose is remarkably vigorous.[4]

---

[1] Feder, p. 209; *Anal. Hymn.* l, p. 4.
[2] Ebert, i. 142.
[3] This line is corrupt; Dreves reads 'gloriam'; Dr. Mason suggests 'Adae cernuata gloria et caduci corporis'; Meyer reads 'gloriosa', which Feder adopts in his text, and I have followed him.
[4] Norden, *Antike Kunstprosa*, ii. 583.

PRUDENTIUS, A.D. 348–405 (*circa*).

§ 1. *The Cathemerinon.*

THE first great Christian poet was a fellow countryman of Seneca and Lucan. Aurelius Prudentius Clemens[1] was born in Spain, probably at Saragossa, in the year 348. In the verses, which he composed as a kind of preface to his collected works, he gives some scanty information about the events of his life.[2] He tells how in boyhood he wept under the rod of the schoolmaster, learning no doubt his Virgil and Horace, how when he had put on the manly toga, he acquired, like Augustine, the deceitful rhetoric of the schools and followed the wanton ways of youth; how he became twice a magistrate, 'dispensing civil justice to the good and terrifying evil doers'. So his life proceeded quietly in prosperous Spain, while great things went on in the world outside. His memory reached back to the days of Julian the Apostate,[3] and he witnessed part of the impressive change from the pagan to the Christian Empire. He may possibly have been called to Rome when Theodosius honoured him with an office at court.[4] In any case, we know that he paid a visit to the capital and that the imperial city with its monuments and memories of the past, its new Christian basilicas, and above all its sacred places of pilgrimage, the tombs of apostle and martyr, profoundly im-

---

[1] *Carmina*, ed. J. Bergman, *C.S.E.L.*, xli; ed. M. Lavarenne, Paris, 1943–51; ed. H. J. Thomson, vol. i, London, 1949; on Prudentius see Boissier, *Fin du paganisme*, ii. 105 sqq.; Glover, *Life and Letters in the Fourth Century*, pp. 249 sqq.; F. St. J. Thackeray, *Translations from Prudentius*, Texts, Introd., and notes, London 1890, is worth consulting.

[2] Manitius, *Christl. lat. Poesie* (p. 62), calls it 'Der lebendige und mit rhetorischem Pathos wohl versehene Prolog'; M. Boissier, *Fin du paganisme* (ii. 123),

finds it 'mélancolique'.

[3] *Apotheosis*, 449 sqq. For an analysis of the Prologue, with full discussion, see J. Bergman, *Aurelius Prudentius Clemens*, pp. 31 sqq.

[4] *Prologus*, 19 'militiae gradu evectum'; cf. Manitius, p. 63; Glover (p. 252) suggests that *militia* simply means the civil service and that the office was not military. The view is now generally accepted that it was a civil office. See Bergman, op. cit., pp. 40 sqq., where the point is dealt with in detail.

pressed him. He is filled with the sense of the superiority of Rome as compared with the barbarian world :

> sed tantum distant Romana et barbara, quantum
> quadrupes abiuncta est bipedi vel muta loquenti,
> quantum etiam, qui rite dei praecepta sequuntur,
> cultibus a stolidis et eorum erroribus absunt.[1]

Now, in his fifty-seventh year, he looks back upon it all, and sadly realizes, with old age upon him, that most things are vanity :

> numquid talia proderunt
> carnis post obitum vel bona vel mala,
> cum iam, quidquid id est, quod fueram, mors aboleverit?

So, before he dies, he will praise God, if not by virtuous deeds, at least in song :

> hymnis continuet dies,
> nec nox ulla vacet, quin dominum canat.

The lyrical poems of Prudentius are collected under the titles *Cathemerinon* and *Peristephanon*. The former is a series of 'hymns for the Christian's day', which are much too long ever to have been, like those of Ambrose, intended for congregational use, though the first six might well have served for private devotion. Parts of them, however, found their way into Church use, and have become one of the glories of the Catholic hymnary.

In the *Cathemerinon* Prudentius shows an easy mastery of familiar classical metres. The great merit of the poems is their vigour and grace, even where the subject-matter might seem to be somewhat tedious. Now and again, in reading them, we seem to breathe the air of an earlier time, when the faith was young and full of hope. In the *Hymn for the Burial of the Dead* the bright clear atmosphere of hope is that which Walter Pater imagined when he pictured the Christian children chanting the *Laudate pueri dominum!* over the grave of their dead companion.[2] These verses of Prudentius remain, as a lover of Christian hymns has said, 'the crowning glory' of his verse.[3]

> iam moesta quiesce querela,   sic semina sicca virescunt,
> lacrimas suspendite, matres,   iam mortua iamque sepulta,
> nullus sua pignora plangat,   quae reddita caespite ab imo
> mors haec reparatio vitae est.   veteres meditantur aristas.

[1] *Contra Symm.* ii. 816–19.
[2] *Marius the Epicurean*, ii. 188.
[3] Archbishop Trench, *Sacred Latin Poetry*, London 1874, p. 287 ; *Cathemerinon*, x.

nunc suscipe, terra, fovendum,
gremioque hunc concipe molli :
hominis tibi membra sequestro,
generosa et fragmina credo.

nec, si vaga flamina et aurae,
vacuum per inane volantes,
tulerint cum pulvere nervos,
hominem periisse licebit.

animae fuit haec domus olim,
factoris ab ore creatae,
fervens   habitavit in istis
sapientia principe Christo.

sed dum resolubile corpus
revocas, deus, atque reformas,
quanam regione iubebis
animam requiescere puram ?

tu depositum tege corpus,
non immemor ille requiret
sua munera fictor et auctor,
propriique aenigmata vultus.

gremio senis addita sancti
recubabit, ut est Eleazar,
quem floribus undique septum
dives procul aspicit ardens.

veniant modo tempora iusta,
cum spem deus impleat omnem,
reddas patefacta necesse est,
qualem tibi trado figuram.

sequimur tua dicta, Redemptor,
quibus atra morte triumphans,
tua per vestigia mandas
socium crucis ire latronem.

non si cariosa vetustas
dissolverit ossa favillis,
fueritque cinisculus arens
minimi mensura pugilli :

patet ecce fidelibus ampli
via lucida iam Paradisi,
licet et nemus illud adire,
homini quod ademerat anguis.

nos tecta fovebimus ossa
violis et fronde frequente,
titulumque et frigida saxa
liquido spargemus odore.

In connexion with this poem we may note some points of religious interest. The resurrection of the *flesh* had become a Christian dogma and the pious care of the bones of the dead was enjoined as a matter of supreme importance, for the self-same body, laid in the earth, must rise again at the last day. The fear lest the violation of a grave should hinder the resurrection was very real to Christians who were brought up under the influence of heathen ideas of the importance of burial for securing entry into the home of the dead.   Hence the following pathetic inscription on a Christian tomb: 'Adiuro vos omnes christiani ... per domino et per tremenda die iudicii ut hunc sepulchrum violari nunquam permittatis sed conservetur usque ad finem mundi ut possim sine impedimento in vita redire cum venerit qui iudicaturus est vivos et mortuos.'[1]   Another fear was lest the destruction of the corpse by fire should likewise

[1] Le Blant, *Mémoire sur les martyrs chrétiens et les supplices destructeurs du corps : Mémoires de l'Institut National de* *France, Académie des Inscriptions et Belles-Lettres*, Tome 28 (1876), p. 87 (quoted in Lucius, *Heiligenkult*, p. 25, note 3).

hinder resurrection in the day of the Lord. But the Church laid this fear at rest, and Prudentius in these verses maintains the Christian hope; it is the power of God which will call back the fragile body out of the dust and make it once more a dwelling for the soul.

This care for the dead was dictated, in part, by the old feeling that they were very near, and did not wholly forsake the place where their body was laid.[1] Like the heathen, the Christians were apt to regard their dead as beings to be propitiated or capable of aiding their former friends and relations.[2] While some believed that the dead departed to an intermediate state, the more common belief was that the departed souls were received at once into heaven, 'in domo aeterna dei', as an inscription says.[3] The orthodox view is set forth by Prudentius in a manner which suggests that his aim is to allay the possible doubts of. any of his readers and to present for their assurance the Catholic doctrine of the resurrection. Indeed, all through the poem runs the thread of doctrine, but not with sufficient intrusiveness to affect the beauty of the verse. It would be true, indeed, to say that the whole of the poetry of Prudentius is coloured by this doctrinal intention. He is first a Catholic, and only in the second place a poet. In the ' Hymn for every Hour ',[4] he sets forth the Christ of Theology, the Saviour sung by the prophets, the Alpha and Omega, the creative Word who took upon Himself our nature, healed the sick and raised the dead; who fed the hungry with earthly and with heavenly bread; who suffered on the Cross, descended into Hades, rose from the dead, and is to come again to judge the world. This attractive poem, written in trochaic tetrameters which move with a solemn measure, has given a famous Christian hymn to the Breviary. The best known verses are:

corde natus ex parentis, ante mundi exordium
Alpha et Ω cognominatus, ipse fons et clausula
omnium, quae sunt, fuerunt quaeque post futura sunt.
    ipse iussit et creata, dixit ipse et facta sunt
terra, caelum, fossa ponti, trina rerum machina
quaeque in his vigent sub alto solis et lunae globo.
. . . o beatus ortus ille, virgo cum puerpera
edidit nostram salutem feta sancto spiritu
et puer redemptor orbis os sacratum protulit.

[1] Lucius, *Heiligenkult*, p. 28. [3] ib., p. 31, note 1.
[2] ib., p. 32. [4] *Cath.* ix.

> psallat altitudo caeli, psallite omnes angeli,
> quidquid est virtutis usquam psallat in laudem dei:
> nulla linguarum silescat, vox et omnis consonet.
>   ecce quem vates vetustis concinebant seculis,
> quem prophetarum fideles paginae spoponderant,
> emicat promissus olim: cuncta conlaudent eum.

The *Hymn for the Epiphany* [1] is known for those pathetic verses which picture the Innocents, the first martyrs of Christ, gathered up to heaven, and there by the side of God's altar, playing, childlike, with the palms and crowns which are the tokens of their reward.

> salvete flores martyrum,
> quos lucis ipso in limine
> Christi insecutor sustulit,
> ceu turbo nascentes rosas:
>
> vos prima Christi victima,
> grex immaculatorum tener,
> aram ante ipsam simplices
> palma et coronis luditis.

One interest of the *Cathemerinon* arises from the fact that it shows how Christian poetry was learning to make use of the new 'mythology' which was derived for the most part from Old Testament legend. The masters of Prudentius were the classical Roman poets, but their mythology was forbidden to a Christian singer, though later poets, like Fortunatus and Ennodius, born in days when it might seem to be less harmful, could not refrain from using it in their more secular verses. The Old Testament supplied an immense fund of material for the construction of a new mythology, especially as the Christian imagination, since the days of Paul, had learned to see everywhere in the book of the old covenant the type and symbol of the new. Mythology and symbolism go hand in hand in the *Cathemerinon*.[2] In the *Hymn at Cock-crow* the cock is the symbol of Christ, who awakes us to life;[3] the sparrows twittering under the eaves before the dawn are the figure of the Judge; sleep is the type of death and darkness represents

---

[1] *Cath.* xii.

[2] Cf. Manitius, *Christl. lat. Poesie*, p. 65, who indicates the indebtedness of Prudentius to Ambrose; and Ebert, i. 252 and 254; Ambrose in turn had borrowed largely from Clement and Origen.

[3] *Cath.* i. 1; cf. i. 29–32 ; also verse 2 of Ambrose's hymn *Aeterne rerum conditor*; on the cock as a symbol in early Christian art, see Kraus, *Gesch. der christl. Kunst*, i. 111; Kaufmann, *Handbuch der christlichen Archäologie*, p. 287.

the dreadful night of sin. In the *Morning Hymn*[1] the light of day is the symbol of Christ, the *oriens ex alto*, the dayspring from on high. In the third hymn the dove and the lamb are types of Christ,[2] who appears again (*Cath.* viii. 33-52) as the Good Shepherd, clothed with all the youthful beauty of the famous picture from the Catacombs. Recounting the miracle of the loaves, Prudentius reminds us that Christ is the true Bread:

> tu cibus panisque noster, tu perennis suavitas.[3]

The water and the blood of the crucifixion are signs, the water of cleansing, the blood of the martyrs' crown.[4] The familiar symbolism of the gifts of the Magi is expounded in the *Hymn for the Epiphany*:

> regem deumque adnuntiant
> thesaurus et fragrans odor
> turis Sabaei, ac myrrheus
> pulvis sepulcrum praedocet.[5]

The most detailed symbolic exposition occurs in the last hymn.[6] There Moses is shown as the perfect type of Christ. His escape as a child from the decree of Pharaoh prefigures the flight of Jesus from Herod; like Christ, he was a priest; like Christ, the giver of the Law; he saved Israel from the yoke of Pharaoh, Christ saved us from the bondage of death; Moses, upon the mountain, defeating with outstretched arms the hosts of Amalek, prefigures the Christ who stretched out his arms upon the Cross for the salvation of men.

Viewing the *Cathemerinon* as a whole, we are impressed with its *literary* character. As Ebert has said, Prudentius took the Ambrosian hymn and gave it the character of a Christian ode, divorcing it from a merely liturgical aim and making it a literary product.[7] In this, as in the *Peristephanon*, which we have next to consider, Prudentius showed a measure of originality which separates him from the mass of Christian poets.

---

[1] *Cath.* ii. 4; cf. v. 153.
[2] ib., iii. 166.
[3] ib., ix. 61; this is already symbolic in John vi; see Schmiedel, *The Johannine Writings*, pp. 97-8 (London 1908).
[4] ib., ix. 87.
[5] ib., xii. 69.
[6] ib., xii. 144 sqq.
[7] Ebert, i. 291; cf. Boissier, *Fin du paganisme*, ii. 146.

§ 2. *The Peristephanon and the Cult of the Martyrs.*

Less beautiful than the *Cathemerinon*, but considerably richer in historical interest, is the *Peristephanon*, a collection of fourteen poems, chiefly in well-known lyric metres, in honour of Spanish, African, and Roman martyrs. Its importance arises from the fact that it presents a new genus of poem, a combination of the epic and lyric which can almost be described as a ballad. If we except Pope Damasus, whose epigrams were known to our poet, and Ambrose, who wrote hymns in honour of several martyrs, Prudentius was the first to praise them in verse. He celebrates in detail, and with all the additions suggested by tradition and popular imagination, the miracles and the sufferings of the Christian martyrs. The poems were obviously not intended for liturgical purposes, though some of them appear in full in the Mozarabic Breviary. Written for the most part in com-plicated lyrical metres, they could only have been intended for educated readers of the middle class, who had been trained to appreciate the classical poets and needed a Christian literature to wean them away from the corrupting influences of the pagan authors. Prudentius wrote them for a literary public, and for his fellow countrymen, since he concerns himself mainly with Spanish martyrs and those whose tombs he had visited in a journey to Italy and whose cults he was anxious to see established in the cities of Spain.[1] But, more than once, the personal note appears. The poet hoped, by celebrating the deeds of the martyrs and by helping to further their cult, to secure their powerful aid and intercession in this world and the next. So he addresses S. Laurence, the 'eternal consul' of heavenly Rome, and begs that he too may be included in the protection which the saint affords to the children of his persecutors :

> hos inter, O Christi decus,
> audi poetam rusticum
> cordis fatentem crimina
> et facta prodentem sua.
> . . . audi benignus supplicem
> Christi reum Prudentium,
> et servientem corpori
> absolve vinclis seculi.[2]

---

[1] Cf. *Peristeph.* xi. 233.
[2] ib., ii. 573–85 ; cf. x. 1136 ; ix. 3 ; iii. 206.

In his devotion to the martyrs, Prudentius was a true child of his age, and it is to his zeal for their honour that we owe the welcome light which his poems throw on one of the most important developments of post-Constantinian Christianity.

Like so many other characteristic features of Christian worship and practice, the cult of the martyrs has its roots far back in the second century. Already in the Apocalypse a special position is assigned to the witnesses of the faith who have given their lives for its sake. 'Therefore are they before the throne of God, and serve Him day and night in His temple, and He that sitteth upon the throne shall dwell among them.' But the Christian imagination as yet busied itself but little with the stories of their sufferings. Such accounts as have survived, like those of the martyrdom of Polycarp, the Acts of Perpetua and Felicitas, or the letter of the Church at Lyons, are, on the whole, faithful accounts, written too closely under the shadow of the terror to wander far into the miraculous or the wonderful.[1] It was the persecution of Diocletian which created out of the sufferings of the martyrs the Christian legend. The new conception of the martyr, which was to dominate the whole middle ages, was the creation of the post-Constantinian Church. The persecution of Diocletian, so wide and far-reaching in its effects, made a profound impression on the Christian imagination. It became the type after which all persecutions were imaged; the whole pre-Constantinian epoch was envisaged by its light.[2] The intensity of the persecution and the sufferings of the victims were exaggerated, and the whole period of the life of the Church from its beginnings was regarded as full of persecution and prolific in martyrdoms. 'Repleta est terra martyribus', says Augustine. The calm demeanour of the historical martyr, typified by the noble figure of Polycarp, gives place to a new conception; the martyr of the Christian legend took on those features which the Middle Ages loved and cherished. The martyr has become the aggressive soldier of the faith. Fearless, uncompromising, proud, and violent, he is always master of the situation. He is strong; his enemies are feeble. No torture can daunt him; the malice of his judges is powerless even to devise a torture which can produce more than a contemptuous

---

[1] The same is true of the early and 'authentic' *Acts* of the martyrs, in general, e.g. the Passion of Perpetua and Felicitas; see H. Günter, *Legenden-Studien*, p. 7, Köln 1906; also the minute studies of A. Dufourcq, *Les Gesta martyrum romains*, especially i. 67 sqq., Paris 1900.
[2] Lucius, *Heiligenkult*, pp. 79–80.

smile.   In the agony of death, he calmly addresses his tormentors, often at tedious length.   Miracle follows miracle, and the
end comes only when he has said enough and is anxious to
depart and claim his crown.[1]   The martyr is the warrior of
God.[2]   His enemies are not the judges and the heathen crowd.
They are the demons, the perpetual enemies of the Christian
flock ; the powers whom Christ came to destroy.   Following
Paul, each generation of Christians knew that the apparent
struggle with flesh and blood was not the real struggle.   The
true battle was with the unseen powers, surrounding the believer
night and day.   So, quoting Paul, Prudentius says, in his
Hamartigenia :

> errat, ait, qui luctamen cum sanguine nobis
> et carne et venis ferventibus et vitioso
> felle putat, calidisque animam peccare medullis !
> . . . sed cum spiritibus tenebrosis nocte dieque
> congredimur, quorum dominatibus humidus iste
> et pigris densus nebulis obtemperat aer.[3]

The devil is therefore one of the protagonists in this immense
conflict, and God is the other.   They are the leaders each of
an army, the one of demons and the other of martyrs, and the
victory of the latter is a victory over the heathen gods, who,
as always, are identified with the powers of darkness.   This
presentation of the story of the Christian martyrs, embodied
to some extent in the panegyrics of great Christian rhetoricians,
like Basil and Chrysostom, and fully developed in the later *Acts*,
is closely followed by Prudentius, who in some instances has
merely translated into poetry the text of what Delehaye has
described as ' epic ' passions,[4] for in them the martyr is the hero
of an epic conflict.   There is the same picture of the cruel
judge [5] ; the long dialogue between the latter and his victim ;
the series of unavailing torments, each more terrible than the
last ; but always the martyr mocks his tormentors, encourages
them to persevere in their hopeless task, and, after the usual
miracles, his soul is taken to heaven.

---

[1] On the lack of historical sense shown
in the accounts of the martyrdoms see
Allard, *L'hagiographie au IVᵉ siècle*
(*Revue des Questions historiques*, 1885,
xxxvii, p. 356).

[2] Cf. *Peristeph.* ii. 17.

[3] *Hamartigenia*, 509-16 ; so, Perpetua
fights with the devil in a dream, *Passio*

Perpetuae et Felicitatis, 10 (*Texts and
Studies*, i. 76, Camb. 1891).

[4] Delehaye, *Les Passions des Martyrs*,
pp. 238, 312 ; Lucius, *Heiligenkult*, p. 83,
note 4 ; 185, note 3 ; Allard, *L'hagiographie au IVᵉ siècle*, p. 355 ; *Peristeph.*
v. 347 ' ut fert vetustas conscia ' ; xiv. 57.

[5] *Peristeph.* vi. 34.

Laurence, the Roman deacon, while being roasted on the gridiron, makes a grim joke to his tormentors:

> converte partem corporis
> satis crematum iugiter,
> et fac periclum, quid tuus
> Vulcanus ardens egerit.
>   praefectus inverti iubet.
> tunc ille: 'Coctum est, devora,
> et experimentum cape,
> sit crudum an assum suavius.'
>   haec ludibundus dixerat.[1]

Romanus, after his tongue has been torn out by the roots, continues to speak and at great length declaims against the iniquities of heathen superstition, and especially against the *Taurobolium* of the priests of Attis.[2]

By virtue of their sufferings and death the martyrs enter at once victoriously into their reward and obtain their crown. Their place is by the throne of God and they 'follow the Lamb'. Hence they are able to succour with their prayers those who call upon them for deliverance from sin, for earthly benefits, or for forgiveness in the day of judgement. This idea naturally established itself more deeply when, with Constantine's conversion, the Empire became Christian, and the Church received into its fold the great masses of the population who had been reared in heathendom and were familiar with the cult of the dead and of heroes.[3] In entering the new religion they demanded of it and obtained more than they had demanded of the old. Instead of their gods and heroes, they had recourse to the martyrs in all their troubles and their affairs of everyday life. The actual grave of the martyr, or the place where one of his relics was laid, formed a centre of supernatural power, the spot where he was specially present and able to hear and answer the prayers of his supplicants. Hence the great vogue of pilgrimages which had begun already in the days of Prudentius. He himself visited the tombs of the Apostles and of the Roman martyrs, and poured out his prayers and tears before the altar of S. Cassian, the martyred schoolmaster of Imola.[4] The remains

---

[1] ib., ii. 401-9.

[2] *Peristeph.* x. 1011; the *Taurobolium*, or bath of bull's blood, was a rite of initiation. Here the reference is to a public and annual ceremony; see Loisy, *Les mystères païens*, pp. 117 sqq. A similar attack on the *Taurobolium* is contained in a fourth-century poem, printed in Riese, *Anth. Lat.* i. 13 sqq.

[3] Lucius, pp. 105 sqq.

[4] *Peristeph.* ix. 99.

of Fructuosus,[1] Augurius, and Eulogius, the martyrs of Tarraco, were seized, after the martyrdom, by their faithful friends, who wished to keep them as relics and charms against the power of the demons. But the body of a martyr was sacred, and the bones must be collected together, for without them he could not appear at the last day. So, says Prudentius, the martyrs appeared to their friends, clad in white robes, and bade them restore the relics and place them together in a marble tomb.[2] So important, from the point of view of the cult, was the possession of the martyr's body, and so great was the fame which accrued to a church from the presence of such a source of miracle and wonder, that graves of all kinds were opened in the hope of discovering bodily remains which, by any possible stretch of the imagination, could be held to belong to those who had suffered for Christ.[3] Prudentius lived in the full tide of this popular devotion to the martyrs, and from his *Peristephanon* alone the main lines of its development could be laid down. These poems are particularly interesting because they throw a vivid light on the Spanish Christianity of his day. How proud he is of the Spanish martyrs, the spiritual protectors and patrons of the cities he loved and knew!—of Calahorra, Saragossa, Tarragona, and Merida. Spain is for him Christian Spain, and the number of martyrs each city can boast is the best guarantee of its safety in the day of judgement. Above all the cities of Spain, rivalling Carthage and Rome itself, Saragossa,

Caesaraugusta studiosa Christi,

where 'Christ dwells in every street, Christ is everywhere', shall appear at the last day, with the other cities, bearing the relics of its martyrs, and shall obtain a special grace.[4] Side by side with this Spanish patriotism goes that feeling for Rome, the mother and ruler of the human race, once great under her kings and conquerors, now rendered more venerable than ever by the reflected glory of apostles and martyrs.[5]

---

[1] See Harnack, *Mission*, ii. 300; Delehaye, *Les Passions*, p. 144, where the *Passio Fructuosi*, which Prudentius and Augustine knew, is signalized as a document containing some valuable and contemporary elements.

[2] *Peristeph.* vi. 130 sqq.; see also the *Acts* of S. Fructuosus in *Bibliotheca hagiographica Latina*, 3196, no. 6, Brussels 1899.

[3] Lucius, *Heiligenkult*, p. 150; Delehaye, *Les Passions*, p. 108.

[4] *Peristeph.* iv. 1 sqq.; cf. vi. 157; on the Spanish martyrs and the hagiographical value of the *Peristephanon*, see Delehaye, *Les Passions*, pp. 412 sqq.

[5] *Peristeph.* ii. 1–15, 541; cf. Allard, *Rome au IVe siècle, Revue des Questions historiques*, xxxvi. 10–11; Delehaye, *Les Passions*, p. 309.

vix fama nota est, abditis
quam plena sanctis Roma sit,
quam dives urbanum solum
sacris sepulchris floreat.

In his poem on the Passion of Peter and Paul, Prudentius describes the crowds which flocked to Rome to celebrate their festival,[1] and in the verses on the Passion of Hippolytus he tells how, at the yearly feast, the martyr was honoured by a vast concourse, from Rome and Alba and Tuscany.

exultant fremitus variarum hinc inde viarum,
    indigena et Picens plebs et Etrusca venit.
concurrit Samnitis atrox habitator et altae
    campanus Capuae iamque Nolanus adest.[2]

But Rome, 'aurea Roma',[3] as Prudentius calls her, was still involved in her pagan past. In the fourth century, she stood at the parting of the ways. The old temples still dominated the city in their imperial splendour and existed side by side with the Christian basilicas.[4] Prudentius longed for the time when Christ would be the undisputed king of Rome, and the demons, with Jove at their head, would finally be cast forth. This explains the long polemics against the heathen gods which he has inserted in the *Peristephanon*. The poem devoted to the martyrdom of Romanus contains a long defence of the Christian position against paganism, with its sacred chickens, its immoral *Lupercalia*, its degrading fables of gods and goddesses, the indecency of its mystery cults and the prostitution of its beautiful art in the cause of idolatry and error.[5]

It will be gathered from what has been said that the main interest of the *Peristephanon* lies in its value as an historical document which throws a vivid light on the critical period of change from the pagan to the Christian world. In these poems

[1] *Peristeph.* xii.

[2] ib., xi. 205–8 ; on Prudentius' account of Hippolytus, see A. d'Alès, *La théologie de S. Hippolyte*, pp. xi sqq., Paris 1906. The original Hippolytus, celebrated at Rome on Aug. 13, is the famous author of the *Philosophoumena*; but, in the confused traditions recorded by Damasus and reflected by Prudentius, he became Bishop of Porto and a temporary adherent of the Novatian schism. Actually, he was Antipope, 217–235, and rehabilitated himself by martyrdom.

[3] On the epithet *aurea*, which Ausonius and many medieval writers applied to Rome, see Graf, *Roma nella memoria del medio evo*, i. 6, Turin 1882.

[4] Cf. Allard, *Revue des Quest. hist.* xxxvi. 5 ; cf. *Contra Symm.* i. 225.

[5] *Peristeph.* x. 123–271.

the student of hagiography can sometimes trace the original tradition,[1] while the student of religions is grateful for details such as those which Prudentius affords concerning the *Taurobolium* and other religious ceremonies. The topographical details, scattered over the poems which deal with the Roman martyrs, are of great archaeological interest, because they come from one who had wandered devotedly among the monuments of Christian Rome—the Basilica near the grave of Hippolytus, the catacombs, the churches of Peter and Paul, the Baptistery of the Vatican. The description of Cassian's *martyrium* at Forum Cornelii, with its picture of the unhappy schoolmaster stabbed to death by the *stili* of his revengeful pupils, is extremely vivid. The poet had halted at Imola, Forum Cornelii, a colony of Sulla's, on the way to Rome, and he visited the martyr's tomb to make his prayers to Christ for a prosperous journey. As he knelt before the tomb, he looked up and saw the brilliant mosaic which depicted the sufferings of the saint. The verger approached him and told him the story represented above. 'I embrace the tomb, my tears flow, the altar and stone are wet with my weeping. . . . I murmur my hopes and fears, my home so far behind me, and my desire of good fortune to be. My prayers are heard, I reach Rome in safety, all goes well: I see my home again and give praise to Cassian.'[2]

But such lively and personal touches are rare. The *Peristephanon* is laden with rhetoric, and rarely rises to passages of lyrical beauty like those which are the charm of the *Cathemerinon*. The same skill, the same mastery of metre are there, but the plainer treatment of a narrative, the more popular qualities required by what is almost a ballad, make the *Peristephanon* less attractive from the purely literary standpoint than the *Cathemerinon*. But, as M. Boissier says, in a brilliant chapter of his *Fin du paganisme*,[3] there are, in the *Peristephanon*, lines of splendid poetry which possess 'the amplitude and purity of the masterpieces of classic verse'. Such a passage, says that distinguished historian, is found in the opening of the poem on the martyrs of Saragossa :

---

[1] Allard, *Revue des Quest. hist.* xxxvii. 359.

[2] ix. 99–106; Delehaye, *Les Passions*, pp. 407 sqq., suggests that Prudentius was the first to codify the tradition which had grown up round the basilica at Imola, thus fixing the version which made Cassian a schoolmaster martyred by his pupils. His poem was used as a basis for later prose passions of Cassian.

[3] ii. 125.

cum deus dextram quatiens coruscam
nube subnixus veniet rubente,
gentibus iustam positurus aequo
    pondere libram.

orbe de magno caput excitata
obviam Christo properanter ibit
civitas quaeque pretiosa portans
    dona canistris.[1]

It is the picture of the last judgement painted in 'hues of earthquake and eclipse', and if the verse has classical qualities of form, the spirit is Catholic and medieval. This is true of those lines in the *Cathemerinon* which ring like an earlier *Dies Irae*, for all their classical form :

cum vasta signum buccina
terris cremandis miserit,
et scissus axis cardinem
mundi ruentis solverit.[2]

We have already pointed out the literary character of the *Cathemerinon*. This character is shared equally by the *Peristephanon*, and indeed by all the poetry of Prudentius. In an age when, at any rate for those who had been brought up in the public schools, poetry was literature *par excellence*,[3] Prudentius was the first great representative of a real Christian literature. Juvencus indeed preceded him, but the *Historia Evangelica* is the work of a facile versifier and has no claim to intrinsic literary importance.[4] Prudentius, on the other hand, is an artist with sure command over his form and material. His poems are the self-conscious products of a literary age, a blending of the poetical form derived from generations of aesthetic activity with the new content of Christian thought, itself rooted in a strange and manifold development from the past. Hence the two elements which stand out in his poetry, which we may call the classical and the catholic. The classical is derived from the educational tradition in which he was brought up, the tradition of the schools of grammar and rhetoric. But as a Catholic, he is thoroughly a man of the new order. For him art is the minister of truth, and truth is nothing but the orthodox faith. For him Photinus and Arius are 'grim wolves',[5] and heresy

---

[1] *Peristeph.* iv. 9–16.
[2] *Cath.* xi. 105–8.
[3] Cf. Boissier, *Fin du paganisme*, ii.
146.
[4] See Ebert, i. 117.
[5] Cf. *Psychomachia*, 794.

is worse than heathendom. The first requirement, therefore, is that his verses shall express sound doctrine and tend to the edification of the faithful. It is significant that his other poems, the *Psychomachia*, the *Apotheosis*, the *Hamartigenia*, and the *Contra Symmachum*, are all either polemical or theological in character, and it is these that we have next to study.

§ 3. *The Apotheosis, Hamartigenia, Psychomachia, Contra Symmachum, and Dittochaeon.*

The *Apotheosis* is devoted to the true doctrine of the incarnation and the refutation of heretical opinions on the nature of Christ. It seeks to establish the divinity of Christ as the guarantee of salvation and the assurance of the redemption of soul and body at the last day. This long poem, of more than a thousand hexameters, is prefaced by a lyrical introduction of alternate iambic trimeters and dimeters, in which the poet addresses Christ on the difficulty of following the true faith without wandering into heresy. In the main poem, Prudentius attacks in turn the Patripassians who held that God had suffered on the Cross; the Sabellians who did not distinguish the Son from the Father; the Jews who refused to recognize their Saviour; the Ebionites who saw in Jesus only a virtuous man and a prophet; the hated Manichees whose docetism deprived the redemption of its reality.

The material of the poem is not promising, but the vigour and passion of the poet relieve it of any tendency to dullness. There are passages of great rhetorical power, such as that in which he calls Lazarus from the tomb to bear witness to the divinity of Christ, and summons Death to confess the name of his master;[1] and that in which he paints the triumph of Christianity over the fierce barbarians and the gods of Greece and Rome.[2] He tells how the oracles ceased and the temples fell, and the Emperor adored the standard of the Cross:

> ex quo mortalem praestrinxit spiritus alvum,
> spiritus ille dei, deus et se corpore matris
> induit, atque hominem de virginitate creavit;
> Delphica dampnatis tacuerunt sortibus antra,
> non tripodas cortina tegit, non spumat anhelus
> fata Sibyllinis fanaticus edita libris.

---

[1] *Apotheosis*, 741-81.   [2] ib., 424-47.

perdidit insanos mendax Dodona vapores,
mortua iam mutae lugent oracula Cumae,
nec responsa refert Libycis in Syrtibus Ammon:
ipsa suis Christum Capitolia Romula maerent
principibus lucere deum destructaque templa
imperio cecidisse ducum: iam purpura supplex
sternitur Aeneadae rectoris ad atria Christi,
vexillumque crucis summus dominator adorat.[1]

Then follows his celebrated judgement on Julian, the Emperor
of his boyhood, a judgement of surprising fairness, in which
the poet's patriotism is balanced against his abhorrence of the
apostate :

principibus tamen e cunctis non defuit unus,
me puero, ut memini, ductor fortissimus armis,
conditor et legum, celeberrimus ore manuque,
consultor patriae, sed non consultor habendae
relligionis, amans tercentum milia divum.
perfidus ille deo, quamvis non perfidus urbi.

It is a true portrait, for Julian's superstition, like that of his
neo-Platonic masters, embraced a multitude of gods, and he was,
in spite of all his pettiness and pedantry, a follower of the
best imperial tradition.   Prudentius, at any rate, did not begin
the process of defamation which enabled the Middle Ages to
regard Julian as a cruel persecutor, a renegade monk, and a
thief.[2]

At the end of the poem Prudentius returns to his pre-occupation, the resurrection of his body in Christ :

veniam, quibus ille revenit
calcata de morte, viis,

and eagerly he expresses his faith in the power of his risen
Lord to restore it whole and perfect, freed from the mutila-
tions of accident, and the disfigurements of disease, old age,
and pain.

The next poem, the *Hamartigenia*, deals, as its name implies,
with the origin of sin.   In a preface of sixty-three iambic
trimeters, Prudentius moralizes in a curious way on Cain and
Abel.   Abel is a type of Christ, but Cain, the parricide, is the
forerunner of Marcion who taught that there were two Gods,
the God of the Old and the God of the New Testament, and

---

[1] ib., 435–48.   [2] See below, p. 198.

so profanely divided the divine substance. The *Hamartigenia* is a bitter attack on the man who built upon a perverse study of Paul a new religion and founded a new Church which had a long history, especially in the East. By the middle of the third century the Marcionite Church had surrendered its heritage in the West to the rising sect of the Manichees, but in Syria, in Cyprus, in Palestine and Egypt it survived a long time, and Theodoret in the fifth century converted whole villages of Marcionites.[1] We need not follow the polemics of Prudentius, whose acquaintance with the details of Marcion's system was probably superficial,[2] but it is interesting to note that, in describing the true origin of sin, he gives a Miltonic picture of Satan, the ruined Archangel,[3]

> vertice sublimis, cinctum cui nubibus atris
> angiferum caput et fumo stipatur et igni,

with traits as well, which rather suggest the devil of the Middle Ages. This, he says, is no God, but the ' Charon of the World '; there is one supreme and only God who is omnipotent. But if God is all-powerful, why does he not forbid the existence of evil ? Here Prudentius appeals to the freedom of the will, as the necessary accompaniment of reason, and he shows by the examples of Lot and his wife, and of Ruth and Orpah, with what issues the choice between good and evil is fraught. For God in his wisdom has appointed eternal punishment and eternal reward, in separate places; but he has ordained that the damned and the blessed suffer and rejoice in each other's sight across the 'great gulf'. Again the poet thinks of his own salvation. He dare not ask for a mansion among the saints and martyrs, but he humbly prays that he may escape the torments of the fiends :

> cum flebilis hora
> clauserit hos orbes et conclamata iacebit
> materies oculisque suis mens nuda fruetur,[4]

and that a place of lesser punishment may be found for him where he shall expiate for ever the sins which he has committed in the body :

---

[1] See Harnack's admirable study, *Marcion : das Evangelium vom fremden Gott*, Leipzig 1921.

[2] Harnack, *Marcion*, pp. 312 sqq.; K. Holl, *Berlin. Sitzungsber.*, 1918, pp. 514 sqq. A later poet, whose name is unknown, composed a similar poem, *Carmen*, or *Carmina adversus Marcionem*, but he had studied Irenaeus, Tertullian, and Hippolytus; Harnack, p. 314.

[3] Lines 130 sqq.

[4] Lines 943-5.

esto: cavernoso, quia sic pro labe necesse est
corporea, tristis me sorbeat ignis averno:
saltem mitificos incendia lenta vapores
exhalent aestuque calor languente tepescat:
lux immensa alios et tempora vincta coronis
glorificent: me paena levis clementer adurat.[1]

The *Psychomachia*, which comes next in the group of didactic
and polemical poems we are now considering, has been described
by Ebert[2] as aesthetically the weakest, but the most important
from the literary and historical standpoint.   For it presents the
first poetical Christian allegory, an original creation, which
caught the fancy of the Middle Ages and inspired many imitations.   The subject of the poem is a series of epic combats
between personified Virtues and Vices: Faith against the Worship of the Ancient Gods, Modesty against *Sodomita Libido*,
Patience against Anger, Pride against Humility, &c.   The
detail of each combat is ingeniously worked out in order to
avoid monotony, and the Warriors on either side follow the
epic tradition of making speeches before or after the battle.
Thus *Pudicitia*, a virgin in bright armour, appears on the grassy
field and is attacked by *Sodomita Libido*, who would blind her
with the smoke of her sulphurous torch; but with a stone the
'fearless maid' wards off the blow and pierces the disarmed
enemy with her sword:

> tunc exarmatae iugulum meretricis adacto
> transfigit gladio, calidos vomit illa vapores
> sanguine concretos caenoso, spiritus inde
> sordidus exhalans vicinas polluit auras.[3]

A long speech follows in which *Pudicitia* develops those ideas,
so dear to Prudentius, which centre round the redemption of
our flesh by Christ.   Judith is presented as an example of the
victory of chastity, but as she lived under the old law (though
actually she foretells the Christian struggle), *Pudicitia* over-
whelms her dying foe by the supreme instance, the virgin birth,
which glorified our flesh:

> inde omnis iam diva caro est, quae concipit illum,
> naturamque dei consortis foedere sumit.

---

[1] Lines 961–6.
[2] i. 271; there is a separate edition of
the *Psychomachia*, ed. by J. Bergman,
Upsala 1897.
[3] *Psychomachia*, 49–52.

In the peroration, Lust is consigned to the abyss: 'Trouble no more the worshippers of Christ, O greatest of the Furies, that their bodies, henceforth pure, may serve their king.'[1] But the sword was stained by the foul blood of the dead Fury; so Modesty washed it in the 'Waves of Jordan'—the symbol of baptism—

> expiat ergo aciem fluviali docta lavacro
> victricem victrix abolens baptismate labem
> hostilis iuguli.[2]

and dedicated it at the altar of the 'Catholic temple', where it shines with everlasting splendour.

The last and worst enemy of all is Discord, also known as Heresy, whose teacher is Belial, and she is the scourge of the world.[3] 'God to me', she says, 'takes different shapes, now less, now greater, now double and now single; now a phantom of air and now an inborn soul.' When Heresy is disposed of by Faith, it is time to celebrate the peace by building a temple to Christ, four square like the New Jerusalem of the Apocalypse, where Wisdom, the true regent of the human soul, is enthroned, holding her sceptre, which blossoms with lilies and roses.

Personification of abstract qualities was not, when Prudentius wrote, a new thing in Latin literature. It was, indeed, part of the stock-in-trade of the later poets, and Apuleius had inserted in his *Metamorphoses* a complete allegory, *Cupid and Psyche*, in which such figures as *Solicitudo* and *Tristities*,[4] *Sobrietas*[5] and *Consuetudo*[6] appear. A moralizing poem, if it were also an allegory filled with such personifications, made a peculiar appeal to the medieval mind, and the *Psychomachia* provided what has been called a 'moral iconography'[7] for religious art. In the ninth century, M. Bréhier tells us, the virtues are still depicted in the miniatures as allegorical figures with attributes. In the Autun Sacramentary, for instance:

'Prudence holds a book and a cross, Temperance an urn and a cornucopia, Justice her scales, Courage a sword and a shield. From the tenth century we possess an illustrated manuscript of the *Psychomachia*. On the monuments of the eleventh and twelfth centuries, the battle of Vices and Virtues appears as a current motive, and a long catalogue could be drawn up of these *Psychomachiai*. They are found in

---

[1] *Psychomachia*, 96-7.   [2] ib., 102-4.   [5] ib., v. 30.   [6] ib., vi. 9.
[3] ib., 709 sqq.   [7] Bréhier, *L'art chrétien*, p. 203.
[4] *Metamorph.* vi. 9.

paintings, on mosaic pavements, on miniatures, and on capitals and sculptured doorways. . . . At Clermont-Ferrand (Notre-Dame du Port) a capital serves to illustrate three episodes of the poem: on the south-east front *Largitas* and *Caritas*, designated by the inscriptions on their shields, in coats of mail and helmets, lower and cross their pennoned lances, while they tread under foot the heads of two vices. On the north side, in agreement with the text, Anger, in rage at her failure to strike at Patience, plunges her javelin in her own breast, *Ira se occidit*: she is a naked woman with dishevelled hair and wild eyes. . . . Finally, on the north-west front, Mercy brandishes her great sword and clashes her shield against the shield of Avarice, a bearded demon.'[1]

The artists had not themselves read the *Psychomachia*, and they do not follow its episodes with any exactness, but the poem of Prudentius was the final source of these subjects which lent themselves so excellently to a decorative and moral art.

The last long poem by Prudentius, the *Contra Symmachum*, is a polemic against the heathen gods, which centres round the affair of the Altar of Victory. Constantius, although he allowed the old cults to continue, had removed the altar with its statue from the chamber where the Roman Senate met. Julian had, in his turn, restored the figure of the goddess. But Gratian, the first of the 'most Christian emperors',[2] had yielded to the representations of Pope Damasus and of the Christian Senators, and commanded that the altar should be finally removed. An embassy, headed by Symmachus, a noted orator, and the leader of the pagan aristocracy, went to Milan[3] to implore the Emperor to reverse his decree. But Gratian refused to see them. This was in the year 382; in 384 a new emperor, Valentinian II, sat on the throne, and a fresh effort was made. Symmachus, now City Prefect, was again the chosen speaker, and in a long oration, in which rhetoric was mingled with real pathos, he pleaded for the ancient gods. But Ambrose was at hand with a written answer; he reminded the Emperor of his responsibility as a Christian and overwhelmed him with stern admonition at a time when his other advisers showed signs of wavering. Prudentius had read and admired both the speech and the answer of Ambrose. He was generous in his recognition of

---

[1] ib., pp. 203–5, with abbreviations.
[2] Cf. Costa, *Religione e politica nel impero romano*, pp. 304 sqq.; the facts of the affair of the Altar of Victory are conveniently summarized in Geffcken, *Der Ausgang des griechisch-römischen Heidentums*, pp. 146 sqq.
[3] Hodgkin, *Italy and her Invaders*, I. i. 398, note 3, suggests Verona rather than Milan.

the oratory of Symmachus, whose mouth would truly have been golden if he had chosen to praise God instead of the demons. He fears to set himself against such a master of words and argument, but at least he may be allowed to stand firm and ward off with his shield the darts which threaten him.[1]   For at the beginning of the next century the heathen party in the Senate had raised the issue again, with the sons of Theodosius, and it was at this time, about the year 402, that Prudentius took up the task of Ambrose, addressing himself not so much to the emperors, as to the world at large.[2]   The first book of his poem has a preface in asclepiads, in which the experience of Paul, safe in harbour after shipwreck, but at the very moment of deliverance attacked by a viper, is compared with the condition of the Church, delivered from persecution, but now exposed to an envenomed assault which was to have a like happy issue.   The whole of the first book is directed against the heathen gods, and, if Prudentius is inclined to follow the Christian apologists in attacking myths in which no one any longer believed,[3] he does give a realistic and striking picture of the way in which religious usages or, as he calls them, empty superstitions, once established, grow by habit and become bound up with domestic life.   It is the reverse of the enchanting picture which Pater draws in *Marius the Epicurean* of the patriarchal religion of Rome with its antique air, its puritanic beauty, and its pastoral peace.   Tibullus might write as a poet:

> at mihi contingat patrios celebrare Penates,
> reddereque antiquo menstrua thura Lari,

but Prudentius reaches the root of the matter, even if we throw aside the polemic and look only at the historical fact.

> ut semel obsedit gentilia pectora patrum
> vana superstitio, non interrupta cucurrit
> aetatum per mille gradus: tener horruit haeres,
> et coluit quidquid sibimet venerabile cani
> monstrarunt atavi: puerorum infantia primo
> errorem cum lacte bibit: gustaverat inter
> vagitus de farre molae, saxa inlita ceris
> viderat unguentoque lares humescere nigros.
> formatum Fortunae habitum cum divite cornu

---

[1] *Contra Symm.* i. 650 sqq.
[2] In 393 Eugenius had restored the altar, but Theodosius certainly removed it when he overthrew Eugenius in 395.
[3] Cf. Cumont, *Oriental Religions in Roman Paganism*, p. 203.

sacratumque domi lapidem consistere parvus
spectarat matremque illic pallere precantem.
mox humeris positus nutricis trivit et ipse
impressis silicem labris, puerilia vota
fudit, opesque sibi caeca de rupe poposcit,
persuasumque habuit, quod quis velit, inde petendum.[1]

He goes, too, to the root of the matter by attacking the live beliefs of the day—the sun-worship, the astrology, the paralysing fear of Fate. This carries us into the second book, which has its preface also where Christ, who saved Peter struggling in the waves, is called upon to aid the poet against the orator, whose eloquence is like the stormy sea. Like the early apologists, Prudentius presents Christianity as a monotheism,[2] and on the sole almighty power of God he rests his belief in immortality. Without this belief, he says, God is nothing, and there is no reason to observe the moral law. With rhetorical exaggeration, he proceeds to a catalogue of the sins which follow from such an unhappy state:

ibo per impuros fervente libidine luxus:
incestabo toros, sacrum calcabo pudorem,
inficiabor habens aliquod sine teste propinqui
depositum, tenues avidus spoliabo clientes,
longaevam perimam magico cantamine matrem.

The real attack on Symmachus begins when Prudentius refutes the argument that old customs are worthy of reverence because our ancestors have handed them down to us. He preaches the law of progress and points out at length that Rome herself brought in new gods with each fresh victory and has not been faithful to her past. If Symmachus wishes to appeal to antiquity, let him go back to the original worship of one God revealed to the first men. But, the orator says, Rome is ruled by her genius. A variable genius, answers Prudentius, since it was always changing the form of government, and now, by God's providence, Rome is the servant of Christ, ' cultus exosa priores'. Again, Symmachus argues, the gods gave Rome her victories. Did Jupiter then betray his own Crete, and Pallas her own Argos, Diana her own Ephesus to the conquerors?

perfidiane deum indigenum cecidere tot urbes,
distructaeque iacent ipsis prodentibus arae?

[1] i. 197-211.
[2] See J. Lortz, *Das Christentum als Monotheismus in den Apologien des II.*

Jahrhunderts, in Ehrward's *Festgabe*, Bonn 1922, pp. 301 sqq.

What are we to make of the valour of the Fabricii, Curii, Drusi, and Camilli, if it was really the gods who were responsible? The final cause is quite different; it was God's purpose to join the nations together in a union of peace, in order to prepare the way for the true religion :

> deus undique gentes
> inclinare caput docuit, sub legibus isdem,
> Romanosque omnes fieri, quos Rhenus et Ister,
> quos Tagus aurifluus, quos magnus inundat Hiberus,
> corniger Hesperidum quos interlabitur et quos
> Gangis alit tepidique lavant septem ostia Nili.
> ius fecit commune pares et nomine eodem
> nexuit et domitos fraterna in vincla redegit.[1]

Here the intense patriotism of Prudentius breaks out as he celebrates the strength of Christian Rome, who is still able to quell her enemies; he brings her forward to praise Stilicho and his recent victory over the Goths at Pollentia, which is the triumph of Christ himself. Then he turns to that strange sentence of Symmachus, which does not express, as we are apt to think, a dreamy mysticism, but what seemed the plain truth to a later neo-Platonist—*uno itinere non potest perveniri ad tam grande secretum*[2]; and he affirms that there is only one way, the narrow way, which does not turn or divide.[3]

The remainder of the poem answers the final complaint of Symmachus that the Vestal Virgins had been deprived of their allowance of the public corn, and that in consequence the harvests had failed. After an easy refutation, Prudentius closes his poem by referring to the presence of the Vestals at the Roman games, where they sate and shared with the people the frenzy of bloodshed, condemning—*converso pollice*—the miserable victims of the arena. The noblest thing in the whole poem is his final appeal to Honorius to free 'golden Rome' of this disgrace and forbid the slaughter of men for pleasure :

> tu mortes miserorum hominum prohibeto litari.
> nullus in urbe cadat, cuius sit poena voluptas.[4]

Two years later this prayer was answered. In 404 the Colosseum was for the last time the scene of a gladiatorial show. According to Theodoret, an eastern monk, Telemachus, went into the arena to part the gladiators, and was murdered

---

[1] ii. 602–9.
[2] *Epist. Lib*.x, ed. Seeck, *M. G. H.*, *Auct. Antiq.* VI. i, p. 282.
[3] ii. 843 sqq.
[4] ii. 1125–6.

by the crowd. The horror of this event induced Honorius to put an end to such exhibitions for ever. Telemachus was remembered as a martyr and a saint.

Apart from the rest of the work of Prudentius stands the *Dittochaeon*,[1] a collection of forty-nine hexameter tetrastichs, of which the first twenty-four deal with scenes from the Old, and the remaining twenty-five with scenes from the New Testament. It is probable that they were inscriptions for mosaics or pictures in a Spanish basilica. One side of the great arcade would contain the twenty-four scenes of the Old Testament, and the other side twenty-four from the New, while the apse might be crowned with the elders of the Apocalypse praising the Lamb who alone was worthy to 'take the book and to open the seven seals '.

> bis duodena senum sedes pateris citharisque
> totque coronarum fulgens insignibus agnum
> caede cruentatum laudat, qui evolvere librum
> et septem potuit signacula pandere solus.

It has been pointed out[2] that a number of these tetrastichs are evidently related to pictorial compositions which represented a series of Palestinian scenes, such as are described in early pilgrim-literature. By a curious but not uncommon anachronism, the picture would represent, for instance, the Beautiful Gate of the Temple[3] in its existing ruined state, while in the foreground Peter was shown performing his miracle. This is the key to the understanding of the following tetrastich :

> porta manet templi, speciosam quam vocitarunt,
> egregium Salomonis opus: sed maius in illa
> Christi opus emicuit, nam claudus surgere iussus
> ore Petri stupuit laxatos currere gressus.

So Prudentius either had before him a cycle of mosaics or pictures, which were based on Palestinian prototypes, or he himself composed his verses under the same Palestinian influence, in order that they might be attached to a series of pictures which were to follow the scheme of his *Dittochaeon*.[4]

<hr />

[1] This has been interpreted as 'twofold nourishment', that is, of the soul, but the spelling may be corrupt, and F. Ogara, *El Dittochaeum de Prudencio, Estud. Eclesiast.*, i (1922), pp. 132 sqq., suggests that it is derived from διστοιχος, 'bi-mural';

see also A. Baumstark, *Byzant. Zeitschr.* xx (1911), p. 179, note 3.
[2] Baumstark, pp. 179 sqq.
[3] i.e. the relic pointed out to the pilgrims as being the original Beautiful Gate.
[4] Baumstark, p. 187.

§ 4. *General remarks on Prudentius.*

In his prologue to the *Cathemerinon* Prudentius tells us that his poems are the work of a middle-aged official, who wishes to make amends for the uselessness of his past life by singing the praises of God, fighting heresies, unfolding the Catholic faith, trampling on heathen rites, overturning idols, and celebrating the martyrs and the apostles. This is the bald summary of his work, but after fifteen centuries he is the most esteemed of the Christian-Latin poets and is read with interest and often with pleasure by lovers of Catullus and of Virgil. Like his Pagan contemporaries, he could not forget his rhetorical training, but rhetoric is never of the essence of his work, as it tends to become with Claudian, and, more certainly, with Ausonius. For Prudentius uses his material as a craftsman who is making something that it is his own. He does, indeed, overload his poems with lengthy speeches, he is too fond of alliteration, of playing on words, and there is a good deal of possibly conscious assonance and rime;[1] but when we have allowed for this and for the freedom of his prosody, we have still a body of verse which is strongly and confidently constructed, and has a freshness and originality which were gifts derived from a new outlook. For the Christian idea dominates Prudentius entirely, and there is no half-regretful backward glance to antiquity. Christianity had reached a stage in its development when it was capable of providing ample material for poetry, and poetry was now almost the only department of pure literature. The Christian ode was Prudentius' happiest creation. In the *Cathemerinon* he chooses as his subject a Christian practice or belief, and illuminates it by the teaching of the Church, by the parallelism of the Old Law and the New, and by a practical or a mystical appeal which is often his own contribution. While others had attempted with limited success to create a literary epic out of sacred history, Prudentius saw how much more 'current' was the material afforded by the Acts of the martyrs, and he wisely chose the variety of lyrical measures instead of the somewhat ponderous uniformity of the hexameter. There was nothing remarkable in his use of poetry for polemical and didactic ends; for Commodian and others had done this before him, and polemical

---

[1] Cf. Manitius, *Rhein. Mus.*, xlv, p. 490; *Christl. Lat. Poesie*, p. 98.

subjects, at any rate, lay very near to hand.   But the Christian allegory was a new creation, and, if we measure its success by its influence, it was his greatest achievement.

Prudentius is marked out from the mass of the Christian poets who succeeded him by the fact that he was and remained a layman.   In all his poems he assumes the position of a simple believer, but, like Dante, he had made deep, and, so far as a layman can judge, accurate theological studies.   It seems clear that he had the rare advantage of a sound knowledge of Greek, and it is reasonable to assume that he had turned it to account by a study of the Greek fathers.   He knew the Bible thoroughly both from the literal and from the doctrinal point of view, and of the writers of the Western Church he certainly knew Tertullian, Cyprian, and Lactantius, and he must have known something of the work of Ambrose.   Perhaps no one before him had such a clear and direct sense of the surrounding heathendom in its age of decline.   Certainly we do not find elsewhere such a living picture of the old religion in operation.   At the same time he stands alone among the Christian poets as a patriot, deeply impressed with the material power of Rome, seeing the Christian city still as the destined ruler of the nations and the mistress of unconquerable armies. He had been brought up on the classical historians, and he viewed, more clearly perhaps than Symmachus, the course of Roman history as a natural progression, and the successive conquests by which the Roman state became an Empire, as the victory of a vigorous stock over the less virile peoples of the East:

> sed nec difficilis fuit aut satis ardua genti
> natae ad procinctus victoria frangere inertes,
> molliaque omnigenum colla inclinare deorum
> num cum Dictaeis bellum Corybantibus asper
> Samnitis Marsusque levi sudore gerebat?[1]

And again he emphasizes his argument, with a patriotic intensity, against Symmachus, who would ascribe the Roman victories to the gods :

> non fero Romanum nomen sudataque bella
> et titulos tanto quaesitos sanguine carpi.
> detrahit invictis legionibus et sua Romae
> praemia diminuit, qui, quidquid fortiter actum est,
> adscribit Veneri, palmam victoribus aufert.[2]

---

[1] *Contra Symm.* ii. 512–16.   [2] ib , ii. 551–5.

But he has nothing to say of the great names in Roman poetry; for he could only have confessed that they were enslaved to the superstition which he hated. Yet they were the foundation of his technique and they even provided models for some of his most telling scenes. It is unnecessary to speak of his general dependence on Horace and Virgil. His imitations of Seneca and Lucan afford more striking examples of the manner in which he went to work. In Seneca's *Hippolytus*,[1] the messenger tells the story of how the young prince was dragged to death by his horses, and Prudentius in the *Peristephanon* constantly borrows from this narrative when he is describing the similar end of his own Hippolytus.[2] The *Hercules Furens*, besides providing Prudentius with the phrase, 'noctis aeternae chaos',[3] gave him suggestions, in the scene where Hercules murders his children, for his lines on the Innocents;[4] and for the harrowing of hell a parallel was found in the story of the hero who 'broke down the doors of infernal Jove'.[5] Lucan's *Pharsalia* supplied material for scenes of horror and bloodshed, but also for one more pleasing description which shows how Christianity had adopted the astrological *Weltbild* given by the East to the West.[6] In the hymn on the martyrdom of Agnes, the released soul soars above the earth into the upper air, and wonders at the world beneath her feet. She looks and laughs at the darkness of terrestrial things as she mounts to the heavens.[7] Here Prudentius found his model in the ninth book of the *Pharsalia*, where Lucan describes the soul of Pompey passing upwards from the earth to the same local heaven:

> at non in Pharia manes iacuere favilla,
> nec cinis exiguus tantam compescuit umbram:
> prosiluit busto, semustaque membra relinquens
> degeneremque rogum, sequitur convexa tonantis,
> qua niger astriferis conectitur axibus aer,
> quodque patet terras inter lunaeque meatus,
> semidei manes habitant, quos ignea virtus
> innocuos vita patientes aetheris imi

[1] Lines 1000 sqq.
[2] *Peristeph.* xi. 85 sqq.
[3] *Herc. Furens* 610 = *Cath.* ix. 81.
[4] *Herc. Furens* 1002 sqq.; *Cath.* xii. 109 sqq.
[5] *Herc. Furens* 47; *Cath.* ix. 70 sqq.
[6] See Cumont, *Astrology and Religion among the Greeks and Romans*, New York 1912.
[7] *Peristeph.* xiv. 91 sqq.:

> exutus inde spiritus emicat
> liberque in auras exilit, angeli
> sepsere euntem tramite candido.
> miratur orbem sub pedibus situm,
> spectat tenebras ardua subditas
> ridetque, solis quod rota circuit,
> quod mundus omnis volvit et implicat,
> rerum quod atro turbine vivitur,
> quod vana secli mobilitas rapit.

fecit , et aeternos animam collegit in orbes.
non illuc auro positi, nec thure sepulti
perveniunt. illic postquam se lumine vero
implevit, stellasque vagas miratus et astra
fixa polis, vidit quanta sub nocte iaceret
nostra dies, risitque sui ludibria trunci.[1]

But in such imitations Prudentius did not go beyond the license
which had always been assumed by the Latin poets. 'A good
idea was considered common property, and a happy phrase
might be adopted without theft.'[2]   Where Prudentius shows
his originality is in his vocabulary ; he is pre-eminent as a
coiner of new words.[3]   But he coins them after the manner
of his contemporaries, a manner which was developed more
particularly by Christian writers and can be best studied in the
Old Latin and the Vulgate.   Thus he was fond of nouns constructed with the ending -amen (creamen, cruciamen, luctamen),[4]
or -trix (enuntiatrix, peccatrix, strangulatrix) ;[5] of diminutives,
substantival and adjectival (aetatula, turbidulus) ;[6] of adjectives
in -alis and -ilis (carceralis, vitiabilis).[7]   These and similar constructions found a permanent place in the Christian Latin of
the Middle Ages and were accepted by the Carolingian poets
for whom Juvencus and Prudentius were included among the
classical authors.

In his own day Prudentius seems to have enjoyed a small
reputation, except perhaps in his native Spain.   But towards
the end of the fifth century he became 'a living factor in the
spiritual life of Christendom';[8] both Sidonius Apollinaris and
Alcimus Avitus held him in high esteem, and the Spanish
Church made great use of his poetry in its hymnary, while the
other Western Churches drew consistently, if more sparingly,
upon both the *Cathemerinon* and the *Peristephanon*.

---

[1] *Pharsalia* ix. 1–14.
[2] Cruttwell, *History of Roman Literature*, p. 304.
[3] *Manitius, *Rhein. Mus.* xlv, p. 487 :
'Prudentius ist ein Neubildner ersten
Ranges. Eine grosse Anzahl von substan-
tivischen und adjectivischen Weiterbil-
dungen gehört ihm an und ist durch die
weite Verbreitung seiner Werke Gemein-
gut der christlichen Poesie geworden.'
[4] Rönsch, *Itala und Vulgata*, pp. 25 sqq.,
for examples from Tertullian and other
Christian writers and from Latin Bible.
[5] ib., pp. 62 sqq.
[6] ib., pp. 93 sqq., 140 sqq.
[7] ib., pp. 109 sqq.
[8] Schanz, iv. 255.

THE CHRISTIAN POETS OF GAUL AND AFRICA IN THE FOURTH, FIFTH, AND SIXTH CENTURIES

§ 1. *Ausonius and the end of the old order.*

AT an early date the Gauls began to take kindly to Roman civilization. They adopted the Roman scholastic system with eagerness and application, and in the time of Tiberius the schools of Autun had a reputation which extended beyond the borders of Gaul.[1] In the fourth century Gaul holds a foremost place as a home of letters, pagan and Christian. Each important town had its schools of grammar and rhetoric where the classical poets were read and imitated, and the art of the rhetorician was studied under the best masters of the day. An examination has already been made of the merits and limitations of the programme of studies which was common to the Roman schools. For the present purpose it is important to remember the emphasis which was laid on the close study of the Roman poets, a study which was intended to mould both the prose and the poetical style of the student.

The Romanized aristocracy of Gaul had looked upon the education provided by the schools as an equipment for the official life which was the only becoming activity remaining to the upper classes. But the rapid Christianizing of all ranks of society, a process which had strikingly advanced by the middle of the fifth century,[2] opened out new possibilities, whether by presenting the episcopate in the light of a public office to which an able and intelligent noble could aspire, or by offering the spiritual rewards of a life spent in the service of religion apart from the tedium of a world devoted to idleness or pleasure. For the moment, however, while the political

---

[1] On the Gallic schools see Boissier, *La fin du paganisme*, ii. 42 sqq.; Dill, *Roman Society in the Last Century of the Western Empire*, pp. 167 sqq., 385 sqq.

[2] Harnack, *Mission*, ii. 269; on the Gallic Church see T. S. Holmes, *The Christian Church in Gaul during the first six centuries*, London 1911.

troubles of the Empire were merely gathering force for a fresh outbreak, the spirit of disillusion was not unduly prominent. The picture of society which is gathered from the writings of Ausonius shows the Church living on peaceful terms with the old Roman civilization. The spirit of the schools remains as pagan as ever, although the professors were Christian at least in name. Decimus Magnus Ausonius,[1] the *doyen* of Gallic rhetoricians, whose talents had raised him from a humble professorship to the supreme honour of the consulate, is the type of this lukewarm Christianity which found room by the side of Christ for Apollo and the Muses. He was born at Bordeaux about A. D. 310, and received his education in the schools of his native town. In 364 he became tutor to Gratian, the son of Valentinian, and when the pupil became emperor, Ausonius was rewarded with the office of *Praefectus Galliarum*, and in 379 with the consulship. He spent his old age in retirement in his beloved Aquitaine, among a circle of friends devoted to letters and in enjoyment of the pleasant life of the country villa.

The mass of rhetoric and pedantry which lies over the verses of Ausonius cannot always obscure a glimmer of charm and natural expression. All the faults of imitation and tasteless ingenuity, a study of form which is not the scrupulousness of the true artist, and an absence of content which only reveals the more the defects of the form—these are the vices of his poetry. But, here and there, when he is describing a journey along the Moselle or the landscape of his dear Garonne, the poet is a little, but only a little, less the rhetorician.

The extent to which Ausonius was moved by the claims of the Christian religion is sufficiently indicated in the *Ephemeris*, a poem which relates the events of his usual day. The swallows wake him, and he calls his servant to bring his clothes and water. He has no need of incense, cake, or fire; he can pray to God without such heathen aid. But, the prayer over, he says :

> satis precum datum deo :
> quamvis satis nunquam reis
> fiat precatu numini.

Then after his formal orisons, he proceeds to the business of the day.

---

[1] For Ausonius' poems, ed. Schenkl, *M.G.H.*, *Auct. Antiq.*, V. ii; on Ausonius see Dill, *Roman Society in the Last Cen-* *tury of the Western Empire*, pp. 167 sqq. ; Glover, *Life and Letters in the Fourth Century*, pp. 102 sqq.

But the easy and leisured life of the Gallic aristocracy was not to last. A new order of things was already preparing. In 406 the Vandals, Suevi, and Alans broke through the Rhine frontier [1] and overran the north of Gaul, while the south was soon distracted by civil war. In the meantime, Italy was experiencing the terror of Alaric's three marches on Rome, and the sack of 410 which sent a thrill of horror throughout the Christian world. Before the middle of the century, the south-east of Gaul was occupied by Burgundian invaders, and the Alans had established themselves farther west. In the Bordeaux of Ausonius, the Visigoths were masters, and their kingdom extended from the Loire to the Pyrenees. The Roman administration was shaken to its foundations. Profound economic and social changes accompanied the political dissolution. Then in 451 Attila and his Huns swept across the country leaving destruction and devastation in their train, until Aetius defeated them at the ' Mauriac plain '.[2]

In Italy, likewise, the old political order passed. First Odoacer with his mixed barbarian army, and finally the Ostrogoths under Theodoric assumed *de facto* the authority of the emperors which as yet they dared not claim *de iure*.

The period which witnessed the political transformation of the West witnessed as well the laying of the strong foundations of the medieval Church. The medieval world begins with Augustine and Jerome, with the *De Civitate Dei* and the Vulgate. The one contained in outline the theory of the medieval Church, which was being constructed on the ruins of the Western Empire ; the other finally provided the liturgical and to a large extent the ecclesiastical language of Latin Christianity.[3]

If Augustine and Jerome stand out as the great teachers of the earlier Middle Ages, their immediate importance lies in the immense impulse which their writings and example gave, throughout the whole of the Christian west, to the practice of the ascetic and monastic life. Their influence went all the deeper in view of the reaction, both moral and spiritual, that was already making itself felt throughout a society which had relied too pathetically on the stability of the old order. In Gaul the reaction was guided most conspicuously by the

---

[1] Hodgkin, *Italy and her Invaders*, I. ii. 739.
[2] ib., ii. 124.
[3] Cf. Milman, *Latin Christianity*, i. 95, London 1883.

influence of a monasticism based on the severer Eastern and Egyptian models. Cassian and Cesarius of Arles compiled a monastic code which allowed no lukewarm compromise with the past, no concessions to the pride of life, and left no room for the culture of an Ausonius or a Sidonius Apollinaris.

The full note of the new order is struck in Salvian's *De Gubernatione Dei*,[1] that impetuous tract which laid bare the judgement of God on a sinful society in which Christian and Pagan, sunk in vices, might take an example from the virtues of the heathen or, at any rate, heretical, barbarians.

The complete disappearance of the public schools in Gaul in the course of the fifth century[2] struck a fatal blow at the study of letters for their own sake. What studies continued were pursued in private, and education, such as it was, became more and more the monopoly of the Church. But in spite of the political upheaval and the progress of asceticism, the fifth century is the great age of Christian poetry in Gaul. The forces of dissolution did not reach their full extent until the close of the century. Men were still alive whose youth had been spent in the old schools, and on whose minds the liberal studies had made an indelible impress. It is true that they were Christians and no longer Christians after the order of Ausonius. They had definitely broken with Apollo and the Muses, and their hearts were dedicated to Christ:

> negant Camenis nec patent Apollini
> dicata Christo pectora.

They turned to poetry, sometimes to express their deepest feelings in measures which once they had used to describe the trivialities of the schools or subjects taken from the pagan myths; more often, they used the language of Virgil to set forth for didactic purposes the Bible story or the Trinitarian faith.

§ 2. *Poets of the fifth century.*

The most important in the group of thoroughly Christian poets who owed their education to the Gallic Schools is Paulinus of Nola,[3] the brilliant pupil of Ausonius; he stands apart from the others both in the fame which he acquired by his saintly

---

[1] Written *c.* 440-50; see Dill, *Roman Society in the Last Century of the Western Empire*, pp. 137 sqq.

[2] Roger, pp. 56, 82.

[3] On Paulinus see below, pp. 101 sqq.

asceticism, and in the range and quality of his religious poetry. The other poets followed, for the most part, what can best be described as the epic tradition.[1] Virgil was their model, and their subjects were taken, as a rule, from sacred history. Their aim was didactic and moral, and in an age when the lettered public was more easily persuaded to read verse than prose, they saw that greater possibilities of edification lay in the presentation of religious truth and the facts of Christian history in a medium which the Spanish Juvencus had already used with such success. If the Gospels did not lend themselves so admirably to epic treatment, the story of the Old Testament was rich in scenes of romantic and dramatic possibility, which could be made to minister, in the highest degree, to the cause of Christian edification. The appeal of this poetry was directed to men of some culture and leisure, who, like the poets themselves, owed the whole atmosphere of their education to the public schools, and whose lukewarm Christianity might be transformed into something more serious and genuine by a method of instruction which would appeal to their aesthetic sense.

The *Heptateuchos* of Cyprian, a fifth-century fragment of an epos which was designed to embrace the whole course of the Old Testament, is a versification of biblical history from Genesis to Judges.[2] Its essentially instructional character is indicated by the fact that the poet adheres closely to the *Itala*, the pre-Vulgate version, and does not allow himself to be tempted into poetical excursions in search of descriptive beauty. The picture of Paradise, which with its trees and rivers offered an opportunity for at least a rhetorical digression, is formal and bare; but in the hymn of Moses and other lyrical passages, Cyprian allows himself to break into hendecasyllabics, which he manages, however, with all restraint :

> cantemus domino deoque nostro,
> cui gloria cum honore pollens.
> sese magnificis decorat actis,
> dum currus celeres Aegyptiorum
> iunctis equitibus gravique turba
> rubri marmoris enecat fluentis.[3]

Still more summary in its treatment, though not unadorned with poetical touches, is the versification of *Genesis* which Hilary

---

[1] Manitius, *Christl. Lat. Poesie*, p. 161.

[2] Text, ed. Peiper, in *C. S. E. L.* xxiii.

[3] Peiper, p. 74.

of Arles dedicated to Pope Leo.[1]   Claudius Marius Victor is a
poet of a higher order. According to Gennadius he was a rhetor
in Marseilles, much addicted to secular literature and versed
but little in the divine scriptures.[2]   The unfavourable verdict
of Gennadius on Marius Victor's poetical paraphrase of *Genesis*,
due perhaps to its lack of dogmatic and moralistic ornament,[3]
is reflected in the neglect which it suffered during the Middle
Ages. It was, however, expressly intended by its author to
be used for the purposes of Christian edification and especially
to instruct the young : [4]

> quae sit origo poli vel quae primordia mundi,
> arcanamque fidem qui toto excusserit aucta
> pestis et in mores penitus descenderit error,
> quaque iterum redeat verum ritusque profanos
> pellat et aeternae reseret sacra mystica vitae.[5]

The three books of the *Alethias* are a paraphrase of *Genesis*
as far as the destruction of Sodom. The poet ventured to treat
his material with more freedom than had appeared possible to
his predecessor Cyprian. He gives a highly wrought picture
of Paradise, a garden of eternal spring, with

> Groves whose rich trees wept odorous gums and balm,
> Others whose fruit, burnished with golden rind,
> Hung amiable, Hesperian fables true.

Here the *Georgics* provided him with flowers to gather, and
the success of the description attracted Avitus, Bishop of
Vienne,[6] who, towards the end of the fifth century, chose the
same subject for a didactic poem. Isidore of Seville, in his
notice of Avitus,[7] says, 'Avitus the Bishop, a man learned in
secular letters, composed five books in heroic metre, of which
the first deals with the origin of the world, the second with
original sin, the third with the judgement of God, the fourth
with the deluge, the fifth with the crossing of the Red Sea.
He wrote also a book for his sister Fuscina on the praise of
virginity, a most beautiful poem.'
Alcimus Ecdicius Avitus came of an aristocratic family and

[1] Text, ed. Peiper, *C.S.E.L.* xxiii, pp. 231 sqq.
[2] *De Script. Eccles.* 60, Migne, lviii, col. 1094.
[3] Cf. Manitius, *Christl. Lat. Poesie*, p. 182.
[4] Text, ed. Schenkl, *C.S.E.L.* xvi, pp. 359 sqq.
[5] Schenkl, p. 363.
[6] Works, ed. Peiper, *M.G.H.*, *Auct. Antiq.*, VI. ii.
[7] *De Viris illustr.* 36, Migne, lxxxiii, col. 1101.

succeeded his father about 490 in the Bishopric of Vienne. He was an able defender of the Catholic faith against heretics of all kinds. Such of his polemical writings and letters as have survived are in the usual rhetorical prose, but his verses surprise the reader by their clearness and strength.[1] His intention was, not to compose an easy paraphrase of the Old Testament, but to present to cultured readers a philosophic and romantic poem, adorned with all the beauties of style which he was able to command. The five 'books' into which the poem is divided carry the story from the creation to the crossing of the Red Sea, not in continuous narrative, but dealing only with outstanding events and digressing to explain the allegorical reference of the subject or to develop an elaborate description of a romantic or dramatic scene. Thus the picture of Paradise is full of colour :

> hic ver adsiduum caeli clementia servat ;
> turbidus auster abest semperque sub aere sudo
> nubila diffugiunt iugi cessura sereno.
> nec poscit natura loci quos non habet imbres,
> sed contenta suo dotantur germina rore.
> perpetuo viret omne solum terraeque tepentis
> blanda nitet facies, stant semper collibus herbae
> arboribusque comae : quae cum se flore frequenti
> diffundunt, celeri confortant germina suco.
> nam quidquid nobis toto nunc nascitur anno,
> menstrua maturo dant illic tempora fructu.
> lilia perlucent nullo flaccentia sole
> nec tactus violat violas roseumque ruborem
> servans perpetuo suffundit gratia vultu.
> sic cum desit hiems nec torrida ferveat aestas,
> fructibus autumnus, ver floribus occupat annum.[2]

In spite of rhetorical embellishment and excessive alliteration, the whole passage reveals a poetical talent above that of Juvencus or indeed of any of the 'epic' poets of the Church. The deliverance of the children of Israel is treated in the fifth book in a manner approaching the grand epic style. The crossing of the Red Sea and the destruction of Pharaoh's army offered a subject which allowed the poet to bring out the whole epical apparatus of a Virgilian battle scene, and Avitus made full use of his opportunity, adding, however, the Christian moral for the reader's edification :

[1] Cf. Manitius, *Christl. Lat. Poesie*, p. 242.   [2] Peiper, i. 227 sqq., p. 209.

o si compunctas humana superbia mentes
ante obitum mutare velit ! quid denique prodest
tunc finem posuisse malis, cum terminus urget,
praesentis vitae spatium dum ceditur aevo ?
'confitearis'! ait sanus scriptura valensque.
si tunc peccatum quisquam dimittere vovit,
cum peccare nequit, luxu dimittitur ipse.[1]

The appeal which Avitus made to his own generation is sufficiently demonstrated by the concluding lines of his epitaph :

orator nullus similis nullusque poeta ;
clamant quod sparsi per crebra volumina libri,
quis vixit, vivit perque omnia saecula vivet.[2]

Apart from this group of 'epic' poets stands one who belongs in spirit to an older tradition, Sidonius Apollinaris,[3] the Bishop of Clermont, whose letters and poems throw such a vivid light on what remained of the old society amid the successive shocks of the barbarian invasions. Those invasions did not lead at once to the destruction of the leisured life of the literary aristocracy. In the letters of Sidonius we see its members living in the same graceful and easy fashion, their days divided between the library, the open air, and literary *causeries* at the dinner table. They felt that they were the last heirs of a dying tradition. Upon them was laid the hopeless task of preserving, in an age of indifference and political disaster, the 'meram linguae Latiaris proprietatem' as Sidonius phrased it in a letter to a friend, whose love of letters was the source of Sidonius' own affection for him.[4] The manner in which private studies continued in spite of the disappearance of the schools is shown in the charming picture which Sidonius draws of himself and his son engaged together in reading the *Hecyra* of Terence, which the father illustrated by reference to the *Epitrepontes* of Menander.[5] But the end of such studies was approaching. The monastic schools of Arles and Lérins took the place of the schools of grammar and rhetoric, and the shadow of ecclesiastical Latin was over all the studies. Sidonius is therefore the representative of a dying order.

C. Sollius Sidonius Apollinaris, to give him his full name,

[1] ib., v. 676 sqq., pp. 272–3.
[2] ib., p. 186.
[3] Works, ed. Lütjohann, *M.G.H.*, *Auct. Antiq.*, viii.
[4] *Epist.* ii. 10, p. 33 'Amo in te quod litteras amas '.
[5] *Epist.* iv. 12, p.64 ; Allard, *S. Sidoine Apollinaire*, p. 128 sq., dates the letter from the early years of his episcopate.

was born at Lyons about 430 of a high official family, and
he was educated for an official career. He became an accomplished rhetorician and easily acquired all the fashionable
literary vices. His marriage to a daughter of Avitus, an
important official who rose to the purple in 455, set him at
once on the road of political advancement. For the panegyric
which he delivered on his father-in-law at Rome he was rewarded with a statue in the Forum of Trajan. But the downfall
of the phantom emperor at the hand of Ricimer the master
of soldiers put an end to his immediate hopes. He allowed
himself to compose a flattering panegyric on the new emperor,
Majorian, whose favour he was on the way to win when Ricimer
brought about Majorian's fall.[1]   After a few years of retirement
at Lyons and at his villa in Auvergne, Sidonius returned to
Rome, and delivered a panegyric on the Emperor Anthemius,
who rewarded him with the City Prefecture.[2]   But, before long,
he prudently retired, with the title of Patricius, to his country
estates.   In 471 or the following year, he accepted the office of
Bishop, which was urged upon him by the clergy and people,
and he held it honourably and modestly, amid great difficulties
and dangers, until his death.

He was the most distinguished literary figure of his day.
He had won fame by his panegyrics on successive emperors;
his occasional poems were read with delight and wonder, and
his letters were regarded as the most precious of literary treasures. The poems themselves are poor in content and deficient
in sincerity of feeling, obscure in expression and overladen with
recondite allusions. The hendecasyllabics which he wrote for
the new Church of Bishop Patiens at Lyons, 'quae imaginarie
tantum et quodammodo umbratiliter effingimus ',[3] may serve as
a specimen of his Christian verse :

> quisquis pontificis patrisque nostri
> conlaudas Patientis hic laborem,
> voti compote supplicatione
> concessum experiare quod rogabis.
> aedes celsa nitet nec in sinistrum
> aut dextrum trahitur, sed arce frontis
> ortum prospicit aequinoctialem.

[1] On the events of these years see Bury,
Hist. of the Later Rom. Emp. i. 323 sqq.;
Allard, *S. Sidoine*, pp. 47 sqq.
[2] The real motive was perhaps the con-
ciliation of Gallo-Roman sentiment. See
Bury, i. 338 ; Allard, *S. Sidoine*, p. 90.
[3] *Epist* ii. 10, p. 34. He is really speaking of his verse in general.

intus lux micat atque bratteatum
sol sic sollicitatur ad lucanar,
fulvo ut concolor erret in metallo.
distinctum vario nitore marmor
percurrit cameram solum fenestras,
ac sub versicoloribus figuris
vernans herbida crusta sapphiratos
flectit per prasinum vitrum lapillos.
huic est porticus applicata triplex
fulmentis Aquitanicis superba,
ad cuius specimen remotiora
claudunt atria porticus secundae,
et campum medium procul locatas
vestit saxea silva per columnas.
hinc agger sonat, hinc Arar resultat.
hinc sese pedes atque eques reflectit
stridentum et moderator essedorum,
curvorum hinc chorus helciariorum
responsantibus alleluia ripis
ad Christum levat amnicum celeuma.
sic, sic psallite, nauta vel viator;
namque iste est locus omnibus petendus:
omnes quo via ducit ad salutem.[1]

These verses still, with all their ineffectual ingenuity, exercise a fascination over the wearied inheritors of a long literary tradition.[2] But the truth is that Sidonius shows best as a bishop and a Roman; in his defence of his city against the Visigoths, in his fatherly care of his people, and in his struggles against the administrative injustices which accompanied the decline of the Empire. The people and country of the Auvergne were handed over to the Visigoths against their will, and the bishop found it difficult to maintain his position with the alien and heretical conquerors. He was, indeed, for a time imprisoned by the Goths. He died soon after his release, to the grief of his people, in whose memory he lived as a father and a saint. The last of the Gallo-Romans who had loved the humane letters

[1] Text, *Epist.* ii. 10, p. 34; for a verse rendering see Hodgkin, *Italy and her Invaders*, ii. 328; in prose, Dalton, *Letters of Sidonius*, i. 54–5, from whom I venture to give the rendering of a few words: 'bratteatum . . . lucanar' = 'coffered ceiling'; lines 14, 15, 'and mosaic green as a blooming mead shows its design of sapphire cubes winding through the ground of verdant glass', referring (Dal-ton, ii. 226) not to windows but to 'glass wall-mosaics'; 'amnicum celeuma' = 'river-chant'.

[2] See J.-K. Huysmans, *À Rebours*, p. 48, Paris 1899; de Gourmont, *Le Latin mystique*, p. 57; Bury, *Later Roman Empire*, i. 346, says, 'He could write good verses, occasionally approaching Claudian, and bad verses, which remind us of Merobaudes'.

G

for their own sake, he could not forget that he was a Roman citizen, and his eyes turned in a way that at the end of the century such eyes could no longer turn, to Rome, 'the home of laws, the school of letters, the source of honours, the summit of the world, the home of freedom, in which city, peerless in all the earth, barbarians and slaves alone are foreigners.'[1]

Paulinus of Périgueux was a contemporary of Sidonius. At the request of Perpetuus, Bishop of Tours (A.D. 458–88), he put into verse an account of the life and miracles of S. Martin.[2] He naturally made great use of the popular work of Sulpicius Severus, while the bishop provided him with a collection of miracles. He is full of admiration for the saint and he hoped by celebrating him to win such good will that he might be healed from some physical infirmity with which he was inflicted. The poem consists of more than three thousand verses; it makes tedious reading and the modest excuses contained in the dedication which precedes it are more necessary than possibly the poet actually recognized.[3]

Auspicius, Bishop of Toul, was likewise a contemporary of Sidonius. Arbogast, the Frankish Comes at Trier, once asked Sidonius to explain the meaning of a theological treatise. The Bishop of Clermont referred him to two other bishops—Lupus of Troyes and Auspicius of Toul. The only poem of Auspicius which we possess is addressed to this same Arbogast,[4] but it is noteworthy not on account of its literary quality or its content, but because it is the earliest example (*circ.* 470) of a rhythmical imitation of the 'Ambrosian' stanza. It was used by Brandes in an attempt to demonstrate that rhythmical poetry from the beginning, followed the principle of the regular substitution of accent for quantity, for at first sight a stanza like the following might appear to show a clear recognition of the developed rules of rhythmical verse :

> praecelso et spectabili
> his Arbogasti comiti
> Auspicius, qui diligo,
> salutem dico plurimam.

But Meyer has shown that Auspicius has produced this effect simply because he is observing a caesura after the third or the

[1] *Epist.* i. 6, p. 9.
[2] Text, ed. Petschenig, *C. S. E. L.* xvi, pp. 1 sqq.
[3] Cf. P. Lejay, in *Revue critique d'hist.* *et de litt.* xxv. (1888), p. 286.
[4] Text, ed. W. Meyer, *Die rythmischen Jamben des Auspicius, Gött. Nachr.,* 1906, pp. 194 sqq.

fifth syllable (sometimes after both), and not because he consciously aimed at the construction of iambic ' accent-feet '.[1] It is
simply a question of taste and not a law of metre.

The *Eucharisticos*[2] of Paulinus of Pella, a poem of thanksgiving in which he reviews the chances and changes of a varied
life, is a document of considerable importance for the historian
of the fifth century.   The author was a grandson of the great
Ausonius; he was born in Pella, while his father was Prefect of
Macedonia.   He received his education, he tells us, in the
school of Bordeaux.   He had mastered Greek in childhood
from the Macedonian servants, but his Latin studies were a painful
task.   A succession of misfortunes turned his heart to religion,
and in the eighty-fourth year of his age he wrote this poem
of thanksgiving and reconciliation.   The verses betray reminiscences of Virgil, Ausonius, Paulinus of Nola, Marius Victor, and
possibly, of Juvencus.[3]   They are undistinguished, but show
how natural it was in those days for a man who had followed
the schools, to turn to account, even in old age, the studies
of his youth.

Orientius was likewise an old man when he composed, in
moderately good elegiacs, a moral *Commonitorium*[4] exhorting
to virtue and pointing the way to salvation.   The first two
distichs set forth the subject of the poem :

> quisquis ad aeternae festinus praemia vitae,
>   perpetuanda magis quam peritura cupis,
> quae caelum reseret, mortem fuget, aspera vitet,
>   felici currat tramite, disce viam.

Of greater interest are two hymns (all that remain of a
collection of over twenty), which, unlike those of Ambrose, are
in iambic trimeters with stanzas of five verses. They can hardly
have been composed for liturgical purposes, but were suitable,
perhaps, for private devotion. The subject of the first is nature's
praise of the Creator :

> te solis astrum cum sorore menstrua,
> Vergiliae Iugula Vesperugo Lucifer,
> omnesque guttae praemicantes invocant.
> et nos imago consonantis cantici
> amen sonamus, alleluia dicimus:

---

[1] ib., p. 211 ; for the literatuie of this
controversy see *Bibliography*.
[2] Text, ed. Brandes, *C.S. E.L.* xvi,
pp. 289 sqq.

[3] See Manitius, *Christl. Lat. Poesie*,
p. 218.
[4] Ed. Robinson Ellis, *C.S. E.L.* xvi,
pp. 205 sqq.

> aer aquosus sive sudus invicem,
> simulque venti pluviae grando flumina,
> ritu suomet conditorem concinunt.
> et nos imago consonantis cantici
> amen sonamus, alleluia dicimus.[1]

The other surviving hymn is a 'canticum deprecandi', the object of which is to ensure that no one should add to or take away from the words of these metrical 'prayers':

> postremo dico deprecandi canticum,
> id facio quantum per viginti cantica,
> sed ne quis audax interpellet quippiam,
> anguem magistrum falsitatis increpo,
> ut non adiciat neve demat litteram.

The prayer has miscarried, not by the fault of a scribe, but by the uncaring hand of time.

Tiro Prosper,[2] the last of the group of Gallic poets whom we are considering, was born in Aquitaine about the beginning of the fifth century. He was a prominent defender of the Augustinian doctrine against the Pelagians, and he devoted his life to the great controversy. He also visited Rome, where he attacked the Eutychians.[3] His poetry is wholly dogmatical, dealing like all his works with polemical and doctrinal subjects, and the prosody is poor. The long poem περὶ ἀχαρίστων, or *De Ingratis*, is directed against the Semipelagians:

> unde voluntatis sanctae subsistat origo,
> unde animis pietas insit, et unde fides:
> adversum ingratos falsa et virtute superbos,
> centenis decies versibus excolui.[4]

The Middle Ages loved all poetry which possessed a moral or a dogmatic content, and although the *De Ingratis* is mentioned at a later date only by Hincmar of Reims,[5] Prosper's long book of *Epigrams*, which are versifications of short *sententiae* from Augustine, was apparently popular in the medieval schools, and Vincent of Beauvais admired it.[6] But the epigrams are dreary reading,[7] and the shortest possible specimen must be given here.

---

[1] Ellis, p. 251.
[2] His works are contained in Migne, li ; see *Hist. Litt.* ii. 369 sqq.
[3] Holder-Egger, *Neues Archiv*, i. 59.
[4] Migne, li, col. 91 ; for the argument

of this tedious poem see Manitius, *Christ. Lat. Poesie*, pp. 203 sqq.
[5] Manitius, *Christl. Lat. Poesie*, p. 210.
[6] Manitius, ib., p. 202.
[7] Text, Migne, li, col. 497 sqq.

The sentence of Augustine,

> ' Ordo temporum in aeterna Dei Sapientia, sine tempore est, nec aliqua
> sunt apud deum nova, qui fecit quae futura sunt ',

is thus versified :

> artifice in summo sine tempore temporis ordo est,
>   inque deo rerum non variat series.
> aeterno auctori simul adsunt omnia semper,
>   cum quo in factorum est ordine, quidquid erit.[1]

Prosper stands apart from the other Gallic poets.   In him the
' medievalization' of letters, which showed itself in the absence
of care for form, and the extreme of emphasis on dogma and
morals, holds full sway.   Compared with Avitus or Marius Victor
he hardly deserves the name of poet.   They, at least, while
professing the same high didactic purpose, had laboured, without
relenting, after what they conceived to be perfection of form.
With Prosper the didactic content is everything, and the form
is but an accident.   He wrote in verse because he followed
the theory, which held its own throughout the Middle Ages,
that verse was a snare by which an indifferent reader might
be captured.   But his was the ecclesiastical mind, and if in his
youth he had been taught in the schools to compose secular
verses after the favourite classical models, the temper of his
mind was changed by his close contact with ecclesiastical politics
and his nature was contracted by his absorption in doctrinal
battles.

   With the end of the fifth century, the disruption of the Gallo-
Roman civilization brought to a close a brilliant period of
Christian literature.   The schools had fallen, and with them
departed every opportunity for the serious study of the old
classical language and literature.   It was the first great break
with the wonderful past, and it implied for a time the end of
literature properly so called.   In Italy, Arator palely reflects in
the sixth century the ancient tradition, and Venantius Fortunatus
appears in a barbarian Gaul bringing the last break of secular
culture.   But Fortunatus belonged equally to the new order,
of which he is the lonely herald.   On his death darkness settled
down on Gallic letters until the light broke again in the eighth
century.

[1] Migne, li, col. 515.

§ 3. *Venantius Fortunatus,* A.D. 540–600.

Venantius Honorius Clementianus Fortunatus,[1] Bishop of Poitiers, was born near Treviso in Italy about the year 540. He was educated at the imperial Ravenna, where he learned the rudiments of grammar, rhetoric, and law. Healed by the miraculous intercession of S. Martin of a disease which affected his eyesight, he undertook a pilgrimage of gratitude to the tomb of the saint. So, about the year 565, he crossed the Alps, and entered the realm of the Franks, who were suffering under the chaotic rule of the sons of Chlothar. At the court of Metz he was well received by Sigibert of Austrasia, whose marriage to Brunhildis he celebrated in a somewhat tedious *Epithalamium.*[2] Here Cupid and Venus consent to play their parts again, as though they had never been exorcized by the Christian priests. Cupid extols the virtues and achievements of the king, while Venus praises the beauty and modesty of the bride, and the poem closes with a recognition of their equal and unsurpassed renown.

> ite diu iuncti membris et corde iugati,
> ambo pares genio, meritis et moribus ambo,
> sexum quisque suum pretiosis actibus ornans.

At the court of Sigibert, Fortunatus began to discover his talent. He made many friends among the Frankish and Gallo-Roman nobles and, what was not less important, among the bishops. He travelled with the king along the Moselle, and went with the court to Reims and other places; it is evident that he was attached to the royal train, not merely as a poet, but as a man of education and ability whose services could be put to good use. It was he who was chosen to celebrate in a studied speech the conversion of Brunhildis to catholicism, and on other occasions he was made the 'public orator' of the court. He praised in flattering verses the bishops who were at various times the guests of the king. It has been conjectured that the modest bishops were compelled to listen to their praises in the mouth of the young poet as they sat at table, and to hear the catalogue of their virtues in a succession of superlatives.[3] Then there were nobles to be celebrated: Duke Lupus, who

---

[1] *Venanti Fortunati Carmina,* ed. Leo and Krusch, *M. G. H., Auct. Antiq.,* iv.

[2] vi. 1, pp. 124 sqq.

[3] Meyer, *Der Gelegenheitsdichter Venantius Fortunatus,* p. 34; Köbner, *Venantius Fortunatus,* p. 27.

surpassed Scipio, Cato, and Pompey; Gogo, who is compared with Orpheus for charm; and Duke Bodegisel, whose very presence was ravishing, and whose wife was like the morning star. Fortunatus entered into the 'cult of personality and friendship'[1] which ruled at the Austrasian court, and found its expression in demonstrative letters, in prose and verse.

But in 567 he had left the court for ever. He remembered and fulfilled his ancient vow to S. Martin, but first he made a stay at Paris, where Sigibert's brother Charibert was king. Fortunatus felt that he was a man without a home;[2] the Lombards had overrun the north of Italy, and he made up his mind to settle at last in Poitiers, the city which was to be his home until his death. It was a fortunate choice, for here he found a circle of friends whose devotion crowned with happiness and contentment the best years of his life. Radegunde, the daughter of the king of Thuringia, married against her will to the blood-thirsty Chlothar, the murderer of her brother, had fled from her husband, and found a refuge from her troubles in the peace of her monastery of the Holy Cross at Poitiers. This cultured lady, and the Abbess Agnes, became the firm friends of the now celebrated poet, who was persuaded to take up his abode in the neighbourhood of the monastery. The intimacy and charm of this new friendship is revealed in a series of epigrams and epistles in which the poet renders grateful thanks for gifts of food and fruit, and even for dinners of many courses with which the queen had loaded his table. Fortunatus was now in priest's orders, but he could depict with broad humour his delight in the lavish array of good things, which he describes after the manner of a true *bon vivant*.[3]

Before his death, about the year 600, Fortunatus became Bishop of Poitiers, and when he died he was prosperous and famous, having won the good things of this life. But he had won in addition a new world, the supernatural world of religion as it revealed itself in the life of the nunnery at Poitiers. For the real attraction that held the bishop was the holy life of renunciation which raised his friends above the level of this world. This almost superstitious reverence for the religious life fills the long poem which he composed for the installation of Agnes as abbess. He was moved to express himself in the terms of that erotic mysticism which became more common

---

[1] Köbner, p. 32.   [2] vii. 9, p. 163.   [3] cf. xi. 9, 10, p. 262.

at a later date. In another poem he places the virgins next
to the martyrs, among the apostles and prophets :

> inter apostolicas acies sacrosque prophetas
>   proxima martyribus praemia virgo tenet.
> splendida sidereo circumdata lumine pergens
>   iungitur angelicis casta puella choris.
> fruge pudicitiae caeli dotanda talento
>   aeterni regis ducitur in thalamis.[1]

It was at Radegunde's command that he wrote the verses, *De
excidio Thoringiae*,[2] which were to be addressed to her cousin
Amalfrid, who was in the service of the emperor at Constantinople. The poet was to tell in pathetic verses of the ruin of
their royal house, and the horrors through which both had lived.
Radegunde recalls the friendship of their youth, and she hopes
that the cousin will renew it by some message to show that
he is alive and remembers her. But he was dead, and so
Fortunatus must write another letter, this time to her nephew
Artachis, who was perhaps the son of her murdered brother.[3]

Among the mass of the poetry of Fortunatus—epitaphs,
epigrams, panegyrics, metrical epistles and trifles—a few purely
religious pieces stand out as the true expression of his genius.
His imagination turned, under the influence of the mysticism
of Poitiers, to the Cross, the tree upon which was hung, as in
a balance, the Ransom of the world. For the medieval Catholic
the Cross had become the Tree of salvation. As sin and death
had entered the world by the Tree in the Garden, so by a Tree
the redemption of the world was achieved. Nay, the Tree of the
Garden had been miraculously preserved, and from its wood, by
the poetic justice of God, was formed the Cross, that Tree which
bore a better fruit for the healing of the nations.[4] The fascination of such a theme was enhanced, for Fortunatus, by the fact
that the Emperor Justin II and his wife had sent, most precious
of relics, a piece of the true Cross to be the glory of Radegunde's
monastery at Poitiers.[5] In a long elegiac poem, addressed to
Justin and his wife Sophia,[6] Fortunatus celebrates the authors
of this marvellous gift. Apart from those curious poems, half
picture and half acrostic, 'in honour of the sacred Cross', the

---

[1] viii. 4, p. 192.

[2] *App.* i, p. 271.

[3] *App.* iii, p. 278; this is Meyer's con-
jecture, p. 137, of his monograph on
Fortunatus.

[4] On this notion see Émile Mâle, *L'art
religieux du XIIIᵉ siècle en France*,
p. 223; Bréhier, *L'art chrétien*, p. 239.

[5] Gregory of Tours, *Hist. Franc.* ix. 40.

[6] *App.* ii, p. 275.

second book of his *Carmina* contains four poems on this same subject. The first, in elegiacs, is full of that strange and novel beauty with which Christian mysticism was learning to adorn the measures borrowed from the ancient world :

> crux benedicta nitet, dominus qua carne pependit
>   atque cruore suo vulnera nostra lavat,
> mitis amore pio pro nobis victima factus
>   traxit ab ore lupi qua sacer agnus oves,
> transfixis palmis ubi mundum a clade redemit
>   atque suo clausit funere mortis iter ;
> hic manus illa fuit clavis confixa cruentis,
>   quae eripuit Paulum crimine, morte Petrum.
> fertilitate potens, o dulce et nobile lignum,
>   quando tuis ramis tam nova poma geris !
> cuius odore novo defuncta cadavera surgunt
>   et redeunt vitae qui caruere diem.
> nullum uret aestus sub frondibus arboris huius,
>   luna nec in noctem sol neque meridie.
> tu plantata micas, secus est ubi cursus aquarum,
>   spargis et ornatas flore recente comas.
> appensa est vitis inter tua brachia, de qua
>   dulcia sanguineo vina rubore fluunt.[1]

These verses, like those of Paulinus, go back to classical models, but they have, nevertheless, a medieval flavour.[2] What is most insistent in them is not the classical form, but the wholly Christian idea, the emotion of Catholic mysticism which speaks in lines like these :

> fertilitate potens, o dulce et nobile lignum
>   quando tuis ramis tam nova poma geris !

This triumph of the medieval idea is seen, with an effect even more striking, in the *Vexilla regis prodeunt*, which the Church has adopted as one of her great Passion hymns. Written in iambic dimeters, with a free use of rime, this famous poem is one of the first creations of purely medieval religious feeling :

> vexilla regis prodeunt,   confixa clavis viscera
>   fulget crucis mysterium,   tendens manus, vestigia
>   quo carne carnis conditor   redemptionis gratia
>   suspensus est patibulo.   hic immolata est hostia.

---

[1] ii. 1, p. 27.
[2] For the contention that the latinity of Fortunatus was improved by his more learned Carolingian transcribers see H.

Elss, *Untersuchungen über den Stil und die Sprache des Venantius Fortunatus,* Heidelberg 1907.

quo vulneratus insuper
  mucrone diro lanceae,
  ut nos lavaret crimine,
  manavit unda et sanguine.

impleta sunt quae concinit
  David fideli carmine,
  dicendo nationibus :
  regnavit a ligno deus.[1]

arbor decora et fulgida,
  ornata regis purpura,
  electa digno stipite
  tam sancta membra tangere!

beata cuius brachiis
  pretium pependit saeculi!
  statera facta est corporis
  praedam tulitque Tartari.

fundis aroma cortice,
  vincis sapore nectare,
  iucunda fructu fertili
  plaudis triumpho nobili.

salve ara, salve victima,
  de passionis gloria,
  qua vita mortem pertulit
  et morte vitam reddidit.

But superior in execution and inspiration to the *Vexilla regis*, is the *Pange, lingua*, another Passion hymn, written in the metre of the Roman soldiers' songs, the trochaic tetrameter. Here the talent of Fortunatus is at its best : [2]

pange, lingua, gloriosi proelium certaminis
  et super crucis tropaeo dic triumphum nobilem,
  qualiter redemptor orbis immolatus vicerit.

de parentis protoplasti fraude factor condolens,
  quando pomi noxialis morte morsu conruit,
  ipse lignum tunc notavit, damna ligni ut solveret.

hoc opus nostrae salutis ordo depoposcerat,
  multiformis perditoris arte ut artem falleret
  et medellam ferret inde, hostis unde laeserat.

quando venit ergo sacri plenitudo temporis,
  missus est ab arce patris natus orbis conditor
  atque ventre virginali carne factus prodiit.

vagit infans inter arta conditus praesepia,
  membra pannis involuta virgo mater adligat
  et pedes manusque, crura stricta pingit fascia.

lustra sex qui iam peracta tempus inplens corporis,
  se volente natus ad hoc, passioni deditus
  agnus in crucis levatur immolandus stipite.

---

[1] Ps. xcvi. 10. In the *Psalterium Romanum* the reading was, ' Dicite in gentibus quia dominus regnavit a ligno '. This is Jerome's first revision of the ' old Latin ' psalter, and in this instance he retained the old text. The first revision soon became official in Italy. In the second revision, or *Psalterium Gallicanum*, ' a ligno ' has disappeared. The reading was a Christian addition to the LXX ; Justin (*Dialogus cum Tryphone*, 73) accused the Jews of maliciously cutting it out from their texts.

[2] ii. 6, p. 34. Attempts have been made to ascribe this hymn to Claudianus Mamertus, a priest of Vienne, but the oldest ascriptions are to Fortunatus ; see *Anal. Hymn.* l, p. 73, note ; for a suggestion by Dr. A. J. Mason that Fortunatus, in composing this hymn, was much influenced by Hilary's trochaic hymn, see *J. T. S.* v. 429 sq.

hic acetum fel harundo sputa clavi lancea,
    mite corpus perforatur, sànguis, unda profluit,
    terra pontus astra mundus quo lavantur flumine.

crux fidelis, inter omnes arbor una nobilis
    (nulla talem silva profert flore fronde germine),
    dulce lignum, dulce clavo dulce pondus sustinens!

flecte ramos, arbor alta, tensa laxa viscera,
    et rigor lentescat ille quem dedit nativitas,
    ut superni membra regis mite tendas stipite.

sola digna tu fuisti ferre pretium saeculi
    atque portum praeparare nauta mundo naufrago,
    quem sacer cruor perunxit fusus agni corpore.[1]

'Chef-d'œuvre de poésie théologique', says M. Remy de Gourmont.[2] But, beyond the theological symbolism, lie a pathos
and pity by virtue of which the poetry—and this is rare in
a medieval hymn—achieves a triumph over the dogmatic
intention :

> Faithful Cross! above all other,
>   One and only noble Tree!
> None in foliage, none in blossom,
>   None in fruit thy peer may be;
> Sweetest wood, and sweetest iron!
>   Sweetest weight is hung on thee.
>
> Bend, O' lofty Tree, thy branches,
>   Thy too rigid sinews bend;
> And awhile the stubborn hardness,
>   Which thy birth bestow'd, suspend;
> And the limbs of heav'n's high Monarch
>   Gently on thine arms extend!

Here we seem to catch something of the pathos, the 'dispiritedness' of medievalism,[3] which the Church has bequeathed to the
modern world.

The same qualities which we have already noted in his
religious poetry, appear in another hymn. *Quem terra, pontus,
aethera*, a poem in honour of the Virgin, which has been ascribed
to Fortunatus, but is almost certainly the work of another poet.
As in the *Vexilla regis*, rime is used as a conscious artistic
device. The metre is again the iambic dimeter.

[1] ii. 2, p. 28.
[2] *Le Latin mystique*, p. 74.

[3] Bury, *Later Roman Empire*, i. 358,
London 1889.

quem terra, pontus, aethera
colunt, adorant, praedicant,
trinam regentem machinam
claustrum Mariae baiulat.

benedicta caeli nuntio,
fecunda sancto spiritu,
desideratus gentibus
cuius per alvum fusus est.

cui luna, sol et omnia
deserviunt per tempora,
perfusa caeli gratia
gestant puellae viscera.

o gloriosa domina
excelsa super sidera,
qui te creavit provide
lactasti sacro ubere.

mirantur ergo saecula
quod angelus fert semina,
quod aure virgo concipit
et corde credens parturit.

quod Eva tristis abstulit
tu reddis almo germine ;
intrent ut astra flebiles,
caeli fenestra facta es.

beata mater munere,
cuius supernus artifex,
mundum pugillo continens,
ventris sub arca clausus est.

tu regis alti ianua
et porta lucis fulgida.
vitam datam per virginem
gentes redemptae plaudite.[1]

Though Fortunatus loved best the hexameter, and the elegiac, which he had learned to handle with a smooth facility, his ear and the ears of his imitators were pleased with the new music of rime which could produce such novel effects as in the sixth stanza of this hymn, or in the second of the *Vexilla regis*. After the pale effort of Sedulius,[2] such lines must have contained for the contemporaries and successors of Fortunatus an ineffable charm.

Of the remainder of the religious poems of Fortunatus, we have only to note the elegiac piece addressed to Bishop Felix on the subject of the Easter festival.[3] It begins with a beautiful description of the spring of the year, when the days grow longer and brighter and the flowers begin to make glad the meadows :

> mollia purpureum pingunt violaria campum,
>   prata virent herbis et micat herba comis.
> paulatim subeunt stellantia lumina florum
>   arridentque oculis gramina tincta suis.

The leaves begin to bud, the bees appear, the birds are singing again, and the voice of the nightingale makes sweeter the

---

[1] *M. G. H.* iv, p. 385. Leo classes this among the *Carmina spuria.* Dreves, *Hymnologische Studien zu Fortunatus und Raban* (cf. *Anal. Hymn.* l, p. 88), tries to show that it is by Fortunatus. Strecker in his review of Dreves (*Anzeiger für deutsches Altertum, &c.*, xxxiii, p. 45) points out that MS. authority is wanting, and that the hymn is rather an imitation of Fortunatus. See also Köbner, p. 147, note 1. I observe that, in spite of Strecker, von Schubert, *Gesch. d. christl. Kirche im Frühmittelalter,* Tübingen 1921, p. 170, holds to Fortunatus's authorship.

[2] See below, p. 110.

[3] iii. 9, p. 59.

echoing air. It is the resurrection of nature, which is the
symbol of the resurrection of Christ:

> ecce renascentis testatur gratia mundi
>   omnia cum domino dona redisse suo.

The *Salve, festa dies,* once famous as an Easter processional,
is a cento from this splendid poem. The selection most commonly used is the following: [1]

Sabbato Sancto.
Ad Processionem.

R°. salve, festa dies, toto venerabilis aevo,
    qua deus infernum vicit et astra tenet.

ecce renascentis testatur gratia mundi
    omnia cum domino dona redisse suo.

namque triumphanti post tristia tartara Christo
    undique fronde nemus, gramina flore favent.

legibus inferni oppressis supra astra meantem
    laudant rite deum lux, polus, arva, fretum.

qui crucifixus erat, deus, ecce, per omnia regnat,
    dantque creatori cuncta creata precem.

nobilitas anni, mensum decus, arma dierum,
    horarum splendor, scripula puncta fovent.

Christe, salus rerum, bone conditor atque redemptor,
    unica progenies ex deitate patris,

qui genus humanum cernens mersisse profundo,
    ut hominem eriperes, es quoque factus homo.

funeris exsequias pateris, vitae auctor et orbis,
    intras mortis iter dando salutis opem.

pollicitam sed redde fidem, precor, alma potestas,
    tertia lux rediit, surge sepulte meus!

solve catenatas inferni carceris umbras
    et revoca sursum, quidquid ad ima ruit.

redde tuam faciem, videant ut saecula lumen,
    redde diem, qui nos te moriente fugit.

eripis innumerum populum de carcere mortis,
    et sequitur liber, quo suus auctor adit.

hinc tumulum repetens post tartara carne resumpta
    belliger ad caelos ampla tropaea refers.

[1] *Anal. Hymn.* l, p. 79.

In estimating the poetical achievement of Fortunatus, those critics who have refused to see in him anything more than a 'last and feeble representative of classical poetry',[1] have naturally arrived at an unfavourable conclusion. To such critics Fortunatus is merely the unworthy successor of those poets of the fifth century, who, with all their faults, were steeped in the classical tradition, and had caught something of the manner of their great models. These were, at any rate, men of education, trained in the Imperial Schools, while Fortunatus, who, on his own confession, knew little 'grammar' and less rhetoric,[2] was hardly less than a barbarian among barbarians. 'Le poëte épicurien, l'abbé gastronome'; so M. Ampère dismissed with contempt the author of the *Vexilla Regis*.[3] But when, in the true historical spirit and laying classical prejudice aside, we are content to regard Fortunatus as a poet to be judged in the setting of his own age, we recognize at once that he draws his inspiration from the material of his own experience, and refuses to remain a mere versifier of worn-out themes.[4] And so it is that his verses, tedious as many of them doubtless are, reflect the real man, his lively interest in the common things of life, his delight in nature, his good humour, and most of all, his relation to what was deepest and best in the religious life. This 'occasional' poet, who wrote about trifles—a supper, a gift of flowers, a garden, a journey along the Moselle—could also celebrate in noble verse the passion of Christ, or the world's resurrection in the spring. It is far truer, therefore, to regard Fortunatus, not as the last of the Roman, but as the first of medieval poets. His hymns are steeped in the Catholic spirit, in Catholic symbolism and mysticism. The form may be classical at bottom, but in his use of rime and even more in the quality of his inspiration, he is in the great line of liturgical poets who were the creators of a new tradition, a tradition out of which was to issue the lyrical poetry of the modern world. Further, in his secular verses, he expresses the spirit of a new civilization, which was being raised on the ruins of the Gallo-Roman past. For a time he was a court poet, and it is surprising to find that

---

[1] Ampère, *Hist. lit. de la France*, i. 312.

[2] In his versified *Life of S. Martin*, i. 29–30 (p. 296):
parvula grammaticae lambens refluamina guttae,
rhetorici exiguum praelibans gurgitis haustum.

[3] ii., op. cit., 346.

[4] Cf. Meyer, *Venantius Fortunatus*, p. 31: 'Fortunatus schildert nur, was wirklich um ihn ist, und das mit Gedanken, welche den Menschen seines Gleichen nahe liegen'; so Manitius, pp. 439, 469. Cf. also Meyer, *Rythmik*, i. 41.

among the rude Franks he found many who appreciated his poems as well as their author.[1]   There was at Sigibert's court a circle of men of noble birth who were united in friendship and formed a kind of spiritual, if not an intellectual aristocracy, and it was their ideal which Fortunatus attempted to express. Bishops and Gallo-Romans of high birth or importance brought with them something of the old tradition from the days of Sidonius, and their Frankish friends did their best to imitate their manners and tastes.   But this was only one stage in the poet's progress, and it was fortunate that he turned away from the courts and settled finally at Poitiers.   For it was there that he made a more profitable friendship and, coming once for all under the spell of the Church, became a great Christian poet.

§ 4. *Christian Poetry in Africa.*

Reference has already been made to the great part which the African provinces played in the beginnings of Christian-Latin literature.   But the African temperament would seem to have been, on the whole, unfavourable to the production of verse.[2] Towards the end of the second century, Fronto and Apuleius were setting the fashion in prose for the whole Roman world, but no poet of any note had come from Africa since the days of Terence.   Yet the schools of Carthage remained famous until the time of Augustine, and the country was covered with prosperous cities.   The fifth century, however, subjected the African provinces to the same troubles which had already fallen on Western Europe.   In 429 the fatal invitation of Count Boniface had brought the Vandals into Africa.[3]   They crossed from Spain under Gaiseric, their able and cruel king, whose Arian faith made him the implacable enemy of the Catholic Church.   Eighty thousand Vandals and Alans broke into the wealthy and peaceful provinces, plundering and destroying as they went.   Augustine died in the third month of the siege of Hippo, and with him ended the long line of Christian men of letters which included such names as Tertullian, Minucius Felix, Cyprian, Arnobius, and Lactantius.   In 439 Carthage fell, and the Vandals were masters of the greater part of Roman

[1] Köbner, *Venantius Fortunatus,* pp. 28 sqq.
[2] Cf. Mommsen, *Roman Provinces,*
ii. 373, London 1909.
[3] Bury, *History of the Later Roman Empire,* i. 245, London 1923.

Africa. The landowners were dispossessed; the Catholic bishops suffered persecution and their Churches were handed over to the Arians.[1] Yet the power of the old Roman culture was not exhausted. It was not long before the Vandal kings admitted men of letters to the Court, and the barbarians sent their children to the schools, where they learned grammar and rhetoric with the children of the well-to-do provincials. It was under the Vandal domination that Africa produced her most important Christian poet, Blossius Aemilius Dracontius,[2] whose verses are worthy of comparison with those of Avitus or Marius Victor. From the poems of Dracontius and a little group of other poems which by some strange chance have escaped the ravages of time, we learn that the cultured classes were unable to surrender their old passion for the making of verses.[3] Most of these verses deal with purely secular subjects, although the authors were obviously Christian. Like Ennodius in Italy, these poets cultivated the epigram, sometimes with a satirical bent which recalls the obscenities of Martial, at other times with a more pleasing fancy.[4] Luxorius, to whom a number of these poems is attributed, shows a vicious taste for the cento and for epanaleptic verses. Some of the African epigrams are on Christian themes. Thus Calbulus composed some verses, of which the following were frequently used for inscription on medieval crosses:

> crux domini mecum, crux est quam semper adoro,
>   crux mihi refugium, crux mihi certa salus.
> virtutum genetrix, fons vitae, ianua caeli,
>   crux Christi totum destruit hostis opus.[5]

The *Carmen ad Flavium Felicem de Resurrectione Mortuorum* has already been mentioned.[6] This poem may be an African production of the sixth century. It is chiefly remarkable for its use of rime and for the evidence which it affords of the decline of the feeling for quantity; it has, indeed, a vigour of its own, especially in the description of the last judgement and the pains of hell.

---

[1] On the Church under the Vandals see Duchesne, *Hist. de l'Église*, iii. 625 sqq.; *Cambridge Medieval History*, i. 304 sqq.

[2] Text, ed. Vollmer, in *M. G. H., Auct. Antiq.*, xiv, Berlin 1905; Migne, lx, col. 595 sqq.; Bährens, *Poet. Lat. Min.* 126 sqq. (re-edited by Vollmer, *P. L. M.* v, Leipzig 1914, whose text I have used).

[3] Cf. Manitius, *Christl. Lat. Poesie*, p. 340.

[4] Texts, in Riese, *Anthologia Latina*, i. 208 sqq., Leipzig 1869; Bährens, iv. 386 sq.

[5] Riese, *Anthol. Lat.* i. 246; Bährens, iv. 429-30.

[6] p. 24; text in *Cypriani Opera*, *C. S. E. L.* iii. 308 sqq.

But Dracontius easily occupies the first position among the African poets.   He is the best witness to the survival in Africa of the old school of cultured and aristocratic Christianity.   Of high birth and a lawyer by profession, he had a facile talent for verse, which he exercised unwisely to his lasting sorrow.   For he made the mistake of celebrating the Roman Emperor instead of Gunthamund, the Vandal king.[1]   For this fault, which was magnified into a political offence, his property was confiscated, and he and his family were thrown into prison.   His misfortunes turned his heart to God, and in an elegiac poem called the *Satisfactio*, he implored forgiveness, first of God and then of the king.   He humbly confessed his fault, even to the length of comparing himself to a dog.   The dog's tongue can lick and heal its sores, but alas! for himself, his tongue had been the cause of his own misfortune :

> ast ego peccando regi dominoque deoque,
>   peior sum factus, deteriorque cane.
> vulnera vexati curat sua lingua molossi,
>   heu! mea quippe mihi vulnera lingua dedit.[2]

But this humble plea for pardon was all in vain, and the unhappy prisoner turned once more to his muse.   In the long hours of imprisonment he composed, this time in heroic measure, a lengthy didactic poem in which he endeavours to justify the ways of God to man.[3]

> qui cupit iratum placidumve scire tonantem,
>   hoc carmen, sed mente legat, dum voce recenset.

The omnipotence of God is his first theme; to which the creation bears witness.   In lively verses he describes the opening story of Genesis, and he paints the earthly paradise in dazzling colours with a skill which equals that of Avitus :[4]

> ver ibi perpetuum communes temperat auras,
> ne laedant frondes, et ut omnia poma coquantur.
> non apibus labor est ceris formare cicutas :
> nectaris aetherii sudant ex arbore mella,
> et pendent foliis iam pocula blanda futura,
> pendet et optatae vivax medicina salutis ;
> dependent quis dat sollers pictura figuras.[5]

---

[1] Gunthamund became king in A.D. 484 and died in A. D. 496.

[2] Vollmer, p. 96.

[3] *Carmen de Laudibus Dei*, Vollmer,

p. I.

[4] Cf. Manitius, *Christl. Lat. Poesie*, p. 331.

[5] Vollmer, p. 9.

He describes the Fall, and the coming of sin and death, which have involved the whole human race. Dracontius here digresses to praise the greatness and power of God, and in the second book he shows how God revealed His grace in the incarnation of His Son, that the world might not perish without hope of redemption. He briefly touches on the miracles of Christ, but returns, with greater interest, to those favourite wonders of the Old Testament which prefigured the redemption—the passage of the Israelites through the Red Sea, the manna in the wilderness, the water from the rock. Then once more he takes up his old theme of God's greatness, and proceeds to the story of the Flood and its failure to cure the evil race of men of their manifold sins. The destruction of the Cities of the Plain was equally without effect. But the mercy of God was not exhausted; He sent His Son to redeem the world:

> pietas tamen alma parentis,
> indulgere volens cito quam punire parata,
> misit ab arce pium caeli per sidera Christum,
> qui virtute sua serpentis frangeret artes,
> per vexilla crucis hostis populando cohortes,
> praecipiti iactu quas celsa palatia caeli
> exsilio trusere gravi sub perpete culpa.[1]

It is not necessary to follow Dracontius into the third book, in which he celebrates the wonderful dealings of God with man. At the close he returns to his own troubles and his own sins. He implores the mercy of God (for the mercy of man had failed him), and he looks for the peace of heaven after the misery of life:

> sit sine tormentis post corpus vita futura.
> noxia mens non sit, non sit rea, non sit iniqua,
> et requies animae, quae mox purgata quiescet.
> iudicio, deus alme, tuo detur inde triumphus,
> inter odoratas flores et amoena virecta
> ad nemus aeternum veniam, sedesque beatas
> et grates exceptus agam de fasce malorum,
> additus insonti populo sub sorte piorum.[2]

Whether Dracontius was finally released from prison we cannot tell. His religious poetry does not appear to have made any considerable appeal to later ages, but his verses as a whole are an important evidence for the culture of his time.[3] A group of secular poems, most of which must belong to his younger

[1] Vollmer, p. 54.
[2] ib., p. 94.
[3] Cf. Manitius, *Christl. Lat. Poesie*, p. 331.

days, show that Dracontius did not confine his talent to religious subjects. Some of these are mere school versifications[1] on common themes, like Hylas and the nymphs; a soliloquy of Hercules when he was fighting the Hydra; the Rape of Helen; a deliberation of Achilles over the body of Hector. Dracontius had formed his style on good classical models. He knew his Virgil and Ovid well, but he could not escape the faults of his age. It is sufficient praise to say that his longest poem can fairly challenge comparison with those of the 'epic' poets of Gaul in the fifth century.

The kingdom of the Vandals came to an end in 534, and Africa was reunited to the Empire. About the same year the priest Verecundus was made Bishop of Junca in Byzacene. He had lived through many difficult years and might well have expected to end his days in peace. But he became involved in the dispute between Justinian and Pope V gilius about the Three Chapters. The Emperor had seized the Pope and transported him to Constantinople, where he was compelled to condemn the writings of Theodore of Mopsuestia, Theodoret, and Ibas, although they had been approved by the Council of Chalcedon. The African bishops protested, and the Pope recanted to the extent of demanding a council. Justinian adopted strong measures and Verecundus was among the bishops who were brought to Constantinople to be dealt with in the manner of the East. He was by the side of Vigilius in the Church of St. Peter in Hormisda when the Emperor's soldiers used violence against the Pope, seizing him by the beard and feet in a struggle which horrified the crowd that had followed the soldiers into the Church. Vigilius escaped with his life and fled with Verecundus and a few others to Chalcedon, where they took refuge in the Church of S. Euphemia. But Justinian would not relent. The unfortunate Pope had to yield once more. Verecundus, we may guess, would have resisted to the last, but death overtook him before he could incur the punishment—prison or exile—which Justinian meted out to the surviving rebels.

The experiences of Verecundus are sufficient to account for the gloomy outlook of his verses 'de satisfactione poenitentiae', a 'lamentabile carmen' as Isidore calls it,[2] though in it the

---

[1] Texts in Bährens, pp. 126 sqq.; Vollmer, pp. 108 sqq.

[2] Isidore, *De viris illustribus*, 7; the text of the poem is in J. B. Pitra, *Spicilegium Solesmense*, iv, pp. 138 sqq., Paris 1858.

author laments his own sins rather than those of others.   He
wishes that he might weep rivers of blood, and in the words
of Job, he curses the day on which he was born :

> saeva dies pereat, ea quae me protulit orbi
> materna effusum muliebris viscera ventris,
> contenebrata suo societur noctibus ortu!
> lumine subtracto, radios abscondat anhelos, .
> ut matutinae iungantur vespera luci!
> turbidus implicitis tenebretur nubibus aer,
> condensusque diem pluat imber flammeus illum!
> mensibus ablatum pereat sine nomine tempus!

This lamentation is a prelude to a picture of the coming doom,
when the world will be consumed, and the sea, the earth, the
sky will be involved in one furnace of destruction, along with
beasts and men and birds :

> et quaecumque simul latentia saecula gestant.

The world will be at once its own pyre and its own corpse.[1]
Three books, the poet says, will be unrolled before me in that
day, containing my works, my words, and my wandering thoughts.
They will accuse me, and I must answer them.

The poem, which in places is reminiscent of the spirit of
Commodian, has the sombre vigour of the African tradition.
The prosody is not good and the literary reminiscences go back
to the Bible rather than to heathen or Christian poets.[2]   But
the lament of this sixth-century bishop is one of the last
voices that reach us before the final eclipse of Latin culture
in Africa.

---

[1] p. 143, ' Mundus erit rogus ipse sibi,   [2] Cf. Manitius, *Christl. Lat. Poesie*,
mundusque cadaver '.   p. 406.

IV

THE CHRISTIAN POETS OF ITALY IN THE FOURTH, FIFTH, AND SIXTH CENTURIES

§ 1. *Paulinus of Nola*, A. D. 355 *circa*–431.

PONTIUS Meropius Anicius Paulinus,[1] who shares with Prudentius the honour of being the creator of Christian lyrical poetry in the West,[2] was born at Bordeaux about A. D. 355, of noble and wealthy parents who were attached to the Christian faith. At Bordeaux, he received under the famous Ausonius, who conceived a great affection for his brilliant pupil, the best education which his age was able to afford. There he acquired the art of composing those elegant verses on trifling themes which Ausonius regarded as the perfect fruit of a liberal education. Paulinus might well have continued to the end of his days in the enjoyment of an easy and luxurious life, in the midst of the cultured society of Aquitaine, obtaining one by one the public honours which were due to his noble birth, his education, and his intellectual endowments. It is not clear that, like his master Ausonius, he attained the dignity of the consulship, though he did become governor of the province of Campania, but his interests did not lie in the direction of a public career, and he preferred the quiet ease of the country side on one of his vast estates, to the distractions and disappointments of public life. He married a wealthy Spanish lady, named Therasia, whose piety and strength of character soon gained an ascendency over a nature already attracted by the Church. He was deeply moved by the religious revival which, under the influence of Martin of Tours, was then sweeping over the south of Gaul, and he came into contact with

---

[1] For the poems of Paulinus, *Paulini Nolani Carmina*, ed. von Hartel, *C.S.E.L.* xxx ; besides the special works on Paulinus and the notices in the usual literary histories, see Boissier, *Fin du paganisme*, ii. 49 sqq. ; Dill, *Roman Society in the last* century of the Western Empire, pp. 396 sqq.; Bigg, *Wayside Sketches in Ecclesiastical History*, pp. 27 sqq.

[2] i. e., apart from writers of hymns, like Hilary and Ambrose.

the best minds of his age, with Sulpicius Severus, with Ambrose, and with Amandus of Bordeaux.

About the year 389 he was baptized, and soon after he retired with his wife to Spain. There, under the influence of some bitter experience, and after the death of a long desired child, Paulinus and his wife decided to forsake the world and devote themselves to the religious life near his family estates at Nola in Campania. In 394 they settled at Nola near the tomb of S. Felix, a popular Italian saint, whom Paulinus had always regarded as his especial patron.[1] In the course of time, a monastic community sprang up round their dwelling, and crowds of pilgrims came each year to celebrate the festival of S. Felix in the basilicas at Nola. Happy and peaceful years followed, broken only by rumours of the invasion of Radagaisus and the terrible experiences of 410. The monasticism of Nola bears that idyllic impress of freedom and simplicity which preceded the era of organization and of rules. Paulinus died in 431. Humane and tolerant,[2] beloved by the common people, he was respected and honoured by the leaders of the Church, by Ambrose, by Augustine, and by Jerome.

His conversion to the life of religion called forth the wonder and the indignation of the easy-living cultured society in which he had spent his earlier years, and the Romans were astounded to see the man who had once been accompanied by lictors appearing in their streets in the garb of a monk. His old master Ausonius felt most keenly the conversion of his beloved pupil, and in a series of poetical epistles, in which he used all the resources of his rhetoric, he endeavoured to persuade him to abandon his ascetic practices and return to the old manner of life at Bordeaux. At this time Paulinus was in retreat in Spain. In a poem of much beauty and singularly free from those rhetorical touches which disfigured the verses of Ausonius, he replied that he had forsaken the old life for ever, and was henceforth wholly devoted to Christ. But throughout the whole poem he is careful to insist that his affection for his master remains undiminished :

---

[1] On the popularity of S. Felix see Lucius, *Heiligenkult*, p. 174, note 2 ; on Paulinus and his devotion to Felix, p. 301 sq.

[2] Cf. M. Boissier's charming estimate of the character of Paulinus (*Fin du paganisme*, ii. 1c2–3) : ' Malgré l'ardeur de sa foi, il sut conserver jusqu'à la fin les vertus les plus précieuses et les plus rares, la tolérance et l'humanité ! C'est le plus bel éloge qu'on puisse faire de lui: c'est par là qu'il a mérité l'honneur d'être mis, à côté de son maître saint Martin, au premier rang des saints français.'

gratia prima tibi, tibi gloria debita cedit,
cuius praeceptis partum est quod Christus amaret.[1]

It is in vain that Ausonius counsels him to return to the Muses
and to the vanities of pagan mythological lore.   Forsaking the
elegiacs with which his letter began, Paulinus proceeds in iambic
measure of charming beauty to tell his master that the heart
which is vowed to the service of Christ can never again welcome
Apollo and the Muses:

> quid abdicatas in meam curam, pater,
>   redire Musas praecipis?
> negant Camenis nec patent Apollini
>   dicata Christo pectora.
> ... nunc alia mentem vis agit, maior deus,
>   aliosque mores postulat,
> sibi reposcens ab homine munus suum,
>   vivamus ut vitae patri.

His heart, he says, is fixed on the things which are unseen—' for
the things which are seen are temporal, and the things which are
not seen are eternal':

> namque caduca patent nostris, aeterna negantur
> visibus, et nunc spe sequimur quod mente videmus,
> spernentes varias rerum spectacula formas
> et male corporeos bona sollicitantia visus.[2]

He has before his eyes the terror of the final judgement, when
it will be too late to repent and seek forgiveness for a life which
has been squandered on trifles:

> huius in adventum trepidis mihi credula fibris
> corda tremunt gestitque anima id iam cauta futuri,
> praemetuens ne vincta aegris pro corpore curis
> ponderibusque gravis rerum, si forte recluso
> increpitet tuba vasta polo, non possit in auras
> regis ad occursum levibus se tollere pinnis,
> inter honora volans sanctorum milia caelo,
> qui per inane leves neque mundi compede vinctos
> ardua in astra pedes facili molimine tollent
> et teneris vecti per sidera nubibus ibunt,
> caelestem ut medio venerentur in aëre regem
> claraque adorato coniungant agmina Christo.[3]

The talent of Paulinus did not lie in the direction of theological
speculation.   He remained to the end what Ausonius had made

---

[1] *Carmen* x. 145-6 ; cf. 89 sqq. ;   *de Nole.*
Carmen xi. 8-9, 44 sqq. ; see Labriolle,   [2] *Carmen* x. 174-7.
La correspondance d'Ausone et de Paulin   [3] ib., x. 304-15.

him, the cultivated poet and man of letters. But for his conversion, he would have employed his poetical gifts upon trifling subjects and rhetorical themes; now that he had devoted himself to religion, he used his talent to express those ideas and emotions which had really mastered his life. In short, he became a true poet. The long series of poems written at the festivals of his beloved Felix are full of interest, not merely for their poetical qualities, but because they give a vivid picture of the popular devotion of the age, a devotion with which, as at the present day, many survivals. of pagan sentiment were inextricably mingled.[1]

In one of these poems[2] Paulinus describes the crowds of country folk assembling for this their great festival and holiday of the year. Inside the church the altar blazes with lights, so that 'night is as bright as day, and day itself is rendered more bright by the glow of innumerable candles'. The people bring their gifts in kind and ask the protection of the saint for themselves and their goods through the coming year.

In another poem[3] on the same theme, Paulinus begins with a description of spring time, for although the festival of Felix takes place in the winter, it is for him the true spring-time of the year:

> ver avibus voces aperit, mea lingua suum ver
> natalem Felicis habet, quo lumine et ipsa
> floret hiems populis gaudentibus.

He prays that he may be inspired to sing like the nightingale which hidden in the deep leaves of the wood pours forth an always changing melody:

> adnue, fons verbi, verbum deus, et velut illam
> me modo veris avem dulci fac voce canorum,
> quae viridi sub fronde latens solet avia rura
> multimodis mulcere modis linguamque per unam
> fundere non unas mutato carmine voces,
> unicolor plumis ales, sed picta loquellis.
> nunc teretes rotat illa modos, nunc sibila longis
> ducit acuta sonis, rursum quasi flebile carmen
> inchoat et subito praecidens fine querellam
> adtonitas rupto modulamine decipit aures.[4]

---

[1] Cf. Boissier, *Fin du paganisme*, ii. 96; Paulinus had dedicated his beard to the saint, *Carmen* xxi. 377.

[2] ib., xiv.
[3] ib., xxiii.
[4] ib., 27–36.

In these charming poems, Paulinus, like his contemporary Prudentius, helped to create a new *genre*, the poem in praise of the saint and martyr ; but he has the honour as well of being the author of the first Christian elegy.[1] His elegiac verses on the death of the boy Celsus, in which, recalling his own earlier sorrow, he attempts to console the heart-broken parents, contain none of that pathetic sadness 'at the doubtful doom of human kind' which filled the elegies of the pagan world. Pity, he says, inclines him to weep, faith to rejoice. He weeps because the little one has been granted for so short a space to his parents, but he rejoices the more when he thinks of the rewards of eternal life which God has prepared for the innocent child who has known so little of the contagion of earthly life :

> tam modicum patribus tam dulci e pignore fructum
>   defleo in exiguo temporis esse datum.
> rursus ut aeternae bona volvo perennia vitae,
>   quae deus in caelo praeparat innocuis,
> laetor obisse brevi functum mortalia saeclo,
>   ut cito divinas perfrueretur opes,
> nec terrena diu contagia mixtus iniquis
>   duceret in fragili corporis hospitio.
> sed nullo istius temeratus crimine mundi
>   dignius aeternum tenderet ad dominum.[2]

Finally, he pictures the child in heaven, in the groves of paradise, where with the innocent victims of Herod, he plays in the sweet-smelling gardens, and weaves the crowns for the martyrs :

> aut cum Bethlaeis infantibus in paradiso,
>   quos malus Herodes percutit invidia,
> inter odoratum ludit nemus atque coronas
>   texit honorandis praemia martyribus.[3]

In the elegiac poem, written for the marriage of Julianus and Titia,[4] Paulinus composed the first Christian *epithalamium*. There is no trace of the mythological adornment which Sidonius Apollinaris and Venantius Fortunatus employed on such occasions. Juno, Cupid, and Venus are vanished, and in their place 'peace, modesty, and piety' are summoned to grace this Christian marriage :

> concordes animae casto sociantur amore,
>   virgo puer Christi, virgo puella dei.

---

[1] Boissier, *Fin du paganisme*, ii. 89.
[2] *Carmen* xxxi. 11–20.
[3] ib., 585–8.

[4] *Titia*, not *Ia*, is the correct form ; Schanz, iv, i. 264.

Christe deus, pariles duc ad tua frena columbas
et moderare levi subdita colla iugo.
namque tuum leve, Christe, iugum est, quod prompta voluntas
suscipit et facili fert amor obsequio.
invitis gravis est castae pia sarcina legis,
dulce piis onus est vincere carnis opus.
absit ab his thalamis vani lascivia vulgi,
Iuno Cupido Venus, nomina luxuriae.
sancta sacerdotis venerando pignora pacto
iunguntur; coeant pax pudor et pietas.[1]

This Julianus, whose marriage received so remarkable a celebration, became a bishop, and in after years Paulinus had the
sorrow of seeing him a prominent supporter of the heresy of
Pelagius.   Among the other poems of Paulinus may be noted
an elegant ode in sapphics addressed to Nicetas, Bishop of
Remesiana, who had paid a visit to Nola;[2] a long and rhetorical
panegyric on John the Baptist;[3] and three interesting paraphrases from the Psalter.[4]   The last of these paraphrases, that
of Psalm cxxxvii, shows how unsatisfactory a medium the
Virgilian hexameter was for such a purpose, but we must
not suppose that the contemporaries of Paulinus would have
agreed with this view.   The prose of the Vulgate had indeed
acquired something of the Hebrew spirit and there is a pathos
in the lament of the exiles.   'Super flumina Babylonis, illic
sedimus et flevimus: cum recordaremur Sion: in salicibus in
medio eius suspendimus organa nostra.'   Expanded and adorned
with Virgilian rhetoric, the version of Paulinus is far less
successful than the attempts of Racine to translate into French
verse the poetry of the Roman breviary:[5]

sedimus ignotos dirae Babylonis ad amnes
captivi, Iudaea manus, miserabile flentes,
cum patrium memori traheremus pectore Sion
et meritum iusta suspiraremus ab ira
exilium, lentis qua consita ripa salictis
hospitibus populis umbras praebebat amicas.
illic Assyriae mediis in moenibus urbis
obliti laetas per maesta silentia voces
de salicum ramis suspendimus organa nostra.[6]

---

[1] *Carmen* xxv. 1–12.
[2] *Carmen* xvii; Remesiana in Dacia;
on this remarkable man see E. Burn,
Nicetas of Remesiana, Cambridge 1905.
He wrote hymns, none of which has survived, though the *Te Deum* has been
ascribed to him.
[3] *Carmen* vi.
[4] *Carmina* vii–ix.
[5] For another judgement see Schanz,
iv, i. 265.
[6] *Carmen* viii. 1–9.

The high talent and the spiritual gifts of Paulinus could still invest with charm a theme which was given in the course of the life of every day. Thus the elegy on the death of Celsus, the *Epithalamium*, and the descriptive passages in the poems which he dedicated to S. Felix provided subjects which could be treated with some success in hexameters or elegiacs. But where the deeper Christian emotion was concerned, such an emotion as the faithful found already expressed in the Hebrew psalter, the Catholic poets had yet to discover by a process of experiment, a verse-form adequate to their need.

§ 2. *Severus Sanctus Endelechius, Honorius Scholasticus, and Sedulius.*

Paulinus of Nola had a friend named Endelechius who appears to have been a rhetorician and a poet. He is not improbably the author of an *Eclogue* in asclepiads, in which Aegon, Bucolus, and Tityrus hold talk together.[1] Bucolus has lost his flocks by pestilence; one by one his oxen have fallen, and there is no remedy. But the beasts of Tityrus have escaped and he is asked why the plague has passed him over. He answers that the sign of the cross,

signum quod perhibent esse crucis dei,

made over the foreheads of the oxen has saved them. This is why they call Christ the Saviour. The sign, and a prayer as well, are efficacious if faith is added. There is no need of altars dripping blood; only a pure heart is necessary to win an answer to prayer. 'If this is so', says Bucolus, 'I will join the true religion at once and gladly forsake my old superstition.' Tityrus offers to go with him to the 'temple of the supreme God', and Aegon ends the *Eclogue* by offering to join them, for a sign which overcomes the pestilence must also be of help to men.

In this poem we catch a glimpse of the borderland between Paganism and Christianity, and are able to see how easy the transition was; for in spite of its artificial and traditional setting, the poem is an instructive document for the historian.

Another fifth-century poet is Honorius Scholasticus, whom Jordanes, probably Bishop of Ravenna, had exhorted, in letters composed after the manner of Seneca, to forsake the world and to embrace 'the true philosophy'. Honorius replied with

[1] Riese, *Anthol. Lat.*, no. 893, pp. 314 sqq.

an elegiac poem, *Contra Epistolas Senecae*,[1] in which he exalts the superiority of the Catholic faith over heathen philosophy and of Jordanes himself over Seneca.

These are solitary voices, and, with the exception of Sedulius, there is little more than a series of names to fill out the story of the Italian poets of this century.

Caelius Sedulius[2] was born, perhaps in Rome, in the early part of the fifth century. Of his life we know little more than the meagre details which he supplies in a prefatory letter to his most important poem, the *Carmen Paschale*. From it we gather that he received the usual education in the public schools, but there is no reason to doubt that he was always, at any rate in name, a member of the Christian Church. He relates how by the mercy of God he was led to turn his talents away from the idle ends of worldly wisdom to the glory of their author and to accept the mild yoke of Christ—' onus Christi quod leve nimis est, humili pronus devotione conplectens'. So he was led to compose in heroic verse his long *Carmen Paschale*, with the aim of attracting to the love of divine things the cultivated classes of his day, whose taste for poetry found its sole satisfaction in the verses of the pagan poets. Like Juvencus before him, he wished to show that the Gospel history contained a whole Christian 'mythology' which was capable of pleasing as well as edifying those who had hitherto delighted more in the fables of Ovid than in the miracles of Christ. The first book of the *Carmen Paschale* relates those miracles of the Old Testament which set forth the power of God and foretold the coming Saviour. The remaining books are devoted to the miracles of Christ, and the poem ends with the Resurrection and Ascension. The *Carmen Paschale* is a free treatment of the Gospel story from the standpoint of the miraculous. It is full of characteristic Christian allegory and symbolism,[3] and there are

---

[1] Riese, no. 666, p. 124 sq.

[2] The praenomen Caelius is uncertain, and we cannot be sure that he was an Italian; the works of Sedulius (ed. Huemer) are in vol. x of *C.S.E.L.*

[3] On its use of symbolism cf. Manitius, *Christl. Lat. Poesie*, pp. 306 sqq.; Ebert, i. 378. The gifts of the Magi, according to Sedulius, are three, because there are three persons in the Godhead, and because God lives in three 'times'—past, present, and future, ii. 95-101:—

aurea nascenti fuderunt munera regi,
thura dedere deo, myrrham tribuere sepulchro.
cur tria dona tamen? quoniam spes maxima vitae est
hunc numerum confessa fides, et tempora summus
cernens cuncta deus, praesentia, prisca, futura,
semper adest, semperque fuit, semperque manebit
in triplici virtute sui:

curious rhetorical touches, as, for instance, in the line on the dying thief :

> abstulit iste suis caelorum regna rapinis.

His last robbery was the theft of the kingdom of heaven! Like Juvencus, Sedulius uses throughout Virgilian turns of expression, but unlike Juvencus, he is not careful to retain where possible the literal Gospel language. At a later date, he put the matter of the *Carmen Paschale* into prose under the title *Opus Paschale*. Boissier has remarked that a comparison of the two works proves that in the fifth century prose and poetry did not speak the same language. The language of verse naturally remained more faithful to the past, and imitated as closely as possible such a classical model as Virgil. Prose, called by Sedulius ' stylus liberior ', was more open to the influences of contemporary life and had suffered greater change. To us the verse is easier to read, but we are not entitled to assume that the contemporaries of Sedulius thought the same.[1]

Along with the *Carmen Paschale*, two hymns are the only poems of Sedulius which have survived. The first is in epanaleptic elegiacs, that is to say, the latter part of the pentameter simply repeats the first part of the preceding hexameter. The theme of the hexameter in each case is complemented by the pentameter which follows. Thus,

> unius ob meritum cuncti perierunt minores :
> salvantur cuncti unius ob meritum.
> sola fuit mulier, patuit quae ianua leto :
> et qua vita redit, sola fuit mulier.

It is unnecessary to comment on this exercise of perverse ingenuity. More interest attaches to the second poem from the fact that it has provided the material for two well-known hymns in the Roman Breviary. It is an alphabetical poem, written in quantitative iambic dimeters, but there is a significant tendency for accent and *ictus* to fall together. Rime also appears in every stanza but one, an indication of the transition to the characteristic medieval hymn. The mediocre quality of the

---

Cf. Juvencus, *Evangelica Historia*, i. 284:
    tum munera trina,
thus, aurum, myrrham regique homini-
    que deoque
dona dabant.
Mone, *Lateinische Hymnen*, ii. 81 :

aurum regi regnaturo,
thusque sacerdoti puro,
myrrha datur morituro.
[1] Boissier, *Revue de Philologie*, &c., vi (1882), p. 34.

verses will be gathered from the following extract, which represents the Christmas hymn in the Breviary[1]:

> A solis ortus cardine
>   adusque terrae limitem
>   Christum canamus principem,
>   natum Maria virgine.
>
> B eatus auctor saeculi
>   servile corpus induit,
>   ut carne carnem liberans
>   non perderet quod condidit.
>
> C lausae parentis viscera
>   caelestis intrat gratia
>   venter puellae baiulat
>   secreta quae non nouerat.
>
> D omus pudici pectoris
>   templum repente fit dei,
>   intacta nesciens virum
>   verbo creavit filium.
>
> E nixa est puerpera
>   quem Gabrihel praedixerat,
>   quem matris alvo gestiens
>   clausus Iohannes senserat.
>
> F aeno iacere pertulit,
>   praesepe non abhorruit,
>   parvoque lacte pastus est,
>   per quem nec ales esurit.
>
> G audet chorus caelestium,
>   et angeli canunt deum,
>   palamque fit pastoribus
>   pastor creatorque omnium.

The thoroughly didactic character of the poetry of Sedulius, which reveals itself as much in this hymn as throughout the *Carmen Paschale*, made him one of the favourite poets of the Middle Ages. He became a Christian classic, cited by the grammarians, read as a model of style, and imitated by generations of versifiers.[2]

---

[1] Text, pp. 163 sqq., in *C. S. E. L.* x ; stanzas H, I, L, N form the Epiphany hymn.

[2] Boissier, *Journal des Savants*, 1881, p. 566.

§ 3. *The Sixth Century. Boëthius, Ennodius, Arator.*

In Italy the barbarian invasions had failed to bring about that disruption of society which, as we have seen, had produced in Gaul results so disastrous to the pursuit of letters. The invasions of Alaric and of Gaiseric left no trace of permanent ruin behind them, and when in 476 the barbarian Odoacer made himself master of Italy, he found it desirable to have his title confirmed by the Roman Senate, and by the Emperor at Constantinople. When Odoacer's short-lived government disappeared, Theodoric the Ostrogoth [1] made no attempt to destroy the Roman administration, and, although an Arian, he refused to persecute his Catholic subjects. He was enlightened enough to continue the imperial protection of the schools, which were still an avenue to political advancement,[2] and his successor Athalaric followed the same policy. The age of the Ostrogothic domination is not on the whole remarkable for literary achievement; but the reign of Theodoric is rendered illustrious by the names of Cassiodorus and Boëthius.

Cassiodorus Senator (A.D. 490–583), the adviser of Theodoric, is an example, in sixth-century Italy, of the love of classical learning. Like Ennodius and like Boëthius, he was an accomplished rhetorician, and like Boëthius, he had a reputation for encyclopaedic learning. But his face is set towards the future and not to the past. In the dark days which followed the death of Theodoric, when the armies of Belisarius were reducing to ruins the kingdom of the Goths, Cassiodorus retired to his native Squillace in the Calabrian hills and laid down the burdens of statesmanship. Here he devoted himself to the religious life in the first of those monasteries where the Greek and Latin authors were assiduously copied in the *Scriptorium* and libraries were founded which preserved throughout the dark ages the literary treasures of the ancient world. His ideal was that of a Christian school in which by the side of sacred studies the liberal arts should have their place. These arts are the servants of religious studies and are not to be pursued for their own sake. But Cassiodorus gave to the study of profane letters so great a part in his educational plan and conceived that plan in such a large and liberal spirit that he stands apart in a time

[1] On Theodoric see Hodgkin, *Theodoric the Goth*, London 1900; *Italy and her Invaders*, iii; Bury, *Later Roman Empire*, i and ii.

[2] On the schools under Theodoric and Athalaric see Roger, pp. 170 sqq.

when Churchmen were beginning to show a more or less open hostility to any studies which did not minister directly to religion and the Christian life.[1]

His contemporary and friend, Boëthius, is usually regarded as a last representative of classical letters, and he is not always included in a history of Christian literature. But the Middle Ages claimed him as their own and he has his place in Dante's *Paradise*. The claim was just, for if he was the last of the Roman philosophers, he was also 'the first of the scholastic theologians'.[2] The story of his life is too well known to require retelling in detail. He was a Roman, born about A.D. 480, and he belonged to the great Anician family. He achieved the public honours which were due to his birth and ability, for he was consul in 510 and, twelve years later, Theodoric conferred the same honour upon his children. But the end of his good fortune was near, and his enemies prevailed. He was falsely accused of treason and suffered a cruel death in 524. In his prison at Pavia he composed the *Consolation of Philosophy*, a book which, in spite of its unpromising structure—it is a mixture of prose and verse—deals with the permanent problems of philosophy with a hardness and definition in which he equals the best of the Neo-Platonists and joins hands with the great medieval scholastics. But the scholastic temper is clearest in the *Theological Tractates*. The *Consolation* belongs to literature as well as to philosophy. As philosophy, it does not wander into the sphere of theology, but it accepts no conclusions which conflict with the Catholic faith. 'The fundamental aim of the work is to make the language of philosophy approach as closely as possible to the meaning of faith; Boëthius was neither a pagan nor a cold eclectic, nor a dilettante reviser of others' texts, but the first of the Scholastics.'[3] The writer whose words we have quoted proceeds to say, 'The work is an apocalypse of the general type of the Poimandres, but an apocalypse combined with Menippean satire, Stoic diatribe, and Platonic dialogue, with such a skill that like all great works of art it transcends the categories, and itself stands forth almost as a new literary type.' The type is new indeed, because the elements of which

---

[1] On the relation of Cassiodorus to learning see Grisar, *Rome and the Popes in the Middle Ages*, ii. 314 sqq.

[2] Boëthius, *The Theological Tractates and the Consolation of Philosophy*, ed. H. F. Stewart and E. K. Rand, London 1918,

p. x. This is the best edition, pending the appearance of Engelbrecht's critical text of the *Consolatio*.

[3] Cf. E. K. Rand, in *American Journal of Philology*, xliv (1923), p. 83 sq.

it is composed, derived as they are from the Hellenistic-Roman past, had never been combined before in such a fashion, and the apocalypse is the revelation of reason, and not of esoteric teaching given under a feigned seal of secrecy.[1]

When Philosophy appears to the prisoner in the guise of a majestic woman, she sees the 'poetical muses' standing about his bed. 'Who', she says, 'hath permitted these tragical harlots to have access to this sick man, which will not only not comfort his grief with wholesome remedies, but also nourish them with sugared poison? For these be they which with the fruitless thorns of affections do kill the fruitful crop of reason, and do accustom men's minds to sickness, instead of curing them.' But Philosophy uses verse herself and the poetical muses henceforth speak the language of reason. The poetry is inserted to relieve the tedium of the common reader; for after the long argument concerning providence and evil,[2] Philosophy says: 'But I see that long since burdened with so weighty a question, and wearied with my long discourse, thou expectest the delight of verses; wherefore take a draught, that, being refreshed, thou mayest be able to go forward.'

The poems are thirty-nine in number, and there is a great variety of metres. The style of the prose is studied, but, judged by classical standards, it fails here and there in formal correctness, where the author is carried away by his argument.[3] Similarly, in the poetical part of the work, there are sins against the strict rules of prosody which cannot be put down to the corruption of the text.[4] But the sureness and evenness of the whole series of poems is not more than could be expected in one of the last of the Romans to possess a profound knowledge of his own language and of its literature as well as of the language and literature of Greece. Boëthius knew and estimated Plato in a manner which was beyond the reach of his contemporaries or his Neo-Platonic predecessors. In a few memorable lines, beloved of medieval commentators, he summarizes the first part of the *Timaeus*:[5]

o qui perpetuo mundum ratione gubernas
terrarum caelique sator qui tempus ab aevo

---

[1] As in the Hermetic teaching; see Reitzenstein, *Poimandres*, Leipzig 1904; W. Scott, *Hermetica*, Oxford 1924, i, Introd.

[2] iv. 6, p. 352.

[3] Engelbrecht, *Die Consolatio philosophiae des Boethius*, p. 16 (*Wiener Sitzungsber.*, cxliv, iii).

[4] Engelbrecht, *Die Consolatio*, p. 53.

[5] *De Consol.* iii. ix, p. 262, and note 2.

ire iubes stabilisque manens das cuncta moveri,
quem non externae pepulerunt fingere causae
materiae fluitantis opus, verum insita summi
forma boni livore carens, tu cuncta superno
ducis ab exemplo, pulchrum pulcherrimus ipse
mundum mente gerens similique in imagine formans
perfectasque iubens perfectum absolvere partes.
tu numeris elementa ligas ut frigora flammis
arida conveniant liquidis, ne purior ignis
evolet aut mersas deducant pondera terras.
tu triplicis mediam naturae cuncta moventem
conectens animam per consona membra resolvis.
quae cum secta duos motum glomeravit in orbes,
in semet reditura meat mentemque profundam
circuit et simili convertit imagine caelum.
tu causis animas paribus vitasque minores
provehis et levibus sublimes curribus aptans
in caelum terramque seris quas lege benigna
ad te conversas reduci facis igné reverti.
da pater augustam menti conscendere sedem,
da fontem lustrare boni, da luce reperta
in te conspicuos animi defigere visus.
dissice terrenae nebulas et pondera molis
atque tuo splendore mica ! tu namque serenum,
tu requies tranquilla piis, te cernere finis,
principium, vector, dux, semita, terminus idem.

About four hundred manuscripts of the *Consolation* are known, none of which is older than the ninth century.[1] It is often quoted by innumerable writers throughout the Middle Ages, and, in the Psalter of Louis the German, some of the verses are set to music.[2] Translations are numerous; in England, by Alfred the Great, Chaucer, and Lydgate; in Provençal by an unknown poet of the tenth century; in the eleventh century by Notker the German. The commentaries are too numerous to mention. As the character of Theodoric was darkened until he became a heretic who persecuted the true believers, so Boëthius assumed the merit of a martyr who died for the Catholic faith. Therefore Dante places him among the Doctors in Paradise, in the company of Aquinas, Albert, and Dionysius. He is 'the sainted Soul, which unmasketh the deceitful world to whoso giveth it good hearing. The body whence it was chased forth, lieth down below in Cieldauro and itself from martyrdom and exile came unto this peace'.[3]

[1] Engelbrecht, *Die Consolatio*, p. 6.
[2] Manitius, *Gesch.* i. 33.
[3] *Paradiso* x. 124–9 ; Wicksteed's translation, London 1899.

Magnus Felix Ennodius[1] was a contemporary and a relative of Boëthius, but it would be difficult to imagine a greater contrast between two men who were scholars and poets. Ennodius was born at Arles in 474, of aristocratic parents, indeed, but he was soon under the necessity of making his way in the world. He seems to have spent a great part of his youth in Pavia, where he was betrothed to a rich lady; but she lost her money and he did not marry her. The Church offered a career for one who had the Gallic facility in rhetoric and knew how to parade his learning. It appears that his friends persuaded him to take orders. He was ordained deacon at Milan, but he was still absorbed in secular studies and directed the education of the young on lines which would not have met with the approval of Jerome. His motto was: Rhetoric rules the world,[2] and he kept this opinion until his death. He was always busy making verses. In his pompous *Confession*, written after his conversion, he says, 'Delectabant carmina quadratis fabricata particulis et ordinata pedum varietate solidata.'[3] But he did not hold himself apart from the life of the Church. He was present in Rome at the Synod of 502 which was convened to end a troublesome schism. He supported the cause of Pope Symmachus in his *Libellus contra eos qui contra Synodum praesumpserunt*, and elaborated the argument that the head of the Church is subject only to the divine Judge.[4] The pope was pleased, for in 507 he was chosen to compose a long and very flattering panegyric on the Arian king Theodoric.[5]

In the midst of his success, he was attacked by a sudden illness and he trembled at the thought of the coming judgement. 'But the Lord did not fail me', he says, 'who killeth and maketh alive again, who bringeth down to hell and raiseth up again; whose is the promise: while yet the words are in thy mouth, Here am I, saith the Lord.'[6] He invoked the intercession of S. Victor, and made a vow that, if the Lord spared his life, he would renounce the wisdom of this world and devote himself to the Christian life. His prayer was answered, and in 513[7] he was made Bishop of Ticinum. If his renunciation was not as complete as he had promised, he yet made a good and

[1] Works, *C.S.E.L.* vi, ed. von Hartel; *M.G.H.*, *Auct. Antiq.*, vii, ed. Vogel (my references are to the latter).
[2] *Opera*, p. 314 'Qui nostris servit studiis, mox imperat orbi'.
[3] p. 301.
[4] See Grisar, *History of Rome and the Popes in the Middle Ages*, ii. 245.
[5] *Opera*, p. 203.
[6] ib., p. 302.
[7] The date is not quite certain.

orthodox bishop, trusted by the Pope Hormisdas who twice
sent him to Constantinople on troublesome missions connected
with the peace of the Church.   He died in 521, and was buried
at Pavia in the Church of S. Victor, which he himself had built.
His epitaph is still preserved, with its curious orthography,
at S. Michele, in the same city.[1]

The poems of Ennodius consist mainly of occasional pieces,
including a whole series of epitaphs and epigrams, a marriage
poem, and a collection of hymns.   The profane and even
questionable character of many of the epigrams is sufficiently
indicated by such titles as the following—*De Adultero et Molle,
De Eunucho, De Anu quadam, De Cauco cuiusdam habente
Pasiphae et Taurum.*   The *Epithalamium*, written after Ennodius had taken orders, shows no trace of the Christian ideal
of marriage which Paulinus had set forth a century before.
Cupid and Venus are the presiding deities, and Ennodius puts
into the mouth of Cupid a complaint against Christian chastity
and the monastic ideal of virginity :

> frigida consumens multorum possidet artus
> virginitas fervore novo, sublimia carnem
> vota domant, mundus tenui vix nomine constat.
> primaevi tremulos fractis imitantur ephebis.[2]

These verses of a Christian deacon read like the complaint
of a lover of the old gods, regretting the victory of the Galilean.
It is no wonder therefore that Ennodius found little inspiration
when he began to compose a series of hymns for the Milanese
liturgy.   His effort resulted in a dozen rather prosaic compositions which failed to secure a place beside the hymns of Ambrose
and found small acceptance in the other churches of the West.[3]
The following hymn on the Virgin Mary is a fair specimen
of his talent :

> ut virginem fetam loquar,   exposcit, ipsa suggerat.
> quid laude dignum Mariae?   sint verba ceu miraculum,
> det partus ornet exigat,   quid mens, requiras? ordinem
> quod clausa porta, quod patens   natura totum perdidit.

[1] *Opera*, p. lviii.
[2] ib., p. 278.
[3] See *Anal. Hymn.* l, p. 61, where, from the fact that he celebrates only Milanese saints and carefully chooses subjects which his great predecessor had left untouched, it is argued that Ennodius can have had no other aim than the insertion of his hymns beside those of Ambrose in the Milanese liturgy. Like Ambrose, he composed each hymn in eight strophes.

hoc est salus, quod vincimur.   sed nec minor creante fit.
cum sola virgo degeret,   fons dicta clausus adcipit,
concepit aure filium.   fons membra clausus egerit ;
stupente factum corpore   nec rima cessit artior,

turgescit alvum spiritu.   et vera proles emicat.
quod lingua iecit semen est,   dic, mater et virgo, precor,
in carne verbum stringitur.   quisquamne claudit exiens,
de matre cunctus noster est.   artantur exta fetibus.

de patre nil distans deus :   vinclum pudoris natus est.
utrisque partus integer,   q[uae se]de Christi dignior
quae gignit et qui praecipit.   quam sunt superna crederis,
nil maior ille servulis, ·   nostri memento praepotens.[1]

The work of Ennodius is of interest because it shows how
at the end of the fifth century the pagan tradition in Italy was
strong, and that Ausonius and Sidonius Apollinaris were not
without successors, though the barbarian invasions had swept
away the pagan schools in Gaul.   Ennodius is perhaps the last
representative of the futile attempt to reconcile a radically
pagan culture with the profession of the Christian religion.   In
his *Libellus* in defence of Pope Symmachus, he pictures the
Imperial City lamenting the fate of her famous and mighty
sons, the Curii, Torquati, and Camilli, who, unredeemed by the
Church, were doomed to hell, because they had lived before the
coming of Christ.[2]   There can be no question of his thorough
orthodoxy, but he lacked the high earnestness of his friend
Boëthius, who, while a true Christian, found his purest consolation in the noblest aspirations of the ancient world.

Arator is the last important Italian poet of the sixth century.[3]
In his early youth he had known Ennodius, and had received
the usual education of a member of the Italian provincial
aristocracy.   He found a career in the law ; his talents brought
him to the notice of Theodoric, and he held high office under
Athalaric.   But the troubles of Italy began when the kingdom
of Theodoric fell into weaker hands, and the destiny of Arator
was changed under the stress of the political misfortunes of his

[1] *Opera*, p. 254; *Anal. Hymn.* l,
p. 68.
[2] *Opera*, p. 66 ' quae Curios Torquatos
Camillos, quos ecclesia non regeneravit, et
reliquos misi plurimae prolis infecunda
mater ad tartarum, dum exhaustis emarcui
male feta visceribus, quia Fabios servata
patria non redemit, Deciis multo sudore

gloria parta nil praestitit. profligata est
operum sine fide innocentia : criminosis
iunctus est aequi observantissimus.'
[3] Arator's works are in Migne, lxviii,
col. 63 sqq., which reproduces Arntzen's
edition, Zutphen 1769. There is now a
better text in G. L. Perugi, *Aratore*,
Venice 1909.

country. In 534 the armies of Justinian under Belisarius had completed the destruction of the Vandal kingdom in Africa, and in the following year the Ostrogoths abandoned Sicily. Naples soon fell. The Goths deposed the useless Theodahat and elected the almost equally useless Witiges in his place. In 536 Belisarius entered Rome, but early in 537 Witiges made an attempt to recover it. The Goths advanced to storm the mausoleum of Hadrian, but they were driven back by the Imperial troops, who hurled upon their heads the marble statues which crowned the building.[1] It was, it seems, during this siege, that, at the instance of Pope Vigilius and under the pressure of these startling events, Arator turned his thoughts to religion and took orders. As he says in a dedicatory poem, after having saved his body, he began to think about saving his soul. He left the bar for the Church :

> corporeum satis est sic evasisse periclum,
>   at mihi plus animae nascitur inde salus.
> ecclesiam subeo dimissa naufragus aula ;
>   perfida mundani desero vela freti.
> transferor ad niveas Petri, sine turbine, caulas,
>   et fruor optati iam statione soli.[2]

Arator wrote no more profane verses, but turned his talent to the celebration of Christian themes. In an epic poem of two books he versified the Acts of the Apostles from the Ascension of the Lord, describing the events of Pentecost, the story of Ananias and Sapphira, the passion of Stephen, the Conversion of Paul, the imprisonment of Peter, and the other events told by St. Luke up to the visit of Paul to Rome and his appeal to Caesar.

When the poem was finished, he offered it to the Pope with great ceremony. The clergy of S. Peter's and a few bishops gathered before the *Confessio*. Pope Vigilius listened to a part of the poem and ordered it to be kept among the papal archives. But the Romans were not content. The learned among them continually besought Vigilius to agree to a public recitation, and he allowed Arator to read his poem in the basilica of S. Peter *ad vincula*. There was a large gathering of clergy and nobles as well as of the common people. The reading required four separate sessions, not merely on account of the length of the

[1] Hodgkin, *Italy and her Invaders*, iv. 180.

[2] Migne, lxviii, col. 76-7, the dedication of his poem to Pope Vigilius.

poem, but because the enthusiastic audience continually demanded ' encores '.   It is interesting to note that the Romans still
retained something of their love of public declamation, and that
even in the stress of the Gothic War (544) they could welcome
what seemed to them a literary masterpiece.   The visitor to
Rome, as he stands beneath the Doric columns of the somewhat
gloomy church, may try to picture the scene where Arator,
referring to their present perils, promised the Romans deliverance by the virtue of Peter's chains.[1]   How his hearers must
have applauded the words !—

> manet omne per aevum
> pignoris huius apex, et sideris obtinet instar,
> corpore quod Petrus sacravit, et angelus ore.
> his solidata fides, his est tibi, Roma, catenis
> perpetuata salus ; harum circumdata nexu
> libera semper eris : quid enim non vincula praestent,
> quae tetigit, qui cuncta potest absolvere ? cuius
> haec invicta manu, vel religiosa triumpho
> moenia non ullo penitus quatientur ab hoste.
> claudit iter bellis, qui portam pandit in astris.[2]

In choosing as his subject the Acts of the Apostles, Arator
had avoided a comparison with Juvencus or Sedulius, who had
related the Gospel history in verse.   He selected instead a field
in which he had no predecessors ; but Sedulius is evidently his
poetical model.   Like Sedulius he handled his subject-matter
with some freedom, and loved to extract the mystical and
symbolical meaning from the course of events.[3]   Thus he explains
the significance of the number of the twelve apostles by multi-
plying three by four, the three representing the Trinity, and
four the cardinal points :

> quatuor est laterum discretus partibus orbis ;
> trina fides vocat hunc, quo nomine fonte lavatur.[4]

The poem is badly constructed, and it can hardly fail to weary
a modern reader ; but the Middle Ages loved it precisely for
its mysticism and allegory, as they loved the *Psychomachia* of
Prudentius and the *Carmen Paschale* of Sedulius.   Arator shows
none of that feeling for style which links a Prudentius or a
Paulinus of Nola to the classical poets, and in its lack of

---

[1] Cf. Grisar, *History of Rome and the Popes in the Middle Ages*, ii. 341.
[2] i. 1067 sqq.
[3] Cf. Manitius, *Christl. Lat. Poesie*, p. 369.
[4] i. 113–114.

structure, its faults of prosody, and its intellectual feebleness, the work is a prelude to the decline of culture which made the seventh century the darkest period of the Middle Ages.

It is probable that Arator lived to witness some of the political events which hastened the destruction of the old order. We may assume that he survived the Gothic pillage of Rome in 546, and that he was a spectator of the re-entry of Belisarius. Perhaps he lived to see the arrival of Narses, and the final destruction in 553 of the Gothic kingdom which had begun so hopefully under Theodoric. The calamities of Italy were not yet complete; for the Lombards quickly replaced the Goths, and the old anarchy renewed itself for many years. In those days there were few who had leisure or security for the pursuit of letters.[1] The old order had been shattered, and a new was to begin. The pontificate of Gregory the Great ushers in the full Middle Ages.

[1] Arator seems, however, to have had at least one contemporary who worked on similar lines, Rusticius Helpidius Domnulus, author of an hexameter poem, called *De Christi Iesu beneficiis*, which deals with the incarnation and miracles of Christ. The prosody is good, the poet had read his Christian as well as heathen predecessors. Text in Migne, lxii, col. 545 sqq., and W. Brandes, *Gymnasialprogr. v. Braunschweig*, 1890; see also Manitius, *Rhein. Mus.* xlv, pp. 153 sqq.

V

THE TRANSITION TO THE MEDIEVAL WORLD

§ 1. *The Age of Gregory the Great.*

WITH the beginning of the seventh century the medieval spirit may be said to have finally dominated the West.[1] The Christian religion in its Catholic form was everywhere established, and it had now no rival. Benedict of Nursia, by founding the monastic order with which his name is associated, had already given the impulse to an ascetic ideal of life throughout the West in a form in which it was destined to affect powerfully the human outlook for several centuries. The monastic theory despaired of the world and pictured it as a stormy sea upon whose waves floated the ark of the monastery, the only hope of safety and of shelter.[2] In abandoning the world the monk must abandon all pride in secular learning and all pride of the intellect; his whole being is to be consecrated to obedience and to the demands of the religious life. Political and social conditions encouraged men to seek the seclusion and comparative safety of the monastery. The Gothic and Lombard invasions left behind a train of economic ruin, and suggested to many whose hearts had failed them for fear that these catastrophes were signs of the approaching end of all things. Gregory, in his *Dialogues*, tells the story of Redemptus, Bishop of Ferenti, who, on the eve of the Lombard invasions, saw the martyr Euthicius standing over him in a vision, and crying out three times, 'The end of all flesh is come'.

In those troubled times a strange darkness fell over the human spirit. The universe became irrational again, and the wildest superstitions were accepted as the truth about the nature of things. The veneration of relics and images, the belief in their magical power, the immense growth of stories of miracles

---

[1] On the general aspects of the age, see Grisar, *History of Rome and the Popes in the Middle Ages*, vol. iii.

[2] Gregory the Great, Epistle dedicatory to his *Moralia*, 'ex huius vitae naufragio nudus evasi', Migne, lxxv, col. 511.

which went side by side with the increasingly popular worship of the saints, the systematization of demonology, that terrible science which revealed an unseen world of horror—all these were forces powerful in forming the intellectual and emotional character of the first centuries of the Middle Ages.   Gregory the Great is the man of this new outlook ; in him all these forces and tendencies meet.   He is the complete medievalist.   Roman by birth, of the old Anician house, trained in grammar and rhetoric, he rose to the high office of Praetor Urbanus ; but his heart was set on religion and he turned his palace on the Coelian into a convent where he lived as a humble monk. As Bishop of Rome (590), he showed all the qualities of an able statesman and administrator ; [1] he laid the foundations of the temporal power of the Papacy, withstood the Lombard invaders, and was the upholder of orthodoxy against Emperor and Patriarch.   Yet no secular interest had a place in his inner life ; the whole man, body, soul, and intellect, was to be consecrated to religious ends.   'Contemplativae vitae pulchritudinem velut Rachelem dilexi sterilem'.[2]

If this had been the attitude of Augustine, in Augustine at least there still remained something of the classical tradition, and his interests remained the wider for his conversion to a religious life. Gregory is Augustine without the classical tinge.   Augustine had once loved Cicero and the pathos of Virgil had moved him to tears ; but Gregory upbraided a Gallic bishop[3] for his interest in grammar and in a celebrated passage asserted a preference for a barbarous style to one which observed the rules of Donatus.[4] This is, of course, a characteristic exaggeration, and as Renan says in his inimitable manner, 'il n'y a que le pédantisme qui

[1] This mixture of the intensely practical with the speculatively fantastic is not uncommon.   Benedict's rule is a model of practical wisdom ; Gregory was as wise and moderate as Paul in his regulation of the English Church in the days of Augustine's mission.   It is also to be noted that Benedict adopted no definitely hostile attitude to learning, but left the way open to the fortunate developments of the future ; see Hörle, *Frühmittelalt. Mönchs- und Klerikerbildung in Italien*, p. 48.   For Gregory as an administrator, see Spearing, *The Patrimony of S. Peter*, Cambridge 1918.

[2] *Epist.* i. 5, Migne, lxxvii, col. 449.

[3] ib., xi. 54, Migne, lxxvii, col. 1171 ; it is amusing to contrast the conduct of Honorius III some six centuries later, who, according to Salimbene, 'deposuit episcopum qui Donatum non legerat'.

[4] Epistle dedicatory to *Moralia* ; 'unde et ipsam loquendi artem, quam magisteria disciplinae exterioris insinuant, servare despexi.   Nam sicut huius quoque epistolae tenor enuntiat, non metacismi collisionem fugio, non barbarismi confusionem devito, situs modosque et praepositionum casus servare contemno, quia indignum vehementer existimo, ut verba caelestis oraculi restringam sub regulis Donati' ; Migne, lxxv, col. 516 ; on Gregory's attitude to learning see Hörle, *Frühmittelalt. Mönchs- und Klerikerbildung in Italien*, pp. 13 sqq.

puisse prendre en mauvaise part ce passage célèbre. . . . Cette
haute fierté du pontife, cet orgueil de la foi surnaturelle, sont des
traits de caractère d'une si précieuse originalité qu'il serait de
mauvais goût de les critiquer avec trop d'amertume.'[1]   Yet the
general tendency of Gregory's mind was against the old culture,
with its still recent association with the hateful memories of
paganism.   His favourite reading was the Vulgate, over which
he pondered long and profoundly, drawing out with the aid
of his sombre imagination the mysteries hidden in the sacred
text.   His world was a world 'without any order', in which
natural law was unknown, a world of demons and witchcraft, of
miracles and wonders, and over it all was spread the horror
of that day,

> When, shrivelling like a parchèd scroll,
> The flaming heavens together roll,

for the evil and misery of the world were growing and the end
was near.   'Quia enim mundi iam tempora, malis crebrescen-
tibus, termino propinquante turbata sunt.'[2]   His outlook on the
world was to hold sway, at any rate until the twelfth century,
and his shadow is over ecclesiastical literature until the days of
Abélard.   The popularity of Gregory's writings gave an impulse
to the 'barbarization' of Latin which had long been developing.
It set the seal on the change which the Latin Bible had begun,
for although the Latin of Gregory does not descend to the
'vulgarisms' of the Rule of Benedict[3] and of the writings of
Gregory of Tours, it has lost all flavour of classicism, and has
definitely become the Latin of the Middle Ages.   Gregory the
Great did not need to confess like the historian of the Franks
that he did not know the gender of nouns or the cases which
prepositions govern.[4]   He had retained in some degree the
stamp of the Italian schools, which yet remained the depositories
of the classical tradition.   That tradition, preserved in Italy,
was to recover strength in the revival of learning in the days of
Charles the Great, and, after a second period of darkness, in the

---

[1] *Mélanges religieux et historiques*,
p. 334.
[2] Migne, lxxv, col. 511.
[3] Cf. Grisar, *History of Rome and the
Popes in the Middle Ages*, iii. 243 ; and
especially Wölfflin, *Die Latinität des
Benedikt von Nursia, Archiv f. lat. Lex.
und Gramm.* ix (1896), pp. 493 sqq., and
the other works mentioned by Grisar.
[4] See Roger, p. 105 ; it is possible to

exaggerate the ignorance of Gregory of
Tours ; he knew some Virgil, Sallust,
Aulus Gellius ; see Kurth, *Grégoire de
Tours et les études classiques au VIe siècle*
(*Revue des questions historiques*, xxiv. 586,
1878) ; Teuffel-Schwabe, ii. 539 ; and
Manitius, *Neues Archiv*, xxi, pp. 549 sqq.,
who remarks that he wrote poetry ; if it
had survived, we should have a better idea
of his Latin (p. 552).

renaissance of the eleventh and twelfth centuries. Further, the new language of the Church was not to be absorbed by the vulgar Latin, but both were to develop and progress. The one, formless and crude in the hands of monkish Chroniclers, could be invested with perverse strength and a strange and glowing colour in the periods of a Peter Damiani or a Bernard of Clairvaux; the other was already giving birth to the romance languages from which was to issue a wonderful and varied literature.

The circumstances of the age of Gregory could hardly be regarded as favourable to the production of verse, but a number of hymns in the Roman Breviary have been associated with his name.[1] But it is not possible definitely to connect with Gregory or with any one else the authorship of any of this group of hymns, including such well-known compositions as the *Primo dierum omnium*, and the *Audi benigne conditor*, which if their quality is poor, have won the respect due to their venerable age and their place in the Catholic hymnary. For the literary historian they illustrate the decline of culture and the attempt at the construction of a new verse form, in which a frequent rime appears, with absence of elision, and less constantly the avoidance of hiatus. The *Lucis creator optime* will serve as an example of these compositions:

1. lucis creator optime,
   lucem dierum proferens,
   primordiis lucis novae
   mundi parans originem,

2. qui mane iunctum vesperi
   diem vocari praecipis,
   taetrum chaos illabitur,
   audi preces cum fletibus,

[1] On this question see Dreves, Art. *Hymnology* in Hastings' *Encycl. of Religion and Ethics*, vii. 18, and in *Theologische Quartalschrift*, Tübingen 1907, p. 548 sq.; 1909, p. 436 sq.; Blume, in *Anal. Hymn.* li, Introd., and p. 364, and in *Gregor der Grosse als Hymnendichter* (Stimmen aus Maria-Laach, 1908, iii), tries to argue for Gregory's authorship, but, as Dreves says, 'he seems scarcely satisfied with his own arguments'. The earliest witness to Gregory's supposed authorship is Clichtoveus in his *Elucidatarium Ecclesiasticum*, Bâle 1517, says Dreves, *Die Kirche der Lateiner in ihren Liedern*, p. 31; but Blume has found other references (e.g. one of thirteenth century). But his main argument from the Irish *Liber Hymnorum*, which states that Gregory sent 'the hymns of the week', or 'a hymn for every night in the week', to the Irish Church, can only, if the statement is true, show that the collection in question owed its use in the Irish Church to Gregory, not that Gregory was the author. But as these hymns are said to have been sent in return for Columba's *Altus Prosator*, and as they are different from the cycle of hymns which he assumes to have been in Benedictine use at the time, Blume suggests that Gregory was more probably the author than the mere transmitter of the hymns. Columba's gift of the *Altus Prosator* could be suitably rewarded only by an equally distinguished gift. But as I have tried to show (p. 38 above), the thesis of Blume on the *Cursus* of S. Benedict is a mere fiction, and I agree with Dreves (*Theologische Quartalschrift*, 1909, p. 442) that no reliance can be placed on the supposed evidence of the *Liber Hymnorum*.

3. ne mens gravata crimine
vitae sit exsul munere.
dum nil perenne cogitat
seseque culpis illigat ;

4. caelorum pulset intimum,
vitale tollat praemium.
vitemus omne noxium,
purgemus omne pessimum.[1]

For the moment the life had gone out of Italian poetry, and there was hardly a spark of learning in Rome. The city itself was a mournful symbol of the intellectual decline. The palaces, the forums, the baths, and the aqueducts stood grandly at the beginning of centuries of decay, but the life which once gave them meaning and a use had departed.

§ 2. *Spanish Poets and the Mozarabic Hymnary.*

In 412 the Visigoths left Italy and made their way to Gaul. From Gaul they spread into the provinces of Spain, where Vandals, Alans, and Sueves had preceded them, and they set up a large and loosely organized kingdom with Toulouse as their capital. In 531 the Franks drove them beyond the Pyrenees, and although they recovered the province of Narbonne, their destiny was henceforth to be associated with the Spanish peninsula. Their Arian faith hindered the Gothic kings from gaining the willing obedience and support of the provincials, and the power of the nobles rendered the monarchy feeble and ineffectual. A Byzantine army landed in the south, and maintained its hold for many years. Under Leovigild, however (570–86), the monarchy was strengthened and the kingdom reorganized. Toledo became a brilliant capital, and Romans and Sueves were defeated in battle. Reccared son of Leovigild (586-601) took a step of decisive importance when he deserted the Arian for the Catholic faith, and his people willingly followed his lead. The Church rose to unexampled power and ecclesiastical synods eclipsed the authority of the state. The Roman element reappeared in political life ; the Goths took to letters and kings composed verses. But the nobles were turbulent, the kingship was insecure, and the Church was wealthy and intolerant.

Since the time of Prudentius, Spain had produced no Christian poet of note, if we except Merobaudes, the soldier rhetorician who composed a panegyric on Valentinian III in a style which entitles him to be compared with Claudian. He won the honour of a statue in Trajan's forum. We must cease to regard him, with Bury, as almost a pagan at heart ; he was merely a Christian

[1] *Anal. Hymn.* li, pp. 34-5.

using the old mythology.[1] The Christian poetry of the Spanish Middle Ages begins with King Sisebut and Isidore of Seville. Sisebut (612–20) loved the Church and persecuted the Jews. He found time, when not engaged in subduing his unruly nobles, or in attacking the Byzantine garrisons, to write a history, to describe the passion of S. Desiderius, and to compose Latin verses. Two of his poems have survived, a curious composition on the eclipses of the sun and moon which he sent to Bishop Isidore, and a congratulatory poem addressed to Teudila, a Goth who had become a monk.[2]

Isidore of Seville[3] (*circ.* 570–636) is the great father of the Spanish Church. Of Spanish provincial origin, he had the advantage of possessing a brother who occupied the high position of Bishop of Seville, and had been honoured by the friendship of Gregory the Great. Isidore succeeded his brother as bishop and astounded his contemporaries by the extent of his learning and the brilliance of his eloquence. His learning is embedded in the twenty books of his *Etymologies*, an encylopaedia of the whole of human knowledge after the manner in which it presented itself to his age. Of the various poems ascribed to Isidore, the *Versus in bibliotheca*[4] alone are probably genuinely his. They bear an interesting witness to the extent of his library, of which they form a kind of metrical catalogue, but they do not impress us with his skill as a versifier. Beginning with the Bible, he mentions in turn Origen, Hilary of Poitiers, Ambrose, Augustine, Jerome, Chrysostom, and Cyprian. Then come the pagan poets, but if you do not relish them, you will find Prudentius, Avitus, Juvencus, and Sedulius equally good.

> si Maro, si Flaccus, si Naso, et Persius horret,
>   Lucanus si te, Papiniusque tedet,
> par erat eximio dulcis Prudentius ore,
>   carminibus variis nobilis ille satis.
> perlege facundi studiosum carmen Aviti,
>   ecce Iuvencus adest, Seduliusque tibi.

No hymns can be ascribed with any certainty to Isidore, and the two rhythmic poems, *Exhortatio poenitendi* and *Lamentum*

---

[1] Text, Riese, *Anthologia Lat.* I. ii, p. 301 sq. ; see Bury, *Later Roman Empire*, i. 251 sq.; also *M. G. H., Auct. Antiq.*, xiv, ed. Vollmer, pp. 3 sqq.

[2] Text, Riese, I. ii, pp. 9 sqq.; p. 13, note ; see Manitius, *Christl. Lat. Poesie*, p. 410.

[3] Gams, *Kirchengeschichte von Spanien*, ii. 2, pp. 102 sqq.

[4] Migne, lxxxiii, col. 1107 sq.; Manitius, *Gesch.* i. 69, discusses the question of authorship. If they are not Isidore's, they belong to his circle.

poenitentiae,[1] which were once supposed to be his, belong to a later date.

Braulio, Bishop of Saragossa[2] (d. 651), follows next on the list of poets. He is the author of a hymn in iambic trimeters on S. Aemilianus, in which rime occurs with frequency.[3] It begins:

> o magne rerum, Christe, rector inclite,
> parent olympi perpetim cui sidera,
> tu vota festis annuis faventia
> largire nobis, casta praebe et sobria,
> placare possint quae tuam clementiam.

Eugenius III, Bishop of Toledo, 646–58, seems to have been of Gothic origin.[4] He forsook his parents to become a monk at Saragossa, where Bishop Braulio made him his archdeacon. It was with great reluctance that the bishop complied with King Chindaswinth's wishes and allowed him to be promoted to the see of Toledo. Eugenius was weak in body, but he was an industrious student. He reformed the singing and the offices of the Spanish Church, but none of his hymns found its way into ecclesiastical use. At the royal request, he re-edited and revised that part of the poem of Dracontius which deals with the creation, and in order to remedy what was lacking in the story, he added an account of the seventh day, ending

> haec tibi, rex summe, iussu compulsus herili,
> servulus Eugenius devota mente dicavi.[5]

His verses, with their metrical faults, their barbarism of phrase, their poverty of content, their characteristics of acrostic, telestich, and epanalepsis, illustrate the declining culture of the seventh century.[6] His lines, *de brevitate huius vitae,*[7] illustrate as well that medieval pessimism which we have already remarked in Gregory the Great:

> mundus, ecce, nutat aeger et ruinam nuntiat,
> tempora grata fugantur, ingeruntur pessima,
> omnia mala propinquant, et bona praetervolant.

---

[1] Migne, lxxxiii, col. 1251 sqq.; see *M.G.H., Poet. Kar.* iv. ii, p. 760, for discussion and text. The poems are not later than the ninth century.
[2] Gams, *Kirchengesch. von Spanien,* ii. 2, pp. 145 sqq.
[3] Text, *Anal. Hymn.* xxvii, p. 125.
[4] Gams, *Kirchengesch. von Spanien,* ii. 2, pp. 132 sqq.; poems in Migne, lxxxvii, col. 359 sqq.; *Anal. Hymn.* l, pp. 89 sqq.; *M. G. H., Auct. Antiq.* xiv, ed. Vollmer, pp. 231 sqq.

[5] Migne, lxxxvii, col. 388.
[6] See Vollmer, *Neues Archiv,* xxvi, pp. 394 sqq.; Manitius (*Rhein. Mus.* xliv, p. 548) is more indulgent. Poetry, he says, had almost disappeared in Gaul and Italy, but in Spain, as in Anglo-Saxon England, it had a kind of *Nachblüte.* The sense of the antique tradition still lingers in Isidore and Eugenius, even if the execution is inferior to that of the Carolingians.
[7] *Anal. Hymn.* l, p. 91.

Eugeni miselle, plora ; languor instat improbus.
vita transit, finis urget, ira pendet caelitus,
ianuam pulsat ut intret mortis, ecce, nuntius.[1]

Ildefonsus, who succeeded Eugenius as bishop (658–69), wrote epigrams, epitaphs, and hymns of little merit. Much the most important group of Spanish religious poetry is contained in the Mozarabic hymnary.[2] Like the Irish hymns which we shall consider in the following section, they are of great interest as the product of what may be called a national Church. The so-called Mozarabic liturgy is the liturgy of the old Spanish Church, but the name is more particularly attached to the period of the Arab domination. The hymns contained in the Mozarabic breviaries have been re-collected and re-edited in a critical manner in the twenty-seventh volume of *Analecta Hymnica*, and they form the raw material for an important research which would help to elucidate the state of religious and intellectual culture during the obscure centuries of the early Middle Ages. The hymns exhibit great diversity of style and form. The earlier hymns are based on classical models, others show the transition from quantity to accent and rime, while others, again, manifest in the words of Dreves,[3] all the ' linguistic barbarism of the tenth century '. Variety of style is accompanied in the Mozarabic hymnary by an immense variety of subject-matter. There are hymns for all occasions, for a royal or an episcopal birthday, for the new year, for the setting out of the army, *pro varia clade*, for a wedding for rain, and for fine weather. But Blume was wrong in considering that all these hymns were of Spanish origin. It can be proved that several of them originated in Italy as early as the fifth century and were taken over by the Spanish Church from Ambrosian hymnaries.[3] Among them is a fine hymn written in time of invasion:

tristes nunc populi, Christe redemptor,
pacem suppliciter cerne rogantes,
threnos et gemitus, cerne dolorem,
maestis auxilium desuper adfer.

dire namque fremens, en, furor atrox
gentis finitimae arva minatur
saeve barbarico murmure nostra
vastari, perimens ut lupus agnos.

---

[1] Vollmer, *M.G.H., Auct. Antiq.*, p. 235.
[2] On the Mozarabic liturgy see Gams, *Kirchengesch. von Spanien*, ii. 2, 186 sqq. ; for Mozarabic hymns, *Anal. Hymn.*, vol. xxvii, with *Introduction*.
[3] **Raby,** *Medium Aevum*, **xvi (1947),** pp. 1 sqq.

salva ergo tua morte redemptos,
salva suppliciter pacta petentes,
disrumpe frameas, spicula frange,
confringe clipeos bella volentum.[1]

The marriage hymn is a kind of Christian *Epithalamium*,
adorned with the rude device of a continuous assonance in *a*.
Mixed with the grave admonitions of the Church is the noise
of joyful instruments and of song:

choreis, tympanis exsulta, musica
et redde domino vota perennia,
qui crucis gloria eruit animas,
  quas coluber momorderat.

pusilla copula, assume fistulam,
lyram et tibiam, perstrepe cantica,
voce organica carmen, melodia
gesta psalle Davidica.[2]

The alphabetical form of hymn, the fashion for which was set
by Augustine, Hilary, and Sedulius, was a favourite with the
Spanish poets. In the hymn at Lauds for the first Sunday after
Epiphany, as in other cases, the *a* is doubled for structural
reasons, and the lines instead of the strophes are alphabetical.

altissimi verbum patris
almaeque, Iesu, virginis,
bis nostro natus gaudio
carnisque factor et caro.[3]

In a hymn on Saints Simon and Jude, the ingenious poet
attempted an elaborate acrostic, the perfect execution of which
was, however, beyond his powers.[4] On the whole, the hymn-
writers were most successful when they kept as closely as they
could to the classical metres, as in the Sapphic verses of the
vesper hymn for the second Sunday after Epiphany:

Christe, lux mundi, salus et potestas,
qui diem solis radiis adimples
noctem et fulvam faciens corusco
  sidere pingis.[5]

But the Spanish spirit is shown most characteristically in the
subject-matter of the hymns, especially in those which treat

---

[1] *Anal. Hymn.* xxvii, p. 281.
[2] ib., p. 284.
[3] ib., p. 71; cf. also pp. 66 and 68,
where the writer resorts to devices such
as 'Berbum' for verbum, 'Had' for
ad, 'fYdes' for fides, and, dispensing

with the double *a*, has an odd line at
the end.
[4] ib., p. 242; cf. also p. 169, hymn on
S. Eulogius.
[5] ib., p. 73.

K

of the sufferings of the martyrs. Here Prudentius was their
model, and the method of his realistic narratives is followed,
often at a length which a non-Spanish congregation would have
found tedious. The happily brief description of the torments
of S. Hippolytus will give an idea of the style of these hymns:

> tunc Caesar rabido fervidus impetu
> os sanctum lapide scindere praecipit;
> longe dissiliunt fragmina dentium,
> sed vox ingeniti praedicat unicum.
>
> ferro praecalidis ignibus artifex
> format spiniferi spicula cardui,
> quo rupta penitus viscera martyris
> profundunt rosei flumina sanguinis.
>
> hinc ad cornipedum terga ferocium
> innexum religant, tractus in aspera
> vitalem subito linquit anhelitum,
> dirum quo valuit vincere saeculum.[1]

But on other occasions, as in a Lenten hymn, the sombre temper
of the poet produces a grave and lofty piece of liturgical verse:

> verbum patris, quod prodiit factum caro,
> agnus dei peccata mundi auferens,
> ad te venimus cernui, ut inclitum
> bibamus almae passionis sanguinem.
>
> ostende vulnerum sacrorum stigmata,
> exsurgat insignis crucis fortissimum
> signum, quod in vigore perpetim manens
> credentibus salvationem conferat.
>
> arundo, clavi, sputa, potus murreus,
> corona spinarum, flagella, lancea
> impressa sunt damnationis verbere;
> iam nostra pro his cuncta dele crimina.
>
> fons vulneris sacri riget praecordia,
> lavet cruor malitiae contagia,
> sit vita praesens absque omni crimine,
> futura detur in beato munere;
>
> ut cum resurgendi dies effulserit
> orbique regni claritas illuxerit,
> sequamur aetheris viam, quae nos trahat
> in se receptos iam perennes incolas.[2]

---

[1] *Anal. Hymn.* xxvii, p. 183.   [2] ib., p. 83.

The Mozarabic liturgy continued in use as the national liturgy of Spain until the end of the eleventh century, when Gregory the Seventh decided to impose the Roman use. But the Spanish Church did not easily allow the old order of prayer and praise, consecrated by patriotism and the memories of heathen domination, to pass wholly away. It was still in partial use when Cardinal Ximenes at the beginning of the sixteenth century caused it to be re-edited by Alfonso Ortiz and, for the first time, printed.[1] In a Romanized form, the Mozarabic liturgy may still be heard at Toledo and in a chapel at Salamanca.

§ 3. *Irish Poets.*

When Britain was incorporated in the Roman Empire, the Latin language was brought thither by officials and traders, and it was, of course, the language of the Church, when Christianity crossed the channel from Gaul. The Roman occupation possessed a distinctively military character, and only the east and south were Romanized to any considerable extent.[2] After the Edict of Constantine, Britain became rapidly a Christian country, but neither Christianity nor Roman culture took such a firm hold as in Gaul and Spain. What schools existed in Britain must have taught the elements of Latin, and the Christian bishops would have made some provision for clerical instruction. The Gallic Church fed the British, and men like Pelagius and Faustus acquired their theological and other learning abroad.[3] But, when the troubles of the Empire removed the legions, the Church remained, a depository, perhaps, of some slender knowledge of Latin letters.   From Britain and Gaul Christianity had passed to Ireland before the days of S. Patrick, but it was, nevertheless, to him that the conversion of the greater part of the island was due.[4]   A British Christian, about the age of seventeen, he was taken a captive to Ireland, where, in bondage, he experienced a call to spiritual things.   In his *Confessio*, he relates his escape to Gaul, and the events of his life until his return to Ireland as a missionary bishop.   He brought with him little learning, but much practical ability and the spiritual qualities of a saint.   The Irish Church was his creation, and soon

---

[1] *Anal. Hymn.* xxvii, p. 6.
[2] See Prof. Haverfield, in *Cambridge Medieval History*, i. 370 sqq.
[3] Cf. Roger, p. 214 ; Harnack, *Mission*,
ii. 272 sqq.
[4] On Patrick see *Life of S. Patrick*, by J. B. Bury.

after his death the country was thickly sown with monasteries and their schools. The Latin tongue was firmly established as the ecclesiastical language; the grammar was taught in the monastic schools, and the Scriptures were studied according to the methods current in the Latin Church.[1]   How far, in addition to the fathers, the classical authors were studied, it is difficult to say.   To picture the Ireland of the fifth century as a home of liberal studies and of Greek and Latin learning is to go far beyond the warrant of the scanty amount of reliable evidence which is available.   Certainly Patrick brought with him no tinge of classical culture, and if, here and there, some small pursuit of letters accompanied the grammatical and theological studies, it was the exception rather than the rule.

Similar conditions existed in Britain, where the Celtic Churches, under the stress of the Anglo-Saxon invasion, were being steadily pressed back to the West and South.   Gildas (*circ.* 547) stands out as a solitary figure, the product of monastic schools whose history it is hard to separate from legend and in which it is possible that some, at any rate, of the classical authors were studied.   For Gildas knew Virgil and perhaps a few other writers such as Juvenal and Claudian.

A poem called the *Lorica*[2] is ascribed to him.   It was said that he composed it to drive away the demons which assaulted him.   'An angel came to him and the angel said to him : If any man shall use this prayer, seven years shall be added to his life, and a third part of his sins shall be wiped out.   In whatsoever day he shall chant this prayer, his persecutors, men or demons, and his enemies shall not be able to hurt him, and death in that day doth not touch him.'   The author of the poem had learned the fantastic Latin of the *Hisperica Famina*[3] and he was clearly a Celt.   It is impossible to be certain that Gildas was the author,[4] but he may have composed a prayer *pro itineris et navigii prosperitate*, which has a similar structure and is likewise intended as a charm against misfortune.[5]   Both poems are rhythmical, and observe the rule of syllabic equality; they are also rimed throughout.   The beginning of the second poem is as follows :

[1] Roger, pp. 216 sqq.; Bury, S. *Patrick*, p. 184.   It is thought that Gallic rhetoricians found their way to Ireland.

[2] Text, *Anal. Hymn.* li, pp. 358 sqq.; *Irish Liber Hymnorum* (*Henry Bradshaw Society*, London 1898, 2 vols.), i. 206 sqq.

[3] See below, p. 133.

[4] W. Meyer, *Gött. Nachr.*, 1912, p. 53, and Mommsen doubt it, after a comparison with Gildas' prose.

[5] Text, Meyer, *Gött. Nachr.*, 1912, pp. 56-7.

dei patris   festinare maximum
mihi cito   peto adiutorium.
Iesu Christi   imploro suffragia
qui natus est   ex virgine Maria.
sancti quoque   spiritus praesidio
fungar semper   hic vel in exilio.

It is, as we have said, unlikely that there was much study
of the classical poets in Britain or Ireland. What studies there
were, must have been regarded merely as aids to the main and
final study of the Scriptures. But the chief obstacle to classical
learning in the Latin countries—their too obvious association
with a paganism which still retained some of its fatal charm—
did not exist in the Western islands.[1] There the mythology of
Greece and Rome had no life and no allurement which might
imperil the soul. In the sixth century, Ireland, free from the
troubles that had invaded the sister island, enjoyed a period,
which, although it was one of isolation, was at the same time
one of comparative peace. The great age of the monastic
schools of Clonard, Clonfert, Clonmacnoise, and Bangor had
begun.[2] Of the nature of the studies we know little beyond the
fact that the Scriptures and the fathers were read with diligence.
But the preliminary study of Latin grammar may easily have
been accompanied by some severely practical reading of profane
authors, against whom the continental prejudice might in Ireland
be held to possess a weakened force.

The fact remains, however, that the studies in the monastic
schools produced in the sixth century neither prose nor poetry
that shows decisively the influence of anything other than the
ecclesiastical Latin of the day. If Columba, who was educated
at Clonard and died at Iona in 597, is the author of the celebrated hymn *Altus prosator*, his verses betray no classical
reminiscences beyond references to Cocytus, Charybdis, and
Scylla, and no considerable acquaintance with the profane
poets. It seems beyond doubt that the hymn is a Celtic composition; its curious Latin has affinities with other Celtic and
British productions of the period, and, in particular, with the
strange eccentric speech of the *Hisperica Famina*, which was
written in south-west Britain in the sixth century.[3] For the rest,

[1] Roger, p. 229.
[2] Bellesheim, *Geschichte der katholischen Kirche in Irland*, i. 81; also
Hauréau, 'Les Écoles d'Irlande' in *Singularités historiques et littéraires*, Paris
1861, but this essay must be read with
caution.
[3] See Zimmer, *Nennius Vindicatus*,
pp. 291 sqq.; and Jenkinson, *The Hisperica Famina*, for these, the strangest of
Latin curiosities; also Roger, pp. 238 sqq.

the hymn is in ecclesiastical Latin, with a sprinkling of the usual Hellenisms and Hebraisms; it is rudely rhythmical and alphabetical in form (*more Ebreo* says the gloss). It tells the story of the Creation, the fall of the angels and of man, and ends with a terrible *Dies Irae*, reminiscent of Zephaniah's 'day of clouds and thick darkness, day of the trumpet and alarm':

> regis regum rectissimi prope est dies domini,
> dies irae et vindictae tenebrarum et nebulae,
> diesque mirabilium.tonitruorum fortium,
> dies quoque angustiae, meroris ac tristitiae,
> in quo cessabit mulierum amor ac desiderium,
> hominumque contentio, mundi huius et cupido.
>
> stantes erimus pavidi ante tribunal domini
> reddemusque de omnibus rationem effectibus,
> videntes quoque posita ante obtutus crimina
> librosque conscientiae patefactos in facie,
> in fletus amarissimos ac singultus erumpemus
> subtracta necessaria operandi materia.
>
> tuba primi archangeli strepente admirabili,
> erumpent munitissima claustra et poliandria
> mundi presentis frigora hominum liquescentia,
> undique conglobantibus ad compagines ossibus
> animabus ethrialibus eisdem obeuntibus
> rursumque redeuntibus debitis mansionibus.[1]

Of this hymn the Irish gloss says, 'There are in sooth many graces upon this hymn, viz. angels present during the recitation; no demon shall know the path of him who shall recite it every day, and foes shall not put him to shame on the day he shall recite it; and there shall be no strife in the house where its recitation shall be customary; aye, and it protects against every death "save death on pillow"; neither shall there be famine nor nakedness in the place where it shall be oft recited.'[2]

The other Latin hymns of Celtic origin contained in the manuscripts of the Irish *Liber Hymnorum* possess similar characteristics to those of the *Altus prosator*. The oldest of all is the hymn ascribed to S. Sechnall or Secundinus, in honour of his master Patrick.[3]   He is said to have been Patrick's nephew, but the evidence for this assertion is, in Professor Bury's opinion,

---

[1] For the text see Bernard and Atkinson, *The Irish Liber Hymnorum*, i. 66 sqq. (*Henry Bradshaw Society*, London 1898); also in *Revue Celtique*, v. 207. Dr. Bernard's prose translation and notes are valuable.   Text also in *Anal. Hymn.* li, p. 275.

[2] *Liber Hymnorum*, ii. 26.

[3] On Sechnall see Bury, *S. Patrick*, p. 117.   He died *c.* A.D. 447.

not decisive. If, as is probable, he is actually the author of the hymn, that poem is the earliest known example of Irish Latin verse. It is alphabetical, with a trochaic rhythm, and its form shows that the characteristics of Latin poetry in Ireland belong to its beginnings. The first verse runs:

> audite omnes amantes deum sancta merita
> viri in Christo beati Patricii episcopi,
> quomodo bonum ob actum simulatur angelis
> perfectamque propter vitam aequatur apostolis.[1]

In the other hymns, beside alliteration, a free use is made of assonance and rime. This fact suggests at once the problem of the relation of these Latin hymns to the Irish hymns contained in the same collection. Without venturing into such a special field of study, we may say here that the continental rhythmical poetry and, with it, rime, seems to have influenced the structure of the Irish religious verse, but that in the native Irish verse there was already existent a kind of assonance, which 'involved *harmony* rather than *identity* of the consonants'.[2] Examples of this assonance are to be found in many of the Latin hymns. As an example, a specimen of the hymn, *Noli Pater*, ascribed to S. Columba, in which both rime and assonance occur, may be given:

> noli pater indulgere tonritua cum fulgore
> ac frangamur formidine huius atque uridine.[3]

Another collection of Irish Latin hymns is the so-called *Antiphonary of Bangor*, which exists in a single manuscript now in the Ambrosian Library at Milan. Internal evidence places its date at the close of the seventh century, and the manuscript is clearly Irish in character. It is certain indeed that it came from the monastery at Bangor on the southern shore of Belfast Lough, and it wandered from Ireland to Bobbio in the Apennines, whence Cardinal Borromeo removed it in 1606 to his great library at Milan.[4] Some of the hymns contained in this manuscript are not of Irish origin, and belong to the continental tradition of quantitative verse. If the poetical quality of the remaining hymns is not, in general, higher than

[1] For text see *Liber Hymnorum*, i. 7 ; see also Engelbrecht, *Zeitschr. f. d. österreich. Gymnas.*, lix, p. 593. There is no elision, but hiatus is frequent.
[2] For a discussion of the metrical systems of these hymns see *Liber Hymno-* *rum*, ii, pp. ix sqq., xxxi sqq.
[3] ib., i. 88.
[4] *The Antiphonary of Bangor*, ed. F. E. Warren, 2 vols., 1893, 1895 (*Henry Bradshaw Society*).

that of other Irish Latin hymns, they have an important place in the history of medieval verse-forms. Like the poems in the *Liber Hymnorum*, the Bangor hymns show the free use of rime, and a rhythm based on numbered syllables rather than on accent, and there is, likewise, plentiful alliteration. A striking example of the use of two-syllabled rimes is seen in the *Versiculi Familie Benchuir*, a hymn of praise commemorating the monastic rule of Bangor. Here the rimes are most elaborate. Not only does each verse end on the same letter, but there are excellent *alternate* two-syllabled rimes, as in the following verses, where the monastery is described as

> navis nunquam turbata,
>> quamvis fluctibus tonsa,
> nuptiis quoque parata
>> regi domino sponsa.
>
> domus deliciis plena,
>> super petram constructa,
> necnon vinea vera,
>> ex Aegypto transducta.
>
> certe civitas firma,
>> fortis atque munita,
> gloriosa ac digna,
>> supra montem posita.[1]

In these verses *nuptiis* and *deliciis* are to be pronounced as disyllable and trisyllable respectively, an accommodation common in Irish hymns.

Of earlier date, as its absence of rime indicates, is the sacramental hymn:

> sancti, venite, Christi corpus sumite,

which is said to have been sung by angels at the mass of Secundinus. Sechnall or Secundinus had accused Patrick of preaching charity too little, and Patrick in his wrath had attempted to ride his chariot over him. Now Sechnall had left the Offering on the altar, having been saying his mass in the church near by. As the two saints made peace in the graveyard, they heard angelic voices within the church chanting the *Offertorium*,

> sancti, venite,
>> Christi corpus sumite,
> sanctum bibentes,
>> quo redempti, sanguinem.

Text, Warren, ii. 28; *Anal. Hymn.* li, p. 356.

The saints obeyed the command and entered to receive the Body of Christ. 'Wherefore', says the legend, 'from that time forward, this hymn is sung in Ireland when they go to Christ's Body.'[1]

The hymn *In Natali Martyrum*, the Irish origin of which has been needlessly doubted, is also of early date. The opening verse shows a strength and fervour, which give it a distinctively poetical quality:

> sacratissimi martyres summi dei,
> bellatores fortissimi Christi regis,
> potentissimi duces exercitus dei,
> victores in caelis deo canentes: alleluia.[2]

It calls to memory Crashaw's beautiful lines:

> Those thy old soldiers, great and tall,
> Ripe men of martyrdom, that could reach down
> With strong arms their triumphant crown;
> Such as could, with lusty breath,
> Speak loud into the face of death.

The *Hymnus Apostolorum*[3] is a versified confession of faith. Its structure offers no particular interest, being similar to that of the 'Sancti, venite', but the expression is simple and direct. The incarnation and birth of Christ are described in the second part:

> in fine mundi
>   post tanta mysteria
> adest salvator
>   cum grandi clementia; . . .
>
> natus ut homo
>   mortali in tegmine
> non deest caelo
>   manens in trinitate.
>
> vagit in pannis,
>   veneratur a magis,
> fulget in stellis,
>   adoratur in caelis.
>
> statura vili
>   continetur praesepi,
> cuius pugillo
>   potest orbis concludi.[4]

---

[1] Warren, ii. 44; *Anal. Hymn.* li, p. 298.
[2] Warren, ii. 12; *Anal. Hymn.* li, p. 313.
[3] Warren, ii. 4; *Anal. Hymn.* li, p. 271.
[4] Warren, ii. 5; *Anal. Hymn.* li, p. 272.

The *Liber Hymnorum* and the *Bangor Antiphonary* do not exhaust the catalogue of extant Celtic hymns. In volume li of *Analecta Hymnica*, Blüme has collected a number of early hymns which he classifies, together with the hymns which we have already considered, under the comprehensive title of *Hymnodia Hiberno-Celtica*. These additional hymns, which are of 'insular' origin, possess the same characteristics of rhythm and alliteration, and often show rich and fairly perfect two-syllabled rimes. When we find a stanza like the following from a ninth-century manuscript,

> sancte sator suffragator,
> legum lator, largus dator,
> iure pollens, es qui potens,
> nunc in aethra firma petra,[1]

we recognize the beginnings of the conscious manipulation of the two-syllabled rime, which was to issue in the poetry of Hildebert of Le Mans and Adam of S. Victor. To the Irish poets must be given the credit of being the first important innovators in the use of rime, and it is possible to trace a progressive development from the rimeless hymns of the fifth century, through the middle period of incipient rimes in the sixth, to the richer and more exact rimes of the seventh and eighth centuries.[2]

In considering the Irish Latin hymns, collected in the *Liber Hymnorum* and the *Bangor Antiphonary*, we have found no evidence of the influence of classical poetry, but the possibility that a few more eager students may have carried their studies of profane authors farther than the limits imposed on theological education would strictly warrant, cannot, of course, be excluded. The writings of Columbanus (540 *circ.*–615), who was a monk at Bangor under Comgall, show a considerable acquaintance with classical letters. It is possible, but hardly probable, that he may have acquired this knowledge during his long sojourn on the Continent, but, in any case, he deserves the honourable title of the first Irish man of letters.[3] Reminiscences of Virgil, Ovid,

---

[1] *Anal. Hymn.* li, p. 299.
[2] See ib., p. 263: 'Irland ist in dieser Hinsicht allen Anzeichen nach die vorbildliche Urstätte'; for interesting speculations on the influence of Celtic rhythmic verse on Provençal and French poetry see K. Bartsch, '*Ein keltisches Versmass im Provenzalischen und Französischen*', *Zeitschrift für roman. Philol.* ii. 195 sqq.,

1878; also iii. 359 sqq., 1879, on which see Meyer's criticism, *Rythmik*, i. 286.
[3] On Columbanus see Hauck, i. 251 sqq.; Roger, p. 230; Holmes, *Church in Gaul*, pp. 540 sqq.; and Hodgkin's charming sketch in *Italy and her Invaders*, vi. 105 sqq. On his learning see Hörle, *Frühmittelalt. Mönchs- und Klerikerbildung in Italien*, p. 55 sq.

Horace, Juvenal, Claudian, and Sallust, to say nothing of Prudentius, have been detected in his prose or his verses, and his are the first metrical poems of Irish origin.[1] Two of these are in hexameters with a slight tendency to leonine rimes ; they are sententious in character and betray the ascetic monk, who despises the world and its riches for eternal things. Most interesting is the long metrical epistle, addressed to his friend Fedolius. It is composed in adonics, a metre, which says the poet, was used by Sappho.

> Graiugenarum
> inclyta vates
> nomine Saffo
> versibus istis
> dulce solebat
> edere carmen.

And he proceeds to explain, in verse, that the metre is composed of a dactyl followed by a spondee or a trochee. The theme of the poem is the vanity of earthly treasures and the evil power of gold. Columbanus recalls from pagan mythology the Golden Fleece, the Apple of Discord, the Stories of Polydorus, Pygmalion, and Danaë :

> odit iniqui
> munera Christus.
> haec sapienti
> dispicienda,
> qui fugitivae
> atque caducae
> cernere debet
> tempora vitae.

'Frivola nostra'—so Columbanus styles this pleasing composition, a diversion of his extreme old age ; for he tells us in the six hexameters with which it concludes that he was seventy-two when he wrote it. May we, therefore, imagine the 'venerable' monk, finding amid the stress of his endless labours in France and Italy, a consolation in literary compositions of this lighter, if religious, sort ?[2] But Columbanus did

---

[1] Texts in Migne, lxxx, col. 285 sqq.; ed. Gundlach, *M. G. H.*, *Epist.* iii, pp. 182 sqq.

[2] Gundlach'(*Neues Archiv*, xiii, pp. 499 sqq.) regards four poems as authentic (pp. 514 sqq.): (1) The hexameter acrostic addressed to Hunaldus, 'casibus innumeris'; (2) the hexameters to Sethus, 'suscipe, Sethe'; (3) the adonics to Fedolius, 'accipe, quaeso'; (4) the rhythmic verses to a young friend, 'Mundus iste'. Gundlach adduces parallels to the phraseology, &c., of the verses from the prose writings of Columbanus. The model for Columbanus's adonics was

not come to Europe as a humanist; he came from Ireland with his twelve companions, driven by the Irish *Wanderlust,* to set up a severe monasticism in a corrupted Church, and to be an apostle and prophet.   The foundations which bore witness to his labours were long in becoming homes of liberal study; they were houses of hard discipline, daily toil, and strict obedience. First Anegray was founded on Burgundian soil; then Luxeuil, as the number of monks increased, and, later, Fontaines. Driven from Burgundy by Brunhildis, whose hatred he had incurred by his outspoken denunciation of her son's evil life, Columbanus desired to make for Italy.[1]   After wanderings in France under the custody of Burgundian soldiers and a short missionary labour in Germany, the final fruit of which was the foundation by his disciple Gallus of the famous monastery which was to be S. Gall, he carried out his design, and under the Apennines arose the Cloister of Bobbio, which was destined to become a house of learning and a repository of many precious manuscripts of the classical authors.   But the time for the revival of learning was not yet; the young monasteries were full of monks obeying a harsh and uncompromising rule, which tamed the will and crushed the spirit.   Not until the Carolingian revival and under influences which mainly came from Anglo-Saxon schools did classical studies begin to make a real advance on the Western mainland.

§ 4. *Anglo-Saxon Poets : Aldhelm, Aethelwald, Bede, Boniface, Lul, Aethelwulf, Frithegode, Wulfstan.*

In 597 Augustine and his companions landed in Thanet and began the conversion of the kingdom of Kent.   Gregory the Great, the prime mover of this Roman mission, was not, as we have seen, a friend to learning; and, in any case, the work of preaching and of organization could leave no room for any but the smallest educational activities.   So far as literary studies were concerned, the full harvest of the new contact of Britain with Rome was not to be reaped until a later date.   Meanwhile, the Celtic monks from Ireland and Iona were establishing Churches among the Saxons of the north.   In 635 Oswald, king of Northumbria, sent to Iona for a bishop to evangelize his heathen

---

Boëthius.   The rhythmical verse begins :
      mundus iste transibit
      cotidie decrescit.

                  nemo vivens manebit,
                  nullus vivus remansit.
[1] Hauck, i. 325.

subjects.[1] The monks finally sent Aidan, whose name and works have made illustrious the island and monastery of Lindisfarne. There a school was set up, and according to Bede, 'inbuebantur praeceptoribus Scottis parvuli Anglorum una cum maioribus studiis et observatione disciplinae regularis.'[2] What these *maiora studia* consisted of, it is hard to say; but, probably, they went little farther than the elements of grammar and the reading of the Scriptures.[3]

The rise of heathen Mercia in the seventh century, under Penda, set back the course of Christianity in both north and south. Oswald was slain by him at Maserfelth in 642, but thirteen years later his terrible career was ended at the river Winwaed. The triumph of Oswiu was at the same time the triumph of the Church, which was reflected in the revived prosperity of the northern monasteries. The main influences were still Irish, and English monks continually visited Ireland in search of sacred learning.

But at the Synod of Whitby (664) the Celtic Church in England stood face to face with Rome; and Rome, by her superior tradition and uncompromising show of authority, brought the Celtic Church to submission. Three years later the kings of Northumbria and Kent asked Pope Vitalian to send them an Archbishop to set their disorganized Churches in order. Theodore of Tarsus was chosen, and with him came Hadrian. Both were monks and both were men of learning. Theodore [4] had studied at Athens. He had a perfect command of Latin and Greek, and possessed a remarkable knowledge both sacred and profane. Hadrian, an African by birth, knew Latin and Greek, and had made extensive theological studies. These two men, in a happy hour, were charged with the reorganization of the English Church. Bede testifies abundantly to the new spirit which they introduced into the monastic schools. They taught, he says, the art of metre, of astronomy, and of arithmetic, and 'to-day some of their disciples are still alive, who know Latin and Greek as well as their own mother tongue'.[5]

[1] Bede, *H. E.* iii. 3; on the history of the Anglo-Saxon Church see W. Hunt, *History of the English Church, 597–1066*; see also *Cambridge History of English Literature*, vol. i, 1907; for biographies of Anglo-Saxon poets see Wright, *Biographia Britannica Literaria* (*Anglo-Saxon Period*).

[2] *H. E.* iii. 3.

[3] See Roger, p. 277.

[4] Hunt, *Hist. of the Eng. Church, 597–1066*, p. 126; *H. E.* iv.; see Hörle, *Frühmittelalt. Mönchs- und Klerikerbildung in Italien*, p. 29, for interesting remarks on the influx of 'Orientals' into the West about this time.

[5] *H. E.* iv. 2.

Under Theodore and Hadrian the School at Canterbury provided secular and religious learning for the south and west.   In
Northumbria, Benedict Biscop's (d. 690) foundations at Wearmouth and Jarrow performed a like service for the north.
Benedict was one of King Oswiu's thegns, but in early manhood
he forsook the world.[1]   He journeyed to Rome, became a monk
at Lérins, and made the acquaintance of Theodore in Gaul.
Theodore placed him in charge of S. Augustine's at Canterbury
and won him to take a profound interest in the practical life of
monastic England.   At Wearmouth and Jarrow he set up
monasteries with schools, where authors both sacred and profane
were studied, and Latin versification was taught.   Benedict
made many journeys to Rome and to Gaul, bringing back with
him always some treasure, books and relics, vestments and
pictures, or a teacher to instruct his monks in the manner of
the Roman *schola cantorum.*   So, in both north and south, there
were homes of learning, and the possibility of literary production.
With all the eagerness of children the Anglo-Saxons flung
themselves into the new studies.   They had already developed
a vigorous literature in their mother tongue, a literature richly
poetical and fully self-conscious, and when they had painfully
mastered in the schools the strange Roman tongue, they were
eager to show their newly-acquired skill, whether in prose or
verse.   In theory, the new studies were regarded by ecclesiastical authority as mere preliminaries to the pursuit of sacred
knowledge.   But the Anglo-Saxon monks, while formally
acknowledging the superiority of Scripture and the fathers,
were delighted to obtain possession of a knowledge which an
Aldhelm could parade with pedantry and a Bede could employ
to create a clear and adequate prose.

Aldhelm [2] (b. *circ.* 650) was the first important man of letters
who owed his education to Theodore's school at Canterbury.
He studied first under the Irishman Maeldubh, but it was to
Hadrian that he owed his thorough knowledge of Latin and
his acquaintance with Greek and Hebrew.   He became a monk
at Malmesbury, where he rose to be Abbot.   In 715 he was
made bishop of the newly created see of Sherborne.

The extent of his knowledge of the Latin authors has been

[1] On Benedict see Hunt, *Hist. of the
Eng. Church,597–1066,* p. 107 ; especially
Bede's *Historia Abbatum* (in Plummer,
Baedae Opera Historica, Oxford 1896, i.
364 sqq.).

[2] On Aldhelm see Bede, *H. E.* v. 18 ;
Hunt, *Hist. of the Eng. Church, 597–1066,*
p. 202 ; Roger, pp. 290 sqq. ; Works, ed.
Giles, Oxford 1844 ; the best edition is
now Ehwald's, in *M. G. H. auct. antiq.* xv.

carefully investigated.[1]   The influence of Christian writers is at
least as profound as that of the ancients.   Of the poets Virgil
and Sedulius were his favourites; but he knew also Ovid,
Horace, Terence, Persius, Juvenal, Lucan, and Juvencus.
Then follow Paulinus of Nola, Ausonius, Prudentius, Claudian,
Prosper, and Sidonius Apollinaris.   Like Bede, he possessed
no sense of historical or literary perspective; all these poets,
pagan and Christian, had become classics, and to that extent
they were models for imitation.   Aldhelm employed great
diligence and considerable talent in the composition of verses
in words whose appropriate quantity was indicated by some
older poet or grammarian.[2]   Hence his metrical verse has
a certain formal correctness which gives it an advantage over
his extravagantly artificial prose.

His long didactic poem in hexameters, *De laudibus virginum*,
is a versification of his elaborately-constructed prose treatise on
the same subject.   'Librum eximium', Bede styles this double
production,[3] which, as he says, was an imitation of Sedulius'
Opus and *Carmen Paschale*.   The poem is excessively laboured
and obscure, but it was much admired by Aldhelm's contemporaries; so also was his curious collection of metrical riddles,[4]
a form of composition which the Anglo-Saxon loved, as the
example of Tatwine (Archbishop of Canterbury, 731), and of
Eusebius (Hwaetbercht), the friend of Bede, clearly demonstrate.
It is hardly necessary to give at length specimens of these
literary curiosities,[5] but an example from Aldhelm will convey
an idea of their childish nature.   The subject, as can easily
be guessed, is the rainbow:

> Taumantis proles priscorum famine fingor,
> ast ego prima mei generis rudimenta retexam :
> sole ruber genitus sum partu nubis aquosae ;
> lustro polos passim solos, non scando per austros.[6]

The remaining poems of Aldhelm are in honour of the Virgin
and of various Apostles to whom churches or altars were
dedicated.   The first will serve as an example; it refers to
a church of S. Peter and S. Paul, presumably the ancient
church at Malmesbury, which Aldhelm himself restored.[7]

---

[1] For the authors read by Aldhelm see Manitius, *Zu Aldhelm und Beda, Wiener Sitzungsber.*, 1886, pp. 535 sqq. ; Roger, p. 293.

[2] See Roger, p 299.

[3] *H. E.* v. 18.

[4] Wright, *Satirical Poets of the Twelfth Century*, ii. 535 sqq., *Rolls Series*.

[5] For Tatwine's riddles see Wright, *Satirical Poets*, ii. 525 sqq.

[6] Ehwald, p. 100.

[7] See Wright, *Biographica Britannica Literaria*, p. 213.

hic celebranda rudis florescit gloria templi,
limpida quae sacri signat vexilla triumphi ;
hic Petrus et Paulus, tenebrosi lumina mundi,
praecipui patres, populi qui frena gubernant,
carminibus crebris alma venerantur in aula.

claviger aetherius, portam qui pandis in aethra,
candida caelorum recludens regna tonantis,
ausculta clemens populorum vota precantum,
marcida qui riguis umectant imbribus ora :
suscipe singultus commissa piacla gementum,
qui prece flagranti torrent peccamina vitae !

maximus et doctor, patulo vocitatus ab axe,
cum cuperes Christo priscos praeponere ritus,
Saulus, qui dictus mutato nomine Paulus
post tenebras claram coepisti cernere lucem,
vocibus orantum nunc aures pande benignas
et tutor tremulis cum Petro porrige dextram,
sacra frequentantes aulae qui limina lustrant,
quatenus hic scelerum detur indulgentia perpes
larga de pietate fluens et fonte superno,
dignis qui numquam populis torpescit in aevum ![1]

The poems of Aldhelm maintain this uniform level of dullness. It is known that he also tried his hand at rhythmical
compositions, but the little group of rhythmical poems which
used to be ascribed to him is more probably, wholly or in part,
the work of his disciple Aethelwald.[2]   These verses are directly
related to the similar compositions long current in the Irish
monasteries, which we have already examined in discussing
the *Liber Hymnorum*. Further, they form a link between the
Irish rhythmical hymns and those which were composed on the
Continent in Carolingian times. The favourite metre is a line
of sixteen syllables in which the eighth and the sixteenth
syllable rime together, as in the *Altus prosator* of Columba.
There is no elision, and the rimes and assonances are often
as rich as those contained in the Irish *Liber Hymnorum*, while
the language has much in common with that of the Irish poets
and the *Hisperica Famina*. The first, in a lively, but obscure
and florid manner, tells of a journey in Cornwall and an escape
from danger in a storm. 'Ymnista carmen cecini', says the

---

[1] Ehwald, pp. 11–12.
[2] See the note on *Some Poems ascribed to Aldhelm*, by Henry Bradley, *E. H. R.*, 1900, xv, p. 291 ; also Ehwald, p. 524. Bradley ascribed them all to Aethelwald, but Ehwald shows that the first is by an unknown clerk, and he assigns the remainder to Aethelwald ; see also Traube, *Karolingische Dichtungen*, pp. 130 sqq.

jesting poet, who addresses the verses to a friend. The storm is thus described :

> elementa inormia atque facta informia
> quassantur sub aetherea convexi caeli camera,
> dum tremet mundi machina sub ventorum monarchia.
> ecce, nocturno tempore, orto brumali turbine,
> quatiens terram tempestas turbabat atque vastitas,
> cum fracto venti federe bacharentur in aethere
> et rupto retinaculo desevirent in saeculo.[1]

As it was the festival of S. Paul, the travellers were saved from destruction by the triune deity, to whom the concluding doxology is addressed :

> ergo Christo in commune adempti a discrimine,
> grates dicamus dulciter manenti immortaliter.
> doxa deo ingenito atque gnato progenito,
> simul cum sancto superna flatu regenti saecula.

The other poems are in the same manner. The third is a hymn proper, a prayer for peace and for the destruction of the wicked. Here the rime and alliteration, familiar in the Irish hymns, are fully present :

> summum satorem, solia sedit qui per aethralia,
> alti Olimpi arcibus obvallatus minacibus,
> cuncta cernens acumine caelorum summo lumine,
> alta poli et infima telluris latae limina.

And so the hymn continues, and demands the destruction of the wicked in the place where Typho, the giant whom Jupiter buried under Aetna, lies in torment :

> illos, illos omnipotens trudat aeternis tenebris,
> ubi Typo, teterrimis tostis globorum gremiis,
> girat, torquens gurgitibus atri ignis ultricibus.

It is difficult to understand the fascination which these poems appear to have exercised over Aethelwald's contemporaries, but their importance in relation to the later developments of Latin rhythmical poetry on the Continent is considerable.

Bede,[2] who was born in 673 and so belongs to the next generation of Anglo-Saxon scholars, is one of the greatest names in medieval ecclesiastical literature. His uneventful life-story is best given in his own words. 'I, Baeda, a servant of Christ and priest of the monastery of the blessed apostles,

---

[1] Ehwald, p. 524 sq.
[2] On Bede see Plummer, *Baedae Opera Historica* (Oxford 1896), i, Introduction.

S. Peter and S. Paul, which is at Wearmouth and at Jarrow . . . was born in the territory of the said monastery, and at the age of seven I was, by the care of my relations, given to the most reverend Abbot Benedict (Biscop), and afterwards to Ceolfrid, to be educated.   From that time I have spent the whole of my life within that monastery, devoting all my pains to the study of the Scriptures; and amid the observance of monastic discipline and the daily charge of singing in the Church, it has been ever my delight to learn, or teach, or write.   In my nineteenth year I was admitted to the diaconate, in my thirtieth to the priesthood, both by the hands of the most reverend Bishop John, and at the bidding of Abbot Ceolfrid.   From the time of my admission to the priesthood to my fifty-ninth year, I have endeavoured, for my own use and that of my brethren, to make brief notes upon the holy Scripture, either out of the works of the venerable fathers, or in conformity with their meaning and interpretation.' [1]

Bede spent the greater part of his life at Jarrow, hardly leaving the monastery.   There is, indeed, a notice of a brief visit to Ecbert's school at York, and perhaps of one to Lindisfarne, but for the most part he remained like a true monk, wedded to his cloister.

His was not a poetical nature.   He was above all a student of history and theology, and a teacher, whose aim it was to equip his pupils with the knowledge necessary both to salvation and to the understanding of Christian theology and history. To this end he wrote a series of text-books and treatises which were used in the schools of Western Europe for many centuries. The study of Latin was the basis of the instruction, which included besides, the rules of metre and rhythm, some natural history, chronology, and arithmetic, and the established methods of biblical interpretation.   His treatise De Arte Metrica, an elementary study of metres, was still the basis of the instruction in versification given by Fulbert at Chartres in the eleventh century.[2]   It is founded on an uncritical study of the old grammarians, and the poets, Christian and profane.   Bede was no purist.   He is ready with Sedulius to shorten the first syllable of spiritus, if it will enable him to celebrate more easily the glory of the Trinity.   In this treatise he deals also with

---

[1] I use Dr. Plummer's rendering (pp. ix and x of his edition of the H. E., text, i. 357).
[2] Taylor, Mediaeval Mind, i. 300; text of the De Arte Metrica, in Migne, xc, col. 149 sqq.; see Roger, p. 367, for a criticism.

rhythmical verse, describing rhythm as *modulatio sine ratione*, and he makes it clear that the characteristic of this kind of verse is equality in the number of syllables.

The work by which his fame has extended to our own day, is, of course, his *Ecclesiastical History of the English People*, an admirably arranged and straightforward account of the foundation and growth of the Christian Church in England.   Here his qualities of candour, simplicity, and carefulness are exhibited in a style which never strains after effect or wanders in search of rhetorical embellishment.   He had read the ancient authors to good purpose, and if he shares the hagiological leanings of his day, he did no more than accept what he already found in his sources, and he gives the miraculous no undue emphasis.

The nature of Bede's classical studies has been investigated by Manitius,[1] who shows that, unlike Aldhelm's, his writings betray more reminiscences of Christian than of classical poets, although Virgil, Ovid, Persius, and Lucan, are quoted or imitated.   Juvencus, Sedulius, and Paulinus of Nola, were especial favourites, and Avitus, Arator, and Fortunatus, were well known to him.

The most important of Bede's poems which has survived is in hexameters, on the life, or more accurately, on the miracles of Cuthbert, the famous Bishop of Lindisfarne.[2]   It is dedicated to his friend John, a priest who was journeying to Rome.   The dedication contains the promise of a prose life of Cuthbert, a work which is extant, and is a valuable source for the history of the saint.   The verses of the poem are formally correct, and show a knowledge of the Christian poets, Arator, Juvencus, and Sedulius.[3]

In a poem entitled *Hymnus de die iudicii*, also in hexameters, the poet describes how he sat, in the flowering country side, under the shade of a tree,

> arboris umbriferae moestus sub tegmine solus,

and meditated on his sins, on death and judgement, and the pains of the wicked.   Repentance alone can save a man at the last, as it saved the penitent thief.

> cur, rogo, mens, tardas medico te pandere totam ?
> vel cur, lingua, taces, veniae dum tempus habebis ?

---

[1] *Zu Aldhelm und Beda*, pp. 616 sqq. (*Wiener Sitzungsber.*, 1886).

[2] Text in Migne, xciv, col. 575.

[3] Cf. Manitius, *Christl. Lat. Poesie*, p. 498.

Then follows a description of the terrors of the judgement, the trembling of the earth, the melting of the mountains, the falling of the stars, and the whole apparatus of the 'last assize' as the medieval imagination conceived it, and has many times represented it in stone over the doorways of the churches :

> felix o nimium, semperque in saecula felix
> qui illas effugiet poenarum prospere clades,
> cum sanctisque simul laetatur in omnia saecla !

The poem ends with a pious prayer for grace. Its merits are small and it displays nothing half so well as the piety of its author.

In his Ecclesiastical History, Bede mentions the fact that he is the author of a *Liber hymnorum diverso metro sive rhythmo*, that is, a book containing both metrical and rhythmical hymns. Unfortunately, it has not survived, but Dreves holds that a number of his genuine hymns have been preserved and he includes no less than sixteen in the fiftieth volume of *Analecta Hymnica*.[1] The poem in honour of S. Etheldreda of Ely is certainly the work of Bede, for he inserts it as his own composition in his Ecclesiastical History.[2] It is an alphabetical poem in epanaleptic elegiacs like those of Sedulius. The first few verses are sufficient to show that its poetical quality is not high :

> Alma deus trinitas, quae saecula cuncta gubernas,
>   adnue iam coeptis, alma deus trinitas.
> Bella Maro resonet, nos pacis dona canamus :
>   munera nos Christi, bella Maro resonet.
> Carmina casta mihi, foedae non raptus Helenae.
>   luxus erit lubricis, carmina casta mihi.
> Dona superna loquar, miserae non proelia Troiae,
>   terra quibus gaudet : dona superna loquar.

Nearly all the other hymns attributed to Bede are in iambic dimeters. Best known is the hymn on the Holy Innocents, with its curious refrain :

> hymnum canentes martyrum
> dicamus innocentiam,
> quos terra flentes perdidit,
> gaudens sed aethra suscipit.
>
> vultum patris per saecula
> quorum tuentur angeli
> eiusque laudant gratiam
> hymnum canentes martyrum.[3]

---

[1] pp. 98 sqq.   [2] *H. E.* iv. 20.   [3] *Anal. Hymn.* l, p. 102

The *Soliloquy on Psalm XLII*[1] is written in hexameters and shows how the classical tradition was maintained in the English schools when it was all but dead in the rest of Europe. The verses, however, lack the strength and skill which Fortunatus showed a century before :

> cervus ut ad fontes sitiens festinat aquarum,
> sic mea mens ardet te, conditor alme, requirens
> viventemque sitit te cernere libera lucem.
> o quando optati veniat mihi tempus amoris,
> quando tuam liceat faciem speciemque tueri ?

Here it is not merely the fact that, as in the case of Paulinus of Nola, the poet's inspiration failed to overcome the difficulty of fitting Christian sentiment to classical phrase. Both Aldhelm and Bede were writing a language which could never have for them the familiarity which it possessed for a Prudentius or a Fortunatus. The Anglo-Saxon poets wrote according to rules painfully acquired, and with the grammarians and the poets always at their elbow. As a consequence, their verses wavered between the tasteless elaborations of Aldhelm and the plainer manner of Bede, which gives the impression of a schoolboy's exercise.

The famous missionary of the Germans, Boniface (or, to give him his Anglo-Saxon name Wynfrith),[2] was educated, like Aldhelm and Bede, in the English monastic schools, and he made the usual studies. Called to a life of arduous missionary labours which ended in 755 in his martyrdom in Frisia, he could beguile himself with the composition of metrical riddles, and he loved to append his verses to his numerous epistles. Thus he concludes a letter to the new Pope Zacharias with the lines:

> te deus altithronus sancta conservet in aede
> sedis apostolice rectorem tempora longa,
> melliflua gratum populis doctrina per orbem
> perficiatque deo dignum pia gratia Christi.
> splendida percipiat florens sua gaudia mater,
> atque domus domini laetetur prole fecunda.[3]

These verses have the flavour of the Anglo-Saxon schools, and Boniface also amused himself in the Anglo-Saxon fashion with

---

[1] *Anal. Hymn.* l, p. 114.
[2] On Boniface see the admirable account in Hauck, i. 432 sqq.; poems in Jaffé, *Monumenta Moguntina*; ed. Dümmler, *M. G. H., Poet. Kar.*, i. 1–23 ; M. Tangl, *Die Briefe des heiligen*

Bonifatius und Lull, M. G. H., Epist. Select., i, Berlin 1916. My references are to Tangl.
[3] Tangl, p. 86 [Letter No. 50]; cf. also p. 227 [Letter No. 103].

rhythmical verse.   The following lines which conclude a letter
to a religious lady are more probably (and the letter itself) the
work of Lul, his pupil and friend : [1]

> vale Christo virguncula,   Christi nempe tiruncula,
> mihi cara magnopere   atque gnara in opere,
> tibi laudes contexero   atque grates ingemino.
> teque rogo cum tremore,   agna, Christi pro amore :
> vota redde cum fervore   altissimo in aethere
> quae pepigimus pariter,   memorare vivaciter.

But writing to the youthful Nithard to urge him to liberal and
religious studies, Boniface breaks into rime :

> vale, frater, florentibus
> iuventutis cum viribus,
> ut floreas cum domino
> in sempiterno solio,
> qua martyres in cuneo
> regem canunt aethereo,
> prophetae apostolicis
> consonabunt et laudibus,
> qua rex regum perpetuo
> cives ditat in saeculo.[2]

If the call to missionary labour in 716 had not transported
Wynfrith into an active life where his great practical talents
found scope and development, he might have earned like Bede
the reputation of a famous teacher.   He had all Aldhelm's love
of the Latin poets, and that *penchant* for acrostics and riddles
which Anglo-Saxon scholars were to convey to the Carolingian
schools.   He is a typical child of the Anglo-Saxon literary
movement, a movement which, at the end of the eighth century,
found its consummation in the revival, on a large scale and
mainly under the influence of Alcuin, of classical studies in the
Palace school at Aachen.

While Bede was yet alive, a new school arose at York, which
soon eclipsed the fame of Canterbury and Jarrow.   There
Archbishop Egbert (752–66), a pupil of Bede, and Aelbert,
who succeeded to the archiepiscopal chair, supervised the first
systematic study of the liberal arts in England.   Grammar,
rhetoric, with prose and verse composition, astronomy, arithmetic, and law, formed part of the curriculum, which culminated
in the usual theological studies.[3]   The most famous of Aelbert's

[1] Tangl, p. 280 [Letter No. 140] ; see
note 1, p. 279
[2] ib., p. 6 sq.

[3] See Roger, p. 313 ; Gaskoin's *A. .tin*,
pp. 33 sqq.

pupils was Alcuin, whose life and labours belong more properly to the history of the Carolingian renaissance.

To the same period (the beginning of the ninth century) belongs the interesting poem of Aethelwulf, a monk who lived in a cell of Lindisfarne.[1] The subject is 'the Abbots and the miracles of his Church'. It is dedicated to Egbert, Bishop of Lindisfarne (802–19), who receives the dutiful praise of the poet in the opening verses :

> sume, pater, placidus modulantis vota poetae,
> quatinus aeterno capias cum rege quietem.

Then Aethelwulf tells of the history of his monastery, how Osred of Northumbria shaved the head of Eanmund and compelled him to become a monk ; how the monastery of S. Peter rose and flourished until the poet's own day. He describes the virtues of the monks, their diligence and piety, and makes special mention of Ultan, the Irishman,

> comtis qui potuit notis ornare libellos,

who after long years spent in these labours and in the instruction of his brethren, departed this life, leaving the virtue of a saint in the relics of his body. Then there was Abbot Sigwine, good to the poor and a lover of music ; Iglac, who had the gift of second sight ; and Eadfrid, Aethelwulf's old master, who appeared to him in a vision and showed him the wonders of a great Church. This poem of Aethelwulf's throws a glamour of piety and peaceful industry over the monasticism of the north, but evil days were already near.

After the rich promise of its early bloom, the Latin literature and especially the Latin poetry of the Anglo-Saxons fell into a decline which lasted until after the Norman Conquest. This is partly to be explained by the strength and popularity of the vernacular literature, and by the essentially artificial relation of the Latin language to the general culture of the age. But, most decisively, the instability of political conditions and the devastation wrought by the Danish invasions, aimed a deadly blow at the progress of learning and of letters. In 793 the Vikings sacked Lindisfarne ; in 867 York and its famous library went up in flames. Minster after minster suffered a like fate. The Church was thoroughly demoralized, and all the efforts of

---

[1] Text of the poem in *Rolls Series*, vol. lxxv, 1, *Symeonis Opera*, i. 265 sqq., London 1882 ; also *M. G. H., Poet. Kar.*, i, pp. 583 sqq.; see Wright, *Biogr. Brit. Lit.*, pp. 370 sqq.; also Traube, *Karolingische Dichtungen*, pp. 7 sqq.

Alfred could accomplish little. The able and pious king gathered learned men to his court, Bishop Werfrith from Worcester, Plegmund from his retreat near Chester, Grimbald from S. Omer, John the old Saxon from Corvey, and Asser from S. David's. There was a court school in which the children of the nobles could learn Latin grammar, and there were schools in the monasteries which the king had begun to restore. But the level of ecclesiastical culture remained low. Alfred himself was no great scholar, but with marvellous perseverance and competent aid, he translated, with omissions and additions, books which he conceived to be of value for the edification of his people— Gregory's *Pastoral Rule*, Bede, Orosius, and Boëthius' *Consolation*.

In the tenth century, Dunstan owed his early education at Glastonbury to Irish scholars. The monastic revival associated with his name and more particularly with that of Aethelwald of Winchester, was inspired by the example of the continental Benedictines. At Winchester, Bishop Aethelwald himself taught in the school, and the Abbot of Ramsey borrowed the master of the school of Fleury for two years.[1] During this time of brief revival, Latin verse was again cultivated. In 947, when the Minster at Ripon was burned in the course of the Northumbrian rebellion against King Eadred, S. Wilfrid's body was brought to Canterbury. Frithegode, who was tutor to the Archbishop's nephew, celebrated the event by composing a metrical account of the chequered career of the great champion of Roman orthodoxy.[2] The poem[3] is merely based on a prose life of the saint and is of little historical interest. Frithegode had read Virgil, but he had also acquired all the pedantic mannerisms of the Celtic School. The same Graecisms occur in abundance (*imeras* for ἡμέρας; *dynami* for δυνάμει, &c.), with occasional Hebraisms, and a sprinkling of classical allusions, such as we meet in the Irish poets.

Another Anglo-Saxon poet of the same period is Wulfstan, a pupil of Aethelwald's at Winchester, and cantor of S. Swithin's.[4] He versified Lantfred's *Life and Miracles of S. Swithin*. His description of Aethelwald's new Church at Winchester is of great interest, and the account of the organs which S. Elphege added

[1] Hunt, *Hist. of Eng. Church, 597–1066*, pp. 367, 377.
[2] ib., pp. 340–1 ; Wright, *Biogr. Brit Lit.*, p. 433 sq
[3] Text in Migne, cxxxiii, col. 979 sqq.

[4] On Wulfstan see Ebert, iii. 497 sqq.; Wright, pp. 471 sqq.; *Anal. Hymn.* xlviii, p. 9; for his verse, ib., pp. 9 sqq. ; *Anal. Hymn.* li, p. 164.

is not a little amusing. The bellows required the combined labour of seventy able-bodied men :

> brachia versantes multo et sudore madentes
> certatimque suos quique monent socios,
> viribus ut totis impellant flamina sursum,
> et rugiat pleno capsa referta sinu.

The keyboards were operated by two of the brethren and the noise must have been appalling.[1]

Wulfstan's literary activity appears to have been considerable. He composed several hymns, at once alphabetical and epanaleptic, after the manner of Bede's hymn on S. Etheldreda. They are in honour of English saints, Aethelwald, Birinus the missionary of the West Saxons, and S. Swithin. As a specimen of their style, the beginning of the hymn to S. Aethelwald will serve :

> alma lucerna micat, sol aureus arva serenat,
> summus Adelwoldus alma lucerna micat.
> belliger iste dei fortissima bella peregit
> acer in arma ruit belliger iste Dei.[2]

Three other hymns, all on S. Augustine of Canterbury, are probably the work of Wulfstan.[3] One is epanaleptic and alphabetical, the others show a fondness for continuous rime, which in one stanza at least is trisyllabic.

> aveto, placidis praesul amabilis,
> aveto, celebri laude notabilis,
> aveto, salubri luce capabilis,
> Augustine placabilis.

Frithegode and Wulfstan are almost solitary voices. The eleventh century brought further political troubles, and the conquest of England by the Danes. And when at last an English king occupied the throne in the person of Edward the Confessor, the days of English independence were numbered.

---

[1] See the long quotation, Ebert, iii. 498, and in Wright, pp. 472-3.
[2] *Anal. Hymn.* xlviii, p. 9.
[3] ib., li, p. 164, nos. 141-3.

VI

THE CAROLINGIAN RENAISSANCE

§ 1. *Charles the Great and the revival of classical studies.*

AT the end of the sixth century, Irish missionaries, among whom the most famous is Columbanus, had attempted the reform of Gallic monasticism, which was a necessary preliminary to the reform of the Church at large. Monasteries of Irish foundation, like Luxeuil and Fontaine, became seminaries of religious study, whence issued many future Abbots and Bishops.[1] But little attention was given to secular letters; though here and there the profane authors may have been read.

With the eighth century there are signs of a change. During the mayoralty of Charles Martel, Boniface had begun the conversion of Germany. Under Pippin and Carloman, he commenced the reformation of the Frankish Church. Abuses and irregularities were strenuously attacked, and enough order was introduced to create the possibility of further progress, when Charles the Great took in hand the formidable task of the reorganization of the kingdom as a whole. The work of Pippin and Boniface, as Hauck has pointed out,[2] restored the external organization of a Church that had well-nigh fallen into ruin. The task that remained was the restoration of the inner life of the Church by renewing its spiritual and intellectual activities. This was the task which Charles the Great, in his vision of an ordered commonwealth, regarded as of first importance from the political as well as from a more ideal point of view. Any success in the effort towards reconstruction must have as its presupposition an educated clergy and an intelligent class of laymen, from which administrators and judges could be drawn.

The court school, under Charles Martel and Pippin, had provided some kind of education for the royal family and the

[1] Cf. Roger, pp. 406 sqq.   [2] Hauck, ii. 120.

aristocracy,[1] and it was there that Charles received his education. The nature of the studies there pursued is not wholly clear; but they must have included the elements of grammar. Charles himself never became a scholar in spite of his boundless curiosity, and his eagerness for information on subjects of every kind. He could say his prayers in Latin and read a little Greek. He dearly loved to have learned men about him, and it grieved his heart to see the ignorance and illiteracy of the Frankish clergy. He rightly decided that only by raising the level of ecclesiastical education could he hope to lift the Church out of the low spiritual level to which it had fallen. But for this task teachers were needed, and they could not be found at home. Here and there, signs of literary activity bore witness to some advance in education at the more important monastic centres. At Tours, S. Gall and Fulda, at Mainz, Echternach, and Utrecht, seed. was being sown for a future harvest. But only a systematic application of educational methods as under-stood in Anglo-Saxon and Lombard schools could be expected to achieve any definite and permanent results. It is not the least of the services of Charles to the cause of civilization that he realized not merely the problem but the manner of its solution. By his agency the light from English, Irish, and Italian schools was made to shine on the Frankish darkness. The men by whose labours the renaissance of learning was accomplished were united by their admiration of the great king, who was at once their munificent patron and their loyal friend. He himself formed the centre of a literary circle closely related to the royal school. The court and the school moved about together, and Charles enlisted his family, male and female, among the scholars. He was the David and Solomon among this group of learned friends, each of whom assumed a literary sobriquet. Alcuin was Flaccus, Angilbert Homer, Theodulf Pindar, and Einhard, the builder of Churches, Bezaleel.[2] They amused themselves with versified riddles, acrostics and epigrams, and occasional poetry of the lightest sort.

In the school proper, the studies were serious and systematic; for Alcuin, as master, reproduced the orderly curriculum which Aelbert had established at York. The liberal arts were not unduly overshadowed by the final science of theology, and the authors were read with a diligence which could not fail to result

---

[1] Hauck, ii. 131.   *and her Invaders*, viii. 136; Manitius,
[2] For a fuller list see Hodgkin, *Italy*   *Gesch.*, i. 249.

in a sense, however dim and imperfect, of their beauty of form and charm of content.   At the same time, the idea which underlay the efforts of the School was essentially ecclesiastical. If the old ascetic view of secular studies was no longer emphasized, and the rights of a secular culture obtained a measure of recognition,[1] the religious end of learning was never denied, and the Christian poets were read with the same care which was devoted to Virgil.   The true mind of Alcuin is to be observed in his reconstitution of the school at Tours, where liberal studies were carefully directed to theological ends, and, for Charles himself, the success of the new education was to be judged by the measure in which it tended to the quickened spirituality of an educated clergy.

For the historian of literature, the success of the revived learning is well marked by the merits of Einhard's *Life of Charles*, which, both in style and in arrangement of matter, shows an immense advance on the work of Gregory of Tours. It is marked, too, by the cultivation of letters and poetry for their own sake, and in almost a humanistic spirit.[2] This revival of versification bore little fruit as yet in definitely religious or liturgical poetry.   In the close imitation of classical models, the poets followed the manner of the non-liturgical verse of Fortunatus rather than that of Prudentius or Avitus.   They made their verses as secular as possible by choosing their themes from subjects close to their hands—the amenities of learned intercourse or the affairs of their daily lives.   The secular tone of the bulk of this poetry is to be explained by the fact that the impulse directing the Carolingian renaissance did not come from the monasteries, or from the official Church, but from a secular school.[3]

The shadow of the Church is nevertheless over each and all of the poets, and they reckoned themselves, amid their pastorals, acrostics and riddles, as beyond all else Churchmen and theologians, the servants of Christ and not of the Muses.   So, in their moments of recollection, they would have assented to the position of Aldhelm, at the beginning of his verses, *De laudibus virginum* :

> non rogo ruricolas versus et commata Musas
> nec peto Castalidas metrorum cantica nymphas,
> quas dicunt Helicona iugum servare supernum. . . .
> sed potius nitar precibus pulsare tonantem,
> qui nobis placidi confert oracula verbi.

---

[1] Cf. Hauck, ii. 183.
[2] The bulk of the Carolingian poetry is collected in *M.G.H., Poetae Latini Aevi*

Carolini, 4 vols., Berlin 1881–1923.
[3] Cf. Ebert, ii. 7.

Alcuin and Theodulf are the most important of the poets whose works have in any large measure survived. Next come Paul the Deacon, Peter of Pisa, and Paulinus of Aquileia. Of Angilbert, who appeared to his contemporaries to be a ' divine poet ',[1] only a few poems have survived; but it has been con- jectured that he is the author of a fragment of a long historical poem on the events of his time.[2] He grew up at the court and was entrusted by the king with important diplomatic missions, but his poetical talents appear to have been mediocre. Amalar of Metz has left an amusing account of an unpleasant sea- voyage to Constantinople,[3] and Joseph the Irishman,[4] a few slight verses and several elaborate acrostics.

Modoin, whom Louis the Pious created Bishop of Autun, was the Naso of the court circle of Charles the Great. He was a friend of Theodulf and of Angilbert, and later of Florus of Lyons. He dedicated an Eclogue to Charles,[5] which ends with the praises of the King :

> dilectus domini, David, benedictus in aevum,
> suscipe nunc famuli munera parva tui.
> ille ego Naso tuus tibi carmina mitto pusillus,
> quem sua paupertas vix sinit arcta loqui.
> haec tu si capias animo vultuque sereno,
> ordine cuncta volo gesta referre tua.
> nec te forte piget nostrum percurrere carmen,
> nam precor, ad finem, rex pius, usque legas.
> ex tua si quid erit vitium clementia factum
> corrigat augusto hoc opus ore meum.[6]

Modoin wrote many poems, but two only have survived.

Beside this more or less learned poetry of the court, there must have existed a considerable amount of purely religious verse, which represented the inspiration of humbler scholars in the monastic centres. An example of this is probably to be found in the ' Hymn of Charity ', which, so Dom Wilmart suggests, was used by the Benedictines, to be sung at their peculiar ceremony of the weekly Maundy or washing of feet according to the commandment (*mandatum*) of the Saviour. If this beautiful hymn—*Ubi caritas et amor, Deus ibi est*—is

---

[1] Dümmler, *M. G. H., Poet. Kar.*, i. 77 ; for his verses see i. 358 sqq., although a layman, he was abbot of S. Riquier.

[2] Manitius, *Neues Archiv*, viii, pp. 11 sqq. ; but Simson, *Forsch. zur deutsch. Gesch.*, xii, pp. 569 sqq., doubts Angilbert's authorship.

[3] *M. G. H., Poet. Kar.*, i. 426.

[4] ib., 150 sqq.

[5] Dümmler, *Neues Archiv*, xi, pp. 81 sqq.

[6] *Neues Archiv*, xi, p. 91.

of Italian origin, it was, at any rate, produced in the Empire of
Charles, and probably during his lifetime.[1]   A few strophes
will give an idea of the charm of the whole, with the recurring
refrain of the fifth verse :

> congregavit nos in unum   Christi amor,
> exultemus et in ipso   iucundemur,
> timeamus et amemus   deum vivum
> et ex corde diligamus   nos sincero.
> ubi caritas est vera,   deus ibi est.
>
> qui non habet caritatem,   nihil habet,
> sed in tenebris et umbra   mortis manet ;
> nos alterutrum amemus   et in die,
> sicut decet ambulemus   lucis fili !
> ubi caritas est vera,   deus ibi est.
>
> clamat dominus et dicit   clara voce :
> ubi fuerint in unum   congregati
> meum propter nomen simul   tres vel duo,
> et in medio eorum   ego ero.
> ubi caritas est vera,   deus ibi est.

The same author, it would seem, composed a less successful
piece on the Resurrection [2] with the refrain :

> de sepulchro resurrexit   pastor bonus.

But this sincere and unpretentious poetry has been inevitably
overshadowed by the ambitious productions of the contemporary
classical revival.   Yet the hymn of Charity is still sung in
fragmentary form on Maundy Thursday, and we know that
in the eleventh and twelfth centuries it was in use at Monte
Cassino and elsewhere in Italy.[3]   The admirable hymn, *O redem-*
ptor, sume carmen, which does not seem to be older than Carolingian times,[4] is still used at the blessing of the holy oils.   The
author evidently took as his model the *Corde natus ex parentis*
of Prudentius, with the refrain ' saeculorum saeculis ' which is
added to it in the hymnaries.[5]

[1] A. Wilmart, *L'hymne de la charité*
pour le jeudi-saint, in *La vie et les arts*
liturgiques (April 1924), pp. 250 sqq. ;
text, *M. G. H., Poet. Kar.*, iv, pp. 526 sqq.;
Anal. Hymn. xii, p. 24 ; see also Meyer,
Rythmik, i. 219. For a late rimed paraphrase of part of this hymn see *Anal.*
Hymn. xxiii, p. 26.

[2] Wilmart, p. 256 ; see also *Anal. Hymn.*
xix, p. 20 ; text, p. 19.

[3] Wilmart, p. 252.

[4] *Anal. Hymn.* li, p. 80.

[5] Cf. stanza 7 :

corde natus ex parentis, alvum implens
  virginis,
praesta lucem, claude mortem chrisma-
  tis consortibus ;
o redemptor, sume carmen temet con-
  cinentium.

§ 2. *Alcuin* (735 *circa*–804) ; *Paul the Deacon* (730 *circa*–99) ; *Paulinus of Aquileia* (d. 802).

Alcuin [1] was born about 735, of a noble Northumbrian stock. When a mere child, he was sent to the Cathedral school at York, where he studied a fair number of classical writers from Cicero to Lucan, and became acquainted with the works of the Fathers.[2] His affection for his master Aelbert he has celebrated in his *Versus de Sanctis Euboricensis Ecclesiae*, in which he recalls how he had learned the rudiments of poetical composition from the master himself :

> illos Aonio docuit concinnere cantu,
> Castalida instituens alios resonare cicuta.[3]

When in 781 he met Charles at Parma, Alcuin had been for three years head of the school at York. The king determined to entice him to Aachen (782) and to give him the charge of the Palatine school. Alcuin yielded, but did not forsake his own country finally until 793. At the court of Charles, he was associated with all the scholars of the day, with Paul the Deacon, with the aged grammarian Peter, with Theodulf the Goth, the builder of churches, the lover of the arts and the best poet of them all. But his special friend was Paulinus the future Patriarch of Aquileia.

Alcuin appears to have won the affection of Charles,[4] who delighted in the riddles, which—true to the English tradition— the scholar knew well to propound ; but Charles honoured him above all as a master of that learning which he was enlightened enough to prize, and which he desired to see in the possession of his Frankish clergy. In Alcuin, Charles had found the man he needed ; a skilful teacher capable of introducing into the Frankish schools the methods of English learning. His *compendia* of grammar, rhetoric, and dialectic exerted a profound influence in systematizing the studies of the schools, and in raising the level of education in Western Europe.

[1] Alcuin's poems are in *M. G. H., Poet. Kar.*, i. 160 sqq. ; see also Jaffé, *Monumenta Alcuiniana* (Berlin 1873), for useful documents.
[2] Cf. his account of the library at York, in his *Versus de Sanctis Euboricensis Ecclesiae, M. G. H., Poet. Kar.*, i. 200 ; among the authors are Jerome, Hilary, Ambrose, Augustine, Athanasius, Orosius, Gregory the Great, Basil, Cassiodorus,

Chrysostom, Aldhelm, Bede, Boëthius, Pliny, Aristotle, Cicero, Sedulius, Juvencus, Prudentius, Paulinus, Fortunatus, Virgil, Statius, Lucan, Donatus. But Alcuin can have known Aristotle only through Boëthius.
[3] *M. G. H., Poet. Kar.*, i. 201.
[4] Cf. *Vita beati Alchuini Abbatis*, vi (*Mon. Alcuiniana*, p. 17) 'quem tenens rex loco patris amplectitur'.

Charles himself looked impatiently for the fruits of Alcuin's labour. He wished that his priests might be suddenly transformed into Jeromes and Augustines. Why should he not possess twelve clerks as learned and holy as they? 'The Lord of heaven and earth', answered Alcuin, 'has not many such as they, and thou wouldst have twelve!'[1] The master of the school was expected to satisfy the endless curiosity of the king, which prompted questions of every kind, extending to every branch of learning. And, indeed, Alcuin, without any originality and with no desire beyond the mastery of the inherited wisdom of the past, was the most learned man of his day. Like the rest of the palace circle, Alcuin practised the composition of verses, and they won the admiration of all. Theodulf celebrated his friend as

> . . . Flaccus nostrorum gloria vatum,
> qui potis est lyrico multa boare pede.

With a few possible exceptions, Alcuin uses classical metres.[2] His hexameter poems—such as the verses *De Sanctis Euboricensis Ecclesiae* and the *Vita S. Willibrordi*—are full of Virgilian reminiscences, and, for the most part, the prosody is formally correct. Like Fortunatus, he had a taste for epigrams, poetical epistles, and occasional poetry, mainly in elegiacs, which show a careful study of Ovid, the most facile of poets. In the following piece, which is given as an example of his occasional verse, he is 'Flaccus' praising his 'David', and he speaks from the heart:

> ad nos quippe tuus famulus veniebat Homerus[3]
> nuntia laeta ferens, David, ab ore tuo.
> fecerat et Flaccum gaudentem in pectore vestrum,
> deque salute tua, de sobolisque tuae.
> o mihi dulcis amor, dulcis praesentia Christi,
> dulce tuum studium, et dulcis ab ore sonus.
> tuque tuique simul per saecula semper amici
> pervaleant, vigeant, David ubique vale!
> hunc iterum puerum vestrae pietati remisi,
> serviat ut vobis carmine, corde, manu.

The pastoral piece called the *Contention of Winter and Spring* has been described as 'the most notable' of all Alcuin's poems,[4]

---

[1] Notker, *Gesta Caroli*, i. 9.

[2] Strecker, in *M. G. H., Poet. Kar.*, iv. 903 sqq., has edited three rhythms which may be Alcuin's; Strecker thinks that Alcuin was certainly the author; W. Meyer (*Gött. Nachr.*, 1916, pp. 645 sqq.) is not certain; see C. Weyman, *Hist. Jahrb.*

xli, p. 76 sq.

[3] 'Homer' is Angilbert, *M. G. H., Poet. Kar.*, i. 237; cf. i. 257, 'David amor populi, David laus, gloria plebis', &c.; also i. 300 sq.

[4] W. P. Ker, *The Dark Ages* (London 1904), p. 152; but Winterfeld (*Rhein. Mus.*

and this description would be true if it were certain that Alcuin himself composed it. The shepherds with Daphnis and Palaemon preside over a contest between the two seasons. The question is : Shall the cuckoo come or no ?

' Here, as in Anglo-Saxon poetry, it is the cuckoo that breaks the silence of winter, a bird of good omen, though Winter in the dialogue does not think so. Winter loves the rest, the good cheer, the fire in hall, and is slow to wake to the business of Spring. There is no peace when once the voice of the cuckoo has been heard.' [1]

But the shepherds decide for the cuckoo :

> desine plura, Hiems; rerum tu prodigus, atrox.
> et veniat cuculus, pastorum dulcis amicus. . . .
> tu iam dulcis amor, cunctis gratissimus hospes :
> omnia te expectant, pelagus tellusque polusque,
> salve, dulce decus, cuculus, per saecula salve !

A pleasing poem addressed to the pupils of his school at York begins with a description of the spring. The cuckoo's note resounds in the woods ; the flowers appear in the meadows ; the vine bursts forth, and the nightingale sings without ceasing. Alcuin sends the brethren greeting, and encourages them to take up their studies with ardour :

> aetheriis sophiae feliciter utere donis,
> ut tibi permaneat merces et gloria semper.[2]

Alcuin has left little purely religious verse. The following, an inscription for a bedroom, is a good example in the epigrammatic style :

> hoc deus, in lecto fautor sis, posco, cubanti,
>   dormiat ut tutus, Christe, sub umbra tua,
> ne sibi subripiat hac fur nocturnus in aula
>   ac sibi sis proprius semper, ut opto, deus :
> namque tuis famulis latum tu, Christe, per orbem
>   fidus ades custos, rex pius atque pater.[3]

A little *Oratio in nocte* is almost charming, but its quality is perhaps derived more from the feeling than the manner of its expression :

> qui placido in puppi carpebat pectore somnum,
>   exurgens ventis imperat et pelago :

lx, p. 35) denies that Alcuin is the author; the poem comes out of Charles the Great's circle, and may be the work of an Irishman, as the writer knew Horace. Winterfeld says that Horace was unknown on the Continent before the middle of the ninth century.

[1] Ker, *Dark Ages*, pp. 152–3.
[2] *M. G. H., Poet. Kar.*, i. 273.
[3] ib., p. 267.

fessa labore gravi quamvis hic membra quiescant,
    ad se concedat cor vigilare meum.
agne dei, mundi qui crimina cuncta tulisti,
    conserva requiem mitis ab hoste meam.[1]

Alcuin wrote a hymn in sapphics in honour of S. Vedast. It begins :

Christe salvator hominis ab ore
hostis antiqui superantis Adam,
nostra clementer, domine, precamur
    suscipe vota.[2]

An evening hymn, in the same metre, is neither more nor less remarkable for poetical quality.[3]

On the whole, Alcuin was a mediocre poet. His real talents lay elsewhere. He was pre-eminently a teacher, who was at his best when trying to introduce order and system into the minds of his students. In 796 he had retired from the court to become Abbot of the great monastery of S. Martin at Tours. There, repenting of his earlier, and as it might appear, excessive devotion to letters, he attempted to instil into the minds of his young pupils the love of the sacred writings, and he strove to induce a studious affection for the fathers of the Church in the place of the 'luxuriosa facundia' of Virgil.[4]

It was at Tours that Alcuin made his reputation for holiness, and after his death he won the usual fame of miraculous powers. To-day he is chiefly remembered for his great services to the cause of learning. With all his limitations, he stands out as a great educator, and, after his royal master, as the most prominent figure of the Carolingian Renaissance.

It has already been said that that Renaissance derived its impulse from the two countries in Europe where the tradition of letters yet lingered. Alcuin represents the learning of the Anglo-Saxons, and Paul the Deacon,[5] the celebrated historian of the Lombards, brought to the court of Charles the contribution of Italian scholarship. Paul was a Lombard of noble birth

[1] *M. G. H., Poet. Kar.*, i, p. 350.
[2] ib., p. 313.
[3] ib., p. 349. The first stanza is:
luminis fons, lux et origo lucis,
tu pius nostris precibus faveto;
luxque, peccati tenebris fugatis,
    nos petat alma.
[4] *Vita Alchuini*, x, p. 24. This does not mean, of course, that he advocated the abandonment of secular studies. They were still necessary as preparations for the

supreme study of theology.
[5] On Paul's learning see Hörle, *Frühmittelalt. Mönchs- und Klerikerbildung in Italien*, pp. 44 sqq., 'er war ein feiner Kenner antiker Literatur'; cf. Neff, *Die Gedichte des Paulus Diaconus*, p. 144 sq. Of the poets, Paul knew Virgil, Ovid, Lucan, Fortunatus, Sedulius, Juvencus, Arator, and many prose writers. Yet he compared the heathen poets to dogs, *M. G. H., Poet. Kar.*, i. 49; Neff, p. 65.

who was fortunate enough to belong to a family where learning was prized. He received a good classical education, but he seems to have had no idea of seeking a career in the Church. He came to the court of King Desiderius, where he found a welcome as a scholar, and interested himself in the studies of Princess Adelperga, to whom he dedicated a poem on the chronology of world history. The date of the poem, as we learn from stanza 8, is 763; the princess was then the wife of Duke Arichis, and had settled in Beneventum, but it would seem that she had persuaded Paul to follow her to a court at which learning was cultivated with the same lively interest as at Pavia. In this poem, Paul divides the history of the world in the traditional manner, though with some variations. He chose a rhythmical measure and separated the verses into twelve stanzas of three lines each, with the added ornament of an acrostic—*Adelperga pia*—in honour of his patroness. At the end of the poem, after praising the peace and prosperity of Italy under Desiderius and his son-in-law, he speaks of the coming judgement of the world, and prays that Arichis and Adelperga may find grace in the last day:

> iudex veniet supernus velut fulgor caelitus,
> dies sed et hora quando non patet mortalibus,
> felix erit quem paratum invenerit dominus.
>
> ante tuum, iuste iudex, dum steterit solium
> Arechis benignus ductor cum praeclara coniuge
> dona eis cum electis laetari perenniter.[1]

But the end of this quiet life was at hand. The Franks invaded the country, and the Lombard kingdom fell. Paul was banished to Monte Cassino, and might have found there the happiness which he had lost. But his brother Arichis was involved in the national revolt against the conquerors; he was taken, and flung into a Frankish prison, and his goods were confiscated. For years this sorrow embittered the life of Paul. At length, in 782, he addressed a pathetic elegy to Charles, in which he pictured the plight of his family, his brother in prison, the wife and children begging their bread, and his sister, 'consecrated to Christ from her earliest years'; weeping until

wellnigh with constant tears quenched is the sight of her eyes.[2]

[1] Neff, p. 10.
[2] See Hodgkin's rendering, *Italy and* her *Invaders*, viii. 137; text, Neff, pp. 53 sqq.

It appears that Paul actually made his way to Aachen to plead his brother's cause. If the verses did not at once achieve their aim, they convinced Charles of the necessity of retaining their author at his court.

Paul's knowledge of Greek, which he was inclined to minimize,[1] gave him at once a place of distinction among the other scholars. Peter of Pisa willingly admitted the superiority of the new comer, who brought another breath of the free Italian spirit, and made an added contrast to the harder and more serious Alcuin. Paul had little of the exclusively theological temper, though he seems to have interested himself in Gregory's *Letters* and he composed a history of the bishops of Metz. His verse, for the most part, is 'occasional', and the number of poems which it is possible with any degree of certainty to ascribe to him is small.[2] Some epanaleptic verses on Lake Como give us an idea of his earlier work in the days before the fall of the Lombard kingdom.[3] After praising the beauties of the lake, he says that if only Jesus had walked on its waters as on the Sea of Galilee, it would excel all the lakes in the world:

> ordiar unde tuas laudes, o maxime Lari.

So he begins the poem, and he adapts the same verse for the commencement of a longer piece in praise of S. Benedict:[4]

> ordiar unde tuos, sacer o Benedicte, triumphos?

Here again he uses the epanaleptic form which Sedulius and others had employed before him. This poem and a hymn on the same subject belong to the year of his first retirement to Monte Cassino (after 774),[5] and he appended them both, the former (in a revised version) to his brief account of Benedict in his *History of the Lombards*, modestly introducing his elegiacs in these words—'pro parvitate ingenii mei ad honorem tanti patris singula eius miracula per singula disticha elegiaco metro contexui'. The hymn is in iambic dimeters, a mere paraphrase

---

[1] To Peter of Pisa he says (Neff, p. 66):
Graiam nescio loquellam, ignoro Hebraicam:
tres aut quatuor in scolis quas didici syllabas.
ex his mihi est ferendus maniplus ad aream.
[2] For criticism and text we now rely on K. Neff, *Die Gedichte des Paulus Diaconus, kritische und erklärende Aus-*
gabe, Munich 1908 (see also *M.G.H., Poet. Kar.*, i. 27 sqq., 625 sqq.). Winterfeld (*Neues Archiv*, xxix, pp. 468 sqq.) assigns to Notker Balbulus the three poems which in *M.G.H., Poet. Kar.*, i. 62 sqq. (Nos. 27–29), stand under the *Carmina Petri et Pauli*, but Neff, p. 192 sq., contests this ascription.
[3] Neff, pp. 4 sqq.
[4] ib., p. 27.   [5] ib., p. 25.

of the longer poem and nothing more than a catalogue of
miracles from the second book of Gregory's *Dialogues*.[1] To
the same period belongs a poem of ampler spirit in which he
complains to a friend of the contrast between the former life at
the Lombard court and the constraint of the cloister. The
Muses shun the monastic prison and prefer the 'rosulenta prata'
of the outside world:

> quapropter nobis aversae terga dederunt
> et comitem spernunt me vocitare suum.[2]

For this reason he excuses his bad verses, and takes refuge
in a pious wish directed to the next life.

The time was now at hand, however, when he was to leave
his prison and the misery which was rendered more bitter by
the misfortunes of his brother and of his family. As we have
seen, he addressed himself to Charles in verses which obtained
his release from the cloister, and gave him the position due to
his merit as a scholar and a poet. Prompted by Charles, Peter
of Pisa praised him to the skies in long trochaic lines, which
were doubtless meant for communication to the whole court
circle. In the coldness of Paul's reply it is possible to detect
the shadow of a disappointed hope. It would appear that
Charles had not accorded him the satisfaction which he desired,
the rehabilitation of his brother and the restoration of the family
estate. But he was not a silent and churlish member of the
court. He contributed his share of versified riddles[3] for the
amusement of the king, and he composed 'grammatical hymns'
to be used in the schools as an aid to memory in the study of
Latin grammar. As time went on, he seems to have changed
his attitude towards Charles; he praises him in terms of loyal
affection, as 'maxime princeps, deliciae populi, summus et orbis
amor'.[4] In this poem, Charles is 'no longer the enemy of his
nation, but the king appointed by God Himself to be the ruler
of Christendom'.[5] It may be that Paul had at last obtained
the favour for which he had waited so long. In any case, when
he received permission to return to the monastery which he had

---

[1] One stanza will give an idea of the rest:
> vitrum resistit cautibus,
> manant olivo dolia,
> vinctum resolvit visio,
> vitam recepit funera.

[2] Neff, p. 39.

[3] Neff, p. 83, prints a riddle in rhythmical hexameters which may be Paul's. It consists of six verses, containing the acrostic PAULUS; see Meyer, *Rythmik*, ii. 161 sqq.

[4] Cf. Neff, p. 101.

[5] ib., p. 102.

once been glad to leave, but the memory of which haunted him always like the memory of home, he still addressed his verses to the ' summo apici rerum regi dominoque potenti ',[1] and the king got his scholars to answer him and to ask for his prayers and those of his brethren at Monte Cassino.

The court poems and a few epitaphs exhaust the limited scope of Paul's achievement.   He was first of all a grammarian, and his piety was not of the ardent kind which bears fruit in religious poetry.   It is only a late and uncertain testimony which makes him the author of a famous hymn in honour of the Baptist.[2]   But as this remarkable ode is a product of the Carolingian age, it may properly be noticed here.   It is interesting to observe that, although the poet had obviously given close study to the sapphics of Horace, he admits hiatus at the end of verses ; but, in the first two books of the *Odes*, Horace had permitted himself a similar licence.   He follows Horace, however, in placing the caesura definitely after the fifth syllable.

ut queant laxis resonare fibris
mira gestorum famuli tuorum,
solve polluti labii reatum,
    sancte Iohannes.

nuntius celso veniens Olympo
te patri magnum fore nasciturum,
nomen et vitae seriem gerendae
    ordine promit.

ille promissi dubius superni
perdidit promptae modulos loquelae,
sed reformasti genitus peremptae
    organa vocis.

ventris obstruso positus cubili
senseras regem thalamo manentem;
hinc parens nati meritis uterque
    abdita pandit.

antra deserti teneris sub annis
civium turmas fugiens petisti,
ne levi saltem maculare vitam
    famine posses.

praebuit hirtum tegimen camelus
artubus sacris, strophium bidentes,
cui latex haustum, sociata pastum
    mella locustis.

ceteri tantum cecinere vatum
corde presago iubar adfuturum,
tu quidem mundi scelus auferentem
    indice prodis.

non fuit vasti spatium per orbis
sanctior quisquam genitus Iohanne,
qui nefas saecli meruit lavantem
    tingere lymphis.

o nimis felix meritique celsi,
nesciens labem nivei pudoris,
praepotens martyr eremique cultor,
    maxime vatum !

serta ter denis alios coronant
aucta crementis, duplicata quosdam,
trina centeno cumulata fructu
    te, sacer, ornant.

---

[1] Neff, p. 133.

[2] Petrus, *de viris illustr. Casinens.* viii ; see *Anal. Hymn.* l, p. 122, where Dreves argues for Paul's authorship against Dümmler, *M.G.H., Poet. Kar.*, i. 28,

and Neff., p. 152. It is equally doubtful whether, as Dreves asserts, we are also to ascribe to Paul a hymn on the Assumption, beginning, ' Quis possit amplo famine praepotens ' (*Anal. Hymn.* l, p. 123).

nunc potens nostri meritis opimis
pectoris duros lapides repelle,
asperum planans iter et reflexos
    dirige calles,

ut pius mundi sator et redemptor
mentibus pulsa livione puris
rite dignetur veniens sacratos
    ponere gressus.

laudibus cives celebrant superni
te, deus simplex pariterque trine,
supplices ac nos veniam precamur,
    parce redemptis.[1]

With Paul the Deacon we naturally associate Peter of Pisa, his friend and fellow grammarian, the first Lombard scholar to enter the service of Charles the Great.[2] If Charles was at pains to induce them to versify for his pleasure, he prized them mostly for their grammatical learning and their services to his educational reforms. As we have seen, it was Peter's duty to compose for Charles the poetical letters which he addressed to Paul,[3] though it has been suggested that Charles himself ventured on occasion to send his own compositions, which he had laboriously pieced together from the work of other poets.[4] If, indeed, Charles got so far with his study of Latin, he owed it to Peter, who taught him grammar and, we may suppose, read the authors with him. The old grammarian dedicated to the king a grammatical work, to which he prefaced a brief elegiac poem, explaining that it was composed 'by Peter for love of his master'.[5] In another poem, he praises Charles as the conqueror of the Lombards, who builds churches, converts the heathen, and punishes evil-doers. He prays that the king may inherit the eternal kingdom, and then, in verses which bring the poet out of his dull and pedantic round, he describes the city of God:

in quo nulla famis lacerans nec pestis habetur
nullaque maeroris servantur vincula cordis.
non dolor aut gemitus fragilis nec iurgia linguae,
nulla senectutis metuendae toxica saeva
mortifero poterunt iaculo disperdere quemquam,
sed sine fine manens celebratur vita beata
angelicumque canit productis vocibus agmen
et nunquam fessi spoliantur cantibus aptis.[6]

Then he recalls to Charles the great examples of old, Noah,

---

[1] *Anal. Hymn.* l, p. 120; *M.G.H.*, *Poet. Kar.*, i. 83.
[2] See Hauck, ii. 155.
[3] They are printed in Neff's edition of Paul's poems.　[4] Cf. Neff, p. 136.
[5] ib., p. 157.　[6] ib., p. 161.

Samson, Gideon, and David, and prays that Christ may help him in the future :

> qui populi duros descendit pellere morbos,
> frigida qui pedibus calcavit pectora ponti,
> vos regnare polo faciat sine fine superno.

Another Lombard grammarian, and one who earned the special affection of Alcuin, was Paulinus, who was born about 730, and after the destruction of the Lombard kingdom entered the service of the conqueror.   Charles showed him great favour and made him a teacher of grammar in the royal school.   He was, with Alcuin, the tutor of Angilbert, and continued at the school until, in 787, Charles promoted him to the Patriarchate of Aquileia.   Deprived of the presence of his much loved companion, Alcuin sent him frequent letters and verses, and in one touching poem he begs that he will remember him before the altar of God :

> sis memor Albini sacris altaribus adstans,
> et dulces inter lacrimas super ora fluentes
> dic : miserere, deus, nostro clementer amico,
> criminibusque suis veniam largire benignus,
> ut te cum sanctis liceat laudare per aevum.[1]

At Aquileia, Paulinus found work to his hand beyond the compilation of theological treatises, and poetry, occasional and religious.   He associated himself with the political schemes of Charles, and aided in the missionary campaigns which were then being conducted among the heathen Avars.   Duke Erich of Friuli was here his lay adjutant, a man of remarkable intelligence—' potens in armis, subtilis ingenio ',[2] at whose request Paulinus composed an unoriginal moral treatise, the *Liber Exhortationum*.   After Erich's death in battle, Paulinus honoured his memory in a rhythmical dirge, the last two stanzas of which deserve quotation on account of their facility and strength :

> deus aeterne, limi qui de pulvere
> plasmasti tuam primos ad imaginem
> parentes nostros, per quos omnes morimur,
> misisti tuum sed dilectum filium,
> vivimus omnes per quem mirabiliter.
> sanguine cuius redempti purpureo
> sumus, sacrata cuius carne pascimur,

---

[1] *M. G. H., Poet. Kar.*, i. 240.
[2] So Paulinus describes him ; *M.G.H., Poet. Kar.*, i. 131.

Herico tuo servulo mellifluo
concede, quaeso, paradisi gaudia
et nunc et ultra per immensa secula.[1]

In spite of his grammatical studies, Paulinus was a careless
prosodist, and in a prose epilogue to his metrical *Regula Fidei*,
an hexameter poem on the Christian faith, he humorously asks
the reader's pardon if 'per incuriam' he may have written
'short for long or long for short'.[2] He felt more at ease in
his rhythmical compositions, where he need trouble himself only
with accent and the number of the syllables. His verses on the
raising of Lazarus [3] are in rhythmic trochaic tetrameters, with
occasional and apparently unsought rimes. The poem is simply
a versification of the Gospel narrative, but there is a sense
of the pathos of the story in the description of Jesus weeping at
the tomb. The poet is, however, careful to add that the Master
wept as a man ; as God, he could not weep.

> quod ut Martham vidit flere ac Mariam dominus,
> tactus cordis est dolore benigno clementia
> semet ipsum mox turbavit, fremuit in spiritu,
> lacrimatus est et ipse totus dulcis dominus.
>
> nostra tamen miseratus flevit de substantia,
> quam suscepit pietatis exigente viscere,
> in quo deus erat verus flere nunquam potuit,
> nec turbari potest illa dealis essentia.

The verses on the festival of Peter and Paul are in a higher
strain, and rise at times to a note of lyrical beauty, as in the last
stanzas which celebrate the Rome of the martyrs :

> o Roma felix, quae tantorum principum
> es purpurata precioso sanguine,
> excellis omnem mundi pulchritudinem,
> non laude tua, sed sanctorum meritis,
> quos cruentatis iugulasti gladiis.
>
> vos ergo modo, gloriosi martyres,
> Petre beate, Paule, mundi lilium,
> caelestis aulae triumphales milites
> precibus almis vestris nos ab omnibus
> munite malis, ferte super aethera.[4]

---

[1] *M. G. H., Poet. Kar.*, i. 132–3.
[2] ib., i. 130.
[3] ib., i. 133 sqq.; the ascription to
Paulinus is uncertain ; but Dom Wilmart
(*Revue Bénédictine*, xxxiv (1922), pp. 27
sqq., where a new text is given) is inclined to decide for him as author ; for

similar rhythms of the same period see
M. G. H., Poet. Kar., IV. ii, pp. 459 sqq.
Wilmart suggests that these might be
assigned to Paulinus as well.
[4] *M. G. H., Poet. Kar.*, i. 137 ; there is
no direct evidence, however, that these
verses are the work of Paulinus.

A poem on the Resurrection, in the same rhythmical scheme, shows, like the verses on Lazarus, a fondness for the Gospel narrative, but it cannot be ascribed with certainty to Paulinus :

> venit Maria Magdalene sabbato,
> Maria venit altera diluculo
> ad monumentum, portantes aromata,
> ut valde mane corpus sacratissimum
> Christi linirent redolenti crismate.[1]

Three other rhythmical poems have been assigned to Paulinus. The first is an alphabetical *planctus* on the destruction of Aquileia by Attila. This complaint for ' old, unhappy, far-off things' is evidently intended as a warning against the sins and perils of the present. In vigorous verses it tells of a proud city brought low, of massacre and outrage, the destruction of Churches, the murder of priests :

> o quae in altum extollebas verticem,
> quomodo iaces despecta, inutilis,
> pressa ruinis, numquam reparabilis
>   tempus in omne !

> pro cantu tibi, cithara et organo
> luctus advenit, lamentum et gemitus,
> ablatae tibi sunt voces ludentium
>   ad mansionem.[2]

Was the poet thinking of the Hungarians who were in years not distant to descend on Italy and renew the days of Attila, when he subjoined a prayer for mercy ?

> Christe rex noster, iudex invictissime,
> te supplicamus, miseratus respice,
> averte iram, tales casus prohibe
>   famulis tuis.

The other poems in the same collection are a hymn on the Nativity and an alphabetical *Confessio*. The former, which alone possesses any interest, is in narrative form, and tells of the birth of Christ, the adoration of the shepherds and magi, and the massacre of the Innocents. The failure alike of form and content is too conspicuous when the verses on the Innocents

---

[1] *M. G. H., Poet. Kar.*, i. 138.   [2] ib., i. 143.

are compared with the great examples, the hymn of Prudentius, which, here, is basely imitated :

> salvete flores martyrum candiduli,
> respersi tamen rore sed purpureo;
> felices nati hac in luce rosuli,
> pulchri, tenelli.[1]

These rhythmical poems are of interest because they show a departure from the Carolingian tradition without following the Irish and Anglo-Saxon systems which combined alliteration with frequent assonance and rime.   There is more attention to the word-accent than is shown in the Irish and English rhythmical pieces, while the influence of classical studies is seen in the more careful choice of words and the finer sense of form.

§ 3. *Theodulf of Orleans, circa* 760–*circa* 821.

Theodulf of Orleans [2] is the most important poet of the royal school.   He was of Gothic race, and it is now established that he was born in Northern Spain.   His education was the most complete that the resources of the day could offer.   In an interesting poem he gives a list of the authors over whose works, in his student days, he had loved to ponder, 'by night and day' :

> saepe et Gregorium, Augustinum perlego saepe,
>   et dicta Hilarii seu tua, papa Leo.
> Hieronymum, Ambrosium, Isidorum, fulvo ore Iohannem,
>   inclyte seu martyr te, Cypriane pater.[3]

But, besides the fathers, those fountains of sound doctrine, he loved the heathen writers with a passionate love :

> legimus et crebro gentilia scripta sophorum,
>   rebus qui in variis eminuere satis.

Like others among his contemporaries, he had not neglected the study of the Christian poets whose works had now acquired the position of classics.   Juvencus, Sedulius, Avitus, Paulinus, and Fortunatus are mentioned, but a special place is given to Prudentius, whom elsewhere he styles 'disertissimus atque

---

[1] *M. G. H., Poet. Kar.*, i. 146.
[2] On Theodulf see B. Hauréau in *Singularités historiques et littéraires,*
pp. 37 sqq.   The poems of Theodulf are in *M. G. H., Poet. Kar.*, i. 437 sqq.
[3] ib., i. 543.

Christianissimus poeta'.[1] The only heathen authors to whom
he refers by name are Pompeius, Donatus, Virgil, and Ovid :

> in quorum dictis quamquam sunt frivola multa,
> plurima sub falso tegmine vera latent.

This distich contains Theodulf's whole theory of the study of
pagan authors. He refused to take up the extreme position
of Alcuin, who, in his later years, had forbidden his pupils to
court the perilous enchantments of Virgil. Theodulf endeavoured to exorcize the latent evil by the familiar method
of allegory. So Proteus could be explained as Truth, the
Virgin of the fourth Eclogue as Justice ; Hercules was an
example of conquering Virtue, while Cacus taught the wickedness of Theft. Similarly, the nature and attributes of Cupid
furnished Theodulf with the materials for endless moralizing.
He says :

> mens prava in pharetra, insidiae signantur in arcu,
> tela, puer, virus, fax tuus ardor, amor.[2]

Keeping always in mind the application of the allegorical
method, the Christian reader—so Theodulf seems to say—
may listen unharmed to the wistful music of Virgil, and, what
is the more surprising, he may wander without fear through
the dangerous and alluring tales of Ovid. For Theodulf found
his chief delight in Virgil and the 'loquacious' Naso.[3] If his
affection for Prudentius went so far that he styled him his master,
it was to the close study of the elegiacs of Ovid that he owed
the merits as well as the defects of his verse. It will hardly
surprise a student of the Middle Ages to learn that among the
numerous allusions and imitations which make this influence
plain, many are derived from the *Ars Amatoria* and the
Remedium Amoris.[4]

Theodulf, then, was not willing to endure the deprivation
to which Alcuin had been ready to consent for the salvation of
his soul. Nevertheless, like a true child of the Middle Ages, he
felt that his love for the pagan poets required some formal
excuse or plausible justification, and, in his later years, he
confessed that his other passion, the composition of verses,
might tend to obscure the all-important issue of life. It was

---

[1] *M. G. H., Poet. Kar.*, i. 543, note 2.
[2] ib., i. 544.
[3] 'Naso loquax', ib., p. 543.
[4] On the vogue of Ovid in the Middle
Ages see E. K. Rand, *Ovid and his In-*
fluence, Lond. 1925, and Sandys, *History*
of Classical Scholarship, i. 638 sqq. ; 'even
the *Art of Love* was allegorized for the
benefit of nuns ', i. 639 ; Graf, *Roma nella*
memoria del medio evo, ii. 296 sqq.

in such a mood (but in verse) that he wrote to his scholars at Orleans, who had proudly sent him their painfully laboured school-compositions :

> non amor ipse meus Christus mea carmina quaeret,
> sed mage commissi grandia lucra gregis.[1]

But this is the disillusion of age. About 781 he appeared at the court of Charles, and became the ' Pindar' of a literary circle which he delighted with his lively and elegant verses. The king rewarded him with the see of Orleans, and soon possessed no more zealous and energetic bishop in the whole of his kingdom. Theodulf carried out with thoroughness the royal injunction that schools were to be established in connexion with monasteries and cathedrals. He went further and set up in towns and villages free schools where the children of the poor were to receive instruction under the supervision of the priests. At Germigny he built an elaborate little church, most of which still survives.[2] He busied himself with the reform of religious houses in his diocese, he was the true shepherd of his flock, and he exercised a strict discipline over his clergy. No wonder, therefore, that Charles selected this able and enlightened bishop as one of his *Missi Dominici* in the year 798. The feelings of Theodulf overflowed into verse. In a lengthy poem he describes the experiences of his tour ; the innumerable bribes which he had to refuse, the corruption of the local judges and even of one of the royal *Missi*.

During these years of eager and useful labour, Theodulf passed his days between the pleasures of the court and the business of his spiritual office. The great king died in 814, and Louis the Pious succeeded. Four years later occurred the revolt of Bernard, the son of Pippin. It was a hopeless failure ; Bernard was blinded, and punishment was meted out to his followers.[3] Among the sufferers was Theodulf, who, in spite of his protestations of innocence, was deposed from his bishopric and shut up in the monastery of S. Aubin at Angers. There he poured forth his sorrows in pathetic verses addressed to his friend the Bishop of Autun. He bids his muse speed forth and seek his friend, and say: 'I am the muse of Theodulf, come from the dungeon of his prison-house, where he is consumed

---

[1] *M. G. H., Poet. Kar.*, i. 542.
[2] See R. de Lasteyrie, *L'architecture religieuse en France à l'époque romane*, Paris 1912, p. 143.

[3] See Simson, *Jahrbücher des fränkischen Reichs unter Ludwig dem Frommen*, i. 117 sq. on the revolt ; on Theodulf's punishment, i. 122.

with love for thee. There he lies, an exile, helpless and poor,
sad, troubled, and in want, despised and cast down ... He reads
nothing, he cannot teach, he cannot fulfil his duty of praise to
the Lord, the father of all, the king of heaven and earth.'[1]
In 821, however, Theodulf was set free and he may have
returned to his bishopric. But he did not long survive his
release. The place of his burial is unknown.

As a poet Theodulf stands easily supreme among his contemporaries, and to find his equal we must go back as far as
Venantius Fortunatus. For Theodulf, his muse was his companion and his consolation. Poetry and art were for him
necessities of life. He delighted in sumptuous books and in
costly works of art. His love for the classical poets was deep
and untainted by pedantry. But, like Fortunatus, he is under
the darkening shadow of the Middle Ages. So he is constrained
to discuss in verse the coming of Antichrist, and to depict in
a melancholy elegy the approaching end of the age. The
winter seasons, he says, have grown more severe, the summers
less full of the sunshine that ripens corn and vine; the spring is
less pleasant, and autumn less abundant than of old :

> nil modo terra boni sic fert velut ante ferebat,
> effaetum et sterilem semet inesse docet.

The world is growing old, and it is given over to all manner
of evil :

> dira cupido viget, sordes, periuria, luxus,
> livor edax, falsum, iurgia rixa dolus.[2]

Already we hear the accents of the monk of Cluny in the
De contemptu mundi.

The best of Theodulf's religious poems is the celebrated
Gloria laus et honor, part of which has found its way into the
liturgy as the Palm Sunday processional. The verses which
compose the hymn are selected from the opening lines of the
poem :

> gloria laus et honor tibi sit, rex Christe, redemptor,
> cui puerile decus prompsit Hosanna pium.

> Israel es tu rex, Davidis et inclyta proles,
> nomine qui in domini, rex benedicte, venis.

---

[1] *M. G. H., Poet. Kar.,* i. 563.
[2] ib., i. 469. It is true that centuries
before Cyprian (*Ad Demetrianum*, ii)
drew a similar picture and foretold the
imminence of judgement.

coetus in excelsis te laudat caelicus omnis
    et mortalis homo et cuncta creata simul.

plebs Hebraea tibi cum palmis obvia venit,
    cum prece, voto, hymnis adsumus ecce tibi.

hi tibi passuro solvebant munia laudis,
    nos tibi regnanti pangimus, ecce, melos.

hi placuere tibi, placeat devotio nostra,
    rex bone, rex clemens, cui bona cuncta placent.

gloria laus et honor tibi sit, rex Christe redemptor,
    cui puerile decus prompsit Hosanna pium.[1]

These remarkable verses are the crown of Theodulf's poetry, and round them has grown an interesting legend. The main feature of the Palm Sunday festival was the great procession after the solemn blessing and distribution of the palms. At Orleans, it was in later times an occasion of special magnificence, as we learn from a manuscript now in the library of that city.[2] 'At the head of the procession were borne the Gospels, the dragon, the cross, and the banners; then followed a living representation of Jesus seated on the ass; last came a throng of people, carrying branches in their hands and singing the Hosanna. When the gates of the city were reached, they were closed, the procession halted while the Gospel was sung, and a prayer was said for the city and its inhabitants. Then a choir of children sang, from the city walls, the *Gloria laus et honor*, and the refrain was taken up by the crowd. The gates were then opened and the ceremony ended at the Cathedral.' The story runs that the Emperor Louis was at Angers on Palm Sunday.[3] The procession moved through the city and halted beneath the tower where Theodulf was imprisoned. Suddenly, from above was heard the *Gloria laus*, chanted loudly and melodiously. The Emperor was charmed and asked the name of the unknown singer. He was told that it was Theodulf, his own prisoner. 'Then the merciful and gentle monarch was moved with compassion, and from that hour he delivered and pardoned him and sent him back to his Church, quit and absolved of the crime whereof he had been accused.' There is no reason, however, to suppose that the story is more than a pious legend invented by the people of Orleans for the glory and justification of their beloved bishop.[4] It is at the same time a testimony to the

---

[1] *Anal. Hymn.* l, p. 160 ; for the whole poem see *M. G. H., Poet. Kar.*, i. 558.
[2] Cuissard, *Théodulfe*, pp. 136-7, from which the following description is taken.
[3] ib., pp. 134-5.
[4] Simson, i. 169.

popularity of this magnificent hymn, which was one of the last
to enter the liturgy.   The other devotional poems of Theodulf
hardly possess the same qualities.   The epanaleptic verses on
the Resurrection [1] do not challenge a comparison with the *Salve
festa dies* of Fortunatus.   They are hardly more than a poetical
curiosity, an exercise of misplaced ingenuity, like the picture
poem addressed to Charles, in which Theodulf imitated the bad
example set by Fortunatus.[2] When, immediately after his
accession, the Emperor Louis visited Orleans, he was received
with much ceremony, and Theodulf greeted him with a loyal
poem in sapphics, full of religious feeling and courtly flattery :

> en adest Caesar pius et benignus,
> orbe qui toto rutilat coruscus,
> atque prae cunctis bonitate pollet
>   munere Christi.[3]

So the poem begins and continues with the praise of Louis'
virtues; he is humble, wise, and merciful, just and brave, the
father of the Church, and a triumphant warrior.   The poet
wishes him long life and success in battle, and prays that his
wife and children may prosper, and ends the poem with a
doxology :

> sit patri et nato, tibi, spiritusque,
> splendor aeternus honor atque perpes
> nunc ut in praesens, ita et in futura
>   saecula semper.

The following example—an inscription to be placed above the
entrance to a house—shows the epigrammatic style of Theodulf, in which, like many of his contemporaries, he follows
Fortunatus :

> qui stas quive sedes, qui rura et tecta peragras,
>   tempora consumis actibus et variis,
> nil gere turpe, quod hac celsa quis spectet ab aede.
>   est hoc, est aliud quod mage tu timeas :
> est super astra deus, quid agat humana propago
>   laturus librae pondera iusta videt.[4]

Theodulf's poems are a mirror of the Carolingian age, and
represent the highest achievement of an effort after learning
which it is easy to despise for its limitations, and difficult to
praise too highly for its disinterested aspiration after the things

[1] *M. G. H., Poet. Kar.,* i. 553.
[2] ib., p. 482.   It is an acrostic in the
form of a parallelogram which contains
a square divided by diagonals.
[3] ib., p. 529 ; see Simson, i. 12.
[4] *M. G. H., Poet. Kar.,* i. 555.

of the mind. It shows a dim, half-conscious humanism struggling with the insistent temper of medievalism, a mixture of freedom and tradition, the secular and the religious. And Theodulf, the scholar and the churchman, represents the best side of his age. His poetry is not always a mere imitation; he chose his subjects from his everyday experience, his hopes and fears, his joys and his sorrows. The proof of this lies in the fact that he lives again in his verses, as a noble and enlightened man, the friend of the poor and oppressed, who taught a barbarous age the responsibilities of power and reminded the rich that they shared a common humanity with the poor; 'for you are blessed by the same holy baptism, anointed with the same oil at the last, and fed by the Flesh and Blood of the Lamb. And as the giver of life died for them as well as for you, so He calls each according to his deserts to receive of His bounty.'[1]

§ 4. *Characteristics of the Literary Movement after Charles the Great.*

The course taken by the literary movement after the death of Charles the Great in 814 proves clearly the debt which that movement owed to the largeness of his views and to his personal inspiration.[2] The generation of scholars which followed Alcuin and Theodulf shows indeed great industry and erudition, but less productivity and a more definitely theological outlook. Those who still shared something of the humanistic spirit which had marked the earlier renaissance, now spoke regretfully of the decline of studies. In his preface to Einhard's life of Charles, Walafrid Strabo contrasted the brilliant age of its author with the decadence of his own generation. 'Now, Charles was beyond all kings most eager in making search for wise men and in giving them such entertainment that they might pursue philosophy in all comfort. Whereby, with the help of God, he rendered his kingdom, which, when God committed it to him, was dark and almost wholly blind (if I may use such an expression), radiant with the blaze of fresh learning, hitherto unknown to our barbarism. But now once more men's interests are turning in an opposite direction, and the light of wisdom is less loved, and in most men is dying out.'[3]

---

[1] *M. G. H., Poet. Kar.*, i. 517.
[2] See Hauck, ii. 604 sqq.

[3] Prologue to Einhard's *Vita Caroli* (trans. by A. J. Grant, London 1905).

If the court school still existed under the Irish Clement, it had lost its commanding influence, and was no longer the main centre of literary production. Clement, an industrious and uninspiring grammarian, and Benedict of Aniane,[1] the zealous monastic reformer, are the men of the new age. Louis the Pious had been trained by his father in all the arts which might fit him to become a Christian prince. He was a good Latin scholar, knew some Greek, and was interested in theology as well as the chase. But for letters in their wider sense he had none of his father's love; he leaned to the theological studies which flourished best in the monastic schools, and the asceticism of Benedict of Aniane attracted him more than the secular spirit of the scholars who had thronged his father's court. Thus the ecclesiastical character of learning becomes more pronounced. Ermoldus Nigellus,[2] in his four books of tedious elegiacs in honour of Louis, made some attempt to continue the old courtly tradition, but the centre of culture had definitely shifted to the monasteries of the Eastern part of the Empire, to Germany and Lorraine.

Although Wandalbert (b. 813) was probably of West-Frankish birth, he was brought up in the monastery of Prüm in Lorraine. He composed a versified *Martyrology*, enlivened by the addition of various poems of differing content and metre.[3] He is an example of the eastward trend of learning after the death of Charles the Great.

In the Benedictine houses, the rule was now enforced that schools within the monasteries should be reserved for oblates alone;[4] laymen and those who were destined to become secular clergy were to go to the 'external' school, a separate establishment. Thus a narrower aim of religious education won acceptance, and this aim is reflected in the monastic literature, which tends more and more to consist of books of instruction intended for practical scholastic use.[5] The schools of Fulda and Reichenau, which had been famous in the time of Charles, continued their activity under Louis, but, although the presence at Fulda of Raban Maur, and of Walafrid at Reichenau was a guarantee of the retention of classical studies, theological pursuits held, as at Tours, a dominant place. If Abbot Baugulf at Fulda himself

---

[1] On Benedict see E. Bishop, *Liturgica Historica*, pp. 211 sqq.
[2] For his poems see *M. G. H.*, *Poet. Kar.*, ii. 4 sqq.
[3] See ib., ii. 569 sqq.
[4] *M. G. H., Leges*, i 202.
[5] Hauck, ii. 608.

transcribed the *Bucolics*,[1] and if Raban boasts of the great stores of books both sacred and profane,

> quicquid sapientia mundi
> protulit in medium temporibus variis,[2]

the decline of classical studies is apparent in the lessened command of literary Latin, and the poverty of the poetical output. Of the three most important poets of the time, Raban, Walafrid, and Gottschalk, only Walafrid is a true spiritual child of the earlier renaissance. Raban is the monk and theologian, with hardly a spark of poetical feeling, and Gottschalk, partially abandoning the classical tradition, owes less to the schools.

§ 5. *Raban Maur* (780–856); *Walafrid Strabo* (809 *circa*–849).

Magnentius Rabanus Maurus is the commanding figure among the ecclesiastics of his age, a great churchman and the first German theologian.[3] As a boy he went to school at Fulda, the monastery where the bones of Boniface reposed, and where the classical studies which the saint had loved, were still pursued. But as he showed exceptional promise, he was dispatched to Tours to the care of the most distinguished master of the day. Alcuin loved him and gave him the name of Maurus, after Benedict's dearest disciple. Raban's passion was knowledge in every form, but theological studies were nearest his heart, and he was, above all, an excellent teacher. On his return to Fulda, and even after his elevation to the rank of Abbot (822), he continued to teach and followed Alcuin's example in the composition of various *compendia* for use in the school. Strict, and not too sympathetic by nature, he ruled the Abbey well, caring little for politics and testing all things by a high standard of duty. When in 842, for personal and political reasons, he resigned his Abbacy, he sought a solitary retreat where he could devote himself to the mastery of the universal knowledge which he embodied in the encyclopaedic *De Universo*, a treatise based on Isidore of Seville, explaining the universe of things both mystically and historically. In a world of change, it appeared to him that the written word alone had a chance of survival, and that knowledge had an abiding value not subject to vanity.

---

[1] Hauck, ii. 614.   [2] *M. G. H., Poet. Kar.*, ii. 187.   [3] Hauck, ii. 627.

nullum opus exsurgit, quod non annosa vetustas
    expugnet, quod non vertat iniqua dies:
grammata sola carent fato, mortemque repellunt,
    praeterita renovant grammata sola biblis.[1]

So he wrote to Eigil, his predecessor at Fulda, and in this faith
he laboured until, in 847, Louis the German, recognizing his
work, in spite of their political differences, persuaded him in
his old age to undertake the charge of the Archbishopric of
Mainz. Raban was now involved in worldly cares and theological controversies. His sense of duty gave him no rest. He
stood out as the upholder of order in a time of social disintegra-
tion, and as the zealous supporter of sound doctrine against
heretics like Gottschalk, his old pupil, whose condemnation he
pronounced at the Synod of Mainz.

As a writer, Raban conveys the impression of immense industry. He contented himself, in all modesty, with garnering
in the harvests of his predecessors. He created nothing, and
what he collected from Jerome, from Isidore, or from Bede,
he did not attempt to stamp with the mark of his own personality.
It can, therefore, be hardly expected that he should show any
great aptitude for poetry.

Although his prosody is, on the whole, poor, his training at
Fulda and Tours had given him a certain facility in the composition of occasional verses and poetical epistles. Several of
the latter are addressed to his friend Samuel, the future bishop
of Worms. In them may be discerned, perhaps, a trace of
warmer feeling than it was his wont to display, but the verses
are austere and simple enough.

te deus aeternus, hominum sanctissimus auctor,
stelligeram caeli summus qui continet arcem,
perspicit atque omnem fortis dominator abyssum,
exaltet, salvet, servet te, diligat, ornet.
concedatque tui omonimi meritumque locumque,
exstitit ut templi typici hic servitor, amator,
utque habeas omnem Samuel Samuelis honorem,
esto memor proprii quem nominis ultima notet
syllaba;[2] hic cordis laus sit, hic fervor amoris.
sit tibi vita salus, tibi sit via gloria virtus,
protector, rector per secula cuncta valeto.[3]

---

[1] *M. G. H., Poet. Kar.*, ii. 186.   [2] i.e. El, the name of God.
                [3] *M. G H., Poet. Kar.*, ii. 189.

The same simplicity and piety, stern with monkish rigour, are shown in Raban's poetical prayers, prayers for mercy :

> eripe me miserum, flenti et miseratus adesto,
>   qui graviter peccans aeger in orbe dego.
> eripe me his, invicte, malis, procul omnia pelle,
>   quae mentem et corpus crimina dura tenent,[1]

or litanies to God and the saints :

> agnus sancte dei, qui tollis crimina mundi,
>   semper in aeternum tu miserere tuis.
> tu nos, Christe, audi, tu exaudi, Christe, precamur,
>   te sequimur, Christe, te volumus, cupimus.
> o domine, salva, quia vitam quaerimus abs te,
>   redde tuum vultum, sic erit atque satis.[2]

If we search for charm, personal or poetical, in Raban's verses, the nearest approach to it is, perhaps, in the lines which he prefaced to a treatise on virtues and vices, dedicated to Louis the Pious :

> rure morans flexo decerpsi pollice flores,
>   qui mixtim spirant nectar odoriferum.
> arboribus celsis evulsi ex cortice ramos,
>   qui foliis myrram, balsama rore dabunt.
> haec quoque collecta calathis cum, lector opime,
>   cernas, non spernas, sed relegens teneas.
> hic quoque virtutum redolet gratissimus ordo,
>   sordidus et foetor pellitur arte procul.
> his tu deliciis frueris si, rite placebis
>   altitrono et felix regna beata capis.
> collectoris enim nomen si noscere quaeris,
>   Maurus dicor ego : tu sine fine vale.[3]

His pupil Rudolf, at any rate, was an admirer of Raban's verses, for he describes him as 'sui temporis poetarum nulli secundus'.[4] But Raban wrote for the most part as though he were composing school exercises, borrowing freely from his Christian predecessors Sedulius, Fortunatus, and Alcuin, as well as from Virgil and Ovid. The most conspicuous example of such plagiarism is the long rhythmical poem on the Catholic faith, which incorporates, with appropriate adaptations, the *Altus prosator* of Columba. This instance is important for the demonstration of Irish, and with it Anglo-Saxon, influence on the development of rhythmical and rimed poetry on the Continent ; for, as we have already seen, it was among the Irish

[1] *M. G. H., Poet. Kar.*, ii. 171.
[2] ib., ii. 218.   [3] ib., ii. 169.
[4] Dümmler, *Hrabanstudien*, p. 25 (*Berlin. Sitzungsber.* 1898).

poets that the possibilities of rime and rhythm were most significantly recognized.   Raban's poem begins :

> aeterne rerum conditor,
> et clarus mundi formator,
> deus in adiutorium
> intende tu humilium :
> cordeque tibi devotûm,
> festina in auxilium.[1]

It expounds first the Trinitarian faith, then the story of the Creation, the Fall, and the Flood, showing how the wickedness of men, in spite of punishment and warning, had grown, and death had dominion over them :

> regnabat mors latissime
> super omnes durissime.

But God, in His mercy, sent His only Son to free a fallen world from the power of sin.   The poem proceeds to tell the story of Jesus from the birth to the death and resurrection.   Then the last judgement is described, with large borrowings from Columba's powerful and gloomy verses, but the personal application at the end is Raban's own, and here we reach the severe and simple piety—evangelical as we should call it—which marks so much of his religious verse.

> quo me tum possum vertere
> et suffragia quaerere,
> cum contra me sententia
> profertur in angustia ?
> accusor reus criminis,
> cum non sit favor operis. . . .
> cerno tremens quod feceram,
> et diu quod celaveram,
> nec adiuvant solatia,
> patris et matris famina,
> turba nec amicabilis
> praestat iuvamen debilis.

Raban's other hymns, if indeed they are his, possess the smallest measure of merit or of interest.   There are some poor elegiacs in honour of S. Boniface,[2] and a hymn on SS. Marcellinus and Peter,[3] beginning :

> claras laudes ac salubres, posco, fratres dicite,
> quas proferre cogit apte nunc sanctorum gloria.
> o victores gloriosi his ovate laudibus !

---

[1] *M. G. H., Poet. Kar.,* ii. 197.   [2] ib., ii. 234.   [3] ib., ii. 235.

Many other hymns are attributed to Raban, but without any clear justification.[1] Thus an uncertain tradition assigns to him the famous *Veni, Creator Spiritus*, the solemn hymn of consecration sung when pontiffs and kings are crowned, at the election of bishops and at the translation of holy relics.[2] If, however, it cannot be proved that this splendid hymn is the work of Raban, it is certain that it belongs to the ninth century, and is a fruit of the Carolingian Renaissance.

1. veni, creator spiritus,
   mentes tuorum visita,
   imple superna gratia,
   quae tu creasti, pectora.

2. qui paraclitus diceris,
   donum dei altissimi,
   fons vivus, ignis, caritas
   et spiritalis unctio.

3. tu septiformis munere,
   dextrae dei tu digitus,
   tu rite promisso patris,
   sermone ditans guttura.

4. accende lumen sensibus,
   infunde amorem cordibus,
   infirma nostri corporis
   virtute firmans perpeti.

5. hostem repellas longius,
   pacemque dones protinus,
   ductore sic te praevio
   vitemus omne noxium.

6. per te sciamus, da, patrem,
   noscamus atque filium,
   te utriusque spiritum
   credamus omni tempore.

From Raban Maur we pass to his pupil Walafridus Strabus or Strabo (809 *circa*–849), a poet of genuine gifts, a lover of nature, and a man of tolerant sympathies and humane learning. He was born of humble parents, who devoted him to the Church in his childhood. He received his first instruction in letters at Reichenau under Haito, Grimald, Wettin, and Tatto. Affectionate and gentle by nature, the clever boy strove hard to please his masters, whom he remembered with gratitude to the end of his brief career. At the age of fifteen he had acquired a remarkable facility in the composition of verses, and at eighteen he wrote a long poem in which he recounted the

[1] Dreves, *Hymnologische Studien zu Venantius Fortunatus und Rabanus Maurus*, endeavours to prove Raban's authorship of a group of hymns (see *Anal. Hymn.* l, pp. 180 sqq.), but Strecker, *Anzeiger f. deutsch. Alt.* xxxiii, p. 51, is sceptical.

[2] Text, *Anal. Hymn.* l, p. 193 ; on its authorship see A. Wilmart, *L'hymne et la séquence du Saint-Esprit* in *La vie et les arts liturgiques*, July 1924, pp. 395 sqq., and Julian, *Dictionary of Hymnology*, 2nd edit., pp. 1212 and 1720. A manuscript of Fulda of the tenth century did indeed ascribe this hymn to Raban, but it equally ascribed to him others that plainly are not his (Wilmart, p. 396). The hymn was assigned to Charles the Great on the authority of Ekkehard V (*c.* 1220), who, however, makes Charles and Notker contemporaries. The Charles of the tradition can only be Charles the Fat, who is known to have had friendly relations with Notker, but can hardly be the author. There is no evidence to support the attribution of the hymn to Ambrose or to Gregory the Great. Dryden's fine paraphrase is well known.

visions of his dying master, Wettin, who in his delirium visited hell, purgatory, and paradise, and saw the torments of sinners and the joys of the saints.[1] Haito had already set forth in prose the strange story which had filled the monks of Reichenau with wonder and fear, and at Grimald's request the young poet unfolded it in heroic verse with appropriate reminiscences of Ovid and Virgil.

The death of Wettin,

> celebri rumore magister
> artibus instructus septem de more priorum.[2]

occurred in 824. It was, perhaps, in 827 that Walafrid was sent to Fulda to complete his theological studies under Raban, who had made the school the first in Germany.[3] Here he found good friends, among them the noble and highly gifted Gottschalk, to whom he appears to have become warmly attached. But their ways soon divided. Gottschalk became a persecuted wanderer, and Walafrid went to court as tutor of the young prince Charles, the son of Louis the Pious by Judith, his second wife. This remarkable woman, eminent for learning as well as beauty, gave her patronage to Walafrid, who rewarded her appropriately in courtly verses, tinged at the same time with monastic piety :

> omnia qui solus rerum secreta tuetur,
> praemia qui fidei devotis mentibus offert,
> illius arbitrio factum nutuque fatebor,
> ut, qui corde humili vobis fidissimus esse
> iam pridem statui, tandem quo nescio casu,
> servitio attraherer vestro prolisque beatae,
> quam vestris regnique simul profectibus huius
> alma dei pietas concessit surgere magni.
> vos vestrosque dei semper miserata potestas
> protegat, exaltet, firmet, regat, armet, adornet.
> Augustae haec humilis mittit munuscula Strabus
> pignora multorum domino transmissa sequestro.

> pacis amatrix,   lucis amica,   quae bona cuncta
> mente tueris,   haec mea clemens percipe scripta.[4]

It was during this happy period, when he enjoyed the friend-ship of the accomplished 'Augusta', that Walafrid composed many of those occasional poems which are worthy to rank

---

[1] *Visio Wettini, M. G. H., Poet. Kar.*, ii. 303 sqq.

[2] ib., p. 309.

[3] See J. M. Clark, *The Abbey of S. Gall*, p. 60.

[4] *M. G. H., Poet. Kar.*, ii. 378.

beside the best productions of the court circle of Charles the Great. The most interesting as well as the most curious is the long poetical dialogue[1] between the poet and his *Scintilla*, his muse or genius, the scene of which is placed outside the palace of Aachen, before the statue of Theodoric, which Charles the Great had brought from Ravenna in 801. Walafrid asks *Scintilla* why in the season of spring, when

> ver floriferis laetum se subrigit austris,
> magnus et ardentem gradibus legit aethera Phoebus,
> iam spatiis crevere dies, dulcescit et umbra,

she will not answer his desires and inspire him to song. She answers that the old poets sought solitude, and that the noise of the city is not pleasing to the Muses. Then follows a dialogue, beginning with a discussion on Theodoric, who appears as the type of the cruel tyrant, the persecutor of Catholics and the murderer of Boëthius. The consideration of his vices leads naturally to the main subject of the poem, the praise of the Carlings, and especially of the pious Louis, who is restoring to earth the age of gold, making up by his piety for all other defects:

> aurea, quae prisci dixerunt saecula vates,
> tempore, magne, tuo, Caesar, venisse videmus.
> tu pietate reples quicquid minus esse putasti;
> thesauris alii, meritis tu comptior esto,
> tu bonitate places, aliique tyrannide gaudent.[2]

Louis rewarded the poet at last by making him abbot of his beloved Reichenau, where amid the labours of his office and the compilation of theological treatises, he could exercise a delightful leisure in the cultivation of the little monastic garden which provided herbs and plants of medicinal virtue and flowers of actual and symbolic beauty. The joys of these pleasant hours Walafrid has gathered up in verses which charm us by their strange flavour and the sense of ten long centuries between us and the poet and his garden.[3] Laden with the fragrance of herb and flower, they describe, one by one, the beauties, the virtues, and the uses of the plants of the *Hortulus*, the little garden of Reichenau. Here, as in the garden where poppy and

---

[1] *De Imagine Tetrici*, M.G.H., *Poet. Kar.*, ii. 370 sqq.; for a hermit's vision of Theodoric's soul cast into a crater of Lipari see Gregory the Great, *Dialogues*, iv. 30; Graf, *Roma nella memoria del medio evo*, ii. 361.

[2] *M.G.H., Poet. Kar.*, ii. 373.

[3] Text of the *Hortulus*, M.G.H., *Poet. Kar.*, ii. 335 sqq.

rose grew together, are mingled flowers from the *Metamorphoses* and the *Georgics* with the roses and lilies of the martyrs and saints. Sage and rue and southernwood, pumpkin, gherkin and wormwood, horehound, fennel and orris, lovage, chervil, fleawort and parsley grow with lily and poppy and rose. Here, too, is ambrosia (eupatory):

> sed an ista sit illa,
> cuius in antiquis celeberrima mentio libris
> fit, dubium est multis.[1]

But the supreme praise is reserved for the chaste flowers of the Church's garden, the roses which are the blood of the martyrs on earth, and the lilies which are the reward of the saints in heaven:

> haec duo namque probabilium genera inclyta florum
> ecclesiae summas signant per saecula palmas,
> sanguine martyrii carpit quae dona rosarum,
> liliaque in fidei gestat candore nitentis.
> o mater virgo, fecundo germine mater,
> virgo fide intacta, sponsi de nomine sponsa,
> sponsa, columba, domus regina, fidelis amica,
> bello carpe rosas, laeta arripe lilia pace.
> flos tibi sceptigero venit generamine Iesse,
> unicus antiquae reparator stirpis et auctor,
> lilia qui verbis vitaque dicavit amoena,
> morte rosas tinguens, pacemque et proelia membris
> liquit in orbe suis, virtutem amplexus utramque,
> praemiaque ambobus servans aeterna triumphis.[2]

In these closing verses, the Church is celebrated in imagery derived from the *Song of Songs*.

> O virginal mother! O Store of ripe seed!
> Inviolate maid, wed to Heaven indeed.
> Dove of purity, bride, Heaven's queen, faithful friend,
> O pluck Roses in war, but when wars have an end.
> Pluck Lilies for joy![3]

The political troubles which brooded over the Empire broke into the peace of Reichenau. In 840, Louis the Pious died, amid the disasters of civil war and a dismembered Empire. Walafrid was one of the victims of Louis the German, who drove him from Reichenau. He returned, indeed, in 842, by the intervention, perhaps, of his old master Grimald, who was

---

[1] *M.G.H., Poet. Kar.*, ii. 348.   [3] R. S. Lambert, *The Little Garden*,
[2] ib., ii. 349.   London 1924, p. 37.

now the royal chancellor;[1] but he died in 849, and was buried in the monastery. His epitaph tells of the warm affection which his gentle nature was capable of winning from those who knew him,[2]

> deseris ah rapide caros, carus super omnes,
> moribus ac dulcis, doctus et aptus homo,

and his lovable character shines through his verse. There we see him gentle and studious, pure and modest, but always a monk who found his greatest consolation in the regular round of school and cloister. If he had learned to love the dangerous beauties of Virgil and Ovid, he did not neglect the graver volumes of the classical Christian poets. He had read Prudentius well, for his hymn *De Agaunensibus Martyribus*,[3] in praise of the Theban Legion, is closely modelled on the *Felix Tarraco* of the Spanish poet. It begins,

> felix Gallia, fortibus trophaeis,
> ubertate soli, virum nitore,
> regni nomine purpurata magno
> Romanae soror urbis atque consors.

The story follows quite in the vein of the *Peristephanon*. The Theban legion, led by Maurice, Candidus and Exsuperius, were Christians to a man, and when the Emperor,

> quem nec carmine nominare dignum,

ordered them to sacrifice to idols on pain of death, they refused to obey. Their leader drew them up and exhorted them to be firm, fear naught, and follow God. With perishable arms they had cast down many a foe; now a greater foe was to be vanquished and a greater garland won:

> stant inflexibiles, manentque fixi,
> non dant liba diis genuve ponunt,
> rex et conditor est quibus per aevum
> Christus, vivere commorique lucrum.

The 'fierce and impious lictor' conveys the news of their resolve to the 'cruel lord' Diocletian, who in his rage swears that he will make them an example for ever. First he orders

---

[1] See Ebert's suggestion, ii. 148.

[2] *M. G. H., Poet. Kar.*, ii. 423.

[3] ib., ii. 367 ; Agaunum, now S. Maurice in Valais, where according to the legend this Christian legion was destroyed by order of the Emperor Diocletian in 285.

Gregory of Tours (*De gloria martyrum*, xlviii) relates how the martyrs revealed their relics in a vision ; quoted by Delehaye, *Origines du culte des martyrs*, p. 104.

the legion to be decimated, but when the remainder hold firm, they are all condemned to death. 'They are slain with the sword, the very valleys are filled with corpses, and rivers of sacred blood are shed, and Rhone flows past, its waters consecrated by the blood of the saints':

> o quam nobilis unda, quae beatas
> solvens exequias, lavare plagas
> et secum meruit sacrata ferre
> et se corpora possidere circa.

While the butchers were feasting beside the scene of slaughter, an old man, named Victor, passed by and questioned them, and learned the story of the dreadful scene which lay before him. He sighed, and said, 'Why have I lived so long? Gladly would I lay aside the burden of age among these blessed dead.' The soldiers seized and slew him, and so he became

> martyr sociusque candidati
> coetus.

None of Walafrid's hymns possesses an equal measure of vigour or assurance. The sapphics *De Natale Domini*,[1] and those on S. Januarius,[2] and those on S. Gall[3] are not remarkable for felicity of execution or of phrase. The adonic versification of the *Song of the Three Children*[4] is not much superior:

> omnipotentem semper adorent
> et benedicant omne per aevum:
>   omnipotentem.
>
> astra polorum cuncta chorique,
> solque sororque, lumina caeli
>   omnipotentem.
>
> sic quoque lymphae quaque supernae,
> ros pluviaeque, spiritus omnis
>   omnipotentem.
>
> ignis et aestas, cauma geluque,
> frigidus et ardor atque pruinae
>   omnipotentem.
>
> nix glaciesque, noxque diesque,
> lux tenebraeque, fulgura, nubes
>   omnipotentem.
>
> arida, montes, germina, colles,
> flumina, fontes, pontus et undae
>   omnipotentem.

---

[1] *M. G. H., Poet. Kar.*, ii. 381.   [2] ib., ii. 415.   [3] ib., ii. 411.   [4] ib., ii. 394.

omnia viva, quae vehit aequor,
quae vehit aera, terraque nutrit,
omnipotentem.

cuncta hominum genus Israhel ipse
omnipotentem.

This poem with its tripping measure, well adapted for singing,
was used in some places as a 'Tract' on various occasions.

Walafrid's fame has rested mainly on his supposed authorship
of the *Glossa Ordinaria*, the brief commentary which filled the
margins of the medieval bibles; but this attribution is now dis-
proved, although it is known that he composed commentaries
on the opening books of the Old Testament.[1]

The humanistic element, not inconspicuous in Walafrid, shone
out more clearly in the work of another pupil of Raban, the
famous Servatus Lupus, who became Abbot of Ferrières in
842. 'In his literary spirit', it has been said, 'he is a precursor
of the humanists of the Renaissance'.[2] In his inexhaustible
curiosity, his feeling for style and his love of books for their
own sake, he stood alone and played an important part in the
preservation of classical manuscripts. His hymns on S. Wigbert
deserve to be mentioned.[3]

§ 6. *Gottschalk of Fulda*, 805 *circa*–869.

To the same generation as Walafrid belongs Gottschalk of
Fulda,[4] the wayward monk and impetuous disputant, whose life
was filled by a long and unequal contest with his old master
Raban Maur. He was the son of noble parents who dedicated
him from childhood to the religious life. He entered the Abbey
School of Fulda, and against his will he was compelled by Raban
Maur to take the vows. At Fulda he learned grammar and music,
and won the affection of the warm-hearted Walafrid. But
Gottschalk chafed under the restraints of monastic life. In 829
he appeared before a synod at Mainz, and obtained release from
his vows on the ground of the compulsion which Raban had
exercised, when he was a young oblate. But the Abbot was

---

[1] *M. G. H., Epist.* v. 515 sq., contains
prefaces to his commentary on *Exodus*
and *Leviticus*.

[2] Sandys, *History of Latin Scholarship*,
i. 486.

[3] *Anal. Hymn.* xxiii. 292.

[4] For Gottschalk's poems see *M. G. H.,
Poet. Kar.*, iii, and G. L. Perugi, *Gottschalc*, pp. 123 sqq.; on Gottschalk see
pp. 707 sqq. of *Poet. Kar.* iii; Dümmler,
Geschichte des ostfränkischen Reichs, i.
311 sqq.

not content to accept this adverse decision. He appealed to a synod presided over by Louis the Pious, and the former decision was reversed to the extent that Gottschalk remained a monk, but was transferred to the cloister of Orbais in the diocese of Soissons. There he devoted himself to theological studies and sought in the pages of Augustine an answer to the perplexing problems of predestination. Treatises flowed from his pen, and before long he fell under the suspicion of heresy. His was a restless and inquiring spirit;[1] not content, like Raban and Walafrid, to copy the tradition of the past, he shared the new speculative impulse then manifesting itself in Erigena, Radbertus, and Ratramnus, which began the religious philosophy of the Middle Ages.

At Orbais Gottschalk appears to have begun composing verses, but all his thoughts were directed to the propagation of his theological doctrines. In order to be free to preach, he somewhat irregularly obtained ordination at the hands of the chorepiscopus of Reims. Then he fled from his cloister and wandered to Italy, preaching as he went. Whether urged by spite or by a real fear of the consequences of heresy, Raban pursued his old pupil and obtained his expulsion from the court of Eberhard of Friuli. From Italy Gottschalk passed to Dalmatia and Pannonia, and finally appeared again in Germany. At the council of Mainz he paid dearly for his rashness in venturing to place himself again in the power of Raban Maur. He was convicted of heresy, soundly beaten, and handed over for further correction to Archbishop Hincmar of Reims. In 849 a provincial assembly deprived him of his orders, and shut him up in the monastery of Hautvillers. But he continued his theological labours and made many friends and disciples. Then, at the last, as his health declined and he was near death, he desired to receive the Sacrament and the absolution of the Church. Hincmar consulted Raban, but Gottschalk's old enemy was unrelenting. Hincmar sent the dying man a confession of faith, which he must accept, or die without absolution. Gottschalk was now *in extremis*, but he would not subscribe to a confession which he could not faithfully accept. He died without the last consolation. 'Sicque', said Hincmar, 'vitam digna morte finivit et abiit in locum suum.'

---

[1] Hincmar of Reims, an adversary, says 'ab ineunte aetate semper vocum novitates exquisivit'; he said himself, 'Nemo fuit mihi dux' (*M.G.H., Poet. Kar.*, iii. 735).

Theology had furnished the master interest of Gottschalk's eventful life. Under happier circumstances he might have acquired fame as a poet, for one at least of his poems shows some feeling for the musical possibilities of rhythmical verse. It is addressed to a youth [1] who had begged him to write a 'sweet song'. He replies that he is an exile in a far country, more ready to weep than to sing. 'How shall we sing the Lord's song in a strange land?'

1. ut quid iubes, pusiole,
   quare mandas, filiole,
     carmen dulce me cantare,
     cum sim longe exsul valde
       intra mare?
     o cur iubes canere?

2. magis mihi, miserule,
   flere libet, puerule,
     plus plorare quam cantare
     carmen tale, iubes quale,
       amor care.
     o cur iubes canere?

3. mallem, scias, pusillule,
   ut velles tu, fratercule,
     pio corde condolere
     mihi atque prona mente
       conlugere.
     o cur iubes canere?

4. scis, divine tiruncule,
   scis, superne clientule,
     hic diu me exsulare,
     multa die sive nocte
       tolerare.
     o cur iubes canere?

5. scis, captivae plebeculae
   Israeli cognomine
     praeceptum in Babylone
     decantare extra longe
       fines Iudae.
     o cur iubes canere?

6. non potuerunt utique
   nec debuerunt itaque
     carmen dulce coram gente
     aliena nostrae terrae
       resonare.
     o cur iubes canere?

7. sed quia vis omnimode,
   consodalis egregie,
     canam patri filioque
     simul atque procedente
       ex utroque.
     hoc cano ultronee.

8. benedictus es, domine,
   pater, nate, paraclite,
     deus trine, deus une,
     deus summe, deus pie,
       deus iuste.
     hoc cano spontanee.

9. exsul ego diuscule
   hoc in mare sum, domine,
     annos nempe duos fere,
     nosti fore, sed iamiamque
       miserere.
     hoc rogo humillime.

10. huic cano ultronee
   interim cum, pusiole,
     psallam ore, psallam mente,
     psallam die, psallam nocte,
       carmen dulce,
     tibi, rex piissime.[2]

[1] But see G. L. Perugi, *Gottschalc*, p. 56, who suggests that 'pusiole' refers to the past, while the 'sodalis' of strophe 7 refers to the present. The former pupil has become his equal. On the metre see Perugi, p. 73 sq.

[2] *Anal. Hymn.* l, p. 227; *M.G.H., Poet. Kar.*, iii. 731.

Sincerity of feeling, so rare in an age when poetry was manufactured according to the precepts of the schools, seems here to have made a brief appearance. But the rhythm is not handled with assurance, and the principle of the two-syllabled rime is not mastered. The following lines from another poem illustrate the principles of rime as understood by Gottschalk:

> erue servum
> valde misellum,
> pelle piaclum,
> tolle reatum,
> dirige gressum,
> redde paratum.[1]

The rhythmical scheme is:

> érue sérvum
> válde miséllum.

The rime, therefore, falls on an unaccented syllable, and the verse which follows, although it presents to the ear the effect of a two-syllabled rime, does so by accident:

> atque clientem
> suscipe flentem
> teque timentem;
> da mihi mentem
> fraude carentem,
> prava caventem.

But it could not be long before the pleasing appeal of such verses led to the composition of poems with a perfect and continuous two-syllabled rime.

In his poem to Ratramnus,[2] Gottschalk employs the hexameter but, with a characteristic departure from the classical tradition, he uses the leonine rime. The rime is single, in the form in which it became so popular in the following century, and Gottschalk's poem is one of the earliest important examples of the leonine hexameter.[3]

---

[1] *M. G. H., Poet. Kar.*, iii. 724.

[2] ib., iii. 733; he uses rime too in a sapphic prayer to Christ, in iii. 727.

[3] Manitius (see *Gesch.* i. 572) is inclined to attribute to Gottschalk a curious poetical dialogue, the *Ecloga Theoduli*. Theodulus (θεοῦ δοῦλος) = Godescalc or Gottschalk, and is a pseudonym. Osternacher (*Neues Archiv*, xl, pp. 331 sqq.) supports this attribution, but Strecker (*Neues Archiv*, xlv, p. 18) denies it on the ground that there is nothing in common between the manner of Gottschalk and that of this poem. The *Ecloga* was very popular in the Middle Ages, and was used in schools. It is a contest between Alithia and Pseustis, ended by Fronesis.

§ 7. *Sedulius Scotus, Florus of Lyons, and others.*

Of the numerous other versifiers of the later Carolingian age it is not necessary to mention more than a few names. Paschasius Radbertus is better known as the author of the treatise *De Corpore et Sanguine Domini*, than for the slight collection of his verse which has survived.[1] Similarly, John the Irishman, known as Scotus Erigena, stands apart, not as a poet, but as a bold thinker, philosopher rather than theologian, who asserted, but not without qualifications, the supremacy of reason over authority. It can hardly be said that the verses[2] of either possess any distinctive merit; the interest of their poetry lies in its association with the names of distinguished pioneers of medieval thought, whose careers are a fitting close to the Carolingian renaissance.

John, as befitted an Irish scholar, was not content to allow his remarkable knowledge of Greek to be proclaimed only by his translation of the Pseudo-Dionysius; he not only composed verses in Greek, but habitually introduced words, phrases, and whole lines of Greek into his Latin poems.[3]

Another Irishman, who was rather a man of letters than a theologian, and who combined a lively humour with an adequate amount of piety was Sedulius Scotus.[4] Like many others of his countrymen who had been educated in the Irish schools, he was tempted to cross the sea to find a career on the Continent. Cold and hungry, in the midst of winter, he arrived at Liége with his companions, and implored the Bishop Hartgar (840–54) to give them,

doctos grammaticos presbiterosque pios,

a refuge at his school.[5] In a playful ode, in which earnest was mixed with jest, Sedulius points out to the Bishop the contrast between the episcopal palace, with its brilliant ornaments and its alluring luxuries, and the miserable smoky lodging, with its leaky roof and its darkness as of the cave of Cacus or the

---

[1] Poems in *M. G. H.*, *Poet. Kar.*, iii. 38 sqq.

[2] Erigena's poems, ib., iii. 518 sqq.

[3] Cf. p. 527, 'Eroumque μάχαc dicere ludus erat'.

[4] Sedulius's poems are in *M G. H.*, *Poet. Kar.*, iii. 151 sqq. The name is not Irish, as has been supposed by those who would make Caelius Sedulius also an Irishman, but the name, like that of Virgil, was adopted in Ireland as a result of the popularity of those authors; see Traube, *Sedulius Scottus*, in *Abhandl. d. kgl. Bayer. Akad.*, Munich 1891, p. 339. On the chronology of the poems see pp. 341 sqq.

[5] *M. G. H.*, *Poet. Kar.*, iii. 168. Sedulius may have come over with an Irish mission to King Charles in 848. Traube, pp. 342 sq.

labyrinth of Crete, which was deemed good enough for him and his fellow grammarians. His wretched lodging is only fit for night-ravens and moles:

> non haec apta domus, crede, sophistis,
> qui splendentis amant munera lucis—
> sed haec apta domus nicticoraci
> talparumque gregi mansio digna.[1]

On several occasions Sedulius had to address a begging verse to his patron, asking for wine or meat or honey:

> ast his versicolis risit pius ille relectis
> ac sophicis votis prospera cuncta dedit.[2]

The Bishop smiled at these poetical complaints, and attended to the wants of the Irish scholars. On his death, Sedulius found a protector in his successor Franco (854–901), whom he celebrated in the best sapphics that he could command.

Sedulius had a careless and happy temperament. He spent his time, he says, reading, writing, teaching, saying his prayers regularly, eating and drinking his fill, and invoking the muses. He slept soundly at night, and recognized that he was a sinner:

> aut lego vel scribo, doceo scrutorve sophian:
> obsecro celsithronum nocte dieque meum.
> vescor, poto libens, rithmizans invoco musas,
> dormisco stertens: oro deum vigilans.
> conscia mens scelerum deflet peccamina vitae:
> parcite vos misero, Christe Maria, viro.[3]

He wrote many poems in a great variety of classical metres; he regarded himself as in some sort a priest of the muses and not as a mere versifier. His reminiscences are mainly from Virgil and Ovid, but he knew, of course, the favourite Christian poets, Juvencus, Prudentius, and Caelius Sedulius. His religious verse, in its classical technique, reminds us of Theodulf, but it has also an Irish impress in its curious use of words which had originally a pagan significance. Thus in an Easter hymn he writes:

> Titan gemmigeri centrum conscendit Olimpi,
> ardens flammivomis emicat ecce rotis.[4]

[1] *M. G. H., Poet. Kar.*, iii. 169.
[2] ib., p. 178.
[3] ib., p. 225.
[4] ib., p. 218.

Here also, like Theodulf, he expatiates on the beauty of spring, when the earth renews 'her winter weeds outworn':

> tellus florigeras turgescit germine bulbas,
> floribus et pictum gaudet habere peplum.
> nunc variae volucres permulcent aethera cantu,
> produnt organulis celsa trophea novis.

His sapphic ode, *De strage Normannorum*,[1] is a vigorous song of triumph and thanksgiving over a defeat of those dreaded invaders, the Danes. The Irish fighting spirit was awakened and Sedulius exulted in the slaughter of the enemy:

> quem sitiverunt varios per annos
> sanguinem sumunt rabidi tyranni:
> dulce fit cunctis satiare pectus
> caede virorum.

We must pass by the many occasional poems composed by Sedulius, mentioning only the 'debate' between the Rose and the Lily,[2] a charming Eclogue in which the dispute between the flowers is settled by the intervention of the reconciling Spring. The rose boasts of her bright colour, the purple of kings, and reproaches the lily for her pallor, the pallor of want and misery. 'The fair Apollo loves me,' says the lily; the glory of the rose is like the blush of conscious guilt. 'I am the sister of the dawn,' replies the rose,

> et me Phebus amat, rutili sum nuncia Phebi;
> Lucifer ante meum hilarescit currere vultum.

So the dispute continues, until the Spring, a youth reclining on the grass, his head garlanded with flowers, reminds them that they are twin sisters of the earth, their common mother. Finally, as in Walafrid's *Hortulus*, the religious note is struck. The rose typifies the blood of the martyrs and the lily is the symbol of virginity:

> tu, rosa, martyribus rutilam das stemmate palmam,
> lilia, virgineas turbas decorate stolatas.

Then the poet in person ends the Eclogue on the appropriate note:

> et tunc ver genitor geminis dans oscula pacis
> concordat dulces patrio de more puellas.
> lilia tunc croceae dant oscula grata sorori,

---

[1] *M. G. H., Poet. Kar.*, iii, pp. 208-9.   [2] ib., pp. 230-1.

illa sed huic ludens spinetis ora momordit.
lilia vernigenae ludum risere puellae,
ambroseo bibulum potant et lacte rosetum.
at rosa puniceos calathis fert xenia flores
ac niveam largo germanam ditat honore.

It is only recently that Sedulius has been recognized as one of the founders of the political literature of the Middle Ages. His *Liber de rectoribus Christianis*,[1] written *circa* 855-9, sets forth for the benefit of Lothair II the duties and responsibities of kings. In this book he adopts the common medieval expedient, suggested by Martianus Capella and Boëthius, of interspersing his prose with verse. The verses recapitulate, with much ingenuity and a great variety of classical metres, the argument of the preceding passage of prose. 'Sed haec quae breviter stilo prosali diximus, aliqua versuum dulcedine concludamus'—so he apologizes for his first interpolation.[2]

Considering the poetry of Sedulius as a whole, we are bound to place him with Theodulf and Walafrid in the front rank of the poets of the Carolingian age. While he shared with them the inevitable defects both of taste and of execution, like them he sought his subjects in experience and in life, and conveyed into his verses the impression of a lively personality. It is for reasons of this kind that modern readers are able to find pleasure in the occasional verses of Fortunatus or Sedulius, while the Middle Ages, true to their peculiar standard, delighted most in poems of extravagant moral or theological allegory, which modern readers can hardly approach without an effort.

A poet of the medieval order was Florus, master of the Cathedral School at Lyons, who lived about the middle of the ninth century.[3] Walafrid Strabo had heard of his fame and praised him in verse,[4] and Wandalbert of Prüm, another poet, praised him in prose for his knowledge of the Scriptures. Florus was a man of some learning, and he belonged to that conservative school of theology, which looked askance on the bolder speculations of their contemporaries, and relied on the Bible and the fathers. This spirit prompted his refutation of John the Irishman, *Libellus adversum cuiusdam vanissimi*

[1] Ed. Hellmann, in *Sedulius Scottus*, pp. 19 sqq.
[2] ib., p. 24.
[3] Florus's poems are in *M. G. H., Poet. Kar.*, ii. 509 sqq., and selection in *Anal.*

Hymn. li, pp. 210 sqq.
[4] *M. G. H., Poet. Kar.*, ii. 357 'Nam hic Florus florem sequitur de germine Iesse'.

hominis, qui cognominatur Iohannes, ineptias et errores. A conservative in religion, Florus was a conservative in politics. He lamented the division of the Empire of Charles the Great, and he depicted in moving verses the disastrous results of this division, the decay of morals, the increase of lawlessness, the departure of the glory of the Franks, who had succeeded the Romans as the arbiters and protectors of the Christian world. The long poem, *Querela de divisione imperii*,[1] is not merely a cry of distress uttered from the heart of a patriot; it is the expression of a practical idealism, which saw in the union of the Frankish Empire with the Papacy the best guarantee of political order and of material and spiritual progress:

> o fortunatum, nosset sua si bona, regnum,
> cuius Roma arx est et caeli claviger auctor,
> tutor et aeternus caelorum in saecula rector,
> qui terrestre valet in caelum tollere regnum.

Once the Frankish name was renowned throughout the world, Greeks, barbarians, and Latins sent their envoys to the Frankish court. But all that glory has passed away like a garland cast off by its wearer and trampled under foot. In a pregnant line, Florus bitterly sums up the whole matter:

> pro rege est regulus, pro regno fragmina regni.

In conclusion, he prays God that all these evils, all this chastening may purge the hearts of men, that they may pluck a sweet fruit from this bitter seed and attain to the salvation of their souls.

Among the longer religious poems of Florus are some versifications of the Scriptures—a bald summary of Matthew in hexameters, a similar version of John, and a metrical prayer, with an effective refrain, on the miraculous exhibitions of divine power as described in the Old Testament, beginning with the Creation, and ending with a forecast of the Judgement, in which the contrast of the lot of the evil and the good is set forth in a manner which cannot but lead the medieval writer to close with a prayer for personal salvation in that great day:

> illic laetitiae voces et cantica laudum,
> hic dolor et gemitus totum resonabit in aevum.
> hinc me, quaeso, reum peccati labe piatum
> eripe, Christe potens, clementi numine Florum.[2]

---

[1] *M. G. H.*, *Poet. Kar.*, ii. 559 sqq.   [2] ib., ii. 529.

Similar in character is another poem, which is a versified preface to a homiliary for the Catholic year.[1] More pleasing are a few versions from the Psalms, one of which is in the Ambrosian iambic dimeter, and might well have been used as a hymn, or, at any rate, for private devotions :

> ad te, polorum conditor,
> clamore supplex intimo
> votum precemque dirigo;
> aurem benignus commoda.[2]

This is the twenty-seventh Psalm : 'Ad te Domine clamabo, Deus meus ne sileas a me.'

Florus likewise versified the *Song of the Three Children*, and wrote a curious elegiac hymn for the festival of St. Michael.[3] The hymn *In Natale sanctorum Iohannis et Pauli*[4] is in honour of two martyrs who suffered under Julian, and whose memory is perpetuated by their basilica in Rome. It is interesting to observe the figure of the emperor, clothed in the dark hues of apostasy by the ecclesiastical tradition, becoming to the medieval writers, the type of a fierce and ungodly tyrant, who preferred an idol to the true God.[5] When Christ looked down from heaven and heard the cry of innocent blood, he avenged his saints by the tragedy of the Persian desert. Dying of his wounds the unrepentant Emperor breathed a last blasphemy against his Maker and Lord :

> ebibe nunc nostrum, quem quaeris, Christe, cruorem,
> atque avidus loeto iam satiare meo.
> ille quidem tales iusto sub iudice poenas
> exsolvit, post haec Tartara caeca petens.

Like the rest of his contemporaries, Florus found his poetical models in Ovid and Virgil, and like them, he did not neglect the Christian classics, Juvencus, Prudentius, Sedulius, and

---

[1] *M. G. H., Poet. Kar.*, ii. 530 sqq.
[2] ib., ii. 537.   [3] ib., ii. 540.
[4] ib., ii. 541–2.
[5] See the account of Julian in the *Golden Legend*. He was supposed to have been at one time a monk; cf. Johannes de Garlandia, *De Triumphis Ecclesiae*, ed. Wright, London 1856 (*Roxburghe Club*), p. 19:

> exemplum sceleris Iulianus apostata saepe
> ponitur, exuerat qui monachale decus.

By a base trick he robbed a woman of her money, and used it to be made consul and, finally, emperor. John adds the comment :

> cuius in exitium tota Gehenna coit.

The best account of medieval legends concerning Julian is in Graf, *Roma nella memoria del medio evo*, ii. 121 sqq. I may refer also to the anonymous *Carmen de Sancto Cassiano*, a product of the Carolingian age, in which Julian is depicted as a savage persecutor ; *M. G. H., Poet. Kar.*, iv, p. 183.

Fortunatus. If he read the pagan authors privately with pleasure, in his public profession he contrasted the Castalian rills unfavourably with the clear streams of Jordan, and the laurel of Apollo with the palms which were strewn in the path of Jesus. The pagans have Parnassus, but what is Parnassus to the holy hill of Sion, to Tabor and Hermon, to Lebanon with its cedars, to Carmel with its memory of Elijah, to Sinai and Horeb with their thunders? Job has sung his battles in heroic measure, David is a lyric poet, and as for Solomon :

> quid loquar insigni tumidum Salomona cothurno,
> qui thalamos Christi psallit et ecclesiae?

The conclusion of the argument, which is addressed to Moduinus, Bishop of Autun, is

> hos, reverende pater, pleno sectemur amore,
> hinc sensus nostri verbaque cuncta fluant.[1]

A contemporary of Florus, Milo, a monk of S. Amand near Tournai, was equally a man of learning, a theologian, and a poet.[2] He had charge of the education of two of the children of Charles the Bald, and when they were taken away by an untimely death he composed their epitaph.[3] Besides two amazing *carmina figurata* or picture-acrostics, and a few occasional verses, Milo composed two long hexameter poems, one a life of S. Amand, the other a curious and amusing treatise in two books, *De Sobrietate*. The latter is tedious enough, but it is an excellent example of the didactic manner that medieval readers always loved. The argument is admirably summarized in the metrical preface :

> sobrietas caput huius erit finisque libelli,
> pro qua distinctas acies ad bella vocavi,
> telaque divinis collegi plura pharetris.[4]

By many examples, mainly from the Old Testament, Milo shows the merit of sobriety and the awful results of *Gastrimargia*, its opposing vice. Noah and Lot and Esau fell victims to this vice, but Samson, Daniel, Judith, Esther, and the Maccabees,

[1] *M. G. H., Poet. Kar.*, ii. 554.
[2] Milo's poems are in *M. G. H., Poet. Kar.*, iii. 561 sqq.
[3] ib., iii. 678.
[4] ib., iii. 613; M. Schedler, *Die Philosophie des Macrobius und ihr Einfluss auf die Wissenschaft des christlichen Mittelalters*, p. 113, points out that in this poem Milo makes use of the *Saturnalia* of Macrobius, a book which was well known throughout the Middle Ages.

conquered through abstinence. The New Testament affords the poet, in the second book, more splendid and exalted types. First, the Virgin Mary is praised, as

> fons signatus aquae, purissima vena salutis,
> hortus conclusus quo fons processit honestus,
> caedrus cypressus platanus nux myrtus oliva,
> myrra storax calamus thus balsama cassia nardus,
> onyx cristallus prasius berillus iaspis.[1]

Then Anne is praised for her chaste widowhood, and the Baptist for his austerity and the manner of his end. Finally Milo chastises the vices and intemperance of his day. These remind him of the judgement, and he asks that the reader will pray that he may receive pardon for his sins.

A poet of similar outlook and equal talent is Heiric,[2] a monk of Auxerre, who composed in hexameters a life of S. Germain, the patron of his convent. Heiric was born in 841, and he entered the monastery at the age of eight. He had the unusual advantage of learning profane letters from the great scholar, Lupus of Ferrières, and he added to the study of theology a knowledge of astronomy and chronology. He appears to have known a little Greek, which he may have learned from Irish teachers. His metrical life of S. Germain presents some points of historical interest, but it is based mainly on a prose life which is still extant. It is preceded by a dedicatory ode in hendecasyllabics addressed to the Trinity. The mixture of Latin and Greek is a curious feature which recurs in many ninth-century poems, the fashion having been set by Irish scholars who appear to have practised it in their own country :

> o fecunda *ΤΡΥΑΣ ΜΟΝΑΣ*que simplex,
> seu te distribuant *ΕΛΛΗΝΑΣ ΚΑΤΑ*
> *ΟΥΣΙΑΝ ΜΙΑΝ ΕΙΣ ΤΡΕΙΣ ΥΠΟΣΤΑΣΕΙΣ.*
> seu sicut latius fatetur orbis
> *ΜΙΑΝ ΥΠΟΣΤΑΣΙΝ ΤΡΙΑ ΠΡΟΣΩΠΑ :*
> idem semper es, idem ipse constas.[3]

In concluding this survey of later Carolingian poetry, we must mention the name of Hincmar of Reims, the great ecclesiastic whose work belongs far less to letters than to the politics of Church and State. The Archbishop, whose long career fills a great part of the ninth century, was a man of

---

[1] *M. G. H., Poet. Kar.*, iii. 645. *Kar.*, iii. 427 sqq.
[2] Heiric's poems are in *M. G. H., Poet.* [3] ib., iii. 432.

imperious will, determined to defend his high position against Pope or King, and he had a large share in the work of consolidating the Western part of the Old Frankish Empire. His political and theological writings do not concern us here, but he left a little verse,[1] a few epigrams, and an elegiac poem in honour of the Virgin, ending with an invocation:

cum moriar, caeli claris praelata ministris,
    Christo conregnans, sis pia, quaeso mihi,
ut partem merear cum his, quos gratia salvat,
    in lucis, pacis sorte, quietis. Amen.

The poem contains one hundred verses, because if you multiply the number of the commandments by ten, you arrive at that total. 'And as this same decalogue is fulfilled by the love of God and of our neighbour, so by this twofold love we attain to everlasting life, which is signified by the number of a hundred.'

[1] *M. G. H., Poet. Kar.*, iii. 409 sqq.

VII

GERMAN RELIGIOUS POETRY IN THE TENTH AND ELEVENTH CENTURIES

§ 1. *The Tenth Century.*

THE most important political events in the West after the break-up of the Empire of Charles the Great centre round the severance of the Eastern and Western parts, and the separate developments of the French and German nations. Out of the disasters of heathen invasion and civil disruption, the German peoples emerged with the impress of Christianity fixed upon them, and the capability of absorbing the civilization of the Latin races without losing the remarkable characteristics derived from their own vigorous Teutonic ancestry.[1] The Saxons were the leaders in the mighty struggle against the heathen Danes, Slavs, and Hungarians, and the people whose conversion and conquest had cost such pains to the great Charles, were destined to be the instrument by which the triumph of Christianity in the north and east of civilized Europe was finally to be attained. Henry the Fowler began the difficult task of restoring the conditions which made civilization, culture, and the settled life of town-communities again a possibility. To Otto I, his greater son, is due a larger achievement. He made the German name the first in Europe. He subdued the heathen, restored order in Church and State, and looking towards distracted Italy, he dreamed the old dream of the Christian Empire. In 951 he was acknowledged as overlord of Italy, and in 962 he entered Rome and received the imperial crown at the hands of John XII. The Germans were now brought into close contact with Italy, and with what remained of culture in the chief centres of the old Latin civilization. Rome herself may have had little to give, but in the eloquent phrase of Giesebrecht, 'if the mouth of wisdom

---

[1] On the civilization and letters of the age of the Ottos see Giesebrecht, *Deutsche Kaiserzeit*, i, and especially pp. 761 sqq.; Hauck, iii. 275 sqq.; Taylor, *Mediaeval Mind*, i. 308 sqq.; also, for a useful summary, von Keller, *Die lateinische Sprache im deutschen Mittelalter* in *Deutsche Rundschau*, Aug. 1907, pp. 263 sqq.

is silent, the very stones cry out; the tomb of S. Peter was more eloquent than the men who called themselves the successors of the Prince of the Apostles.'[1]

Like Charles the Great, Otto saw the importance of securing for his own people the best culture of his time, and with less success and a vision less keen, he encouraged the efforts of German and Italian scholars. Like Charles, too, he made a tardy effort to learn the Latin tongue, and his brother Bruno, the Archbishop of Cologne, endeavoured to make the royal court a centre of liberal studies and intellectual intercourse.[2] But the cultivation of letters remained throughout the whole period of the Ottos an ecclesiastical and mainly monastic monopoly. The studies pursued at the great monasteries had a severely practical bent. At S. Gall, Reichenau, Fulda, Lorsch, or Gandersheim, the classical authors were read, but with hardly a trace of humanistic feeling. It is true that the court gave a welcome to foreign and especially to Italian scholars, such as Liutprand of Cremona, Ratherius of Verona, and Gunzo, the pedantic Novarese who excited the ridicule of his German hosts.[3]

Gerbert of Aurillac, who stands out above his contemporaries as a lover of classical letters, was recognized by the three Ottos as a man of genius whose talents were of the utmost value to Church and State. The most remarkable man of the tenth century was born of poor parents, somewhere in Auvergne, and received his early education from the Benedictines of Aurillac. A lucky chance took him to Christian Spain, where religious learning still flourished, and he made important mathematical studies. A journey to Rome brought him into contact with John XIII and Otto I. His learning won the admiration of all. Otto would not hear of his departure from Rome, and he appears to have employed him as tutor to his son, the young 'Augustus'. Next Gerbert is found at Reims, adding lustre to the episcopal school and superintending as *Scholasticus* a vast range of studies, among which the humanities were prominent. In 980, Otto II and Gerbert met at Ravenna, where the Emperor listened to a long and curious controversy between the French scholar and a rather pedantic professor of Magdeburg.[4] A few years later his

---

[1] *Deutsche Kaiserzeit*, i. 767.
[2] Bruno did not read the classics for their content, but for their language and style; see Eicken, *Mittelalterliche Welt-anschauung*, pp. 675-6; cf. also p. 591.

[3] Hauck, iii. 285 sqq.
[4] On the discussion between Gerbert and Otric see Picavet, *Gerbert*, pp. 143 sqq.

imperial patron nominated him Abbot of Bobbio, but after Otto's death he withdrew to the safer and calmer atmosphere of Reims, devoting himself to the collection of books and to studies which were limited only by the scientific range of the day.

But he was soon involved in the storm of French politics and he had a considerable share in the elevation of Hugh Capet to the throne of France. The part which he took in the deposition of the Archbishop of Reims, and his own irregular election as metropolitan of that important see, brought him into sharp conflict with the Papacy, and led to his excommunication. These troubles flung him into the arms of Otto III, for whom he had the warmest affection. He became the political adviser as well as the tutor of the young emperor, who was eager for knowledge of every kind. In a letter to Gerbert Otto ventured to transcribe some of his own verses in which the feeling is more obvious than the inspiration :

> versus nunquam composui
> nec in studio habui.
> dum in usu habuero
> et in eis viguero
> quot habet viros Gallia
> tot vobis mittam carmina.[1]

In 998 Otto rewarded Gerbert with the Archbishopric of Ravenna, and a year later the same influence raised him to the Papacy as Sylvester II. There at Rome, with the memorials and memories of the past, the old scholar and his youthful pupil, the two lords of the world, talked of the restoration of the Christian Empire and a new order of peace and religion. But death carried them both away, and the great Pope's memory survived only in a perverse and fantastic legend. Rehabilitated by history, he now appears as a humanist who sought after the learning of the ancient world with the ardour of a Renaissance scholar ; as a mathematician and astronomer who attempted to solve the riddles of nature ; as a man of high purposes and great political ideals—in short, as a rare genius in an age of darkness and confusion. But Gerbert's influence had been exercised mainly at Reims. His relations with the Ottos had been merely personal, and they were not competent to take the measure of his educational ideal.

---

[1] Quoted by Picavct, p. 105 ; see *Lettres de Gerbert*, ed. Julien Havet, Paris 1889, p. 172.

What seed of culture could be sown in Germany fell inevitably on ecclesiastical and especially on monastic soil.   Town
life beyond the Rhine had hardly begun; the nobles were
compelled to live for the arts of war; only in episcopal and
monastic centres was the study of letters provided for as a prime
necessity of life.   It is mainly to the monasteries that we must
look for the scanty literary productions of the time.

Widukind, a monk of Corvey, wrote a history of the Saxons,
Res gestae Saxonicae,[1] but he is almost a solitary figure in this field.
Latin verse still formed part of the exercises of the cathedral
and monastic schools, but the study of the classical poets was
not pursued with the same seriousness as in the age of Charles
the Great.   The composition of verses is now a painful task,
the observance of quantity is poor, the style and taste are
barbarous, and there is a growing fondness for the leonine rime.
The most important monastic productions of the time are the
liturgical sequences which were the glory of the school of
S. Gall.   These are reserved for fuller discussion in the following section, for they are the most important and the most
fruitful invention of the medieval Latin poets.   We have now
to describe in brief the series of versifiers who were connected with the school of S. Gall.   Their verses are for the
most part in classical metres, following the old Carolingian
tradition.   Ratpert (d. *circ.* 884), born at Zurich, lived at
S. Gall in the days of Grimald and Hartmut.   His verses,
mainly elegiac, show a love of the leonine rime, and are
obviously much-laboured productions of the school.[2]   His
Begrüssungshymnus in honour of Queen Richgard shows his
limitations and his merits, and may serve as an example of
the average S. Gall composition:[3]

> aurea lux terrae, dominatrix inclita, salve,
>   quae domibus nostris nunc benedicta venis.
> larga maneto tuis semper, clarissima, servis
>   qui tibi mente canunt carmen et ore ferunt.
> plus hodie solito radiat sol clarus in alto,
>   cumque, serena, venis, nubila cuncta teris.

---

[1] See Hauck, iii. 311; Ebert, iii. 428 sqq.
His ninth-century predecessors, like the
Poeta Saxo (*De Gestis Caroli Magni*)
and Abbo of S. Germain-des-Prés (*Bella
Parisiacae Urbis*), preferred to write their
history in verse. Texts of both in *M.G.H.,*
Poet. Kar., iv. i, pp. 1 sqq.

[2] Texts, ib., iv. i, pp. 321 sqq.; *Anal.
Hymn.* l, pp. 237 sqq.

[3] ib., p. 240.   He wrote in German
a poem on S. Gall, which we possess
only in the Latin version of Ekkehart IV.

floribus arva nitent, quia te nos visere cernunt,
    foetibus atque solum germinat omne bonum.
gloria magnificae rutilas celsissima Romae
    atque Italos radiis comis amoena tuis.

at tibi se famulam praebet Germania fidam
    saepius et facie te cupit aspicere.
Caesaris ipsa decus populorum corrigis actus
    pluribus et validis imperitans populis.
nunc sine fine vale, miserans et nostra tuere,
    sit tibi magna salus, laus, honor atque decus.

Waldrammus, another monk of S. Gall, wrote in a style which is indistinguishable from that of his contemporary Ratpert,[1] while Abbot Hartmann (d. 925) the younger was an equally laborious composer and, likewise, a lover of the leonine (one-syllabled) rime.[2]   A few lines from his hymn on the Innocents will show that he is no Prudentius:

salve, lactans exercitus,
flores sanctorum martyrum,
ad aram summi numinis
qui laeti semper luditis.

nos vos laudantes pueros
semper iuvate precibus,
vobiscum uti iugiter
possimus laeti psallere.

Ekkehart I (900 *circa*–973), Dean of S. Gall, is a figure of much greater importance.   Born of noble parents, he entered S. Gall in his boyhood and mastered his studies so well that he became a celebrated teacher.   He is described for us as 'natura et studio caritatis dulcedine plenus', and he appears to have won the affection of the monks for the sweetness of his character, as well as their admiration for his learning.   Under Abbot Craloh he became Dean, and when Craloh died (958) he was elected Abbot; but a fall from his horse rendered him lame, and he renounced his office.   Of his religious verses we possess at least one hymn and a group of sequences.   The

---

[1] *Anal. Hymn.* l, pp. 244 sqq.; *M.G.H.,*
Poet. Kar., iv. i, pp. 328 sqq.

[2] *Anal. Hymn.* l, pp. 250 sqq.; *M.G.H.,*
Poet. Kar., iv. i, pp. 317 sqq.

hymn is for the Festival of a martyr. It shows a mixture of rime and assonance :

o martyr aeterni patris,
invicte miles filii,
athleta fortis spiritus,
nobis fave poscentibus.

nunc ergo nobis quaesumus
praesens adesto comminus
omne impetrando commodum
et post perenne gaudium.

Christi crucem tu baiulas
Christoque confixus cruci,
iucunda spernens saeculi,
gaudes modo in regno dei.

praesta, pater piissime
patrique compar unice,
cum spiritu paraclito
in sempiterna saecula.

Ekkehart's claim to the authorship of the *Waltharius*,[1] a long hexameter poem, which he was supposed to have composed in his boyhood, is now contested. It is a stirring tale, based on German national legend, of adventure and battle in the days of Attila. The metrical and artistic skill displayed in this poem is remarkable, even if we believe that it was revised by another hand.[2] The narrative is full of life and the interest of the tale rarely flags. Modestly, at the end, the poet pleads for the indulgence of the reader.

The last words betray the monk:

haec quicumque leges stridenti ignosce cicadae,
raucellam nec adhuc vocem perpende, sed aevum,
utpote quae nidis nondum petit alta relictis.
haec est Waltharii poesis; vos salvet Iesus.

Throughout the poem, the leonine rime appears again and again, as indeed in most of the German metrical verse of the tenth century. In the anonymous *Ecbasis captivi*[3] which belongs to a later period, the leonine rime (mainly of one syllable) is a recurring feature. This strange allegory in which a monk, describing himself under the figure of a calf which has escaped from its mother, relates his adventures and misfortunes outside his monastery, is a 'beast-epic' in which lion and leopard, wolf and fox, nightingale and swan, all take their part. For our present purpose we have merely to note that, while it shows acquaintance with Horace, Virgil, and Prudentius, the

[1] Text of the *Waltharlied*, ed. K. Strecker, Berlin 1947.
[2] Ekkehart IV says in his *Casus S. Galli* that he corrected a life of 'Waltharius manu fortis' by Ekkehart I, but this may not be the Waltharius epic.
[3] Text, in Grimm and Schmeller, *Lat. Gedichte des X. und XI. Jahrh.*, Göttingen 1838, pp. 243 sqq.; also edited by Voigt, Strassburg 1875; see Ebert, iii. 276 sqq.

style is laboured, barbarous, and obscure, and far below that of the *Waltharius*.

A similar lack of metrical skill is apparent in the verses of Hrothswitha, the nun of Gandersheim, who is best known as the author of several dramas in rimed prose, a style of composition suggested to her by a rather unintelligent study of Terence.[1] Hrothswitha, who was of noble Saxon blood, was born about 935. She went to Gandersheim as a girl, and made her studies under Riccardis, whom she calls her *magistra*, and Gerberga, niece of Otto the Great. She studied the classical authors, especially the poets, and learned something about dialectic, music, and arithmetic. But she was taught to shun the enticements of the profane writers, and she rebukes those catholics who ' pro cultioris facundia sermonis gentilium vanitatem librorum utilitati praeferunt sacrarum scripturarum '.[2] Her comedies and her verse are written for edification : the former are of considerable interest, but the verses display the smallest degree of talent, though they must have cost much pains. Her series of Christian legends in leonine hexameters and elegiacs is dedicated to Gerberga. As a favourable specimen of her style, we may give part of the invocation to the Virgin with which the first poem, a life of Mary based on the Apocryphal Gospel of James, begins :

> unica spes mundi dominatrix inclita caeli
> 　sancta parens regis, lucida stella maris,
> quae parens mundo restaurasti pia virgo
> 　vitam, quam virgo perdiderat vetula !
> tu dignare tuae famulae clementer adesse
> 　Hrothsvithae votis carminulisque novis,
> quae tibi femineae studio famulante camoenae
> 　iam supplex modulis succino doctilicis,
> exoptans, nec summatim attingere saltim
> 　laudis particulam, virgo, tuae minimam,
> ortus atque tui primordia clara beati
> 　necnon regalem pangere progeniem.[3]

Hrothswitha attempted also the difficult task of setting forth in verse the deeds of Otto the Great, who appeared to her

---

[1] It is only fair to say, however, that she had no idea of rivalling the art of Terence (though she professes to write, *eodem dictationis genere*), but to provide a wholesome substitute for such dangerous reading ; cf. Strecker, *Hrotsvit von Gandersheim, Neue Jahrb.*, xii, 1903, p. 584.

[2] Works, ed. P. von Winterfeld, *Script. Rer. German.*, Berlin 1902, p. 106.

[3] Works, p. 5.

as a second David. Her narrative has often been examined by historians, but it adds little to our knowledge of the period.[1]

Enough has been said to show the comparative poverty of the metrical poetry of the tenth century, the poetry of the schools which was based on classical models. The knowledge of quantity is defective, and indeed the sense of style has almost gone. The need for some additional embellishment was supplied by rime, either one-syllabled leonine or tailed. Occasionally, that is to say by chance, the rime may be of two syllables, but it was not until the following century that the possibilities of the two-syllabled leonine and tailed rimes in the hexameter were fully realized.

There are other German poets of less importance who belong to the tenth century, but much of their verse is not definitely religious. Froumond of Tegernsee, who was born about 960, is a typical product of the German monastic schools. Like many another man of letters, he was a teacher and wrote verses for his scholars. He made a collection of letters and poems[2] which give a good picture of monastic life in Germany about A.D. 1000. Mingled with occasional verses, some of which display a sour humour,[3] are some religious pieces, compositions on biblical themes for school purposes. Such are the following lines, *In Crucifixo*: [4]

> germinis aeterni ramos hos vitis adornat,
> de qua fonte novo redduntur pocula mundo,
> dextera quem victrix invictaque brachia Christi
> amplexu rapuere pio de faucibus hostis,
> lividulus serpens peritura et tartara cernit
> et caput ignavum lutulenta et terrea lambit.

It was a monk of Tegernsee who, about 1050, composed the *Ruodlieb*, a wonderful romance in Latin verse,[5] which was once ascribed to Froumond, but is clearly not his work. Walther of Speier, towards the end of the tenth century, composed a life of S. Christopher in prose and verse,[6] and Ekkehart IV of S. Gall (b. *circ.* 980) wrote a *Liber Benedictionum*, religious

---

[1] Hrotswitha also composed a poem on the beginnings (*Primordia*) of the monastery at Gandesheim.

[2] He can now be studied in K. Strecker's edition, *Die Tegernseer Briefsammlung (Froumond)*, *M. G. H.*, *Epist. Select.* iii, Berlin 1925, with an excellent Introduction.

[3] Cf. the lines on p. 21 beginning: tempus enim nunc est, 'hu hu' quo dicimus omnes.

[4] p. 27. [5] Edited Seiler, Halle 1882; Manitius, *Gesch.* ii. 547.

[6] ib., p. 502; edited K. Strecker and N. Fickermann, *M.G.H., Poet. Lat. Med. Aevi*, v, pp. 10 sqq.

verses for school use.[1] But it would be a mistake to regard
the tenth century in Germany as a barren period so far as
religious verse is concerned. That century saw a new development of the *Sequence*, which was to lead to the most important
rhythmical invention of the Middle Ages, and this is the subject
of the following section.

§ 2. *The Origins of the Sequence.*

In the Mass, according to the Roman rite, there are inter-
posed between the Epistle and the Gospel, two chants, the
Gradual, and the Alleluia coupled with the verse of a psalm.
In the singing of the Alleluia, it was customary to prolong the
final *a*, in what was known as a *Jubilus*, a lengthy melody,
the singing of which required considerable musical skill. This
Jubilus or prolongation of the last syllable followed the melody
of the Alleluia, and is properly called a *Sequentia* or a Sequence.
Sequentia was therefore originally a musical term and could be
used indifferently with *melodia, neuma,* or *jubilus* to describe
the melody on the final *a* of the Alleluia. This melody was
itself divided into parts (*clausulae*) each of which could be termed
a *Sequentia*. The practice grew up, apparently in the eighth
century, of adapting a text or Prose to some of these divisions,[2]
but the Prose or Sequence proper began when a text was,
for the first time, set to the whole of the melody. The correct
description of such a production would be *Sequentia cum Prosa*
(i.e. a melody with a text). In France the term Prose was
employed, while in Germany the less correct and later designa-
tion of Sequence was used to describe the whole composition.

The question of the origin of the Sequence is beset with
difficulty. Wilhelm Meyer and Wagner, who observed the similarity between Western Sequences and Greek Troparia, argued
for a Byzantine origin;[3] but, in any case, the musical structure
of the Alleluia belongs to a type that was 'introduced from the
East, from the Churches of Syria and Palestine'.[4] The Roman
Church had shortened the Jubilus, but its original form was

[1] E. Dümmler, *Zeitschr. f. deutsch. Alt.*
ii, pp. 1 sqq.; J. Egli, *Der liber Benedictionum Ekkeharts IV*, S. Gallen 1909.
[2] See *Anal. Hymn.* xlix, pp. 515–30, for
examples; these are all English or French,
not one is German.

[3] E. Wellesz, *Eastern Elements in
Western Chant*, p. 156; W. Meyer, *Die
lateinischen Sequenzen*, in *Rythmik*,
ii. 94 sqq.; P. Wagner, *History of Plain-
Chant*, p. 223.
[4] Wellesz, p. 182.

preserved in the Ambrosian, Gallican, and Mozarabic spheres of influence, that is, in Churches which had conspicuous Eastern affinities. Now, from earliest times, in the East, in the Churches of Syria and Palestine, psalms and canticles were sung between the Epistle or Lesson and the Gospel, or after it, and in the Syrian Church there was the Memrâ, or poetical homily after the Gospel, a form of composition out of which, along with similar Syrian poetical compositions, the Mâdrâshâ and the Sôgithâ, came the Greek Kontakion in all its manifold splendour.[1]

It was, therefore, natural that the embellishment of the Mass in the West by the introduction of a new kind of hymn should take place between the Epistle and the Gospel, and it was to the long melisma of the Alleluia that, by gradual process, words were added until a composition resulted which was adapted to the whole of the melody.

It used to be supposed that the invention of Sequences or Proses was due to Notker Balbulus (*circa* 840–912), a monk of S. Gall, who passed his whole life in that famous cloister under the rule of two illustrious pupils of Raban Maur, Grimald and Hartmut. Notker himself is a figure of such importance and interest that we must say something about the man and his reputation before dealing with the problem presented by his Sequences. He owed a good deal to two masters, Iso, who made a commentary on Prudentius, and Moengal (known as Marcellus), an Irishman who had been Abbot of Bangor. In spite of a defect in speech, Notker was for long years a teacher in the school at S. Gall, and generations of scholars passed through his hands. He was listened to with fear and fascination, for he joined to his learning and to his accomplishments in poetry and in music a rough German humour and an endless store of reminiscence. He composed a life of S. Gall in the form of a dialogue, the *personae* of which were Hartmann, Ratpert, and himself. The surviving fragments and Notker's own account indicate that it was a mixture of verse and prose.[2] He busied himself also with a martyrology and with musical theory, with poetical riddles, and with hymns and occasional verses, including a poem on the free arts. But one of his most important works is the *Gesta Karoli*, a prose account, in his gossiping manner, of the deeds of his hero Charles. 'Balbus et edentulus', he

[1] Wellesz, *Byzantine Music and Hymnography*, pp. 157 sqq. and the literature there mentioned.

[2] Text, ed. Strecker, *M. G. H.*, *Poet. Kar.* iv, pp. 1093 sqq.

calls himself,[1] in this rambling collection of anecdotes, marked by the garrulousness of age and a love for a good story especially when it is told at the expense of a Frankish bishop. He wrote for the amusement of Charles the Fat, and had no care for accuracy or even for probability; he was rendering into Latin the beginnings of the legend of Charlemagne as it was being told in the German of the common people.

The story of the manner in which Notker came to compose his Sequences is told in the *Prooemium* to the *Liber Hymnorum Notkeri*,[2] which purports to be addressed by Notker to Liutward, Bishop of Vercelli, and Chancellor of Charles the Fat. The substance of the letter is as follows. In his boyhood Notker had found it hard to commit to memory the long melodies in, which the *a* of the Alleluia was prolonged, and he had often desired to find some means of aiding his 'unstable little memory' (*instabile corculum*). One day a monk appeared at S. Gall from Jumièges, after the sack of his monastery by the Northmen (A. D. 851). He brought with him an Antiphonary in which verses were, apparently, set to an Alleluia-Jubilus, but to Notker the verses were crude and unsatisfactory. 'Quorum ut visu delectatus, ita sum gustu amaricatus', he says. He set to work to write a Sequence in imitation,[3] but his master Iso told him that each syllable ought to correspond to a note of the melody. So he tried again, and produced the *Psallat Ecclesia, mater illibata*, a prose for dedication of a church:

1. psallat ecclesia,
   mater illibata
   et virgo sine ruga,
   honorem huius ecclesiae.

2. haec domus aulae
   caelestis
   probatur particeps

3. in laude regis
   caelorum
   et ceremoniis

4. et lumine continuo
   aemulans
   civitatem sine tenebris

5. et corpora in gremio
   confovens
   animarum, quae in caelo vivunt.

6. quam dextra protegat dei

7. ad laudem ipsius diu!

---

[1] *Gesta Karoli*, ii. 7 (ed. Jaffé, *Bibl. rerum German.* iv).

[2] Text, Migne, cxxxi, col. 1003; *Anal.*

Hymn. liii, Introd.

[3] The *Laudes Deo concinat orbis*; text, *Anal. Hymn.* liii, p. 93.

8. hic novam prolem
   gratia parturit
   fecunda spiritu sancto;

9. angeli cives
   visitant hic suos,
   et corpus sumitur Iesu;

10. fugiunt universa
    corpori nocua;

11. pereunt peccatricis
    animae crimina;

12. hic vox laetitiae
    personat;

13. hic pax et gaudia
    redundant;

14. hac domo trinitati
    laus et gloria
    semper resultant.[1]

Now it is clear from this account that Notker himself makes no claim to be the inventor of Sequences. He got the impulse from the Antiphonary of the monk of Jumièges; both he and his master Iso were clearly familiar with this kind of composition, and Iso, at any rate, knew its rules and was able to put Notker on to the right lines.[2]

Where, then, must we look for the origins of the Sequence? Dreves tried to establish the claim of S. Martial of Limoges, but without success. J. Handschin[3] mentions, with great reservations, the possibility of an English origin, but it is not practicable as yet to arrive at any reliable conclusions. What is certain is that by Notker's time the composition of Sequences on French soil had already reached an advanced stage, especially at such centres as Luxeuil, Fleury, and Moissac.

The older French Sequences begin with the Alleluia and all the verses often end in *a*, while in the S. Gall Sequences there is no sign of this close relation of the text to the final syllable of the Alleluia, but assonance and rhythm appear, sure signs of a later date. In the French Sequences, the words are set to the melody of the Jubilus, whereas in the S. Gall Sequences the first strophes are set to the melody of the Alleluia.[4]

From what has been said, it will be clear that, in considering the origin of the Sequence, it is necessary to begin with the Alleluia-Jubilus, and Blume held that the phrase *versus ad sequentias*

---

[1] ib., p. 398.
[2] Wellesz, *Eastern Elements*, p. 158, points out that Notker saw in the Sequence or Sequences in the Jumièges book an older model which was out of date; see also W. von den Steinen, *Die Anfänge der Sequenzendichtung, Zeitschr. f. schweiz. Kirchengesch.* i (1946), pp. 195 sqq.
[3] *The Two Winchester Tropers, J. T. S.* xxxvii (1936), pp. 34 sqq.; 156 sqq.; cf. p. 48.
[4] Wellesz, *Eastern Elements*, p. 161.

used by Notker, described a penultimate stage in its development.[1]
The final stage is reached when verses are adapted to the whole
melody. The original Sequences, therefore, were texts or proses
fixed to an existing melody. This melody was divided into
parts, which (except, in most cases, the first and last) were
repeated by alternate choirs usually of men and boys. So the
structure of the text was bound to follow the structure of the
melody, and the text was, in fact, a piece of unrhythmical prose,
written, as a rule, in corresponding double strophes of equal length.

The following is an early Sequence of the French type, in
which the *a* ending is conspicuous. The text begins with the
Alleluia, whereas the Notkerian Sequences show a developed
stage in which the first strophe merely follows the Alleluia.

Alleluia

1. qui regis sceptra
    forti dextra
    solus cuncta,

2. tu plebi tuam
    ostende magnam
    excitando potentiam;

3. praesta dona illi salutaria.

4. quem praedixerunt prophetica
    vaticinia,
    a clara poli regia
    in nostra,
    Iesu, veni, domine, arva.[2]

In this example the strophes of the melody were not repeated,
and hence there is no parallelism of the strophes of the text, but
in other cases repetition occurs in the melody involving a similar
repetition in the text. It is probable that sequences without
parallel strophes represent an earlier stage in the development
of the Sequence, and, if this is so, the priority of France is once
more evident.

The detailed study of Notker's Sequences now rests upon the
work of Prof. Wolfram von den Steinen.[3] He discusses what he
considers to be the genuinely pre-Notkerian Sequences, fourteen
in number, a mixed collection in all respects as chance has
preserved them.[4] These Sequences take us back mostly to
France, and we are asked to distinguish between 'lyrical Sequences', less liturgical in character, and liturgical Sequences proper.[5]
A remarkable example of the former is the *Stans a longe*[6] on the
subject of the publican in the Temple. The lyrical impulse is visible

---

[1] Cf. *Anal. Hymn.* liii, p. xxi; this stage
is that at which a text is attached to
certain parts of the melody.
[2] ib., p. 8.
[3] *Die Anfänge der Sequenzendichtung*,
Zeitschr. f. schweiz. Kirchengesch., i
(1946), pp. 190 sqq.; ii (1947), pp. 19 sqq.;

122 sqq.; and *Notker der Dichter*, 2 vols.,
Bern 1948.
[4] *Zeitschr. f. schweiz. Kirchengesch.*,
ii, p. 42 sq.   [5] ib., p. 139.
[6] *Anal. Hymn.* liii, p. 158. It dates
from 850 at the latest. There is also the
beautiful Swan-Lament, ib., vii, p. 253.

here, as it is in many of Notker's Sequences. But Prof. von den Steinen's great achievement is the reconstruction, after so many other attempts, of Notker's *Liber Hymnorum*, with a critical text and all the apparatus for the scholar's use. We can now fully realise Notker's genius and the extent of his achievement.

The tradition of the Sequence at S. Gall was continued by Ekkehart the Old, whose other poetical productions we have already discussed. His Sequences show no advance over Notker's, whose style they follow, except that assonance and rime are more frequent.[1] The Sequence on S. Columbanus is a good example of the German type with an independent strophe at the beginning and the end.

1. a solis occasu
usque ad exortum

2. est cunctis nomen tuum, deus, laudabile,	3. qui inde novum solem mittis mira lege,
4. qui lustret orbem radiis	5. et foetu terras vegetet.
6. hic Columbanus nomine columbinae vitae fuit,	7. dignus habere spiritus sancti pignus in hac vita.
8. hic terram cum Abraham reliquit et cognatos propter deum.	9. hic cum Iohanne regis incestum increpare non metuit.
10. huic partum dat deus in deserto cum Moyse.	11. huic caelum obsequi est paratum cum Iosue.
12. hic feras mansuefacit et corvos ut Elias et Daniel.	13. hic persecutiones cum apostolis Christi perpetitur.
14. huic ipse veritatis hostis nutu dei	15. testatur, quod hic veritatis cultor foret.

16. nos ergo tete poscimus,
beate, quo nos domino
tu commendes.[2]

The introduction of these Sequences added much to the beauty of the services. 'The melodies', says Prof. Wagner,[3] 'exhibit a taste for imposing and sonorous strains, boldness in

---

[1] ib., l, pp. 272 sqq.   [2] ib., p. 274.   [3] *History of Plain-Chant*, p. 231.

melodic development, the frequent occurrence of wide intervals, and an extended compass, such as was made possible by the use of boys. In consequence, the Sequences often extend to a pitch which men's voices cannot reach. All such features are foreign to the older liturgical chants of the Latin Church, especially to the choral chants.' These earlier Sequences owed much of their beauty and impressiveness to the melody, but in some of them, as in the famous Alleluiatic Sequence, a German composition of the tenth century, the text itself has a measure of independent merit.[1]

1. cantemus cuncti melodum
    nunc *Alleluia.*

2. in laudibus aeterni regis
    haec plebs resultet
    Alleluia.

3. hoc denique caelestes chori
    cantant in altum
    Alleluia.

4. hoc beatorum
    per prata paradisiaca
    psallat concentus
    Alleluia.

5. quin et astrorum
    micantia luminaria
    iubilant altum
    Alleluia.

6. nubium cursus,
    ventorum volatus,
    fulgurum coruscatio
    et tonitruum sonitus
    dulce consonent simul
    Alleluia.

7. fluctus et undae,
    imber et procellae,
    tempestas et serenitas,
    cauma, gelu, nix, pruinae,
    saltus, nemora pangant
    Alleluia.

8. hinc, variae volucres,
    creatorem
    laudibus concinite cum
    Alleluia;

9. ast illinc respondeant
    voces altae
    diversarum bestiarum
    Alleluia.

10. istinc montium
     celsi vertices sonent
     Alleluia;

11. illinc vallium
     profunditates saltent
     Alleluia.

12. tu quoque, maris
     iubilans abysse, dic
     Alleluia,

13. necnon terrarum
     molis immensitates:
     Alleluia.

14. nunc omne genus
     humanum laudans exsultet
     Alleluia.

15. et creatori
     grates frequentans consonet
     Alleluia.

[1] *Anal. Hymn.* liii, p. 60. I would draw attention, however, to W. Meyer's remark in *Fragmenta Burana*, p. 37: ' Notker's Sequenz [en] würdigt man nicht richtig, wenn man die hohe rhetorische Ausdrucksweise nicht verücksichtigt'. This remark applies also to the earlier Sequences in general.

16. hoc denique nomen audire
    iugiter delectatur
    Alleluia.

17. hoc etiam carmen caeleste
    comprobat ipse Christus
    Alleluia.

18. nunc vos, o socii,
    cantate laetantes
    Alleluia,

19. et vos pueruli,
    respondete semper
    Alleluia.

20. nunc omnes canite simul
    Alleluia domino,
    Alleluia Christo
    pneumatique *Alleluia.*

21. laus trinitati aeternae:
    Alleluia, Alleluia,
    Alleluia, Alleluia,
    Alleluia, Alleluia.

Here the whole Sequence is constructed in parallel form except for the opening strophe, but there is no independent final strophe as in the *Psallat Ecclesia* which has been quoted above, and together with the *A solis occasu* may serve as an example of the normal German type.

While Proses continued to be adapted to already existing melodies, it was not possible for any advance to be made in the direction of artistic form. But, when once the text and melody were composed together, the Prose tended to become the determinant part of the production, and the development of a rhythmical form based on accent easily followed. To rhythm was added assonance and then rime. Delivered from the bondage imposed by a pre-existing melody, the Prose was free to assume a regular poetical form, with a rhythmical structure and, ultimately, a fully developed system of rime.

The eleventh century saw the transition from the earlier or Notkerian type of Sequence to the regular Sequence of the twelfth century. An example of the transitional type in which an occasional rime occurs, though the structure of the Sequence is Notkerian, is the famous *Victimae Paschali*,[1] which tradition assigns to Wipo (d. 1050), a Burgundian or perhaps a Swabian, priest and chaplain to the Emperors Conrad II and Henry III.

1. victimae paschali laudes
   immolent Christiani.

2. agnus redemit oves,
   Christus innocens patri
   reconciliavit
   peccatores.

3. mors et vita duello
   conflixere mirando,
   dux vitae mortuus
   regnat vivus:

[1] Text in *Anal. Hymn.* liv, pp. 12–3; p. vi of Introduction for observations on its structure; see also Meyer, *Fragmenta Burana*, pp. 49 and 76, for the relation of this Sequence to the Liturgical Drama.

4. dic nobis Maria
   quid vidisti in via?
   sepulchrum Christi viventis
   et gloriam vidi resurgentis.

5. angelicos testes
   sudarium et vestes.
   surrexit Christus spes mea
   praecedet suos in Galilaea.

6. credendum est magis
   Mariae veraci
   quam Iudaeorum turbae fallaci.

7. scimus Christum surrexisse
   a mortuis vere,
   tu nobis, victor rex, miserere!

In two Processionals of the fourteenth century, belonging to the Church of S. John the Evangelist, Dublin, this Sequence appears as a dramatic finale to a dialogue, which was sung at Easter to represent the scene of the visits to the empty tomb.[1] Its great popularity in succeeding centuries led to several imitations, notably to one (ascribed to Adam of S. Victor) in a Sequence in honour of that saint, which was sung at Easter. The refrain is:

> dic, in agonia—quid vidisti, athleta?

In another Sequence, in honour of the Virgin, the refrain runs:

> dic nobis, Maria—virgo clemens et pia,—
> —quomodo facta es genetrix.[2]

The *Victimae Paschali* was deprived of its sixth strophe when the Roman Missal was revised in the sixteenth century.

Wipo was a person of some importance and of considerable learning.[3] His life of the Emperor Conrad II shows that he had read the old historians Sallust, Suetonius, and Sulpicius Severus, and he was acquainted with the poets Horace, Lucan, Ovid, Persius, Statius, and, of course, Virgil. Along with the Easter Sequence, a few of his other verses have survived. His collection of *Proverbia*,[4] with constant use of rime, as in

> qui per ardua vadit, saepissime cadit,

and

> viri mites renuunt lites,

was very popular. The lament on the death of Conrad shows the same fondness for the two-syllabled rime which also appears in the Sequence:

---

[1] Frere, *Winchester Troper*, p. xvii; the dialogue is as described below, pp. 221–2.

[2] Adam of S. Victor, sequences lviii and xci; cf. *Anal. Hymn.* liv, pp. 27 sqq.

[3] See Manitius, *Gesch.* ii, pp. 318 sqq.; H. Bresslau, *Die Werke Wipos, Script. Rer. German.*, Hanover and Leipzig 1915, Introd.

[4] *Werke*, pp. 66 sqq.

qui vocem habet serenam,   hanc profert cantilenam
de anno lamentabili   et damno ineffabili,
pro quo dolet omnis homo   forinsecus et in domo.[1]

Lastly, the *Tetralogus*,[2] which Wipo presented to Henry III[3] at Strassburg in 1024, is a dialogue in which the Emperor is praised, and is exhorted to encourage the legal studies of the German youth, and also to restore peace in Burgundy. The hexameters are correct, but more than half are rimed.

§ 3. *Tropes.*

The addition of Sequences to the liturgy was not the only attempt made in the later Carolingian times to adorn the services of the Church. Another form of composition, known as the Trope, is also associated traditionally with S. Gall and with the age of Notker; although the available evidence tends to show that, as with the Sequence, its origin must rather be sought in France. A Trope has been defined by Léon Gautier as 'l'interpolation d'un texte liturgique',[4] but it is better to attempt a more comprehensive definition, and say that a Trope is a text which is employed (with the accompaniment of music) as introduction, intercalation, or addition to a portion of the liturgy, such as the Introit, the Kyrie, the Gloria, &c.[5] It is not advisable to class the Prose or Sequence as a kind of Trope, since it is of the essence of the latter that it is bound to a liturgical text whose meaning it either completes or expands by way of commentary. An example will make this definition clear. It is a Trope to the Kyrie, which is found in S. Gall manuscripts of the tenth century:[6]

---

[1] ib., pp. 60 sqq.   [2] ib., pp. 76 sqq.
[3] The monk Arnulf, probably of French birth, was also connected with the court circle of Henry III. He dedicated to the Emperor and his wife Agnes a poem called *Delicie cleri*, which consists mainly of versified proverbs from the Wisdom books of the Old Testament, including Ben Sirach, as well as from classical sources. Like Wipo, Arnulf loved the leonine rime, and the dialogue form, for he concludes his poem with a dialogue between himself, the poet, and his book.

Text of *Delicie cleri*, ed J. Huemer, *Zur Geschichte der mittellateinischen Dichtung, Arnulfi delicie cleri, Romanische Forschungen*, ii (1886), pp. 211 sqq.; see also Manitius, *Gesch.* ii. 588 sqq.

[4] *Histoire de la poésie liturgique au moyen âge. Les tropes*, p. 1.

[5] Cf. Gerbertus, *De Cantu et musica sacra*, S. Blasien, 1774, i. 340, 'Tropus in re liturgica est versiculus quidam, aut etiam plures, ante, inter, vel post alios ecclesiasticos cantus appositi'.

[6] *Anal. Hymn.* xlvii, p. 48 sq.

omnipotens genitor lumenque et lucis origo,
de nihilo iussu verbi qui cuncta creasti,
humano generi, peccati pondere presso,
    kyrie eleison.

ad caenum terrae missus genitoris ab arce
indueras carnem, casta de virgine natus,
et mundi culpam mundasti sanguine fuso;
    Christe eleison.

aequalis patri seu nato, spiritus almus,
trinus personis, deus, in deitate sed unus,
    kyrie eleison.

Gautier and others have seen fit to ascribe this Trope to Tutilo or Tuotilo, the friend of Notker. Ekkehart IV, in *Casus S. Galli*,[1] does indeed tell us that Tutilo composed the Tropes *Hodie cantandus* and *Omnium virtutum gemmis*, and presented them to Charles III, who, when Tutilo had also composed the *Viri Galilei*, urged him ' to add verses which were, it is said, "Quoniam dominus Iesus Christus cum esset; omnipotens genitor, fons et origo", with the following: "gaudete et cantate", and others as well'. But the Trope referred to by Ekkehart is quite different from the Trope which we have quoted, and there is no reason to ascribe the latter to Tutilo. Neither can we accept the view that he is to be regarded as the inventor of Tropes, for a study of the manuscripts shows that S. Gall appears with comparative infrequency as a source, and then usually at as late a date as the thirteenth century.[2] On the other hand, the oldest Tropers of France and England provide rich material, and North Italy also followed the fashion. The German development was less plentiful, but Middle and South Italy contributed their share; in the thirteenth century Tropes became less popular, and they died a gradual death.

The oldest French Troper which has survived, that of S. Martial at Limoges (middle of the tenth century), contains no Kyrie-tropes, and no Sequences, but has a number of Tropes for the Gloria, the Introit, Gradual, Offertory, and Communion. As, therefore, Tropes were so well known in France, and as the Antiphonary of Jumièges, which the monk brought to S. Gall,[3] contained at any rate Alleluia-tropes, is it likely that Tutilo was the first to conceive the idea of 'troping' other texts of the liturgy? This is the question put by the editors of the forty-

---

[1] iii. 46.   [2] *Anal. Hymn.* xlvii, p. 16.
[3] See above, p. 211.

seventh volume of *Analecta Hymnica*,[1] and they consider that
the probabilities are against an affirmative answer.   Unfortunately there is nothing to show whether the Jumièges Antiphonary contained Tropes to the Introit, the Kyrie, &c.   If
Tutilo had invented such Tropes before the monk arrived, why
did not Notker get at an earlier date the impulse for his Sequences? It is quite clear that both Notker and Tutilo had French
predecessors, and it is a tempting suggestion that Tutilo found
in the Norman Antiphonary some Tropes at least to the Introit.
In any case, the *Hodie cantandus*, a S. Gall Trope (whether or
no Ekkehart is right in ascribing it to Tutilo), belongs to the
Introit,[2] and its dramatic form gives it a great interest, as it
affords a glimpse of an early stage in the growth of the religious
drama.   It will be seen that it forms rather an introduction to
the Introit than a Trope proper.

> 1. hodie cantandus est nobis puer,
>   quem gignebat ineffabiliter ante tempora pater,
>   et eundem sub tempore generavit inclita mater.

> 2. *Interrogant:*   3. *Respondent:*
>   quis est iste puer,   hic enim est,
>   quem tam magnis praeconiis   quem praesagus et electus
>   dignum vociferatis?   symmista dei ad terras
>   dicite nobis,   venturum praevidens
>   ut collaudatores   longe ante praenotavit
>   esse possimus.   sicque praedixit:

> *puer natus est nobis et filius datus est nobis*, etc.

Still more dramatic is the Easter Trope, *Quem quaeritis in
sepulchro?*, the oldest manuscript of which comes from S. Martial
(*circa* 933–6);[3]

> 1. quem quaeritis in sepulchro,   2. Iesum Nazarenum crucifixum,
>   o christicolae?   o caelicolae.

> 3. non est hic;   4. alleluia, resurrexit dominus,
>   surrexit, sicut praedixerat.   hodie resurrexit leo fortis,
>   ite, nuntiate,   filius dei.
>   quia surrexit.   deo gratias: dicite, eia,

> *resurrexi et adhuc tecum*, etc.

---

[1] p. 17.

[2] *Anal. Hymn.* xlix, p. 7; the *Omnium virtutum gemmis* (S. Stephen's Day) is an Offertory-trope (ib., p. 283), but the *Omnipotens genitor fons et origo* (Easter) is an Introit-trope (see ib., xlvii, p. 50), as are the *Quoniam Dominus* (ib., xlix, p. 19), and the *Gaudete et Cantate*

(Clark, p. 195); though the *Omnipotens genitor* seems also to have been used as an Offertory-trope (Clark, p. 195).

[3] *Anal. Hymn.* xlix, p. 9; the group of German (among them S. Gall) manu-scripts omits strophe 4, and strophe 3 ends 'quia surrexit, dicentes', or 'sur-rexit de sepulchro'. The latter is perhaps

Here, as in Wipo's Easter Sequence, we can see how short the step is to the later Easter plays.   At Winchester[1] and in many other places the Trope formed the dialogue of the dramatic Easter ceremonial at Matins.   On Good Friday the cross was veiled, a representation of Christ in the tomb.   Then on Easter Sunday the cross was removed, and a monk wearing an alb and holding a palm branch in his hand sat by the side of the sepulchre. Three brethren approached, in copes and swinging censers, 'ad similitudinem querentium quid'.   The seated brother then took up the angel's part in the words of the Easter Trope, and the others gave the reply of the holy women.   At the end the angel sang *Venite et videte locum*, and, rising, removed the veil, which showed the empty tomb.[2]

So far we have given examples only of metrical and prose pieces, but it was inevitable that use should be made of rime, as in the following Kyrie-trope:[3]

> summe pater rerum, lumen super omnia verum,
>   eleison; *kyrie eleison.*
> omnia concludens, auctor per singula prudens,
>   eleison; *kyrie eleison.*   etc.

End-rimes and assonances also appear in lines of free construction, as in this Trope to the *Gloria*:[4]

> *gloria in excelsis deo et in terra pax*
> *hominibus bonae voluntatis.*

> 1.   o siderum rector,
>   angelorum creator.

> 2.

a. *laudamus te*	b. *adoramus te*
laude perenni,	trinum et unum,
celsa voce reboanti;	maiestate praecelsum:
benedicimus te	*glorificamus te*
sanctum	gloriosum
ac benedictum	ac venerandum
patrique coaeternum;	arva regentem et polum.

the oldest form of the Trope ; see K. Young, *Origin of the Easter Play, Modern Language Assoc. of America*, xxix, pp. 1 sqq.

[1] Frere, *Winchester Troper*, pp. xvi sqq.; Clark, p. 205.

[2] See *Anal. Hymn.* xlix, pp. 11 sqq. for examples which show how these Introit-tropes or introductions to the Introit led to independent dramatic pieces and plays.

[3] ib., xlvii, p. 123 sq.

[4] ib., xlvii, p. 250.

The Trope, like the Sequences, is the result of an attempt to find an outlet for the impulse to create new musical adornments for the liturgy without changing the sacred text. That text indeed, in the Roman rite, might seem somewhat cold or austere to ' the more . . . effusive or imaginative genius of the nations ' which had adopted it,[1] and they did succeed in introducing changes which gave it dramatic enrichment and endless variety. Rome sanctioned the changes, but, conservative as ever, imposed at last her final uniformity which brought an end to Tropes, and, as we have seen, abolished nearly all the Sequences.

§ 4. *Other Eleventh-century Sequences and Religious Verse.*

The general characteristics of eleventh-century verse in Germany show no change from those of the tenth. The metrical poetry bears the stamp of the monastic schools, and is of little interest. But the influence of the Sequence grew in attraction and power. The admiration which this new form of composition, linked inseparably with music, aroused in Germany and elsewhere is seen in the secular imitations in which love-themes and other popular subjects are set, in the manner of the Sequence, to already-existing melodies. In the *modus Otinc* [2] the three Ottos are celebrated, and there are several other patriotic pieces in a similar strain. More popular are the farcical pieces like the *mendosa cantilena* in the *modus florum*, which tell how a king gives his daughter in marriage to the man who tells the most successful lie, or the less respectable story in the *modus liebinc*, which relates :

> quomodo suevum mulier et ipse illam defraudaret.[3]

Henceforth, the popular Latin poetry of lyrics and folk-songs was to follow closely the development of the Sequence, until, in the twelfth century, it reached its full and perfect structure.

Among eleventh-century religious poets we have first to notice Heribert and Othloh. Heribert studied in the school of Würzburg, and in 1021 became Bishop of Eichstädt. Of him a contemporary says, ' egregia dictandi dulcedine in tantum enituit, ut tunc temporis hac in arte nulli secundus fuerit'.[4]

---

[1] E. Bishop, *Liturgica Historica*, p. 16.
[2] Text in *The Cambridge Songs*, ed. Breul, Cambridge, 1915, pp. 49 sqq.; also in *Carmina Cantabrigiensia*, ed. Strecker, (*M. G. H.*; Berlin, 1926), pp. 33 sqq.

[3] *Cambridge Songs*, p. 56; *Carmina Cantabrigiensia*, p. 41 ; Meyer, *Rythmik*, i. 44–5 ; *Fragmenta Burana*, p. 175.
[4] *Anal. Hymn.* l, p. 290.

He was fond of rhythmical verse with assonance and rime, but the few hymns of his composition which remain give no impression of skill or inspiration. Yet his contemporaries appear to have admired verses like the following :

> deus, deorum domine,
> rex sempiternae gloriae,
> rex invictorum militum,
> carmen exaudi supplicum.

Othloh of S. Emmeram (*circa* 1010–72) shows hardly more ability as a poet, but his life of Boniface and other biographies are of some importance to the historian.[1] He preferred the classical metres in his verse, above all the hexameter and the sapphic, but in the former he could not dispense with the then popular leonine rime. In some lines on the Resurrection he expands, in a curious exercise of imitation, the *Victimae Paschali* of Wipo :

> agnos exemit exinde suosque redemit,
> nos miseros vero simili pietate supremo
> patri placavit, miserando reconciliavit.
> mors contra vitam pugnam confert inimicam,
> dux regnat vitae vivus mortis sine lite.
> dic, dic ergo pia nobis dulcisque Maria,
> quid vidisti flens prope tumbam quando stetisti ?
> angelicos testes, sudaria, lintea, vestes.
> unica spesque mea surrexit et hoc Gallilaea
> approbat, est visus ibi nam multis redimendus.
> an vis Iudaee tibi credamusve Mariae ?
> illius sanis verbis tu falsificaris.
> qui vivis vere, tu nobis, rex, miserere.[2]

With Gottschalk of Limburg (b. *circa* 1010; d. 1098) we reach a composer of some originality and power. Little is known about the circumstances of his life beyond the fact that he was a monk of Limburg who became Provost of Aachen and Court Chaplain to the Emperor Henry III. He was learned in theology, and had some considerable acquaintance with the Latin classics. His book of Proses was dedicated to Henry IV. Though holding fast to the Notkerian tradition, Gottschalk at times succeeds in making his inspiration breathe through the difficult material with which he has to work. To a modern writer he appears as a 'poet of tenderness and mysticism', and 'an inveterate dreamer who relates after the Gradual the divine

---

[1] Hauck, iii. 938 sq.   [2] *Anal. Hymn.* l, p. 325.

dreams which have visited his hours of meditation '.[1] However this may be, there is a certain tenderness in his description of the pity of Christ for the Magdalene :

> pedes amplectitur
> dominicos,
> lacrimis lavat,
> tergit crinibus
> lavanda,
> tergenda,
> unguento unxit,
> osculis circuit.
>
> haec sunt convivia,
> quae tibi placent,
> o patris sapientia,
>
> natus de virgine
> qui non dedignaris
> tangi de peccatrice.
>
> a pharisaeo
> es invitatus
> Mariae ferculis
> satiatus.[2]

Occasional rime and use of assonance are features of the Proses of Gottschalk. In some instances, as in the quotation just given, the rime is two-syllabled, but never does he carry his assonance throughout a Prose on a single vocable.[3] Gottschalk, therefore, remains true to the S. Gall tradition. He did not possess the genius of Notker, neither did he make experiments of his own.

Herimannus Contractus (1013–54),[4] a contemporary of Gottschalk, and a monk of Reichenau, was also a composer of Sequences. Of noble birth, he went to the cloister school of Reichenau, and ended by becoming a monk. He was a cripple, who passed a life of pain and trial, and though he could hardly raise his voice above a whisper, he was able to make his mark as a teacher and a man of universal learning. He is the author of the *Chronicon Augiense*, and he pursued mathematical and astronomical studies. His Sequences followed the tradition of Notker, except that they appear to possess a more rhythmical

[1] Remy de Gourmont, *Le latin mystique*, p. 122.
[2] *Anal. Hymn.* l, p. 347.
[3] See Dreves, *Gottschalk Mönch von*
Limburg, p. 37.
[4] *Anal. Hymn.* l, p. 308 ; Hauck, iii. 943 sq.

character. Rime and assonance are characteristic features, and he loves to introduce Greek words, as in the Prose *De Sancta Cruce* :

1. grates, honos,
   hierarchia
   et euphonizans tibi
   interminabiliter
   hymnologia,

2. sacrosancta
   tu patris hostia,
   Iesu Christe, rex monarchos,
   omnium antistes et
   εὐλογούμενε.[1]

It has been usual to ascribe to Hermann two splendid antiphons in honour of the Virgin, which have found a place in the Roman Office. The *Alma redemptoris* borrows some of its phrases from that lovely early hymn on the Annunciation :

ave, maris stella,
dei mater alma
atque semper virgo,
felix caeli porta.

sumens illud Ave
Gabrielis ore,
funda nos in pace
mutans nomen Evae.[2]

The *Alma redemptoris* is sung at the end of Compline during Advent and Christmas :

alma redemptoris mater, quae pervia caeli
porta manes et stella maris, succurre cadenti,
surgere qui curat, populo, tu quae genuisti
natura mirante tuum sanctum genitorem,
virgo prius ac posterius, Gabrielis ab ore
sumens illud Ave, peccatorum miserere.[3]

The other antiphon, the *Salve Regina*, is of equal beauty :

salve, regina misericordiae,
vita, dulcedo et spes nostra, salve!
ad te clamamus exsules filii Evae,
ad te suspiramus gementes et flentes
in hac lacrimarum valle.
eia ergo, advocata nostra,
illos tuos misericordes oculos ad nos converte
et Iesum, benedictum fructum ventris tui,
nobis post hoc exsilium ostende,
o clemens, o pia,
o dulcis Maria.[4]

---

[1] *Anal. Hymn.* l, p. 310; Gottschalk of Limburg vouches for Hermann's authorship of this Sequence; see Dreves, *Gottschalk von Limburg*, p. 105.

[2] *Anal. Hymn.* li, p. 140; note on p. 142.
[3] ib., l, p. 317.
[4] ib., l, p. 318.

There is not, however, sufficient evidence to prove that Hermann is the author of either of these antiphons.[1] Jacobus de Voragine, in the *Golden Legend*, says that Hermann composed the *Alma redemptoris* and Bishop Peter of Compostella the *Salve Regina*. But his evidence is worthless. The author of the *Alma redemptoris* remains unknown; as for the *Salve Regina*, J. de Valois has shown that the piece goes back to the eleventh century,[2] and is associated with Le Puy in France. Further, Alberic of Trois-Fontaines[3] says explicitly, ' It was called the antiphon of Le Puy (de Podio), because Aimar, Bishop of Le Puy, composed it '.[4] It is highly probable, therefore, that Aimar is the author, and it is clear, in any case, that it is to Le Puy rather than to Reichenau that we must look for the origin of the antiphon.

There is an office of S. Afra, which may, however, be Hermann's. It is in prose, with the exception of the following *Responsorium* : [5]

> *R.* martyr sancta dei, quae flagrans igne fidei
> flammas sprevisti tortorum, victima Christi,
> que foedant mores, precibus restingue calores,
> *V.* crescat ut in nobis divini fervor amoris.

It will be observed that the leonine rime, which was so popular in the eleventh century, is used.

There is a long poem, *De octo vitiis principalibus*, which is certainly Hermann's. It seems that he continued it in a *liber de virtutibus*, which has not survived. The poem is addressed to nuns, and by making Melpomene his *Sprecherin* he is able to speak plainly on the disorders and dangers of convent life.[6] First, Hermann invokes the Muse in trochaic tetrameters :

> musa mi dilecta, surge, dulce quiddam concine,
> carmen, oro, pange metro seu canore rithmico,
> mulce et odis, queso, caras, cara, mis sororculas.

---

[1] See J. de Valois, *En marge d'une antienne—Le ' Salve Regina* '; Manitius, *Gesch.* ii. 777.

[2] Op. cit., p. 48.

[3] 1130; Alberic wrote in the early thirteenth century, and seems to reflect a twelfth-century tradition, op. cit., p. 57.

[4] ib., p. 56 ; Aimar was born *circa* 1050,

and took possession of his see in 1087.

[5] *Anal. Hymn.* l, p. 319; a twelfth-century manuscript of Reichenau ascribes it to Hermann.

[6] Text, ed. Dümmler,*Zeitschr. f. deutsch. Alt.*, xiii, pp. 385 sqq.; see Manitius, *Gesch.* ii. 767.

The Muse replies in adonics :

mene vocari	Melpomene assum.
auribus hausi ?	carmina possum,
anne et amicum	raucida quamvis
mis Herimannum?	uoce loquar vix.
en tua certe,	dic modo, quae vis
frater amate,	psallier ollis.

Then the Muse addresses the sisters, and they the Muse, who in turn speaks to Hermann, and Hermann replies. At last the poem gets under way, when the Muse begins, in iambic dimeters, her *Carmen exhortatorium ad sorores de contemptu mundi*. The nuns are admonished concerning the fragility of this life and the vanity of human praise and glory. The transitoriness of human pleasure is demonstrated ; death is certain, and after the death of the body may follow the death of the soul. The snares of the devil and the seven deadly sins are expounded, and the homily ends with an account of the present joy of the wicked and their eternal torment hereafter.

The immense number of medieval Sequences which have survived gives some idea of the popularity of this form of liturgical composition. The production of Sequences received a great impetus through the increasing interest in music, and the greater technical knowledge of a subject which now possessed a recognized place among the Seven Arts.[1] We have already seen how the vogue of the Sequence at S. Gall was intimately related to musical studies. Elsewhere, especially in France, the musical art made progress ; at S. Amand, Hucbald (b. 840), the monk who sang the praise of baldness for Hatto, Archbishop of Mainz,[2] wrote treatises on music, and similar studies went on at Cluny under the famous Odo (879–943). But the fixing of the music of Mass and Offices according to the Gregorian tradition had left open but few avenues for new developments. One of these, however, was afforded by the Sequence, and the popularity of Proses was due to a great extent to the growing interest in musical composition.[3] We have seen that the Sequence had its beginnings in France, and it was there that it was finally, in the eleventh and twelfth centuries, brought to its full perfection. In Germany, the Notkerian tradition stifled its development, and it never advanced beyond more or less

---

[1] Cf. Ronca, *Cultura medievale e poesia latina in Italia nei secoli XI e XII*, i. 198.

[2] For Hucbald's poems see *M. G. H., Poet. Kar.* iv. i, pp. 265 sqq.

[3] Cf. Frere, *Winchester Troper*, p. vi.

rhythmical prose, with assonance and occasional rime. The 'metrical' or fully developed rhythmical Sequence, the most characteristic creation of the poets of the Latin Church, is the work of the French genius. As Dr. Frere remarks, 'all the great metrical sequences of the twelfth and thirteenth centuries are linked on to the French school, even if they do not actually spring from it'.[1]

In the eleventh century the use of Sequences was widely spread among the Churches of the West. France, Germany, England, and Italy welcomed them gladly, England inclining to the French, Italy rather to the German model. As the regular metrical Sequence evolved, it approximated more and more in its structure to a rhythmical hymn.

The output of Sequences continued throughout the Middle Ages, but their quality inevitably declined as they grew in number. The doom of the Sequence was sealed in the sixteenth century, and only four—the *Veni, sancte spiritus*, the *Victimae Paschali*, the *Lauda Sion Salvatorem*, and the *Dies Irae*—were retained in the Roman Missal of 1570. The *Stabat Mater* was not added until the eighteenth century.[2]

---

[1] ib., p xiii. As regards Germany, it is inevitable that the contribution of S. Gall should loom large, but as a recent writer remarks (J. M. Clark, *The Abbey of S. Gall*, p. 119), 'when the history of hymnology comes to be written . . ., justice will be done to such centres as Fulda and Cologne, and the contribution of S. Gall will be accurately circumscribed'.

[2] Frere, *Winchester Troper*, p. xxiii.

VIII

ITALIAN RELIGIOUS POETRY OF THE NINTH, TENTH, AND ELEVENTH CENTURIES

§ 1. *The Ninth and Tenth Centuries.*

AT the death of Gregory the Great Italy appeared to have lost for ever her proud supremacy as the mother of the arts and the leader of civilization. As time went on, the memory of the past became dim; the vast material monuments, which once expressed the luxury and splendour of imperial Rome, fell slowly into ruin before the eyes of men for whom they had neither beauty nor meaning. If, in the days of Fortunatus, Virgil was still declaimed in Trajan's forum, and the sub-deacon Arator found an audience in S. Pietro in Vincoli for his *De Actibus Apostolorum*, the barbarization of style and thought continued without a check, and such lay schools as survived the shock of the Lombard invasion served only to keep alive some scanty knowledge of the Latin language and literature. But while these schools remained, the position of culture could not be wholly desperate. As the Lombards began to establish themselves in firmer possession of their conquests, and deserted the Arian for the Catholic faith, the life of the cities became more settled; schools revived in Pavia, in Milan, and in Benevento.[1] Adalberga, the cultivated daughter of King Desiderius, lent her patronage to Paul the Deacon, and when in 787 Charles the Great visited Rome, he took back men of learning to adorn his court. The extent to which the Lombards had assimilated the language and culture of the Italian people is reflected in the careers of Paul the Deacon and Peter of Pisa, the chief representatives of Italian learning

---

[1] Giesebrecht, *Deutsche Kaiserzeit,* i. 348; Renan, *Mélanges religieux et his-toriques,* p. 328, says, referring to the con-tinuity of the Italian schools, 'Il n'y a pas eu de moyen âge pour l'Italie; il y a eu décadence de la civilisation ancienne, et renaissance de cette civilisation aux lieux mêmes où elle était tombée en poussière.'

at the court of the Frankish king.[1]   But the Carolingian renaissance produced no appreciable results in Italy.   There the level of culture was hardly raised, and Rome produced little beyond epitaphs in barbarous Latin, unworthy successors of the verses of Pope Damasus.[2]

During the ninth century Italy, like the rest of Western Europe, was involved in a succession of calamities.   The unstable empire of Charles the Great dissolved amid civil dissensions and external invasion.   Saracens, Moors, and Hungarians fell upon an almost defenceless population.   As in the days of the Lombard invasion, monasteries were sacked and cities went up in flames.   In 846 the Saracen fleet sailed up the Tiber.   The Church of S. Peter, outside the Aurelian city, and not yet protected by the Leonine walls, was violated, and its fabulous treasures were carried away.   Still, in the midst of the universal distress and gathering anarchy, the Emperor Lothair and successive Popes are found endeavouring to reconstitute the schools and restore the study of grammar and the all-but-forgotten liberal arts.[3]

The record of the tenth is a reproduction of that of the preceding century.   Roman learning reached its lowest point when the city and the Papacy were controlled by Theodora and Marozia, and John XIII, an illiterate youth, sat in the chair of Peter.   The scandal of Roman ignorance and barbarism was so notorious that it roused the indignation of a synod of Gallic bishops at Reims.[4]   The apostolic answer to their protest was an avowal of the charge of ignorance and an impudent reference to the foolishness of the Gospel.   The vicars of Peter would not have Plato, Virgil, or Terence for their masters, for 'ab initio mundi non elegit deus oratores et philosophos, sed illiteratos et rusticos'.

Of poetry at Rome in the tenth century there is little sign beyond the usual epitaphs and inscriptions ;[5] but a few poems have survived, which prove that poetical inspiration had not quite deserted Italian soil.   The verses of Liutprand of Cremona and the anonymous *Gesta Berengarii*[6] show a keen study of

---

[1] Cf. Giesebrecht, op. cit., i. 349.

[2] Gregorovius, ii. 412 ; Hörle, *Frühmittelalt. Mönchs- und Klerikerbildung in Italien*, p. 31.

[3] Gregorovius, iii. 138-9.

[4] ib., iii. 499.

[5] The lament for the ill-fated Crescentius

(given in Gregorovius, iii. 434) is of interest as showing a sporadic leonine rime ; for other epitaphs, see Gregorovius, *The Tombs of the Popes*, London 1903 ; *M. G. H., Poet. Kar.* iv. ii, pp. 1019 sqq.

[6] ib., iv. i, pp. 354 sqq.

the classical poets.　But, as Giesebrecht says, they share with the rest of the Italian literature of this age less of the imprint of a Christian civilization than of a degenerate return to antiquity. A curious pagan revival which appears to have manifested itself in an outburst of religious indifference, sensuality, and luxury, in a time when the very foundations of society were being shaken, is reflected in the story of a grammarian named Wilgard, who lived at Ravenna in the middle of the tenth century.　This Wilgard, who was excessively proud of his learning, was visited one night by three evil spirits in the guise of Virgil, Horace, and Juvenal, who promised him immortal fame for his service in keeping alive their name and memory among men.　Whereupon the grammarian's conceit grew until it passed all bounds, and when he began to teach that the words of the poets were to be believed in all things he was convicted of heresy and condemned.[1]　These secularized scholars, who were a product of the lay schools, were probably a fairly numerous class, and one of them no doubt was the author of the well-known love song *O admirabile Veneris idolum*, which belongs perhaps to the tenth century.[2]　Religious or semi-religious poetry is represented by two remarkable pieces which stand out far above the rest of the productions of the time.　The first, with its mixture of pagan and Christian allusion, of classical reminiscence and catholic piety,[3] is the work of a citizen of Modena who knew Virgil, and perhaps Livy, and, at the same time, regarded Christ and Mary and John as the true protectors of his city.　The song was composed in the later ninth or in the early tenth century, when the walls of the city had just been rebuilt, and the Hungarians were beginning their inroads.　It is an exhortation to the defenders of the city to stand firm and keep a sleepless watch : [4]

o tu, qui servas armis ista moenia,
noli dormire, moneo, sed vigila.
dum Hector vigil extitit in Troia,
non eam cepit fraudulenta Graecia.
prima quiete dormiente Troia
laxavit Synon fallax claustra perfida.

---

[1] See Comparetti, *Virgil in the Middle Ages*, p. 93; Giesebrecht, i. 357; the story is told by Radulf Glaber (Bouquet, *Recueil des historiens*, x. 23).

[2] Text in Traube, *O Roma Nobilis* (*Abh. d. Bayer. Akad.*, 1891), p. 301.
[3] Cf. Ebert, iii. 174.
[4] Text in *M. G. H., Poet. Kar.* iii, p. 703.

. . . nos adoremus celsa Christi numina :
illi canora demus nostra iubila.
illius magna fisi sub custodia
haec vigilantes iubilemus carmina.
divina, mundi rex Christe, custodia,
sub tua serva haec castra vigilia

. . . sancta Maria, mater Christi splendida,
haec cum Iohanne teothocos impetra.
quorum hic sancta venerantur pignora
et quibus ista sunt sacrata limina.
quo duce victrix est in bello dextera
et sine ipso nihil valent iacula.

fortis iuventus, virtus audax bellica,
vestra per muros audiantur carmina.
et sit in armis alterna vigilia,
ne fraus hostilis haec invadat moenia.
resultet echo ' comes, eia vigila '
per muros ' eia ' dicat echo ' vigila '.

The second poem is the famous *O Roma nobilis*, which has
formed the subject of a special study by Traube.[1]   In these
stirring verses, by some happy chance, an unknown singer has
risen into poetry.   It is a song for the pilgrims who, in those
days and throughout the whole Middle Ages, came from every
country of Europe to win at the tombs of the apostles forgiveness of sins and the assurance of heaven.   Men, women, and
children, kings and princes, men stained with crime or disfigured
by disease, thronged at the grave of S. Peter, with their vows,
their offerings, and their prayers.[2]   The romantic fascination of
Christian Rome, the Rome of the apostles and martyrs, which
had taken the place of that other Rome of the Caesars, burns
with a glow of devotion and piety in these admirable verses :

o Roma nobilis, orbis et domina,
cunctarum urbium excellentissima,
roseo martyrum sanguine rubea,
albis et virginum liliis candida,
salutem dicimus tibi per omnia,
te benedicimus ; salve per secula.

---

[1] Traube, *O Roma nobilis*, pp. 299–
392 ; where the text is given, as also in
Anal. Hymn. li, p. 219.

[2] For a highly eloquent account of
the pilgrimages, see Gregorovius, iii.
76 sqq.

Petre, tu prepotens caelorum claviger,
vota precantium exaudi iugiter.
cum bis sex tribuum sederis arbiter,
factus placabilis iudica leniter,
teque petentibus nunc temporaliter
ferto suffragia misericorditer.

o Paule, suscipe nostra precamina,
cuius philosophos vicit industria ;
factus economus in domo regia,
divini muneris appone fercula,
ut, quae repleverit te sapientia,
ipsa nos repleat tua per dogmata.[1]

Late in the tenth century, perhaps,[2] these verses were written, when the political conditions favourable to the progress of culture were once more in process of restoration. By 916, indeed, the heroic efforts of John X and Alberigo of Camerino had dislodged the Arabs from the neighbourhood of Rome and from Central Italy.[3] Otto the Great restored order in Germany, crushed the Hungarians at the Lechfeld, and began the reform of the Papacy. The brief career of his grandson was spent in the pursuit of dreams, but his successors continued the work of reconstruction, and made the Empire once more a power and a reality. The Cluniac reform and a succession of able popes brought new strength to the Church, making her once more the leader of Western civilization and culture. The partial restoration of order was accompanied by natural and organic changes in European society. The growth of towns and the expansion of commerce brought into increasing importance the lay element. In Italy, the home of an ancient city civilization, education had never become entirely an ecclesiastical monopoly. The official and legal classes, and to some extent, perhaps, the merchants, gave their sons at least the rudimentary education afforded by the schools of grammar, though doubtless a smaller number proceeded to the study of the arts, of law, or of medicine.[4] In France the cathedral schools had risen to prominence. There

[1] It will be observed that each verse has twelve syllables, equally divided by a caesura ; the lines are mono-rimed and the structure is modelled on the iambic trimeter ; there are no elisions.

[2] But Blume would prefer to place these verses in the late eleventh or early twelfth century. The earliest MS. (Vatic. lat. 3227) he says is twelfth century ; see *Ein Jahrtausend lateinischer Hymnendich-*

tung, ii. 347 ; Traube, p. 300, puts the date of the MS. at the end of the eleventh century, and Dr. E. A. Lowe, *Beneventan Script*, p. 17 and elsewhere, in the early twelfth.

[3] Giesebrecht, i. 352 ; Gregorovius, iii. 267.

[4] Novati, *L'influsso del pensiero latino sopra la civiltà italiana del medio evo*, p. 72 ; Giesebrecht, i. 358.

the intellectual movement had begun, which was to continue without interruption until the dawn of the Renaissance. Italy, too, felt the awakening, but while the pagan poets were studied and imitated at Reims and at Chartres, the Italians won fame in the severer studies, and produced a Lanfranc, an Anselm, and, later, a Peter Lombard.[1] The great conflict of Empire and Papacy, the moral ferment aroused by the preaching of the Hildebrandine enthusiasts, turned the minds of ecclesiastics towards the polemics of faith and of politics, while the eager life of the nascent communes left little room for other than practical studies, including medicine and law.[2] Hence, in Italy, the eleventh century was not fruitful in poetry, religious or profane. Yet it would be a mistake to undervalue the significance of the Italian revival. The 'sense of the past' gained life once more; here and there liberal arts were pursued in a humanistic spirit, and they were, in any case, a necessary preliminary to the study of theology, medicine, or law; the lay schools flourished, and verses were written in classical metres.

Anselm the Peripatetic, who flourished about the middle of the eleventh century, is an instance of the strength of the secular spirit. In his prose work, the *Rhetorimachia*,[3] he records a vision in which he found himself among the blessed in Elysium, 'ubi sanctorum et iustorum requiescunt animae'. There he embraced the holy throng, but three most beautiful virgins suddenly appeared, crying, 'Why dost thou desert us, Anselm? Why dost thou leave us desolate?' They were Dialectic, Rhetoric, and Grammar. They threw themselves on the youthful scholar in spite of the efforts of the saints. 'The youth is ours,' the holy ones protested. 'Ours rather,' the virgins replied. Dialectic argued that the corporeal had nothing to do with the incorporeal, nor the mortal with the immortal, and Grammar clinched the argument with, 'nec in Elysiis quidem sunt declinandi loca, non masculini vel feminini hic debentur genera, potius vero in exelsis osanna'.[4] Anselm woke and crossed himself, praying: 'miserere mei, Deus; mira enim videram'. From the circle of rhetoricians such as Anselm, with their studied obscurity and parade of learning, came a number of secular poems like the love dialogue which Dümmler edited

[1] But see Novati, *Comptes rendus*, 1910, *Acad. des Inscr.*, pp. 169 sqq.
[2] Ronca, *Cultura medievale e poesia* *latina in Italia nei secoli XI e XII*, i. 214.
[3] E. Dümmler, *Anselm der Peripatetiker*, Halle 1872. [4] ib., p. 40 sq.

under the title of *Versus Eporedienses*.[1]   The more popular poetry, such as it was, celebrated the striking events of civic life, a memorable victory, or a desolating defeat.

Only religious poetry was slow in emerging from the cloud which had covered it; but, finally, it reappears in the gloomy but moving rhythms of Peter Damiani, and the colder metrical compositions of Alphanus of Salerno.

§ 2. *Poets of Monte Cassino in the Eleventh Century;*
Guaiferius and Alphanus, d. 1085.

In his panegyric on the Emperor Henry III, Wipo exhorted that prince to issue an edict 'per terram Teutonicorum' that each noble should send his sons to school that they might be instructed in letters, as was the universal custom in Italy:[2]

> moribus his dudum vivebat Roma decenter,
> his studiis tantos potuit vincire tyrannos.
> hoc servant Itali post prima. crepundia cuncti,
> et sudare scholis mandatur tota iuventus.

Doubtless the expression 'tota iuventus' need not be taken too literally, but there was sufficient difference of practice between Germany and Italy to strike the imagination of Wipo, and later of that keen observer Otto of Freising. The Bishop noted the urbane and cultivated manner of the Italians, and observed that the schools were open even to the 'mechanical'.[3] The private schools, institutions then peculiar to Italy, were numerous.   An eleventh-century writer [4] talks of thirty-two *philosophi* (students of profane letters) at Beneventum, some of whom were laymen.   The profession of teaching was lucrative. Peter Damiani forsook it for the Church, but one William of Aversa found it a road to riches and honour.[5]

On the basis of these liberal studies, the study of law and of medicine progressed with great rapidity to meet the demands

[1] E. Dümmler, *Anselm der Peripatetiker*, pp. 94 sqq.

[2] *Tetralogus*, p. 81 (ed. Bresslau). Wipo is referring especially to legal studies, but a general education was a necessary basis. Yet we must not imagine that the upper classes and laity generally went as a matter of course to the schools in Italy.

This has been shown clearly by Dresdner, *Kultur und Sittengeschichte der italien. Geistlichkeit*, pp. 219 sqq., 373 sqq.

[3] *Gesta Federici*, ii. 13.

[4] *Anon. Salern. c.* 122, *M. G. H., Scriptores*, iii. 534.

[5] Cf. the verses of Alphanus to William, Migne, cxlvii, col. 1260.

of the growing civilization of the cities. For Italy was now covered with rich and populous cities. The prosperity of the south was immense; the soil was fertile; the fleets of Bari, Tarento, and Amalfi exported corn, and brought back from Byzantium the treasures of the East.[1] It was the day of prosperity for the southern Lombards. The princes of Benevento, Salerno, and Capua, on the eve of the advent of the Normans, lived in luxury and splendour. In Calabria a monkish culture lingered among the Greek cloisters, and when, as at Naples in the tenth century, two civilizations met and mingled, Greek influences affected Latin letters. But the appearance of Norman adventurers in Italy about the year 1017 was destined to bring decisive changes in its train. The Greek hegemony was to disappear; the Saracens were to be expelled from Sicily, and over the wreck of the Lombard States the Normans were to extend their rule almost to the gates of Rome. The foundation of Aversa in 1030 was due to a Norman settlement. Within a few years Alphanus is celebrating its schools of arts and philosophy as the rivals of ancient Athens.

> Aversum studiis philosophos tuis
> in tantum reliquos vincis, ut optimis
> dispar non sis Athenis.[2]

So he addresses Gosfrit the Bishop, who directed the studies. But before the Norman invasion the renaissance of studies had begun on what was still Lombard soil. It was the last flowering of Lombard culture, a culture in which laymen and churchmen had an equal share.

The schools of Salerno by the end of the tenth century had won European fame.[3] Patients travelled from remote parts to avail themselves of the skill of the Salernitan physicians. It is not strange to find that some of the latter were equally skilled in grammar and poetry, since the liberal arts were the necessary basis of all studies. Alphanus the Archbishop, an eager lover of the classical authors, was known for his skill in medicine.

The true centre of humane studies was, however, the great monastery of Monte Cassino, which in the eleventh century,

[1] J. Gay, *L'Italie méridionale et l'empire byzantin*, Paris 1904, pp. 580 sqq.
[2] Migne, cxlvii, col. 1259.
[3] Rashdall, *Universities in the Middle Ages*, i. 75 sqq. for schools of Salerno.

after many misfortunes, rose again into more than its ancient riches and splendour. Abbot Theobald (1022–35)[1] had super-intended the transcription of many codices, and the German, Frederick of Lorraine (1056–58), the future Stephen IX, while encouraging learning in its various forms, had directed the intellectual activities of the monks towards theological and kin-dred studies, which could be used for the defence of the Papacy in the conflict with the temporal authority. But it was during the Abbacy of Desiderius (1058–87) that the monastery of S. Bene-dict reached the height of its glory. Desiderius,[2] a Lombard by birth, never became an accomplished scholar. He appears to have first applied himself seriously to letters in middle age, and he even ventured to compose verses, but none of them has survived. His real talents were of another order. He was formed by nature to superintend great designs and to direct the knowledge and zeal of other men. Zealous for the Church, he strove to exalt her by exalting the great house committed to his charge. He raised new and splendid buildings at Monte Cassino, and repaired the dilapidation of the old. The Basilica was rebuilt and adorned with priceless Greek mosaics. From Byzantium came the great doors of bronze which bore in silver letters the names of the abbey's vast possessions. The new library was filled with a splendid array of codices, many of which had been transcribed by the monks. Here were pagan poets—Homer, Terence, Virgil, Horace, Ovid, and Seneca ; by their side were the poets of the Church—Hilary, Juvencus, Sedulius, Paulinus, and Paul the Deacon.[3]

The dedication of the Basilica on Oct. 1, 1071, in the presence of the Pope, who was accompanied by Hildebrand and the Cardinals, was a scene of great splendour, not lacking in symbolical significance.[4] Here, in one place, were gathered together the different forces, temporal and spiritual, which were being enlisted in the service of the Papal idea. The might of the Normans, the learning of the Lombards, the zeal of the ascetic, and the skill of the ecclesiastical diplomat—these were present in the persons of Richard of Capua, Alphanus of Salerno, Peter Damiani, and Hildebrand. A prescient spectator might

---

[1] Giesebrecht, *L'istruzione in Italia nei primi secoli del medio evo*, p. 51.

[2] On Desiderius, see F. Hirsch, *Deside-rius von Monte Cassino als Papst Victor III (Forsch. zur deutsch. Gesch.* vii, pp. 3 sqq.); Gregorovius, iv. i. 63 ; Tosti, *Storia della badia di M. Cassino*, i. 310 sqq. ; Ozanam, *Documents inédits pour servir à l'histoire littéraire de l'Italie*, p. 42.

[3] Giesebrecht, *L'istruzione*, p. 61.

[4] Gregorovius, iv. i. 163.

have read a strange meaning into the words inscribed upon the apse of the new Basilica :

haec domus est similis Synai sacra iura ferenti :
ut lex demonstrat : hic quae fuit edita quondam,
lex hinc exivit mentes quae ducit ab imis,
et vulgata dedit lumen per clymata saecli.[1]

Alphanus celebrated the great event in a lengthy ode,[2] in which he reviewed the history of Benedict's foundation. The poet does his best to achieve a lofty style. He tells how a temple of Apollo stood on the hill-top, and how Benedict expelled the demons and built a monastery to the praise of Christ. The restoration under Desiderius is described ; how he brought columns from Rome, plundered from the inexhaustible ruins of the ancient city : [3]

marmoreo foris est lapide
intus et ecclesiae paries
splendidus. hic tamen haud facile
ducta labore vel arte rudi
omnis ab urbe columna fuit ;

how the mosaics were made by 'Thracian' craftsmen—' nec Hesperiae sufficiunt satis artifices '—and how the interior was adorned with precious workmanship The works of Cyrus, of Solomon, or of Justinian were not fairer, and the monastery is a second Eden,

ut paradisus amoenus Eden,
omne soli superas specimen,
eius aromatibus redoles :
deliciae tibi non aliae
sunt nisi forte suae pariles.

Indeed, the monastery was a house of prayer and labour. It is not necessary here to describe in detail the relation of the studies at Monte Cassino to the great ecclesiastical movement of reform. It is, however, important to remember that the pursuit of letters was intended to subserve the theological and doctrinal studies, whose importance was now more prominent than ever. But, happily, the demands of sacred studies were not able to stifle entirely the delight in letters, and especially in poetry, for their own sake. There was time to transcribe Virgil

[1] Tosti, op. cit., i. 333.
[2] Migne, cxlvii, col. 1234.
[3] Lanciani, *The Destruction of Ancient Rome*, p. 185, London 1899.

and Horace, and time for the composition of verses which show a real feeling for the beauties of classical form, and an attempt at elegance and wit in the rare moments of relaxation from severer studies.

Peter the Deacon and his continuator[1] have left an account of the illustrious men of Monte Cassino about this time. Alberic the Deacon is mentioned as a writer of metrical verses and rhythms, but his works have perished. Constantinus Afer, who was born at Carthage, and studied medicine among the Arabs, became a monk at Monte Cassino, and translated medical works from Arabic and Greek. But Guaiferius and Alphanus, both sons of Salerno, were the chief glories of Monte Cassino in the eleventh century. Both were poets who delighted in classical letters, and their verses were regarded as marvels of elegance and beauty. Guaiferius,[2] whom Leo of Ostia proudly describes as 'the flower of wisdom and eloquence', was of noble Lombard birth. Like many another youth, he was caught by the ardour of asceticism, much to the sorrow of his parents, who made vain efforts to keep him in the world. He was persuaded to abandon a hermit's life, but he left Benevento, his native city, and entered the monastery of La Cava. Under renewed pressure from his parents he returned, and joined the Benedictines of S. Sophia, whose Abbot was Desiderius. The Church had the care of his education. He learned to love the liberal arts, but he loved, above all, the austere regularity of the monastic life. Though he rose to be Abbot of Salerno he had no longing for the responsibilities and dangers of power. The troublous times drove him at last to seek a refuge in Monte Cassino, where he could more easily combine the life of saint and scholar. What remains of his verses is contained in a manuscript still preserved in the monastery. The most important poem[3] is an account, full of Virgilian reminiscence, of a poor pilgrim to Compostella, whom the evil one, appearing in the guise of the saint, persuaded to commit suicide as the shortest way to the joys of heaven. The demons, of course, seized his soul:

> miseram mox turba ferorum
> spirituum capiunt animam, rapiuntque trahuntque,
> per summas valles agitantes atque per imas.

[1] Migne, clxxiii, col. 1037.
[2] On Guaiferius, see Giesebrecht, *L'istruzione*, p. 53; Ozanam, op. cit., p. 115; Manitius, *Gesch.* ii. 484 sqq. His poems are in Migne, cxlvii, col. 1283 sqq.; see also Tosti, i. 416, and Ozanam, pp. 271 sqq.
[3] Migne, cxlvii, col. 1285; Ozanam, p. 275.

They draw near Rome,[1] when a great voice cries, 'Let be', and the devils loose their hold. A fair youth—this time the real James—leads the soul over S. Peter's, while an Olympian vision appears in the sky,

> in aethere mater
> virgineis stipata choris astare videtur.

The Virgin, in response to the prayers of the saint, decrees that unless the soul can regain the body and make amends for the mortal sin, it is lost for ever. Thereupon James performs the necessary miracle, and the soul regains its body.[2] The versification of the poem is remarkable; Tosti's enthusiastic comment—'Non vedi, o lettore, come corre in questi versi una certa vena Virgiliana? e sotto quella veste Longobarda caldeggi anima latina?'—has its measure of justification. The treatment is, however, of greater interest than the trivial subject. The opposite is true of the long hexameter poem in praise of the Psalms of David. The form is undistinguished, but the subject possesses a peculiar interest. Then, as now, the Psalter was the chosen book of the Christian spiritual life. There the Christian could see as in a mirror the diversities of spiritual and temporal experience, the joys and sorrows of the soul, as well as the foreshadowed dogmas of the Catholic faith. 'The Psalmes are the Manna of the Church. As Manna tasted to every man like that that he liked best, so doe the Psalmes minister Instruction, and satisfaction, to every man, in every emergency and occasion. *David* was not onely a cleare Prophet of Christ himselfe, but a Prophet of every particular Christian; He foretels what I, what any shall doe, and suffer, and say. . . . The whole booke of Psalmes is *Oleum effusum*, (as the spouse speaks of the name of Christ) an Oyntment powred out upon all sorts of sores, A Searcloth that souples all bruises, A Balme that searches all wounds.' So Donne puts, in his own wonderful manner, what Guaiferius, so lamely, would tell us:

> ecce rudimentum sperandi, norma cavendi.
> peccasti, reus es, defle cum rege reatum :
> saucius es graviter, spera cum vate salutem.
> iustus es, inde cave : quis enim vel iustior isto

---

[1] So Dante, *Purgatorio*, ii. 100–5.

[2] This story was known to Guibert of Nogent (d. 1124), who tells it in his autobiography, with an additional detail which it would be unbecoming to reproduce here. He ends the tale by saying that the old man who related it to him assured him that he had heard it from a man who had actually seen the pilgrim (*Guiberti vita*, lib. iii. 19, ed. Bourgin, Paris 1907, pp. 219 sqq.).

iustitieque fuit dilectior omnipotenti.
de cuius fructu ventris, cui sidera sedes
sede super propria iuravit se positurum.
et posuit ; quem precipuo testatur amore
servum sepe suum proprioque oleo se unguente perunctum?
sed magna tantus vir corruit iste ruina :
mox tamen unde ruit merore levante resedit.[1]

The elegiacs in praise of S. Secundinus, Bishop of Troia, are elegant enough, and show some acquaintance with Ovid.[2] There is also a poem in sapphics in praise of the same saint, but it possesses very little merit beyond a certain rhetorical ingenuity.[3]

Christe rex regum, pretium piorum,
nostra qui digne tibi militantis
res Secundini canimus secundas,
vota secunda.

From these poems we may picture the monk Guaiferius, studious and a lover of peace, glad to escape from the cares of his abbey to the irresponsible calm of Monte Cassino, where he could read his books in peace, and fulfil at the same time the strict demands of the contemplative life.   If he was a humanist, he was a monk before everything else, and all that he wrote he wrote for edification and not for love of the Muses.

Alphanus, his friend,[4] a man of more impressive personality and endowed with greater gifts, is truly described by Ughelli as 'Salernitanae ecclesiae et urbis egregium ornamentum'.[5] Like Guaiferius, he was a Lombard of noble blood.   From his earliest years he was devoted to the Church.   An ardent student, he won renown not only for his mastery of sacred and profane letters, but also for his skill in medicine.   It was Desiderius who, after making his acquaintance on a visit to the physicians of Salerno, persuaded him to forsake the world and join the order of S. Benedict.   But Alphanus could not fulfil that intention at once.   He had vowed a pilgrimage to Jerusalem, and the two friends parted for a time.   Alphanus appears

---

[1] Ozanam, p. 272.
[2] ib., p. 281.
[3] ib., p. 284.
[4] The poems of Alphanus are in Ughelli, *Italia Sacra*, x. 47 sqq. (Venice 1722); Migne, cxlvii, col. 1219 sqq. ; his hymns will be found also in *Anal. Hymn.*, vols. xxii, xxiv, and l (see *Anal. Hymn.* l, p. 330, for a list and references) ; Ozanam, pp. 259 sqq., contains some of the poems ; there are transcriptions also in M. Schipa, *Alfano, arcivescovo di Salerno*, and in his article in *Archivio storico per le provincie napoletane*, xii. pp. 767 sqq.
[5] op. cit , vii. 380.

to have been privy to a successful conspiracy of murder against the Salernitan prince Guaimar, and, in order to escape from the danger which pursued the conspirators, he fled with the aid of Desiderius to Benevento. The projected pilgrimage was abandoned, and the friends resolved never to part. The two companions went north to meet the Pope (Victor II), who, with the Emperor Henry IV, was thought to be coming south in order to avenge the murder. They were well received in Florence (1055), but they tired of the Papal court, and at last got leave to betake themselves to Monte Cassino, where they were received into the Order of S. Benedict. But before long the friends had again to separate; Alphanus went to be Abbot and finally Archbishop at Salerno, while Desiderius was sent to rule the monastery of S. Benedict at Capua, and became apocrisiarius of the Holy See. Not long after, Desiderius returned to Monte Cassino as Abbot. In 1058 Alphanus had been raised to the see of Salerno; he now took an important share in the politics of Church and State. The Lombard prince Gisulf took Alphanus and Bishop Bernard of Palestina with him when he went to Byzantium to obtain Greek aid against the encroaching Normans. They travelled in disguise as pilgrims bound for the Holy Sepulchre. The treaty was made, and the two Bishops went their way to Jerusalem. So, at last, Alphanus fulfilled his vow; but Gisulf left them both at Constantinople as hostages for the carrying out of the treaty. Bernard died in the foreign city, and Alphanus composed his epitaph in elegiacs :

> Bernardus nomen, Beneventus patria, sedes
>   Prenestis, celebris laus mihi Roma fuit.
> hostes ecclesiae contrivi : cuncta relinquens,
>   ivi Ierusalem solvere crimen idem.
> iamque dies mensem retinebant quinque Decembrem,
>   cum rediens illinc mortuus hospitor hic.[1]

Alphanus returned at last, bearded and strange. He made a friend of the Norman Duke, Robert Guiscard, whom he dared to visit before he reached Salerno. The Archbishop was by temperament a student and a lover of peace. The Norman menace filled him with dread, and as he did not see how it could be effectively resisted, he was tempted to regard it as a judgement of God that could not be averted. In 1077 the invaders were

---

[1] Giesebrecht, *L'istruzione*, p. 68; Schipa, *Archivio storico per le provincie napoletane*, xii. 767.

at the gates of Salerno. Alphanus played his part as the shepherd of his flock. He distributed bread and comforted the people, but when the fight was clearly hopeless, he went over to the Norman camp, where the Duke received him with kindness. The great event of these years was the discovery of the bones of the Apostle Matthew. Robert Guiscard, with true Norman piety, helped Alphanus to build a grand basilica to contain them, and the Archbishop wrote several elegant odes in honour of the saint. The best of these is undoubtedly the *Apostolorum nobili victoria* : [1]

> apostolorum nobili victoria
> et retributa pro labore gloria
> caeli solique laeta fit respublica,
> ut summa laudum conferant praeconia,
> quibus decora mater est ecclesia.
>
> hic est senatus, rege qui cum gloriae
> die supremo praesidebit arbiter
> ad iudicandum omne semen Israel,
> cuius potestas novit altas claudere
> seras itemque clave linguae pandere.
>
> in hoc beato principum collegio
> Matthaeus almo gloriatur praemio,
> qui mox relicto merito negotio
> Christum secutus eius a primordio
> humanitatem scripsit omnibus prior.
>
> auriga currus primus est mirabilis,
> servat Phisonis et figuram fluminis
> evangelista, cui datur prae ceteris
> formam supremae ferre pulchritudinis,
> nam solus ex his est homo notabilis.
>
> trina refulget dignitate munerum,
> refert ut omne concinendo saeculum,
> evangelista, martyr et apostolus,
> quod tale nulli de suis consortibus
> videtur unquam contigisse praemium.
>
> gentes propinquo solis ustas climate
> intusque tinctas criminum fuligine,
> ne mortis atra vergerent caligine,
> nitere fecit mente dum fideliter
> signis et almo liberavit famine.

[1] *Anal Hymn.* xxii, p. 188.

Matthaee, grates debitas, apostole,
digne tuorum civium iam suscipe,
quos fac ab omni esse tutos crimine,
ut se futuro sentiant examine
tali patrono paruisse strenuo.

The verses were composed for singing, and the metre, adorned
with occasional rime, lends itself well to the purpose.

The Cathedral Church of S. Matthew remains, much altered,
to this day.   It contains, besides the bones of the learned
Archbishop, the body of Hildebrand, who passed his last bitter
days of exile at Salerno.   The Pope died in May of 1085.   In
October of the same year Alphanus followed him.   Over his
grave, in the apse above, was placed the inscription :

da, Matthae pater, hoc det et innuba mater,
ut pater Alphanus maneat sine fine beatus.[1]

Alphanus appears to us as the most remarkable figure in the
humanistic revival in eleventh-century Italy.   His poems were
for Renan, ' un dernier souffle de l'antiquité ',[2] and, indeed, what
is chiefly notable in them is their dependence on the classical
tradition.   But that tradition appears with an air not of pedantry
but of freshness and renewal, with a breath of humanism not
inexplicable in one who had made such wide studies, embracing
subjects so secular as law and medicine, as well as the traditional
theology.   The humanistic and secular note is not, indeed,
always dominant.   Alphanus blames the young Transmundus—
in elaborate verse, it is true, and with pagan reminiscence—for
visiting the monks of Casauria in his ardent pursuit of profane
letters and profane philosophy, and the rebuke is not insincere
for all its Horatian flavour :

sic, Transmunde, mihi credis, amice,
his uti studiis desine tandem ;
fac cures monachi scire professum,
ut vere sapiens esse puteris.[3]

Yet, at the same time, he was ready to invoke the example of
Cyprian, who

ardet in antiquis ut stella retrograda libris,[4]

[1] *Anal. Hymn.* l, p. 329.
[2] *Mélanges religieux et historiques,*
p. 348.
[3] Migne, cxlvii, col. 1260.
[4] ib., col. 1221.

and had adorned his pages with the flowers of rhetoric :

> fas ibi rhetoricis fuit eius floribus uti,
>   atque coloratis ludere saepe iocis.
> nunc licet, ut licuit scribentibus, atque licebit,
>   usus et hic, morem legis habere solet.
> solvi non poterit res haec rationibus ullis,
>   si non solvuntur caetera iura simul.

Alphanus is not ashamed to acknowledge his love of the Muses, and he delighted to compose in those lyric measures which had been, for the most part, beyond the skill of his medieval predecessors. He is careful of quantity; in his great ode on the re-dedication of Monte Cassino, he begs permission to change the quantity of a syllable in order that he may introduce the otherwise unmanageable name of Desiderius,[1] and, in his poem on the twelve brother-martyrs, he explains that there are two whose names cannot be accommodated to the laws of metre :

> de reliquis duo sunt, quos posse venire
>   lex pedis in carmen prohibet.

Yet it can hardly be said that the poems of Alphanus are remarkable for beauty or charm.   They are the productions of a studious humanist, who can convey in sapphics a dry jest to Atto the Bishop of Chieti,[2] or turn into Horatian odes the praise of the Prince of Salerno, raising him above Cato, Scipio, and Caesar, and the rest of the heroes of the antique world.[3]

It is easy to observe that the Roman past thrilled him as it thrilled Hildebert, and was in the next century to thrill Arnold of Brescia.[4] In a poem to the Archdeacon Hildebrand he recalled the days of old and the lesson which the long and marvellous Roman past should teach the Roman of the present :

> quanta gloria publicam
> rem tuentibus indita
> saepe iam fuerit, tuam,
> Hildebrande scientiam
> nec latere putavimus.
>
> nec putamus.   idem sacra
> et Latina refert via,
> illud et Capitolii
> culmen eximium, thronus
> pollens imperii, docet.[5]

---

[1] Migne, cxlvii, col. 1237; Critias, the Athenian politician-poet, boldly changed a pentameter into an iambic trimeter in order to bring in the otherwise unmanageable name of Alcibiades; see W. Nestle, *Kritias*, in *Neue Jahrb. f. d. klass. Alt.* xi. i, p. 94.
[2] Migne, cxlvii, col. 1259.
[3] ib., col. 1256.

[4] It is worth mentioning here that another poet of Monte Cassino, Amato (d. 1093), celebrates the glories of Rome in verses in honour of Peter and Paul; see Graf, *Roma nella memoria del medio evo*, i. 15, for a quotation from Dümmler's transcript.
[5] Migne, cxlvii, col. 1262; Schipa has given a better text in *Versi di Alfano*,

The Rome of the Church is to be more just and great than the Rome of the Caesars; the apostolic anathema shall accomplish more than the proscriptions of Marius or the campaigns of Julius :[1]

quanta vis anathematis!
quidquid et Marius prius,
quodque Julius egerant
maxima nece militum,
voce tu modica facis.

Roma quid Scipionibus
caeterisque Quiritibus
debuit mage, quam tibi?
cuius est studiis suae
nacta iura potentiae.

qui probe, quoniam satis
multa contulerant bona
patriae, perhibentur et
pace perpetua frui
lucis et regionibus.

te quidem potioribus
praeditum meritis, manet
gloriosa perenniter
vita, civibus ut tuis
compareris apostolis.

These were prophetic words, beyond flattery, foretelling the new ecclesiastical imperialism, which Alphanus boldly associates with the powerful Archdeacon who had yet to rise to the throne of Peter.[2]

But, in another mood, Alphanus voices that gloom and despair which filled the medieval soul before the prospect of death and judgement. His long metrical ' confession ', in elegiacs, is an acknowledgement of sin and a prayer for grace and salvation :[3]

quid faciam, quid agam, quo me, pater optime, vertam?
    ultimus ecce dies ille tremendus adest.
quid faciam, quid agam, cum non qui liberet adsit,
    dum sua facta nocens nemo negare potest!
quid faciam, quid agam, cum tanti iudicis ira,
    omnes perpetuo damnet in igne reos.
tu mihi quid faciam, tu consule, consiliator
    unice, qui veniae totus haberis iter.
tu mihi quid faciam, tu dic, qui condita quaeque
    a te sunt, facere nulla fuisse potes.
tu mihi quid faciam tu dic, qui fluminis undam
    astra, solum, pelagus, unde laventur habes.

To this, the eternal preoccupation, Christ answers with words of admonition and comfort; and the poem ends with a prayer to the Saviour, first for the sinner, and then for the whole race of men; in especial for Gregory, seventh of that name, their

Archivio storico per le provincie napo-letane, xii (1887), pp. 768 sqq.; also in his *Alfano, arcivescovo di Salerno*, p. 35 sq.

[1] See Graf, *Roma nella memoria del medio evo*, ii. 420.
[2] Cf. Schipa, *Alfano*, p. 37.
[3] Migne, cxlvii, col. 1250.

Shepherd and Bishop; next for Agnes the Queen, who gave up the pomp of this world for the hope of the next; then for the *domicilium Benedicti*, the monastic home which Alphanus loved; and, finally, for the ministers of the Church and the whole body of the clergy:

> omnes conveniunt, et noctibus atque diebus,
>   horis, momentis, te sine fine canunt.
> Christus pro manibus, Christus pro lumine, Christus
>   pro labiis, Christus pro lare cordis habent.

Alphanus was a prolific writer of hymns. Besides the hymns on S. Matthew, the patron of his church, he wrote a metrical office on S. Sabina, the martyr,[1] and a hymn in praise of the same saint.[2] The latter has some attractive lines on the beauties of Paradise:

> illic purpureus rosae
> flos et nardus inest, vernat amaracus,
>   floret cum violis crocus,
> spirant thura thymus, lilia balsamum.
>
> hymnos angelici chori,
> condignum resonant carmen apostoli,
>   psallant quem pie martyres,
> et plectro feriunt tympana virgines.

Like many another poet he was tempted by the Christian epic of the passions of the martyrs. It was perhaps while he was still a youthful monk at Monte Cassino that he composed a long hexameter poem on the life and passion of the twelve brothers who suffered at Beneventum under Maximian. The poem has been called 'a romance in verse',[3] and, indeed, it treats in all the elaborate detail of romance, with mythological and learned excursions, a theme which could not otherwise have been expanded into so many hundred lines. It tells also how Arichis, Prince of Beneventum, translated the bones of the martyrs into the Church of S. Sophia, and the opportunity is taken of praising the Lombard ruler in terms of exaggerated flattery.[4] The following lines from the dedication to his friend and fellow monk Roffridus will give an idea of Alphanus' hexameters, as well as of the scope of the poem:

[1] *Anal. Hymn.* xxiv, p. 274 sq.; Migne, cxlvii, col. 1263 sqq.
[2] *Anal. Hymn.* xxii, p. 242 sq.
[3] Manitius, *Gesch.* ii. 622.
[4] Texts in *Acta SS. Sept. 1*, 144 sqq.; of the *Translation* only, ed. Waitz, *M. G. H., SS. Rer. Ital.*, pp. 574 sqq.

praecipis historiam duodenum scribere fratrum
versibus herois veterem ; sint unde creati,
et generis titulos, fideique celebria facta :
inde tyrannorum cum quo fortissima bella
conseruere, quibusque locis, quo tempore palmam
martyrii, dignas et suscepere coronas :
postque quod Arechis magnus princeps Beneventum
corpora, diversis sparsimque iacentia terris,
transtulerit, nunc et quâ sunt, sepeliverit aede.
. . . tu prece continua multo studiosius insta,
ut qui martyribus fuerat dux spiritus, idem
horum me faciat tandem pro laude disertum.

The sapphics on S. Maur are a tribute of more intimate piety
to the favourite disciple of Benedict,[1] and so is a fine ode, which
likewise relates his miracles—how Maur healed Arderadus and
Sergius, restored sight to Linus, and raised the dead :

gaudere, fratres, nos hodie decet
et quaeque cordis tristia spernere
summa beati laetitia viri,
his cuius odas pangimus organis.

For all these hymns are odes, in lyric metres, handled with
something of the severity and restraint of his classical models.
And so we have again to recognize the true character of
Alphanus the poet.   His poems take a high place in the
medieval attempt to return to antiquity.   The Italian movement
had indeed its counterpart in France, where the Cathedral
Schools produced poets of considerable talent, like Fulbert of
Chartres and Hildebert of Le Mans.   But, in Alphanus, the
literary renaissance sounds a clearer note of humanism, and
the predominance of the secular element in Italian life made it
easier to escape from an entirely ecclesiastical outlook.   Yet in
Italy, as in France, theology was to overshadow the other studies,
and discourage the ardour of those who loved the authors of
antiquity.   At the same time, the new rhythmical verses were to
eclipse almost entirely, both for ecclesiastical and popular uses,
the learned and intricate measures of the Roman poets.[2]

[1] *Anal. Hymn.* xxii, p. 198.

[2] Alphanus is probably the author of the hymn, *de omnibus sanctis*, which begins 'Gaudete, iusti, mites et pacifici' (*Anal. Hymn.* l, pp. 336 sqq.), and is a rhythmical composition ; Dreves, p. 338, says the doubts as to its authenticity are on that account only too well founded. G. Falco, *Bulletino dell' istituto storico italiano*, No. 32, 1902, p. 4, gives good reasons for accepting Alphanus' authorship. If, as we ought, we read,
Vos, Oderisi, Tudine, Transmundule,
in stanza 9, line 2, we have additional reason for believing that Alphanus is the author.

§ 3. *Peter Damiani*, 1007–72. *The Poetry of Asceticism.*

The tenth century had seen the life of the Church at a low ebb. Otto the Great and his successors had attempted to purge the Papacy and to lift it from the unhappy state into which it had fallen in the days of the Crescentii, but the evils of secularization, rendered most apparent by the prevalence of simony and the marriage of the clergy, still threatened to destroy the spiritual nature of the Church's authority, and to make the Church a worldly organization inextricably bound up with and subject to the secular society which had always been regarded as its antitype.[1] The sense of danger produced a strong movement towards reform from within the Church. It was a movement whose driving force was the monastic ideal of the separation of the Church from the world as understood by the monks of Cluny. The Church, the divinely constituted authority, ruled by the successors of S. Peter, was to assert itself as superior, in origin and aim, to all earthly kingdoms; the secular power was to serve the spiritual, and the Church was to become by its moral authority and the virtues of its rulers what it had always been ideally, the supreme earthly shepherd of the souls of men.[2] This great ideal, in the hands of that imperious genius Hildebrand,[3] who was raised to the chair of Peter as Gregory VII, developed from an ideal of freedom into one of universal domination, from a spiritual movement of reform to a political movement which shook the foundations of society. But while the movement of reform was still in its earlier stage, it profoundly affected the religious life of Italy. There the religious awakening had taken a characteristic form, that of a return to the hermit ideal,[4] and all over Italy little groups of solitary ascetics, with leaders like Nilus and Romuald of Ravenna, led a life of incredible hardship and practised the most barbarous austerities in the hope of saving their souls in a world which was clearly drawing near its term. Famous among these was Peter Damiani, who was born at Ravenna in

---

[1] Augustine's *De civitate Dei* is the classical exposition of the relation of the divine to the human society.

[2] See Gierke, *Political Theories of the Middle Ages*, Cambridge 1900, pp. 11 sqq.

[3] On Gregory VII, see W. Martens, *Gregor VII, sein Leben und Wirken*, 2 vols., Leipzig 1894. In Gregory's own words, his programme was 'ut ecclesia, ad proprium rediens decus, libera, casta et catholica permaneret', Martens, i. 238.

[4] See Sackur, *Die Cluniacenser*, i. 323 sqq.; Gregorovius, iv. i, pp. 101 sqq.

the year 1007, and died at Faenza in 1072.[1] In his youth he
had imbibed most of the learning of his day; he had studied
at Ravenna, Faenza, and Parma, and at Ravenna he opened
one of those secular schools which were still a characteristic
mark of Italian culture.[2] But the religious life called him, and
he left the world for the hermitage of Fonte Avellana. His
virtues brought him fame. In 1057 Pope Stephen X compelled
him to accept the Cardinal-Bishopric of Ostia, and henceforth,
employed on the business of the Church, he saw his soul daily
and hourly in peril from this fresh contact with a doomed world.
Hildebrand, at first Subdeacon and then in 1059 Archdeacon,
was the most influential man in Rome;[3] he saw in Peter's fiery
zeal against ecclesiastical corruption the invaluable instrument
of his great designs. His powerful will and imperious temper
fascinated the wild imagination of Peter Damiani, who, moved
at the same moment by love and fear, could not tear himself
away from an influence which he felt was fraught with peril to
his soul. His bitterness of spirit found vent in those strange
ironical epigrams in which he satirized the almost magical
influence of the man whom he once described as his 'Holy
Satan':

> papam rite colo, sed te prostratus adoro:
> tu facis hunc dominum; te facit iste deum.

and again:

> vivere vis Romae, clara depromite voce:
> plus domino papae quam domno pareo papae.[4]

Peter's ideal was that of a life of thorough renunciation, in
which scourging, penance, and abstinence were a ceaseless
preparation for death. His activities as a reformer were directed
mainly against the simoniac and married clergy. Hildebrand's
schemes of ecclesiastical imperialism filled him with horror, and
he was always the unwilling, helpless tool of that consummate
politician. The real man is expressed in the large body of
letters, treatises, and poems, in which he reveals the ferocity

---

[1] Sackur, ii. 279 sqq.; there is a good
account of Damiani in Lea, *History of
Sacerdotal Celibacy*, i. 216 sqq., 3rd edit.,
London 1907.

[2] On the lay schools in Italy, see Ronca,
Cultura medievale, i. 73 sqq.; Dresdner,
Kultur und Sittengesch. der ital. Geist-
lichkeit, p. 233.

[3] Biron, *S. Pierre Damien*, p. 92.
Hildebrand was also abbot of S. Paolo
fuori le mura.

[4] i.e. I am more obedient to the Pope's
master than to the lord Pope; Migne,
cxlv, col. 967, 961, for the two epigrams.

mingled with gentleness, morbidity verging on madness, and that mystical piety which made up his unhappy and tormented soul.

He lived in a world of phantasms, where the natural order did not exist, where the devil went forth as a raging lion,[1] and the wickedness of men was ripe for judgement.   In the *Liber Gomorrhianus* he inveighs in terrible language against the unnatural vices of men.   It is a book of unrelieved horror beside which Alan of Lille's *De Planctu Naturae*, on a similar subject, is the merest trifling.   The learning of this world, even the study of grammar, was sinful ; the foolishness of the Gospel was the one thing necessary, all else was superfluous and evil.[2] Salvation could be achieved only, and that hardly, by following the path of complete renunciation, which was in his eyes the way set forth by Jesus and by the whole company of apostles and martyrs.   'Say then', he says in his treatise *De laude Flagellorum*, 'whoever thou art who proudly makest mock of the passion of Christ ; who, disdaining to be stripped naked and to be scourged with Him, holdest in derision His nakedness and all His sufferings as trifles and foolish tales and the dreams of madmen ; say, what wilt thou do when Him, who in the sight of all was made naked and hanged upon the cross, thou beholdest in His glorious majesty, surrounded by the hosts of angels, girt with the might of incomparable splendour, and ineffably glorious above all things, visible and invisible ?   What, I say, wilt thou do when thou shalt see Him, whose ignominy thou dost now despise, sitting upon the fiery throne of judgement, and judging terribly the whole race of men with justice ?   Then the sun shall be darkened, the moon shall not give her light, the stars shall fall from heaven, the foundations of the hills shall tremble, . . . and thou, decked out with fair adornment, thou softly and shamelessly clad, what shalt thou do amid these terrible things ? With what effrontery, with what boldness of presumption shalt thou hope to share in His glory, whose reproach and ignominy thou didst disdain to endure ?'[3]

The terror of the Judgement oppressed him ; the flames of the last day seemed to be already kindled against a world of sinners. So in gloomy verses, full of this horror, but majestic in their

---

[1] Cf. *De Castitate*, Migne, cxlv, col. 715.

[2] See Dr. J. A. Endres, *Petrus Damiani und die weltliche Wissenschaft*. Yet Damiani sent his nephew abroad to study the liberal arts, and he is obviously proud of his own rhetoric ; cf. Dresdner, op. cit., p. 226.

[3] Migne, cxlv, col. 682.

music, he gives utterance to the preoccupation of his soul.   The
de die mortis is one of the most remarkable poems of the eleventh
century.   It is written in a rhythm based on the trochaic tetrameter, which is handled with great assurance and competence :

> gravi me terrore pulsas, vitae dies ultima,
> moeret cor, solvuntur renes, laesa tremunt viscera,
> tui speciem dum sibi mens depingit anxia.

> quis enim pavendum illud explicet spectaculum,
> cum, dimenso vitae cursu, carnis aegrae nexibus
> anima luctatur solvi, propinquans ad exitum ?

> perit sensus, lingua riget, resolvuntur oculi,
> pectus palpitat, anhelat raucum guttur hominis,
> stupent membra, pallent ora, decor abit corporis.

> . . . torquet ipsa reum suum mordax conscientia,
> plorat acta corrigendi defluxisse tempora ;
> plena luctu, caret fructu sera poenitentia.

> falsa tunc dulcedo carnis in amarum vertitur,
> quando brevem voluptatem perpes poena sequitur :
> iam, quod magnum credebatur, nil fuisse cernitur.

> . . . quaero, Christe, rex invicte, tu succurre misero,
> sub extremae sortis hora, cum iussus abiero :
> nullum in me ius tyranno praebeatur impio.

> cadat princeps tenebrarum, cadat pars tartarea :
> pastor, ovem iam redemptam tunc reduc ad patriam,
> ubi te videndi causa perfruar in saecula.[1]

The same note of terror and fearful expectation is struck in
another long poem, which Peter composed in the same measure :

> o quam dira, quam horrenda voce iudex intonat,
> cum paratis mergi flammis maledictos imperat ;
> mox deglutiens viventes Stygis olla devorat.

> vaporantur infelices intus, et extrinsecus,
> crepitantes strident flammae, velut ardens clibanus :
> ore, naribus, et ipsis profluunt luminibus.

> immortalis mors occidit, nec omnino perimit :
> ignis urit, non consumit, nec defectum recipit :
> vita moritur, mors vivit ; finis semper incipit.

---

[1] Migne, cxlv, col. 977 ; also *Anal. Hymn.* xlviii, p. 62.

Then follows the catalogue of torments appointed for the wicked.

> illic dolor, cruciatus, fletus, stridor dentium,
> adsunt fremitus leonum, sibili serpentium :
> quibus mixti confunduntur ululatus flentium.[1]

In the same metres, once more, is Peter's beautiful rhythm on the glories of Paradise, a famous poem which was once ascribed to Augustine :

> ad perennis vitae fontem mens sitivit arida,
> claustra carnis praesto frangi clausa quaerit anima :
> gliscit, ambit, eluctatur exsul frui patria,
>
> . . . nam quis promat, summae pacis quanta sit laetitia,
> ubi vivis margaritis surgunt aedificia,
> auro celsa micant tecta, radiant triclinia ?
>
> solis gemmis pretiosis haec structura nectitur,
> auro mundo tanquam vitro urbis via sternitur :
> abest limus, deest fimus, lues nullus cernitur.
>
> hiems horrens, aestas torrens illic nunquam saeviunt :
> flos perpetuus rosarum ver agit perpetuum :
> candent lilia, rubescit crocus, sudat balsamum.
>
> . . . avidi et semper pleni, quod habent desiderant :
> non satietas fastidit, neque fames cruciat :
> inhiantes semper edunt, et edentes inhiant.[2]

The sweetest, the strangest, and the most mystical of the compositions ascribed to Peter is a poetical commentary on part of the Song of Songs : [3]

> quis est hic qui pulsat ad ostium,
> noctis rumpens somnium ?
> me vocat : ' o virginum pulcherrima,
> soror, coniux, gemma splendidissima !
> cito surgens aperi, dulcissima.
>
>   ego sum summi regis filius,
> primus et novissimus ;
> qui de caelis in has veni tenebras,
> liberare captivorum animas :
> passus mortem et multas iniurias.'

---

[1] Migne, cxlv, col. 980; also *Anal. Hymn.* xlviii, p. 65.
[2] Migne, cxlv, col. 980; Mone, i. 422 ; *Anal. Hymn.* xlviii, p. 66.

[3] An interpretation to which line 10 lends colour is that the subject is the visit of Jesus to the human soul.

mox ego dereliqui lectulum,
cucurri ad pessulum :
ut dilecto tota domus pateat,
et mens mea plenissime videat,
quem videre maxime desiderat.

at ille iam inde transierat,
ostium reliquerat.
quid ergo, miserrima, quid facerem?
lacrymando sum secuta iuvenem,
manus cuius plasmaverunt hominem.

vigiles urbis invenerunt me,
exspoliaverunt me,
abstulerunt et dederunt pallium,
cantaverunt mihi novum canticum
quo in regis inducar palatium.[1]

The rhythmical scheme of these verses is curious. It follows roughly the principle of equality of syllables, and the rhythm proper is somewhat rudimentary. If the first three syllables of each strophe are separated so as to form by themselves a strophe, as Dreves arranges them,[2]

quis est hic,
qui pulsat ad ostium,
noctis rumpens somnium, etc.

the rhythmical principle of syllabic equality is rendered more clear, but the rudeness of the rhythm at once reminds us of the earlier rhythmical verse before the rule of alternate stresses had been fully discovered. If, therefore, we conclude that Peter, the author of the splendid and perfect rhythms which we have quoted, can hardly have composed these formally undeveloped verses, we are bound also to conceive a doubt of his authorship of some other verses which show a knowledge and mastery of the two-syllabled rime. These verses are a descant on the 'Ave Maria':[3]

ave, David filia,
sancta mundo nata,
virgo prudens sobria,
Ioseph desponsata,

[1] Migne, cxlv, col. 939.
[2] Anal. Hymn. xlviii, p. 76.
[3] Migne, cxlv, col. 939; Anal. Hymn. xlvii, p. 74; Meyer, Rythmik, i. 308, would place these verses later than the eleventh century, see Anal. Hymn. li, pp. 238 sqq. for a list of the poems of Peter according to the earliest (eleventh-century) MS. Neither this poem nor Quis est hic is included.

ad salutem omnium
in exemplum data,
supernorum civium
consors iam probata.

None of Peter Damiani's other poems possesses anything like the power and beauty of the three great rhythms from which we have quoted. In his sapphic hymns he shows a curious love of the internal rime, a tasteless experiment which his contemporaries may well have admired. So, in the first strophe of a hymn to S. Januarius, which is marked by a play on the name of the saint:

clare famosi titulis triumphi,
raptor aeterni violente regni,
sit tuis per te via, Ianuari,
ianua caeli.[1]

Most of the other hymns are in a measure based on the iambic dimeter, rimed in couplets throughout, and perhaps intended for liturgical use. When Peter celebrates the Virgin Mary he can say no more than this:

o singularis domina,
sola virgo puerpera,
praeclara vitae ianua,
qua caeli patent atria.[2]

The truth is that he was at his best when he was denouncing the wrath of God against men, and examining their wickedness in the light of the Last Judgement. Yet for the sake of his three long rhythms we cannot rank him among the lesser poets of the Middle Ages.

[1] *Anal. Hymn.* li, p. 242; cf. also ib., xlviii, p. 60.   [2] ib., xlviii, p. 36.

IX

FRENCH POETS OF THE CATHEDRAL SCHOOLS: ELEVENTH CENTURY

§ 1. *The Cathedral Schools ; Fulbert of Chartres* (975 *circa–* 1028) *and Berengar of Tours* (999–1088).

IT has already been explained how, on the disappearance of the municipal schools in Gaul, their place was taken by the monastic and cathedral schools. Charles the Great, deploring the ignorance of both regular and secular clergy, had endeavoured to encourage the establishment of schools attached to monasteries and cathedrals, and in spite of the social and economic disorder which accompanied the break-up of his empire, the continuity of the schools remained unbroken when the restoration of order towards the end of the tenth century created once more conditions which were favourable to civilization and culture. As in the eighth century, the extent to which it was possible to restore the direct study of the Latin classics was the measure of literary and intellectual progress. But then, as before, there were forces which made against the disinterested study of letters, and, as in the days of Jerome, those forces owed their strength to the prevalence of the ideals of monasticism. The monastic schools had now completed their contribution to the cause of learning. Cluny set the example of austerity by somewhat discouraging the study of profane authors.[1] The aim of education was on the whole narrowed down to the provision of the minimum required for the everyday routine of the

---

[1] See Ch. Pfister, *Études sur le règne de Robert le Pieux*, p. 3; but as Sackur, *Die Cluniacenser*, ii. 330, shows, Pfister goes too far in asserting that the study of profane authors ceased altogether. That the composition of religious verses with rhythm and rime was not discouraged, we know from the *Vision* of Ansellus Scholasticus, a Cluniac monk. This long and curious poem (printed in Du Méril, *Poésies populaires lat. ant. au 12ᵐᵉ siècle*, p. 200) was written at the request of Odo of Cluny, himself a poet. The author had clearly read Virgil and Horace. Under Abbot Odilo (*circa* 1042) Livy was prescribed for reading in Lent, see Wilmart, *Le convent et la bibliothèque de Cluny*, *Revue Mabillon*, 1921, p. 91.

monastery—reading, writing, arithmetic, and music. In the tenth and eleventh centuries the cathedral schools were the most conspicuous homes of liberal studies; they were the true fore-runners of the universities of the thirteenth century. Under their influence a revival of classical studies began, a movement of great but unfulfilled promise,[1] which was to be overshadowed in the twelfth century by the all-attractive power of the dialectical and theological studies of Paris. But, slight as its achievement may appear, the eleventh-century revival bore permanent fruit in a general raising of Latin style, which, if its results are seen more clearly in the prose of John of Salisbury, of Wibald of Corvey, or of Otto of Freising, had some effect also in raising the technical standard of poetical composition. The word 'composition' aptly describes, for the most part, the character of the poetry of the cathedral schools: for the verses of Fulbert, Hildebert, and Marbod are precisely such compositions as formed part of the grammatical studies included in the *Trivium*. John of Salisbury[2] describes how prose and verse compositions were part of the daily curriculum at Chartres, and in Fulbert's time the same practice must have existed. For Latin was now studied as a dead language, and grammar and syntax were learned by the medieval student in the same way as by the modern schoolboy.

Gerbert of Aurillac taught at Reims from 972 to 982, and he raised the cathedral school of that city to the first place among the houses of learning in France. At Reims the scholars were not allowed to content themselves in their grammatical studies with mere handbooks and compendia; they went behind the *artes* to the *auctores*, and especially they studied the Latin poets. Gerbert regarded this study of the poets as essential to the art of oratory. Virgil and Horace, Lucan and Statius, Terence and Juvenal were in the cathedral library, and Gerbert was untiring in his efforts to collect new treasures. The tradition of Reims was followed at Chartres, where Fulbert made the cathedral school the intellectual glory of eleventh-century France. Chartres became a flourishing school, where not only the arts, but theology itself—the whole sum of a medieval educa-tion—were taught by the best masters of the day. Fulbert himself exercised a magical influence over his pupils, and of

---

[1] Rashdall, *The Universities of Europe in the Middle Ages*, i. 66 sqq.   [2] Quoted, ib., p. 69.

their profound devotion to their learned and saintly teacher there is abundant evidence.

He was born about the year 975, possibly in Aquitaine, and of poor parents.[1] He says, in a curious poem, addressed to himself:

te de pauperibus natum suscepit alendum
Christus, et immeritum sic enutrivit et auxit,
ut collata tibi miretur munera mundus,
nam puero faciles providit esse magistros,[2]

from which it may also be inferred that the Church had the care of his early education.[3] It would appear that he studied under Gerbert at Reims, where he made the acquaintance of Robert, afterwards King of France, who was his fellow pupil. From Reims Fulbert moved to Chartres, to become Master and Chancellor. In 1007 he was consecrated Bishop, in spite of his fears and honest reluctance, which he has expressed in a naïve poem:

mi factor, mea vita, salus, fiducia sola,
da mihi consilium et votum viresque sequendi,
ambiguus quid agam, quo tandem fine quiescam :
nam vereor temere suscepto pontificatu
servandis ovibus, mage quam prodesse, nocere ;
atque ideo puto cedendum melioribus esse.
sed recolens quod non opibus, neque sanguine fretus,
conscendi cathedram, pauper de sorde levatus,
arbitror hoc a te factum sicut tuus est mos,
nec mutare locum, nisi significaveris, ausim.
quamvis illaesae moneat mens conscia vitae,
tu scis, sancte pater, quid sit tibi gratius horum,
utiliusque mihi : precor inde tuam pietatem,
ut mihi digneris hoc inspirare labenti,
consilium, praesensque iuves ad perficiendum.[4]

But his fears were groundless. Alike as Master and as Bishop, he was pre-eminent in his generation. His noble character, his untiring patience, his exquisite charity won the love and respect of kings and princes, clergy and scholars. His pupil, Adelman of Liége, celebrates his fame and virtues in a rhythmic poem, the merits of which are less conspicuous than its genuine feeling.

[1] On Fulbert, see Clerval, *Écoles de Chartres*, pp. 29 sqq. ; Manitius, *Gesch.* ii. 682 sqq.

[2] Migne, cxli, col. 347.
[3] Cf. also Letter, iii, col. 195.
[4] Migne, cxli, col. 346.

Carnotenae decus urbis, memorande pontifex,
te primum, pater Fulberte, dum te conor dicere,
sermo fugit, cor liquescit, recrudescunt lacrimae.[1]

The same pupil has left a charming description of long evening
conversations in the shadow of Fulbert's new cathedral, when
their 'venerable Socrates' opened his heart to his disciples on
the deep things of God.[2]

The nature of the grammatical studies at Chartres[3] is of
particular interest and importance when it is considered in
connexion with the group of poets who are particularly the
product of the French cathedral schools.   We have seen how
Fulbert continued at Chartres the example set by Gerbert at
Reims.   The study of grammar included the greater part of the
'humanities', and much attention was paid to composition not
only in prose but in verse.   These compositions were based on
models provided by the study of the ancient authors.   M. Clerval
points out[4] that the library at Chartres appears to have been
much richer in poets than in prose writers.   Of the poets, he
mentions Virgil, Ovid, Horace, Terence, Statius, Fortunatus,
Sedulius, Arator, Prudentius, Boëthius.

So the Christian poets were read side by side with the great
poets of antiquity, and Fortunatus and Sedulius were doubtless
accepted as models equally with Virgil and Horace.   As in the
other cathedral schools so at Chartres, the new system of
versification was practised by the side of the old.   Accentual
and rimed compositions were part of the school exercises as
well as hexameters and sapphics.   Three of the most important
poets who owed their education to the cathedral schools, Fulbert,
Hildebert, and Marbod, are equally at home in either manner
of composition; but their quantitative verse bears perhaps more
obviously the scholastic mark, while in rhythm and rime they
found a more plastic medium for the expression of the mysticism
which was the basis of their religious thought.[5]   This is less
true perhaps of Fulbert than of Hildebert or Marbod.   For
Fulbert is less a poet than a teacher, and of the slender body of
his verse which survives the best is contained in those poems
where he did not wander far from classical traditions.   He has

---

[1] Clerval, pp. 59 sqq.
[2] Text ib., p. 98.
[3] For what follows, see ib., pp. 108 sqq.
[4] ib., p. 110.
[5] Cf. Gröber, *Grundriss der romani-* *schen Philologie*, ii. i. 124 : 'Die rhyth-mische Dichtung übertrifft die metrische im Allgemeinen an Gehalt; sie ist mehr Poesie des Inhalts, die metrische mehr Poesie des Wortes.'

left an *Epiphany Hymn* and a *Hymn to the Holy Ghost*, both
in sapphics, and a longer hexameter poem *On the Cross*.[1]   His
responses for the feast of the Nativity of the Virgin are pleasing
enough :

> solem iustitiae, regem paritura supremum.
> stella Maria maris hodie processit ad ortum ;
> cernere divinum lumen gaudete, fideles.
>
> stirps Iesse virgam produxit virgaque florem,
> et super hunc florem requievit spiritus almus ;
> virgo dei genetrix virga est, flos filius eius.
>
> ad nutum domini nostrum ditantis honorem
> sicut spina rosam genuit Iudaea Mariam,
> ut vitium virtus operiret, gratia culpam.[2]

Most interesting of all is a quantitative poem, which celebrates
the joys of peace.   The verses show a curious metrical combination based, it seems, on Horace's *Solvitur acris hiems* :

> sanctum simpliciter patrem cole,
>   pauperum caterva,
> quantumque nosti, laudibus honora,
>
> ad normam redigit qui subdita
>   saecla pravitati,
> potens novandi sicut et creandi.
>
> et, grave damnate, longi tibi
>   subvenit laboris
> opem ferendo pacis et quietis.
>
> iam proceres legum rationibus
>   ante desueti,
> quae recta discunt, strenue capessunt.
>
> praedo manum cohibet furcae memor,
>   et latrone coram
> inermis alte praecinit viator,
>
> dente saturnali restringitur
>   evagata vitis
> cultuque tellus senta mansuescit.
>
> gaudet lancea falx, gaudet spata
>   devenire vomer,
> pax ditat imos, pauperat superbos.

[1] *Anal. Hymn.* l, pp. 283, 285, 284 ;   [2] *Anal. Hymn.* l, p. 286 ; Migne, cxli,
Migne, cxli, col. 350, 351, 345.   col. 345.

salve, summe pater, fer et omnibus
    integram salutem,
quicumque pacis diligunt quietem.

at qui bella volunt, hos contere
    dextera potenti,
tradens gehennae filios maligni.[1]

We now turn to Fulbert's rhythmical verse. Of the mono-rimed poem on the nightingale, Archbishop Trench says: 'Surely with all its rudeness and deficiencies this poem has the true passion of nature, and contains in it the prophecy and pledges of much more than it actually accomplishes'.[2] And we need hardly quarrel with this judgement. The rudeness and the deficiencies are obvious, but the poem is so clearly the expression of spontaneous feeling that it becomes something more than a conventional exercise, and wants nothing but an adequate form to pass into the realm of true poetry. As an illustration of medieval emotion in the face of nature it is worth quoting in full :

cum telluris vere novo, producuntur germina,
nemorosa circumcirca frondescunt et brachia :
fragrat odor cum suävis florida per gramina,
hilarescit Philomela, dulcis sonûs conscia,
et extendens modulando gutturis spiramina,
reddit veris et aestivi temporis praeconia.
instat nocti et diei voce sub dulcisona,
soporatis dans quietem cantûs per discrimina,
necnon pulchra viatori laboris solatia.
vocis eius pulchritudo clarior quam cithara ;
vincitur omnis cantando volucrum catervula :
implet sylvas atque cuncta modulis arbustula,
gloriosa valde facta veris prae laetitia.
volitando scandit alta arborum cacumina,
ac festiva satis gliscit sibilare carmina.
cedit anceps ad frondosa resonans umbracula,
cedit olor et suävis ipsius melodia ;
cedit tibi tympanistra et sonora tibia ;
quamvis enim videaris corpore permodica,
tamen cuncti capiuntur hac tua melodia :
nemo dedit voci tuae haec dulcia carmina,
nisi solus rex coelestis qui gubernat omnia.[3]

[1] *Anal. Hymn.* l, p. 288 ; Migne, cxli, col. 349 ; Manitius, *Gesch.* ii. 690, points out that the metrical scheme of the first two lines of each stanza is derived from Boëthius, with the addition of the iambic trimeter.
[2] *Sacred Latin Poetry*, p. 48.
[3] Trench, pp. 47–8 ; Migne, cxli, col. 348 ; Migne's text has one or two errors.

Here the mystical note is lacking which makes the charm of Pecham's *Philomena praevia*, but these lines of Fulbert are remarkable as exhibiting that new feeling for nature which was to enter so deeply into the vernacular poetry of Europe.

The verses on the Resurrection are by far the best known of Fulbert's poems, for they found their way into some of the breviaries and, in translation, into modern hymnaries.

chorus novae Ierusalem
novam meli dulcedinem
promat colens cum sobriis
paschale festum gaudiis.

triumphat ille splendide
et dignus amplitudine,
soli polique patriam
unam fecit republicam.

quo Christus invictus leo,
dracone surgens obruto,
dum voce viva personat,
a morte functos excitat.

ipsum canendo supplices
regem precemur milites,
ut in suo clarissimo
nos ordinet palatio.

quam devorarat improbus,
praedam refundit tartarus,
captivitate libera
Iesum sequuntur agmina.

per saecla metae nescia
patri supremo gloria
honorque sit cum filio
et spiritu paraclito.[1]

But we should form a false impression of Fulbert if we thought of him only as poet and scholar. It was as the Bishop of a great city in a time when the royal power was struggling with difficulty against the forces of political disruption that he stood forth the protector of his flock and of the rights of the Church, a man who pursued, without respect of persons, noble or ecclesiastical, the path which was followed, for the good of their own and of future generations, by so many medieval bishops who were called from the schools to the care of the churches.

One of the ablest of Fulbert's pupils was Berengar of Tours (999–1088), who won notoriety by an incautious and rationalistic examination of the doctrine of transubstantiation. He was compelled to retract his opinions; Lanfranc of Canterbury was his opponent, but neither had achieved a mastery of the dialectical weapons, and, if Berengar was obstinate and self-assertive, the Archbishop, in refuting him, had to resort to 'transparent sophisms'.[2] What concerns us here, however, is the fact that Berengar is the author of a hymn to Christ in which he uses

[1] *Anal. Hymn.* l, p. 285; Migne, cxli, col. 352.

[2] Poole, *Medieval Thought and Learning*, p. 90.

the same rhythmical forms and simple rime as his master Fulbert.[1] It begins :

> iuste iudex Iesu Christe, regum rex et domine,
> qui cum patre regnas semper et cum sancto flamine,
> nunc digneris preces meas clementer suscipere.
>
> tu de caelis descendisti virginis in uterum,
> unde sumens veram carnem visitasti saeculum,
> tuum plasmum redimendo sanguinem per proprium.
>
> tua quaeso, deus meus, gloriosa passio
> me defendat incessanter ab omni periculo,
> ut valeam permanere in tuo servitio.
>
> assit mihi tua virtus semper et defensio,
> mentem meam ne perturbet hostium incursio,
> ne damnetur corpus meum fraudulenti laqueo.
>
> dextra forti qua fregisti Acherontis ianuas,
> frange meos inimicos nec non et invidias,
> quibus volunt occupare cordis mei semitas.[2]

The prayer continues with recurring appeals against the malice of his enemies until it ceases to be certain whether Berengar is asking for protection against his ghostly foes or against his theological opponents, who ultimately silenced him.

Berengar had a pupil and friend, Eusebius Bruno, Bishop of Angers (d. 1081), who composed a group of rhythmical prayers, the most popular of which is addressed to S. Stephen : [3]

> 1. sancti dei pretiose,
>   protomartyr Stephane,
>   qui virtute charitatis
>   circumfultus undique.
>
> 2. dominum pro inimico
>   exorasti populo,
>   funde preces pro devoto
>   miseroque famulo.
>
> 3. ut tuo propitiatus
>   interventu dominus
>   me purgatum a peccatis
>   iungat caeli civibus.

Berengar had been Archdeacon at Angers before he went back to his native Tours to be the head of the school of S. Martin. The school at Angers must have deserved its good reputation, for among its scholars were such important men as Marbod of Rennes, Baudry of Bourgueil, and Geoffrey of Vendôme.

---

[1] See *Anal. Hymn.* xlviii, p. 79; *Hist. Litt.* viii. 90 sqq.

[2] Mone. i. 359 sqq. ; also Dreves-Blume, *Ein Jahrtausend lateinischer Hymnendichtung*, i. 176.

[3] Texts, *Anal. Hymn.* xlviii, pp. 79 sqq.

§ 2. *Hildebert of Lavardin*, 1056–1133.

Hildebert of Lavardin,[1] one of the most important literary figures of the Middle Ages, a master of classical Latin, whose verses were read with delight throughout Western Europe, and whose letters were used as models in the schools, was born in 1056, and died in 1133. Tradition affirms that he was a pupil of Berengar of Tours.[2] He appears, at any rate, to have studied at Le Mans, where in due course he rose to the headship of the cathedral school. In 1091 he became Archdeacon, and in 1096 the clergy elected him to the vacant bishopric. But William Rufus, who was feudal overlord, refused to recognize Hildebert's election, and when, a few years later, the king entered Le Mans at the head of an army he ordered the Bishop to raze the towers of his cathedral. Hildebert refused, and was carried to England to be tried by the English bishops. He managed, however, to return to his diocese, where William's hatred still pursued him, and only the king's death in 1100 saved him from worse things. Henry I became his friend, but Hildebert's experience of ecclesiastical promotion had disillusioned him. He made a fruitless journey to Rome with the object of inducing the Pope to allow him to lay down his office. The sight of the imperial city moved him to admiration, and musing on that spectacle of grandeur and ruin he composed his two elegies on the pagan Rome of the past and the Christian Rome of the present.

Returning sadly to his pastoral cares, he busied himself with the rebuilding of his cathedral, which was consecrated in April 1120. But these were years of trouble. In 1112 he suffered from feudal violence, and was unlawfully imprisoned at Nogent-le-Rotrou. In 1116, as he was setting forth on his second

---

[1] On Hildebert, see *Notice sur les mélanges poétiques d'Hildebert de Lavardin*, by Hauréau, in xxviii. ii. 289 sqq. of *Notices et extraits des mss.*, and especially A. Wilmart, *Le Florilège de Saint-Gatien. Contribution à l'étude des poèmes d'Hildebert et de Marbode*, *Rev. Bénéd.*, xlviii (1936), pp. 3 sqq.; 147 sqq.; 235 sqq. It is worth noting that three, at least, of the poems usually included among Hildebert's are to be attributed to Peter, surnamed the Painter, a canon of St. Omer (twelfth century). These are (1) the piece on the Eucharist; Migne, clxxi, col. 1193 sqq., beginning, 'si deus elegit tria quae sibi sacrificentur'; (2) another piece on the same subject, ib., col. 1198 sqq., with a prologue beginning, 'quisquis nostri redemptoris vestiris imagine'. On these two pieces, see Hauréau, pp. 357 sqq.; (3) verses on the Trinity, Migne, clxxi, col. 1417 sq., ending in *esse* (Hauréau, p. 345).

esse quod est ex se deus est, per quod
 datur esse,
quod non est ex se, deitatis non habet
 esse.
esse quod est deus est, cui verum competit esse, etc.

[2] Hildebert composed his epitaph.

journey to Rome, he unwisely allowed Henry the monk, a follower of Peter de Bruys, free licence to preach in his diocese.
Henry's fierce attacks on the clergy inflamed them against their
bishop, who had the greater sorrow of seeing many of his people
given over to what could only be described as heresy.[1]   With
much difficulty he restored both clergy and people to order, and
in 1123 he was able to proceed once more to Rome, where he
was probably present at the Lateran Council.   In 1125, sorely
against his will, he was elected to the Archbishopric of Tours,
and there, in his old age, he found himself again in conflict with
authority, represented this time by the formidable Louis the Fat,
of France.

A few theological treatises are attributed to Hildebert, and
he has left a collection of letters whose sincere and lively
character lends them a considerable interest.   Not more than
four sermons survive which can be assigned to him with any
degree of probability,[2] and they employ the usual method of
allegory.   Herein Hildebert was the true child of his age,
but, like John of Salisbury, he showed himself pre-eminently
above it in his deep love and knowledge of classical letters,
and, even more than John, in his sense of the glory and beauty
of the inheritance of the Roman past.   So he records the
emotions with which he saw the ruined city after the ravages
of the German soldiers of Henry IV, and the Normans and
Saracens of Robert Guiscard :

> par tibi, Roma, nihil, cum sis prope tota ruina ;
>   quam magni fueris integra fracta doces.
> longa tuos fastus aetas destruxit, et arces
>   Caesaris et superûm templa palude iacent.
> ille labor, labor ille ruit quem dirus Araxes
>   et stantem tremuit et cecidisse dolet ;
> quem gladii regum, quem provida cura senatus,
>   quem superi rerum constituere caput ;
> quem magis optavit cum crimine solus habere
>   Caesar, quam socius et pius esse socer,
> qui crescens studiis tribus, hostes, crimen, amicos
>   vi domuit, secuit legibus, emit ope ;
> in quem, dum fieret, vigilavit cura priorum :
>   iuvit opus pietas hospitis, unda, locus.
> materiem, fabros, expensas axis uterque
>   misit, se muris obtulit ipse locus.

[1] Tocco, *L'eresia nel medio evo*, p. 160.   *Notices et extraits des mss*, xxxii. ii,
[2] Hauréau, *Notice sur les sermons* pp. 106 sqq.
attribués à Hildebert de Lavardin,

expendere duces thesauros, fata favorem,
artifices studium, totus et orbis opes.
urbs cecidit de qua si quicquam dicere dignum
moliar, hoc potero dicere : Roma fuit.
non tamen annorum series, non flamma, nec ensis
ad plenum potuit hoc abolere decus.[1]

In March 1084 Henry IV had entered Rome, seized the
Lateran, and was crowned in S. Peter's by his Anti-pope, while
Gregory VII held out in Hadrian's mausoleum. The Septizo-
nium was defended by the papal troops against the German
soldiers, and the stately columns erected by Septimius Severus
fell before the battering machines. The capitol was a scene
of desolation when Henry at last succeeded in storming it.
S. Angelo still held out when Robert Guiscard came to relieve
the worn and anxious, but still indomitable Pope. The Emperor
retired in haste and left the rebellious Romans, who had trusted
to his promises, to the mercy of the Normans. S. Angelo was
soon relieved, and the Pope embraced his deliverer, but the
helpless city was wasted with fire and sword. The chronicler
relates [2] how many thousand Romans were sold ' like Jews ',
and others were carried away as prisoners. Churches were despoiled
or went up in flames ; precious monuments of antiquity, which
had been spared by Goths and Vandals, were utterly destroyed.
In the words of Gibbon, 'a spacious quarter of the city from
the Lateran to the Coliseum was consumed by the flames and
devoted to perpetual solitude'.[3] The desertion and desolation
which five centuries later filled with wonder the soul of Joachim
du Bellay date from this pillage by the Normans and Saracens
who followed the standard of Robert Guiscard.

In another poem Hildebert celebrates the Christian Rome of
the Popes, richer in her poverty and ruin than in the days of
her splendour, more glorious under the standard of the Cross
than when the eagles flew, more exalted under Peter than in the
days of the Caesars. In the poem it is Rome herself that
speaks and confesses :

---

[1] Hauréau, pp. 331-2 ; so thoroughly classical in execution are these and other verses of Hildebert that, before their authorship was known, they found their way into anthologies of classical Latin verse ; see Norden, *Antike Kunstprosa*, ii. 722. Norden remarks, ' Die Augen dieses Mannes haben auf den Ruinen schon mit jener sentimentalen Sehnsucht geruht, die seit Petrarcha gewöhnlich war' ; see also Gregorovius, iv. i, p. 248 sq.

[2] Bonizo, quoted by Gregorovius, iv. i. 247.

[3] *Decline and Fall*, vi. 205 (Bury's edition) ; cf. Giesebrecht, *Deutsche Kaiserzeit*, iii, p. 565.

dum simulacra mihi, dum numina vana placerent,
    militia, populo, moenibus alta fui;
at simul effigies arasque superstitiosas
    deiiciens, uni sum famulata deo,
cesserunt arces, cecidere palatia divûm,
    servivit populus, degeneravit eques.
vix scio quae fuerim, vix Romae Roma recordor,
    vix sinit occasus vel meminisse mei.
gratior haec iactura mihi successibus illis;
    maior sum pauper divite, stante iacens.
plus aquilis vexilla crucis, plus Caesare Petrus,
    plus cinctis ducibus vulgus inerme dedit.
stans domui terras, infernum diruta pulso;
    corpora stans, animas fracta iacensque rego.
tunc miserae plebi, modo principibus tenebrarum
    impero; tunc urbes, nunc mea regna polus.[1]

These remarkable poems display the two dominant influences in the life of Hildebert. His sense of history and his affection for those ancient masters of the world[2] whose material, intellectual, and artistic achievements seemed so stupendous, led him back to the pagan past, unfettered by revelation, confident in itself, delighting in natural impulse, chafing under no restraint. But over all this the Cross had cast its shadow; the wisdom of the wisest was after all only a charming folly, and the material might of Rome was only an empire over men's bodies. The empire of souls was Peter's and not Caesar's. It is only against the Church that the gates of hell cannot prevail. So, first and foremost, Hildebert is a Churchman, and if in his poems he shows again and again how closely he has studied his Virgil and Ovid, he is drawn irresistibly to adapt his classical forms to a Christian theme.

Hildebert is at his best in the long poem *De exsilio suo*,[3] in which he laments the misfortunes of his life, beginning after the style of the pagan poets, and ending piously with unshaken faith in providence:

si fas est credi te quidquam posse vel esse,
    o fortuna, quid.es? quod potes ipse dedit.

[1] Hauréau, p. 334.

[2] On the feeling of Hildebert and of the Middle Ages generally for the grandeur of the ruins of Rome, see Graf, *Roma nella memoria del medio evo*, i. 33 sqq.; ii. 419. Graf quotes these two poems in full, and ii. 421, two verses on the same text as that of the second poem:

Roma vetusta fui, sed nunc nova Roma vocabor;
eruta ruderibus, culmen ad astra fero.

[3] Hauréau, p. 347.

pace tua, fortuna, loquar: blandire, minare ;
  nil tamen unde querar aut bene laeter ages.
ille potens, mitis, tenor et concordia rerum,
  quidquid vult in me digerat, eius ero.

Two examples of epigrams, in leonine elegiacs, on Christian themes, however trivial they may appear, were no doubt warmly admired by his contemporaries.

De Virgine Maria.

lacto creatorem, salvum mihi crede pudorem.
  res nova : virgo parens, et caro patre carens.

Super Crucem.

crux finis legis, via vitae, passio regis,
  cui dedit interitum gratia, non meritum.[1]

But Hildebert experimented also in the new accentual verse, and showed himself able to attain a mastery of the two-syllabled rime only equalled by Adam of S. Victor. He has left an admirable hymn, which has the form of a prayer addressed to the three Persons of the Trinity.[2]   It begins :

Alpha et Ω, magne deus,
Heli, Heli, deus meus,
cuius virtus totum posse,
cuius sensus totum nosse,
cuius esse summum bonum,
cuius opus quidquid bonum.

super cuncta, subter cuncta ;
extra cuncta, intra cuncta.
intra cuncta, nec inclusus ;
extra cuncta, nec exclusus ;
super cuncta, nec elatus ;
subter cuncta, nec substratus.

But before the end the poem loses its scholastic flavour and becomes an inspired lyric which ranks as one of the few masterpieces of the mystical verse of the Middle Ages.

me receptet Sion illa,
Sion David urbs tranquilla,
cuius faber auctor lucis,
cuius portae lignum crucis,
cuius claves lingua Petri,
cuius cives semper laeti,
cuius muri lapis vivus,
cuius custos rex festivus,

in hac urbe lux solennis,
ver aeternum, pax perennis :
in hac odor implens caelos,
in hac semper festum melos ;
non est ibi corruptela,
non defectus, non querela ;
non minuti, non deformes,
omnes Christo sunt conformes.

---

[1] Migne, clxxi, col. 1407 ; Hauréau, p. 326, is ready to admit Hildebert's authorship.

[2] Text, Migne, clxxi, col. 1411 sqq. ; see

Hauréau, p. 340; the pause after the fourth syllable is observed, with one exception, throughout; see Meyer, *Rythmik*, i. 318.

urbs caelestis, urbs beata	quis affectus eos stringat,
super petram collocata ;	aut quae gemma muros pingat,
urbs in portu satis tuto,	quis calcedon, quis iacynthus
de longinquo te saluto :	norunt illi qui sunt intus.
te saluto, te suspiro,	in plateis huius urbis
te affecto, te requiro.	sociatus piis turbis
quantum tui gratulantur,	cum Moyse et Elia
quam festive convivantur,	pium cantem Alleluia.

Amen.

This is the true medieval appeal, from the earthly city to the heavenly, from this world to the next ; and it is perhaps a personal cry if the poem was composed, as has been suggested, during Hildebert's exile in England.[1] For he felt his misfortunes keenly. Deserted by friends, deserted by his clergy, he had often to fight alone. In one of his letters, which is a kind of confession of faith, he describes the pathos of his position and his unshaken faith in the guidance of God. It was written at the time of his conflict with Louis the Fat. 'I will cast my thought upon the Lord, and He shall give me the desire of my heart. The Lord remembered Joseph, whom Pharaoh's butler, in his time of prosperity, forgot, and failed to intercede for him. He remembered also David His servant when he was abandoned even by his own son, and He lifted him up in triumph and exalted him to be king. Perchance He will be mindful even of me, and will bring my wave-tossed ship into the haven where I would be. For it is He who regardeth the prayer of the humble, and doth not despise their supplications. It is He

---

[1] An English poet of the early seventeenth century has admirably rendered these closing lines. W. Crashaw, *Manuell for True Catholics*, 1611 :

In Sion, lodge me, Lord, for pity—
Sion, David's kingly city,
Built by Him that 's only good ;
Whose gates be of the Cross's wood ;
Whose keys are Christ's undoubted word ;
Whose dwellers fear none but the Lord.
Whose walls are stone, strong, quick and bright,
Whose keeper is the Lord of Light :
Here the light doth never cease,
Endless Spring and endless peace ;
Here is music, heaven filling,
Sweetness evermore distilling ;

Here is neither spot nor taint,
No defect, nor no complaint ;
No man crookèd, great nor small,
But to Christ conformèd all.
Blessed town, divinely gracèd
On a rock so strongly placèd,
Thee I see and thee I long for,
Thee I seek and thee I groan for,
O what joy thy dwellers taste
All in pleasure first and last !
What full enjoying bliss divine;
What jewels on thy walls do shine !
Ruby, jacinth, chalcedon,
Known to them within alone,
In this glorious company
In the streets of Sion, I
With Job, Moses, and Eliah
Will sing the heavenly Alleluia.

Amen.

in whose hands the hearts of kings are as wax.'[1]   It is not too much to say that it is by virtue of his sense of the pathos of his numerous experiences that his verses are often raised above the level of formal exercises, and sometimes reach the height of true poetry.

Hildebert is the reputed author of another lengthy poem, *Lamentatio Peccatricis Animae*, the lament of the sinful soul, a long-drawn-out *Dies Irae*, a hymn of the terror of judgement :

cum dies mortis venerit,
cum mors urgere coeperit,
tunc mihi risus deerit,
tunc sero luctus aderit.
. . . nunquam me caste colui,
sed foede nimis pollui,
virgo putari volui,
pudicus esse nolui.

. . . amara dies veniet,
qua iustus iudex veniet,
per quem omnis recipiet
iuxta quod modo faciet.
tuba clangens ab aethere
omnes iubebit surgere,
ad tribunal occurrere,
iacta, dictaque promere.[2]

The pains of the wicked are described minutely :

si tunc damnatus fueris,
si, quod absit ! perieris,

flebis quod natus fueris,
quod una hora vixeris.

But for the good remain the joys of the heavenly Jerusalem :

o Sion ! sancta civitas
in qua sic ardet caritas

quanta tua felicitas,
quanta in te tranquillitas !

Then, as in the *Dies Irae*, the note changes, and the appeal is to the eternal compassion of God :

tu, pro salute hominis,
alvum intrasti virginis
ut nostri praedam germinis
saevis auferres dominis.
tu, propter nos, ludibria,
tu, sputorum opprobria,

crucis quoque supplicia
mira tulisti gratia.
. . . illa, rex Christe, passio
fiat mihi redemptio,
peccatorum remissio,
paradisi regressio.

And yet the poet of noble elegies and hymns joined the monks in their ill-mannered attack on the other half of the human race.   Hildebert was, it seems, the author of the lines entitled ' Quam nociva sint sacris hominibus femina, avaritia,

[1] *Epistolae*, ii.33 ; Migne, clxxi, col. 257.
[2] Migne, clxxi, col. 1339; Dreves, *Anal. Hymn.* l, p. 409, is, however, unwilling to ascribe this hymn to Hildebert. On account of the two-syllabled masculine rime he prefers to place it in the thirteenth century, or at the earliest at the end of the twelfth, and he is probably right.

ambitio'.[1] It is in these terms that he assails the female sex:

> femina res fragilis, nunquam sine crimine constans,
> nunquam sponte sua desinit esse nocens,

But this is a mere poetical declamation, a commonplace of medieval rhetoric, and it did not hinder the author from treating individual women with all courtesy. Indeed, Hauréau tells us that Hildebert in this respect was beyond reproach,[2] and he cites for proof the verses with which he answered a young girl [3] who had sent him in his exile a poem composed in Latin, in which she expressed her sympathy for him in his misfortune. Hildebert's reply is well turned in his best 'classical manner', but it displays as well what Hauréau so aptly calls 'les raffine-ments de son exquise urbanité'.[4]

> tempora prisca decem se iactavere sybillis
> et vestri sexus gloria magna fuit;
> unius ingenio praesentia saecula gaudent
> quod non ex toto virgine vate carent.

The verses continue in this tone of courteous flattery, and so Hildebert makes amends for the bad taste of his other poem. At the time of his election to the see of Le Mans, his enemies accused him of living a life of great disorder, and Ivo, Bishop of Chartres, took it upon himself to warn Hildebert, in very plain terms, of the report that he was constantly surrounded by a crowd of women, even when he was exercising the office of Archdeacon, and that he was said to be the father of several natural children. But this is merely an example of the manner in which it was common to defame the character of a man whose reputation it was desired, for particular reasons, to injure, and if the censorious Geoffrey of Vendôme wrote to him as 'Hildebertus beatae vitae',[5] and if Bernard of Clairvaux addressed him, 'magno sacerdoti et excelso in verbo gloriae', it is possible that the veiled accusations of Ivo were without serious foundation. Hildebert was buried beside the high altar in his metropolitan church, and, as his body was said to have displayed miraculous power, attempts were made to claim him

---

[1] Hauréau, pp. 365 sqq., with text.
[2] ib., p. 364.
[3] Perhaps, however, we are wrong in assuming her youth.
[4] Hauréau, p. 385.
[5] *Hist. Litt.* xi, p. 260.

as a saint. The mention of his name by medieval writers often leads them to quote two verses which form his fitting epitaph :

> inclitus et prosa, versuque per omnia primus
> Hildebertus olet prorsus ubique rosam.[1]

§ 3. *Marbod of Rennes,* 1035 *circa*-1123.

Of almost equal literary eminence in his day was Marbod of Rennes,[2] whose scholastic and ecclesiastical career is curiously similar to that of his friend Hildebert. Marbod was born at Angers about the year 1035, and he studied in the cathedral school of his native town under a pupil of Fulbert of Chartres. Like Hildebert, he rose to the headship of his school, and became an archdeacon. In 1096 he was made Bishop of Rennes, and in his eighty-eighth year he retired to the Benedictine cloister of S. Aubin at Angers, where he died on September 11, 1123. Like Hildebert's, his intellectual interests were divided between the classical and the Christian world, but he was fascinated above all by the symbolism which, for him as for his contemporaries, lay hidden in nature, and by the mysterious virtues and qualities of gems and precious stones. In his youth he wrote light verses, of which he duly repented in a poetical confession :

> quae, iuvenis scripsi, senior, dum plura retracto,
> poenitet, et quaedam vel scripta, vel edita nollem,
> tum quia materies inhonesta levisque videtur,
> tum quia dicendi potuit modus aptior esse.[3]

We do not know what kind of verses the Bishop was thinking of when he referred to the indiscreet and badly composed productions of his thoughtless youth. They were perhaps school-exercises in which a certain amount of licence was allowed. Or they may have been harmless love-poems or epigrams in imitation of classical models. An epigram on the stock theme of the deceitfulness of woman has been ascribed to him, but it may not be his. Indeed, the manuscript evidence would appear to be decidedly against such an attribution :

---

[1] Hauréau, p. 290 ; the verses are taken from a poem by a monk of Rievaulx.

[2] The works of Marbod are in Migne, vol. clxxi; see also *Poèmes de Marbode,*

evêque de Rennes, ed. (with translation) by S. Ropartz, Rennes, 1873.

[3] Migne, clxxi, col. 1693.

> quisquis eris qui credideris fidei mulieris,
> crede mihi, si credis ei, quia decipieris.[1]

And in his terrible verses *De Meretrice*, he tells us that ' among the countless snares which the crafty foe has spread over all the hills and plains of the world the greatest is woman ; scarce any can escape that snare ',

> femina, triste caput, mala stirps, vitiosa propago.[2]

But it is only fair to add that Marbod devoted another poem to the praises of virtuous women, the sober matrons whose lives were ruled according to the laws of Christ.[3]

The poems of Marbod's riper years have mostly a didactic character ; they lack the finer qualities of Hildebert's, but they are the work of a man of intelligence who was not a mere juggler with words.[4] The *Liber Lapidum* or *Liber de Gemmis*,[5] which gathers into small compass the fantastic theories of the ancient and the medieval world on the symbolism of precious stones, gained such immense popularity that it was speedily translated into French. The account of the mysterious stone called *Allectorium* is an amusing instance of the credulity which Marbod shared with the finest minds of the Middle Ages.

> ventriculo galli, qui testibus est viduatus,
> cum tribus, ut minimum, factus spado, vixerit annis,
> nascitur ille lapis, cuius non ultima laus est,
> et per bis binos capit incrementa sequentes,
> mensuramque fabae crescens excedere nescit.
> crystallo similis, vel aquae, cum limpida paret.
> huic allectorio nomen posuere priores.
> invictum reddit lapis hic quemcunque gerentem,
> exstinguitque sitim patientis in ore receptus.
> . . . hic circa Veneris facit incentiva vigentes.
> commodus uxori quae vult fore grata marito.
> ut bona tot praestet clausus portatur in ore,[6]

of the Jasper, Marbod says :

> appositusque iuvat mulierem parturientem,

---

[1] Migne, clxxi, col. 1684. [2] ib., col. 1698.
[3] *De matrona*, col. 1699.
[4] Cf. Hauréau, in *Journal des savants*, 1881, p. 474.
[5] Migne, clxxi, col. 1738 ; for another poem on the same subject, which has been attributed to Marbod, see Hauréau in *Notices et extraits des mss.*, xxxiii, pp. 194–6.
[6] Migne, clxxi, col. 1742.

and he tells us that the onyx excites nightmares if worn on neck
or finger, while he who wears the sapphire is proof against all
fraud and envy, and need not fear any kind of terror.   Nay, of
such virtue is the sapphire that it leads the captives out of prison,
and makes God Himself favourable and compels Him to listen
to prayer ! [1]

The *Liber Lapidum* is written in quantitative hexameters,
but the following poem demonstrates that Marbod had, like
Hildebert, attained a considerable mastery of the two-syllabled
rime.   The verses are taken from a penitential poem, which is
almost an anticipation of the *Dies Irae* :

cum recordor, quanta cura
sum sectatus peritura
et quam dura sub censura
mors exercet sua iura.

cum singultu preces fundo,
flecto genu, pectus tundo,
ore loquens tremebundo
ad te clamans de profundo.

in interiori meo,
quod est patens soli deo,
dans rugitum sicut leo,
pro peccatis meis fleo.

Iesu Christe, fili dei,
consubstantialis ei,
factor noctis et diei,
quaero, miserere mei.

cum recordor transiturum
me per mortis iter durum
et, quid de me sit futurum
post examen illud purum,

per parentis primae morsum
lapsi sumus huc deorsum,
gravant nobis culpae dorsum,
quas commisimus seorsum.

mentis anxius tumultu,
quae virtutum caret cultu,
tristi corde, tristi vultu,
preces fundo cum singultu.

per secundum genetricem,
saeculi reparatricem,
veterem converte vicem
corpus lavans atque psychen.

sit laus Christo, nostro patri,
sit laus suae sanctae matri,
qui nos tueantur atri
a suppliciis barathri.[2]

Hymns which may be Marbod's were used at Rennes, as for
instance the beautiful verses on Mary Magdalene which were
sung at Lauds.   The rime is simple and the measure is accentual.

---

[1] ib., col. 1744.   Serious doubts have
been raised as to Marbod's authorship of
this poem, but the MS. evidence is decisive ; see L. Pannier, *Les lapidaires français du moyen âge*, p. 19.   It need not be
assumed that he composed it after he
became a bishop.

[2] Migne, clxxi, col. 1651 ; *Anal. Hymn.*
l, p. 402, where the question of Marbod's
authorship is left unresolved. But Wilmart,
on good evidence, ascribes it to Marbod.

omnes immundi, currite,	pedes, quos nudat dominus,
fons patet indulgentiae,	tergamus nostris crinibus,
nullus desperet veniam,	superfluis ex opibus
qui servat patientiam.	ministremus pauperibus.
exemplum dei filius	augebit nobis gratiam,
ostendit peccatoribus,	qui praestat indulgentiam,
Mariam, vas spurcitiae,	ut nostra ex fragrantia
septeno plenam daemone.	redoleat ecclesia.
qua quondam nulla turpior,	peccatrix haec sanctissima
qua nunc vix ulla sanctior,	nostra propulset crimina,
quae Christi pedes abluit,	eius nobis oratio
sed mox et caput imbuit.	sit virtutum largitio.
abhorret Christus neminem,	sit laus patri ingenito
deus non spernit hominem,	et eius unigenito
agamus illi gratias	cum spiritu paraclito
pias fundendo lacrimas.	nec nato nec ingenito.[1]

But the rimed hexameter was Marbod's favourite metre, especially the leonine form. The *Verses on S. Laurence*, those on the *Passion of S. Victor*, and a whole series of minor poems are in leonine hexameters.[2] The musical effect which was obtained by the use of the two-syllabled rime in the hexameter must have helped a great deal to make that form of rime popular in accentual verse. Hence from the end of the eleventh century onwards that rime is used by all the foremost poets. The verses *De Annuntiatione Domini* show the measure of skill which Marbod attained in a metre which was always too monotonous to lend itself to free expression.

> missus ad egregiam Gabriel tulit ista Mariam :
> innuba semper ave, flos pulcher, o ensque suave,
> Christum ventre feres, benedicta super mulieres ;
> solus erit salvus, tua quem salvaverit alvus ;
> ex te nascetur qui sceptra David moderetur,
> de fructu cuius spes germinis exiet huius,
> nunc et in aeternum gerit hic diadema paternum,
> Iesus erit dictus super omnia rex benedictus.[3]

Another poem, addressed also to the Virgin, is an interesting metrical experiment in hexameters, with an internal and a tailed

---

[1] Migne, clxxi, col. 1649 ; *Anal. Hymn.* l, p. 399.

[2] The long 'metrical history of Theophilus' is wrongly ascribed to Marbod; see Meyer, *Rythmik*, i. 97-8. Dom Wil-mart's investigation of the manuscript tradition of the poems of Marbod (see above, p. 265, n. 1) is invaluable in determining questions of authenticity.

[3] Migne, clxxi, col. 1661.

(two-syllabled) rime, which recalls the metre of Bernard of Cluny's famous satire. Marbod's poem begins :

> stella maris, quae sola paris sine coniuge prolem,
> iustitiae clarum specie super omnia solem,
> gemma decens, rosa nata recens, perfecta decore,
> mella cavis inclusa favis imitata sapore
> omnimodos tuus almus odos praecellit odores,
> exsuperat, quos ver reserat, tua gratia flores.[1]

While Hildebert of Lavardin was a poet by nature, who expressed in verse the content of his rich experience, Marbod of Rennes was always the maker of verses and the didactic bishop. We have seen how the elegies of Hildebert recall the best qualities of classical verse without losing the excellence which belongs to originality, and how, in his religious poetry, he handled the new accentual verse with splendid effect. The two-syllabled rime is used with great skill and assurance, and it was largely from Hildebert that the poets of the twelfth century must have learned the secret of their smooth versification. Marbod is as far behind Hildebert in technical excellence as in inspiration. He was cast in a smaller intellectual mould, and his poetry is not always above the level of exercises which continue the lessons he learned in his cathedral school. Nevertheless, he was accounted by his contemporaries a finished scholar and a most illustrious poet,[2] and his friend Hildebert referred to him as the ' Orpheus of our age '.

§ 4. *Baudry of Bourgueil*, 1046–1130, *and Geoffrey of Vendôme*, 1070–1132.

Baudry of Bourgueil was once better known for his history of the conquest of Jerusalem than for his verse, but M. Léopold Delisle,[3] by printing a selection of his poems, caused his merits to be recognized, and at length a complete edition, after the Vatican manuscript, is available.[4]

Baudry was born in 1046 at Meung-sur-Loire, near Orléans.

---

[1] ib., col. 1652.

[2] Cf. the letter sent by the monks of Angers, announcing his death ; quoted by Ropartz, pp. 1–3.

[3] *Notes sur les poésies de Baudri, abbé de Bourgueil, Romania*, i. 23 sqq.

[4] *Les œuvres poétiques de Baudri de Bourgueil*, ed. Phyllis Abrahams, Paris 1926; with good notes, analyses of the poems, and a study of Baudry's style and grammar.

He began his studies in his native town, and seems to have continued them at Angers, where he may have come into contact with Berengar of Tours, for whose abilities he had the greatest admiration.[1] Like Hildebert and Marbod, he became a skilful versifier, but with him the making of verses became an over-mastering passion. He left the world for the monastery, and in 1089 he was made Abbot of Bourgueil. He still pursued his studies, and he still made verses, but he did not neglect the affairs of the house entrusted to his charge. In 1107 he was elected to the see of Dol in Brittany. But he was not happy among his unruly and somewhat barbarous flock, and he went overseas to England, visiting the well-disciplined and prosperous Benedictine houses, where he received hospitality and enjoyed the society of scholars. In Normandy, too, and especially at Bec and Fécamp, he found the monastic houses to his taste. He loved to make his retreat in Normandy at a small possession of his cathedral church, whence he could visit his monastic friends at Fécamp, Fontenelle, and Jumièges. On January 7, 1130, he died, old and famous.

Now that his work can be studied as a whole we are, for the first time, in a position to estimate his importance as a man of letters. For it is as a man of letters, even more truly than Hildebert and Marbod, that he must be considered. In spite of the years which he spent in a monastery, he is the mature product of the eleventh-century cathedral schools. He has an attitude towards the business of letters which makes him the precursor of the literary men of the twelfth century.[2] He took his work and that of his contemporaries seriously; he sent his poems for their criticism, and he treasured the friendship of men with whom he hoped to share a literary immortality.[3] So he writes in verse to Godfrey, a poet who was the glory of the school of Reims, praising him as one who had the 'gravity' of Virgil and the 'levity' of Ovid, and asking him to make the name of Baudry immortal by mentioning it in his verse.[4]

[1] Cf. Baudry's epitaph for Berengar, *Œuvres*, p. 82.

[2] See Miss Abrahams's remarks, p. xliv.

[3] Cf. Wattenbach, *Lateinische Gedichte aus Frankreich im elften Jahrhundert*, *Berlin. Sitzungsber.*, 1891, p. 98, ' Es erin-nert an das Zeitalter der Humanisten, wenn wir sehen, wie hoch diese Dichter und ihre Freunde von sich und ihren Werken denken, wie sie sich als Lieblinge der Musen darstellen und unbedenklich einander Unsterblichkeit und ewigen Ruhm versprechen.'

[4] *Œuvres*, p. 153; on Godfrey of Reims, see Wattenbach's article cited above, where specimens of his verse will be found.

o utinam per te meruissem perpetuari,
meque perennaret musa canendo tua.

Baudry also approached the great Marbod, the 'divine poet',[1] who shared with him an 'ingens dictandi ardor', asking him to read his verses and not to spare his criticism. If Marbod praises him, envy and malice will be silent. Hildebert he had never seen, but from his poems he judged him the equal of the great masters, and worthy of mention by the side of Virgil.[2] He ventures to ask Hildebert to send him some poems and receive him into the circle of his friends. But Baudry never attempted to imitate the gravity of Hildebert; he continued his light verse to the end, and never felt those prickings of conscience which troubled so many of his contemporaries.[3] There were, of course, unkind critics ready to accuse him of wasting on frivolous verses the time which ought to have been devoted to sermons or to his soul. But he had an answer which satisfied himself, if it did not silence his critics. He had written an edifying poem on Moses, he had composed lives of the saints, and he had many sermons to his credit. His verse was the relaxation of his leisure, written at night or while he was travelling.[4] He did not spend much of his time on it. It is true that a good deal of it is light and trifling, but he does what he can do best. He ought to be more serious, but — *qu'y faire?* He writes to be read by the young of both sexes,

ergo quod pueros demulceat atque puellas
scripsimus, ut pueris id consonet atque puellis,
sicque meum relegatur opus volitetque per orbem
illud dum relegent pueri relegentque puellae.[5]

There are, he goes on to confess, love-dialogues among his poems, but his own life is pure, and he is using only for amusement the characters who speak their own words and not his.[6] And, after all, as he says to Godfrey,[7] is it wrong to write about love if it gives pleasure, and one's own life is above reproach? No clergyman, who was really in love, would publish the fact in his verse :

non est in triviis alicuius amor recitandus,
quisquis amat, cautus celet amoris opus.

[1] *Œuvres*, p. 124.   [2] ib., p. 126.   [5] ib., p. 123.
[3] Cf Miss Abrahams's remarks, p. 17,   [6] Baudry is perhaps referring to his love-
note 7.   letters of Paris and Helen, pp. 29 sqq.
[4] *Œuvres*, p. 14.   [7] *Œuvres*, p. 156.

It was his muse that made life pleasant for him, and his ideal, which he expressed in a charming idyll, *de sufficientia votorum suorum*,[1] was that of a peaceful existence in a country house, with a boy to look after him, a garden, a small farm, enough books, and some good wine—but, with all this, he would wish for a greater poetical gift, such as Marbod's, or Godfrey's, or Hildebert's. Baudry had caught the spirit of the pastoral, and had learned the conventions of the bucolic poet. His is a rustic muse, because he lives in the country, in a place where the onion is more appropriate than the stilus and the tablets :

> rustica dicta mihi quia rusticus incola ruris,
> Magduni natus, incolo Burgulium.
> Burgulius locus est procul a Cicerone remotus,
> cui plus caepe placet quam stilus et tabulae.[2]

Yet the spot might well have been beloved of poets in days when the solitary Muses haunted the woods :

> nam prope prata virent illimibus humida rivis,
> prataque gramineo flore fovent oculos.
> et virides herbas lucus vicinus amoenat,
> quem concors avium garrulitas decorat.

Of the Latin poets, Ovid was his master and his favourite. Once he lent a precious volume to a friend who had persuaded him to part with the book by cunning words and against his better judgement. He hopes that he may see it again :

> o utinam verum iuraverit, ut mihi reddat
> quem male decepto sustulit Ovidium.[3]

The elegiac is, naturally enough, Baudry's favourite metre, but he could not hold out against the lure of rime, whether in the form of hexameter couplets :

> in rotulo multi cum sollicitudine quadam
> dicendi seriem semper metantur ad Adam.[4]

or of leonine elegiacs :

> abbas Natalis, flos abbatum specialis,
> signat quod sit homo factus humus sub humo.[5]

---

[1] *Œuvres*, pp. 183 sqq.
[2] ib., p. 271 sq.   [3] ib., p. 165.
[4] ib., p. 57 ; a piece written for the *rotulus* of Abbot Natalis, which announced his death. Baudry is complaining that authors of these compositions begin with a wearisome similarity by describing the fall of Adam ; see note 1, p. 57 ; also Pasquier, *Baudri, abbé de Bourgeuil*, pp. 109 sqq.   [5] *Œuvres*, p. 59.

But for his longer poems he preferred the classical elegiac or the hexameter. He chose the elegiac for his long epistles [1]—Florus to Ovid and Ovid to Florus—in which the misery of the poet's exile and the chances of his release are discussed; but when he imitated the *Heroides*, more obviously in the letters of Paris and Helen, he strangely chose the hexameter.

Baudry took care that his verses were handsomely 'produced'. He loved to adorn them with initials in gold and red and green:

> praecepi fieri capitales aere figuras,
>   ut quod non sensus res tribuat pretium.
> ad nos miserunt Arabes huc forsitan aurum,
>   materiarum quo signa priora micant ;
> introitus alios minio viridique colore,
>   ut mirabilius omne nitescat opus ;
> ut quos allicere sententia plena nequibit,
>   hos saltem species codicis alliciat.[2]

Then he tells us that he has a youth who is a skilled copyist, Walter by name, and a gilder, Gerard of Tours, who limps like Jacob, but is an excellent craftsman :

> claudicat ut Iacob, quoniam pede claudicat uno,
>   scriptor sed recto praevalet ingenio.

We get another glimpse of Gerard in a little epigram humourously urging him to his task of making fair copies on parchment of the verses which his master had scribbled on his tablets of wax :

> sic, Girarde meus, tibi sit pes unus ut alter,
>   quodque tibi cupio, carmina scribe mea.
> carmina carminibus nostris super apposuissem,
>   si super apposita susciperent tabulae.
> implevi nostras, dum tu pigritare, tabellas,
>   dum scriptum in cera lentus es excipere.
> ut vero ceram vacues, opus excipe nostrum ;
>   ut probus, a solita te excute pigritia.[3]

On another occasion Baudry is praising a gift of some tiny tablets, made of eight leaves with fourteen 'pages' of green wax, with room enough for only eight verses on each, but of beautiful workmanship. These, enclosed in an embroidered case and accompanied by a finely wrought stilus, were the gift

---

[1] ib., pp. 141 sqq.   [2] ib., p. 15.
[3] ib., p. 51; on the continued use of wax-tablets, especially for first drafts and for notes, during the Middle Ages, see Wattenbach, *Das Schriftwesen im Mittelalter*, Leipzig 1871, p. 38 sq.; on Baudry's tablets, p. 52 ; Pasquier, op. cit., pp. 66 sqq.

of the Abbot of Séez, to whom in charming fashion Baudry returns his thanks.   He is in love with the delightful gift:

> a tabulis nunquam scilicet amovear.
> vivam vobiscum ! vos autem vivite mecum :
> tandem nos unus suscipiat tumulus.   Amen.[1]

The most remarkable of all Baudry's poems is addressed to Adela, Countess of Blois, the daughter of William the Conqueror.[2]   It is in the form of a vision;[3] he imagines that he sees the bedroom of the Countess, and he describes it at great length, with an accumulation of all the details which his imagination can create.

> at plus quod decuit quam quod erat cecini,

he says towards the end of the poem.[4]   He pictures first the great tapestries.   One relates the story of creation, paradise, and the deluge; then follows the tale of Noah, with other scenes of Old Testament history.   On the third wall are pictures from Greek mythology, including Deucalion and the deluge, the Hermaphrodite which puzzled the Middle Ages so much, Orpheus, the siege of Troy, and the story of Rome.   But above the bed was the most wonderful tapestry of all; it represented the battle of Hastings in a series of lively episodes.[5]   On the painted ceiling the heavens were depicted, with the signs of the Zodiac and the planets.   The floor was a marvellous *mappa mundi* with seas and rivers, continents and towns.   Lastly, the statues which surrounded the bed represented Philosophy with the Seven Arts and Medicine.   Baudry lingers to describe the scope of each art with the aid of reminiscences from Martianus Capella.   What was the aim of this long poem and the object of its flattery?   The poet tells us at the end.   He wanted the Countess's protection, and he also wanted her to give him a cope.

---

[1] *Œuvres*, p. 53.

[2] ib., pp. 196 sqq. ; also ed. by Delisle, *Poëme adressé à Adèle, fille de Guillaume le Conquérant par Baudri, abbé de Bourgueil, Mémoires de la Société des Antiquaires de Normandie*, 3ᵉ série, viii (1871), pp. 187 sqq.

[3] The vision motive was very common (e. g. Godfrey of Reims used it in his *Sompnium Godefridi de Odone Aurelianensi*; Wattenbach, *Lat. Gedicht. aus Frankr.*, p. 101).   But, as Miss Abrahams points out (p. 233), the genre, with which we have to do here, is that of the description of buildings, which has a long history.

[4] *Œuvres*, p. 231.

[5] The relation of this description to the Bayeux tapestry is difficult to determine. A comparison hardly leads one to think that Baudry had ever seen this work; but Lauer, *Le poème de Baudri . . . et la date de la tapisserie de Bayeux*, believes that his description was based on the tapestry. It seems that Baudry was ignorant of Guy of Amiens, *Carmen de Hastingae praelio*, an interesting historical poem written *circ.* 1068 ; text in Michel, *Chroniques anglo-normandes*, iii. 1 sqq. (Paris 1840).

The cope was long in coming; so Baudry reminded her of her promise in a short epistle.[1] It was no ordinary cope, but a magnificent festal garment, stiff with gold and bright with jewels.

Another poem is addressed to a young friend named Gerard,[2] with the object of persuading him to become a monk at Bourgueil. Baudry here speaks as one who has renounced the world and its vanities, and he catalogues for Gerard's benefit the incurable defects under which the external world labours. First, there are the imperfections of Nature; the inconstancy of the seasons, the poor harvests, winter without frost, spring bitterly cold, summer like a showery spring, and autumn scorching the grapes with heat. A similar blight has striken human life; riches are worthless, women are a curse, there is no remedy against the temptation to sin. But in the monastery at Bourgueil there is safety and leisure, with books and all that is needed for study,

> libros et cartas, et cuncta studentibus apta.

The gardens are watered by a river, and there are meadows to walk in, with a wood beyond. Here is the 'leisure of the sanctified life', and, if any other arguments are wanted, there is the religious appeal:

> sis mecum pauper, immo cum paupere Christo;
> cum Christo vives, cum Christo divite dives.

But the religious appeal, supported by a quotation from Paul, seems a little strained. Yet, if Baudry relied most on the arguments from practical advantage, his love for the religious life was probably quite sincere. He writes to Muriel,[3] a girl who was a good reciter, and was therefore well educated, and praises her intention to remain a virgin. His verses to Agnes are in the same strain, but here he dwells on the theme of virginity with a directness borrowed from Jerome:

> omnia, Christe, potes, sed qui potes omnia, Christe,
>   ut loquar audenter audeo mira loqui,
> restaurare nequis violatam virginitatem;
>   ignoscis culpae, virginitas periit.
> virginitas violata semel nequit inviolari,
>   aequa tamen merces restitui poterat.

---

[1] *Œuvres*, p. 254.
[2] ib., pp. 109 sqq.; it is not clear whether he is the Gerard of the preceding poems (pp. 108–9), who is described as a famous scholar, while here he seems to be a young student (see note on p. 378).
[3] ib., p. 256 sq.

> ergo qua polles conserva virginitatem,
>   quam si perdideris, desinis esse quod es.
> desinis esse quod es, amissa virginitate
>   heu fractura gravis quam solidare nequis ![1]

The most thoroughly religious of Baudry's poems is the *Confessio paenitentialis*,[2] which seems to have been influenced by Marbod. He laments his sins, and like Mary he will wash the feet of his Saviour, bathing them with his tears. He will add ointment as well; for he will have pity on the wretched, since he who knows how to be merciful anoints the feet of Jesus :

> flendo rigabo pedes et tergam crine rigatos.
> adiiciam unguentum, miserebor enim miserorum,
> ille pedes unguit Ihesu qui scit misereri.

The proof of this is the parable of the good Samaritan. Yet Baudry is not the good Samaritan, but the wounded victim of sin, who has need of the medicine of salvation. 'I beseech Thee, O God, be my good Samaritan, minister to my wounds with the medicine of salvation; in Thy compassion pour wine and oil upon them. Thou, at whose bidding the rock poured forth water, make mine eyes a fountain of tears. Moses smote the rock twice, smite Thou my heart once only. . . . And I will not cease to weep like another Mary, until the Saviour shall answer with His comfortable word : Thy many sins are forgiven thee, because thou hast loved Me much. Go in peace.'[3]

Baudry's other religious poems consist mainly of a long series of epitaphs and tituli, and of a few liturgical pieces. An example of the former is the epitaph of John, who died at the age of six months, on the day of his baptism :

> intempestiva moritur dum morte Iohannes,
>   a mortis salvo solvitur imperio.
> nam potius vivit qui sic obiisse videtur.
>   nulla voluptatis tacha cohaesit ei.
> aetas ipsius vix annum dimidiarat,
>   ipsa dies lavacri, mortis et ipsa fuit.
> profuit ergo sibi tantummodo gratia Christi,
>   quae tamen et iuste praevenit immeritos.
> ergo laetandum satis est in morte Iohannis,
>   qui nullis moriens indiguit precibus.

---

[1] *Œuvres*, p. 258; Jerome's remark is well known, *Ep.* xxii (*C. S. E. L.*, lv, p. 150), 'audenter loquor ; cum omnia deus possit, suscitare virginem non potest post ruinam ; valet quidem liberare de poena, sed non valet coronare corruptam.'

[2] *Œuvres*, pp. 175 sqq.

[3] ib., p. 176 sq.

The purely liturgical pieces are not of great interest. There is a fragment of a sapphic ode to S. Catherine,[1] and there are two rimed hymns in honour of S. Samson, a former Archbishop of Dol.[2] The first hymn is neither better nor worse than a hundred others in the same metre :

> clarus satus natalibus,
> Samson, nitens virtutibus,
> vivit sacerdos inclitus,
> totus supernis deditus.

The second is a more ambitious attempt with its elaborate system of rimes :

> Samsoni superis associato,
> in caelis etiam glorificato,
> pangamus, socii, cantica grata,
> ut simus domino templa sacrata
> sorde remota.
>
> ergo signipotens atque modestus
> illuxit populis ut vir honestus.
> praesul quippe deo turificabat,
> vel sese potius sacrificabat,
> cordis in ara.
>
> Samson naufragio carnis in isto
> omnino studuit vivere Christo.
> nudo vestis erat, largus egeno,
> fundebatque deo pectore pleno
> congrua vota.
>
> gaude, metropolis aula Dolensis,
> Samson dux tuus est atque Britannis,
> qui nunc in superis iure locatus
> ut sol irradiat mirificatus
> atria clara.
>
> laus individuae sit deitati,
> laus sit summa patri, laus quoque proli.
> laus sit spiritui cuncta replenti,
> laus regum domino cuncta regenti
> omne per aevum.

These hymns were, it has been suggested,[3] written for the consecration of the church of S. Samson-sur-Rille in 1129, on the little Norman estate to which Baudry loved to retire, wearied, as Ordericus Vitalis tells us, by the 'perversity' of his flock.

Nature had not formed him to be a ruler or an administrator ; he had none of that spiritual and intellectual conviction which guided an Anselm or a Hildebert through the dangers and difficulties of high office. Yet he remains an attractive figure, a lover of learning, of order, and of decency in a time when the graces of civilization were being painfully restored.

A man of very different character was Geoffrey, Abbot of the monastery of the Trinity at Vendôme (b. *circa* 1070), who also received his education in the episcopal school at Angers,[4] and

---

[1] ib., p. 10 sq.
[2] ib., pp. 355 sqq. ; also *Anal. Hymn.* xix, p. 252 sq.
[3] Pasquier, op. cit., p. 262.
[4] Compain, *Geoffroi de Vendôme*, p. 21.

was a younger contemporary of Hildebert and Marbod. Elected in his youth to the high position of ruler of a religious house which owned no master but the Pope, he spent his whole life in the service of the Papacy, and in a successful attempt to preserve and extend the possessions and privileges of the monastery and its dependencies, at the expense of his diocesan and other bishops, and against the lay powers. He was continually interfering in the business of the bishops who crossed his path, and he was ready to remind a papal legate with some sharpness that he was not dealing with an ordinary abbot. Sometimes a bishop was able to take a mild revenge, and it was perhaps in mockery of Geoffrey, who, as *ex officio* cardinal-priest of S. Prisca, was allowed to wear the mitre, the ring, the gloves, and the sandals of a bishop, that Marbod composed his epigram *de abbate usurpante pontificalia* : [1]

> abbas sola gerens insignia pontificatus,
> scilicet annellum, guantos, sandalia, mitram ;
> cum super abbatem sit et infra pontificatum,
> esse potest neutrum, vel si dicatur utrumque,
> centauro simile monstrum reor esse biforme ;
> quod si pontificem simulat, sed permanet abbas,
> permanet ergo latens sub pelle leonis asellus,
> aut velut in scena personam fert alienam.

Geoffrey relied on the Pope for protection against all his enemies, and he seldom appealed in vain to the Holy See. But a journey to Rome was a painful undertaking, and whenever he could, he excused himself, for he had the horror of dying 'a pilgrim's death'. 'Jesus Christ', he said, 'commanded us to bear our own cross, but not to dig our own grave.' [2] Cunning and self-righteous, cautious about his health, and anxious to make sure of his own salvation, Geoffrey did not waste much time over poetry. But he has left four hymns, one to the Virgin and three to Mary Magdalene, which show how popular the new rhythmical forms were becoming, and how unskilfully they were still handled by one who had not completely mastered the rules. [3] Geoffrey begins his invocation to the Virgin in a promising, if prosaic, manner :

> o Maria gloriosa,
> Iesse proles generosa,
> per quam fuit mors damnata
> atque vita reparata.

---

[1] Migne, clxxi, col. 1636.　　　　　　　[3] Texts, in *Anal. Hymn.* l, pp. 405 sqq.
[2] Compain, p. 256.

But the rhythm soon becomes imperfect, and he cannot always find a proper rime of two syllables. So he sinks to verses like the following :

> qui assumpsit ex te carnem,
> exaudiet tuam precem ;
> nihil tibi denegabit,
> quem mamilla tua pavit.

The other hymns are even less successful ; they observe the law of syllabic equality, and, where rime fails, they substitute assonance. Geoffrey perhaps considered that the cultivation of poetry was a task fit only for bishops. But he took some interest in the library of his monastery. He ordered manuscripts to be transcribed, though they were probably mainly theological. His own works, besides his letters, were sermons, a commentary on the Psalms, and a few theological treatises. He died at Angers on March 26, 1132, after ruling the monastery of the Trinity for nearly forty years.

X

THE TWELFTH CENTURY

§ 1. *General Survey of Twelfth-century Latin Verse.*

THE twelfth century witnessed remarkable intellectual, political, and social developments in Western Europe. Politically, a great advance was marked by the growing power of centralized government in England, France, and Sicily. In Germany, Henry the Lion and Albert the Bear were carrying Teutonic civilization, and with it ecclesiastical organization, into the Slav lands across the Elbe at a time when the Emperors were ruining both German and Italian unity by their pursuit of the impossible ideal of a Holy Roman Empire. But in Italy the Lombard towns were already developing an active corporate life, and before the end of the century they were well on the way to independence. Outwardly, the power of the Church was at its highest. The Investiture contest had been, in effect, a victory for the Papacy, and for the first half of the century the Empire was its willing subject and protector.[1] The ecclesiastical organization was the only one which still retained a universal character. Roman legates went forth regularly on papal missions, if their activities were restricted in countries like England and Sicily, where Angevin and Norman had modern ideas of state independence; newly elected archbishops came to Rome to receive the *pallium*; ecclesiastics of all kinds made their way to the Curia with appeals; money and riches flowed Rome-wards in the wake of pilgrims from all countries. The strength of the Papacy was revealed when the kings of Europe were seen to sacrifice their interests, their policies, and, above all, their private quarrels, to embark on a Crusade; when Adrian IV compelled Frederick of Hohenstaufen to hold his stirrup, or when the same Emperor knelt before Alexander III in front of S. Mark's.

[1] During the reigns of Lothair II and Conrad III.

If the civilization of Europe presented some homogeneity, due, for the most part, to the universal ecclesiastical order, its real centre in the twelfth century was France.   The great intellectual revival which had its head-quarters in Paris marked the coming of age of the medieval intellect.   With a lamentable poverty of material with which to build, it set itself the task of erecting a systematized structure of knowledge which should explain the universe in terms capable of being harmonized with the truths of revelation.   In the schools of Paris and Chartres the weapon of dialectic was sharpened ready for the warfare of Scholasticism.   The 'credo ut intelligam' of Anselm had become the 'intelligo ut credam' of Abélard.   The rivalry of Nominalist and Realist began, and students came from all countries to the French schools to hear the new philosophers, to listen to Anselm of Laon, William of Champeaux, Roscelin, Gilbert de la Porrée, and Peter Abélard.   Constructive philosophy could not proceed far without meeting the problem of presenting theological doctrine in philosophical form.   In the hands of Abélard it tended towards a suggestion of rationalism [1] which awakened the anxiety and opposition of a mystic like Bernard of Clairvaux, who represented the other extreme in his almost fanatical distrust of the human reason, and his emphasis on submissive faith and contemplation as the surest means of approach to spiritual truth.   Between these two extremes stood humanists like John of Salisbury, who leaned if anything to the side of Abélard, and philosophical mystics like Hugh of S. Victor, who had more spiritual affinity with Bernard of Clairvaux.

The immense intellectual and emotional ferment presented by these varied schools of thought had its influence on the sacred poetry of the time, which naturally found its chief home in France.   Nearly all the greatest hymns and sequences of the twelfth century were composed on French soil and in French monasteries.   French monastic life was active, though the decline of Cluny had begun.   At Cluny, Peter the Venerable, the saintly and beloved abbot; at Clairvaux, Bernard, who was worshipped in his day as an angel from heaven, were the all-dominant influences.   The mysticism of Bernard, with its outpouring of love towards the remembrance of Jesus and in praise of the Virgin, revived a religion of feeling which expressed

---

[1] Cf. Abélard's famous position in the *Sic et Non* (p. 16, Cousin's edition),   'Dubitando enim ad inquisitionem venimus; inquirendo veritatem percipimus.'

itself in lyrical raptures, in verse as well as prose. The school of S. Victor was the home of Adam, the great master of the rimed Sequence, whose verses combine the mystical and doctrinal elements which are characteristic of the Victorine tradition. Abélard, the prince of dialecticians, the master intellect of his age, wrote a volume of hymns of which the least that can be said is that it is worthy of his genius. At Cluny, in the days of Peter the Venerable, Bernard of Morlas expressed in his *De Contemptu Mundi* the typical outlook of monasticism, its 'contempt of the world', and its sense of the 'beyond' as the sole and final reality. The religious poetry of the twelfth century is therefore almost entirely a poetry of monastic origin, and its detailed consideration will lead us mainly to centres of religious life, to Cluny, to Clairvaux, and to S. Victor.

But it would be wrong to imagine that there was in the twelfth century no poetical activity outside these monastic centres. In England we shall find a humanistic movement which produced satire and epigram in greater quantity than purely religious verse.[1] In Italy, where the old city civilization had survived the barbarian invasions, and where the lay-schools still flourished and gave instruction in grammar and in the old classical authors, there was a large variety of poetry on secular themes, written for the most part in classical metres. Henry of Settimello (*circa* 1190), a Tuscan and a student at Bologna, who had to contend with poverty, poured out his woes in a long elegy, *De diversitate fortunae et philosophiae consolatione*, a medieval 'consolation of philosophy', in elegiacs.[2] Henry had read Virgil, Ovid, and Lucan, and he talks about Achilles, Thersites, Hector, and the gods of Olympus. Nestor, Codrus, and Croesus appear by the side of Judas and Pontius Pilate, but, after all, the philosophy which consoles him is a Christian philosophy.

Gunther's *Ligurinus*,[3] a long narrative, based on Otto of Freising, of the deeds of Frederic Barbarossa, is written in hexameters, and so are the anonymous verses on the same subject which were edited by Monaco.[4] The stupendous events which accompanied the visits of the great Emperor to Italy could hardly fail to wake an echo in the poetry of Germany and

---

[1] See below, p. 337.
[2] Text, in Leyser, *Historia Poetarum et Poematum medii aevi*, Halle 1741, pp. 453 sqq.
[3] Migne, ccxii, col. 327 sqq.
[4] *Gesta di Federico I*, ed. Monaco,

Rome 1887 ; on the subject generally, see Ronca, *Cultura medievale*, i. 123 sqq., and i. 251, on the importance of this historical and political poetry as exhibiting the new and civic (and national) tendency of Italian culture.

Italy.   Godfrey of Viterbo celebrated both Frederic and his son, Henry VI.[1]   Godfrey was an Italian of noble birth, whom the Emperor Lothair brought from Viterbo to school at Bamberg, where he learned grammar and theology.   He took orders and became chaplain to successive emperors, Conrad III, Frederick I, and Henry VI.

His constant employment on diplomatic business brought him into close contact with the great movements of his time, and he was an eye-witness of many of the events which he relates.   He appears to have spent the last days of his life at Viterbo, where he died in a ripe old age.   Godfrey loved books, and had closely studied the Roman poets, especially Virgil, Horace, Ovid, and Juvenal.   For his own poetry he invented a curious metrical arrangement, in which an hexameter couplet is followed by a pentameter; sometimes all these verses are rimed together, and generally an effort is made to provide the pentameter with a leonine rime.

Godfrey's vast industry was spent on the composition of historical poems.   The *Speculum Regum*[2] tells, in the first book, the history of the world in its rulers from the deluge to the reign of Tarquinius Superbus; the second continues the story to the days of Pepin, with the aim of showing that Romans and Germans are of one race, derived from Troy, and are therefore properly associated in the Roman Empire, which they regained from the Byzantine rulers in the time of Charles the Great. For the mother of Charles was Roman,[3] and his father a German.

Godfrey's most important work, on which his fame rested, is the *Memoria Saeculorum*, a universal history in prose and verse. The versified part, which is called the *Pantheon*, is a curious mixture of history and legend, covering generally the same ground and at times reproducing the material of the *Speculum Regum*.   It is beyond our scope to give an account of its contents; but room must be found for a specimen of his style, which illustrates as well the religious spirit of the Middle Ages brooding over the great figures of the Roman past.   It is the well-known story of Trajan and the widow, telling how, by the prayers of Pope Gregory, the righteous emperor obtained the rewards of heaven :[4]

[1] *Gotifredi Viterbiensis Gesta Friderici I et Heinrici VI*, ed. Waitz. *Script. Rer. German.*, Hannover 1870.

[2] For Godfrey's works see *M. G. H.*, *Scriptores*, xxii.

[3] Of the Byzantine royal house; see Godfrey's dedication of the *Speculum regum* to Henry VI, p. 21.

[4] Dante, *Purg*. x. 73 sqq., and *Paradiso*, xx. 43 sqq.; on the history of this remark-

Traiano iam defuncto post tempora multa,
Gregorio papa Romana potentia functa,
　　Traiani regis gesta vetusta legit.

prelia gesturus pergebat ab urbe monarchus,
pontis et ad Tiberis properans dum transiit arcus,
obvia stat vidua, mota querela sonat.

' stes ', ait illa, ' meum rediens ulciscere natum,
nam morior, dum sic video cervice necatum.
　　hoc scelus imperium vindicet : ecce caput.'

Caesar ait : ' pugnabo prius, curabo redire '.
illa refert : ' si non redeas, quo vindice fiet ?
　　quam laudem deus hic te meruisse sciet ? '

rex satis iratus, iubet ut vindicta feratur,
post abiit, set non rediit, quia marte necatur,
　　unde virum laudem plus meruisse patet.

hoc pietatis opus dum Gregorio memoratur,
ingemuit pro morte viri, multum lacrimatus,
　　orat, ut alma dei dextera parcat ei.

dum iacet in precibus, stans angelus increpat illum :
' scis, quia non habuit baptismatis ille sigillum,
　　quomodo tu lacrimis dona neganda petis ? '

' ast homo tu pacis opus expetis hoc pietatis,
quo simul indulto, non amplius ista petatis,
　　Traianus requiem, te rogitante, capit.'

excessit papa ; set non permansit inultum :
angelico pulsu femur eius tempore multo
　　claudicat, et pene corpore signa tenet.[1]

The first part of the *Pantheon* is full of legends of this kind ;
but the value of the work is mainly historical, and few readers,
other than historians in search of material, will turn its pages.
It was the fashion in those days to compose history in verse.
When Guibert of Nogent (1053–1124) was preparing the scheme
of his *Gesta Dei per Francos*, an account of the first crusade,
some of his friends advised him to write it in prose, but most
of them were of the opinion that he should write it in verse,[2]
' since they knew that in my youth I had given myself up to such
exercises more than was proper'.[3]　And, although he finally

able legend see Graf, *Roma nella memoria
del medio evo*, ii. 1 sqq.

[1] *M. G. H.* xxii. 161–2.

[2] *Gesta Dei per Francos, Praefatio,
Recueil des historiens des croisades*, iv.
120, Paris 1879.

[3] Cf. Guibert's autobiography (ed. G.
Bourgin, i. 17, p. 64, Paris 1907), where
he tells how, as a young monk at S.Germer-
de-Fly, he wrote erotic verses under the
influence of Ovid.

decided for prose, he could not refrain from adorning his narrative at intervals with appropriate verses of his own composition. The Englishman Joseph of Exeter wrote an epic of the Crusades called the *Antiocheis*, as well as a very good poem in six books on the Trojan War,[1] and Walter of Châtillon celebrated Alexander the Great in ten books, which never become really tedious.[2] Master Peter of Eboli (b. *circa* 1160), a physician who was devoted to the house of Hohenstaufen, related the Sicilian campaigns of Henry VI in a long elegiac poem.[3] He shared the common notion that such a work would appeal to a larger number of readers and have a better chance of surviving than a narrative in plain prose.   Peter seems to have modelled his poem on Henry of Settimello's *De diversitate fortunae*, for he inveighs in the same manner against the instability of fortune, and follows Henry in introducing *Sapientia* as the deliverer.[4]

The best political poetry of the twelfth century makes use of the new verse forms.   A good example is the 'Hymn of the Crusaders', which Roger of Hoveden quotes in his Chronicle:

iuxta threnos Ieremiae
vere Syon lugent viae,
quod solemni non sit die
qui sepulchrum visitet,
vel casum resuscitet
huius prophetiae.

contra quod propheta scribit,
quod de Syon lex exibit:
nunquam ibi lex peribit
nec habebit vindicem,
ubi Christus calicem
passionis bibit.

lignum crucis,
signum ducis
sequitur exercitus ;
quod non cessit,
sed praecessit
in vi sancti spiritus.[5]

The indignation of serious satire could use such measures to admirable effect, when the theme was the corruption of the Roman curia :

---

[1] The only fragment of the *Antiocheis* which has survived is preserved in Camden's *Remaines concerning Britaine*, p. 339, London 1870 ; quoted also in Wright, *Biogr. Brit. Lit., Anglo-Norman*, p. 406, London 1846. For text of *De bello Troiano* see vol. ii of *Dictys Cretensis*, &c., ed. Artopaeus, London 1825 ; text of Book I in J.-J. Jusserand, *De Iosepho Exoniensi*, Paris 1877.

[2] `Alexandreis*, Migne, ccix, col. 463 sqq. ; W. Müldener, Leipzig 1863.
[3] *Petri Ansolini de Ebulo, De rebus Siculis carmen*, ed. E. Rotta, *Rerum Ital. Scriptores*, xxxi. i. Città di Castello 1904.
[4] Cf. Rotta, p. xxxvi ; on Peter's secular outlook, p. lxix.
[5] Hoveden, *Chronica* (ed. Stubbs, *Rolls Series*, 1869), ii. 330. Hoveden names Berter of Orleans as author.

propter Sion non tacebo
sed ruinam Romae flebo,
quousque iustitia
rursus nobis oriatur
et ut lampas accendatur
iustus in ecclesia.[1]

During the twelfth century in Germany, the home of the early sequences, religious and liturgical verse did not flourish. There are indeed a few names to mention—Udalschalk of Maissach, author of hymns and sequences[2] (d. 1149); Hildegarde, the famous mystic, whose sequences are in prose;[3] Herrat, Abbess of Hohenburg (d. 1195), whose rhythms display more piety than talent.[4] For the best Latin poetry we must turn to the *Carmina Burana*,[5] that fascinating collection of satires and student-songs, which shows how poetry was beginning to set itself free from its old dependence on the Church and on religious themes.[6] But the ecclesiastical culture still overshadowed these efforts at freedom. The forms of this secular or quasi-secular verse were borrowed from the poetry of the Church, and although the growth of the towns was accompanied by the appearance of a better-educated middle class, the poets still owed some sort of allegiance to the Church. Some of these poets may have been 'wandering scholars', but of this there is little evidence, unless we include under this description a man like Hugh of Orleans, known as the Primate, a poet of conspicuous ability, a man of learning and a seeker after preferment, or a figure like the German Archpoet,[7] the *vates vatum*, who certainly wandered about from place to place. The songs in these secular collections belong to many nations, but the German origin is unmistakable in some of the lyrics of love and spring, of nightingales and linden-trees. The *Confession of Golias* was written at Pavia, and by the Archipoëta himself. It was addressed by its German author to the great Arch-Chancellor, Rainald of Dassel, Arch-bishop-Elect of Cologne. It 'lays bare the inner nature of a wandering student, describing his vagrant habits, his volatile and indiscriminate amours, his passion for the dice-box, his devotion to wine, and the poetic inspiration he was wont to draw from it.'[8] The object of the poem was to obtain the great

---

[1] Du Méril, *Poésies pop. lat. ant. au XIIme siècle*, Paris, 1843, p. 231.
[2] *Anal. Hymn.* v, pp. 235 sqq.; iv, p. 247; ix, p. 355.
[3] ib., l., pp. 483 sqq.
[4] ib., pp. 493 sqq.
[5] *Carmina Burana*, Hilka-Schumann, Heidelberg 1930–41, 2 vols.
[6] Hauck, iv. 497–8.
[7] Meyer, *Gött. Nachr.*, 1907, pp. 85 sqq.
[8] Symonds, *Wine, Women, and Song*, p. 64.

man's favour, and it was used in an English version to secure
the protection of a Bishop of Coventry.[1] In this poem occur
the celebrated lines, which were afterwards used as a drinking-
song:

> meum est propositum
> in taberna mori,
> vinum sit appositum
> morientis ori,
> ut dicant cum venerint
> angelorum chori,
> 'deus sit propitius
> huic potatori!'[2]

To discuss this secular verse in any detail would take us
beyond the limits of our subject. It is important here to
indicate the profound impress which its form and technique
received from the liturgical verse of the Church.[3] The following
love-song shows how skilfully the profane poet could transfer
the form and language of the sequence from the honour of the
Virgin to the praise of a worldly love:

> ave, formosissima,   ave mundi luminar,
> gemma pretiosa,   ave mundi rosa,
> ave decus virginum,   Blanziflor et Helena,
> virgo gloriosa,   Venus generosa.[4]

Similarly, bacchic ditties were often deliberate parodies of
sacred verse. The *verbum bonum et suave* is the model for
a song in praise of wine.[5]

> vinum bonum et suave,   . . . monachorum grex devotus,
> bonis bonum, pravis prave,   omnis ordo, mundus totus,
> cunctis dulcis sapor, ave,   bibunt ad aequales potus
>   mundana laetitia!   et nunc et in saeculum.
>
> ave! felix creatura,   felix venter quem intrabis!
> quam produxit vitis pura;   felix lingua quam rigabis!
> omnis mensa fit secura   felix os quod tu lavabis,
>   in tua praesentia   et beata labia!

---

[1] Wright, *The Latin Poems commonly attributed to Walter Mapes, Camden Society*, 1841, p. 75.

[2] ib., p. 73; *Carmina Burana*, p. 69.

[3] Cf. P. Lehmann, *Die Parodie im Mittelalter*, pp. 142 sqq.

[4] *Carmina Burana*, p. 142; Dreves, *Anal. Hymn.* xx, p. 8, rightly points out that many of these so-called 'Vaganten-lieder', some of them the pearls of medi-eval poetry, are obviously not the work of wandering students, but are the careful and conscious products of the study, although they may have been sung in student-circles.

[5] Du Méril, *Poésies pop. du moyen âge*, p. 204; Lehmann, *Die Parodie im Mittelalter*, p. 175; cf. pp. 70–1 for a deliberate parody of a hymn.

It would appear from the liveliness and grace of these verses that, just as the new forms of rime and rhythm proved to be by far the most adequate vehicles for the expression of the higher religious emotion of the Middle Ages, so too, the typically human feelings which are common to the popular poetry of all times had to clothe themselves in the same dress. The classical metres, except in the hands of a Hildebert or an Alphanus, were incapable of becoming a really satisfactory medium of poetical expression. During the eleventh and twelfth centuries, after a long series of experiments, rime reached at last its perfection, and the rules of accent were established. The technical difficulties once overcome, there could be no serious question of a return to pale imitations of classical form, especially where liturgical poetry was concerned; from the eleventh and twelfth centuries onward the new forms assume an increasing beauty and capacity for expressing what was most profound and permanent in medieval experience. The history of Latin hymnology after Adam of S. Victor is the history of personal poetry, lyrical in the truest sense, issuing in the thirteenth century in those two perfect and poignant strains in which the Church still voices the pathos of divine and human sorrow and the terror of the final judgement, the *Stabat Mater* and the *Dies Irae*.

§ 2. *French Poets: Philosophers and Men of Letters.*

If the stream of poetry was finally flowing away from classical traditions, there were not wanting, at any rate in the twelfth century, close students of the great masters of Latin prose. Since the days of Gregory of Tours the 'barbarization' of prose had proceeded apace, but the eleventh and twelfth centuries saw a progressive improvement, due in great part, we may suppose, to the influence of the cathedral schools.[1] John of Salisbury stands out in the twelfth century as the master of an admirable Latin style and the dispenser of a humane wisdom which was not to be known again in Europe until the days of Petrarch. Otto of Freising, Wibald of Corvey, and Gerhoh of Reichersperg are German examples of the great progress in latinity, and even Helmhold's *Cronica Slavorum* is an immense advance on the jejune monastic chronicle.

---

[1] Cf. Taylor, *Medieval Mind*, ii. 191.

Further, the influence of the humanism of Chartres, along with the Platonism which was a legacy of that famous school, produced some interesting examples in France of the attempt to express philosophical ideas in poetical allegory. Bernard Silvestris of Tours,[1] who flourished in the middle of the twelfth century, set forth his speculations in an allegorical treatise, half prose, half verse. The *De mundi universitate*[2] is a mixture of Neoplatonic and astrological speculation in the form in which Macrobius[3] bequeathed it to the medieval world. *Natura, Noys, Urania*, and *Physis* appear as actors in the cosmic drama, the theme of which is the creation of the Megacosmus and the Microcosmus (man). There is hardly a hint of Christian dogma, although in the catalogue of mountains Bernard names Lebanon and Sinai, 'quo sacra sub sacro lex Moysete data est,'[4] and in the list of trees he mentions the myrrh which the Persian magus brought to the infant Christ.[5] On the other hand, he affirms the eternity of the world,[6] and speaks disrespectfully of the arguments of the theologians.[7] Bernard's verse, like his prose, is stiff and obscure, although he had read Horace, Virgil, and Ovid; he does not venture to use the Sapphic metre, but he once employs the *alcmanium* and once the measure of Horace, *Odes*, iv. 7.

Bernard found a follower in Master Alanus de Insulis (Alan of Lille), a man of wider learning and a famous teacher, who occupies an important place in the history of medieval philosophy. The Doctor Universalis—so he was styled in later days—was a keen dialectician, a Platonist, and yet an eclectic, like others who had borrowed their Aristotle from Boëthius and a mixture of science and superstition from Macrobius or from Apuleius.[8] It is impossible here to give a sketch of his philosophical system, for which his two allegories the *Anticlaudianus* and the *De planctu naturae* afford material equally with his professedly

[1] Not to be confounded with his namesake, Bernard of Chartres; see Poole, *Medieval Thought and Learning*, p. 101, note 13.

[2] Text, ed. C. S. Barach and J. Wrobel, *Bernardi Silvestris De mundi universitate*, Innsbruck 1876; see M. de Wulf, *Histoire de la Philosophie médiévale*, Louvain 1905, p. 233, who, somewhat unjustly, styles him a pantheist.

[3] See M. Schedler, *Die Philosophie des Macrobius und ihr Einfluss auf die Wissenschaft des christlichen Mittelalters*, pp. 127 sqq. Another twelfth-century poet who knew Macrobius is Godfrey, sub-Prior of S. Victor (d. 1194). His *Fons Philosophiae* is to be found (ed. M. A. Charma) in *Mémoires de la société des antiquaires de Normandie*, i. 27 (3. Sér. i. 7), Caen 1869.

[4] *De mundi Universitate*, p. 20.
[5] ib., p. 24. [6] ib., p. 30.
[7] ib., p. 40; see Poole, *op. cit.*, p. 148.
[8] Schedler, *Macrobius*, pp. 138 sqq.

scientific works.[1]   But the *Anticlaudianus*, at any rate, is such
an important example of a long and elaborately-constructed
poetical allegory that a brief summary of its argument must be
given.   When the reader has accustomed himself to the somewhat monotonous hexameters, with the usual faults of prosody,
he will realize that here is a poet who is master of his material
and has built up a complicated structure, the parts of which are
in due relation to the central idea.   The theme of the poem, as
its title obscurely indicates, is the creation of the soul by God.
For Alan says that Claudianus Mamertus in his *De statu
animae* mentions as one of the errors of Hilary of Poitiers the
opinion that the soul had its origin 'out of something' (ex
aliquo).[2]   Alan holds the view that Nature forms the body out
of the four elements, but that the soul is created from nothing
by the immediate act of God.   There are, indeed, four 'artificers'
who appear and share in the work of man's making and of his
earthly progress—God, Nature, Fortune, and Vice, and their
operations are unfolded in the course of the poem.   Nature is
not satisfied with her works, and desires to make a perfect man ;
but, as perfection implies active virtues, she takes into consulta-
tion the council of her sisters, the Virtues themselves.   The
meeting is held in Nature's own garden, a rare paradise filled
with her bounty of fruit and flower,

> in quo pubescens tenera lanugine florum,
> sideribus stellata suis, succensa rosarum
> murice terra novum contendit pingere caelum.[3]

In the garden is a palace, with a great columned hall, whose
frescoes depict the 'manners' of men; here is Aristotle the
logician, here Plato with his diviner dreams ; Seneca the moralist,
Ptolemy, Cicero, and Virgil; Hercules and Ulysses, Turnus,
Hippolytus, with many others.   Nature expounds her plan to
create a being who shall belong to earth and heaven ; 'on earth
he shall be human, in the stars divine'.[4]   Prudence, whose
beauty is next elaborately set forth, rises and reminds the council
that only God can provide this being with a soul.   Reason
moves that Prudence be dispatched to the court of heaven to
present the petition of Nature and her sisters.   But because

---

[1] On Alan's philosophy see M. Baumgartner, *Die Philosophie des Alanus de
Insulis.*
[2] Baumgartner, p. 97 ; what Claudian
said of Hilary was 'nihil incorporeum

creatum dixit'.
[3] Text, Wright, *Anglo-Saxon Satirical
Poets* (*Rolls Series* 1872), ii. 268 sqq. ;
for this quotation see p. 275.
[4] ib., p. 281.

Prudence modestly shuns this task, Concord adds her persuasions, and a splendid chariot is made which shall bear her through the heavens. The artificers are Prudence's own daughters, Grammar, Logic, Rhetoric, Arithmetic, Music, Geometry, and Astronomy; the five horses are the senses, and Reason is the driver. As Prudence journeys, she learns and marvels at the world of nature—the causes of snow and hail and storm; she sees the demons of air who have fallen from heaven, she passes the planets and the sphere of the fixed stars—'fix'd in their orb that flies'; but Reason can now no longer guide, for the bounds of the world of sense are passed. Here a maiden appears, seated on the summit of heaven, she whose eyes are set on 'extramundane' things, who searches the hidden cause, the beginning and end of all—in short a goddess, whose name is Theology. She will guide Prudence for the rest of the journey; but Reason must stay behind, and all the horses except the sense of Hearing. Now the 'terrene Apollo' must give place to the 'heavenly Muse', and the poet invokes an inspiration for his higher theme.[1] Here in the empyraean the Christian heaven begins; here are the Orders of Angels, here the citizens of God, the saints, the martyrs, and the doctors, all who despised the world, for whom 'God Himself is all in all, the gift and the giver'.[2] But first above all in honour is the Virgin, virgin and mother, reconciling, in a miracle, those discordant names; silencing nature, banishing logic, while 'rhetoric's judgement perishes and reason reels'. At this point Alan must pause to hymn her, 'in the chamber of whose womb the deity made his lodging, and the son of the most high artificer wove a garment for himself'.[3] These are her names of honour:

> haec est stella maris, vitae via, porta salutis,
> regula iustitiae, limes pietatis, origo
> virtutis, veniae mater, thalamusque pudoris;
> hortus conclusus, fons consignatus, oliva
> fructificans, cedrus redolens, paradisus amoenans:
> virgula pigmenti, vinaria cella, liquore
> praedita caelesti, nectar caeleste propinans;
> nescia spineti florens rosa, nescia culpae
> gratia, fons expers limi, lux nubila pellens,
> spes miseris, medicina reis, tutela beatis;
> proscriptis reditus, erranti semita, caecis,
> lumen, deiectis requies, pausatio fessis.

[1] ib., p. 355.   [2] ib., p. 362.   [3] ib., p. 362.

But Prudence cannot bear these dazzling visions, and Faith must now come to her aid, as, with Theology, she reaches the court of the Trinity.   Here her request is granted; for God creates a soul when Noys has presented the perfect *idea* or form (a marvellous summary of the graces of Joseph and Judith, of Job and Phineas, of Moses and Jacob, of Abraham and Tobias) after which it is to be constructed.   God entrusts His creature to Prudence, warning her lest, on the journey to earth, the malevolence of any hostile planet should harm it.   Nature fashions a beautiful body to receive it, and Concord unites the two; the Virtues bestow their gifts, and the Arts follow.   But Nobility, Fortune's daughter, has nothing of her own, and must ask her mother to be bountiful.   Here the poet has to describe the palace of Fortune and the famous wheel.   The gift is offered, but Reason is at hand to see that no malice is mingled with it. Man is complete, but Alecto has heard the news, and is afoot with her army of evil.   It is unnecessary to describe the *Psychomachia* which follows, ending with the triumph of man and his assisting virtues, who rule henceforth a world which has assumed the likeness of heaven.

This mixture of allegory and myth (in the Platonic sense) with elements of an apocalyptic nature shows how the medieval poets had learned to construct, with help from many sources— from Boëthius and Macrobius, the Latin *Timaeus*[1], and Martianus Capella[2]—a literary form which combined the essential element of instruction with the desirable, if not strictly necessary, element of pleasure.   It was not long before the *Anticlaudianus* was translated into French, and it is probable that it was not without its influence on the growth of French vernacular allegory.[3]

The *De Planctu Naturae* was less popular, because it dealt with a subject best 'veiled in the obscurity of a learned language'.   It is a mixture of prose and verse, like the *Consolatio* of Boëthius and the *De Nuptiis* of Martianus Capella.   Nature and the poet hold a dialogue.   The goddess appears in wonderful

---

[1] Alan knew the *Timaeus* from the partial translation of Chalcidius; see Baumgartner, p. 9.

[2] The *De Nuptiis Philologiae et Mercurii* (fifth century), an allegory in prose and verse concerned with the Liberal Arts, which was freely used as a school book in the Middle Ages. It is most easily accessible in F. Eyssenhardt's edition, Leipzig 1866.

[3] See Legrand D'Aussy, *Sur un poème intitulé Anti-Claudien*, in *Notices et extraits des mss.*, v. 546 sqq.   Adam of La Bassée, Canon of Lille (d. 1286), wrote a rhythmical *Ludus super Anticlaudianum* inspired by Alan's work. For the lyrical pieces which are mingled with the main poem see *Anal. Hymn.* xlviii, pp. 299 sqq.

beauty, the vicar of God in this world, who 'surveying the pure
ideas of Nous, stamps the mark of species on to things, clothing
them with form'; she is the ruler of the visible world, control-
ling, under God, its ordered processes, maintaining that constancy
of organic generation by which like always proceeds from like,
performing thus the function of the world-soul as Plato conceived
it in the *Timaeus*, and the Neoplatonists handed it on to the
Middle Ages.   The deification of Nature receives its full
expression in a Sapphic ode addressed by the poet to the *genitrix
rerum* ·[1]

> o dei proles, genetrixque rerum,
> vinculum mundi, stabilisque nexus.
> gemma terrenis, speculum caducis,
>   lucifer orbis.
>
> pax, amor virtus, regimen, potestas,
> ordo, lex, finis, via, lux, origo,
> vita, laus, splendor, species, figura,
>   regula mundi.
>
> quae, tuis mundum moderans habenis.
> cuncta concordi stabilita nodo
> nectis, et pacis glutino maritas
>   caelica terris.
>
> quae noys puras recolens ideas,
> singulas rerum species monetas,
> rem togans forma, chlamidemque formae
>   pollice formas.
>
> cui favet caelum, famulatur aer,
> quam colit tellus, veneratur unda,
> cui velut mundi dominae tributum
>   singula solvunt.
>
> quae diem nocti vicibus catenans,
> cereum solis tribuis diei,
> lucido lunae speculo soporans
>   nubila noctis.
>
> quae polum stellis variis inauras,
> aetheris nostri solium serenans;
> siderum gemmis, varioque caelum
>   milite complens.
>
> quae novis caeli faciem figuris
> protheans mutas, animumque vulgus
> aeris nostri regione donans,
>   legeque stringis,

[1] Wright, p. 458.

cuius ad nutum iuvenescit orbis,
silva crispatur folii capillo,
et sua florum tunicata veste
   terra superbit.

quae minas ponti sepelis et auges,
syncopans cursum pelagi furoris,
ne soli tractum tumulare possit
   aequoris aestus.

Another poem of Alan's[1] is also concerned with Nature, and it affords an instructive contrast to this Sapphic ode, because it shows how the new rhythmical forms could be used to convey a pathos which could never be expressed in imitations of the classic manner. Alan is now concerned, not with Nature as the upholder of the order of law by which the world is sustained and guided, but with Nature the mirror of human fate, reflecting in her own processes of change and decay the unstable fortunes of man. 'Omnis caro foenum, et omnis gloria eius quasi flos agri'.

omnis mundi creatura
quasi liber et pictura
nobis est, in speculum,
nostrae vitae, nostrae mortis,
nostri status, nostrae sortis
fidele signaculum.

ergo spirans flos expirat,
in pallorem dum delirat,
oriendo moriens.
simul vetus et novella,
simul senex et puella,
rosa marcet oriens.

nostrum statum pingit rosa,
nostri status decens glosa,
nostrae vitae lectio :
quae dum primo mane floret,
defloratus flos effloret,
vespertino senio.

sic aetatis ver humanae
iuventutis primo mane
reflorescit paululum.
mane tamen hoc excludit
vitae vesper, dum concludit
vitale crepusculum.

cuius decor dum perorat
eius decus mox deflorat
aetas, in quâ defluit.
fit flos foenum, gemma lutum,
homo cinis, dum tributum
huic morti tribuit.

---

[1] Text, Trench, *Sacred Latin Poetry*, pp. 262 sqq.; also Migne, ccx, col. 579; Hauréau accepts Alan's authorship, see *Notices et extraits des mss.*, xxxiii, p. 204; also Hauréau, *Notices et extraits de quelques mss.*, ii, p. 191, and his note on Alan, *Mémoires de l'Academie des inscriptions*, xxxii, p. 23.

Besides this excellent rhythmical piece three only of Alan's religious compositions have survived.[1]   One has for its subject the Incarnation.   It is dry and scholastic enough in its enunciation of the manner in which this supreme event mocks the power of the human reason, and it uses conceits which did not lose their popularity until the end of the seventeenth century.

> artis suae in censura
>   geometra fallitur,
> dum immensus sub mensura
>   terrenorum sistitur,
> in directum curvatura
>   circuli convertitur,
> sphaeram claudit quadratura
>   et sub ipsa clauditur.

The other hymns are of no special interest or merit, but we know enough of Alan's intellectual and literary quality to wish that more of his rhythmical compositions had survived.

Two French poets of the later twelfth century belong to the new type of the man of letters with an interest in versification. Peter Riga[2] (d. *circ.* 1209), canon of Notre Dame at Rheims, and later canon-regular of S. Denis, earned a great reputation by his *Aurora*, a versification of Old Testament themes, which he undertook at the instance of his fellow-students, who were particularly anxious that he should explain the allegorical meanings which could be drawn from the sacred text.   The most remarkable verses in this collection are those which summarize the two Testaments in twenty-three chapters.   In the first chapter the letter *a* does not appear.

> principio rerum post quinque dies homo primus
>   conditus in sexto creditur esse die.
> exprimit hic Christum, qui sexto tempore mundum
>   ingrediens fit homo nos redimendo cruce.
> fit coniux ex osse viri, dum somnus in illum
>   mittitur, et Christi mors fuit ille sopor.
> ecclesiae signum fuit haec de corpore Christi
>   terreni generis sumpsit origo fidem,
> per ligni vetiti gustum nos ille peremit.
>   in cruce nos redimit ille cruore suo.[3]

---

[1] Texts in Dreves-Blume, *Ein Jahrtausend Lateinischen Hymnendichtung*, i. 286 sqq.; *Anal. Hymn.* xx, p. 42.

[2] *Hist. Litt.* xvii, pp. 26 sqq.; text in part Migne, ccxii, col. 19 sqq.; see also Hau-

réau, *Notices et extraits des mss.*, xxix, ii, pp. 352 sqq., for the poem on *Susanna*, included in the *Aurora*.

[3] Migne, ccxii, col. 31.

In the second chapter *b* is avoided, and so on throughout the alphabet.[1] Misplaced ingenuity could go no farther, but Peter's archbishop, Samson, evidently admired his verses, for he asked him to make a selection of his best for separate publication.[2] Peter was only too ready to comply, and he called his anthology *Floridus Aspectus*, a title which is hardly suggestive of modesty. Here pieces from the *Aurora* were mingled with other compositions, and among them a *Passion of S. Agnes*[3] and a *Life of S. Eustace*.[4] The latter is in hexameters with elaborate leonine and end rimes. Four verses are enough to show what kind of effect Peter was attempting to produce:

> tempore Traiani, studii cultura prophani
> cives Romani sacra spe fraudabat inani.
> hoc regnante duce, fidei subiecta caduce,
> non indigna cruce plebs errabat sine luce.

Matthew of Vendôme[5] was an equally bad poet, but had a wider range of interests. He studied under Bernard Silvestris at Tours, and later went to the school at Orléans. There he wrote an *Ars versificatoria* before he proceeded to Paris. After a period of literary labour he retired to Tours, and no more is heard of him. In a poem which prefaces a collection of model letters he has given us a list of his works. Many of the poems cannot be identified, but they were mainly on secular subjects. His most famous work was a metrical paraphrase of the Book of Tobit, written in elegiacs. It is 'full of digressions and superfluities',[6] in which Matthew gives vent to his love of moral reflections, of long speeches, and drawn-out prayers. He is fond of verbal ingenuities which leave the modern reader gasping, as when he describes the character of his hero in such verses as these:

> odit, amat, reprobat, probat, exsecratur, adorat,
> crimina, iura, nefas, fas, simulacra, deum,
> fas, simulacra, deum, probat, execratur, adorat,
> odit, amat, reprobat, crimina, iura, nefas.
> seminat, auget, alit, exterminat, arguit, arcet,
> dogmata, iura, decus, schismata, probra, dolos.[7]

---

[1] See Hauréau, *Notices et extraits des mss.*, xxix. ii, p. 336.
[2] ib., p. 243.　　[3] ib., pp. 360-1.
[4] C. Fierville, *Notices et extraits des mss.*, xxxi, i, pp. 63 sqq. (text, pp. 64 sqq.). For a political poem by Peter Riga see Hauréau, *Un poème inédit de Pierre Riga*, *Bibl. de l'école des chartes*, xliv, (1883), pp. 1 sqq.

[5] *Hist. Litt.* xv, pp. 420 sqq.; xxii, p. 59; Faral, *Les arts poétiques du XIIᵉ et du XIIIᵉ siècles*, pp. 1 sqq.
[6] *Hist. Litt.* xv, p. 424.
[7] ib., p. 425; Migne, ccv, col. 935; for other similar verses see Hauréau, *Journal des savants*, 1882, p. 282.

'Artifice stérile', is the comment of the Benedictines of S. Maur, 'et même ridicule, qui suffirait pour déprécier le poème entier s'il avait d'ailleurs le moindre prix'. But, if Traube's ascription is correct, Matthew is entitled to honourable renown as the author of one of the most admired Latin epigrams of ancient or modern times, the *Hermaphroditus*, a poem which has found its way into anthologies of classical verse. It is cited here as an example of that humanistic freedom which flowed from the cathedral schools :

cum mea me mater gravida gestaret in alvo,
    quid pareret fertur consuluisse deos.
Phoebus ait 'puer est', Mars 'femina', Iuno 'neutrum' :
    iam, qui sum natus, Hermaphroditus eram.
quaerenti letum dea sic ait 'occidet armis',
    Mars 'cruce', Phoebus 'aqua' : sors rata quaeque fuit.
arbor obumbrat aquas : conscendo, labitur ensis,
    quem tuleram, casu labor et ipse super.
pes haesit ramis, caput incidit amne, tulique
    vir mulier neutrum flumina tela crucem.
[nescio quem sexum mihi sors extrema reliquit :
    felix, si sciero, cur utriusque fui.] [1]

Matthew also wrote a scurrilous *Descriptio senilis nequitiae* [2] and a dull quarrel between Ulysses and Ajax over the arms of Achilles, in which Ajax compares his rival to Verres. It is true that in the manuscript this latter piece is anonymous, but Hauréau has recognized here the accents of 'le plus prolixe, le plus banal des poètes du xiie siècle, le plus laborieux artisan de frivoles antithèses', [3] and it is difficult to believe that he is mistaken.

Lastly, Matthew's *Milo*, a versification of a tale derived from Graeco-Oriental sources, is worthy of mention, because it has a place in the interesting history of the Latin *fabliau* in the Middle Ages, which M. Faral has recently unfolded in a learned study. [4] The genus to which this tale belongs is the *comoedia*,

---

[1] Traube, *Abh. d. Bayer. Akad.*, 1891, ix, 2, p. 317. Matthew in a list of his works tells us that he wrote a poem on this subject. Another poem with the same title is by Peter of Riga (Hauréau, *Notices et extraits des mss.* xxviii, ii, p. 386); it is longer and is clearly an imitation of the epigram quoted above. Hauréau left the authorship of the latter undecided between Hildebert and Matthew, but Wilmart definitely decides in favour of Hildebert.

[2] Migne, ccv, col. 983; Hauréau, *Notices et extraits des mss.* xxix, ii, p. 328.

[3] Hauréau, p. 350.

[4] E. Faral, *Le fabliau latin au moyen âge*, Romania, l (1924), pp. 321 sqq. Text of the *Milo* in M. Haupt, *Exempla poesis latinae medii aevi*, Vienna 1834.

which M. Faral considers to represent a transition between the Latin comedy of antiquity and the French *fabliau*.[1]

Guido or Guy of Bazoches has something in common with Peter of Riga and Matthew of Vendôme. He belonged to the secular clergy, and learned the art of versification according to the routine of the cathedral schools. Although he made use of ingenious and trivial devices like those which are conspicuous in the work of Peter and of Matthew, he reserved them for his metrical compositions, and if his rhythmical pieces contain verbal conceits they are skilfully composed, and will bear comparison with anything except the best liturgical verse of the time.

Guy was a person of some importance. He never forgot that he came of a noble family, which boasted among its members no less a person than the crusader Baldwin II of Jerusalem and he was proud of his paternal uncle, Haimo, who was first Archdeacon and then Bishop of Châlons. Guy's mother had before his birth dedicated him to the Church ; so, at the age of seven, he was taken by his uncle to begin those liberal studies that were to hold him to the end. But the Bishop did not live long enough to secure his nephew's rapid progress in the Church. Guy did not obtain further promotion when he had reached the dignity of Canon and Cantor of Châlons. In 1190 he went on the second crusade with Philip Augustus, was present at the siege of Acre, and came home to die in 1203. His letters[2] give a good deal of information not only about himself and his family, but about the manner of life of those of the secular clergy who had enough money and leisure to do as they pleased.[3] Guy was quite ready to spend his life in an alternation of study and amusement, books, and verses, hunting and hawking, fishing and riding—with no hint of asceticism.

---

[1] Matthew had predecessors in (1) Vitalis of Blois (before 1150), who wrote an *Amphitryon* and an *Aulularia* (or *Querulus*), not derived directly from Plautus, but from late Roman imitators. The form is not dramatic; the title 'comedy' in the Middle Ages depends on the subject and feeling of the piece. Terence and Ovid are equally 'comic' (Faral, p. 327). (2) William of Blois, whose *Alda* (before 1170) is a rather licentious tale, which may go back ultimately to Menander. It was probably read in the schools.

An unknown contemporary emulated Matthew in the *Miles gloriosus* and the *Lydia*, tales of a similar character. An anonymous English piece, the *Babio*, and Geoffrey of Vinsauf's *De clericis et rustico* are tales in dialogue form, but as M. Faral shows (pp. 373 sqq.), they are not dramatic, and rank, with the others, purely as 'contes'.

[2] Wattenbach, *Die Briefe des Canonicus Guido von Bazoches, Berlin. Sitzungsber.*, 1890, pp. 161 sqq.; and *Aus den Briefen des Guido von Bazoches, Neues Archiv*, xvi, pp. 69 sqq., gives a good selection of the letters.

[3] Cf. the lively poem, *Neues Archiv*, xvi, pp. 87 sqq.

His poems are contained in the collection of his letters, which he edited for the benefit of his contemporaries. In one of them he gives a description of Paris, where he was at one time a student. When he wishes to describe the great bridge, he breaks into verse which reminds us of the trivialities of Peter of Riga :

> densus, dives, emax, fervet, suspirat, abundat,
> navigiis, opibus, mercibus innumeris.
> navigiis fervet, opibus suspirat, abundat
> mercibus : ecce parem non habet iste locus.[1]

On two occasions when he was ill and feared that he might die, he composed appropriate verses. On the first occasion he wrote his epitaph and sent it to his mother; it gives a fair picture of his attitude to life :

> Guido mihi nomen, generis Basochis origo :
> qui castri dominus, et pater ille meus.
> in Cathalaunensi sacra protomartyris aula [2]
> officium quintus contulit ordo mihi.[3]
> maior eram brevibus, brevior maioribus, annos
> vir iuvenisque fere, plusve minusve ferens.
> et ludis datus et studiis, sed rarus in illis,
> creber in his, doctus atque docendus eram.
> nec dives nec egens, sed sub moderamine tali
> fortunam medius inter utramque fui.
> septimus instabat media plus virgine mensis,
> cum mihi restabat praeter obire nihil.
> qui legis hos versus, conversus ad aethera pro me
> promere devota mente memento preces.[4]

The second piece was composed when he was with the French army in Syria. He feared that he might not live to see 'the yoke of the heathen broken asunder from the neck of the faithful, and the good things that the Lord would shortly do for Jeru-salem'. After so much toil on land and sea, over mountains and through valleys, rivers, and forests, he had reached 'the native soil of Christ . . . the country dear to God, and to the blessed patriarchs', and he might not live to see its deliverance. He prays to God, who 'wields the sceptre of the threefold realm, of sea and earth and air', that his eyes may not close in death until he has seen the lawless tyrants crushed beneath the heel of the 'unconquered Philip', his king.[5]

---

[1] ib., p. 73.
[2] i.e. S. Stephen of Châlons.
[3] He was then sub-deacon.
[4] *Neues Archiv*, xvi, p. 172.
[5] ib., p. 109 sqq.

The rhythmical pieces[1] contained in Guy's letters consist of songs, sequences, and hymns—for Christmas, for a New Year festival, for the Epiphany, in honour of the Virgin and of various saints, including the Baptist, SS. Stephen, Lupentius, Rufinus and Valerius, and Thomas of Canterbury. Guy had mastered the two-syllabled rime and the sequence-form popularized by Adam of S. Victor, as the following verses from his sequence on John the Baptist show:

1 a. o praecursor, ortu cuius
    gloriosa fulget huius
    diei solemnitas,

1 b. dona nobis, te rogamus,
    ut devote persolvamus
    laudes tibi debitas.

But Guy is at his best in the 'munusculum de meorum flosculis studiorum', as he calls it, which has for its subject the nativity. It is written in a measure admirably adapted for singing, and the arrangement of the rimes is very attractive:[2]

1. qui cuncta condidit
    in sapientia,
  per eius reddidit
    nobis auxilia,
  quae prima perdidit
    insipientia,
      per illam reparans,
    quos serpens perdidit
      a deo separans.

2. haec domum similis
    scrutanti feminae,
  quae testae fragilis
    accenso lumine
  apparens humilis
    drachmam in homine
      repperit decimam,
    regis imagine
      fulgentem animam.

3. sol veri luminis,
    quem virgo concipit
  de carne virginis
    dum carnem accipit,
  naturam hominis,
    non culpam suscipit
    et necessariam
  poenam non recipit
    sed voluntariam.

4. merito numinis
    fit homo socius
  per ipsum luminis
    lumen, ut alius
  non esset hominis
    quam dei filius,
    et idem hominum
  mediator pius
    esset ad dominum.

5. carnem ingenitus
    sumere potuit
  ut unigenitus,
    sed non oportuit,
  quia, qui genitus,
    et non, qui genuit,
    humano generi
  et mitti debuit
    et homo fieri.

6. cur datum filio,
    carnem ut sumeret,
  quae dignos odio
    caros efficeret,
  est item ratio,
    prolis acciperet
    ne nomen alius,
  vel idem fideret
    pater et filius.

[1] *Anal. Hymn.* l, pp. 507 sqq.　　[2] ib., p. 508 sq.

7. illud angelicum
   igitur gloriae
cantemus canticum
   regi iustitiae,
qui misit unicum,
   ut eius hodie
nos a miseria
   redderet gratiae
misericordia.

The same skill is shown in a poem addressed to the Virgin, the second stanza of which follows : [1]

tua nos restituit
   conceptio
quos serpentis obruit
   deceptio ;
de mortis eripuit
   confinio,
et finem imposuit
   exilio,
quod Eva promeruit.

There is a refrain which follows each stanza,

o gloriosa domina,
quorum te laudant carmina,
precamur, dele crimina.

The general survey of twelfth-century verse (for the most part non-liturgical),which is contained in this and the preceding section, is necessarily incomplete,[2] but it illustrates the main tendencies in an age of great intellectual activity and social development. It is clear, in the first place, that the secular element has been decisively strengthened. This is a result of the increasing importance of town life and of the growth of the middle classes, and it is reflected in the position of the cathedral schools, which did so much for the education of the secular clergy, and produced a class of clerical men of letters who tended to neglect the Christian poets, even the Carolingians, and based their

[1] *Anal. Hymn.* l, p. 513.

[2] I have not, for instance, mentioned (1) Peter of Blois, a minor poet (b. *circ.* 1130; d. *circ.* 1200), but a man of great importance in his day, a theologian and statesman who served William II of Sicily and Henry II of England (see *Nouvelle Biogr.Universelle*). The poems attributed to him are in Migne, ccvii, col. 1127 sqq. The first two are in the twelfth-century vein of moralistic satire. (2) Stephen of Bec (d. 1170), whose *Draco Normannicus* (*Rolls Series*, lxxxii, ii. 589 sqq., with selections of his other poems) is a pretentious historical poem of mixed content (Henry II, his mother, Hastings, Duke Rollo, &c.). Of his minor poems, some are poetical epistles ; one is an acrostic containing his name.

versification upon a study of the ancient poets, especially Virgil and Ovid.   At their worst, they were tiresome pedants; at their best, they were poets attempting to exercise their art on the material afforded by life and experience.

Others, under the influence of a revived study of history, or under the impulse of patriotic and political sentiment, turned to the creation of historical epics, or political poems and satires. The philosophical movements of the age were also reflected in verse, and philosophical poems appeared for the first time since Boëthius.   But this poetry was, for the most part, in classical metres.   It was the 'age of Ovid',[1] a poet who was appreciated not only for his easy and elegant versification, but for those keen observations on men and morals which appealed so much to men who were beginning to be interested in themselves as individuals and as members of a civilized society.[2]

Yet religion was still the dominant interest, and the output of religious verse was still undiminished.   Rhythmical verse flourished, and it was not confined to the monasteries, though the best liturgical productions come from S. Victor and from Cluny.   When we admire the great achievements of the Victorine school, we must not forget that all the rhythmical Latin poetry of the Middle Ages was the work of men who had studied the classical poets and had begun their apprenticeship to verse by compositions in the classical metres.

§ 3.   *Poets of Cluny : Odo,* 879–943; *Peter the Venerable,* d. 1156; *and Bernard of Morlas.*

The Abbey of Cluny was founded in 910 by Duke William of Aquitaine.   It was intended to be a model monastic house in which the rule of S. Benedict was to be interpreted with the utmost and unvarying strictness.   It was also to be a centre of reform, and its main business was to preach throughout the countries of western Europe, from monastery to monastery, the ideal of a purified monasticism, freed from secular influences, and consecrated to spiritual ends.   Inspired by this missionary spirit the Abbots of Cluny won over a number of monastic houses and founded others, which henceforth formed part of a great

---

[1] Traube, *Einleitung in die lateinische Philologie des Mittelalters,* p. 113, calls the twelfth and thirteenth centuries the 'aetas Ovidiana'.

[2] See E. K. Rand, *Ovid and his influence,* p. 111.

'congregation' subject to the mother-house at Cluny, and claiming independence of any other ecclesiastical authority. The Abbot himself, who nominated the priors of the dependent monasteries, acknowledged no master beneath the Pope. The Papacy showered privileges upon Duke William's foundation until it became the richest, the most famous, and the most influential monastery in Christendom.

The ideals of ecclesiastical purity which spread from Cluny contributed largely to the movement for ecclesiastical reform which filled the tenth and eleventh centuries ; but they are to be associated rather with practical efforts for the reform of monastic life than with any attempt, such as Hildebrand's, to exalt the spiritual power above the secular by a doctrine of papal imperialism.

The contribution of Cluny to the religious life of the Middle Ages lay, therefore, in setting a practical ideal of monasticism, an ideal of discipline, of labour, and of charity, an ideal of order and obedience, which helped to save the Church in a time of severe crisis, and gave monasticism itself a new lease of life when it was being threatened by internal decay. Though Cluny possessed a school for oblates, it never became a house of learning. The reading of profane authors appears to have been carried only to the degree necessary for the successful pursuit of grammatical studies. This, at any rate, was the theory, and no doubt too close an application on the part of the young novices to the pagan poets was officially discouraged. Yet, besides Virgil and Juvenal, the library at Cluny contained Ovid, the most dangerous and most alluring among the Latin poets.[1] When Odo, the first great Abbot of Cluny, was a student at Tours he fell under the charm of Virgil, until like Jerome he was warned by a dream. A beautiful vase appeared, from which threatening serpents issued. By this dream he learned that out of the beautiful verses of the poet came a poisonous doctrine which was perilous to the soul. Henceforth he would choose the safer study of Gregory's *Moralia.*

The four hymns which he composed in honour of S. Martin, his boyhood's patron, are of no great interest.[2] Three of them are in rhythmic iambic dimeters, and show an intermittent use of rime, while the other is a curious metrical piece which the Abbot appears to have composed on his death-bed. An attempt,

[1] Sackur, *Die Cluniacenser*, ii. 330. See   [2] *Anal. Hymn.* l, pp. 265-9.
also above, p. 257, note 1.

not always successful, is made to preserve an internal rime in each line of the poem :

> tu pacem reparas hic et ad astra migras,
> nunc nos te medio concilies domino
> Odonis famuli, hoc opus qui condidit
> emigrando de saeculo.

But Odo's masterpiece was the *Occupatio* in seven books, a philosophical and moral poem dealing with the creation of the world, the fall of the angels, the making of man, and the origin of sin ; the manifold growth of wickedness, and God's plan of redemption by the incarnation and death of Christ, and the foundation of the Church. But it is no epic in the spirit of Juvencus or Sedulius. It is overladen with the moral and allegorical, and it has a monastic pre-occupation with evil and with the invisible world. Here we move in an intellectual twilight deepened by the obscurity of verses in which the strange verbiage of the *Hisperica Famina* again appears. Occasionally there is almost a gleam of sunshine :

> aere iam sudo tellus hiemale fugato
> frigore, sol placidas cum dat vicinior auras,
> vere novo faciem praetendit ubique venustam,
> quolibet ad varios laxat cum viscera foetus,
> germina cum laeti produnt sibi credita sulci,
> picturant varii cum prata virentia flores,
> frondibus arboreis folio fructuve repletis
> garrula vox avium cum per convallia tinnit,
> hinnulus enixae cum se sugit ubera cervae,
> mater ovis proprium noscit balatibus agnum[1].

Then the winter twilight settles again. The *Occupatio* may have puzzled the brain of many generations of Cluniac monks, but they had glosses to assist them to read the barbarous words. Odo's poem shows reminiscences of Virgil, Horace, and Juvenal, as well as of Sedulius and Prudentius. After his time, too, the profane authors continued to be studied. Maiolus, who was librarian under Odo's successor, and later became Abbot, appears to have loved them ; as priest and archdeacon, before he became a monk, he had taught 'grammar'. But in later years he made it his duty to erase from the manuscripts 'quae superflua, de amore scilicet rerumque saecularium cura'.[2] On

[1] *Odonis Abbatis Cluniacensis Occupatio*, ed. A. Swoboda, Leipzig 1900, pp. 37–8; on the *Occupatio* see Manitius, *Gesch.* ii. 22 sqq.

[2] That is, if we are to take literally the passage in the *Vita Maioli*. Migne, cxxxvii, col. 755, which reads, 'quae superflua, de amore scilicet rerumque

the whole, therefore, the traditions of Cluny were anything but favourable to the study of humane letters, and the abbey contributed little of importance to medieval literature. In the twelfth century there are but two notable names,[1] Peter the Venerable and Bernard of Morlas.

In 1122 after the anarchic reign of the unworthy Pontius, during which discipline had been relaxed and the abbey had been reduced to poverty, Peter became Abbot, and restored the house to its ancient influence and splendour. Peter was a man of singular charm of character; he ruled Cluny wisely, and gained the love of all who knew him. It was he who received Abélard when, broken in spirit and weary of the unequal battle, he left the Council of Sens to find a refuge for his last days. Peter interceded with the Pope on his behalf, and obtained permission for him to remain at Cluny, and when in 1142 the great scholar passed away, the Abbot wrote a touching letter to Héloïse, in which he extolled the fame and the virtues of the man who had won his sympathy, not by his doctrines, but by his misfortunes and sufferings.

Peter was a voluminous writer both in prose and in verse, as his epitaph testifies:

> tractatus scribens nec non volumina multa,
> sermones varios, dictamina prosa metroque,[2]

that is to say, he composed both rhythmical and quantitative verse. Among the rhythmical pieces are a few *proses* of mediocre quality. On the Nativity he begins

> caelum, gaude, terra, plaude,
> nemo mutus sit a laude,
> ad antiquam originem
> redit homo per virginem,

and he proceeds,

> tunc de caeno surgit reus,
> cum in feno iacet deus,
> tunc vile celat stabulum
> caelestis escae pabulum.[3]

saecularium cura, haec quasi venenata radebat et mortifera, his calvitium inducebat, haec unguium more ferro acutissimo disecabat'; the reference being to Deut. xxi. 10-14. The art of erasing MSS. for re-use of the parchment was taught in the monasteries and required some skill; see Wattenbach, *Das Schriftwesen im Mittelalter*, pp. 171 sqq., Leipzig 1871.

[1] In the eleventh century Maiolus' successor, Odilo (d. 1048), a man of strong character and a good ruler, wrote a few hymns: *Anal. Hymn.* l, pp. 298 sqq.; see also G. Morin, *Un hymne inédit de S. Odilon*, *Rev. Bénéd.*, 1926, pp. 56 sqq.
[2] Migne, clxxxix, col. 42.
[3] *Anal. Hymn.* xlviii, p. 234.

The Easter *prose* is a pretty jingle of rhymes :

> mortis portis
> fortis vim intulit,
> trucem ducem
> illius perculit.[1]

A long *Rhythmus in laude Salvatoris* has for its theme the incarnation of Christ ; His redemption of man by His death and resurrection ; the ascension, and the coming judgement. It is a mere rhythmical narrative until it gathers a greater fervour in the contemplation of the last things :

> tunc terror pessimus
> et horror maximus
> orbem concutiet,
> tunc quidquid firmius
> atque stabilius
> erit, diffugiet.[2]

The heavens shall roll together, the earth shall be dissolved as wax, the beauty of flower and fruit and tree shall wither, the stars shall be darkened, and the sulphurous pit shall open its mouth. The trumpet of the archangel shall summon the dead, their souls and bodies joining, before the tribunal of Christ. Even hell is emptied in order that the damned may reassume their bodies ; not to obtain a respite from their pangs, but that they may suffer henceforth a twofold pain :

> o quam terribilis
> et formidabilis
> haec dies irruet,
> heu, heu, quam luridum,
> heu, heu, quam turbidum
> tunc vultum induet ![3]

Then the Judge appears, with the Cross and the symbols of the passion. 'Every eye shall see him, and they which pierced him.' Here Peter's enmity against the Jews, the one unpleasant trait in his otherwise gentle, tolerant character,[4] breaks out into fury. He bids them look upon the Christ whom they have despised and blasphemed. 'Do you believe now that He is God, now that you are to be consigned by Him to hell and shut up in the

---

[1] *Anal. Hymn.* xlviii, p. 236.
[2] ib., p. 248.   [3] ib., p. 250.
[4] See Morison, *S. Bernard*, pp. 374–5, 'damnati damnandique Iudaei,' he calls them. Bernard, on the other hand, so intolerant of the mere suspicion of heresy, protected the Jews.

fiery pit?' Then Peter remembers that, after all, he himself is a sinner, and he trembles for his own condition in that terrible day:

> Christe, deus meus,
> ad te clamo reus,
>   quem spero iudicem,
> ut tunc clementiam,
> non iram sentiam
>   malorum vindicem.

Anxiously, too, he thinks of the fate of the little flock entrusted to his charge and of the great congregation of Cluny:

> Cluniacensium
> sis memor ovium
>   in tanto turbine
> et ad perpetua
> duc ea pascua,
>   benigne domine.

A hymn in sapphics on S. Benedict gives us an idea of Peter's abilities in metrical composition. The poem is quite colourless, and it merely relates with an obscure brevity the life and miracles of the saint as they are told in Gregory's *Dialogues*.

The venerable Abbot is not one of the greater poets of his century. His verse would hardly call for notice if it were not the work of a man of high importance in Church and State, a man of lofty spirit and gentle disposition—in a word, one of the most attractive and saintly ecclesiastics of the Middle Ages.

But during Peter's abbacy the monastery could boast the presence of a remarkable versifier, Bernard of Morlas, who dedicated 'to his lord and father, Peter, the most worthy abbot of the brethren of Cluny', his long satirical poem entitled *De Contemptu Mundi*.[1] Of Bernard's life we know little with any certainty. He was a monk at Cluny under Peter the Venerable, and he appears to have been born at Morlas in the Pyrenees [2] somewhere about the beginning of the twelfth century. His poem is an exposition of the favourite monastic themes of a world given over to wickedness, and an impending judgement:

---

[1] The full text is given in Thomas Wright's *Anglo-Latin Satirical Poets of the Twelfth Century*, vol. ii (*Rolls Series*, London 1872); there is a critical edition by H. C. Hoskier, London 1929.

[2] Not Morlaix in Brittany, as is often supposed.

> The world is very evil ;
>   The times are waxing late :
> Be sober and keep vigil ;
>   The Judge is at the gate.

This is the text of a long denunciation of the evils of a world which seemed to be moving towards the abyss of destruction. The poet takes himself and his art very seriously. In his *Dedication* he shows that he has read the *Ars Poetica,* and explains that he writes in verse because men will read it more eagerly than plain prose, and rimes appeal more easily to the memory and so to the conscience of the reader.[1] 'Materia est mihi vitiorum repraehensio, et a vitiis revocare intentio ', he says, after explaining that his heart grew hot within him at the sight of the vices with which the world was filled, while no voice was raised against them. And indeed he attacks those vices with a savage outspokenness which Juvenal never attempted, and with a minuteness of description which knows neither reticence nor restraint. For him, as for monks in general, woman is the arch-enemy :

> est fera femina, sunt sua crimina sicut arena ;[2]

and again,

> femina perfida, femina foetida, femina foetor.[3]

But he does not spare the unnatural vices of men, the corruption of the clergy and of the civil magistrates, the prevalence of simony, and the venality of the Roman curia. He is of the opinion that Horace, Cato, Persius, and Juvenal would be astonished if they visited the world again in the flesh, and that Lucilius would call his own age golden in comparison with these latter days.[4]

Bernard's satire has become famous of recent years because it contains those mystical visions of the heavenly country which Dr. Neale's translations have introduced into so many English hymnaries.[5] For Bernard, while holding before the wicked the

---

[1] On a similar passion at the Renaissance, for writing in verse on all kinds of subjects, see Burckhardt, *Civilization of the Renaissance in Italy,* London 1878, i. 370–1.

[2] Wright, p. 57 ; on the same page he parodies Pentadius :

> nulla quidem bona, si tamen et bona
>   contigit ulla,
> est mala res bona, namque fere bona
>   femina nulla.

[3] p. 59 ; this part of the satire was imitated by an unknown monk, 'né ou devenu chagrin, mais certainement né sans esprit et sans délicatesse', Hauréau in *Notices et extraits. des mss.* xxviii, 2, p. 364 sq.   [4] Wright, p. 68.

[5] J. M. Neale, *Mediaeval Hymns,* pp. 68 sqq., London 1863 ; *The Rhythm of Bernard de Morlaix on the Celestial Country,* edited and trans. by J. M. Neale, London 1911.

pains of hell, lingers to celebrate the glories of the 'golden city of Syon', in verses of much beauty, full of the elaborate mysticism so dear to the monastic mind :

> urbs Syon aurea, patria lactea, cive decora,
> omne cor obruis, omnibus obstruis, et cor et ora.
> nescio, nescio, quae iubilatio, lux tibi qualis,
> quam socialia gaudia, gloria quam specialis.
> laude studens ea tollere, mens mea victa fatiscit.
> o bona gloria, vincor, in omnia laus tua vicit.[1] . . .
> urbs Syon unica, mansio mystica condita coelo,
> nunc tibi gaudeo, nunc mihi lugeo, tristor anhelo.
> te quia corpore non queo, pectore saepe penetro ;
> sed caro terrea, terraque carnea, nunc cado retro.[2] . . .
> urbs Syon inclita, patria condita littore tuto,
> te peto, te colo, te flagro, te volo, canto, saluto.
> nec meritis peto, nam meritis meto morte perire ;
> non reticens rego, sum meritis ego, filius irae.
> vita quidem mea, vita nimis rea, mortua vita ;
> quippe reatibus exitialibus obruta, trita.
> spe tamen ambulo, premia postulo speque fideque ;
> illa perennia postulo praemia nocte dieque
> me pater optimus atque piissimus ille creavit
> in lue pertulit, ex lue sustulit, a lue lavit. . . .
> dum sua suppleo robora, gaudeo ; dum mea ploro ;
> tum sibi gaudeo, tum mihi defleo, flere laboro.[3]

Of Bernard of Morlas it can be said that no one before him, even the unknown author of the *Urbs beata Hierusalem*, or Hildebert in his *Me receptet Syon illa*, had risen to such heights in describing the longing of the pilgrim for his home. *Non habemus hic manentem civitatem !*—the true monk should have his eyes fixed on the world to come, and Bernard was a true

---

[1] Wright, p. 16.   [2] ib., p. 17.
[3] ib., p. 18. The following lines are taken from a fine free version of these verses by Swinburne, which deserves to be known, as it was never gathered into his collected works. It was printed in the *Academy*, April 2, 1910, and has since been published in Mrs. Disney Leith's *Boyhood of Swinburne*, London 1917, p. 33 :

O land without guilt, strong city safe built
   in a marvellous place,
I cling to thee, ache for thee, sing to thee,
   wake for thee, watch for thy face :
Full of cursing and strife are the days of
   my life, with their sins they are fed,
Out of sin is the root, unto sin is the fruit,
   in their sins they are dead.

No deserving of mine can make answer to
   thine, neither I unto thee;
I a child of GOD'S wrath, made subject to
   death, what good thing is in me?
Yet through faith I require thee, through
   hope I desire thee, in hope I hold fast,
Crying out, day and night, that my soul
   may have sight of thy joy at the last.
Me, even me, hath the FATHER set free,
   and hath bidden come in ;
In sin hath He found me, from sin hath
   unbound me, and purged me of sin.
In His strength am I glad, whom my weakness made sad ; I that slept am awake ;
With the eyes that wept, with the spirit
   that slept, I give thanks for His sake.

monk in an age when, in spite of Cîteaux and Clairvaux, monastic laxity was widespread.   But, as a poet, he could not help a little pride in his poetical achievement; he had written a long poem in a difficult and complicated metre, the dactylic hexameter, with both internal rime and a tailed rime of two syllables.   He reminds us [1] that the great Hildebert himself had managed to compose only a few verses in that metre, and he is of the opinion that 'unless the spirit of wisdom and understanding had been with him and had inspired him he could not have composed so long a work in so difficult a metre'.   It is certainly a remarkable achievement; but, to be critical, the metre is obviously ill-adapted for a long poem.   It is soon monotonous, for it admits of no variations; it fetters the expression throughout, and Bernard would perhaps have been better advised if he had followed the more modest example of Hildebert.

Besides the *De Contemptu Mundi*, Bernard is probably the author of the famous *Mariale*,[2] which has been wrongly attri-buted both to Anselm and to the saint of Clairvaux.   This remarkable poem, which is devoted to the praises of the Virgin, consists of fifteen long 'Rhythms' in the favourite metre of Peter of Cluny.   It begins with a paraphrase of Psalm xlii, *Quemadmodum desiderat cervus ad fontes aquarum* :

> ut iucundas cervus undas
>   aestuans desiderat,
> sic ad deum, fontem vivum
>   mens fidelis properat.
>
> sicut rivi fontis vivi
>   praebent refrigerium,
> ita menti sitienti
>   deus est remedium.

Then the poem proceeds to tell at length the praises of Mary; it is full of that symbolism and allegory which we shall discuss in detail when we come to consider the sequences of Adam of S. Victor.   Already Mary has become the refuge of sinners, for whom she intercedes against the strict justice of her Son, the all but inflexible Judge:

> si te sentis temptamentis,
>   urgeri daemonicis,
> mox respiras, si requiras
>   matrem summi iudicis. . . .

---

[1] p. 6, *Dedication*; on the metre see Meyer, *Rythmik*, i. 90.

[2] *Anal. Hymn.* I, p. 423; Hauréau, *Journal des savants*, 1882, p. 410.

si te doles ferre moles
culparum prementium,
hanc praecare, ut placare
possis eius filium.

nam placatum eius natum
tunc habere poteris,
si fideli menti caeli
reginam rogaveris.[1]

§ 4. *The Hymns of Peter Abélard* (1079–1142).

Among the great hymn writers of the Middle Ages Peter Abélard holds a high place. He was born in 1079 at Palais in Brittany, and, after a boyhood of great promise, abandoned his heritage and became a wandering student. Being possessed of a restless mind which recognized no limits to intellectual inquiry, he determined to devote his whole life to the pursuit of knowledge.[2] He came into notice when he refuted the extreme realist theory of his master William of Champeaux, who was then an important figure in the Paris schools. It was not long before he was attracting a crowd of enthusiastic students to hear his own lectures at Mont Ste. Geneviève. This was his period of dazzling success when his name was on all men's lips; he became known in Paris for his beauty and charm of person as much as for his intellectual supremacy.[3] It was when Abélard was at the height of his fame that the great and destructive crisis of his life occurred. He became the tutor of Héloïse, niece of Canon Fulbert of Notre-Dame, and the most remarkable woman of her age, who had already a reputation for learning which had made her name known throughout the kingdom. The story of their love and of Fulbert's vengeance does not need retelling.[4] Abélard found a refuge at S. Denys, and Héloïse became a nun at Argenteuil. But the scholar could not rest in the seclusion of a monastery. His old labours called him, and in 1120 he was again lecturing to a throng of students at Maisoncelles-en-Brie. But his incautious handling of the doctrine of the Trinity caused him to be called before a Council

[1] *Anal. Hymn.* l, p. 427.
[2] See the account which Abélard gives in his *Historia calamitatum*, Migne, clxxviii, col. 113 sq.
[3] John of Salisbury, who was his pupil, speaks of him as 'clarus doctor et admirabilis'; see *Metalogicus*, ii. 10; iii. 1.
[4] See Charles de Rémusat's *Abélard*; J. Cotter Morison, *S. Bernard*, pp. 258 sqq.; Milman, *Latin Christianity*, iv. 342 sqq.

at Soissons in 1121 ; he was condemned unheard, and immured in the abbey of S. Médard. Thence he returned to S. Denys, where he occupied himself in criticizing the legend of Dionysius the Areopagite, the patron of the abbey. He fled from the wrath of the monks, and built himself a hermitage in the wilds of Champagne. ' He called the place his Paraclete, because it had been his consolation ',[1] and there it seemed likely that he might find rest. But his old scholars sought and found him, and endured the hardships of a hermit's life for the sake of listening again to the fascinating discourses of their master. Not long after Abélard was made Abbot of S. Gildas, an abbey situated on the wild and lonely Breton coast, ' ad horrisoni undas oceani ',[2] where he spent unhappy years among a crowd of insubordinate monks, and wrote the books which established his fame. There, at the end of the earth, he says, in despair of heart, how often he mingled with his prayers the cry of the psalmist, ' From the ends of the earth have I cried unto thee, when my heart was in heaviness '. To S. Gildas came the news that Héloïse and her sister nuns had been dispossessed at Argenteuil ; Abélard at once offered them his old refuge, the Paraclete,[3] which soon became a flourishing religious house with Héloïse as prioress, ' on whom ', says Abélard, ' the Lord bestowed such grace in the eyes of all, that bishops loved her as a daughter, abbots as a sister, lay-folk as a mother '.[4] Abélard visited his ' beloved sister in Christ ', as he called her, and gave advice as to the ordering of the new monastery, but the visits caused some scandal, and their meetings ceased. The ' history of his calamities ', contained in a letter to a friend, came into Héloïse's possession, and prompted her to write to Abélard a letter, warm with more than sisterly love, in which she implored him to ' render himself present in the way he could, to wit, by writing some words of consolation '.[5] This epistle called forth an answer, somewhat cold, monastically reserved, as of one disillusioned of love and dedicated to higher ends. He professed his willingness to give advice ' in the things which pertain to God ', he asked for the prayers of Héloïse and her nuns, begging that when he died his body might find a resting-place in the Paraclete. His advice on matters of rule and discipline was sought and given ; he gave a rule for the nuns, and, most precious of all, sent a collection of hymns and sequences which

---

[1] Newman, *Hist. Sketches*, vol. iii, cap. 16 ; *Hist. calam.*, col. 162.
[2] *Hist. calam.*, col. 165.
[3] ib., col. 169.
[4] ib., col. 173.
[5] ib., col. 189.

he had composed for use in the services at the Paraclete.   In
his youth he had celebrated his love for Héloïse in songs which
had been the delight of Paris, and were heard in every street;[1]
but only hymns and sequences and six remarkable *Planctus* or
Complaints have survived to prove his skill as a maker of verses.[2]
In his dedicatory letter he says, 'At the instance of thy prayers,
my sister Héloïse, once dear to me in the world, now most dear in
Christ, I have composed what in Greek are called hymns (*ymnos*),
in Hebrew *tehillim*'.   He expresses the diffidence with which
he complied with this request, seeing that there were already
in existence so many hymns which had been consecrated by custom
and their antiquity.   Héloïse had pleaded that there was such
confusion among the hymns then in use that it was impossible
to know the names of their authors, and that if, in some instances,
the authorship was capable of being ascertained, as in the case
of Hilary, Ambrose, and Prudentius among the earliest, yet the
syllables are often so uneven that the verses cannot easily be
fitted to melodies, without which they are not hymns at all,
since by definition a hymn is 'laus Dei cum cantico'.   Further,
many festivals had no proper hymns at all (for instance, the
feast of the Innocents and those of the Evangelists).   For these
and for other reasons Abélard says he was led to comply with
the request of Héloïse, and to compose these 'hymns for the
whole cycle of the year'.   'Wherein your prayers being given
on my behalf, we also pray in our turn for you, that you may
lift up in the hands of your prayers the burden which we have
placed on our shoulders, to the end that he who sows and he
who reaps, together labouring, together may rejoice.'[3]
    In these hymns the genius of Abélard created new verse
forms with the same boldness that he had shown in his methods
in the schools.   Thus in the first book he uses verses made up
of rimed couplets, two of eight syllables followed by two of
ten syllables.   The following example is a hymn for the second
nocturn at Matins:[4]

> deus qui tuos erudis
> testamentorum paginis,
> ex eorum intelligentiae
> cantus nostros condis dulcedine.

---

[1] *Hist. calam.*, col. 128; 'Me plateae
omnes, me domus singulae resonabant',
says Héloïse (*Epist.* ii, col. 188).
[2] There is, however, an interesting
'hortatory' poem in elegiacs, addressed
to his son, Astralabius (Hauréau, *Notices
et extraits des mss.* xxxiv, ii, pp. 157 sqq.);
for the hymns, &c., see *Anal. Hymn.*
xlviii, pp. 144 sqq.
[3] ib., p. 144.   [4] ib., p. 145.

> tibi sit acceptabile,
> nobis sic fiat utile
> quod de tuis solvemus laudibus,
> si quod sonat intellexerimus.
>
> triplex intelligentia
> diversa praebet fercula,
> deliciis abundat variis
> sacrae mensa scripturae fertilis.[1]
>
> alunt parvos historica,
> pascunt adultos mistica,
> perfectorum ferventi studio
> suscipitur moralis lectio.
>
> illis fides astruitur,
> ex hac fructus colligitur,
> fructus hic est et consummatio,
> quam det nobis, morum instructio,
>
> haec nobis, deus, fercula
> tua paravit gratia,
> ut his nostra peregrinatio
> sustentetur quasi viatico.

The expression is simple and severe, and the lines move slowly and solemnly like a scholastic exposition. This is the character of the remaining hymns for Matins, which describe the six days of creation, ending with the Sabbath upon which the Creator rested. Then follow hymns for the other canonical hours, from Lauds to Compline, in a fresh metre of twelve-syllabled rimed couplets. The symbolism of Prudentius' morning hymns reappears. Thus in the hymn for Sunday, at Lauds, the dawning light is the symbol of the dawn of truth and of the resurrection of Christ :

> transacto flebili de morte vespere,
> cum vita redditur mane laetitiae,
> resurgit dominus, apparent angeli,
> custodes fugiunt splendore territi.[2]

But the most beautiful application of the symbolism of the hour is given in the hymn for the Sabbath (i. e. Saturday), at Vespers, celebrating the joys of the endless Sabbath which knows no evening.[3]

---

[1] On the three ways of interpreting Scripture see below, p. 357.

[2] *Anal. Hymn.* xlviii, p. 150.
[3] ib., p. 163.

o quanta, qualia sunt illa sabbata,
quae semper celebrat superna curia !
quae fessis requies, quae merces fortibus,
cum erit omnia deus in omnibus !

vere Ierusalem est illa civitas
cuius pax iugis est, summa iucunditas,
ubi non praevenit rem desiderium,
nec desiderio minus est praemium.

quis rex ! quae curia ! quale palatium !
quae pax ! quae requies ! quod illud gaudium !
huius participes exponant gloriae,
si, quantum sentiunt, possint exprimere.

nostrum est interim mentem erigere,
et totis patriam votis appetere,
et ad Ierusalem a Babylonia,
post longa regredi tandem exilia.

illic, molestiis finitis omnibus,
securi cantica Syon cantabimus,
et iuges gratias de donis gratiae
beata referet plebs tibi, domine.

illic ex sabbato succedet sabbatum,
perpes laetitia sabbatizantium,
nec ineffabiles cessabunt iubili,
quos decantabimus et nos et angeli.

The second book contains hymns for the different festivals,
exhibiting a variety of metres.   As an example we give the first
verse of a hymn on the Resurrection :

Christiani, plaudite,
(resurrexit dominus !)
victo mortis principe
Christus imperat,
victori occurrite,
qui nos liberat.[1]

A hymn on the Cross begins :

lignum amaras   omnes agones
indulcat aquas   sunt sanctis dulces
eis immissum.   per crucifixum.

In Book Three (hymns for Saints' Days) more varieties of metre
appear.   The hymns on the feast of the Holy Innocents are

---

[1] *Anal. Hymn.* xlviii, p. 179.

written in a delicate four-syllabled rimed metre, the rhythm of
which is well adapted to the subject.

<table>
<tr><td>est in Rama</td><td>interfecti</td></tr>
<tr><td>vox audita</td><td>sunt inviti,</td></tr>
<tr><td>Rachel flentis,</td><td>sed pro vita ;</td></tr>
<tr><td>super natos</td><td>meritorum</td></tr>
<tr><td>interfectos</td><td>fuit nullum,</td></tr>
<tr><td>eiulantis.</td><td>merces multa.</td></tr>
<tr><td>lacerata</td><td>merces ipsa</td></tr>
<tr><td>iacent membra</td><td>fuit vita,</td></tr>
<tr><td>parvulorum,</td><td>quam et ipsi</td></tr>
<tr><td>et tam lacte</td><td>moriendo,</td></tr>
<tr><td>quam cruore</td><td>non loquendo,</td></tr>
<tr><td>rigant humum. . . .</td><td>sunt confessi.[1]</td></tr>
</table>

The Hymn for the Common of Martyrs shows a variety of
metre within the poem itself:

> scutum, deus, omnium,
> et corona martyrum,
> tam causa certaminum
> quam palma certantium,
> per inermes dimicas,
> et armatos superas.
> intus arma fabricas,
> quibus pugnat charitas.
>
> his confisa bene virtus
> nudum hosti praebet pectus,
>   quam a dextris
>   et sinistris
>   muniunt,
>   a laesuris
>   universis
>   protegunt.
>   in hanc pugnae
>   quantaecunque
>   saeviunt,
>   spes securam,
>   fides certam
>   faciunt . . . [2]

A beautiful hymn or sequence on the Annunciation is ascribed
to Abélard.[3]   It begins :

[1] *Anal. Hymn.* xlviii, p. 205.
[2] ib., p. 200.

[3] *Anal. Hymn.* liv, p. 296; but the
ascription is doubtful ; see ib., p. 298.

> mittit ad virginem
> non quemvis angelum,
> sed fortitudinem
> suam, archangelum
> amator hominis.

The rich variety of verse forms which Abélard devised appears again in the remarkable series of *Planctus* or Complaints on subjects taken from the earlier books of the Old Testament.[1] The rimes are simple enough, but the structure of lines and strophes, as well as that of the poems as a whole, is worthy of the close investigation to which Meyer has subjected them. As their musical notation has been preserved it is clear that they were intended to be sung. The first *Planctus*, one of three on the 'complaint of the virgins of Israel for the daughter of Jephthah the Gileadite', may be quoted as an example :[1]

> ad festas choreas caelibes
> ex more venite virgines !
>   ex more sint odae flebiles
>   et planctus ut cantus celebres !
> incultae sint maestae facies
>   plangentium et flentum similes !
>   auratae sint longe cyclades
>   et cultus sint procul divites !
>
> Galaditae virgo Iephtae filia
> miseranda patris facta victima,
>   annuos virginum elegos
>   et pii carminis modulos
>   virtuti virginis debitos
>   per annos exigit singulos.
>
> o stupendam plus quam flendam virginem !
> o quam rarum illi virum similem !
>   ne votum sit patris irritum
>   promissoque fraudet dominum,
>   qui per hunc salvavit populum,
>   in suum hunc urget iugulum.

Charles de Rémusat, in his romantic life of Abélard, would see in this 'truly poetic elegy' a pathetic and personal meaning. Are not the maidens, the companions of Jephthah's daughter, the 'mournful companions of Héloïse, surrounding with tears and sighs the monastic altar on which the victim is giving herself

---

[1] For text and commentary see Meyer, *Anal. Hymn.* xlviii, p. 223 sqq. *Rythmik*, i. 340 sqq.; they are also in

to sacrifice?'[1]　In the elegies as a whole, Rémusat sees the echo of Abélard's personal sorrows.　In the complaint of Israel for the death of Samson,

> quem primo Dalida sacra caesarie,
> hunc hostes postea privarunt lumine.
> exhaustis viribus, orbatus oculis
> molae fit deditus athleta nobilis,

he hears 'the groanings of the prisoner of S. Médard after his disgrace and fall'.　Does Héloïse speak in the complaint of Dinah, the daughter of Jacob?

> incircumcisi viri rapina
> hominis spurci facta sum praeda.

Abélard stands in a special position as a hymn writer, as he stands alone as a philosopher.　He broke away from tradition, and left no successors.　The hymns bear the mark of an original genius, and would have attracted attention apart from the immense fame of their author.　It will be remarked that the rime throughout is simple and undeveloped; there is no trace either of the two-syllabled rime employed so effectively by Adam of S. Victor in the same century, or of the 'feminine' two-syllabled rime which appears in the *dulcis Iesu memoria* and other poems of the same school.[2]　But Abélard's hymns were written before Adam of S. Victor became famous, and long before the Jubilus on the name of Jesus.　They possess more than any other a romantic interest, because they were sung daily by the nuns of the Paraclete, both during the lifetime of Abélard and after his burial at the Paraclete, whither Peter of Cluny, who had given him a refuge in the later years of his life, sent his body that it might rest in the place where he had once obtained consolation.　Abélard died in 1142; Héloïse lived on for many years, and was buried in the same tomb.

§ 5. *Bernard of Clairvaux and the Poetry of the Name of Jesus.*

Bernard of Clairvaux, the 'doctor melifluus', the mightiest spiritual and political figure of the first half of the twelfth

---

[1] Rémusat, i. 124.

[2] Cf. the remarks of Ronca, *Cultura medievale*, i. 351; also Dreves, *Petri Abaelardi Hymnarius Paraclitensis*, pp. 18 sqq., who remarks on the somewhat careless rimes and on Abélard's failure to make use of the two-syllabled rimes preferred by Hildebert and Peter the Venerable.

century, was born in 1090 at Fontaines, near Dijon. He was the son of a knightly father, but the profession of arms did not attract him, and, from the first, he was devoted to the religious life. He entered Cîteaux, taking with him, by force of his charming eloquence, his uncle, his brothers, and many young men who had been his companions. At Cîteaux, the Abbot, Stephen Harding, guided a newly-formed community which kept with an unsurpassed strictness the old rule of S. Benedict, but Bernard soon outran his fellows in ascetic practices. His presence made Cîteaux famous; the community grew so large that it was necessary to found another house to accommodate the increasing numbers. So Bernard, with twelve companions, went forth and founded Clairvaux.[1] This was in the year 1115. The fame of Bernard's saintliness and of his miracles grew daily, so that the monastery increased and spread its offshoots far and wide.

From Clairvaux Bernard ruled the fortunes of Christendom until his death in 1153. No ecclesiastic, before or after him, wielded an authority so unquestioned, an authority based on his personal charm, his powerful eloquence, and his angelic saintliness. It was sorely against his will that he mingled in the world of politics; but there he was the acknowledged mediator in an age of fierce, blind enmities. It was Bernard only who could join Genoa and Pisa together in alliance with the Pope, who could convert stubborn Milan to the cause of the Church, and, above all, could persuade Saxon and Hohenstaufen to lay aside a quarrel which delayed the healing of the schism then dividing the Church. The discomfiture of the Antipope Anacletus was Bernard's greatest triumph, but his influence reached its height when his old pupil Eugenius III sat in the chair of Peter. Through the mouth of Eugenius he spoke to Christendom.

A pure mystic, Bernard viewed with growing apprehension the intellectual renaissance which was going on in France before his eyes; he profoundly distrusted the rationalism of the philosopher and the subtlety of the theologian. Safety was to be found only in submission to the Church, and the pride of the intellect could lead men only to their destruction.[2] It was in this spirit that he attacked Abélard and Gilbert de la Porrée, the leaders of opposing schools, and launched his violent rhetoric

---

[1] *Vita Prima*, cap. v (Migne, clxxxv); Bernard's works are in Migne, clxxxii–clxxxv.

[2] Cf. Bernard, *Epist.*, 331 and 332 (Migne, clxxxii, col. 336 sqq.).

against Arnold of Brescia; all alike, the dialectician, the theologian, and the reformer, were wolves in sheep's clothing ravening against the Church of Christ.[1]

Bernard's mysticism was of a simple kind; it was rooted in experience, and needed no formulae for its expression. In the spiritual influence which he wielded, Bernard may be compared with Francis of Assisi, but the contrasts are deeper than the apparent similarities. Bernard was always the Churchman, the idealist who would subject ecclesiastical and secular politics to spiritual principles. Francis was troubled not at all by political or doctrinal questions; he was a follower of Jesus, and his model was the primitive apostle. While Francis moved the hearts of the people like Jesus, Bernard was rather another Ambrose, a terror to evil-doers and heretics, and a doctor whose lips distilled honey. But Bernard and Francis both brought a new personal element into Catholicism, a mysticism based on the direct experience of God's love as revealed in His Son. For Bernard, as for Francis, Jesus was clothed again with human flesh; they had rediscovered in the Saviour a human figure who was the centre of the Christian hope. The Bernardine mysticism was thus, in some sense, a monastic anticipation of one aspect of Franciscanism—the personal love of Jesus and the devotion to his Passion. When the Second Crusade was afoot Bernard encouraged recruiting with fiery letters, in which he appealed to the pathos of the situation. ' The earth is moved and shakes ', he said, ' because the God of heaven has begun to lose His own land. His own, wherein He was seen, and for more than thirty years dwelt a man among men. . . . Alas, the heathen covet with sacrilegious eyes the very shrine of the Christian religion, and are attempting to invade and trample under foot that bed whereon for our sakes He who was our Life slept the sleep of death.'[2] So, too, the passion of the Saviour moved him, as it moved Francis. ' The Church', he says in that beautiful treatise *Of the Love of God*, ' beholds the Lord of majesty buffeted and spat upon; she beholds the Author of life and glory fastened by nails, pierced by the lance, overwhelmed with reproaches, and at last laying down that dear life of His for His friends.'[3] This personal devotion to Jesus fills the long series of sermons on the *Song of*

---

[1] Cf. *Epist.*, 188,189, 330 (Migne, clxxxii, col. 351 sqq.).

[2] Otto of Freising, *Gesta Friderici*, i. 41.

[3] *De diligendo Deo*, iii; ed. E. G. Gardner, London 1916; the translation is by Dr. Gardner, p. 43.

Songs. There of Jesus he says,[1] 'none other, whether angel or man, but Himself I ask that He kiss me with the kisses of His mouth'. ' Jesus is honey to the lips, in the ear melody, in the heart joy. Medicine also is that name. Is any sad? Let Jesus come into his heart, and thence leap to his tongue. . . . For when I name Jesus, I set before me a man meek and lowly of heart, kind, sober, chaste, merciful, and adorned with all grace and holiness, and, at the same time, God's self the almighty, who makes me whole by His example and strong by His aid.'[2]

This same devotion is reflected in a series of verses whose sweetness and beauty caused them to be attributed to Bernard's pen. They are known familiarly as the *Iubilus rhythmicus de nomine Iesu*, but one manuscript describes them as *Meditatio cuiusdam sanctae Virginis de amore Christi.* Wilmart[3] has finally shown that it is not by Bernard and that the manuscript evidence points to an English and Cistercian origin about the end of the twelfth century. Bernard's name was not attached to it until the end of the next century. The only hymns of Bernard which we possess are of such mediocre quality that it is impossible to conceive of him as being the author of these beautiful verses. The abbot of the monastery of Montiéramey had once flattered him by asking him to compose a hymn in honour of S. Victor, the patron of the abbey, and he complied with his wish ; 'hymnum composui', he says, ' metri negligens, ut sensui non deessem', proving that he did not look on such compositions with a poet's eyes. But the monks do not appear to have shrunk from singing in the office of S. Victor such lines as these :

> vita Victoris meritis praeclara
> hominem terris, qui non sit de terra,
> velut de caelo datum repraesentat
> ad imitandum.[4]

Bernard's other hymn is on S. Malachy of Armagh, the beloved friend in whose society he had found such delight, and whose death at Clairvaux, described in words of glowing beauty by Bernard in his *Life of Malachy*, left to the monastery the great treasure of his earthly body.

[1] *Sermo*, ii, Migne, clxxxiii, col. 790.
[2] *Sermo*, xv, ib., col. 847.
[3] Wilmart, *Le 'Jubilus' dit de S. Bernard*, Rome 1944. A critical text is given and an account of all the known manuscripts.
[4] Text in *Anal. Hymn.* lii, p. 318.

o Malachia, Claravallis tua,
clarior tui corporis thesauro,
postulat supplex te tuenti frui
pace perenni.[1]

Bernard's poetry is, like that of Augustine, to be looked for in his prose. Yet if he is to be deprived of the fame attaching to the authorship of the *Jubilus*, the inspiration of his mysticism shines through every line.

dulcis Iesu memoria,
dans vera cordi gaudia,
sed super mel et omnia
eius dulcis praesentia.

Iesu, spes poenitentibus,
quam pius es petentibus,
quam bonus es quaerentibus,
sed quid invenientibus ? . . .

nil canitur suavius,
auditur nil iocundius,
nil cogitatur dulcius
quam Iesu dei filius.

nec lingua potest dicere,
nec littera exprimere,
expertus novit tenere
quod sit Iesum diligere. . . .

cum Maria diluculo
Iesum quaeram in tumulo,
cordis clamore querulo
mente quaeram non oculo.

This is truly the voice of Bernard. 'He gave himself to be merited,' says Bernard in the *De diligendo Deo*,[2] 'he keeps himself for reward. . . . Thou art good, O Lord, to the soul that seeketh Thee : then what to her who finds ? (Bonus es, Domine, animae quaerenti te : quid ergo invenienti ?)' : or again, 'Thou art good, O Lord, to the soul that seeketh Thee. If to the soul that seeketh, how much more to the soul that findeth ? If the thought of Thee is sweet, how sweet must be Thy presence ! If honey and milk is sweet beneath the tongue, what will it be upon the tongue ?'[3]

Thus Bernard's rapture bore fruit in poetry. To what extremes the use of earthly love as a simile could go, following the example of Bernard himself,[4] this same poem shows :

quocunque loco fuero,
meum Iesum desidero
quam laetus cum invenero,
quam felix cum tenuero !

tunc amplexus, tunc oscula,
quae vincant mellis pocula,
tunc felix Christi copula,
sed in his parva morula.

---

[1] Text in *Anal. Hymn.* xix, p. 190.
[2] vii. 22.
[3] 'Bonus es, Domine, animae quaerenti te. Si quaerenti, quanto magis invenienti ? Si tam dulcis est memoria, qualis erit praesentia ? Si mel et lac dulce est sub lingua, quid erit super linguam ?'

Sermones de Diversis, iv (Migne, clxxxiii, col. 552) ; cf. *Ecclesiasticus,* xxiv. 27–8, 'Spiritus enim meus super mel dulcis, et hereditas mea super mel et favum : memoria mea in generationes saeculorum'.
[4] Cf. *De diligendo Deo,* iii. 8 ; see Taylor, *Medieval Mind,* i. 476.

But rarely did the poetry of the name of Jesus gather such an intensity of feeling; other medieval hymns devoted to the same theme are mostly pious salutations without any particular merit.[1] It is otherwise with the poetry of the Passion, which, inspired by the devotion of the Franciscans to the crucified Saviour, is full of fervour and profoundly moving. But one anonymous poem of great beauty, intensely mystical and deriving its inspiration from Bernard's beloved Canticles, is worthy of being quoted in full.[2]

tandem audite me,
Sionis filiae!
aegram respicite,
dilecto dicite :
amore vulneror,
amore funeror.

fulcite floribus
fessam languoribus ;
stipate citreis
et malis aureis ;
nimis edacibus
liquesco facibus.

huc odoriferos,
huc soporiferos
ramos depromite
rogos componite ;
ut phoenix moriar !
in flammis oriar !

an amor dolor sit,
an dolor amor sit,
utrumque nescio ;
hoc unum sentio,
iucundus dolor est,
si dolor amor est.

quid, amor, crucias ?
aufer inducias,
lentus tyrannus es ;
momentum annus est ;
tam tarda funera
tua sunt vulnera.

iam vitae stamina
rumpe, o anima !
ignis ascendere
gestit, et tendere
ad caeli atria ;
haec mea patria !

The whole of this poetry is monastic in origin; its mysticism carries with it that flavour of the cloister which clings to the pages of the *De Imitatione Christi*. It is the poetry of men without a home in this world, who held to the maxim ascribed to Seneca, 'As oft as I have been among men, I returned home less a man than I was before'.[3] 'Shut thy door upon thee', says the *Imitation*, 'and call unto thee Jesus, thy Beloved. Stay with Him in thy closet; for thou shalt not find so great peace any where else.'[4] It needed the spirit of a Francis of Assisi to transform the mysticism of Bernard into a gospel.

[1] See Mone, i. 333–56.
[2] Given in Trench, p. 254 ; there is a fine English rendering by Philip Worsley, the talented translator of the *Odyssey* (*Poems and Translations*, London 1863,

p. 202). Mearns (Julian's *Dict. of Hymnology*, p. 1114 *b*) suggests that the poem belongs to the seventeenth century.
[3] Quoted, *De Imitatione Christi*, i. 20.
[4] ib. ; cf. ii. 7.

§ 6. *English Poets under the Norman and Angevin Kings,
Eleventh and Twelfth Centuries.*

When the Norman William invaded England with the
blessing of the Pope, he professed to come as the champion of
the Catholic Church, and with the intentions of a reformer.   In
effect, an attempt at reformation was made.   Norman bishops
were introduced into Anglo-Saxon sees.   The schismatic Archbishop Stigand was deposed, and Lanfranc, Abbot of the
Conqueror's Church of S. Stephen at Caen, was consecrated in
his stead.   With the advent of this Italian lawyer the English
Church was brought into direct relationship with the wider life
of Catholic Europe.   A leaven of learning, gained in French
and Italian schools, was re-introduced into England.   Godfrey
of Cambrai, Prior of S. Swithin's, Winchester, composed some
Latin epigrams after the manner of Martial.   Some are moral,
others are satirical, while a few, of historical interest, are
addressed to great personages such as King William, Matilda,
and Lanfranc.   This is Godfrey's appreciation of the piety and
learning of the Archbishop :

> vixisti, venerande pater, sapienter et aeque,
>   vixisti vivens, mors quoque vita tibi.
> inter divitias pauper, Lanfrance, fuisti,
>   divitiis manans, pauperum amator eras.
> per te florentes artes valuere latinae,
>   Graecia de nobis ecce triumphat ovans.
> tu Latios ortu Gallosque docendo levasti,
>   te sibi primatem cardo Britannus habet.
> in terra degens coelestia mente petebas,
>   exemptus terra sidera liber adis.
> sol geminos denis obsederat igne diebus,
>   prompsit luna diem, nocte solutus abis.[1]

Lanfranc himself does not appear to have composed any
verse, but it was inevitable that an attempt should have been
made to discover some religious pieces with which the name
of his gentle successor, Anselm of Aosta, might be associated.
Dreves [2] believed that a collection of hymns which follow some
prose prayers of Anselm might be the latter's work, but it is
clear that no solid grounds exist for attributing to him these

---

[1] Wright, *Satirical Poets of the Twelfth*   i, p. xvii ;   *Camb. Hist. of Engl. Lit.* i. 191.
Century, ii. 150; on Godfrey, see Wright,   [2] *Anal. Hymn.* xlviii, p. 94 sq.

mediocre compositions, and he, therefore, disappears from the list of medieval hymnographers.[1]

Reginald of Canterbury (d. *circ.* 1109) is a poet of much liveliness and skill. He was born in Poitou in the second half of the eleventh century. Before 1092 he is found at S. Augustine's, Canterbury, having made his studies in France. Besides a few poetical epistles in the manner of the day he composed a great epic in leonine hexameters on the life of the hermit Malchus. His main source is Jerome's life of the saint, and Dr. Lind, who has produced a critical edition of the poem, detects the influence of the *chanson de geste* and the travel tale.[2] Here is an address to the Cross:

> o decus, o clavi suaves in stipite suavi,
> o liber, o lignum divino sanguine dignum,
> o pia crux Christi, quae tincta cruore fuisti ;
> sanguinis hoc sacro sacri nos tinge lavacro.
>
> robora conscendit tua Christus ibique pependit,
> virginei floris honor et flos castus honoris,
> fers, geris ipsa deum, sumis de morte tropaeum ;
> servet ab impura lue nos tua sancta figura.[3]

A similar mastery of the two-syllabled rime is shown by Reginald in other verses addressed to Malchus.

> ergo ille sanctis mille
>   est aequandus meritis,
> quisquis amat deum clamat
>   huius nomen militis
> nec non fandae et amandae
>   suae sacrae comitis.[4]

Reginald sent his verses to Hildebert, who courteously accorded them the warmest praise.

The period from William the Conqueror to the death of Henry I is one of initial promise. The impulse to learning came from abroad, and the scholars and poets are all Normans, Frenchmen, and Italians. With the reign of Henry II a new period opens, an era of great administrative and political growth, of reconstruction, and of consolidation. Henry became the

[1] See Wilmart, *Une prière inédite attribuée à S. Anselme. La recension interpolée des prières*, Rev. *Bénéd.*, 1923, pp. 143 sqq., and especially p. 149, note 2 ; cf. also Wilmart, *La tradition des prières de S. Anselme*, Rev. *Bénéd.*, 1924, pp. 52 sqq.
[2] *Vita Sancti Malchi*, ed. R. Lind, Urbana 1942 ; see p. 18.
[3] *Anal. Hymn.* l, p. 375 ; Lind, p. 142.
[4] *Anal. Hymn.* l, p. 384.

ruler of a vast empire from Scotland to the Pyrenees. The quickening of intelligences, the sharpening of political interest, and the progress of learning are reflected in the admirable chronicles of William of Malmesbury, William of Newburgh, Ralph de Diceto, and Roger of Hoveden. But besides these larger and vaguer influences there were two great centres of intercourse and education which definitely moulded the intellectual life of the learned class. First in importance came the great schools of Paris, to which English students crowded to hear the lectures of Abélard or of their own countryman Robert Pulleyn. The schools of Paris were now more likely to turn the bent of the eager student to dialectic or philosophy than to encourage him to humane studies or the career of a poet. The historian and Dean of S. Paul's, Ralph de Diceto; Adam du Petit-Pont, the philosopher; John of Salisbury, the universal scholar and humanist; Nicholas Brakespear, the monk of S. Alban's who became Adrian IV—all were students at Paris.

But in England itself there was a school with a character all its own, a house of severe studies, of delightful social recreation, a home of wit and of humanism, and a meeting-place of scholars and ecclesiastics from every country in Catholic Europe. This was the household of Theobald, the able, learned, and saintly Archbishop of Canterbury (1139-62). Here we can picture a circle of scholars and students comparable with that which gathered round the venerable Fulbert at Chartres. Here was John of Salisbury, the primate's secretary, a fountain of learning and of common sense; Becket, the ambitious and hard-working Archdeacon; Roger of Pont-l'Évêque, the future Archbishop of York. Under Becket's rule the same atmosphere was preserved, enlivened by the wit and irony of Walter Map, Canon of S. Paul's, afterwards Archdeacon of Oxford, whose *De Nugis Curialium* [1] is a miscellany of gossip, satire, and history. Gerald de Barri, the Archdeacon of Brecon, belonged to the same circle, a rival of Map in his intellectual curiosity, his love of gossip, and his eye for human weakness. Serious students, they were also accomplished men of the world; ambitious, but ready to attack or to satirize abuses; not given to asceticism—for they despised the excesses of the Cistercians, and Map was ready to sneer at S. Bernard—but at the same time faithful sons of the Church and ready to defend her interests.

---

[1] Edited by M. R. James, Oxford 1914.

In those days all who could write a decent Latin prose believed that they could compose equally well in verse. But the scholars of the twelfth century did not turn easily to religious poetry ; their models were the Latin satirists and epigrammatists, and they had no thought for Prudentius or the other Christian classics. This is true more particularly of the English group, although epigram or satire inevitably assumed something of a moral or religious colour. No medieval writer had a more comprehensive knowledge or a deeper appreciation of classical literature than John of Salisbury,[1] and when he composed in verse he naturally followed classical models. The poem which introduces his long prose work, the *Policraticus*, is in grave and ironical elegiacs.[2] It is an address by the author to his book, sending it on its way from Canterbury to Thomas Becket, the royal chancellor, who was abroad with the king.

> ergo quaeratur lux cleri, gloria gentis
>   Anglorum, regis dextera, forma boni.
> quaesitus regni tibi cancellarius Angli,
>   primus sollicita mente petendus erit.
> hic est qui regni leges cancellat iniquas,
>   et mandata pii principis aequa facit.[3]

The long poem called *Entheticus de dogmate philosophorum*,[4] written at the request of Thomas, contains a summary of the opinions of the various schools of philosophy, but in addition it contains admonitions directed in a veiled manner to John's powerful master. As in his *Metalogicus*, John derides those pedantic logicians who thought that logic was the end of all learning. He emphasizes the essential basis of all sound education, the classical studies, and points to the knowledge of God as the supreme end. For philosophy is indeed one with the love of God, since God is wisdom.

> si verus deus est hominum sapientia vera,
>   tunc amor est veri philosophia dei.[5]

He classifies the parts of a liberal education, ending with Theology, the queen of the sciences. We cannot follow John through his account of the ancient philosophers, the Stoics, the Epicureans, the Platonists, the Aristotelians, at the end of which

---

[1] See Schaarschmidt, *Johannes Saresberiensis*, p. 84.
[2] *Ioannis Saresberiensis Policraticus*, ed. C. C. J. Webb, Oxford 1909, i, p. 1 sqq.
[3] ib., p. 2.
[4] Text, *Opera*, ed. Giles, Oxford 1848, v. 239 sqq.; on it see Schaarschmidt, pp. 194 sqq.
[5] *Opera*, v. 248.

he triumphantly asserts the superiority of Christian truth to pagan error.

> sed cur gentiles numero, quos error adegit ?
> omnis enim ratio deficit absque fide.
> Christicolae soli sapiunt, et philosophantur
> vere, quos tibi dat pagina sancta duces.[1]

From philosophy he now abruptly turns to his contemporaries, and expresses his indignation at the evil days in which his lot is cast. He attacks the particular objects of his hatred—the dead tyrant Stephen and his corrupt followers, some of whom were yet alive; and he even hints at the worse side of the character of Henry II and his court. He goes so far as to take the Chancellor to task, though he has to do it carefully by hinting that in conforming himself to the manners of the Court Thomas has doubtless a higher aim in view. Finally, he praises the society of Canterbury,

> quae caput est regni iustitiaeque domus.

It is a home of studies, where knowledge is the general toil, and to be without a book is a great punishment. He goes over the list of his friends, Brito, the sub-prior, Odo, the prior, and others; not forgetting the less desirable inmates of the place, whom he lampoons under the names of Euphorbus, Baccara, Davus, and Thersites. He ends with moral reflections on the contrast between the fear of men and the perfect love which casts out fear, between the bondage of vice and the freedom of philosophy, between the weakness of unaided effort and the power of grace. Not the tonsured head, nor monkish garb of black and white, but grace alone can ensure the gift of life. For fools can perish whatever garb they wear.

> excipit infernus pereuntes veste remota,
> nec minuit poenam tetra vel alba suam.[2]

The whole poem reveals the vigorous mind of a sane and well-balanced scholar, thoroughly English at once in its tolerance, its gravity, and its judicial quality. These characteristics are more abundantly clear in the *Policraticus* and the *Metalogicus*, which contain the whole ripe experience of the author. John's poetry is of interest solely for its content, for its expression of one of the rarest and most admirable types which the Middle Ages produced.

---

[1] *Opera*, v. 279–80. [2] ib., v. 297.

The tendency of the literary movement to satire is well illustrated by the poems of Nigel Longchamp and of John de Hanville. Nigel,[1] Precentor of Christchurch, Canterbury, dedicated to William Longchamp, the powerful Bishop of Ely, his amusing elegiac satire called *Speculum Stultorum*. Under the figure of Burnellus, the ass, who is discontented with his short but useful tail and wants to obtain one of larger dimensions, Nigel satirizes the monk who, not satisfied with the life of the cloister, desires fame and fortune and a high position. The satire includes in its scope the students at Paris, the monastic orders, the secular clergy, bishops, and kings; and the Papal curia is mercilessly assailed for its venality.

> munera si cessent, sine sanguine tempore pacis,
> quod nunquam potuit, Roma subacta ruet.
> munera si cessent, primatum pallia multo
> constabunt levius et meliore foro.
> . . . munera si cessent, deus in cellas Cluniaci
> forte revertetur, et remanebit ibi.
> munera si cessent, Iudam cum Simone clerus
> tollet, et e medio coget abire sui.[2]

The interest of this verse lies in the witness it bears to the wakening of the human intellect from the torpor into which it had sunk. Satire is the fruit of a highly developed society, and if the satire of Nigel is at times crude and obvious, it is the work of a man whose wit had been sharpened by contact with affairs, by observation as well as by study.

John de Hanville[3] flourished towards the end of the twelfth century. His *Architrenius* or *Arch-Mourner* is an allegorical satire addressed to Walter of Coutances, Archbishop of Rouen. Written in hexameters, it is a more tedious, if also a more ambitious, attempt than that of Nigel. The young man who mourns for his weakness of will and his wasted youth rails against lady Nature, and goes to seek her in order that he may lay his case before her. The allegory shows us his visit to the wonderful palace of Venus, to the house of Gluttony, and then to Paris, with the noise and strife and weariness of the schools. The

---

[1] Raby, *Secular Latin Poetry*, ii. 94 sqq. and the Bibliography, ib., p. 373. Bale calls him Nigellus de Werekere, on what authority is not clear.

[2] Wright, *Satirical Poets*, i. 102.

[3] *Works*, Wright, i. 240 sqq. He has hitherto been usually called John de Hauteville, but the MSS. give the forms Hauvilla, Hanvilla, and Havilla. It is probably Hanville, near Évreux; see Faral, *Les arts poétiques du XII⁰ et du XIII⁰ siècles*, p. 34, and note 2.

mount of Ambition suggests a satire on the manners of courts, and the hill of Presumption provokes an onslaught on its inhabitants, monks, clergy, and doctors of the schools. So the allegory continues until the pilgrim reaches lady Nature, who consoles him with a beautiful wife—the virtue of Moderation.

At the end of his elaborately rhetorical *Historia Anglorum*, Henry of Huntingdon (*circ.* 1084–1155) appended a book of satires and epigrams.[1] His satire has no subtlety, it is a frontal attack on simoniacal bishops and rapacious monks, on laymen who refuse the Church its due. Or he composes plain distichs, *De cupiditate, De vero amore, De avaritia*, ending his collection with an admonition addressed to himself:

> sunt, vates Henrice, tibi versus bene culti,
>   et bene culta domus, et bene cultus ager.
> et bene sunt thalami, bene sunt pomeria culta,
>   hortus centimodis cultibus ecce nitet.
> o iam culta tibi bene sunt, sed tu male cultus;
>   se quicunque caret, dic mihi, dic quid habet?[2]

The name of Walter Map has already been mentioned as that of a scholar and a wit. He must have composed a good deal of verse, but the rhythmical pieces to which his name has been attached are not his by right,[3] and the only verses which can be ascribed to him are properly enough in elegiacs. It seems, however, that Map did indulge in metrical satire against the Cistercians, as one bitter and blasphemous line of such a satire has been preserved:

> lancea Longini, grex albus, ordo nefandus.[4]

This hatred, as we have already said, Walter shared with his friend Gerald or Giraldus. Giraldus Cambrensis[5] was the youngest son of the Norman William de Barri and his Welsh wife, Angareth, granddaughter of Rhys ap Theodor, prince of South Wales. His uncle, the Bishop of S. David's, encouraged him in the path of learning. Of his early education Gerald tells us little, but some of his boyish verses have survived. They show a considerable study of classical poetry, in spite of their offences against grammar and prosody. His prose works con-

[1] *Camb. Hist. of Engl. Lit.* i. 191.
[2] Wright, ii. 174.
[3] See Wright, *The Latin Poems commonly attributed to Walter Mapes.* Introd., *Camden Society*, vol. xvi, 1841.
[4] ib., p. xxxv.
[5] On Gerald see *Camb. Hist. of Engl. Lit.* i. 194 sqq.; *Works*, ed. Brewer (*Rolls Series*), poems in vol. i. 341 sqq., London 1861.

tain references to Terence, Horace, Virgil, Ovid, Juvenal, Statius, Cicero, and Seneca.[1]   He studied and even lectured at Paris while still a youth, and he is careful to tell us that he had a reputation for brilliancy in the art of rhetoric; 'praecipuam in arte rhetorica laudem obtinuit', he says of himself, describing himself further as a model of industry and good conduct.[2]   We are able to follow him through all the stages of his long career, and we see him, as it were, through his own eyes—exacting tithes from reluctant Welshmen; suspending an aged archdeacon for concubinage; striving without avail, in England and at Rome, to win the succession to his uncle's see; acting as chaplain to Henry II; visiting Ireland with John, the king's son; and afterwards reading his *Topographia Hiberniae* to an applauding audience of Oxford scholars; preaching the Crusade like a second Bernard, and all but succeeding the saintly Hugh in the see of Lincoln.

His surviving verses are few in number.   There is a pleasant school-exercise which describes the beauty of a young girl, and a pastoral *De subito amore*.   The longest poem is an elegiac piece, *De mundi creatione et contentis eiusdem*,[3] which tells of the creation of the world from chaos, and the ordering of nature animate and inanimate, the planets, the seasons, the climates. The most poetical part is that which tells how the world began in the spring of the year.

> tempore quo mundum mundo produxit origo,
>   et tener in tenero claruit orbe dies,
> ver erat, et veris clementia rebus amica,
>   rebus adhuc teneris dux novitatis erat.
> cum primo carpi coepit spirabilis aer,
>   cum lux hauriri, cum levis aura trahi,
> temperies vernalis erat, mixtusque calori
>   humor, et in rebus vis genetiva tepor.[4]

The whole piece is doubtless nothing more than a school-exercise, but it is a not unpleasing evidence of the care which he must have given to the classical poets.   In his manhood he can hardly have found much time for poetry, but the distich which he is said to have composed for inscription above his stall at S. David's may be genuine:

> vive deo, tibi mors requies, tibi vita labori;
>   vive deo; mors est vivere, vita mori.

---

[1] Brewer, i, p. xiv.
[2] *De rebus a se gestis*, ii, Brewer, i. 23.
[3] ib., i. 341 sqq.
[4] ib., i. 346.

Serlo of Wilton,[1] an Englishman, a scholar and a poet, lived in the memory of Giraldus and of following generations, but not for the same reason. Giraldus met Serlo on the occasion of a youthful visit to Archbishop Baldwin. Serlo, seated at the Archbishop's side, saw the young man approach, modest and charming, and, prolonging his gaze in amazement, cried, 'Think you so fair a youth can ever die?' Giraldus had, therefore, good reason for remembering this flattering visitor, and if the pleasure with which he tells the story of his meeting is hardly becoming, he deserves our gratitude by proceeding to tell us something about this interesting man.[2] Serlo had been a distinguished master in the schools at Paris, where he lived a life of worldly frivolity; but, like many others, he repented and became a Cluniac monk, at La Charité-sur-Loire, but the laxity of the discipline displeased him, so he joined the Cistercians at L'Aumône, where he ultimately became abbot. He remembered with some bitterness the order in which he had made his profession, for Giraldus heard him say in the hearing of the gentle Baldwin, who was shocked by such uncharitableness, that he would 'rather die a black mastiff than a black monk'.

Serlo lived in the popular memory as the hero or subject of an often told tale which furnished a moral lesson for medieval preachers.[3] While still a master at Paris he found a colleague or a pupil at death's door, and begged him, when he died, to return to him and tell him how he fared in purgatory. Shortly afterwards the dead man appeared to him, clad in a gown of parchment covered with the 'sophisms' of the schools. He explained that he was clad in the vain arguments in which he had once delighted, and that the gown weighed him down more heavily than the weight of a church tower. Further, he had to endure the fires of purgatory. Serlo nervously made light of the torment, until the dead man stretched out his hand and touched him. The torture of that touch decided him; he deserted the world, and, entering the cloister, left these verses as the epitaph of his secular life.

---

[1] Walter Map, *De Nugis Curialium*, ii. 4, tells us that he was of Wilton, and therefore an Englishman or, rather, Anglo-Norman.

[2] Giraldus, *Speculum Ecclesiae*, ii. 33 (Brewer, iv. 104 sqq.).

[3] For various versions of the story see Hauréau, *Mémoires sur les récits d'apparitions dans les sermons du moyen âge*, *Mémoires de l'Académie des Inscriptions*, xxviii, ii, pp. 242 sqq.

> linquo *coax* ranis, *cra* corvis vanaque vanis,
> ad logicam pergo quae mortis non timet ergo.

Henceforth he abjured profane verses, if he did not always bridle his sarcastic tongue.   But the memory of his earlier work remained, for verses have been preserved which show that he followed the style and morals of the Goliardic poets.

> cum vinum poto faciem lavo, corpore loto
> tum fundo lacrimas, tunc versificor quasi Primas.[1]

But he made amends later by producing more serious, if less interesting, compositions, such as his 'farewell to the world' when he became a Cistercian monk.[2]   It is a tiresome reiteration of the theme 'mundus abit'.

> mundus abit, res nota quidem, res usque notanda:
> nota tibi mundi sit nota: mundus abit.
> mundus abit (non mundus, id est haec machina mundi,
> dico, sed mundi gloria), mundus abit.

Other verses are addressed to Roger of Gloucester, Bishop of Worcester (d. *circ.* 1177).[3]

> Serlo Rogerio.   Tu par vel nullus Homero:
> tu vel nemo Paris: sapiens animo esse probaris.

But they were composed while Serlo was still in the schools, as were the elegiacs to Louis the Young.[4]   Poor indeed they are, but better than this religious epigram[5] on the masses for Christmas Day:

> in natale sacro sacrae solempnia missae
> quid signent aut cur tunc celebrentur habe:
> nocte prior, sub luce, sequens in luce suprema,
> sub Noe, sub David, sub cruce sacra notant.
> sub Noe, sub David, sub Christo sacra fuere
> nox, aurora, dies, umbra, figura, deus.

Yet the epigram has an interest as an expression of the symbolism with which it was customary to invest the various parts and seasons of the liturgy.   Noah represents the dusk of

---

[1] Hauréau, *Notice sur un MS. de la reine Christine à la bibl. du Vatican, Notices et extraits des mss.* xxix, ii, p. 260, note 3; ib. xxviii, ii, pp. 428 sqq., for text of his *De partibus orationis*; p. 334 for his *De diversis modis versificandi.*
[2] Printed by P. Meyer, in *Archives des missions scientifiques,* 2ᵉ série, v (1868), p. 173.
[3] Hauréau, *Notices et extraits des mss.* xxix, ii, p. 338.   They form part of the *De diversis modis versificandi.*
[4] Hauréau, p. 340.
[5] P. Meyer, p. 173.

revelation, David the dawn which foretells the day; Christ is the full day, the complete revelation—God.

Serlo is a good example of the secular spirit of the twelfth century, which was not ultimately strong enough to defy the stern admonition of the Church against the vanities of the world, and its promise of purgatory or of an unending punishment in hell. He might, indeed, have survived in history in this character alone, and not as a versifier at all, if modern criticism had not been able to restore to his name these verses which others had assigned to another Serlo—a Canon of Bayeux who lived a century before him.[1]

Another Anglo-Norman poet was Geoffrey de Vinsauf, who enjoyed a greater fame in his own day than in succeeding generations.[2] He dedicated to Pope Innocent III his *Poëtria Nova*, a kind of *Ars Poetica*, adapted to the literary *naïveté* of his age, with examples composed by himself of the manner in which various themes might be treated. An example of a religious theme is *Querela crucis*, a fit subject in the age of Crusaders.[2] The Cross complains:

> crux ego rapta queror.   ego crux Christi crucifixi.
> crux ego sancta, salus populi, reparatio mundi.
> crux ego rapta queror, vi rapta, manuque canina,
> et tactu polluta canum.   sum rapta pudenter
> a veteri, nec adhuc extorta, nec ense redempta.
> dic homo! nonne tibi crevi? tibi fructificavi?
> nonne tuli dulcem tibi fructum, nonne salutem?
> dic homo! dic mihi! dic homo perdite, quem reparavi,
> sicne rapi merui, sine vindice? sicne perire?[3]

The quotation is already long enough. The twelfth century in England was not, as we have seen, prolific in religious verse. The classical studies and the pursuit of dialectic and philosophy filled the minds of scholars, and their productions have mainly a secular tinge. Yet it is possible and even probable that, in the latter years of this same century, an English poet produced

[1] Serlo of Bayeux's epigrams are in Wright, *Anglo-Saxon Latin Satirical Poets*, ii. 232 sqq. (see H. Böhmer, *Der sogenannte Serlo von Bayeux und die ihm zugeschriebenen Gedichte, Neues Archiv*, xxii.,703 sqq.).   On the critical question see Hauréau, pp. 231 sqq.
[2] Stubbs, *Learning and Literature at the Court of Henry II*, p.152; *Camb. Hist. of Engl. Lit.*, I. 193; Leyser, *Historia*

Poetarum et Poematum Medii Aevi, Halle, 1741, p. 855 sqq.; his *Poëtria Nova*, p. 862 sqq.; the best text is now that of Faral, *Les arts poétiques du XIIe et du XIIIe siècle*, pp. 194 sqq.; pp. 15 sqq. for his life and works.   The *Poëtria* was composed in the early years of the thirteenth century.
[3] Leyser, p. 887; Faral, p. 211.

one of the masterpieces of catholic liturgical verse.   The great sequence, *Veni, sancte Spiritus*, has been associated with no less a name than Stephen Langton, Archbishop of Canterbury.   It is true that both King Robert the Pious (d. 1031) and Hermann the Lame (d. 1054) have been put forward as having a claim to its authorship, but they cannot be seriously considered; the choice lies between Innocent III and Archbishop Stephen. Ekkehard V, a contemporary, assigns the sequence to the Pope, and he further tells us how Ulrich, the Abbot of S. Gall, visited Innocent and talked with him about the famous Notker.[1]   It might reasonably be supposed that the Pope took the opportunity of bringing his own sequence to the notice of the Abbot, who would introduce it under Innocent's name to his monks at S. Gall.   But we are faced by the fact that an English Cistercian, also a contemporary, a member of an order with which Stephen Langton had close relations,[2] unhesitatingly affirms that the Archbishop composed the sequence.   Now both Pope and Archbishop had met in their student days at Paris, and it may well be that Innocent received the poem from its author, and, admiring it for its striking merit, recommended it to Ulrich and to others.   Whoever the author may have been, 'The Golden Sequence' deserves the praise which has been generally bestowed upon it.

1. veni, sancte spiritus
   et emitte caelitus
      lucis tuae radium ;

2. veni, pater pauperum,
   veni, dator munerum,
      veni, lumen cordium.

3. consolator optime,
   dulcis hospes animae,
      dulce refrigerium ;

4. in labore requies,
   in aestu temperies,
      in fletu solacium.

5. o lux beatissima,
   reple cordis intima
      tuorum fidelium ;

6. sine tuo numine
   nihil est in lumine,
      nihil est innoxium.

[1] For this and what follows see Dom Wilmart's interesting account, *L'hymne et la séquence du Saint-Esprit*, in *La vie et les arts liturgiques*, July 1924, p. 397. Father Thurston, *The Month*, June 1913, pp. 602 sqq., reached the same conclusions. I reproduce Wilmart's argument almost in his own words.   Blume and Bannister, *Anal. Hymn.* liv, pp. 237 sqq., are unable to decide between Innocent and Stephen.

[2] Pitra, *Spicilegium Solesmense*, iii. 130 ; Blume says (wrongly) that Langton was himself a Cistercian, and that, although the Cistercians did not use Sequences, he may have composed the verses for private devotion. The *Veni, sancte Spiritus* does not seem to have come into use in England until towards the end of the thirteenth century ; in Germany and France it won immediate popularity ; see *Anal. Hymn.* liv, pp. 238 sq.

7. lava, quod est sordidum,
   riga, quod est aridum,
      sana, quod est saucium ;

8. flecte, quod est rigidum,
   fove, quod est frigidum
      rege, quod est devium.

9. da tuis fidelibus
   in te confidentibus
      sacrum septenarium ;

10. da virtutis meritum,
    da salutis exitum,
       da perenne gaudium.[1]

At S. Alban's Abbey in the twelfth century the monastic poets celebrated their patron in uninspired rhythm :

ecclesiae prosapies,
veri patris effigies,
melos pangamus humiles
Albani sancti memores.

qui fide plenus catholica
mundum sprevit et idola,
Christi sequens vestigia
arma tempsit barbarica.[2]

and at Ely the Benedictines sang in praise of their royal virgin :

Ethelreda tuos virgo tuere,
noxarum, petimus, vincula rumpe,
virtutum studiis pectora subde,
da, simus nitidi corpore mente.[3]

Westminster too produced its poet in Prior Osbert of Clare, who composed two pieces on S. Anne.[4]   He professed a special devotion to the mother of the Virgin, whose cult had been slow in spreading in the Western churches.   The two rhythms show a competent mastery of the two-syllabled rime.   The first begins :

o praeclara mater matris,
quae concepit verbum patris
non commixtione maris
sed ut virgo singularis.
quem in utero portavit
genetrix de stirpe David,

invocantem te exaudi,
et studentem tuae laudi.
o parentis parens dei,
apud ipsum memor mei :
quibus deprimor meorum
terge sordes peccatorum.[5]

The second piece is written in a woman's name,[6] and was probably intended for a community of nuns.   Osbert does not reach a high flight in these rhythms, but in two prose prayers of elaborate composition, in which he employs rhythmic *clausulae* and constant rimes, he is not altogether unsuccessful.

---

[1] *Anal. Hymn.* liv, pp. 234 sq.
[2] ib., xi, pp. 67 sq.
[3] ib., p. 121.
[4] These pieces are to be found in *Anal. Hymn.* xv, p. 186, and xxxiii, p. 36. A. Wilmart (*Les compositions d'Osbert de Clare, en honneur de Sainte Anne, Annales de*

Bretagne, xxxvii (1926), pp. 1 sqq.) has assigned them to Osbert.
[5] Wilmart, p. 21.
[6] ib., p. 8 ; cf.

et me semper illibatam
sponsam sibi consecratam
homo deus habeat (p. 23).

XI

ADAM OF S. VICTOR AND THE REGULAR SEQUENCE

§ 1. *The Sequence in the Eleventh and Twelfth Centuries.*

THE origin of the Sequence and the beginning of its progress towards a rhythmical structure have already been described. The Sequence began as a composition in unrhythmical prose. In its transitional form the characteristics of rhythm and rime appear in rudimentary fashion, as in the *Victimae Paschali,* which belongs to the early eleventh century. The creation of the regular Sequence, a symmetrical structure in which the rhythm is based on the correspondence of word-accent and verse-accent, and the rime is consistent and regular, was the work of the eleventh and twelfth centuries. Yet Sequences of the irregular transitional type continued to be composed until the end of the Middle Ages.[1]

We have already seen how in the verses of Hildebert and Marbod the two-syllabled rime and regular rhythm had been admirably mastered in the eleventh century. So, in the Sequence a similar progress to greater technical perfection is manifested from the rudimentary structure of verses like

> angelus consilii,
> natus est de virgine,
> sol de stella [2]

to a more ambitious attempt in a Sequence in honour of S. Nicholas, which, in some of the strophes, attains great beauty, and shows considerable technical skill.

1. congaudentes exsultemus
   vocali concordia

2. ad beati Nicolai
   festiva sollemnia,

3. qui in cunis adhuc iacens
   servando ieiunia

4. ad papillas coepit summa
   promereri gaudia.

[1] See *Anal. Hymn.* liv, p. 10, for a fifteenth century example.

[2] ib., p. 5.

5. adulescens amplexatur
   literarum studia

6. alienus et immunis
   ab omni lascivia.

7. felix confessor,
   cuius fuit dignitatis
   vox de caelo nuntia,

8. per quam provectus
   praesulatus sublimatur
   ad summa fastigia.

9. erat in eius animo
   pietas eximia,
   et oppressis impendebat
   multa beneficia :

10. auro per eum virginum
    tollitur infamia
    atque patris earundem
    levatur inopia ;

11. quidam nautae navigantes
    et contra fluctuum
    saevitiam luctantes
    navi paene dissoluta,

12. iam de vita desperantes,
    in tanto positi
    periculo clamantes
    voce dicunt omnes una :

13. 'o beate Nicolae,
    nos ad portum maris trahe
    de mortis augustia ;

14. trahe nos ad portum maris,
    tu qui tot auxiliaris
    pietatis gratia.'

15. dum clamarent nec incassum,
    ecce, quidam dicens : 'assum
    ad vestra praesidia'.

16. statim aura datur grata
    et tempestas fit sedata,
    quieverunt maria.

17. ex ipsius tumba manat
    unctionis copia,

18. quae infirmos omnes sanat
    per eius suffragia.

19. nos, qui sumus in hoc mundo
    vitiorum in profundo
    iam passi naufragia,

20. gloriose Nicolae,
    ad salutis portum trahe,
    ubi pax et gloria ;

21. illam nobis unctionem
    impetres ad dominum
    prece pia.

22. qui sanavit laesionem
    multorum peccaminum
    in Maria.

23. huius festum celebrantes
    gaudeant per saecula,

24. et coronet eos Christus
    post vitae curricula.[1]

In this prose the rime and the rhythm are well developed, but it must obviously be assigned to the 'transitional' style. Yet in the same century Sequence-verses were produced, which are indistinguishable in technical quality from the great Sequences of the twelfth century. The best example of such early compositions is the *Verbum bonum et suave*, which was written in France towards the end of the eleventh century. Rhythm and rime are faultless, and—a further mark of technical quality—the

---

[1] Text in *Anal. Hymn.* liv, p. 95 sq.; the Sequence is French or Italian of the eleventh century. The Mary of verse 22 is, of course, Mary Magdalene. The various legendary allusions are explained by Gautier, *Œuvres poétiques d'Adam de S. Victor*, 1st edit., Paris, 1858, i. 208 sqq.; see also the *Golden Legend*.

caesura is observed after the fourth syllable, and it is always at the end of a word.

1. verbum bonum et suave
   personemus, illud *Ave*,
   per quod Christi fit conclave
   virgo, mater, filia;

2. per quod *Ave* salutata
   mox concepit fecundata
   virgo, David stirpe nata,
   inter spinas lilia.

3. ave, veri Salomonis
   mater, vellus Gedeonis.
   cuius magi tribus donis
   laudant puerperium.

4. ave, solem genuisti,
   ave, prolem protulisti,
   mundo lapso contulisti
   vitam et imperium.

5. ave, mater verbi summi,
   maris portus, signum dumi,
   aromatum virga fumi,
   angelorum domina;

6. supplicamus, nos emenda,
   emendatos nos commenda
   tuo nato ad habenda
   sempiterna gaudia.[1]

Similarly, the *Hodiernae lux diei*, also in honour of the Virgin, is a fine production of the end of the eleventh century. It was once ascribed to Adam of S. Victor,[2] and its almost perfect form shows that Adam was not the first master of an accomplished style. Another admirable composition, formerly supposed to be Adam's,[3] is much more probably the work of an earlier poet.[4] This is the *Laudes crucis attollamus*, which by the middle of the twelfth century had found its way into liturgical use wherever Sequences were in fashion. It is, perhaps, the first of the great Sequences which won an almost universal popularity. Its independent first strophe goes back to the Notkerian type, whereas in later Sequences the tendency was to construct the whole poem of equal strophes. The first three strophes are:

1. laudes crucis attollamus
   nos, qui crucis exsultamus
   speciali gloria.

2. dulce melos tangat caelos,
   dulce lignum dulci dignum
   credimus melodia.

3. voce vita non discordet;
   cum vox vitam non remordet,
   dulce est symphonia.[5]

This progress of the Sequence in the later eleventh and early twelfth century is of great importance for determining the relation of Adam of S. Victor to the development of the regular

---

[1] *Anal. Hymn.* liv, p. 343; the symbolical allusions are explained below, pp. 369 sqq.

[2] In Gautier's 1st edit., ii. 272 sqq.; text *Anal. Hymn.* liv. 346.

[3] In Gautier, 1st edit., i. 348 sqq.; see 3rd edit., p. 253 sqq.; and *Anal. Hymn.* liv, p. xii.

[4] See *Anal. Hymn.* liv, p. 190, and note on p. 192, and also p. xiv.

[5] *Anal. Hymn.* liv, p. 188.

Sequence-form. The characteristics of the regular Sequence in its full development may be summarized as follows :—

1. The rhythm is regular and is based wholly on the word-accent, with occasional transpositions of stress, especially in the short line which ends a strophe.

2. The caesura is regular, and should occur at the end of a word.

3. The rime is regular, and at least two-syllabled.

4. The Sequence measure *par excellence* is the trochaic line of eight syllables, repeated one or more times, and followed by a trochaic line of seven syllables. The initial independent strophe is rare, and the recognizable parallelism hardly distinguishes the composition from a hymn.

§ 2. *Adam and the School of S. Victor.*

The history of the Sequence in the twelfth century centres round the name of Adam of S. Victor, to whom tradition assigns the glory of having brought to perfection this most characteristic achievement of medieval poetry.[1] He appears to have been, like Abélard, a Breton by birth, and about 1130 he entered the Augustinian house of S. Victor, which William of Champeaux had founded in 1108, when he retired from the noise of Paris, and for a time from the tumult of the schools. The abbey flourished and became famous. Before the middle of the century it numbered among its inmates two of the foremost spiritual leaders of the time, Hugh and Richard, who expounded a mystical philosophy midway between the rationalism of Abélard and the pure mysticism of Bernard of Clairvaux. Adam is the third of a trio of famous men. He drew his inspiration from the same spiritual fountain, and set forth in verse what Hugh and Richard expounded in prose.

It is told of Adam that he loved to haunt the crypt of the abbey church, where there was a chapel dedicated to the Virgin. It was here in the gloom and quiet, before the image of Mary, that he meditated on the Sequences which were to be composed

---

[1] Gautier, *Œuvres poétiques d'Adam de S. Victor*, 1st edit., 2 vols., Paris, 1858; 3rd edit., 1 vol., Paris, 1894, containing results of later criticism by Delisle and Misset; *The Liturgical Poetry of Adam of S. Victor*, ed. D. S. Wrangham, Gautier's text of first edition with English verse rendering, and introduction; Misset and Aubry, *Adam de S. Victor, les proses, texte et musique*; for the latest criticism, *Anal. Hymn.* liv, Introduction, and also critical texts of many of the Proses attributed to Adam. Others will be found in vol. lv.

in her honour.   There the inspiration of the *Salve mater salvatoris* came upon him, and he celebrated the mother of God with all the ardent allegory of the *Song of Songs*.

<table>
<tr><td>

5. porta clausa, fons hortorum,
   cella custos unguentorum,
     cella pigmentaria ;

</td><td>

6. cinnamoni calamum
   mirram, tus et balsamum
   superas fragrantia.

</td></tr>
<tr><td>

9. . . . tu convallis humilis,
   terra non arabilis,
     quae fructum parturiit ;

</td><td>

10. flos campi, convallium
   singulare lilium,
   Christus, ex te prodiit.

</td></tr>
</table>

Then, as he reached the crowning strophe of praise and adoration,

<table>
<tr><td>

salve, mater pietatis
et totius trinitatis
  nobile triclinium,

</td><td>

verbi tamen incarnati
speciali maiestati
  praeparans hospitium,[1]

</td></tr>
</table>

the Blessed Virgin appeared before him, and bowed her head in salutation and gratitude.

It is probable that Adam made profound scholastic studies, and he might well have followed in the footsteps of Hugh and Richard.   He chose rather to use his talent for the adornment of the liturgy, but the theological foundation of his proses is a conspicuous feature.   His life must have passed quietly enough at S. Victor in following the offices and composing the Sequences which were sung at the great festivals.   He died towards the end of the century, and was buried in the cloister near the doorway of the chapter house.   His epitaph, which affirms the vanity of human life, and may be in part his own composition, is as follows :

haeres peccati, natura filius irae,
   exsiliique reus nascitur omnis homo.
unde superbit homo, cuius conceptio culpa,
   nasci poena, labor vita, necesse mori ?
vana salus hominis, vanus decor, omnia vana;
   inter vana, nihil vanius est homine.
dum magis alludunt praesentis gaudia vitae,
   praeterit, imo fugit ; non fugit, imo perit.

[1] *Anal. Hymn.* liv, p. 383 sq. ; see Gautier, 1st edit., I, pp. lxxviii sqq. ; the Missal of S. Victor, 1524, says : ' Dum venerabilis Adam sequenti versiculo beatam Mariam Virginem salutaret, ab ea resalutari et regratiari meruit ' ; cf. a similar appearance of the Virgin to Romanos the Greek poet, Krumbacher, *Gesch. d. Byz. Lit.*, Munich (1897), p. 663.

post hominem vermis, post vermem fit cinis, heu ! heu !
   sic redit ad cinerem gloria nostra suum.
hic ego qui iaceo miser et miserabilis Adam,
   unam pro summo munere posco precem :
peccavi, fateor, veniam peto, parce fatenti ;
   parce pater, fratres parcite, parce deus.[1]

In discussing the contribution of Adam of S. Victor to
medieval religious poetry the historian is faced at the outset
with a critical problem. The available documentary evidence
is so fragmentary and uncertain that it is as yet impossible to
draw up a list of proses which are beyond doubt to be ascribed
to Adam.[2] The first piece of evidence is that of William of
S. Lô (d. 1349), an Augustinian, who says of Adam, after
describing his learning and conversation :

valde multas prosas fecit de benedicta Trinitate, de Sancto Spiritu, de
gloriosa Virgine Maria, ad quam specialem devotionem noscitur habuisse,
de apostolis et aliis pluribus sanctis, quae succincte et clausulatim pro-
gredientes, venusto verborum matrimonio subtiliter decoratae, scientiarum
flosculis mirabilibus picturatae, schemate congruentissimo componuntur.[3]

Unfortunately the Abbot does not proceed to give a list of the
proses in question, and the list (Paris Bibl. Nat. 10508) which
Gautier[4] imagined to be the actual list compiled by William is
now recognized merely as a compilation of the early sixteenth
century.[5] The next evidence is afforded by an examination of
the earliest graduals of S. Victor. These belong to the thirteenth century, and are therefore too late to be a sure guide.
But from this source the Abbé Misset has compiled a list of
forty-five Sequences, and it can hardly be doubted that within
this list a number of Adam's Sequences are to be found.[6] All
these Sequences are similar in technical structure, style, and
content, and are more or less easily distinguishable from the other
compositions which have found a place beside them. At the
same time it is, as Blume suggests, going too far to say that
compliance with certain stylistic and structural criteria is sufficient to mark the whole of these forty-five Sequences as defi-

---

[1] Gautier, 3rd edit., pp. 230-1.

[2] See generally the Preface to *Anal.
Hymn.* liv, ed. Blume ; also the works of
Gautier, Aubry, and Misset, already re-
ferred to.

[3] *Anal. Hymn.* liv, p. x (quoted from
Martène, *Amplissima Collectio,* vi. 220).

[4] 1st edit., I, p. lviii.

[5] Cf. Delisle, *Bibl. de l'école des chartes,*
xx. 196.

[6] *Anal. Hymn.* liv. p. xii, where the
list is given in full; Misset, *Essai sur les
œuvres poétiques d'Adam de S. Victor,*
pp. 62 sqq.

nitely the work of no other poet than Adam. The position of
Misset and Gautier may be described generally as this. If a
Sequence is to be ascribed definitely to Adam the rhythm must
show invariable correspondence of word and verse accent; the
caesura must occur at the end of the fourth syllable and at the
end of a word, but in the seven-syllabled line of a strophe when
that line is acatalectic and ends with a masculine rime there
may be a change of stress, as in the line

salutis puerpera.[1]

Further, when these characteristics are present the attribution
must be confirmed by the presence of the Prose in the earliest
graduals of S. Victor. Such formal tests are, however, difficult
to apply with certainty. As Blume has shown, verses which
comply with these rules (e. g. the *Verbum bonum et suave*) had
been composed before the time of Adam, and Misset, by
following strictly his *a priori* method, had wrongly ascribed the
Laudes crucis to Adam, when on manuscript grounds it is
practically certain that it belongs to the end of the eleventh
century.[2] There is, therefore, a possibility that of the forty-five
Sequences ascribed by Misset to Adam several others may not
be actually his, and there is the further consideration that Adam
may be assumed to have followed a structural pattern no less
susceptible to change and experiment than that of other poets.[3]

It is possible, however, by studying the centres in which the
manuscripts indicate that the various proses were in use, to
arrive at fairly certain conclusions as to their places of origin,
and in many cases, as Blume has shown, we have a right to
assume that the Abbey of S. Victor is the place of origin.
Further, if the dates and the quality of the Sequence are satisfactory, we may guess that Adam is the author. It will be clear
that the last word has not been said on this perplexing problem
of criticism. But we shall hardly be wrong in instancing (beside
the *Salve mater salvatoris*) two particular Sequences as masterpieces which have come from the hand of Adam. The first is
in honour of S. Stephen:

1. heri mundus exsultavit	2. heri chorus angelorum
et exsultans celebravit	prosecutus est caelorum
Christi natalitia ;	regem cum laetitia.

[1] Cf. *Anal. Hymn.* liv, p. vii.
[2] Cf. ib., liv, p. 192.

[3] This appears to be recognized by
Blume, *Anal. Hymn.* lv, p. viii.

3. protomartyr et levita,
　clarus fide, clarus vita,
　　clarus et miraculis,

4. sub hac luce triumphavit
　et triumphans insultavit
　　Stephanus incredulis.

5. fremunt ergo tamquam ferae,
　quia victi defecere,
　　lucis adversarii;

6. falsos testes statuunt
　et linguas exacuunt
　　viperarum filii.

7. agonista, nulli cede,
　certa certus de mercede,
　　persevera, Stephane!

8. insta falsis testibus,
　confuta sermonibus
　　synagogam Satanae!

9. testis tuus est in caelis,
　testis verax et fidelis,
　　testis innocentiae;

10. nomen habes coronati,
　te tormenta decet pati
　　pro corona gloriae.

11. pro corona non marcenti
　perfer brevis vim tormenti,
　　te manet victoria;

12. tibi fiet mors natalis,
　tibi poena terminalis
　　dat vitae primordia.

13. plenus sancto spiritu
　penetrat intuitu
　　Stephanus caelestia;

14. videns dei gloriam
　crescit ad victoriam,
　　suspirat ad praemia.

15. en, a dextris dei stantem
　Iesum, pro te dimicantem,
　　Stephane, considera;

16. tibi caelos reserari,
　tibi Christum revelari,
　　clama voce libera.

17. se commendat salvatori,
　pro quo dulce ducit mori
　　sub ipsis lapidibus,

18. Saulus servat omnium
　vestes lapidantium
　　lapidans in omnibus.

19. ne peccatum statuatur,
　his, a quibus lapidatur,
　　genu ponit et precatur
　　condolens insaniae;

20. in Christo sic obdormivit,
　qui Christo sic oboedivit
　　et cum Christo semper vivit,
　　martyrum primitiae.

21. quod sex suscitaverit
　　mortuos in Africa,
　Augustinus asserit,
　　fama refert publica.

22. huius dei gratia
　　revelato corpore
　mundo datur pluvia
　　siccitatis tempore.

23. solo fugat hic odore
　　morbos et daemonia,
　laude dignus et honore
　　iugique memoria.

24. martyr, cuius est iucundum
　　nomen in ecclesia,
　languescentem fove mundum
　　caelesti fragrantia.[1]

In this 'sublime composition', as Archbishop Trench calls it,[2] the Sequence-form reaches a perfection which was never surpassed. Equal in its dignity and facile in its execution is the Easter Sequence, *Zyma vetus expurgetur*. Its ascription to

---

[1] Text in *Anal. Hymn.* lv, p. 341 sq.　　　　[2] *Sacred Latin Poetry*, p. 212.

Adam is confirmed, more or less satisfactorily, by Alan of Lille,[1] his contemporary. The rhythm is good, the caesura is observed, and the changes of stress occur only in the lines of seven syllables.

1. zyma vetus expurgetur,
   ut sincere celebretur
      nova resurrectio.

2. haec est dies nostrae spei,
   huius mira vis diei
      legis testimonio.

3. haec Aegyptum spoliavit
   et Hebraeos liberavit
   de fornace ferrea ;

4. his in arto constitutis
   opus erat servitutis
   lutum, later, palea.

5. iam divinae laus virtutis,
   iam triumphi, iam salutis
      vox erumpat libera.
   haec est dies,
      quam fecit dominus,
   dies nostri doloris terminus,
      dies salutifera.

6. lex est umbra futurorum,
   Christus finis promissorum,
      qui consummat omnia.
   Christi sanguis
      igneam
   hebetavit romphaeam
      amota custodia.

7. puer, nostri forma risus,
   pro quo vervex est occisus,
      vitae signat gaudium.

8. Ioseph exit de cisterna,
   Christus redit ad superna
      post mortis supplicium.

9. hic dracones Pharaonis
   draco vorat, a draconis
      immunis malitia :
   quos ignitus vulnerat,
   hos serpentis liberat
      aenei praesentia.

10. anguem forat in maxilla
    Christus, hamus et armilla
       in cavernam reguli
    manum mittit ablactatus,
    et sic fugit exturbatus
       vetus hostis saeculi.

11. irrisores Elisaei,
    dum conscendit domum dei,
       zelum calvi sentiunt.
    David arrepticius,
    hircus emissarius
       et passer effugiunt.

12. in maxilla mille sternit
    et de tribu sua spernit
       Samson matrimonium ;
    Samson Gazae seras pandit
    et asportans portas scandit
       montis supercilium.

13. sic de Iuda leo fortis
    fractis portis dirae mortis
       die surgens tertia,

14. rugiente voce patris,
    ad supernae sinum matris
       tot revexit spolia.

15. cetus Ionam fugitivum,
    veri Ionae signativum,
    post tres dies reddit vivum
       de ventris angustia.

16. botrus Cypri reflorescit,
    dilatatur et excrescit,
    synagogae flos marcescit
       et floret ecclesia.

---

[1] *Liber in distinctiones dictionum,* Migne, ccx, col. 122 ; see *Anal. Hymn.* liv, p. 229 ; text p. 227 sq. ; for the symbolism of this Sequence see below, p. 359 sq.

17. mors et vita conflixere,
    resurrexit Christus vere,
    et cum Christo surrexere
    multi testes gloriae.

18. mane novum, mane laetum
    vespertinum tergat fletum ;
    quia vita vicit letum,
    tempus est laetitiae.

19. Iesu victor, Iesu vita,
    Iesu vitae via trita,
    cuius morte mors sopita,
    ad paschalem nos invita
    mensam cum fiducia.

20. vive panis, vivax unda,
    vera vitis et fecunda,
    tu nos pasce, tu nos munda,
    ut a morte nos secunda
    tua salvet gratia.

In estimating Adam's poetical achievement we are bound to admire the wonderful facility of his versification, the smoothness of his rhythm, and the skilful handling of rime. In these proses, indeed, medieval rhythmical verse reached its greatest formal perfection. Henceforth, there could be no thought of a serious return to the classical tradition for the inspiration of liturgical verse. A new style had been at last forged and perfected, capable of expressing, in Adam and the poets of his school, the precision of doctrinal truth with a fitting liturgical solemnity. For Adam remains a child of the twelfth century. His main interest is dogmatic, and he is ever expounding those symbolical conceptions which, for the school of S. Victor, were the key to the Scriptures and indeed to the whole world of nature. Hence Adam and the poets of his school rarely reach the highest flights of inspiration. Their poetry contains little or nothing of sheer lyrical beauty, because they are always trammelled by the nature of their subject, the feast of an apostle or martyr, the festivals of the Virgin, or the common imagery, in which, according to custom, the meanings of Christmas, of Easter, of Pentecost were to be given their symbolical expression. Most readers will agree with Remy de Gourmont's criticism of Adam.[1] 'Il lui manque de joindre à son génie d'artiste un peu de la folie de l'amour, un peu de l'envol du mysticisme ; il lui manque encore une originalité réelle de pensée.' But in fairness to Adam it should be said that poetry so strictly and definitely liturgical must necessarily be objective and direct in its expression rather than personal and lyrical. The Franciscan poets of the next century, who used the Sequence-measure to convey all the fervour and exaltation of the gospel of Assisi, had no such regard to liturgical needs, and their poetry is personal and lyrical. Adam and his school are

[1] *Le latin mystique*, p. 263.

the exponents of form, the classical masters of rhythmical verse. From them it was that Thomas Aquinas learned the severe music of the *Lauda Sion* and the *Pange lingua*, verses of a loftier aim but not of a higher execution. On the whole we would say, borrowing the phrase which Matthew Arnold applied so happily to Pope, that Adam was a poet of 'prodigious talent',[1] and we can only marvel when Dr. Neale describes him as 'to my mind the greatest Latin poet, not only of medieval, but of all ages'.

§ 3. *The Victorine Sequences and Medieval Symbolism.*

When we consider the content of the large group of Sequences which can be described most conveniently as Victorine,[2] we recognize that their meaning cannot be understood without reference to the elaborate allegory and symbolism in which the thought of the Middle Ages was rooted. For the Middle Ages, whose ideas of man and of nature owed little to the patient practice of direct observation, the key to the universe of concrete things and the key to history was to be found in a symbolical interpretation, by which the things which were visible existed as a picture or sign of things invisible, that is, of the spiritual and moral universe. In the words of Alan of Lille :

> omnis mundi creatura
> quasi liber et pictura
>   nobis est in speculum,
> nostrae vitae, nostrae sortis,
> nostri status, nostrae mortis
>   fidele signaculum.

The spiritual and moral universe, like the world of Plato's ideas, was the real and intelligible universe, of which the world of phenomena was merely a sign or a shadow.[3] Hence the world of things was worth understanding only as a step towards the understanding of the world of reality. Symbolism is the

---

[1] *On Translating Homer*, i ; for Léopold Delisle's judgement—'l'un des plus grands poètes latins du moyen âge', see *Bibl. de l'école des chartes*, v, IVᵉ série, p. 197, Paris 1859.

[2] The Sequences which are mainly referred to in this section are those which Gautier collected in his first edition of Adam of S. Victor, and which Mr. Wrangham has reprinted in his English edition. For convenience of reference to either volume, I quote the Sequences by number. Other hymns and sequences referred to are largely taken from Mone, *Hymni Latini*, vol. ii, and *Anal. Hymn.*

[3] On the medieval conception of nature see Eicken, *Mittelalterliche Weltanschauung*, pp. 611 sqq.

universal speech of man,[1] but nowhere was it erected into a completer system than in the labours of the symbolists of the twelfth and thirteenth centuries. For them

alles Vergängliche ist nur ein Gleichnis.

From Philo Judaeus, who had borrowed it from the Greeks and used it in the interpretation of Genesis, this method, already known to Paul, passed to the Fathers of the Church—to Clement and Origen, and, in the West, through Hilary and Ambrose, to Augustine, the supreme theological master of the earlier Middle Ages. Industrious compilers like Isidore of Seville, Bede and Raban Maur, explained the Old Testament by its typological and symbolical reference to the New.

The whole visible universe in its smallest details appeared to them as fraught with a hidden meaning. The world of nature in its manifold changes bore witness to spiritual and dogmatic truths. For instance, the renewal of nature in the spring is a visible symbol of the resurrection of Christ.[2] The very beasts of the field may be taken as types and symbols. 'When a lioness gives birth to a cub', says a medieval *Bestiary*, 'she brings it forth dead and watches over it three days, until the father coming on the third day breathes upon its face and brings it to life. So the Father Almighty raised His Son our Lord Jesus Christ from the dead, even as Jacob saith: " Dormitabit tanquam leo, et sicut catulus leonis. Quis suscitabit eum ?"' The unicorn is a type of Christ, and bears witness to the Virgin Birth. In his *Speculum Ecclesiae* Honorius ' Augustodunensis' (second quarter of the twelfth century) says,[3] 'The very beasts

---

[1] See Max Schlesinger, *Geschichte des Symbols*, p. 65 ; on the history of Christian symbolism, pp. 88 sqq., 284 sqq. ; on Greek allegorical interpretations of Homer, Seeck, *Geschichte des Untergangs der antiken Welt*, iii. 53 sq. ; see also Hatch, *Influence of Greek Ideas and Usages upon the Christian Church*, pp. 58 sqq. ; in *Confessions*, vi. 4, Augustine speaks of the method of Ambrose : ' Cum ea, quae ad literam perversitatem docere videbantur, remoto mystico velamento spiritualiter aperiret, non dicens quod me offenderet, quamvis ea diceret, quae utrum vera essent adhuc ignorarem' ; for symbolism in medieval art see Mâle, *L'art religieux du XIII⁶ siècle*, cap. i ; Bréhier, *L'art chrétien*, pp. 175 sqq.

On the sudden renaissance of symbolism in religious art, *circ.* 1140, under the influence of Suger at S. Denis, see Mâle's fine book, *L'art religieux du XIIme siècle*, p. 159.

[2] Fortunatus, *Salve Festa Dies*, supra p. 92 ; Adam of S. Victor, Sequence xiii ; according to another interpretation the winter signifies the times before Christ ; spring the Baptism ; summer eternal life ; autumn the judgement ; and winter again death ; Mâle, *L'art religieux du XIII⁶ siècle*, p. 46.

[3] *Speculum Eccles.*, Migne, clxxii, col. 819 ; on Honorius see J. A. Endres, *Honorius Augustodunensis*, Kempten and Munich 1906. Honorius has nothing to do with Autun, but is to be associated

prefigured this birth. The unicorn is a very fierce beast with only one horn ; to capture it a virgin maid is placed in the field. The unicorn approaches her, and, resting in her lap, is so taken. By this beast Christ is figured ; by the horn his insuperable strength is expressed. Resting in the womb of a Virgin, he was taken by the hunters, that is, he was found in the form of a man by those who loved him.'

If nature is one vast allegory, the same is true of the works of men. The churches of stone are symbols of the Church herself ; their stones represent the living stones out of which the City of God is built. The door of the Church is Christ, through whom we enter into the heavenly Jerusalem ; the pillars are the bishops and doctors ; the towers are the preachers ; the sacristy, where the priest clothes himself in his priestly garments, is the womb of Mary where Christ clothed himself with our flesh.[1] So with every detail of the Church and its services is associated a symbolic meaning which varies with the fancy of the writer, whether it be Honorius in his *Gemma Animae*[2] or Durandus of Mende in his *Rationale Divinorum Officiorum*.

But, further, the whole course of profane and especially of sacred history is one long allegory, a story with a spiritual meaning. In his *De Sacramentis Christianae Fidei*[3] Hugh of S. Victor explains that there are three ways of understanding Holy Scripture—historically, allegorically, and tropologically. 'History is the record of events, and there the meaning is in the literal sense ; allegory exists when by a certain fact is signified another fact either in the present or the future ; tropology exists when what has been done signifies that something ought to be done.'[4] The most fruitful and attractive of these methods to the medieval mind was the allegorical, which saw in the Old Testament the persons and doctrines of the New hidden darkly under temporal forms, 'per speculum in aenigmate'. The

---

with a monastery in Ratisbon. This is Endres's thesis, but R. Bauerreis, *Zur Herkunft des Honorius Augustodinensis, Studien und Mitteilungen zur Geschichte des Benediktinerordens*, 1935, pp. 24 sqq., holds that he was a monk of S. Augustine's Canterbury.

[1] Durandi *Rationale divinorum officiorum*, Lyons 1568, pp. 6 sqq. ; see Taylor, *The Medieval Mind*, ii. 106-7, where an analysis of Durandus is given ; cf. Adam of S. Victor's exposition of the symbolism of a Church, Sequence xxiv :

sed tres partes sunt in templo
Trinitatis sub exemplo
  ima, summa, media:
ima signat vivos cunctos,
et secunda iam defunctos,
  redivivos tertia, &c.

[2] Migne, clxxii, col. 541 sqq.
[3] ib., clxxvi, col. 184 sq.
[4] The three methods are therefore (1) historical, referring to the literal meaning ; (2) allegorical, referring to present or future ; (3) tropological, extracting a moral lesson.

meaning of the Old Testament could be understood only by reference to the New; what was hidden under a veil in the Old was revealed in the New. The dictum of Augustine, 'In vetere testamento novum latet, in novo vetus patet,' expresses concisely the spirit of this interpretation. 'In the passion of Christ', says Honorius,[1] 'the veil of the temple is rent because by His death heaven and the book closed with the seven seals are opened. For, after the resurrection, He took away the veil and opened their understanding that they might understand the Scriptures, and He opened heaven to them that believe.'

To what puerilities the persistent application of this method must inevitably lead, the following example, conceived by no less a mind than Augustine's, shows.[2] David was not merely one of the prophets who had foretold the Christ; he was himself a type of the Saviour who was to be born of the Root of Jesse. For David watching Bathsheba bathing upon the housetop is Christ beholding His Church cleansing herself from the pollution of the world. Bathsheba, married to Uriah, represents the souls in bondage to the devil, who are to be freed by grace and transformed into the Church, that is to say, the Bride of Christ.

Again, to take a more impressive instance, on a doorway at Reims Cathedral Melchisedek, priest and king, is represented offering to Abraham the bread and wine in the form of a communion, which the patriarch receives with adoration.[3] At Chartres the priest-king stands in the northern doorway holding a chalice and paten in his hands.[4] Melchisedek is the type of Christ, the true Priest and King, and his offering to Abraham is a figure of the Eucharistic offering.

This method of interpretation was inherited by the mystics of the school of S. Victor, where Hugh was an accomplished master of the symbolic science. In his *De Sacramentis Christianae Fidei* he regards the visible world as a sign or sacrament under which the invisible was everywhere to be discerned, just as in the Eucharist the visible bread and wine were the signs of the real and invisible Presence.[5] Similarly, with the interpretation

---

[1] *Gemma animae*, Migne, clxxii, col. 657.

[2] *Contra Faustum*, quoted by Taylor, *Medieval Mind*, ii. 71; this symbol is used in Sequence xxiii,

    hic Urias viduatur,
    Bethsabee sublimatur,
        sedis consors regiae.

The attribution to Adam is incorrect, as the Sequence is of the eleventh century; *Anal. Hymn.* lv, p. 34.

[3] Mâle, *L'art religieux du XIII* siècle*, p. 187.

[4] Marriage, *Sculptures of Chartres*, p. 156, Cambridge, 1909.

[5] Migne, clxxi, col. 313 'Sacramentum est sacrae rei signum. Quemadmodum

of Scripture, an allegorical meaning lies hidden beneath the literal fact. In his curious treatise *De Arca Noe morali*,[1] Hugh explains that 'the Church herself is the Ark which the highest Noah, that is, our Lord Jesus Christ, the steersman, and the haven, amid the storms of this life at once guides and brings unto Himself. The length of three hundred cubits signifies this present world, which sails through three ages, that is, the time of the natural law, the time of the written law, and the time of grace, through which ages holy Church from the beginning of the world unto the end tendeth from this present life to the glory hereafter.'

The most beautiful and poetical interpretations of the hidden meanings which underlay Old Testament history were naturally derived from those parts of the sacred Scriptures which were believed to relate to Christ and His Church, and to the Blessed Virgin Mary. And it was here that Adam of S. Victor, bred in the school of Victorine mysticism and a faithful pupil of his master Hugh, found inspiration and material for his liturgical poetry.

The Old Testament was to the medieval imagination full of the types of Christ. Round the north porch at Chartres stand the rows of patriarchs and kings, majestic figures, symbols in stone of the Messiah of whom all the prophets had spoken. In a Sequence for Easter, Adam brings forth a similar array of the great figures of the past who lived under the Old Law, and in their persons unconsciously foretold its fulfilment in Christ. For,

> lex est umbra futurorum,
> Christus, finis promissorum,
> qui consummat omnia.[2]

Thus Isaac appears as a type of Christ, because his name signifies laughter, and Christ brought us joy;[3] Joseph, brought out of the pit, prefigures Christ in His resurrection;[4] Christ is

enim in homine duo sunt, corpus et anima, et in una scriptura duo similiter, littera et sensus, sic et in omni sacramento aliud est quod visibiliter foris tractatur et cernitur, aliud est quod invisibiliter intus creditur et praecipitur.

[1] Migne, clxxvi, col. 629.

[2] Sequence xiv. 19; see Mâle, *L'art religieux du XIII⁰ siècle*, p. 184, for instances of medieval typology in this respect; Adam is the type of Christ, the second Adam (cf. 1 Cor. xv. 45); Abel,

the shepherd, the type of the Good Shepherd; Moses gave the Old Law, and is a type of Christ who gave the New.

[3] Trench, p. 168, note 25; but Isaac carrying the wood for the offering is also a type of Christ bearing His cross.

[4] The *Bobbio Missal* (*Henry Bradshaw Society*, lviii (1919), p. 51) of the seventh or eighth century contains an interesting elaboration of the parallelism of the life of Joseph and that of Christ.

Aaron's serpent which devours the serpents of Pharaoh,[1] He is Moses' serpent which was lifted up in the wilderness—each time for the deliverance of men; Elijah, derided by the children, is typical of Christ mocked by the Jews, and the vengeance of Elijah foretold the woes which overtook them in the days of Vespasian and Titus;[2] David's madness [3] prefigures Christ of whom it was said, ' He is beside himself'; Samson bearing away the gates of Gaza is typical of the rising Lord who breaks the gates of hell; Christ is once more the Lion of the *Bestiary*:

> sic de Iuda leo fortis,
> fractis portis dirae mortis,
> die surgens tertia ;
> rugiente voce patris,
> ad supernae sinum matris
> tot revexit spolia.

Jonah, for three days in the whale's belly, is the sign of the true Jonah who rose on the third day from the depths of the grave;[4] Christ, again, is the grape-bunch trodden in the winepress of the passion, but flourishing again in his resurrection—' Botrus Cypri dilectus meus mihi in vineis Engaddi '.[5]

Sequence vii on the Nativity is filled with the same symbolism. The poet lingers over a curious comparison of Jesus with the nut, whose hull (*cortex*) is the symbol of His passion which closed round His mortal flesh, while the shell represents His bodily frame, the kernel the divinity, and its pleasant savour the sweetness of Christ. But the nut gives light and oil and food; so Christ is light to the blind, ointment to the sick, and His Body is the food of the faithful.

> lux est caecis, et unguentum
> Christus aegris, et fomentum
> piis animalibus.
> o quam dulce sacramentum !
> foenum carnis in frumentum
> convertit fidelibus.

---

[1] Exod. vii. 12.

[2] 2 Kings iii. 23-4; see Trench, p. 170, who quotes Hugh of S. Victor.

[3] 1 Sam. xxi. 14 (Vulgate *I Regum* xxi. 14) ' vidistis hominem insanum'; Mark iii. 21 ' Quoniam in furorem versus est '.

[4] Cf. Matt. xii. 39-40.

[5] Cant. i. 13 (Vulgate) ; cf. Isa. lxiii. 3 ; cf. Mone, ii. 10 (*Anal. Hymn.* v, p. 50), where the Virgin is the Vine which bears the grape-bunch.

> haec est botrum paritura
> virgo plena gratiâ,
> qui in crucis nos pressura
> convivantes debriat.

This nut, with leaf and flower, is borne by the 'dry rod', the rod of Aaron, which is the Virgin Mary.[1] The leaf is Christ, who protects us with His shadow, and the flower is the sign of His sweetness. So the hidden meaning is explored to its smallest detail.

In the Victorine group are four splendid Sequences for the occasion of the dedication of a church,[2] in which a wealth of imagery is employed to celebrate the glories of the building of stone which was the symbol of the spiritual Church, the true temple of which it was written : 'Quam dilecta tabernacula tua, Domine virtutum'.   But his inspiration soon carries the poet far away from the visible edifice, and he sees only the Church, whose walls are built of living stones, the Bride of the Canticles, awaiting the Bridegroom.

> sponsa mea speciosa,
> inter filios formosa,
>   supra solem splendida !
>
> caput tuum ut Carmelus,
> et ipsius comae tinctae regis uti purpura ;
>   oculi ut columbarum,
> genae tuae punicorum ceu malorum fragmina !
>
> collum tuum ut columna, turris et eburnea ;
> mel et lac sub lingua tua, favus stillans labia ![3]

Like the Bride of the Canticles, the Church is 'fair as the moon, clear as the sun, terrible as an army with banners'.[4] So she is represented in many a cathedral, as at Strassburg, a majestic woman, crowned and erect, with the Cross as her staff ; while the Synagogue, blinded and downcast, holds in one hand a broken stave and in the other the shattered Table of the Old Law.[5] If Adam is the type of Christ, Eve is the type of the Church ; for as Eve was taken out of Adam's side and became his wife, so the Church issued from the wounded side of Christ and is His Bride.

> formaretur ut sic ecclesia
> figuravit in pari gloria
> Adae costis formata femina.
>   hostis Eva.[6]

---

[1] Num. xvi. 8.
[2] xxiii–xxvi ; xxiii is not Adam's.
[3] Sequence xxv. 21–32 ; Cant. iv (Vulgate).
[4] Sequence xxvi. 30–2.

[5] See Sauerlandt, *Deutsche Plastik des Mittelalters*, pp. 36–7, for an illustration of the Strassburg statues ; cf. Sequence xxvi. 25–6.
[6] Sequence xxvi. 21–4 ; cf. xxxiii. 11–

The Church is the Ark, both the Ark of the deluge and the Ark of the covenant. As the former she carries her freight, the souls of the faithful, through the deluge of an evil world;[1] as the latter she contains the pot of manna and the Tables of the Law, that is the Bread from heaven and the new covenant of which she is the depository.[2]

> hic est urna manna plena,
> hic mandata legis dena,
> sed in arca foederis.

But the Church is also the Queen of the South, coming from afar to hear the wisdom of one greater than Solomon;[3] she is the ladder of Jacob reaching from heaven to earth and the pathway of angels;[4] she is Rachel, the chosen wife of Jacob, while Leah is the unhappy Synagogue.[5]

The Church on earth is part only of the whole body of God's city, which is composed of the pilgrim city on earth and the city of the blessed in heaven. So one of the Sequences[6] begins by invoking the citizens of both cities,

> Ierusalem et Sion filiae.

the Church triumphant and the Church militant, the Church triumphant which is Jerusalem, 'the vision of peace,' and the Church on earth, which is Syon or 'watching'.[7] So the unknown poet who wrote the loveliest of all hymns for a Church dedication :

> urbs beata Hierusalem, vivis ex lapidibus,
> dicta pacis visio, et angelis coornata,
> quae construitur in caelis ut sponsata comite. . . .

13; for this symbolism in art see Mâle, *L'art religieux du XIIIᵉ siècle*, p. 225, as the Church is shown standing on the right side of Christ at his crucifixion, a queen who receives the blood and water in a chalice.

[1] Sequence xxiii. 14–16; cf. Hugh of S. Victor, *De arca Noe morali*, Migne, clxxvi, col. 629.

[2] Sequence xxiii. 43–6.

[3] ib., xxiii. 56–8; xxvi. 37–9.

[4] ib., xxv. 3–4.

[5] ib., xxiii. 26–31; Rachel and Leah, like Mary and Martha, are favourite types of the contemplative and the active life

respectively; cf. Bernard of Morlas, *De contemptu mundi*, Wright, i. 15 ; Richard of S. Victor, *Benjamin minor*, cap. ii et seqq., in Migne, cxcvi, col. 2 sqq., for a full and varied exposition.

[6] Sequence xxvi.

[7] Durandus, *Rationale*, i. 1, p. 4. Dicitur enim praesens ecclesia, Syon, eo quod ab hac peregrinatione longe posita promissionem rerum caelestium speculatur ; et ideo Syon, id est *speculatio*, nomen accepit. Pro futura vero patria et pace, Hierusalem vocatur : nam Hierusalem *pacis visio* interpretatur.

angularis fundamentum
lapis Christus missus est,
qui compage parietis

in utroque nectitur,
quem Sion sancta suscepit,
in quo credens permanet.[1]

Here the poet clearly draws the distinction between the Church militant and the Church triumphant, but the necessities of metre hindered the medieval singer from always observing it.[2]

§ 4. *Adam of S. Victor and the Symbolism of the Virgin Mary.*

The devotion to the Blessed Virgin Mary, which assumed such importance in the full Middle Ages, can hardly be traced in the earliest centuries of the Christian Church.[3] There are signs, indeed, of an heretical Eastern sect which offered meal and honey in her honour, as the Greeks did to Artemis; and in those Hellenistic-Oriental religions professing devotion to a divine Mother there were doubtless elements which, during the absorption of paganism by Christianity, aided the spread of a cult which was a natural extension of the honour already paid to angels, martyrs, and ascetics as the intercessors nearest to the throne of God and of His Son.[4] The *Protevangelium of James*, by relating in detail the events of her life and affirming her perpetual virginity, helped to increase the position of honour in which Mary was held in the Eastern Church, while Origen and the fathers of the fourth century completed the picture of the mother of the Saviour by presenting her as the ideal ascetic, devoted to fasting and prayer.[5] First the Syrian and then the Greek Church took up her cult. The greatest force in the West which made for its extension was the commanding influence of men like Ambrose, Jerome, and Augustine, the great exponents of the spiritual value of virginity.[6] If Origen had declared

---

[1] *Anal. Hymn.* li, p. 110; the hymn is perhaps of the eighth century.

[2] Cf. Trench, *Sacred Latin Poetry*, p. 318.

[3] See Mâle, *L'art religieux de la fin du moyen âge en France*; Lucius, *Heiligenkult*, pp. 422 sqq.

[4] Lucius, p. 466, ' Den Heiligenkult in der Tat hat der Marienverehrung sowohl die Richtung vorgezeichnet, in welcher sie sich entwickeln, als die Formen geboten, in welchen sie einen festen Bestand gewinnen sollte '.

[5] See ib., pp. 431 sqq.

[6] ib., p. 437, the Nicaean theology, by establishing the position of the Son as of the same essence (οὐσία) as the Father, tended to raise the estimation in which Mary was held. The spread of the cult of Mary in the West and especially in Spain was influenced by the early translations of Ephrem and other Syriac writers into Latin. Cf. Edmund Bishop, *Liturgica Historica*, p. 178, note 3; see also

that Christ had died for Mary's sins in dying for those of mankind, the later fathers, including Ambrose and Augustine, contended that the Virgin who had been counted worthy to be the mother of God was never defiled by sin.[1]   By this time, in the East, Mary was beginning to be called the Θεοτόκος, the Mother of God.   Her worship had gained both officially and popularly a place of first importance.[2]   Her images were everywhere in the churches, in monastic cells, and private houses;[2] and after the failure of Iconoclasm the devotion spread without a check.

In the West, by the eighth century, the cult of the Virgin was universal; churches were raised everywhere in her honour, her praises were celebrated in the offices, and it soon became usual for an altar to be dedicated to her in every large church.   But the monasteries were the great centres where the devotion to Mary grew, and from which it radiated.   Nearly every monastic order professed some kind of special devotion to the Virgin.[3] In the twelfth century Bernard of Clairvaux loved to use his eloquence in her praise. 'What tongue', he said, 'even the tongue of an angel, could extol in praises worthy of her, the virgin-mother, mother not of just any one (*cuiuscumque*), but of God?'[4] Nevertheless, the saint set himself steadfastly against the attempt which was then being made to establish the festival of the Immaculate Conception.   It was Mary's humility and virginity which gained his devotion.[5] 'In perils, in sore straits, in difficulties', says Bernard, 'think on Mary, call on Mary.   Let her not be absent from the lips, let her not be absent from the heart; and that thou mayest obtain the suffrage of her prayer, desert not the example of her conversation.   Following her, thou shalt not stray: praying to her, thou shalt not lose hope: thinking on her, thou shalt not wander.'[6]   So Dante represents the 'doctor mellifluus' seated in paradise, 'his eyes still fixed on his delight', on Mary whom he had celebrated as the 'treasury of God', *thesaurus Dei*.

---

p. 202, note 1 (on Augustine's influence); and the same writer in *The Book of Cerne*, p. 280.

[1] Lucius, pp. 439–40; Origen, *In Luc. hom.* 17.

[2] Lucius, pp. 469–70.

[3] Especially the Cistercians;   see Hauck, iv. 337.   Over the door of Cîteaux the inscription ran :—

Salve, sancta parens, sub qua Cistercius ordo militat.

[4] Bernard, *In Assumpt. serm.*, iv. 5, Migne, clxxxiii, col. 483 ;   see Vacandard, *Vie de S. Bernard*, ii. 79 sqq.

[5] Bernard, *De laudibus Virginis Matris*; Migne, clxxxiii, col. 58 'Pulchra permistio virginitatis et humilitatis'.

[6] ib., col. 70.

In the twelfth century the custom was widespread in the monasteries of reciting the *Little Office of the Blessed Virgin* before the canonical office, and to add to Compline the *Salve Regina* or other anthems in her honour.[1] By this date the cult of the Virgin had assumed such proportions and evoked so much fervour that the figure of the Mother of Christ began to eclipse that of her Son and of all the apostles and saints. It might seem almost true to say that, in the later Middle Ages, the central object of the popular cult was in actual fact the Virgin Mary, exalted to the rank of Queen of Heaven, crowned with the twelve stars,[2] and invested with all those human and tender attributes in which the early Church had first clothed the figure of the Saviour.

It was impossible that the medieval imagination should fail to see on many pages of the Old Testament prophecies and symbols of the Virgin and of the miraculous birth by which she became the mother of the Christ. Such a process had indeed begun long ago, from the time when Irenaeus had seen in the Virgin Mary the second Eve,[3] but it was left to the Middle Ages to establish her position in the symbolic universe.

It was in the *Song of Songs*, so full of rich colour and sensuous beauty, that the most fascinating and mystical prefigurations were found. The Shulamite, interpreted also as the Church, became now the Mother of Christ, and Christ himself the lover, the *dilectus meus*. The whole of the sensuous imagery with which the poet clothes the beauty of the country girl is reproduced, with a spiritual meaning, in the praises of Mary.

> tua sunt ubera
> vino redolentia,
> candor superat lac et lilia,
> odor flores vincit et balsama,[4]

sings an unknown poet of the twelfth century.[5] The lily, the symbol of her purity—'sicut lilium inter spinas, sic amica mea inter filias'[6]—is a favourite figure, and it occurs in the Victorine

---

[1] Vacandard, op. cit., ii. 95 ; *Cath. Encycl.*, art. *Virgin Mary* ; Batiffol, *Histoire du bréviaire romain*, pp. 225, 260.

[2] Cf. *Anal. Hymn.* xvii, p. 25 :
  mulier amicta sole,
    ornata sideribus,
  est Maria digna prole
    regnans in caelestibus.

[3] Iren. v. 19 ; Mary is also the second Judith and the second Esther, *Anal. Hymn.* xvii, p. 25.

[4] Mone, ii. 297 (*Anal. Hymn.* liv, p. 357) ; also *Anal. Hymn.* v, p. 61 ; cf. Cant. iv. 10.

[5] Or perhaps the end of the eleventh ; *Anal. Hymn.* liv, p. 358.

[6] Cant. ii. 2.

Sequences.[1] Mary is also the fountain sealed, the garden enclosed,[2] because the birth of Christ left unbroken the seal of her virginity.[3] So Adam sings:

> haec est ille fons signatus,
> hortus clausus, fecundatus
> virtutum seminibus.[4]

Again the Virgin is the Tower of David, the *Turris David* of the Canticles, the *Fons hortorum*, which flows from Lebanon; and the roe skipping upon the mountains. The tower, because of her strength and inviolable chastity; the fountain, because from her there flowed the fount of Wisdom, the Christ; the roe skipping upon the mountains, when she visited Elizabeth in the hill country before the birth of Jesus.[5] To her were applied the verses of Ecclesiasticus (xxiv.17), 'I was exalted like a cedar in Libanus, as a cypress tree on Mount Sion: I was exalted like a palm tree in Cades, and as a rose-plant in Jericho: as a fair olive tree in the plains. . . . . I gave a sweet smell like cinnamon and aromatical balm. I yielded a sweet odour like the choicest myrrh. And I perfumed my dwelling like storax, and galbanum, and onyx, and aloes, and Libanus not cut; and my odour is as the purest balm.'

She was the Temple of God, because in her body as in a temple, the godhead dwelt for a time; of her, it was written, 'Quam dilecta tabernacula tua, Domine virtutum'. So Adam:

> verbum carni counitum,
> sicut erat praefinitum,
>   sine carnis copula
> virgo parit, dei templum,
> nec exemplar, nec exemplum
>   per tot habens saecula.[6]

---

[1] Sequence iii. 56–8; xcvii, 39; cf. Mone, ii. 297, line 10 (*Anal. Hymn.* liv, p. 357).

[2] Cant. iv. 12 'Hortus conclusus soror mea sponsa, hortus conclusus, fons signatus'.

[3] This had been a matter much discussed by the fathers, Tertullian (anti-Docetic), Irenaeus, and Origen holding a contrary view, but later opinion upheld it, Ambrose arguing (from Ezek. xliv. 2), 'transivit per eam Christus, sed non aperuit'; cf. Hugh of S. Victor, *De B. Mariae virginitate* (Migne, clxxvi, col. 872–3); see Hirn, *The Sacred Shrine*,

pp. 331 sqq.; Lucius, pp. 425 sqq.; cf. Adam of S. Victor, vii. 14:
> nec sigillum
> propter illum
> castitatis perdidit.

[4] Sequence lxxiv, lines 33–5; cf. xliv. 59; cf. Mone, ii. 297 (*Anal. Hymn.* liv, p. 357).

[5] See Canticles, *passim*; Luke i. 39; Hirn, *The Sacred Shrine*, pp. 441–2; on the *Fons Hortorum*, Honorius, *Spec. eccles.*, Migne, clxxii, col. 999.

[6] Sequence v. 7–12; cf. Mone, ii. 196 'Gaude templum deitatis'.

If Mary is the Temple, she is naturally also the Ark of the New Covenant, and likewise the Ark of Noah, by which the world was saved.[1]

> tu es archa Noe viva
> per mundi diluvia,
> tu columba cum olivâ
> verae pacis praevia.[2]

She is the throne of Solomon, that is, of the true Solomon; the ivory is the symbol of her chastity, and the gold of her charity.

> tu thronus es Salomonis,
> cui nullus par in thronis
> arte vel materia ;
> ebur candens castitatis,
> aurum fulvum charitatis
> praesignant mysteria.[3]

Most dear to the medieval imagination was the conception of Mary as the second Eve, who by poetic justice, in the form of a woman, made amends for the sin which, by a woman, had entered the world :

> ut quod ruit per feminam,
> relevetur per feminam.[4]

The first Eve brought forth woe to the human race, the second Eve bore the fruit of life. This contrast is used more than once in the Victorine Sequences to emphasize the joy of Christmas, in which the old Adam and the first Eve are banished for the new.

---

[1] Mone, ii. 72 (*Anal. Hymn.* liv, p. 373),
  archa Noe fabricatur,
  per quam mundus liberatur.
[2] Mone, ii. 400.
[3] Sequence lxxiii. 36-42 ; cf. lxv. 43 ; *Anal. Hymn.* xvii, p. 25, and xxxiii. 323–4; cf. III Regum, x. 18. 'Fecit etiam rex Salomon thronum de ebore grandem: et vestivit eum auro fulvo nimis'; hence the Virgin is usually represented seated holding her Son on her lap. She is the throne of the true Solomon; see Mâle, *L'art religieux du XIIe siècle*, p. 433.
[4] Mone, ii. 10 (*Anal. Hymn.* v, p. 49) ;

cf. Milton, *Paradise Lost*, v. 385 :
    On whom the angel ' Hail'
  Bestowed, the holy salutation used
  Long after to blest Mary, second Eve.
Cf. Bernard, *De laudibus Virginis Matris*, Migne, clxxxiii, col. 62 ; cf. also Sedulius,
  sola fuit mulier, patuit qua ianua leto :
  et qua vita redit, sola fuit mulier ;
also the *Mariale* (*Anal. Hymn.* l, p. 428),
  Evae crimen nobis limen
    paradisi clauserat,
  haec, dum credit et obedit,
    coeli claustra reserat.

> Eva prius interemit,
> sed salvator nos redemit
> carnis suae merito.
> prima parens nobis luctum,
> sed Maria vitae fructum
> protulit cum gaudio.[1]

Another Sequence introduces the well-known pun by which
'Eva', the Latin form of Eve, was transformed into 'Ave', the
greeting of the Angel to Mary. For Gabriel in forming his
'Ave' out of the letters which make up the word 'Eva' was
announcing the redemption of man from the curse of Eve.

> verbum bonum et suave
> pandit intus in conclave
> et ex *Eva* format *Ave*,
> Evae verso nomine.[2]

We have yet to discuss a famous group of symbols which
were used to express the Virgin Birth of Christ, symbols which
most frequently appear both in ecclesiastical art and in all the
liturgical poetry dedicated to Mary. They are all derived from
various passages of the Old Testament, which were regarded as
signifying directly the mystery of the Virgin Birth. Honorius
'Augustodunensis' gives a useful summary of them in his
Speculum Ecclesiae[3] in the course of a sermon on the Annunciation. It will be most convenient to give the commentary of
Honorius by the side of the relative extracts from the Vulgate,
and to illustrate both from various hymns and sequences, and
especially from the sequences of the Victorine group.[4]

---

[1] Sequence vi. 7–12 ; vii. 11–13 ; xcii.
43–8 ; cf. Mone, ii. 196.

[2] xlv. 5–8 ; cf. Mone, ii. 49 (*Anal.
Hymn.* liv, p. 400) :

> lapso namque genere
> humano pro scelere
> matris Evae
> missus ad hanc propere
> Gabriel cum foedere
> promit ave.

Cf. the pun in Mone, ii. 200 (*Anal. Hymn.*
liv, p. 368) :

> tibi dicant omnes 'ave' !
> quia mundum solvens a vae
> mutasti vocem flentium.

[3] Migne, clxxii, col. 901 sqq.; a long
poem (thirteenth century) attributed to

Bonaventura, entitled *Laus beatae Virginis Mariae* (*Opera Omnia*, xiv. 181, ed.
Peltier, Paris 1868), expounds at length
the various Old Testament figures of the
Virgin, adding as well another figure, the
Woman of Rev. xii. For another exposition of this symbolism see Bernard, *Super
Missus est hom.* ii, in Migne, clxxxiii,
col. 63. For a summary of these figures
and symbols, Richard of S. Victor, *Expli-
catio in Cantica Canticorum*, xlii, Migne,
cxcvi, col. 522 ; also col. 517.

[4] The numerous rimed *Offices* in *Anal.
Hymn.* (see below, p. 453 sq.) would provide an inexhaustible source of illustrations, and I have used them to a small
extent.

(1) *The Paradisus Malorum* and *Fons Hortorum.*

Cant. iv. 13 'Emissiones tuae paradisus malorum punicorum cum pomorum fructibus.'

Cant. iv. 15 'Fons hortorum, puteus aquarum viventium.'

Honorius, col. 902, 'She is truly the orchard of pomegranates, the fountain of gardens, because in her arose the tree of life, and from her flowed forth the fount of wisdom (i.e. Christ).'

So a poet celebrates her,

paradisus voluptatis	paradisum hunc quaeramus,
est Maria, praestans gratis	cibum vitae glutiamus,
signum immortalitatis	aquas dulces hauriamus,
ad fontem iocunditatis.	ut feliciter vivamus.[1]

Adam likewise invokes the Virgin as the 'caelestis paradisus.'[2] and the 'fons hortorum',

fons hortorum	cordis prava
internorum,	quaeque lava ;
riga mentes	fons sublimis,
arescentes	munde nimis,
unda tui rivuli :	ab immundo
fons redundans	munda mundo
sis inundans ;	cor immundi populi.[3]

(2) *The Burning Bush (Rubus).*

Exod. iii. 2 'Apparuitque ei Dominus in flamma ignis de medio rubi ; et videbat quod rubus arderet, et non combureretur.'

Honorius, col. 904, 'Moses beheld the bush burning with fire, yet not consumed by the flame. In this bush the Lord appeared, when he delivered his people from the Egyptian bondage. This prefigured the blessed Virgin, whom the fire of the Holy Ghost illuminated with offspring, yet defiled not with the flame of concupiscence. Out of her the Lord appearing visibly visited the world, and freed the people of the faithful from bondage to the devil.'[4]

---

[1] Mone, ii. 72 (*Anal. Hymn.* liv, p. 373).

[2] Sequence lxxiii. 31.

[3] Sequence xliv. 63 sqq.; Adam's authorship cannot be guaranteed ; but see *Anal. Hymn.* liv, p. 309.

[4] See Bernard's interpretation, *Super Missus est hom. II*, Migne, clxxxiii, col. 63.-'What did that bush of Moses in old time, which sent forth flames, yet burned not, portend save Mary giving birth and yet feeling no pangs ?'; cf. the idea of the painless birth in a hymn ascribed to Peter Damiani,(*Anal. Hymn.* xlviii, p. 33),

concepit sine coitu,
emisit absque gemitu.

Cf. *Mariale (Anal. Hymn.* l, p. 432),
aliarum feminarum
proles fletu funditur,
partus iste nil scit triste,
quando deus nascitur.

Also Hugh of S. Victor, *De B. Mariae virginitate* (Migne, clxxvi, col. 873), 'non solum sine libidine concepit, sed neque de semine viri partum accepit ; et ob hoc sine dolore filium edidit'.

The thought of Honorius is exactly expressed in these lines of a Victorine sequence:

rubus quondam exardebat
et tunc ardor non urebat
nec virori nocuit:

sic ardore spiritali
nec attactu coniugali
virgo deum genuit.[1]

(3) *Aaron's Rod.*

Num. xvii. 8 'Sequenti die regressus invenit germinasse virgam Aaron in domo Levi: et turgentibus gemmis eruperant flores.'

Honorius, col. 904, 'Aaron also at the command of the Lord placed a dry rod in the tabernacle, which flowering on the morrow put forth nuts. . . . The dry rod which put forth the nut is the Virgin Mary who bore the Lord Christ.'

'What', says Bernard, 'is the rod of Aaron which flowered without being watered, but Mary who conceived, although she knew not a man?'[2]

Upon this mystery the Victorine poet expends several verses, in which he sets forth at length the mystical meaning of the nut, with leaf and flower, borne by the dry rod, which is the Virgin Mother. We have already dwelt upon this curious and complicated piece of symbolism[3] in discussing the types of Christ which appear in these Sequences.

(4) *The Manna,* Exod. xvi.

Honorius, col. 904, 'The Lord rained down manna from heaven for the children of Israel, and forbade that any should be saved for the morrow. He was willing to give it anew on the morrow, but the manna was kept, and it brought forth worms. By the manna Mary is meant, of whom the worm Christ was born. For he himself saith: *I am a worm and no man* (Ps. xxi). For a man is born by the intercourse of a man and a woman, but Christ was born of a Virgin only, even as a worm is formed out of the mud of the earth.'

This, perhaps the most curious of all symbolic interpretations, can hardly have gained much popularity; but the Virgin is compared in a hymn to the white manna of which 'bread sweeter than honey is made, whereon the court of heaven

[1] Sequence lxxiv. 27-32; cp. v. 13; xlv. 30; lxv. 50; cf. Mone, ii. 9 (*Anal. Hymn.* v, p. 48),
namque rubus incombustus,
Moysen qui terruit,
haec est virgo quae pudore
salvo deum genuit.

[2] *Hom.* ii. 5 (quoted by Mone, ii. 12); cf. Mone, ii. 9 (*Anal. Hymn.* v, p. 48),
virga Aaron fructifera
Mariae typum gesserat,
quae nobis fructum attulit,
famem qui nostram depulit.
[3] supra, p. 360.

feedeth and likewise the Church'.[1]   But the bread is here 'the Bread of Angels', and the manna is not the manna which was preserved in disobedience to the command of the Lord.

(5) *Gideon's Fleece*, Judges vi.

> *Honorius*, col. 904, 'Gideon, the captain of Israel, spread out a fleece on the threshing-floor, into which the dew descended from heaven, while the threshing-floor remained dry.   Again spreading out the fleece, the floor was wet with dew, but the fleece was dry. This was a sign of the victory of the faithful and of the flight of the enemy.   The fleece wet with dew is the holy Virgin, having conceived.   The dry threshing-floor is her inviolate virginity.   The floor was on the second occasion wet with dew, because the Church was pregnant with the gifts of the Holy Spirit. . . . The fleece was dry because the Synagogue was barren and lacked those gifts.'

The fleece of wool, the most famous of all the symbols of the virginity of Mary, is often represented in medieval art; with the Burning Bush, it figures in the thirteenth-century windows at Laon, and on the façade of the Cathedral.[2]   With the story in Judges was associated the verse of Psalm lxxi, which reads in the Vulgate (verse 6), ' Descendet sicut pluvia in vellus '—'he shall come down like rain into a fleece,' and the ' Rorate coeli desuper' of Isaiah—' Drop dew, ye heavens from above, and let the clouds rain down the just one '.[3]

Adam expounds the mystery thus :

> tu, perfusa coeli rore,
> castitatis salvo flore,
> novum florem novo more
> protulisti saeculo.[4]

But here perhaps he is thinking mainly of Isaiah xlv.   In Sequence lxv [5] he combines the symbols of the Fleece and the Burning Bush :

---

[1] Mone, ii. 237 (*Anal. Hymn.* xxxv, p. 193, *Psalterium beatae Mariae*):
      ave manna candidior,
      de qua fit melle dulcior
      panis, quo coeli curia
      vivit nec non ecclesia.
Cf. Mone, ii. 356 (*Anal. Hymn.* l, p. 512, strophe 2), the thought of which is similar. The author is Guido of Bazoches.

[2] Mâle, *L'art religieux du XIIIe siècle*, p. 179.

[3] Isa. xlv. 8.

[4] Sequence lxvi. 25–8.

[5] Lines 49–54 ; cf. lxxiv. 39 ; xcv. 22–4 ; cf. Mone, ii. 10 (*Anal. Hymn.* v, p. 50):
      ut super vellus pluvia
      sic descendit in Mariam.
Cf. also Mone, ii. 35 (*Anal. Hymn.* l, p. 513; this hymn is by Guido of Bazoches) ; Mone, ii. 53 (*Anal. Hymn.* liv, p. 346) ; Mone, ii. 196.

> super vellus ros descendens
> et in rubo flamma splendens,
>   (neutrum tamen laeditur),
> fuit Christus carnem sumens,
> in te tamen non consumens
>   pudorem, dum gignitur.

Similarly a trope,[1] of unknown authorship :

> rore vellus irrigatur,
> rubens ardens non crematur,
> quando verbum incarnatur
> et intacto conservatur
>   puellari gremio.

(6) *The Rod of Jesse.*

Isaiah xi. 1 'Et egredietur virga de radice Iesse, et flos de radice eius ascendet.'

Honorius, col. 904,[2] Jesse was the father of King David, who was the root of this sacred stock. From this root David grew as a tree, of which a noble rod sprung, because the Virgin Mary derived her ancestry from his offspring. This rod brought forth a flower, when the Virgin Mary bore Jesus. For he himself saith : " I am the flower of the field and the lily of the valleys " (Cant. ii). A field is soil untilled, that is, an unwedded virgin. This field produced a precious flower when Christ born of a virgin shone forth on the world.'

Adam uses this symbol in his second Sequence, on the Nativity. 'The rod of Jesse flowered. The root brings forth a rod, the rod a flower, the Virgin brings forth the Saviour, as the law foretold. The root signifies David, the rod is Mary, who descended from his royal seed; the Child who is born unto us is the flower, rightly likened thereunto for his exceeding loveliness.'[3]

Similarly in Sequence lxv (55–60).

> de te virga progressurum
> florem mundo profuturum
> Isaïas cecinit,

[1] Mone, ii. 38 (*Anal. Hymn.* xlix, p. 46).

[2] In another place (*Speculum Eccles.*, Migne, clxxii, col. 1001), Honorius, commenting on the same passage from Isaiah, says, 'Christ was the root of Jesse according to His divinity, but born of the rod which sprang forth from it, according to His humanity.'

[3]
> virga Iesse floruit.
> radix virgam, virga florem,
> virgo profert salvatorem
>   sicut lex praecinuit.
> radix David typum gessit,
> virga matris quae processit
>   ex regali semine ;
> flos est nobis puer natus,
> iure flori comparatus
>   prae mira dulcedine.

> flore Christum praefigurans
> cuius virtus semper durans
> nec coepit, nec desinit.[1]

and in the Sequence, by an unknown author, in Mone,[2]

> felix Iesse gignens prolem,
> virga florem, virgo solem,
> flos designat salvatorem,
> virga florens virginem.

The idea of Honorius that the Virgin is the 'untilled field' is illustrated in a hymn clearly belonging to the later Middle Ages,

> tu campus non arabilis
> tua nunc amoenitas
> rubrum florem protulit.[3]

(7) *The Closed Door of Ezekiel.*

Ezekiel xliv. 2 ' Porta haec clausa erit: non aperietur, et vir non transibit per eam: quoniam Dominus Deus Israel ingressus est per eam.'

Honorius, col. 905, 'Ezekiel beheld a door always shut, through which the King of Kings alone passed and left it shut. The blessed Mary is the gate of heaven, for, before the birth and during the birth, she was a virgin, and remained a virgin after the birth.'

' The Virgin ', says the poet,[4] 'is this closed door, which God, for a hidden reason, had closed unto men.'

> haec est illa porta clausa,
> quam latente deus causa
> clauserat hominibus.

The whole meaning of the vision of Ezekiel, which was one of the main medieval arguments for the perpetual virginity of Mary, is expounded more fully in a twelfth-century rimed Office.[5]

> o Maria clausa porta,
> quam nemo aperuit,
> princeps ille, qui transivit,
> deus et homo fuit,
> nec ingressu nec egressu
> violavit clausulam,
> sed, quam prius non habebat,
> sumpsit carnis fibulam,
> sic togatus tanquam sponsus
> suo processit thalamo.

---

[1] Cf. Sequence v. 18-24; lxxxix. 18-23; xcvi. 1-6; xcvii. 9-12; Mone, ii. 9 (*Anal. Hymn.* v, p. 48).
[2] Mone, ii. 73 (*Anal. Hymn.* liv, p. 377).
[3] Mone, ii. 414.
[4] Sequence lxxiv. 36-8.
[5] Mone, ii. 11 (*Anal. Hymn.* v, p. 49).

The closed door is, therefore, not merely a symbol of the virgin birth of Christ, but of the perpetual virginity of Mary, both before, during, and after the birth. It was so used by Ambrose to refute the contrary opinion, which had been held by such great authorities as Tertullian, Irenaeus, and Origen.[1]

(8) *Daniel's Mountain.*

Daniel ii. 34 'Abscissus est lapis de monte sine manibus.'
Honorius, col. 905, 'The stone which was cut out of the mountain without the hands of any one breaking it off is Christ, born of a Virgin without the hands of any one embracing her.'

Here the symbol merely refers to the Virgin birth, as in Adam's second Sequence.[2]

> quid de monte lapis caesus
> sine manu, nisi Iesus
>   qui de regum linea,
>   sine carnis opere,
>   de carne puerperae
>   processit virginea ?

Similarly in Sequence lxxxix.[3]

> Daniel, dic clara fronte :
> 'hic abscissus est de monte
>   lapis frangens statuam.'
> mons est Virgo, lapis Verbum
> destruens regnum superbum
>   per legem perpetuam.

These examples are sufficient to show that, as the Church found the figure of Christ everywhere in the Old Testament, so it discovered everywhere the types of His mother and the symbols of her virginity. If, therefore, in the divine writings, God had so honoured Mary by manifesting through the prophets her virginity and her destiny as the mother of the Saviour, it is clear that the allegorical exposition of the Scriptures contributed greatly to the position which she occupied in Christian theology. It can have caused no scandal when a Franciscan admirer wrote in her honour a *Te Deum* in this manner :

---

[1] See above, p. 363 sq.; the story of Daniel in the Den of Lions, who is fed by Habakkuk without the seals being broken, is a symbol of the perpetual virginity; cf. Honorius, *Speculum Eccles.*, col. 905.
[2] Lines 17–22.
[3] Lines 24–9; cf. Mone, ii. 65 (*Anal. Hymn.* liv, p. 143).

te matrem laudamus, te virginem confitemur ;
te aeterni patris, stella maris, splendor illuminat ;
tibi omnes angeli, tibi caeli et universae potestates,
tibi cherubin et seraphin humili nobiscum voce proclamant,
virgo, virgo, virgo virginum sine exemplo,
ante partum et in partu et post partum.[1]

This is the veritable apotheosis of Mary, of whom Dante could say, 'Look on the face which is likest Christ's, for its brightness alone can make thee fit to look on His'.[2]   Her final apotheosis is, indeed, in the Paradise of Dante, who sees in her the 'fixed end of the eternal counsel'.

qui sei a noi meridiana face
di caritate, e guiso, intra i mortali,
sei di speranza fontana vivace,

donna, sei tanto grande e tanto vali,
che qual vuol grazia ed a te non ricorre,
sua disianza vuol volar senz' ali.[3]

The swiftest way for a prayer to reach its goal was by an appeal to the womanly sympathy of the Queen of Heaven.

[1] Mone, ii. 229; printed in Bonaventura's works (Paris 1878), xiv. 222, along with a 'parody' of the Psaltery in honour of Mary ; most-curious of all is the version of the Athanasian Creed, beginning 'Quicumque vult salvus esse, ante omnia opus est : ut teneat de Maria firmam fidem,' &c.
[2] *Paradiso* xxxii. 85–7.
[3] ib., xxxiii. 10–15.

XII.

THE THIRTEENTH CENTURY

§ 1. *English Poets in the Thirteenth Century: Alexander Neckham; John Garland; John of Hoveden.*

IN the thirteenth century England experienced to the full the influences, religious, intellectual, and political, which were making that century the culminating point of medieval culture. In political development, indeed, England may be said to have reached a stage far in advance of the rest of Europe. The great Charter, the emergence of political parties and political principles under Henry III, and the progress of 'constitutional mechanism'[1] during the second half of the century are conspicuous signs of national growth. The middle class was now reaching the stage of political self-consciousness, and was testing its capacity for a measure of self-government. The constitutional struggle of Henry III's reign was led, indeed, by the barons, and principally by Simon, Earl of Leicester, but the educated middle class, the lower clergy, and the Franciscans lent their support to what they regarded as the cause of liberty against a lawless tyranny. The divisions of political feeling, the hopes and fears of the men who deplored the corruption of the times and the plight of their country, found expression in a number of political songs and satires, in Latin, in Anglo-Norman French, and in English.[2] The aims of the baronial party are set forth by a clerical supporter, almost certainly a Franciscan of the school of Adam Marsh, who wrote just after the battle of Lewes.[3] The song is full of the praises of Earl Simon, who, like another Mattathias, the leader of the Jews against the tyrant Antiochus, led the English against their oppressors.

> set hanc videns populi deus agoniam
> dat in fine seculi novum Mathathiam,
> qui cum suis filiis zelans zelum legis
> nec cedit iniuriis nec furori regis.[4]

---

[1] Stubbs, *Constitutional History*, ii. 304 sqq.
[2] Wright, *The Political Songs of England from the reign of John to that of Edward II, Camden Society*, 1839.
[3] *The Song of Lewes*, ed. Kingsford, Oxford 1890, p. xviii.
[4] ib., p. 3.

The poem is filled with these scriptural reminiscences, which betray the clerical education of its author. Other verses of the time attack the avarice of the bishops, and the author is again a clerk, who used the measures of the sequence to denounce his unworthy superiors.

> tu qui tenes hunc tenorem,
> frustra dicis te pastorem ;
> nec te regis ut rectorem,
> rerum mersus in ardorem :
>   haec est alia
>   sanguisugae filia,
>   quam venalis curia
> duxit in uxorem.[1]

Some of the satire is more playful and less full of this *saeva indignatio*. The extravagance of foreign fashions in dress, which were imported along with the foreigners into England, gave rise to a *Song on Tailors*, in sequence form.

> ego dixi, dii estis;
> quae dicenda sunt in festis
>   quare praetermitterem ?
> dii, revera, qui potestis
> in figuram novae vestis
>   transmutare veterem.[2]

When Simon died, he was venerated as a saint, and an office was composed for his commemoration by his Franciscan friends. Nor did he appear only as a saint to those who lamented him ; by his death in battle he had suffered a kind of martyrdom, which was confirmed by the miracles wrought at the ' Earl's Well ', near Evesham, and elsewhere.[3] How the violence of his death was transfigured into the likeness of a martyr's passion is shown in the following fragment :

> salve, Symon Montis-Fortis,
>   totius flos militiae,
> duras poenas passus mortis,
>   protector gentis Angliae.
> sunt de sanctis inaudita,
> cunctis passis in hac vita,
>   quemquam passum talia ;

---

[1] Wright, p. 46.
[2] ib., p. 52 ; or perhaps we should rather, with Meyer, *Gött. Nachr.*, 1907, p. 87, regard it as a satire on misers who adapt their old clothes instead of giving them away. He would assign the verses to the ' Primate ', Hugh of Orléans, in the twelfth century.
[3] G. W. Prothero, *Life of Simon de Montfort*, London 1877, pp. 371 sqq.

> manus, pedes amputari,
> caput, corpus vulnerari,
>   abscidi virilia.
> sis pro nobis intercessor
> apud deum, qui defensor
>   in terris extiteras.[1]

Another hymn compares the Earl to Thomas of Canterbury. Both fought against evil laws and both for liberty, one in the State and the other in the Church.

> nunc uterque pugil fortis,
> post occasum dirae mortis
> in agone sacrae sortis
>   migrat ad celestia.[2]

A like honour of popular canonization was paid in the reign of Edward II to Thomas, Earl of Lancaster, whose execution in 1322 ended a selfish career, and won him the temporary fame of a martyr. The *Office of S. Thomas of Lancaster*[3] is the ambitious effort of one of his clerical followers, who, with less justification than in the case of Simon, did not hesitate to compare his death with that of Thomas of Canterbury, and to imitate the eucharistic hymn of Thomas Aquinas in praising his miracles and merits.

> pange, lingua, gloriosi
> comitis martyrium,
> sanguinisque preciosi
> Thomae floris militum,
> germinisque generosi
> laudis, lucis comitum.

Even richer and of greater interest than this Latin poetry is the more popular political and satirical verse in the language of the people, but we may guess that most of it was also written by clerks.

Along with this political awakening, England felt the force of the religious movement which was giving a new life to the Western Church. The great religious event was the coming of the Franciscans in 1224. They soon had a settlement in every important town, and England was not long in providing them with men who rose to eminence in the order. At Oxford they persuaded the great scholar, Robert Grosseteste, to be their lecturer;[4] for in England, as elsewhere, they began the pursuit

---

[1] Prothero, op. cit., pp. 379-80; Wright, p. 124.

[2] Prothero, p. 389.

[3] Wright, pp. 268 sqq.

[4] Thomas [of Eccleston], *De adventu fratrum minorum in Angliam*, p. 60, ed.

of learning both at the Universities and in their provincial houses. While they produced scholars like Adam Marsh and Roger Bacon, they could boast in John Pecham not only a scholar and lawyer, but one who equalled in his expression of the devotional side of the Franciscan mission, the greatest poets of the order. The English contribution to the poetry of the Passion belongs to the general history of Franciscan verse, and here it requires only a passing mention.

It was not merely through the religious revival that England shared in the wider life of Western Europe. In the intellectual movement of the time England, as in the twelfth century, still depended on Paris. There were schools at Oxford and Cambridge, but sooner or later the attraction of Paris drew the student to the most famous centre of learning in Christendom. Not a few of the English scholars at Paris won an international reputation for the depth and variety of their learning. Roger Bacon and Robert Grosseteste stand apart from the rest, but in their own day Alexander Neckham and John Garland, both Englishmen, won, as grammarians and teachers, an enormous reputation. They are not only the representative scholars, but the representative poets in the England of the thirteenth century. They took all learning for their province; in those days of varied accomplishments a man might win a reputation for knowledge in branches of study so far apart as jurisprudence and medicine, and he might easily add a talent for versification, and exercise it with great persistence without suspecting that there is something which lies deeper than the mechanism of syllables.

Alexander Neckham[1] was a man of science as well as a grammarian and poet. He was born at S. Albans in 1157 on the same September night on which the future King Richard was born at Windsor, and he and Richard were foster-brothers. Alexander was educated at S. Albans, and made such progress that he was, it seems, placed in charge of the school at Dunstable. Thence he proceeded to Paris, entering the school of Petit-Pont; but he soon became a teacher himself, lecturing on grammar and rhetoric, including poetry. He went the whole

A. G. Little, in *Collection d'études et de documents . . . du moyen âge*, vii, Paris 1909.
[1] On Neckham see *Camb. Hist. of Engl. Lit.* i. 193 ; Wright, *Introd.* to *De naturis rerum, Rolls Series*, vol. 34, London 1863; Du Méril, *Poésies inédites du moyen âge*, pp. 169 sqq.; but the best account is still Hauréau's article in the *Nouvelle biographie générale*. For a list of Neckham's works see M. Esposito in *E.H.R.*, 1915, pp. 460 sqq.

round of the studies, 'lectio sacra', canon law, civil law, and medicine. Speaking of Paris, he says:

> vix aliquis locus est dicta mihi notior urbe,
>   qua Modici Pontis parva columna fui.
> hic artes didici docuique fideliter, inde
>   accessit studio lectio sacra meo.
> audivi canones, Hippocratem, cum Galieno,
>   ius civile mihi displicuisse neges.[1]

His contemporaries facetiously spelt his name in Latin, Nequam. It is said that when he applied to the Abbot of S. Albans for the headship of his old school, in the words, ' si vis, veniam, sin autem', he received the witty answer, 'si bonus es, venias; si nequam, nequaquam', and that, offended at this reply, he left the Benedictines and joined the Augustinians of Cirencester. Whatever the truth about this incident may be, he certainly became Abbot at Cirencester in 1213. He died at Kempsey in 1217, and was buried in Worcester Cathedral.

This is not the place to discuss the scientific learning of Alexander Neckham. Roger Bacon does not altogether despise his grammatical attainments, but he condemns him for various errors, remarking finally, ' Hic Alexander in multis vera et utilia scripsit ; sed tamen inter auctores (authorities) non potest, nec debet, iusto titulo numerari'.[2] Neckham's best known work is the *De naturis rerum*, a curious prose treatise combining a popular handbook of natural science with a commentary on *Ecclesiastes*. The scientific part is of some interest, but it is the numerous anecdotes and observations collected from popular superstitions and contemporary beliefs which enliven the work for the ordinary reader. Inevitably, the author must find a moral meaning for each scientific fact, whether he is comparing the firmament with the Church, or explaining that the spots on the moon were created by God to remind sinful man of his fallen nature. In dealing with natural history, Neckham produces a complete *Physiologus* and *Bestiary*, with the usual allegorical accompaniment. He tells how the oyster is the type of the monk, safe within its shell as the monk in his cloister; if it ventures out it is devoured by its enemies. This brief description gives a wholly inadequate account of the varied contents of the *De naturis rerum*, which covers all manner of subjects in its

---

[1] *De laudibus divinae sapientiae*, Wright, p. 503.

[2] *Opera inedita*, ed. Brewer, *Rolls Series*, p. 457, London 1859.

meandering course—the art of building, the whole range of studies, the seven arts, the schools, the universities, the classes of society, the vices of the age and of all ages.

In his later years Alexander undertook the labour of setting out, in verse, under the title *De laudibus divinae sapientiae*,[1] the main part of his treatise, omitting most of the anecdotes and making certain additions. He intended to present it, he tells us, to the Abbey of Gloucester, or, failing this, to S. Albans. The ten books into which it is divided treat of the divine wisdom displayed in the creation of the angels and the heavenly bodies, the four elements, and the creatures living in earth, in air, and sea. The poet digresses into geography and meteorology as well as into natural history, and he finds room for the wonders of Stonehenge and of Rome. No less, he delves into the earth and tells of metals and precious stones, and then of plants and herbs and trees. Finally, he reaches the animals and man, science and the seven arts.

His description of Nazareth, the 'city of flowers', will give an idea of the compass of his art.[2]

> Nazareth, urbs florens, salve, qua floruit hortus
> virgineus, florem virgula sicca dedit.
> virgula concepit florem, virguncula fructum,
> flos vernans, fructus deliciosus erat.
> est in flore decor et odoris gratia spirans ;
> fructum commendas, deliciose sapor.
> cerno candorem floris, mirorque ruborem ;
> lacteus est candor purpureusque rubor.

An interesting and almost beautiful passage is one in which he compares the earth, solid and secure in spite of earthquake and storm, with the Church of Christ, which

> looks on tempests and is never shaken.

As the earth is decked with flowers, roses, lilies, and violets, so is the Church adorned with flowers of her own, roses of her martyrs, and lilies of those whose monastic lives yield a sweet savour of innocence and purity. He addresses the Church :[3]

---

[1] ed. Wright, as appendix to *De naturis rerum*, pp. 357 sqq. ; on the defects of this edition see Esposito, *E.H.R.*, 1915, p. 462.

[2] Wright, p. 462.
[3] ib., pp. 442-3.

o mater, quae sublata foecundior extat
  prole, nec ablata, virgo pudica parens.
rursum terra rosis vernantibus est decorata,
  candoris nivei lilia gignit humus.
dat violas dulci pictas ferrugine, sponsa
  Christi floribus est sic redimita suis.
quos rosa martyrii, flos campi, donat honore,
  tanto purpureas dicimus esse rosas,
hos assertores fidei, stabilesque columnas,
  invictosque duces, ecclesiaeque decus.
quis neget? allegant caput hi roseumque cruorem,
  nec pretio procerum mors pretiosa caret,
mors est discrimen huius caliginis atque
  lucis quae nubis nescia semper erit.
lilia sunt quos munditiae commendat honestas,
  quorum cum vita coelibe suavis odor.
angelicam datur his in terris ducere vitam,
  dum mens in casto corpore casta nitet.

Another long poem, the ascription of which to Alexander
Neckham is more than doubtful,[1] is concerned in a semi-satirical
manner with the ideal of monasticism.[2]

quid deceat monachum, vel qualis debeat esse.

It sets before the monks, in the form of severe admonition, what
manner of life they ought to lead.   For it is not the tonsure and
the coarse vestment which make the monk, but strength of soul,
contempt of the world, and a sober and godly conversation.
These form the chariot which will bear them aloft to heaven.
For Christ is not deceived by appearances, and those who have
been false to their vows will receive His condemnation.   The
moral is—let them change their way of life, turn aside from
sloth, and diligently set their face against the manifold tempta-
tions to which a monk is so easily subject.   In that century the
monastic reforms had lost their force, the manners of monks
had become a by-word, and the world was ripe for S. Francis.

The poem is an essay on the contempt of the world.   It
reminds the monks that mortal flesh grows old like a garment,
old age creeps on unseen, the days of man are as a smoke and
a shadow that pass away:

fumus et umbra levis, tota est haec gloria mundi.

---

[1] See Du Méril, op. cit., p. 170 ; Hauréau, *Journal des savants*, 1882, p. 172,
says the author is a monk, perhaps Roger
of Caen, a monk of Bec.
  [2] *De vita monachorum*, Wright, *Satirical Poets*, ii. 175 sqq.

Poverty alone is safe, the judgement alone is certain; before the dread tribunal riches and race can exercise no influence. Again the poem takes up the note of warning against the things of this world, and above all against women :

> occidunt animas, multos ad tartara mittunt,
> et monachis pestis nulla timenda magis.[1]

A discussion of the *Novus Aesopus*, versified fables from Æsop which are attributed to Neckham, would lead us too far,[2] and we must pass now to his religious lyrical pieces in which he uses with skill the rimed and rhythmical measures which suited his subjects best.[3]   There are nine pieces in sequence form dedicated to the Virgin, and four to S. Mary Magdalene. Perhaps the most striking piece is that which begins :

1. in te concipitur,
   o virgo regia,
   rex, a quo regitur
   caelestis regia ;
   in te conectitur
   duplex substantia,
   quibus accingitur
   gigas ad proelia.[4]

2. intra te clauditur,
   qui claudit omnia,
   aeternus nascitur
   pater ex filia ;
   candoris igitur
   non marcent lilia,
   nec ardens patitur
   rubus [5] incendia.

3. succensa radio
   superni luminis
   splendens in medio
   nostrae caliginis ;
   dum incarnatio
   fit in te numinis,
   nostrae corruptio
   cedit originis.

4. verbi conceptio
   nil habet criminis,
   nec flore proprio
   florere desinis ;
   in te fit unio
   matris et virginis,
   in tuo filio
   dei et hominis.[6]

All the verses on the Virgin are filled with those mystical and allegorical allusions which we have seen in the sequences of the Victorine school.   One type which has not been noted before is worth mentioning.   Moses in the ark of bulrushes is a type of the Virgin birth.

---

[1] p. 188.
[2] Text in Du Méril, op. cit., pp. 176 sqq., and full discussion ; see also Hervieux, *Les fabulistes latins*, ii, pp. 392 sqq., Paris 1894.
[3] Text, *Anal. Hymn.* xlviii, pp. 262 sqq.

[4] The reference is to Ps. xix. 5, the supposed double nature of the giant referring to Christ.
[5] The burning bush, see above, p. 369.
[6] *Anal. Hymn.* xlviii, p. 269.

in fiscella scirpea
Moyses reconditur,
facie siderea
victa pie flectitur
Pharaonis filia.[1]

· These liturgical verses of Neckham attain a fair level of
technical excellence such as might be expected from a man of
his abilities, but it would be vain to search his lines on Mary
Magdalene for a sign of that beauty and pathos which Philip de
Grève [2] could give to his *Pange, lingua, Magdalenae.*

Among the curiosities of medieval literature is Alexander's
prose treatise which bears the strange title *Corrogationes Promethei.* M. Paul Meyer has ingeniously explained it as ' les
compilations de Prométhée ',[3] and he tells us that by Prometheus
the author means himself, a man condemned to idleness, like
Prometheus chained to the rock. This explanation throws light
on the title of a poem by Neckham which bears this preface,
' incipiunt metrice corrogaciones Novi Promothei ',[4] though the
subject of the poem is not the same as that of the treatise. The
latter consists of chapters on Latin grammar to which is joined
a verbal commentary on the Bible, whereas the subject of the
poem is apparently ' the general considerations which ought to
guide the conduct of one who intends to become an abbot '.[5]
Did he write it for his own edification while waiting for his
expected preferment ? If so, he shows throughout the course
of the poem an attractive self-complacency which deserved to
be rewarded. He tells us that his ideal is that of a peaceful
community,

quo pacis crescit oliva,
regnat amor concors, gratia, vera fides,

and firmness and caution are to be his guiding principles, while
justice is always to be accompanied by mercy. The phase of
the New Prometheus was short, as is evident if we consider
only his vast treatise on the *Song of Songs*, which is hardly

[1] *Anal. Hymn.* xlviii, p. 265.
[2] See below, p. 399.
[3] *Notices et extraits des mss.*, xxxv,
ii. 652, to which I refer the reader for a
full statement of the reasons for accepting
this explanation of the meaning of the
title.
[4] Text, ed. Esposito, *E.H.R.*, 1915,
pp. 457 sqq.
[5] ib., p. 452.

likely to be disturbed from its resting-place in Oxford libraries.[1] It is not surprising to learn that it deals more with the Virgin Mary and with the mystery of the Incarnation than with the *Song of Songs.*

A scholar, grammarian, and poet like Alexander Neckham was Johannes de Garlandia, or John Garland,[2] an Englishman, whose career was equally distinguished, and whose verses were equally, if not so wisely, acclaimed. John was born about 1180. He studied at Oxford under John of London, and found his way to Paris, where he is supposed to have been a pupil of Alan of Lille.[3] If England was his mother, France, he tells us, was his foster-mother :

Anglia cui mater fuerat, cui Gallia nutrix,[4]

and France more than England was destined to be his home. He was involved in some way in the great crusade which, with the blessing of the Pope, Simon de Montfort was leading against the subjects of the Count of Toulouse. He witnessed part at any rate of that terrible and bloody struggle called the Albigensian crusade, and he was with the army before Toulouse when Simon met his death (1218). Philip Augustus took over the lordship of Toulouse from Simon's feeble son Amaury, and under Louis VIII the crusade was actively conducted by the royal power. In 1229, under the regency of Blanche of Castille, a peace was made at Meaux. The Pope set up two institutions to deal with what remained of heresy in the south—the Inquisition and a University at Toulouse. The Dominicans controlled both institutions, but John Garland was one of the Paris professors selected by the Papal legate to organize the new university. Gregory IX granted to all the students at Toulouse, masters and scholars, 'omnium peccaminum suorum plenariam indulgentiam'.[5] In the first flush of enthusiasm the masters declared, in a circular letter to the other *studia generalia,* that the flowers had appeared in their land and the time of the pruning of vines had come. They admonished the new Achilles not to be

---

[1] ib., p. 463; P. Meyer, *Notices et extraits des mss.,* xxxv, ii. 643.
[2] On Johannes de Garlandia see *Hist. Litt.* viii. 83-99, xxi. 369-73, xxii. 11-13, and 77-103; Johannis de Garlandia, *De triumphis ecclesiae,* ed. Wright, *Roxburghe Club,* 1856, Introd. For a list of his works see Faral, *Les arts poétiques du*

XIIe et du XIIIe siècle, pp. 40 sqq.
[3] Alan died in 1202; Haskins, *Studies in Medieval Science,* p. 359, note 16, denies that Garland could have studied under Alan.
[4] *De triumphis,* p. 59.
[5] ib., p. 96.

detained from Troy by any Deidamia, and they prayed that no
Thersites might deprive Ajax of his laurels.   They boasted the
peace and liberty of their university, free from the restrictions
on study imposed at Paris, and they enlarged on the cheapness
of living and the courtesy of the people.   During the three
years John remained at Toulouse he had leisure to reflect on
the contrast between the brilliant picture drawn by the masters
and the more sober reality presented by experience.   The
university did not fulfil its promise, the salaries of the professors
were not regularly paid, and the courtesy of the people changed
under the combined oppression of the French garrison and of
the Inquisition.   The university naturally suffered as one of the
engines of tyranny; the masters and students dispersed, and
John was one of the first to make his escape.   After a dangerous
journey he reached Paris:

> Parisius venio peregrinus cum peregrinis,
>   gratia sit proli, virgo Maria, tuae.[1]

At Paris he enjoyed at once fame and safety.   His most distinguished pupil was Roger Bacon, who, in his *Compendium Studii*,[2]
pays him the rare compliment of a respectful mention.   John
appears to have died, either at Paris or in England, about the
year 1258, having lived through the minority of S. Louis, and
watched the growing fame of the saintly king, which was not
eclipsed by the disastrous events at Damietta.

John Garland was above all else a teacher.   He composed
a *Dictionnarius* or Latin vocabulary, a *Compendium Grammaticae*, and a versified *Accentuarium*[3] for the use of his pupils.
Of this latter he says complacently that it was received at Paris
with great favour.   Much of his other instructional work is, after
the medieval custom, also in verse.   The *Exempla honestae
vitae*[4] form a book of examples of useful styles for students of
poetry and rhetoric, the subjects being chosen at the same time
for moral edification.   The full title of the work is, *Exempla
honestae vitae, quam debent habere praelati, coloribus verborum et
sententiarum insignita*.   One example, of an 'interrogation', will
show the author's manner:

> dic mihi, detractor: quid garris? quid tibi lingua
>   garrula lucratur? disce silere, loquax![5]

[1] *De triumphis*, p. 101.
[2] ed. Brewer, p. 453.
[3] Hauréau, *Notices et extraits des mss.*
xxvii, ii, pp. 53 sqq.

[4] *Die exempla honestae vitae des
Iohannes de Garlandia*, ed. Habel, in
Romanische Forschungen, xxix. 131 sqq.
[5] ib., p. 139.

The purely religious verse of John Garland is not of much greater interest than his pedagogic pieces. The *De Mysteriis Ecclesiae*[1] is an hexameter poem dedicated to Fulk, Dean of York, and afterwards Bishop of London (d. 1259):

> Anglia quo fulget, quo gaudent praesule claro
> Londiniae, quo Parisius scrutante sophiam
> florebat studium; basis aurea, fulgide Fulco,
> firmae iustitiae, mysteria suscipe sacrae
> ecclesiae, studio distincta metroque Ioannis,
> tutius ut veniant in apertum iudice tanto
> mystica, Parisius licet haec recitata probentur,
> exposcunt subtile tuum, pie pastor, acumen,
> qui sacer instituis sacros ad sacra ministros.[2]

This is the dedication; the poem itself deals with the Church, its buildings, its services, ministers, and vestments, in the usual terms of allegory and symbolism.

A longer poem, called *De Triumphis Ecclesiae*, is in elegiacs. It is valuable for its references to contemporary events, such as the wars of England and France, the third crusade, the campaign against the Albigensians, and the foundation of the university of Toulouse. But its miserable prosody, its lack of form and structure, its meaningless digressions easily discourage a reader who begins it with the expectation of following it to the end. The theme is the triumph of the Church against infidel and heretic, Saracen and Albigeois. The Christian kings of Europe are admonished to make up their quarrels among themselves or against the Church, and to unite under the banner of the Cross against the enemies of the faith. But the theme is obscured by endless digressions, on Dunstan and the devil, on the fate of Theodoric, on the four saints named Julian, and it is only occasionally that the reader obtains a glimpse of the real subject of this disordered epic. But the plea for Christian unity comes in more than once:

> si reges nostros concordia vera ligaret,
> Christo curvaret India tota genu.
> ense Machometus meteretur, te, Dionisi,
> Chaldeus coleret Angligenamque Thomam.[3]

John displays his classical learning when he has a chance, but his versification, like that of others among his contemporaries

---

[1] B. W. Otto, *Comment. crit. in codices biblioth. Gissensis*, pp. 131 sqq., Giessen, 1842; Leyser, *Hist. poet. et poemat. medii aevi*, pp. 339 sqq.
[2] Otto, p. 131.
[3] *De triumphis*, p. 26.

who wrote in classical measures, shows a falling off from the standard set by the schools of Chartres and Le Mans in the eleventh century. In order to fit the name of Pope Innocent into his verse he employs a curious licence, which has, however, a classical parallel:

> Gregorii quartus In papa—nocentius haeres
> hostibus occurrit canonis ense sui.[1]

In another passage he exhibits his skill, and, to us, his bad taste in forming *versus retrogradi* which read the same backwards as forwards:

> Parisius proba non pugnat gens, parcere clero
> provida, non curat perfidiam sua lex.
> lex sua perfidiam curat, non provida clero
> parcere, gens pugnat non proba Parisius.[2]

John Garland wrote hymns and other religious pieces,[3] and, although they do not give us a high idea of his poetical talent, they do not lose much by comparison with the lesser liturgical verse of the Middle Ages. Those in classical metres are poor and undistinguished, but the Sequence on the Virgin Mary is a fair specimen of the later style, of which, after Adam of S. Victor, it was easy for any intelligent versifier to gain a superficial mastery.

1 virgo mater salvatoris. 'stella maris, stilla roris, et cella dulcedinis.	da spiramen veri floris, florem fructus, et odoris, fructum fortitudinis.
2 in hoc mari sis solamen nobis, cymba, dux, tutamen. remex, aura, statio,	aura perfles in hoc mari, quae praefulges singulari semper igne praevio.[4]

A Sequence on S. Catherine of Alexandria follows the same manner. More interest attaches to the piece, *De Licentia puerorum circa natale Domini*, which is a kind of holiday ode addressed by pupils to their master, such an ode as John would have liked himself to have received, for the merits of the master are extolled, and his eloquence is compared with Tully's:

---

[1] *De triumphis*, p. 10; cf. similarly, Geoffrey de Vinsauf's Dedication to Innocent III (Leyser, p. 861):
Divide sic nomen: IN praefer, et adde
  NOCENTI;
efficiturque, comes metri; sic et tua virtus,
pluribus sequatur divisa, sed integra nulli.

[2] *De triumphis*, p. 41.
[3] See *Anal. Hymn.* li, pp. 546 sqq.; Zarncke prints some of these pieces without being aware of their authorship, in *Leipzig. Sitzungsber.* (1871) xxiii. 34 sqq.
[4] *Anal. Hymn.* li, p. 548.

sapit linguam Tullii
   vox oris facundi,
fontem pigmentarium
   pectoris profundi,
doctrinale balsamum
   sermonis iucundi
dictaque mirantum
   magni primordia mundi.[1]

Each verse concludes with a classical quotation adroitly chosen, a witness to a humanistic spirit capable of wearing its learning, for once, lightly and humorously.[2] The Virgilian prophecies of Christ are not forgotten in this Christmas 'breaking-up' song:

regis natalitia
   caelestis exalto,
iam nova progenies
   caelo demittitur alto.

The last quotation is from the *Ars Amatoria*, a favourite medieval source:

inscribat foliis: Naso magister erat.

Both Alexander Neckham and John Garland were mainly conspicuous as grammarians and teachers. Inspired religious poetry was not lacking in the thirteenth century in England, but it is not to be found in their pages. In John Pecham, Archbishop of Canterbury, England possessed one of the greatest of the medieval poets, and by his side may be placed John of Hoveden, or as we should more properly call him, John of Howden, who, now that the whole of his Latin poetry is available in critical editions, is seen to be one of the major religious poets of the Middle Ages.[3] He was born, it would seem, in London, and it appears likely that he was educated at Oxford, as his poetry contains allusions which show a thorough acquaintance with the physical and astronomical theories in vogue at that University. He was the author of a scientific treatise, *Practica Chilindri*,[4] and the Chronicle of Lanercost tells us that he was skilled in astrology. The same Chronicle states that he was a

---

[1] *Anal. Hymn.* li, p. 554.
[2] Cf. *Carmina Burana*, I, 2, p. 173 sq., for a similar device in a profane song, where Ovid is the source.
[3] *Philomena*, ed. C. Blume, Leipzig 1930; *Poems of John of Hoveden*, ed. F. J. E. Raby, *Surtees Society*, cliv, 1939.
[4] Ed. E. Brock, *Essays on Chaucer*, *Chaucer Soc.* 1868, pp. 31 sqq.

Prebendary of Howden, a man of saintly life, given to hospitality and works of mercy; that he began, at his own cost, the new Choir at Howden and that he foretold that it would be completed after his own death, so that 'out of the offerings of the crowds of visitors [at his tomb] we see not only the choir but the spacious and sumptuous nave of the church being completed'. The continuator of William of Newburgh tells us that miracles were wrought at the tomb, and that when the Mass was being sung before the burial of his body, at the elevation the hands of the dead man were seen to be lifted up towards the Host and lowered again when the elevation was over.

John of Howden was clerk or chaplain to Queen Eleanor, the mother of Edward I, and it was for her that he composed in Anglo-Norman French a long poem, which, under the title of *Rossignol*, gave her, not a literal rendering of his great poem, the *Philomena*, but a composition on similar lines in which he could allow himself freedom of invention and of poetical adornment.[1] The death of the poet is probably to be placed in the year 1275.

The *Philomena* is undoubtedly Howden's masterpiece. It contains over a thousand stanzas in a measure which had been often used since the twelfth century; it begins:

> ave, Verbum, ens in principio,
> caro factum pudoris gremio,
> fac quod fragret praesens laudatio
> et placeris parvo praeconio.
>
> et tu stella maris eximia,
> mater patris et nati filia,
> laude, precor, reple praecordia,
> cum sis laudis mira materia.
>
> Virgo, David orta progenie,
> dola linguam hanc imperitiae
> in sonantis lyram placentiae,
> et iam psallas manu munditiae.[2]

The poem is a long personal meditation on the almighty power of love as shown in the incarnation, the life, and the passion of the Saviour. With this passion is linked, as in other poems of Howden, the compassion of the mother of Christ, and Love is

---

[1] See L. W. Stone, *Jean de Howden, poète anglo-normande du XIIIᵉ siècle, Romania*, lxix (1945), pp. 496 sqq.   [2] *Philomena*, p. 3.

invoked as the scribe, to write these sufferings on the heart of the poet:

> fortis Amor, forti conamine
> cordis mei scribas volumine
> carnem natum virenti virgine,
> roris nantem in nati flumine.
>
> Amor scriba, scribe velocius
> cor petrinum et sis notarius;
> scribas ibi ferro profundius,
> agnum ferro confossum fortius.

The poet's power of invention, remarkable as it is, is not always sufficient to remove all sense of tedium, but we recognise here a poem of compelling beauty which did not fail to influence the mystical writers of the next century.[1]

Another long poem, the *Canticum Amoris*, in the same measure, is a kind of first sketch of the *Philomena*.[2] It survives as a lengthy fragment in B.M. MS. Nero C. ix, and it resembles the *Philomena* closely in its subject-matter and its general plan. Like the *Philomena* it is a song of love's omnipotence shown in the birth, the life, the Passion, the Resurrection, and the Ascension of the Lord and in the Assumption of Mary. Love is the almighty instrument of these wondrous events:

> Amor iubet et *ave* mittitur
> flori cuius candor non leditur,
> et cor a ve nostrum eripitur,
> *ave* quando puelle promitur.
>
> Amor videns amaritudine
> nomen Eve plenum in turbine,
> *ave* novum natans dulcedine
> merso promit priori nomine.
>
> . . . Amor matris te fovit gremio
> virginalis lactis edulio,
> et grandescis dierum spacio,
> ut flos vernis sub veris folio,
>
> . . . Amor facit, o princeps unice,
> te cum tuis cenare celice,
> largiturum eis magnifice
> corpus sacrum in panis apice.

---

[1] For its influence on Rolle, see Raby, *Poems of John of Hoveden*, pp. xxiv sqq.;   on William of Rimington, p. xxvi sq.   [2] Raby, p. xlii sqq.; text, pp. 206 sqq.

> . . . Amor crucem adoptat humero
> baiulandum: quod dolens refero,
> luctu certe, cum istud legero,
> si me mergam, non satis fecero.
>
> Amor tandem cruce se cruciat
> crucifigens quo celum radiat:
> lator vite latrones mediat,
> quem acetum ledit, cum siciat.

A long interrogation of Love, the omnipotent Love that nails the Saviour to the cross, is a feature of the *Philomena* as well as of the *Canticum*, and we may guess that the lost ending of the poem contained, like the *Philomena*, an invocation of the Blessed Virgin.[1]

Another long poem is the *Quinquaginta Cantica* of seven hundred and twenty-three stanzas, divided into fifty *cantos* of unequal length and composed in quatrains with feminine rimes of two syllables. The themes are rich and varied,[2] and there is fine poetry mingled with some tedious verses. The following extract from an invocation, headed 'vox fidelium Christum mistice laudancium et orancium quod eis munus amoris impendat', will give an idea of the quality of the poem:

> proles David et domine gloriose,
> flos sempiterne, glorie diadema,
> melleum melos, cantici dulce thema,
> tu lux lucis verissima radiose,
>
> rex mansuetus, regnum preelectum,
> robur eximium, compago petrina,
> ara rubescens, victima vespertina,
> predulce thimiama summis evectum,
>
> preminens pontifex, et sancta sanctorum,
> secundum ritum Melchisedech ordinaris;
> Helyseus vivificans incurvaris
> quo reclinante rumpitur mortis lorum.[3]

Another poem has as its subject the Fifteen Joys of the Glorious Virgin. The first stanza is as follows:[4]

> virgo, vincens vernancia
> carnis pudore lilia,
> materno leta gaudio,
> da tua loqui gaudia

---

[1] Howden's *Cythara* ends in this manner as well, Raby, p. xlv, n. 4.
[2] See the analysis ib., p. xxx.
[3] ib., p. 111 sq.
[4] ib., p. 1 ; on the theme of the Joys, pp. xxvii sqq.

lingue, quam ligant tristia
pre doloris supplicio;
omni digna preconio,
si tuo stillicidio
perfundas iam precordia,
letus hoc refrigerio
te canam cum tripudio,
de te sumens solacia.

This very attractive poem is, as is the *Cythara*, a composition on the love and passion of Christ, in which Howden uses the same elaborate arrangement of two-syllabled masculine rimes that strikes upon the ear with a fascinating music.[1]

The *Quinquaginta Salutaciones* are addressed to the Virgin, and are mainly concerned with her Sorrows.[2] The verses are skilfully constructed with an attractive scheme of rimes:

ave, stella maris,
virgo singularis,
vernans lilio;
que cum salutaris,
veri gravidaris
solis radio,
pectus nunc preconio
reple, que cum replebaris
dudum dei filio,
tactus inexperta maris,
nos replesti gaudio.

The *Viola*,[3] in praise of the Virgin, consists of two hundred and fifty verses divided into mono-rimed sections of fifty verses each. It is, indeed, a *tour de force* and is not altogether unsuccessful. It begins:

Maria, stella maris,
fax summi luminaris,
regina singularis,
sublimitas polaris
tu parens salutaris,
que prole fecundaris,
set inexperta maris;
tu luna transsolaris,
tu via linearis,
lanx perpendicularis;
plus celo sublimaris,
plus melle dulcoraris,
plus sole serenaris.

[1] ib., pp. 118 sqq.   [2] ib., pp. 176 sqq.   [3] ib., pp. 194 sqq.

A short song, the *Lira*, is of interest, because it is found in several important musical collections of the thirteenth and fourteenth centuries. In its musical setting it is a *Conductus* for two voices.[1] Lastly, there is a beautiful poem, clearly meant to be set to music, addressed to the Virgin. The first stanza runs:

> o mira creatura,
> tam magna, tam pusilla,
> mater et virgo pura,
> regina et ancilla,
> amica, sponsa, filia
> et soror creatoris,
> electa super milia,
> flos matrum, mater floris.[2]

When we look at Howden's Latin poetry as a whole, we are struck by the technical competence which it displays, the skilful use and arrangement of rimes, and the original rhythmical schemes. Originality, indeed, is the mark of his verse. He owed very little to his predecessors, though he was, as a scholar of the first rank, acquainted with the literature of devotion in which the Cistercian order, in the person of men like Bernard of Clairvaux and Aelred of Rievaulx, had set what was virtually a new fashion.[3] The extent of his own influence on the fourteenth-century mystical movement in England is shown not only by the fact that Richard Rolle had studied him to good effect, but by the existence in the same century of a paraphrase in English verse of the *Philomena*.[4]

Howden was clearly one of the great men of his day. He was, as has been said, clerk to Queen Eleanor, and he was probably high in the favour of Edward I, for in September 1275, just before his death, he was presented, as king's clerk, to a prebend in the king's free chapel of Bridgnorth. His acquaintance with the philosophical and scientific movement associated with the names of Robert Grosseteste, Adam Marsh, and Roger Bacon appears to have been profound, and we should probably be right in regarding him as familiar with the great musical

---

[1] For a discussion, Raby, pp. xxxvii sqq.; text, pp. 202 sqq.

[2] Text, ib., p. 241 sq.; for Howden's claim to authorship, pp. xlvi sq.

[3] On this movement which begins, in definite form, with Anselm of Canterbury, see A. Wilmart, *Auteurs spirituels et textes dévots du moyen âge latin*, Paris 1932, and Raby, *Poems of John of Hoveden*, pp. xviii sqq.

[4] Ed. C. D'Evelyn, *Meditations on the Life and Passion of Christ*, E.E.T.S. 1921; see Raby, *A Middle English Paraphrase of John of Hoveden's Philomena and the Text of his Viola*, M.L.R., xxx (1935), pp. 339 sqq.

developments of the time which were related to the school of
Notre-Dame in Paris. He was a prolific coiner of new words,
daring in his imagery, and confident in his creative powers. He
was absorbed in the personal mysticism and personal devotion
which, with loss as well as gain, was to be the mark of all later
medieval religion.[1] It was, however, not for his writings so
much as for the holiness of his life and his active charity that
he gained the reputation of a saint. The choir of Howden
Church, still beautiful in its ruined state, ranks with his poetry
as his fitting memorial.

§ 2. *Philip the Chancellor*

Philip of Paris, more usually known as Philip the Chancellor,[2]
was one of the most celebrated men of his time, but it has
been recognized only recently that, besides being an energetic
man of affairs, he was one of the most prolific and important
poets of the thirteenth century. He was born in Paris in the
latter part of the twelfth century, and there he must have
received the best education which his age could offer. In 1217
or 1218 he appears as Chancellor of the Church of Paris, an
office which he held during a period of strenuous activity and
perpetual disputes with the University and the Friars, until his
death in 1236 or 1237. In 1219, the Bishop being absent with
S. Louis on a crusade, he excommunicated the Masters and
Scholars on the ground that they had not obtained his own
and the Bishop's consent to certain regulations which they had
made. The University appealed to the Pope, and Honorius III
decided against the impetuous Chancellor, who was summoned
to Rome, where he seems to have made his peace without much
difficulty; for circumstances had arisen which made it desirable
that the Pope should show some mark of favour to the Church
of Paris. Nevertheless, the Chancellor does not appear to have
renounced his pretensions. Soon after we find him casting the
scholars into a special prison which he had constructed for the
purpose. The next quarrel was with the Mendicants, whom he
forbade to have other pupils than the members of their own
order. But Gregory IX was naturally ready to protect them,

---

[1] On this question, A. Wilmart, *Le
'Jubilus' dit de Saint Bernard*, Rome
1944, Introd.; Raby, *The Poem Dulcis Iesu
memoria*, *Hymn Society Bulletin*, xxxiii,
October 1945.

[2] For Philip's poems see *Anal. Hymn.*
xx, xxi, l, and the list and references in l,
pp. 529–31. He has been wrongly confused
with Philip de Grève.

and the decision again went against the Chancellor.   Then the troubles with the University recommenced.   There were riots consequent on a dispute between the University and the Mendicants, during which Philip had to flee from Paris.   The Papal Bull of 1231 composed the quarrel and upheld the University against the interference of Bishop and Chancellor.

In 1236 or 1237 Philip died, and, according to Thomas of Cantimpré, appeared to his Bishop from the place of torment, to which, he confessed, a woful ghost, he had been consigned for three grave causes—his harshness to the poor, his defence of the plurality of benefices, and worst of all, ' quia abominabili carnis vicio in scandalum multorum multo tempore laboravi '.[1] The story is too evidently the revenge of his Dominican adversaries on his memory ; but, fortunately, a worthier witness, Henri d'Andeli, has recorded in a vernacular poem the virtues, learning, and piety of the great Chancellor.   From this record we learn that he wrote poems,

> et en romans et en latin,

but the only verses which can be recognized as the work of Philip the Chancellor are in Latin.   They show the fullest understanding of the principles of rhythmical versification, an admirable command of rime, and, in some instances, a rare lyrical quality.   A large group of these verses is moral and satirical in character, with a secular rather than a definitely religious tinge. The satires on worldly dignity and the moralizings on the brevity of human life are in the usual medieval vein, while the attacks on ecclesiastical abuses are in the vigorous manner of Walter Map or of *Carmina Burana*.   But when Philip relates at length the favourite fable of the belly and the members, he cannot help recalling that the story can be referred most aptly to Christ and the Church :

> haec sub typo mysterii
> sub uno Christo capite
> geruntur in ecclesia,
> cuius sunt actus varii,
> necessitatis debitae,
> diversa sunt officia.[2]

The best example of his satirical vein is the *Bulla fulminante*, an attack on the abuses of the Curia, which, as the example of

[1] Thomas of Cantimpré, *De apibus*, quoted in P. Meyer, *Henri d'Andeli et le chancelier Philippe, Romania*, i. 194–5.   [2] *Anal. Hymn.* xxi, p. 117.

John of Salisbury proves, a good Churchman might make without scruple or fear of consequences. The bitterness and directness of the satire and the classical allusions relate the piece to the similar compositions which are contained in the *Carmina Burana*:

1. bulla fulminante,
   sub iudice tonante
   reo appellante,
   sententia gravante
   veritas supprimitur,
   distrahitur
   et venditur,
   iustitia prostrante;
   itur et recurritur
   ad curiam, nec ante
   quid consequitur,
   quam exuitur quadrante.

2. papae ianitores
   cerbero surdiores,
   in spe vana plores
   nam, etiamsi fores
   Orpheus, quam audiit
   Pluton, deus
   Tartareus,
   non ideo perores,
   malleus argenteus
   ni feriat ad fores,
   ubi Protheus
   variat mille colores.

3. si quaeris praebendas,
   frustra vitam praetendas,
   mores non commendas,
   nec iudicem offendas,
   frustra tuis literis
   inniteris,
   moraberis
   per plurimas Kalendas,
   tandem expectaveris
   a ceteris ferendas,
   paris ponderis
   pretio nisi contendas.

4. Jupiter dum orat
   Danem, frustra laborat,
   sed eam deflorat,
   auro dum se colorat;
   auro nil potentius,
   nil gratius,
   nec Tullius
   facundius perorat,
   sed hos urit acrius,
   quos amplius honorat,
   nihil iustius,
   calidum crassus dum vorat.[1]

The campaign against simony conducted by Hildebrand had borne little fruit. Along with other disorders this evil had its head-quarters at Rome. Adrian IV, a man of austere life, viewed the abuses of the Curia with cynical tolerance, since they were in his eyes the only possible means of government.[2] Without money no case could move forward at the Papal court. In a lively dialogue, Philip the Chancellor makes Diogenes inquire of Aristippus what is the best way to succeed at Rome. He cannot lie, or fawn upon the great. Aristippus tells him that unless he can lie, and flatter, and share the vices of the great, he has no chance at all.[3]

[1] *Anal. Hymn.* xxi, p. 126; see also *Carmina Burana*, pp. 51-2, where the same poem is given with differences.
[2] John of Salisbury bears witness to this in a conversation which he had with Pope Adrian IV (*Policrat.* vi. 23).
[3] *Anal. Hymn.* xxi, pp. 152-3.

In a more poetical and pietistic vein is the complaint of Christ against the evil prelates of his Church. Christ addresses his vineyard, the Church :

quid ultra tibi facere,
  vinea mea potui ?
quid potes mihi reddere,
   qui pro te caedi, conspui
  et crucifigi volui ?

et tu pro tanto munere
baptismi fracto foedere
  praesumis vice mutui
me rursus crucifigere
  et habere hostem tui.[1]

The clergy wish to enjoy both Christ and the world. They cease not to seek riches, leaving their Master poor ; they care nothing for their sheep, whose blood will be required at their hands. Other verses of Philip have a similar burden :

omnis immunditiae
clerus frons est hodie,
  capita malitiae
    praesules,
nec tot pestis variae
  monstra vidit Hercules.[2]

Another group of poems is concerned with moralizing on the misery of mortal life with its brief passage from dust to dust; on the vanity of riches in the face of the certain end, and the text 'all flesh is grass'.

cum sit omnis caro foenum
et post foenum fiat coenum,
  homo, quid extolleris ?
cerne, quid es et quid eris,
modo flos es, sed verteris
  in favillam cineris.
terram teris, terram geris
et in terram reverteris,
  qui de terra sumeris.[3]

This is doubtless the usual medieval moralizing, repeated a thousand times in sermons and homilies ; well worn, indeed, like the sentence of Homer,

The race of man is as the race of leaves,

but the permanent answer of the moralists of all ages to the bravery of the present world. Like the 'dispiritedness' of Homer or of a Hebrew patriarch, the world-despair of the Middle Ages was based on a reflecting experience, but the Middle Ages

[1] *Anal. Hymn.* XXI, p.141   [2] ib., p. 144.   [3] ib., xxi, p. 95.

returned with a ghastly persistence to the text, 'post hominem vermis,' and exulted in the humiliation of man's fleshly nature from birth to the grave.

Yet, in another mood, Philip could instil into his verse a rare grace and sweetness. The three office hymns on S. Mary Magdalene are full of beauty; they have a Franciscan warmth of feeling, tempered by a conscious art which avoids the extreme. No more admirable rhythmical poem than the *Pange, lingua, Magdalenae*, was produced in France during the thirteenth century.

pange, lingua, Magdalenae
  lacrimas et gaudium,
sonent voces laude plenae
  de concentu cordium,
ut concordet philomenae
  turturis suspirium.

in praedulci mixtione
  nardum ferens pisticum
in unguenti fusione
  typum gessit mysticum,
ut sanetur unctione,
  unxit aegra medicum.

Iesum quaerens convivarum
  turbas non erubuit,
pedes unxit, lacrimarum
  fluvio quos abluit,
crine tersit et culparum
  lavacrum promeruit.

pie Christus hanc respexit
  speciali gratia,
quia multum hunc dilexit,
  dimittuntur omnia.
Christi, quando resurrexit,
  facta est praenuntia.

suum lavit mundatorem,
  rivo fons immaduit,
pium fudit fons liquorem
  et in ipsum refluit,
caelum terrae dedit rorem,
  terra caelum compluit.

gloria et honor deo,
  qui paschalis hostia,
agnus mente, pugna leo,
  victor die tertia
resurrexit cum tropaeo,
  mortis ferens spolia.[1]

The identification of Mary Magdalene with the sinful woman who bathed the Saviour's feet:

> With costly spikenard and with tears,

represents the common medieval view. It reappears in that charming anonymous resurrection hymn which begins:

> pone luctum, Magdalena,
> et serena lacrymas;
> non est iam Simonis coena,
> non cur fletum exprimas;[2]

---

[1] *Anal. Hymn.* l, p. 532, imitated in a late hymn on S. Margaret, *Anal. Hymn.* xxiii, p. 231.

[2] Trench, *Sacred Latin Poetry*, p. 161.

The same theme is treated, with greater beauty and tenderness, by Philip in a resurrection hymn, the third of the series:

o Maria, noli flere,
  iam non quaeras alium;
hortulanus hic est vere
  et colonus mentium,
intra mentis hortum quaere
  mentis operarium.

iam non miror, si nescisti
  magistrum, dum seminat;
semen quod est verbum Christi
  te magis illuminat,
et *Rabboni* respondisti,
  dum *Mariam* nominat.

unde planctus et lamentum?
  quid mentem non erigis?
quid revolvis monumentum?
  tecum est quem diligis;
Iesum quaeris, et inventum
  habes nec intelligis.

pedes Christi quae lavisti
  fonte lota gratiae,
quem ab ipso recepisti,
  funde rorem veniae,
resurgentis, quem vidisti,
  fac consortes gloriae.

unde gemis, unde ploras?
  verum habes gaudium;
latet in te, quod ignoras,
  doloris solacium;
intus habes, quaeris foras
  languoris remedium.

gloria et honor deo,
  cuius praefert gratia
invitanti pharisaeo
  Mariae suspiria,
cenam vitae qui dat reo
  gratiae post prandia.[1]

Many other hymns are attributed to Philip the Chancellor, but the following verses are really by Walter of Châtillon:

dum medium silentium
  tenerent legis apices,
et literae dominium
  regnaret apud simplices,
extendit pater brachium,
  in quo, si recte iudices,
regnum et sacerdotium
  reliquit iudex iudices.
R° de tenebris historiae
  processit sol iustitiae.[2]

Another piece is a kind of carol with a refrain, which reminds us of the manner of those Christmas songs, half Latin, half German or French, which were being composed at this time.

ecce mundi gaudium,
ecce salus gentium,
virgo parit filium
  sine violentia.
  ave, virgo regia,
  dei plena gratia.

natus est de virgine
sine viri semine,
qui mundat a crimine,
  rex, qui regit omnia.
  ave, virgo regia,
  dei plena gratia.

---

[1] *Anal. Hymn.* l, p. 534.   [2] ib., xx, p. 38.

angelus pastoribus:
natus est in gentibus,
qui dat pacem omnibus
  sua providentia.
  ave, virgo regia,
  dei plena gratia.

reges tria praemia
offerentes varia
stella duce praevia
  ad salutis gaudia.
  ave, virgo regia,
  dei plena gratia.

cum nil scire potuit
de nato, rex fremuit,
et tota gens tremuit
  Christi natalitia.
  ave, virgo regia,
  dei plena gratia.

cum mori per gladios
Rachel videt, proprios
moesta plorat filios,
  nulla sunt solatia.
  ave, virgo regia,
  dei plena gratia.[1]

Of a singular grace are the verses on the Virgin, which begin :

o Maria, virginei
  flos honoris,
vitae via, lux fidei,
  pax amoris.

o regina, tu laquei,
  tu doloris
medicina, fons olei,
  vas odoris.[2]

They reveal to us Philip the mystical poet, as the moral and satirical verses show us the hard and upright ecclesiastic, the enemy of vain show in the world and of abuses in Church and State. The composer of sweet songs, the lover of soft cadences and charming rimes, had a very bitter tongue. In the practical affairs of Paris he magnified his office, and would not abate its rights ; in the pulpit he would illustrate his text at the expense of the masters of the University. In an Advent sermon on the crowing of the cock, he compares the doctors of Paris to fighting-cocks, who have forsaken their true calling. They ought to be the heralds of the dawn, waking men from sleep. ' Facti sunt galli pugnaces. Quid enim est ista contentio doctorum, nisi pugna gallorum ? '[3] And he develops the comparison in detail at the expense of the professors. ' Gallus insurgit contra gallum et cristatur contra eum, et sibi commanducant cristas, et effundunt viscera et sese cruentant: sic hodie magister contra magistrum et sese ad invicem corrodunt.'

Hence it was, we may guess, that when Philip came to die there were many enemies ready to assail his memory, and if time had not preserved the *Dit* of Henri d'Andeli and a number of his beautiful verses, the historian might have been compelled to draw severe conclusions from the gossip of Thomas of Cantimpré.

---

[1] ib., xx, p. 95.
[2] ib., xx, p. 141.

[3] Hauréau, *Notices et extraits des mss.*, xxi, ii, p. 193.

§ 3. *Thomas Aquinas* (1225 *circ.*–1274) *and the poetry of the Eucharist.*

Thomas Aquinas, the 'angelic doctor', the most famous, if hardly the most original of medieval thinkers, was born about the year 1225.   His father was the Count of Aquinum in Italy, and in his veins flowed the mingled blood of Norman and Hohenstaufen.   His noble birth and his astonishing intellectual gifts might have marked him out for a distinguished secular career.   But he was brought up under the monastic shadow of Monte Cassino, the mother-house of the Benedictines, and the impressions made during those years of childhood at that venerable house of learning and piety were destined to en-dure.   He left Monte Cassino when the monks were expelled by Frederick II, and continued his studies at Naples.   Then, in his twentieth year, captured by the religious revival which was sweeping over Italy, he joined the brotherhood of Dominic. It can be imagined that the order of the Preachers, with their emphasis on the rational qualities of argument and exhortation, attracted the young scholar more readily than the Brothers Minor, whose sublime follies were then stirring so profoundly the hearts of the Italians.

The intellectual glory of the Dominicans in those days was Albert the Great of Cologne, whose life work was the introduc-tion of Aristotle to the Catholic world.   From 1245 to 1248 Thomas studied under Albert at Paris, and when Albert was transferred to Cologne Thomas followed him.   In Paris and Cologne, in close contact with his master, Thomas laid the foundations of his study of the Aristotelian philosophy, which was to issue later in the *Summa Theologica*.   Albert was proud of this brilliant pupil whose fame was to eclipse his own, and whose doctrines, built on the foundations he himself had laid, he lived to defend after death had carried away the disciple in 1274.   It is difficult to estimate the breadth and depth of the learning of Thomas Aquinas.   His industry was doubtless immense, but he made full use of existing compendia and short cuts to knowledge.   He knew his Aristotle thoroughly, but not, of course, in the original ; he had some acquaintance with Plato, and a full knowledge of Boëthius.   He had read some of the Greek and most of the Latin fathers, and knew his predecessors from Anselm of Lucca to Peter Lombard.   It is not easy to measure the influence of the classical studies, which he must have pursued at Monte Cassino, and, later, at Naples. The fact that his writings contain quotations from Horace and Ovid, Seneca and Terence,[1] throws no light on his possible humanistic leanings, and we are similarly in the dark when we attempt to discover the man behind the scholar and the saint. He lived for philosophy, which he prized as a higher occupation than the care of souls, and on his death-bed he expounded the *Song of Songs* to the Cistercians of Fossanuova, who had given him hospitality when, weary and ill, he was journeying to the Council of Lyons.

Thomas was the first of medieval thinkers to erect, on the basis of a systematic knowledge and the acceptance of Aristotelianism, a philosophical synthesis in which the truths of reason and revelation were harmonized. The *Summa Theologica* is still the classical and authoritative statement of Catholic philosophy. The severe and rationalistic temper, the subordination of detail to the necessities of system, were qualities of an order rare enough in his day. To say that he exhibits these qualities to a full degree is not to deny at the same time that he shows the deep piety of a true son of the Church.

In 1257 John of Fidanza and Thomas Aquinas received at Paris, on the same day, the confirmation of their Doctorate in Theology.[2] Bonaventura, the Seraphic Doctor, true to Franciscan type, was an ardent mystic, who saw that reason helped the soul but a little way upon its journey to God;[3] while admitting that some truths transcended reason, Thomas, like his master Aristotle, saw in the rational principle the most godlike thing in man, though reason must first be sanctified by grace.[4] The emotional leaning of Bonaventura, and his conservatism, led him to follow in the steps of Hugh of S. Victor, and, filled with the Franciscan spirit, he expressed in verse the personal love and pity of the follower of Francis for the 'poor one crucified'. But Bonaventura was a Platonist by preference, and an Augustinian. Thomas had the harder Aristotelian temper; he was always the philosopher and commentator, and when he, in his turn, came to write hymns and sequences, he gave to his compositions the severe dignity and majesty of his own philosophy.

[1] Grabmann, *Thomas von Aquin*, p. 47.
[2] E. Gilson, *La philosophie de S. Bonaventura*, p. 20.
[3] Cf. his *Itinerarium mentis in Deum.*
[4] Yet Aquinas did not lose his liberty of judgement in following Aristotle, and he often shows strong signs of Platonic influence; see P. Rotta, *S. Tommaso e il pensiero classico*, p. 83, in *S. Tommasso d'Aquino, publicazione commemorativa del sesto centenario della canonizzazione*, Milan 1923.

For in 1264 Thomas, who had been summoned to lecture on theology at the Papal court, was entrusted by Urban IV with the task of composing the office for the new festival of Corpus Christi. Hitherto there had been no special celebration of the central mystery of the Catholic faith, the Sacrament of the Altar. Before the thirteenth century, indeed, apart from the controversies which centred round the speculations of Paschasius Radbertus and Berengar of Tours, philosophical discussion had hardly ventured to approach the mysterious subject of the Real Presence. The primitive Church, while regarding the Eucharist with the awe and reverence due to a great mystery of the faith, did not feel the need for any discussion of its theological implications. The main interest centred round the act of worship, and the religious feeling which was evoked by a growing complexity and grandeur of ceremonial. From early times the Lord's Supper had begun to assume the character of a eucharistic sacrifice offered by a priesthood. Later on, the communion of the laity tended to become less frequent, and the supernatural element of the ceremonial was more and more exalted. Legends were widespread as to the miraculous power of the Host, and as to supernatural evidences of the presence of the Body and Blood of Jesus in the consecrated elements.[1] From the second half of the twelfth century the communion of the laity in one kind began to be more general. The sublime and moving character of the ceremonial, with the silence of the secret prayer of consecration broken only by the sound of the sacring bell, the sight of the elevated Host, made the Mass the emotional centre of Catholic ritual, and its doctrine the centre of the Catholic faith.[2]

[1] Cf. the legend of *S. Gregory's Mass* (see *Golden Legend*); also *Annales Palidenses* (*M. G. H.*, *SS.* xvi), 1150, where a woman, who received the sacrament at Easter, carried the wafer home. It turned into bloody flesh ('in cruentam carnem versam'). She confessed her sin to the bishop, who ordered a three days' fast for his flock and had the host brought back to his church 'cum veneratione'. The story forms the subject of a twelfth-century sequence which places the scene at Augsburg: see *Anal. Hymn.* liv, p. 266–7; cf. the story of the Jew and the wafer, quoted p. 157 in Morison's *S Bernard*; see also Thomas Aquinas, *Summa Theologica*, pars iii, *Quaest.* lxxvi, art. viii, 'Utrum quando in hoc sacramento apparet miraculose caro vel puer, sit ibi vere Corpus Christi', where there is a curious discussion.

[2] See J. Wickham Legg, *Ecclesiological Essays*, London 1905, p. 43. The elevation of the host and chalice at the time of consecration, introduced in the twelfth and thirteenth centuries, according to Edmund Bishop, led to great additions to the ceremonial, 'lights and torches, censings, bell ringings, and genuflexions'. Mr. Legg points out that 'before elevation came to be the custom, the Canon must have been recited in profound silence,

Yet not until the thirteenth century was a special festival instituted in honour of the Body of Christ. The story of its institution is well known. To Juliana, a nun at Mont Cornillon in Belgium, who professed an ardent devotion towards the Body of Christ, a vision came of a full moon whose purity was sullied by one black spot. The moon represented the Church whose liturgical year remained incomplete without the addition of a feast in honour of Christ's Body. Robert, Bishop of Liège, to whom the vision was made known, was so impressed that he ordered on his own authority a solemnization of the new festival. In 1258 Juliana died. Three years later a former Archdeacon of Liège, to whom the vision had been revealed at the time, ascended the throne of S. Peter as Urban IV. He was approached with a petition that he would make the celebration of *Corpus Christi* general in the Catholic Church. So the Bull *Transiturus* was issued on 8 Sept. 1264, ordaining the annual celebration of the feast on the Thursday after Trinity Sunday.

To Thomas Aquinas was given the task of composing the office, including the Mass for the day.[1] It is one of the most splendid in the Roman Breviary and Missal. The hymns and the sequence are admirable liturgical compositions; severity of form, economy of expression, scholastic exactness of doctrinal statement are joined to a metrical skill which owes as much to the genius of the poet as to a study of predecessors like Adam of S. Victor.

The sequence in the Mass is the famous *Lauda Sion Salvatorem*, which properly enough is a severely doctrinal exposition of the dogma of the Real Presence. The first strophe is:[2]

> lauda, Sjon, salvatorem,
> lauda ducem et pastorem
> in hymnis et canticis;

---

broken only by *Nobis quoque*; the exact moment of consecration was not evident. Until the schoolmen determined that consecration ensued upon the priest reciting the words of institution, it was not reasonable to elevate the host and chalice at this place.' I notice, however, that Cumont, *Textes et monuments figurés relatifs aux Mystères de Mithra*, Brussels 1899, i. 68, note 2, refers to the discovery of bells in the Catacombs (as in the *Mithraeum* at Heddernheim) and suggests that bells were used in the divine office in the Early Church, but he can hardly be right, as against Edmund Bishop, *Liturgica Historica*, p. 9.

[1] It has been thought that Thomas, in composing the office, borrowed a good deal from the already existing Cistercian Office by John of Mt. Cornillon; see Grabmann, *Die echten Schriften des hl. Thomas von Aquin*, p. 232 sq.

[2] Text in *Anal. Hymn.* l, p. 584; see *Anal. Hymn.* liv, p. 305, for an imitation of this sequence, *Lauda, sponsa, genetricem.*

quantum potes, tantum aude,
quia major omni laude,
nec laudare sufficis.

Sion is the symbol of the whole Church on earth, which is here summoned to sing the praises of the 'living and life-giving bread'.[1] For in this feast the old passover is done away, and the new is instituted; as the daylight chases away the darkness, so the truth puts to flight the shadow. So the ancient passover is the type of the new, the Paschal Lamb is a figure of Christ, as Thomas explains at length in his exposition of the doctrine of the Eucharist in the Third Part of his *Summa Theologica*. 'In this sacrament,' he says, 'we can consider three things; to wit, what the sacrament is by itself, which is bread and wine; and what is both reality (*res*) and sacrament together, to wit, the true Body of Christ; and what is reality (*res*) alone, to wit, the effect (*effectus*) of this sacrament. As regards the sacrament alone, the offering of Melchisedek, who offered bread and wine, was the principal (*potissima*) figure of this sacrament. But as regards Christ himself in his passion, who is contained in this sacrament, all the sacrifices of the Old Testament were its figures, especially the sacrifice of atonement, which was the most solemn. As regards the effect, the manna was the especial figure thereof, which *contained in itself every savour of sweetness*, as is said, *Wisd.* xvi. 20, even as the grace of this sacrament refreshes the soul in all respects. But the Paschal Lamb prefigured this sacrament as regards all the three things aforesaid; the first, because it was eaten with unleavened bread, . . . the second, because it was slain by the whole multitude of the children of Israel on the tenth day of the month, which was a figure of the passion of Christ, who for his innocence is called a lamb; and as regards the effect, because by the blood of the lamb the children of Israel were protected from the destroying angel and brought out of the bondage of Egypt, and as regards this, the paschal lamb is held to be the especial figure of this sacrament, because in all respects it shows him forth.'[2]

In the sequence, Thomas makes use of the figure of the Paschal Lamb, and of the manna, and of Isaac, the familiar type of Christ.

---

[1] Strophe 2.

[2] *Summa, Pars* iii, *Quaest.* lxxiii, *Art.* vi.

in hac mensa novi regis
novum pascha novae legis
   phase vetus terminat ;
vetustatem novitas,
umbram fugat veritas,
   noctem lux illuminat. . . . .

ecce, panis angelorum,[1]
factus cibus viatorum,
vere panis filiorum,
   non mittendus canibus.
in figuris praesignatur,
cum Isaac immolatur,
agnus paschae deputatur,
   datur manna patribus.

The doctrinal exposition follows closely the lines of the *Quaestiones* in the *Summa*. Thus *Quaestio* lxxv, art. 1,[2] is 'Utrum in hoc Sacramento sit Corpus Christi secundum veritatem,'—is the Body of Christ truly and actually in this sacrament ? The answer is : 'That the true body and blood of Christ are in this sacrament cannot be apprehended by sense or intelligence, but by faith alone, which leans upon the divine authority'. So in the sequence,

dogma datur Christianis,
quod in carnem transit panis
   et vinum in sanguinem ;
quod non capis, quod non vides,
animosa firmat fides
   praeter rerum ordinem.

The next strophe, likewise, can be understood only by reference to the *Summa*.

sub diversis speciebus,
signis tantum et non rebus,
   latent res eximiae :
caro cibus, sanguis potus,
manet tamen Christus totus
   sub utraque specie.

In the first quotation from the *Summa* given above, Thomas distinguishes the *species*, i.e. the bread and wine, from the *res*, which together with the bread and wine is the Body of Christ. In another place he says, ' the Body of Christ is present *invisibi-*

---

[1] *Psalm* lxxvii, 2, ' Panem angelorum manducavit homo'; cf. Augustine, *Sermo*, 225, 3 (Migne, xxxviii, col. 1097), ' ut panem angelorum manducaret homo, dominus angelorum factus est homo.'
[2] *Pars* iii.

liter under the *species* of this sacrament'.[1] And the whole Christ is contained under each kind.[2]

Lastly, the whole Christ is contained in every part of the bread or wine, whether the wafer is broken or no.[3]

> fracto demum sacramento
> ne vacilles, sed memento,
> tantum esse sub fragmento,
>   quantum toto tegitur:
> nulla rei fit scissura,
> signi tantum fit fractura,
> qua nec status nec statura
>   signati minuitur.

The last strophe is a prayer that the congregation of the faithful may be gathered together at the heavenly feast above.

> bone pastor, panis vere,
> Iesu, nostri miserere,
> tu nos pasce, nos tuere,
> tu nos bona fac videre
>   in terra viventium.

> tu qui cuncta scis et vales,
> qui nos pascis hic mortales,
> tu nos ibi commensales,
> coheredes et sodales
>   fac sanctorum civium.

This is doubtless the supreme dogmatic poem of the Middle Ages; it never wanders from the correct scholastic terminology, *res* and *signa* are used in the sense of the *Summa*; the thought is hard and closely woven, but it is a poem as well as a dogmatic exposition. The verses have an austerity and grandeur which no Latin poet of the Middle Ages ever equalled.

The hymn at First Vespers is the familiar *Pange lingua*:

> pange, lingua, gloriosi
>   corporis mysterium
> sanguinisque pretiosi,
>   quem in mundi pretium
> fructus ventris generosi,
>   rex effudit gentium.

> nobis datus, nobis natus
>   ex intacta virgine,
> et in mundo conversatus,
>   sparso verbi semine,
> sui moras incolatus
>   miro clausit ordine.

---

[1] *Pars* iii, *Quaest.* lxxv, *Art.* i.

[2] *Quaest.* lxxvi, *Art.* ii, *Utrum totus Christus contineatur sub utraque specie huius sacramenti.*

[3] *Quaest.* lxxvi, *Art.* iii: cf. Mone, i. 258:

> iustis et fidelibus ita manducatur,
> sed ob hoc in aliquo nunquam laceratur,
> totus in particula confracta moratur,
> aliquanta specie deus occultatur.

Similarly, Mone, i. 279:

> mira Iesus operatur,
> cum a multis manducatur,
> totus tamen conservatur,
> nec fracturam patitur.

in supremae nocte cenae
  recumbens cum fratribus,
observata lege plene
  cibis in legalibus,
cibum turbae duodenae
  se dat suis manibus.

verbum caro panem verum
  verbo carnem efficit,
fitque sanguis Christi merum,
  et, si sensus deficit,
ad firmandum cor sincerum
  sola fides sufficit.

tantum ergo sacramentum
  veneremur cernui,
et antiquum documentum
  novo cedat ritui :
praestet fides supplementum
  sensuum defectui.

genitori genitoque
  laus et iubilatio,
salus, honor, virtus quoque
  sit et benedictio ;
procedenti ab utroque
  compar sit laudatio.[1]

Beyond all praise, for its severe and rigid beauty, its precision
of thought and adequacy of content, this splendid hymn should
be heard as the processional in a cathedral on Holy Thursday.
Less purely doctrinal than the *Lauda Sion*, the *Pange lingua* is
one of the most sublime productions of sacred poetry. Here
again the technical excellence of metre and rime, reached by
Adam in the twelfth century, is more than maintained by
Thomas. The beginning of the hymn is an imitation of the
Pange lingua of Fortunatus, and similarly, in the hymn for Lauds,
Thomas borrows his first line from a well-known Ambrosian
hymn on the Advent.[2]

verbum supernum prodiens,
nec patris linquens dexteram,
ad opus suum exiens
venit ad vitae vesperam.

in mortem a discipulo
suis tradendus aemulis,
prius in vitae ferculo
se tradidit discipulis.

quibus sub bina specie
carnem dedit et sanguinem,
ut duplicis substantiae
totum cibaret hominem.

se nascens dedit socium,
convescens in edulium
se moriens in pretium,
se regnans dat in praemium.

o salutaris hostia,
quae caeli pandis ostium,
bella premunt hostilia,
da robur, fer auxilium.

uni trinoque domino
sit sempiterna gloria,
qui vitam sine termino
nobis donet in patria.[3]

---

[1] Text in *Anal. Hymn.* l, p. 586 ; for an
amazing ' parody ' of this hymn, in honour
of Thomas, see *Anal. Hymn.* xliii, p. 294.
Here is a characteristic stanza :

  tantum ergo nos portentum
    veneremur cernui
  et Aquini documentum,
    nostro dispar sensui,

  praestat nostrae supplementum
    virtutis defectui.

[2] verbum supernum prodiens,
    a patre olim exiens,
    qui natus orbi subvenis,
    cursu declivi temporis.

[3] Text in *Anal. Hymn.* l, p. 588 ; it has
been suggested by Dom Morin (*Revue*

The two last stanzas as well as the two last of the *Pange lingua* are sung regularly at the Benediction of the Sacrament. The hymn for Matins is the least familiar of all the hymns which Thomas composed for the office of Corpus Christi. It displays great skill in the handling of a fourteen-syllabled metre. The first stanza is

> sacris sollemniis iuncta sint gaudia
> et ex praecordiis sonent praeconia;
> recedant vetera, nova sint omnia
> corda, voces et opera.[1]

Here the doctrinal expression is all but absent; the picture is more human, Christ appears almost like the Jesus of Leonardo, 'as one taking leave of his friends'.[2]

> dedit fragilibus corporis ferculum,
> dedit et tristibus sanguinis poculum
> dicens: accipite quod trado vasculum,
> omnes ex eo bibite.

Lastly, there is the famous *Adoro te devote*, a pious meditation of incomparable beauty and closely-knit construction, which Wilmart felt unable to assign, on the ms. evidence, to Thomas, but which on other evidence may be regarded as probably his.[3]

> adoro devote, latens veritas,
> te qui sub his formis vere latitas;
> tibi se cor meum totum subicit,
> quia te contemplans totum deficit. . . .

> o memoriale mortis domini,
> panis veram vitam praestans homini,
> praesta meae menti de te vivere
> et te semper illi dulce sapere.

> pie pellicane Iesu domine,[4]
> me immundum munda tuo sanguine;
> cuius una stilla salvum facere
> totum mundum posset omni scelere.

Bénéd., 1910, p. 236 sqq.) that this hymn is S. Thomas's abridged and improved edition of an earlier hymn already in use among the Cistercians; see also the Bishop of Clifton, *The Liturgical Poetry of S. Thomas*, in *S. Thomas Aquinas, Papers from the Summer School of Catholic Studies*, Cambridge 1925, p. 285 sqq.

[1] *Anal. Hymn.* l, p. 357.
[2] Walter Pater, *The Renaissance*, p. 125.
[3] Critical text, A. Wilmart, *La tradition littéraire et textuelle de l'Adoro te devote*, *Recherches de Théologie ancienne et*

médiévale, i. (1929), pp. 21 sqq., 149 sqq. Wilmart, after examining all the manuscripts, concluded that one of them, which ascribed the poem to Thomas, might be based upon a copy which was a little older than 1323; beyond this he saw only 'impenetrable darkness'. But in *The Date and the Authorship of the poem Adoro te devote*, *Speculum*, xx (1945), pp. 236 sqq., I have, I think, shown that the poem was written in S. Thomas's lifetime and that it has the strongest claim to be his.

[4] Christ as the Pelican was a favourite

Iesu quem velatum nunc aspicio,
quando fiet illud, quod tam cupio,
ut te revelata cernens facie
visu sim beatus tuae gloriae ?

The later Middle Ages saw a great growth of eucharistic poetry in the form of sequences, or of hymns to be sung after the Preface or during the prayer of consecration, or compositions which were of the nature of private devotions before or after communion. Perhaps the best known in the *Ave verum corpus natum*, which was sung, says Mone,[1] after the Preface or during the consecration.

ave, verum corpus natum
  ex Maria virgine :
vere passum, immolatum
  in cruce pro homine
cuius latus perforatum
  vero fluxit sanguine,
esto nobis praegustatum
  in mortis examine.
o dulcis, o pie,
  o fili Mariae :
    miserere mei.

Sometimes the hymns are almost wholly doctrinal expositions of the meaning of the 'transubstantiation'. So

coenam cum discipulis affectat coenare,
exemplis sermonibus ipsos informare,
panem in substantiam carnis transformare,
vinum in essentiam sanguinis mutare.[2]

or,

panis et vini mera essentia
carnis suae fit vera substantia.[3]

In one hymn the word 'transubstantiatio' is used :

sicut hoc mysterio
  tam sacro, tam divino
transubstantiatio
  de pane fit et vino.[4]

The verses are an expression of the orthodox theory ; the whole *substantia* or substance of the bread and wine is changed

---

subject of medieval art (Mâle, *L'art religieux au XIIIe siècle*, p. 57). The bird was supposed to feed its young with its life-blood.

[1] i. 279, note ; the best text is in *Anal. Hymn.* liv, p. 257.
[2] Mone, i. 258.   [3] ib. 262.
[4] ib. 289.

into the whole substance of the Body and Blood of Christ,[1] only the *accidentia,* accidents or sensible qualities of the elements, remaining unchanged.[2] 'The accidents which are discerned by the senses are truly there (*secundum rei veritatem*). But the intellect, whose proper object is *substance* (as is said by Aristotle, *De anima,* lib. iii, 29), is saved by faith from being deceived. . . . For faith is not contrary to the senses, but is concerned with things which the senses cannot reach.'[3]

Another hymn exalts the dignity of the priestly office; for neither angel nor saint, but only an ordained priest can offer the sacrifice of the altar.

> hoc nemo valet alius
> sanctus homo vel angelus,
> quod solus potest presbyter,
> formam servans integriter.

> decet ergo presbyteros
> honore tanto praeditos
> se ipsos circumspicere,
> fideliter attendere.

> regale sacerdotium,
> mirificum officium
> his unctio quod contulit,
> character quantum extulit.[4]

'It is not,' says the *Imitation,*[5] within the compass of the deserts of men that man should consecrate and administer the Sacrament of Christ, and receive for food the bread of Angels. Grand is this Mystery; great too is the dignity of the Priests to whom hath been granted that which is not permitted to Angels. For none but Priests duly ordained in the Church have power to celebrate this Sacrament, and to consecrate the Body of Christ.' Upon the possession of this mysterious privilege was based the power of the priesthood; this, and the weapon of excommunication, in an age of faith, were the *arcana imperii* by which the Church attempted to govern an unruly world.

The Franciscan movement, with its tendency to religious subjectivism,[6] to the side of personal emotion, encouraged that devotion to the Sacrament of the Altar which was merely another expression of the love of the Crucified. This is the inspiration of many hymns for private devotion. The following hymn is given by Mone, from a fifteenth-century manuscript:[7]

---

[1] Cf. *Summa, Pars* iii, *Quaest.* lxxv, *Art.* iv.

[2] ib., *Art.* v.   [3] ib., *Art.* v.

[4] Mone, i. 260.

[5] iv. 5. Cf. the *Corpus Christi* Processional, dated before 1384, *Anal. Hymn.* iii. 33:

'non est angelicae naturae tanta potestas
unquam concessa, quanta datur homini,
presbyteris tantum conceditur ista facul-
tas,
Christi conficere corpus ut est hodie.'

[6] Cf. Sabatier, *S. François,* p 387.

[7] i. 294.

o Iesu dulcissime,
  cibus salutaris,
qui sic te tribuere
  intime dignaris;
mala mea deprime
  fletibus amaris
et affectus inprime,
  quibus delectaris.

o Iesu vivens hostia,
  placa maiestatem,
sacramenti gratia
  confer sanitatem,
pauperis substantia
  da aeternitatem
et tua praesentia
  fove caritatem.

vanitatem spernere
  fac me consolator,
hostem dona vincere,
  Christe propugnator,
et, quod doces credere,
  Christe reparator,
per te tandem cernere
  da, remunerator.

But the tenderest and purest expression of this devotion is contained in the *Imitation of Christ*, 'the last voice of monasticism in its pure original form'.[1] Here the voice of dogma is silent; the only voices are those of the Beloved and the Disciple. Thomas à Kempis speaks as if he regarded the disputations of philosophy as dangerous, and to be shunned by those who would follow the path of perfection. 'We shall not be blamed in the Judgement', he says, 'for our ignorance of them. . . . What have we to do with *genera* and *species*? He to whom the Eternal Word speaketh is delivered from a multitude of opinions.'[2] Only when the heart is purged of all other affections can it be ready to receive its Guest. 'For every one that loveth will prepare the best and fairest place for his beloved; for herein is known the affection of him that entertaineth his beloved.'[3] 'For the Lord bestoweth His blessings there where he findeth the vessels empty.'[4] Only by complete renunciation of all things can all things be gained; this is the final message of medieval mysticism, set forth in the *Imitation* in a manner which has impressed itself on the imagination of each succeeding age.

'As it would not suffice thee to have all things whatsoever, besides Me; so neither can it please Me, whatsoever thou givest, if thou offer not thyself.

'Offer up thyself unto Me, and give thyself wholly for God, and thy offering shall be acceptable.

[1] Renan, *Études d'histoire religieuse*, p. 328.
[2] *Imitation*, i. 3; cf. iv. 18.
[3] iv. 12.
[4] iv. 15.

' Behold, I offered up Myself wholly unto My Father for thee ; I gave also My whole Body and Blood for thy food, that I might be wholly thine, and that thou mightest continue Mine to the end.' [1]

So, while for S. Thomas the end of man is the possession of God, a possession which borrowed its intellectual character from the Aristotelian philosophy, for the great medieval mystic the possession of God was mediated by the renunciation of self and by the Sacrament of the Altar. Yet the contrast is perhaps superficial ; for, in practice, the philosopher and the mystic followed the same path and achieved a like illumination.

[1] iv. 8.

XIII

THE FRANCISCAN POETS

§ 1. *Franciscan Christianity.*

THE first half of the thirteenth century marks the height of medieval civilization, the age of its fullest and most perfect growth, luxuriant, manifold in its promise, and bearing within it the seeds from which was to issue the life of the modern world. It was the age of Innocent III and Frederic II ; of S. Louis and Edward I ; of Reims and Westminster and the Sainte Chapelle. It witnessed the enthusiasm and agony of the Crusades in Europe, in Africa, and in Asia ; while in France, Germany, and Italy a brilliant and prosperous communal life sprang up in the cities with the growing importance of the middle classes. The defeat of Frederic Barbarossa at Legnano had set the seal on the liberties of the Lombard cities, and to Italy henceforth was to be entrusted the task which in the twelfth century had fallen to France, the leadership of Europe in the path of civilization, in art, in religion, and in letters. As of old, the power at the head of this common civilization was the Catholic Church, with its hierarchy, its central organ the Curia, and its army of legates and envoys. But powerful forces were at work which appeared to be rapidly undermining the established order. It was not that the universal ecclesiastical corruption, the abuses of the Curia, the prevalence of simony, had awakened the consciences of men to revolt against an intolerable burden ; for centuries the voices of earnest men had been raised against a corruption that was always present, but had tended, if anything, to strengthen the organization of the Church as a centralized body dependent for its direction and control on the Roman Curia.[1]

The real danger arose from heresy ; not from the speculations

---

[1] Cf. Gebhart, *L'Italie mystique*, p. 8, 'La simonie fut alors à Rome le plus efficace moyen de gouvernement' ; John of Salisbury, *Policraticus*, vi. 23 ; Bernard of Clairvaux, *Epist.* 238 (Migne) ; *De Consid.* i. 10 ; cf. Fournier, *Études sur Joachim de Flore*, p. 8 ; on the prevalence of simony generally see Lea, *History of the Inquisition in the Middle Ages*, i. 7.

of the schools, the effect of which was limited to narrow academic circles, but from a series of popular heresies which spread with inconceivable rapidity from one end of Western Europe to the other. Most alarming of all was Catharism, a dualistic system recognizing the existence of two gods, one good and the other evil, whose action was revealed in the course of human history. What took the imagination and sympathies of the common people was the fact that the leaders of the Cathar Church practised that complete renunciation and inhuman asceticism which had always won affection for saints and prophets in the past. The Cathar movement was a lay movement, finding its support in the good will of men whose simplicity made it easy for them to. appreciate the difference between the apostolic poverty enjoined in the gospels and the luxury which surrounded a cardinal legate on a papal mission.[1] When it is realized that this movement, definitely heretical, and violently opposed to the Roman Church, spread over the northern and central parts of Italy, gaining an enormous number of converts, covered the south of France, and extended its ramifications northwards as far as Liège and Cologne, it is possible to estimate the gravity of the danger which threatened not merely Catholicism but the Christian religion.[2] Less dangerous, because it retained in its teaching more of the elements of Catholic doctrine, was the heresy of the Poor Men of Lyons (Vaudois), who went from town to town preaching the gospel in the vulgar tongue, enjoining evangelical poverty, chastity and quietism, and teaching the doctrine, fatal to the whole Catholic system, that a priesthood is not necessary for approach to God, and that a good layman has every priestly qualification, even that of consecrating the body of the Lord. By slow degrees the Vaudois were driven further into heresy, until, like the Cathars, they became the object of ecclesiastical persecution.

The spread of these heresies can only be explained by the fact that the spiritual element of their creed, the insistence on poverty and the gospel teaching, corresponded in some degree to the ideals of the common people. Within the Church, too, Joachim of Flora, the Calabrian prophet, had raised his voice against the corruption of the age, and had foretold the coming

---

[1] On Catharism and on similar heresies see Döllinger, *Beiträge zur Sektenge-schichte des Mittelalters*; Tocco, *L'Eresia nel medio evo*; Lea, *History of the Inquisition*, i.

[2] On the great extent to which the heresy spread see Tocco, pp. 108 sqq.; Döllinger, i. 110, 125; cf. Walter Map, *De Nugis curialium*, i. 30.

of the Third Kingdom, the Kingdom of the Spirit, in which society was to be reorganized on a basis of poverty and monasticism, in the age of the new and Everlasting Gospel.[1]

Thus had the *Beati pauperes !* of the Gospel created a religious fever which threatened to undermine the strength of the Catholic Church precisely at the moment when she had all the appearance of outward solidity and success.

But salvation came, and from the people, from the very classes which had been most deeply tinged with the heresies that were troubling the age. The saviour was Francis, the son of Peter Bernardone, whose gospel of spiritual joy, repentance, and poverty was joined to a delight in nature, an exuberant poetry of feeling, and an intense love for the poor and the oppressed. To his own and the following generations Francis appeared as the special minister of God, the angel of the Apocalypse 'ascending from the sunrising and bearing the seal of the Living God'.[2] Bonaventura relates[3] how Innocent III beheld in a dream the Lateran Basilica about to fall in ruins, 'which a poor little man, mean and despised, supported and upheld on his own back'. The dream expressed in very truth the reality of the situation.[4] Francis and the Brothers Minor gave to the Western world what was almost a new religion. Based like the Cathar and Waldensian, on poverty and renunciation, while retaining a thoroughly personal and evangelical content, it was saved from the charge of heresy by its utter lack of speculation and its simple obedience to the constituted powers of the Church. This spiritual and emotional renewal of Western and especially of Italian Christianity was the main influence which made itself felt in the whole development of later medieval art, and not less in art than in the vernacular and Latin poetry of the thirteenth and fourteenth centuries.[5]

Religion had once more come to find its expression in a personal experience, in an emotion of the heart, in a direct relation between the human soul and Christ. The Franciscan movement was a lay movement; it had sprung up apart from priestly and sacramental traditions. It was no product of the

---

[1] On Joachim see Tocco, p. 261 sq. ; Renan, *Nouvelles études d'histoire religieuse*, p. 217 sq. ; Gebhart, p. 51 sq. ; Fournier, *Études sur Joachim de Flore.*

[2] Bonaventura, *Legenda S. Francisci, Prologus* (Quaracchi 1923).

[3] *Legenda*, iii, p. 31 ; Giotto's fresco on the subject is well known.

[4] Sabatier, *Vie de S. François*, p. 32 ; *Tres socii*, cap. v ; cf. Dante, *Paradiso*, xii. 37-45 ; II Celano, 11.

[5] See Mâle, *L'art religieux de la fin du moyen âge en France* ; A. F. Ozanam, *Les poètes franciscains en Italie.*

E e

cloister, it came from the people, it appealed to the religious
instinct in its simplest and most fundamental form. The
emphasis which was laid on the personal act of renouncing one's
goods and giving them to the poor (there was no other condition
of entry to the new Order) expressed this characteristic in
a practical manner. Francis himself is said to have declared
that he had been sent directly by God 'to be a new covenant
in this world'.[1] For him the whole of religious experience was
summed up in the motto of the Order: ' Mihi absit gloriari nisi
in cruce Domini '. This is the personal note which makes itself
heard in the whole of the religious poetry inspired by the
Franciscan movement, and it is the key to the whole emotional
content of Franciscan literature. Francis himself had the natural
gaiety of one who had wandered for long days in the luxuriant
beauty of an Umbrian spring, but the joyful spirit of the
'jongleur of God' had more affinity with the secular poetry of
the courts, and it was the other side of his nature, the brooding
on the sorrow and passion of Christ, which was to bear fruit in
the mystical verses of his followers. For Francis, indeed, the
ecstasy of gazing on the Passion and the Wounds of Christ was
at once a torment and a delight. The crucifix above the altar
was the symbol of His divine grief, which moved him continually
to tears. ' I weep', he said, 'for the Passion of my Lord Jesus
Christ, for whom I ought not to be ashamed to go mourning
aloud throughout the whole world.'[2] In the solitude of Mount
Alvernus he received the stigmata, the Five Wounds of Christ
'written on his fleshly members by the finger of the living God '.
Now, in the minds of his followers, he was perfectly transformed
into the likeness of Christ; 'as he had imitated Christ in the
deeds of his life, so it behoved him to be conformed unto Him
in the afflictions and sorrows of His passion, before he departed
from this world '.[3]

Christ was now no longer that grave and noble Redeemer,
who appears on the sculptured doorways of Amiens and Chartres;
He is no longer the Logos, all knowing and almost impassive, He
has become the Son of Mary, the Man of Sorrows ; for art and
for poetry, He is henceforth the ' vir dolorum et sciens infirmi-
tatem '.[4]

---

[1] *Spec. Perfect.* cap. lxviii; Sabatier,
p. 108, note 3; p. 390. But we are now
told to read ' novellum pazzum '.

[2] *Tres socii*, v ; cf. II Celano, 90 ; Bonav.
xiii ; *Spec. Perfect.* xcii.
[3] Bonav. xiii.   [4] Isaiah liii. 3.

M. Mâle, in a beautiful and scholarly study,[1] has shown the commanding influence exercised on later medieval art, so sad and so impassioned, by ' Franciscan Christianity', which replaced the old calm theological symbolism by a terrible and sorrowful realism of detail. Precisely the same influence is as profoundly felt in the later Latin religious poetry of the Middle Ages, and we can follow M. Mâle in illustrating the sources of the new emotionalism from a famous specimen of religious literature, which provides a full commentary on the poetry of the Passion of Christ. The *Meditationes Vitae Christi*,[2] long attributed to Bonaventura, and presumably the work of a thirteenth century Franciscan, form a biography of Christ devised as a religious handbook for the followers of the life of contemplation. The treatment of the subject is thoroughly realistic. The author aimed at presenting a living picture of the Man of Sorrows, which, by its neglect of dogma and its emphasis on the human pathos of the story, should appeal directly to the common heart. Where the canonical narratives afforded nothing more than the barest outline of events, and where the apocryphal Gospels suggested no line of elaboration, the author gave himself up to the guidance of a vivid imagination, which was ready to invent and invest with lively colour new scenes and situations as the need arose. The emotional treatment of the subject is most intense when the last days of the Saviour are described, and the climax is reached with long meditations which pursue every detail of the Passion. The old symbolism of the Cross had been dignified and serene; in poetry as in art the Cross had been invested with a theological and symbolical grandeur.[3] In the hymns of Fortunatus, it was the beautiful tree of salvation, on which the ransom of the world had been paid. The grief of the Crucified, in the mature art of the thirteenth century, is godlike

[1] Mâle, *L'art religieux de la fin du moyen âge*; cp. also Bréhier, *L'art chrétien*, pp. 308 sqq.

[2] Bonaventura, *Opera omnia*, Paris 1868, xii. 599 sqq. It would be wrong, however, to suppose that all the motives of this presentation of the Passion appear for the first time in Franciscan literature. As Gilson remarks (*S. Bonaventure et l'iconographie de la Passion*, p. 422 sq.), S. Bernard is a 'capital source of Franciscan mysticism', and many of the dramatic scenes which the Franciscans loved are to be found already in earlier Byzantine art. The Franciscans collected what moved them in Bernard, in Damiani, or in the Victorine mystics, and made ' the devotion to the Passion, which was not in itself new, the centre of everything — mysticism, theology, philosophy, art, and devotion' (Gilson, p. 424).

[3] Bréhier, *L'art chrétien*, p. 81 sq. This tradition goes back to the earlier Christian Art, which even shrank from representing the crucifixion at all.

and restrained;[1] now, in literature as in art, it has become personal, poignant, and full of anguish. It now became a pious exercise to meditate on every ghastly detail which the imagination could add to the picture of the Passion; 'for it ought not to weary us in meditating on those things, which it wearied not the Lord Himself to endure for us.'[2] Bonaventura's *Regula Novitiorum*[3] contains this injunction. 'Have always the eyes of the mind towards Jesus crucified, crowned with thorns, having drunk the vinegar and gall, spit upon and abused, blasphemed of sinners, wearied with the multitude of scourgings, consumed with death most bitter, pierced by the spear, buried of mortal men. And think on this, whether thou eat or drink, or do any other thing, that, thinking on the Creator crucified, thou mayest have sorrow in thy heart all the day long, and in thy body show sadness of countenance, saying with the Apostle: " Far be it from me to glory save in the Cross of our Lord Jesus Christ".' This is the spirit of the *Meditations*, in which we follow, stage by stage, the double passion of Jesus and His Mother. The passion of Jesus grows by feeding on His Mother's sorrow, while her grief is nourished by the sufferings of her Son.[4] The scene of the scourging is pictured in detail. 'He stands naked in the presence of all, that youth so gracious and modest, "fairer than the children of men"; that flesh so innocent, so tender, so pure and so beauteous, endures the rude and dolorous scourges of shameful men. The flower of all flesh and of all human nature is filled with bruises and broken. That royal blood flows on every side from every part of his body.' So each detail of the long agony is dwelt upon, and the growing anguish of the Mother is depicted, until, when the centurion pierces the side of her Son, she faints in the arms of Mary Magdalene. ' Then verily the sword of that spear pierced the body of

---

[1] The Crown of Thorns is absent in the thirteenth century sculptures of the Crucifixion ; it is the constant feature in later art ; see Mâle, *L'art religieux de la fin du moyen âge*, p. 84.

[2] *Medit.* lxxiv, p. 600 ' Sed videamus singula diligenter: non enim debet nos taedere ista cogitare, quae ipsum Dominum non taeduit tolerare' ; cf. *Lignum vitae, Praefatio* ' Verus Dei cultor, Christique discipulus, qui Salvatori omnium pro se crucifixo perfecto configurari desiderat, ad hoc potissimum attento mentis conatu debet intendere, ut Christi Iesu crucem circumferat iugiter tam mente quam carne' ; and the whole treatise.

[3] *Selecta scripta S. Bonaventurae*, Quaracchi 1898, p. 220.

[4] The sorrows of the Virgin began in the house of Simon the Leper: ' Cum Dominus defendens Magdalenam a murmure proditoris dixit: *Mittens haec unguentum hoc in corpus meum, ad sepeliendum me fecit;* an non credis, quod huius verbi gladius matris animam pertransierit ?' *Medit.* lxx (p. 594).

the Son and the heart of the Mother.'[1]   But the sorrows of Mary
are not over.   When Joseph, as the day grows late, would wrap
Jesus in the shroud for His burial, her grief breaks out anew.
' O my friends ', she cries, ' do not take away my Son so quickly,
nay, bury me with Him.'   But the last parting must come.
' Now therefore, O my Son, our companionship is severed, and
I must be parted from Thee, and I thy mother most sorrowful
must bury Thee; but thereafter whither shall I go?   Where
shall I abide, my Son?   How can I live without Thee?
I would more gladly be buried with Thee, that wherever thou
wert, I might be with Thee.   But as I may not be buried with
Thee in the body, I will be buried in the heart; I will bury my
soul in the tomb with Thee, to Thee I give it up, to Thee
I commend it.   O my Son, how full of pain is this separation
from Thee!'[2]

This is the emotional atmosphere in which the poetry of
Franciscan Christianity had its beginnings.   The subjects are
ever the same—the passion of Jesus and the sorrows of Mary.
The Franciscan singers, from Bonaventura to Jacopone, sang
always with their faces set to the scene of this double passion,
where

> Under the world-redeeming rood
> The most afflicted mother stood,
> Mingling her tears with her Son's blood.

The whole of Franciscan poetry is invested with this pathos,
and filled with this compassion.   It is charged with tears for
that suffering divine and human by which the world is redeemed.

§ 2.   The Poetry of the Passion; Bonaventura (1221–74) and Pecham (d. 1292).

A series of hymns and poems, the central theme of which
is the Passion of Jesus, is attributed to John of Fidanza, better
known as S. Bonaventura, the Seraphic Doctor and the official
biographer of S. Francis.   Born in 1221 of humble parentage,

---

[1] *Medit.* lxxx (p. 608).   Bonaventura
himself had already dwelt on the passion
of the Mother ; cf. his Sermon for *Dominica
infra Octav. Epiphaniae*, i, 'non est dolor
sicut dolor suus, excepto dolore filii, ad
cuius exemplar dolor suus assimilatur '.
[2] *Medit.*, p. 610.

at Bagnorea in Tuscany, Bonaventura joined the Brothers Minor when still a boy, and he studied at Paris under the Franciscan doctor Alexander of Hales. Within a few years he was lecturing at Paris and in 1257 he became Minister-General of the Franciscans. He was compelled to take an active part in the great crisis which threatened to dissolve the Order over the question of poverty. The 'spiritual' and 'observant' Franciscans clung to the letter of the teaching of Francis, while the 'conventuals', who formed the greater body of the Friars, interpreted the Rule in a laxer fashion, and held that it was lawful for the Order to build churchès and accept freely the secular learning of the age.[1]   The 'spirituals', and among them John of Parma, Minister-General until 1257, became deeply tinged with the Joachimite doctrines; they saw in Francis the precursor of the Kingdom of the Spirit, and, in their enthusiasm, proceeded to the enunciation of doctrines which laid them open to the charge of heresy.   In 1257 John of Parma was persuaded to resign his ministry, and Bonaventura succeeded him in the office, which he held until his death in 1274.   Bonaventura was a Platonist, or, more exactly, an Augustinian, by intellectual conviction, and emotionally he goes back to the school of Victorine mysticism, seeing the approach to God as a progress made by long stages of contemplation 'through love of the crucified'.[2]

Whether the hymns and poems which have been attributed to Bonaventura are really his or no, they breathe the ardent mysticism and the love of the Crucified which inflame every page of his prose writings.   Best known of all is the *Laudismus de Sancta Cruce*,[3] beginning in the true Franciscan spirit :

[1] Holzapfel, *Handbuch der Geschichte des Franziskanerordens*, pp. 40 sqq.

[2] Cf. Bonav. *Itinerarium mentis in Deum, Prologus* 'Via autem non est nisi per ardentissimum amorem crucifixi, qui adeo Paulum ad tertium caelum raptum transformavit in Christum'; see Ehrle, *Der hl. Bonaventura und seine drei Lebensaufgaben*, p. 124.   Bonaventura tried to retain as much of the Neo-Platonic Augustinian element as he could; see also Rosenmüller, *Religiöse Erkenntnis nach Bonaventura*, pp. 210 sqq., and E. Gilson, *La philosophie de S. Bonaventure*, who shows (pp. 12 sqq.) that Bonaventura was not ignorant of, but opposed to, the Aristotelian system.

[3] *Anal. Hymn.* l, p. 571 ; doubts have been cast by some earlier editors on Bonaventura's authorship of this poem, see Fedele da Fanna, *Ratio novae collectionis operum omnium . . . S. Bonaventurae*, p. 31. Dreves (*Anal. Hymn.* l, p. 577) is inclined to ascribe the poem to Pecham.   It is remarkable that it is the later manuscripts (fifteenth and sixteenth century) which alone name Bonaventura as the author.   The two manuscripts of the fourteenth century wrongly name Bernard.   The editors of the Quaracchi edition, *S. Bonav. Opera Omnia*, x. 20, accept the *Laudismus* as probably genuine.

recordare sanctae crucis,
qui perfectam vitam ducis,
    delectare iugiter.
sanctae crucis recordare,
et in ipsa meditare,
    insatiabiliter.

ama crucem, mundi lucem,
et habebis Christum ducem
    per aeterna saecula ;
cruce corpus circumcinge,
hanc constringe, manu pinge
    consignando singula.

stes in cruce Christo duce
donec vivas in hac luce,
    moto procul taedio,
non quiescas nec tepescas,
in hoc crescas et calescas
    cordis desiderio.

cor in cruce, crux in corde
sit, cum corde sine sorde,
    quae tranquillum faciat ;
lingua crux efficiatur,
crucem promat et loquatur,
    et nunquam deficiat.

The Cross is for Bonaventura,[1] as for every follower of Francis, the centre of all man's hope of salvation, his only consolation, his sorrow and his delight.

quaere crucem, quaere clavos,
quaere manus, pedes cavos,
    quaere fossam lateris ;
ibi plaude, ibi gaude
sine fraude summa laude,
    quantumcunque poteris. . . .

crux est navis, crux est portus,
crux deliciarum hortus,
    in quo florent omnia ;
crux est fortis armatura
et protectio secura
    conterens daemonia.[2]

The second part of the hymn is an exposition of the manner in which a true Franciscan should meditate on the sufferings of Christ. The text is evidently the ' Rule of the Novices ' which we have already quoted, enjoining the continual remembrance of the crown of thorns, the vinegar and gall, the scourge and the spear. Here again that personal appeal, in which we have seen the essence of the Franciscan Gospel, rings out with a deep pathos :

[1] Cf. E. Gilson, S. Bonaventure et l'iconographie de la Passion, Revue d'histoire franciscaine, i. 407 sqq.

[2] Cf. Bonav. De perfectione vitae ad sorores, vi : 'Accede ergo tu pedibus affectionum tuarum ad Iesum vulneratum, ad Iesum spinis coronatum, ad Iesum patibulo crucis affixum, et cum beato Thoma apostolo non solum intuere in manibus eius fixuras clavorum, non solum mitte manum tuam in latus eius, sed totaliter per ostium lateris eius ingredere usque ad cor ipsius Iesu, ibique ardentissimo amore crucifixi in Christum transformata, clavis divini amoris affixa, lancea praecordialis dilectionis transfixa, intimae compassionis transverberata, nihil aliud quaeras, nihil aliud desideres, et nullo alio velis consolari, quam ut cum Christo tu possis mori in cruce ; et tunc cum apostolo Paulo exclames, dicens : Christo confixus sum cruci. Vivo iam non ego, vivit vero Christus.'

quam despectus et abiectus
rex caelorum est effectus,
  ut salvaret saeculum ;
esurivit et sitivit,
pauper et egenus ivit
  usque ad patibulum.

recordare paupertatis
et extremae vilitatis
  et gravis supplicii,
si es compos rationis,
esto memor passionis,
  fellis et absynthii ...

illi oculi beati
sunt in cruce obscurati
  et vultus expalluit ;
suo corpori tunc nudo
non remansit pulchritudo,
  decor omnis abfuit. . . .

The remainder of Bonaventura's verse does not share the
poetical qualities of the *Recordare sanctae crucis*, but all of it
derives its inspiration from the Passion. The poem called
Lignum Vitae contains a series of verses in which each line
begins with the name of Jesus; it is no more than a collection
of the chapter headings of Bonaventura's prose treatise called
by the same name.[1]

The *Office of the Holy Cross* is said to have been written by
Bonaventura at the instance of S. Louis.[2] The hymn for Matins,
in two-syllabled masculine rime, is the most successful of the
eight hymns contained in the Office :

in passione domini,
qua datur salus homini,
sit nostrum refrigerium
et cordis desiderium.

haec omnia nos satient
et dulciter inebrient,
nos repleant virtutibus
et gloriosis fructibus.

portemus in memoria
et poenas et opprobria
Christi, coronam spineam,
crucem, clavos et lanceam.

te crucifixum colimus
et toto corde poscimus,
ut nos sanctorum coetibus
coniungas in caelestibus.

et plagas sacratissimas,
omni laude dignissimas,
acetum, fel, arundinem,
mortis amaritudinem.

laus, honor Christo vendito
et sine causa prodito,
passo mortem pro populo
in aspero patibulo.

---

[1] Text in *Anal. Hymn.* l, p. 559. The
verses on the Passion are as follows :

'Iesus notis incognitus,
  Iesus vultu velatus,
  Iesus Pilato traditus,
  Iesus morte damnatus,

Iesus spretus ab omnibus,
  Iesus cruce clavatus,
  Iesus iunctus latronibus,
  Iesus felle potatus,

Iesus sol morte pallidus,
  Iesus translanceatus,
  Iesus cruore madidus,
  Iesus intumulatus.'

[2] *Anal. Hymn.* l, p. 568, *The Chronicle of
the XXIV Generals* (*Anal. Francisc.* iii.
231), a fourteenth century compilation, contains this tradition ; also a fourteenth century manuscript. The Quaracchi editors
(x, p. 16) consider the office genuine, and
so does E. Gilson, *S. Bonaventure et
l'iconographie de la Passion*, p. 408.

Bonaventura's verse does not reveal so well as his prose the rich poetical clothing with which he could invest his thought. His deeper meditations, the fruit of that inward life of devotion to which he preferred to dedicate himself, are enshrined in his mystical treatises—the *Lignum Vitae*, the *Itinerarium mentis in Deum*, the *Vitis Mystica*, and the *De sex alis Seraphim*. Here the philosopher is inseparable from the saint, and, although Bonaventura is writing for others and will not reveal the inner secrets of his 'interior illumination', he shows us enough of himself to make us understand the saying of Alexander of Hales, reported by Salimbene—'in eo videbatur Adam non peccasse'.[1] He saw in Francis his master in that *Itinerarium mentis*, whose end was an ecstasy to which he gave the name of peace— 'quam pacem evangelizavit et dedit Dominus noster Iesus Christus: cuius praedicationis repetitor fuit pater noster Franciscus, in omni sua praedicatione pacem in principio et in fine annuntians, in omni salutatione pacem optans, in omni contemplatione ad extaticam pacem suspirans, tanquam civis illius Ierusalem, de qua dicit vir ille pacis... rogate quae ad pacem sunt Ierusalem'.[2]

The author of the *Philomena*, one of the loveliest of all the poems of the Passion, is John Pecham, a Brother Minor, who became Archbishop of Canterbury. He appears to have been born at Patcham, near Lewes, and his early studies were made at Lewes Priory and then at Oxford, where he joined the Order of S. Francis. From Oxford he went to Paris, where he listened to Bonaventura, took his doctor's degree, and became a lecturer in Theology. About 1270 he returned to Oxford as lector, and in 1275 he became Provincial of the English Franciscans, in which capacity he attended a General Chapter of the Order at Pavia, proceeding there on foot in true Franciscan fashion. We next find him settled in Rome as 'lector sacri palatii', official lecturer in divinity in the papal schools. Cardinals and bishops were his frequent auditors, and they rose from their seats in his honour when he entered the school. In 1279, after Kilwardby's death, Nicholas III made Pecham Archbishop of Canterbury, in spite of the fact that Edward I supported the candidature of Robert Burnell. Pecham accepted the honour much against his will, but carried out his duties with a fearless

---

[1] Gilson, *La philosophie de S. Bonaventure*, p. 11.
[2] *Itinerarium mentis in Deum, Prolog.*:

cf. Gilson, *op. cit.*, p. 76, and the rest of his brilliant and finely-drawn portrait of Bonaventura.

dignity until his death in 1292. His body was laid to rest in his Cathedral Church, but the Brothers Minor took his heart and buried it in the sacrarium behind the high altar of their Church in London.[1]

The *Philomena*,[2] the greatest of Pecham's poems, is written in four-lined stanzas of thirteen syllables, with a mono-rime. The metre is handled with consummate mastery, and the cadence of the rhythm is exquisite. It is a purely lyrical poem, unfettered by the conditions imposed upon a liturgical composition, personal in its emotion, and filled with the new inspiration which was the secret of the gospel of Assisi. The subject of the poem is the nightingale, the forerunner of the spring, the bird who, ' in her saddest, sweetest plight', sings a song which typifies the crying out of the soul for the heavenly country. For the nightingale, when she perceives that she is near to death, flies to a tree top, and at dawn pours forth her song. When the day begins to break, she sings without pause ever louder at the hour of prime, and at tierce the joy and passion of her song increase, until it seems as if her throat must burst with the torrent of melody. Then at last, when noon arrives, her body can endure no longer ; *Oci, Oci*,[3] she cries, and in the anguish of her song she sinks and fails. At none she dies, her tiny body shattered and broken. The nightingale is the type of the pious soul, which longs for the heavenly country, and, longing, beguiles itself with song. So it lives, as it were, through a mystical day, the hours of which correspond to the stages of its redemption. Dawn is the stage of man's creation ; Prime the season of the incarnation of Christ ; Tierce is the period of His life on earth. Sext represents the hour of His betrayal, scourging, and crucifixion, None of His death, and Vespers of His burial. Stage by stage the soul follows in meditation, and out of its meditation fashions a song. The sweetness and sadness of the meditation increase as the hour of the Passion approaches, and the soul remembers

---

[1] C. L. Kingsford, *The Grey Friars of London*, p. 40, *Brit. Soc. Francisc. Studies*, vi.

[2] For the form *Philomena*, a not uncommon medieval variant for Philomela, see Grimm and Schmeller, *Lateinische Gedichte des X. und XI. Jh.*, p. 322 ; W. Meyer, *Fragmenta Burana*, p. 24, for the form *Filomena*.

[3] On the meaning of *Oci*, see Otto Glauning's edition of the *Two Nightingale*

Poems, by John Lydgate, E. E. T. S., extra series 80, 1900, p. 35 ; also R. Köhler, in *Zeitschr. für roman. Philol.* viii, 1884, pp. 120-2. The word occurs frequently in medieval poems with reference to the song of the nightingale and is either onomatopoeic, or, as in Pecham's poem, is regarded as the imperative of the old French 'occir', to kill. For the latter use sèe Uhland, *Schriften zur Geschichte der Dichtung und Sage*, iv, pp. 97 sqq.

the sufferings of the Redeemer, in which it longs to share, until, at the hour of the *Consummatum est,* it fails and dies in the ecstasy of love and compassion.

The whole poem is filled with this personal devotion to the Crucified, to one who had become a human child in Bethlehem, and had grown up a man amongst men, and had suffered an inconceivable anguish for their sake. The same sense of the reality of the Gospel story, which had led Francis to an exquisite act of devotion when he set up the manger in the wood at Greccio, with ox and ass by its side,[1] wakens a desire in the poet that he might have been deemed worthy to minister to the wants of the child of Bethlehem, to have soothed His cries and to have rocked His cradle :

> heu me, cur non licuit mihi demulcere
> vagientem parvulum, dulciter tenere,
> illos artus teneros sinu refovere
> eiusque cunabulis semper assidere.
>
> credo, pius parvulus hoc non abhorreret,
> immo more parvuli forsan arrideret
> nec se a pauperculo tangi prohiberet
> et petenti veniam facile faveret.[2]

In the meditation at noon, the soul is weeping for the passion of the Saviour; it is pierced with the dart of the divine love, saying, *Oci, oci,* like the passionate nightingale :

> oci, oci anima clamat in hoc statu,
> crebro fundens lacrimas sub hoc incolatu,
> laudans et glorificans magno cum conatu
> Christum, qui tot pertulit suo pro reatu.
>
> . . . plorans ergo respicit agnum delicatum,
> agnum sine macula, spinis coronatum,
> lividum vulneribus, clavis terebratum,
> per tot loca corporis totum cruentatum.
>
> tunc exclamat millies oci cum lamentis,
> oci, oci miseram, quia meae mentis
> turbat statum pallidus vultus morientis
> et languentes oculi in cruce pendentis.
>
> quare sic decuerat, inquit, te benignum
> agnum mortis exitum pati tam indignum ?
> sed sic disposueras vincere malignum,
> et hoc totum factum est ad amoris signum.

---

[1] Bonaventura, *Legenda,* x.
[2] The text of the *Philomena* is in *Anal. Hymn.* l, pp. 602 sqq.

But the soul is not satisfied with gazing on the passion, and on the wounds of the Saviour. It must have its own passion, it too must suffer and die of love and pity:

> plane, nisi moriar tecum, non quiescam,
> *oci, oci* clamitans nunquam conticescam,
> ab hoc desiderio vere non tepescam,
> quantumcunque plus in hoc saeculo vilescam.

> tunc ut demens clamitat: veniant lanistae,
> qui adfigant miseram cruci tuae, Christe;
> erit enim exitus dulcis mihi iste,
> si complectar moriens propriis ulnis te.

Thus crucified with Christ, the soul is made the partaker of His passion, and, finally, of His death.

None of the other poems of Pecham reaches the height of the *Philomena*. The poem *De Deliciis Virginis gloriosae*[1] contains one verse which refers to the sorrow of the Virgin:

> salve, grandi cum dolore
> Iesum madidum cruore
>   cernens in patibulo;

> sed hoc minus doluisti,
> quod hunc pati credidisti
>   pro salvando saeculo.

Here is the grim realism which the Franciscans encouraged in art and proclaimed in their sermons. It appears, too, in the *Philomena*, where the soul desires to be bathed in the wounds of Christ:

> suo quippe corpore languidum te pavit,
> quam in suo sanguine gratis balneavit,
> post hoc suum dulce cor tibi denudavit,
> ut sic innotesceret, quantum te amavit.

> o quam dulce balneum, esca quam suavis,
> quae sumenti digne fis paradisi clavis!
> ei, quem tu reficis, nullus labor gravis,
> licet sis fastidio cordibus ignavis.

Such realism was entirely absent from the literature and art of pre-Franciscan times. On the sculptured jubé at Bourges, Christ is shown carrying His cross, but it is the progress of

---

[1] *Anal. Hymn.* l, p. 598.

a king, and not of a pale and languid sufferer. The cross is a symbol of triumph; it is studded with precious stones. In later medieval art, under Franciscan influence, the symbolism disappears, and Christ is the Victim, worn and weary, the blood streaming from His wounds, the thorns piercing His brow. The pictures of the Passion show the blood pouring from His wounds as He hangs on the Cross; it falls into a fountain beneath, in which a crowd of sinners bathe, as it flows into a winepress, which is a figure of the eucharistic sacrament.

§ 3. *The Laude of Jacopone da Todi* (1230 *circ.*–1306).

It lies outside the scope of the present study to treat of the immense influence upon art, and especially upon Italian art, which was exercised by the Franciscan movement,[1] or to discuss in any detail the popular religious poetry which throughout the whole of Italy began to absorb the Franciscan emotion and the Franciscan realism. But any attempt at describing the true character of the poetry which, in spite of its liturgical form, owed so much to the attitude of Francis to nature, and to the human side of the Gospel story, must take account of the stream of popular verse wherein are mirrored with greater clearness the true Franciscan ideas in their most direct and uncompromising appeal. Apart from any claim which Jacopone da Todi may possess to the authorship of the *Stabat Mater*, that supreme expression of love and compassion for the Mother and her Son, he is the Franciscan poet who has left the most abiding tradition of popularity in those religious *Laude*, composed in the Umbrian dialect, which are a remarkable witness to the manner in which the Franciscan religion had invaded the nascent literature of the people. In the later twelfth century[2] the Provençal poetry had already entered Italy, and created a school of imitators at the Italian courts. In the thirteenth century the Court of Frederic II was a centre of vernacular poetry. But, independently, the humbler poets of the people sang their songs, religious and profane, not of knightly *gestes* or courtly love, but of common happenings and common tales, of heaven and hell, of God and

---

[1] See Thode, *S. François d'Assise et les origines de l'art de la Renaissance en Italie* (French trans. of *Franz von Assisi und die Anfänge der Kunst der Renaissance in Italien*).

[2] Thode, ii. 124 sqq.

the saints.[1]   The religious jongleurs could possibly claim among
their number the founder of the Franciscan movement, who had
sung the praises of God on the Umbrian roads, and had left
that exquisite *Song of the Creatures* which he had made, 'so
that in considering the praise of the Lord, he might forget the
bitterness of his pains and infirmities'.[2]   By the interposition
of Francis, Fra Pacifico, who in the world had composed wanton
songs and had been crowned by the emperor as *Rex versuum*,
turned to religion, and may have used his talents in the service
of his new Master.[3]   The Franciscan Giacomino of Verona
sang of hell and paradise after the manner of the typical Franciscan homily.[4]

In Umbria and elsewhere in Italy, there were lay brother-
hoods of *Laudesi*,[5] whose business it was to sing and act religious
songs and dramas on special occasions.   They gave employment
to those jongleurs and poets who, without desire for more than
passing fame, and with more devotion than art, could frame
rude songs or dramatic pieces on the ever-popular events of the
Gospel story, especially on the Passion, the miracles of the
Virgin, and the joys of paradise.   Of their number was Jacopone
da Todi, known in the world as Ser Jacomo, who excelled all
others in the composition of these *laude*, and came, indeed, to be
regarded as their first inventor.

He was born about the year 1230, and until the age of forty
appears to have lived the life of a respectable and successful
lawyer.   The fifteenth-century life or legend of Jacopone pictures
him as a proud and avaricious man,[6] and relates how his heart
was turned to religion by the tragic death of his young and
beautiful wife in an accident at a public show.   When they
drew the rich and delicate clothing from her dying body, they
discovered a hair-shirt next to the tender flesh.   The pathos of
this discovery worked one of those strange revulsions of feeling,

[1] See D'Ancona, *Jacopone da Todi*,
p. 7.
[2] *Spec. Perfect.* cxix ; the best text of
the Song is in Böhmer, *Analekten zur
Geschichte des Franciscus von Assisi*,
pp. 65 sqq., Tübingen and Leipzig 1904.
[3] II Celano, 106.
[4] Ozanam, *Les poètes franciscains*, pp.
123 sqq. ; Thode, ii. 128 ; text in Mussafia,
Berlin. Sitzungsber. xlvi, pp. 113 sqq.
[5] Ancona, op. cit., p. 12 ; also Ancona,
Origini del teatro italiano, i. 153 sq. ;

Brugnoli, *Le satire di Jacopone da Todi*,
p. cxix sq.
[6] In *Zeitschr. für roman. Philol.* ii.
25 sqq. (*Vita del beato Jacopone da Todi*,
ed. Tobler) ; for his life see also Wadding,
Annales Minorum, v. 407 sqq., vi. 77 sq.,
Rome 1738, 2nd edit. ; there is a notice of
Jacopone in Bartholomew of Pisa, *De con-
formitate vitae beati Francisci ad vitam
Domini Iesu*, lib. i, fruct. viii, par. ii, *Analecta Franciscana*, iv, p. 235, Quaracchi
1906.

so common among the Latin peoples in the Middle Ages. Jacopone sold his goods and gave them to the poor ; he wandered about, clothed in the rough garb of a Tertiary, seeking the perfect poverty of Christ, and manifesting such extravagant excesses of religious devotion and repentance, that he appeared to his fellow-citizens to have parted with his reason.   He became a 'fool for Christ's sake', he exulted in his folly, and gloried in the rude persecutions to which he was subjected :

> senno me pare e cortesia
> empazir per lo bel Messia,[1]

he says at the beginning of a *lauda* in praise of his divine madness.   He is pictured for us as the true Franciscan 'joculator Dei', who, as he wanders about, sings in the Umbrian dialect his love of the Crucified, and the delights of companionship in the sufferings of Christ.   ' He was so inflamed with the divine love', says Wadding, ' that he appeared to have taken leave of his senses ; now he sang, now he wept, and often he would break out into sighs'.[2]   His aim, says the fifteenth-century *Vita*, was to make progress in the way of perfection by achieving a perfect contempt of himself, bearing shame and dishonour 'for the love of Jesus Christ who bore such shame for the human race'.[3]

Some ten years passed before Jacopone definitely became a Brother Minor, but, when he joined the Order, it was inevitable that he should fling himself with all the ardour of his soul on the side of the *spirituali*.   He showed his convictions in the bitterest attacks on the 'relaxed' Friars, and he satirized the worldly passions which were exhibited in the Franciscan family :

> vedete el grand' amore
> che l'un a l'altro ha en core ! [4]

he exclaimed with savage irony.   He hated also the impulse which urged the followers of Francis to crowd into the Universities in pursuit of the ' curiosa et sterilis scientia' of the schools.[5] ' Paris has destroyed Assisi ', he said, in a memorable phrase. For him, as for the other *zelanti*, Francis remained the true and

---

[1] *Lauda*, lxxxiv ; the references are to Ferri's edition of the *laude*, Bari 1915.
[2] Wadding, v. 413.
[3] *Vita*, p. 29.

[4] *Lauda*, xxxi.
[5] Cf. H. Felder, *Geschichte der wissenschaftlichen Studien im Franziskaner- orden*, pp. 378 sq., 519 sq.

only pattern of the perfect Brother Minor, and the very revelation of Christ :

> o Francesco, da Dio amato,
> Cristo en te s'ène mostrato.[1]

Poverty is the desirable Bride—'her wings have so many feathers that the way from earth to heaven is short'.[2]

With such an impetuous temperament, joined to an ardently mystical nature, Jacopone was soon involved in the world of ecclesiastical politics. The election to the Papacy of Pietro da Murrone, a saintly hermit, an aged man without the slightest qualification for such a trust, raised high the hopes of the spiritual party. He was consecrated in August, 1294. Before the end of the year, he had performed an ignominious act of abdication, and the imperious Gaetani took his place as Boniface VIII. The party of the Colonna Cardinals, who were the personal enemies of Boniface, declared against him, and appealed against his election to a General Council. Jacopone was with the rebels when Boniface, after their solemn excommunication, proceeded to storm their stronghold at Palestrina. The poet had attacked the Pope in scurrilous verses :

> o papa Bonifazio,
> molt' hai iocato al mondo : ˙
> penso che giocondo
> non te porrai partire.[3]

'As the salamander lives in the fire, so in scandal thou dost seek thy solace and pleasure. Of souls redeemed thou hast but little care, but when thou art dead thou shalt know thine own place.' Such words could not be easily forgiven. Jacopone was cast into a subterranean prison whence he implored in vain the mercy of the Pope. The jubilee of 1300 passed him by, though it brought freedom to others; not until 1303, at the age of seventy-three, when his great enemy had died of a broken heart after the indignity at Anagni, did he regain his liberty. He passed away on Christmas Eve, 1306, at the moment when, in the neighbouring church, at the first mass the priest intoned the *Gloria in Excelsis*.[4] He was buried at Todi, and his tomb

---

[1] *Lauda*, lxii; cf. *Vita*, p. 31, 'This servant of God was a faithful and true son of S. Francis in all things pertaining to the true observance of the rule of the holy Francis.'

[2] *Lauda*, lix.

[3] *Lauda*, lviii; also *Le satire di Jacopone da Todi*, ed. Brugnoli, p. 305.

[4] Wadding, vi. 78.

bears the epitaph, inscribed in 1596, 'Ossa beati Jacoponi de Benedictis, Tudertini, fratris ordinis minorum, qui stultus propter Christum nova mundum arte delusit, et caelum rapuit'.

The Franciscan authorities had received Jacopone into their Order with some diffidence; but once dead, he grew in reputation as a saint, 'mirandae sanctitatis, et totus ardens in Dei amore'.[1] The devotion of the common people, whom he had loved and served, was lavished on his memory, and he lived long in those *laude*—'laudes magnarum sententiarum et dulcedine plenas',[2] as Bartholomew of Pisa calls them—which set forth in rude measures, rising often to the highest beauty and sweetness, the gospel of Francis and the perfection of poverty. Many of them are songs of the divine love, some simple and clear, others coloured with passion and sensuous imagery, in praise of that 'love whose name is " I love ", but has never a plural'.

> amor c'hai nome amo,
> plural mai non trovamo.[3]

'Once', says Wadding,[4] 'he was asked by a Brother why he so often wept. He replied: I weep because love is not loved.' One of his songs begins : ' In the furnace love has laid me. . . . In the furnace love has laid me. . . . If I die of love, marvel not. For I am smitten with lances of love.'[5]

Of splendid beauty is the *lauda*, beginning *Fiorito è Cristo*. Its theme is the 'flos de flore', on which Bernard had written eloquent pages. ' This sweet flower, its great might humbled, was trodden under foot, surrounded with sharp thorns, and its beauty was veiled. The brightness which lightened the darkness of men was obscured by harsh sorrow, and its light was all hidden in a tomb in a garden of flowers. The flower lay down and slept, but soon awoke and rose again. The pure and blessed body flowered again and appeared in great brightness. . . . He comforted the hearts of his brethren, and raised up many new flowers. He sojourned in the garden with them, singing of love to his lambs.'[6]

Mingled with these songs of divine love are fierce, satirical pieces, denunciations of worldly vanities, of ecclesiastical abuses ; pictures of the Church[7] weeping for her evil estate, complaining

---

[1] *Anal. Francisc.*, iv. 235.   [2] ib.   Brugnoli, however (p. 406), denies that
[3] *Lauda*, lxxxv.   [4] v. 414.   this *lauda* is Jacopone's.
[5] Pacheu, *Jacopone de Todi*, p. 229 ;   [6] *Lauda*, c.   [7] *Lauda*, liii.

that her true sons and brothers are dead, that only bastards are
left who are cowards, lovers of discord, and enemies of poverty,
eager only for silver and gold.   Then, at times, a startling
passage appears, which can only be paralleled in the subtle mind
of Donne, even if it is partly taken from S. Gregory:

> I am the book of life with seven seals;
> Mine open page five miniatures reveals
> Emblazoned with my blood, to all displayed . . .
> This is the scripture all can make their own,
> So plain to read, yet never wholly known;
> Here elephants can swim and lambs can wade.[1]

But always his thoughts were ready to turn to the contemplation of death and corruption, as in the horrible dialogue
between the Soul and its Body,[2] and the still more terrible
Quando t' allegri, an address to the decaying corpse. 'Where
are thine eyes, once so bright?   They are cast forth from thy
head.   I deem that the worms have devoured them.   Of thy
pride they had no fear.' 'I have lost those eyes, wherewith
I have sinned, as they strayed with evil desire.   Woe is me!
I am in torment; my body is devoured and my soul is in fire.'[3]
And so the abominable inquisition proceeds.   Another poem is
an admonition to sinners of the approach of death:

> ecco la pallida morte
> laida, scura e sfigurata.[4]

It is no avail to close the gates of the great fortified towers
against him, for nothing can withstand his onset. 'Consider the
great lords, so feared and high-esteemed, counts, kings and
emperors, to what end they have come.   Death had so well
entreated them, that their delicate flesh, once so well adorned,
is all red beneath their worms.   Death comes and casts down
knights and dames and damsels, priests and friars, fair and foul
alike.   He comes with feet so swift that none may hear his
coming.'

In the same mood of 'dispiritedness' he wrote (if we may
accept the uncertain testimony of Wadding[5]) a Latin rhythm

---

[1] *Lauda*, xl; this excellent rendering
is by Mrs. Theodore Beck, in Miss Evelyn
Underhill's study, *Jacopone da Todi*.
[2] *Lauda*, xv.   [3] ib., xxv.
[4] Pacheu, p. 114: Brugnoli, p. 402,
classifies this *lauda* among the doubtful,

meno improbabili.
[5] vi. 79, 'Valde commendatur illud eiusdem de contemptu mundi canticum, quod
sine auctoris nomine communiter circum-
fertur . . . Cur mundus militat', &c.

De Contemptu Mundi, which for its beauty and pathos has been attributed, but without reason, to Bernard of Clairvaux.   This remarkable poem represents so fully the whole of his mood in the face of human glory and the ignominy of its end that one might be tempted to accept the tradition of Jacopone's authorship.   It is said [1] that these verses, together with the rapturous *Udite nova pazzia*, were the means of persuading the hesitating Friars to accept the eccentric convert as a member of their order :

> cur mundus militat sub vana gloria,
> cuius prosperitas est transitoria ?
> tam cito labitur eius potentia,
> quam vasa figuli, quae sunt fragilia.
>
> plus fide litteris scriptis in glacie,
> quam mundi fragilis vanae fallaciae ;
> fallax in praemiis, virtutis specie,
> qui nunquam habuit tempus fiduciae.
>
> credendum magis est viris fallacibus,
> quam mundi miseris prosperitatibus,
> falsis insaniis et vanitatibus,
> falsisque studiis et voluptatibus.
>
> quam breve festum est haec mundi gloria !
> ut umbra hominis sic eius gaudia,
> quae semper subtrahunt aeterna praemia,
> et ducunt hominem ad dura devia.
>
> o esca vermium ! o massa pulveris !
> o ros, o vanitas, cur sic extolleris ?
> ignorans penitus, utrum cras vixeris,
> fac bonum omnibus, quamdiu poteris.
>
> haec carnis gloria, quae tanti penditur,
> sacris in litteris flos foeni dicitur ;
> ut leve folium, quod vento rapitur,
> sic vita hominis luci subtrahitur.
>
> nil tuum dixeris quod potes perdere,
> quod mundus tribuit, intendit rapere :
> superna cogita, cor sit in aethere,
> felix, qui potuit mundum contemnere !

---

[1] Ozanam, p. 161 ; Pacheu, p. 13: I have been unable to trace any early evidence for this assertion ; Wadding, v. 411, simply mentions a ' libellum brevemque commentarium de mundi contemptu ', in recording the incident, and the *Vita* (p. 29) mentions only the vernacular *lauda*.   But as the Latin verses appear in a work (*Summa Iustitiae*) ascribed to Grosseteste, and certainly older than Jacopone, the latter cannot be the author ; see *British Museum Catal. of Royal MSS.*, i. 221 (1921).

dic, ubi Salomon, olim tam nobilis,
vel ubi Samson est, dux invincibilis,
vel pulcher Absalon, vultu mirabilis,
vel dulcis Jonathas, multum amabilis?

quo Caesar abiit, celsus imperio,
vel Dives splendidus, totus in prandio?
dic, ubi Tullius, clarus eloquio,
vel Aristoteles, summus ingenio?

tot clari proceres, tot rerum spatia,
tot ora praesulum, tot regna fortia,
tot mundi principes, tanta potentia,
in ictu oculi clauduntur omnia.

These verses, 'contemning', as an Elizabethan editor puts it,
'the unstable felicitie of this wayfaring worlde', possess a quality
which lifts them from their theological and religious setting and
gives them something of the more universal meaning of the
greater secular poetry which has in all ages revolved round
a similar theme. When we read a verse in the Elizabethan
paraphrase[1]—

Where is that Caesar nowe, whose hygh renowned fame,
Of sundry conquests wonne throughout the world did sound?
Or *Dives* riche in store, and rich in richely name,
Whose chest with gold and dishe, with daynties did abound?
Where is the passing grace of *Tullies* pleding skill?
Or *Aristotles* vayne, whose penne had witte and w,yll?—

it sounds like a *ballade du temps jadis*, more full of the melancholy of art than of religion.

§ 4.   *The Donna del Paradiso and the Stabat Mater.*

The *Life* of Jacopone[2] tells how 'the servant of God, fra
Jacopone, began to meditate on the passion of Christ as the
sovereign remedy and medicine against every hindrance of the
soul that desires to serve God', and, furthermore, describes
the compassion which he had for the Mother of Christ; 'wherefore he composed that *lauda* which is called *Donna del Paradiso*'.

---

[1] *The Paradyse of daynty devises*, London 1576: reprinted, 1810, edited by Sir
Egerton Brydges; it contains an interesting verse translation of the *Cur mundus militat*; for another version see
E. E. T. S., *Hymns to the Virgin and*

Christ, ed. Furnivall, 1867, pp. 86 sqq.
For another Latin poem on the same subject see Hauréau, *Notices et extraits de
quelques mss.*, iv, p. 332.
[2] p. 33.

It is in this composition that Ozanam[1] and others have found the same inspiration which produced the statelier pathos of the *Stabat Mater*. The characters of this dramatic *lauda*, which D'Ancona has described as 'the most notable monument of the spiritual poetry of the thirteenth century',[2] are the Virgin, Christ, the crowd, and a voice which relates to Mary the cruel details of the Crucifixion. 'Lady of Paradise, thy Son is taken, Jesus Christ the blessed. Run, Lady, and see how they are smiting Him; methinks that they have slain Him; they have scourged Him so much.' 'O Pilate,' cries the Mother, 'do not allow my Son to be tortured, for I can show thee that He is wrongly accused.' 'Madonna,' says the voice, 'behold the cross which the people are carrying, whereon the true Light must be lifted up. . . . Lady, He is stretched on the cross.' And the sword pierces the Mother's heart. She wishes to die with her Son and be buried with Him in one tomb. But Christ replies:

> Mamma col cor aflicto,
> entro a le man te mecto
> de Joanne mio electo ;
> ssia el tuo figlio appellato.
>
> Joanne, esto mia mate,
> tollela en caritate,
> aggine pietate
> ch' ha lo core forato.

And the *lauda* ends with the lament of the broken-hearted Mother.

The *Stabat Mater*, likewise, grew out of the Franciscan devotion to the passion of Mary. The problem of its authorship has been the subject of long and tiresome controversy.[3] The oldest ascription is, indeed, to Jacopone, the claims of Gregory the Great and Bernard of Clairvaux, to whom other famous hymns have been attributed, being easily ruled out. The much favoured attribution to Innocent III has been shown to rest on the purely gratuitous assertion of Louis Jacob, reiterated by Benedict XIV in his book on the 'festivals of our Lord Jesus Christ' printed at Bologna in 1740.[4]

[1] p. 233.
[2] *Origini del teatro italiano*, 2nd ed., i. 162 ; for a text and full discussion see i. 157 sqq. ; text also in Ferri, *Lauda*, xciii.
[3] See Julian, *Dictionary of Hymnology*, p. 1082 ; Ozanam, *Les poètes franciscains*, p. 195 ; Tenneroni, *Lo Stabat Mater e Donna del Paradiso* ; Pacheu, *Jacopone de Todi*.
[4] Pacheu, p. 73.

Before discussing the positive evidence in favour of Jacopone, it is necessary to deal with the argument that the acknowledged author of the *Donna del Paradiso* could not possibly have risen to the loftier style of the *Stabat Mater*. Such a criticism fails to recognize that each is the work of a perfectly self-conscious artist obeying the rules of his craft. The *Donna del Paradiso* is composed as a vernacular *lauda*, following the traditional form with all its roughness and its crude realism. 'In iis' (i.e. in the *laude*), says Wadding [1] with perfect good sense, 'quidem facile liquet eum de industria sermonis stilique elegantiam neglexisse.' Further, the realistic treatment follows exactly the presentation of the passion story as the Franciscan preachers loved to set it forth, and in its details it hardly digresses from the manner of the *Meditationes vitae Christi*. The author knew precisely the effect which he desired to achieve, and he achieved it. The case of the *Stabat Mater* is surely similar. The poet set out, not to compose a *lauda*, but a devotional poem, according to the strict rules of the Latin sequence in its latest manner, and the treatment of the subject is determined by stringent conditions. The Franciscan emotion is there, and the same devotion to Mary, which inspired the *Donna del Paradiso*, but the feeling is personal, not dramatic, and the total impression is necessarily different. There is, therefore, no *a priori* reason why a poet of Jacopone's power, when he turned to Latin verse, should not have produced a liturgical masterpiece like the *Stabat Mater*. But the problem of authorship rests finally on positive documentary evidence. The *Stabat Mater* is ascribed to Jacopone by three mss. of the fourteenth or fifteenth century:

(1) A ms. of the early fifteenth century at the Bibliothèque Nationale [2] (no. 559), which also assigns to Jacopone, *inter alia*, the *Cur mundus militat, Iesu dulcis memoria*, and the *Stabat Mater speciosa*.

(2) A fourteenth-century ms. in the Riccardi Library (no. 1049), which, however, also ascribes the *Recordare sanctae crucis* to Jacopone. [3]

---

[1] *Annales*, vi. 79; Ermini, *Lo Stabat mater e i pianti della Vergine nella lirica del medio evo*, p. 16, goes so far as to assert that the strongest argument for Jacopone's authorship is 'the clear and continuous poetical analogy of thought and style' between the *Stabat* and the Italian *laude* which are known to be his.

[2] Pacheu, p. 80, says it is of the fourteenth century, but Leopold Delisle (Julian, p. 1082) assigned it to the early fifteenth.

[3] A. Lopez, *Codices Riccardianae, Archiv. Franc. Hist.*, iii (1910), p. 744.

(3) A manuscript at Todi apparently of the fifteenth century, which states that Jacopone 'in holy contemplation composed many sacred poems, and, in contemplating how the blessed Virgin Mary stood at the feet of Jesus Christ her Son hanging on the cross, he composed that poem which begins *Stabat Mater dolorosa*'.[1]

As he died in 1306, the earliest ascription of the *Stabat Mater* to Jacopone is considerably later, while the oldest manuscripts are, apparently, not earlier than 1350–80.[2]   Further, a manuscript at the Bodleian, of 1380, states that Pope Boniface (who can be no other than Jacopone's worst enemy) granted an indulgence to all who should recite 'this plaint of the blessed Mary'.   Of course, as Pacheu suggests,[3] the Pope may have been ignorant of its authorship, or he may have been too great to exercise a petty spite.   But the evidence of the Bodleian MS. seems to weigh heavily against that of the other three witnesses. It is impossible, then, to prove that Jacopone composed the *Stabat Mater*, and the evidence of the manuscripts carries no decisive weight.   What is certain is that the poem came from the family of Francis charged with the same devotion which produced the *Donna del Paradiso*, whether or no these two noble spiritual poems of the Franciscan age were the work of one great poet.

Gregorovius relates how at the Capuchin house of Monte Santo, near Todi, the brothers showed him

'with much pride a MS. poem by Fra Jacopone, a profound and mystical poet . . . Todi is very proud of this monk, who died at Collazione in 1304, and is buried in the Church of S. Fortunatus there. The words of the *Stabat Mater*', he adds, 'have been ascribed to him, and perhaps rightly so.   That glorious and celebrated hymn might well confer immortality upon any man.   I found one of the monks at Monte Santo busily occupied with making a transcript of the Codex containing the *Stabat Mater*, as well as other verses by Fra Jacopone.'[4]

The wonder and emotion which this grand and pathetic sequence has gathered for itself since the days when it was chanted by the wandering Flagellants of the fourteenth century, will hardly diminish.   It has inspired in turn Palestrina,

---

[1] Pacheu, p. 79, quoting from Tenneroni.
[2] ib., p. 80.
[3] ib., p. 80.
[4] Gregorovius, *Latian Summers*, p. 353.

Pergolese, Haydn, and Rossini; but it failed to find a place in the Roman Missal or the Breviary until the eighteenth century, though it had long been in use in Germany, England, and France.

Whether or no it owes parts of its inspiration and many of its phrases to older sequences or hymns, the *Stabat Mater* remains, with the *Dies Irae*, a supreme achievement of Franciscan and, indeed, of the religious verse of the Middle Ages:

1. stabat mater dolorosa
   iuxta crucem lacrimosa,
     dum pendebat filius;
   cuius animam gementem
   contristantem et dolentem
     pertransivit gladius.

2. o quam tristis et afflicta
   fuit illa benedicta
     mater unigeniti!
   quae maerebat et dolebat,
   et tremebat, cum videbat
     nati poenas incliti.

3. quis est homo qui non fleret
   matrem Christi si videret
     in tanto supplicio?
   quis non posset contristari,
   piam matrem contemplari
     dolentem cum filio?

4. pro peccatis suae gentis
   Iesum vidit in tormentis,
     et flagellis subditum,
   vidit suum dulcem natum
   morientem, desolatum,
     cum emisit spiritum.

5. eia, mater, fons amoris,
   me sentire vim doloris
     fac, ut tecum lugeam;
   fac ut ardeat cor meum
   in amando Christum deum,
     ut sibi complaceam.

6. sancta mater, illud agas,
   crucifixi fige plagas
     cordi meo valide;
   tui nati vulnerati,
   tam dignati pro me pati,
     poenas mecum divide.

7. fac me vere tecum flere,
   crucifixo condolere,
     donec ego vixero.
   iuxta crucem tecum stare,
   te libenter sociare
     in planctu desidero.

8. virgo virginum praeclara,
   mihi iam non sis amara;
     fac me tecum plangere,
   fac, ut portem Christi mortem,
   passionis eius sortem
     et plagas recolere.

9. fac me plagis vulnerari
   cruce hac inebriari
     ob amorem filii;
   inflammatus et accensus
   per te, virgo, sim defensus
     in die iudicii.

10. fac me cruce custodiri,
    morte Christi praemuniri,
      confoveri gratia;
    quando corpus morietur,
    fac ut animae donetur
      paradisi gloria.[1]

By the side of the *Recordare Sanctae Crucis* and the *Stabat Mater* must be placed the long rhythm *De Passione Domini*,[2]

---

[1] Text in *Anal. Hymn.* liv, pp. 312 sq.
[2] Dreves-Blume, *Ein Jahrtausend lateinischer Hymnendichtung*, i. 323; see É. de Moreau, *L'Abbaye de Villers-en-Brabant aux xii*e* et xiii*e* siècles*, Brussels 1909, p. lix; also 63 sqq.

usually attributed to Bernard of Clairvaux, but really belonging to the Cistercian, Arnulf of Louvain, Abbot of Villers-en-Brabant, 1240–8. It is a prayer to the feet, the knees, the hands, the side, the breast, the heart, and the face of the Saviour on the Cross. The hymn is so full of that ecstatic devotion to the wounds of Christ, it dwells so ardently on the instruments of the Passion, that we might have assumed it to be the cry of one who was a spiritual son of S. Francis. The last division of the poem—*Ad faciem*—is the inspiration of Gerhardt's famous hymn, *O Haupt voll Blut und Wunden*, but it is not part of the original poem :

> salve caput cruentatum,
> totum spinis coronatum,
> conquassatum, vulneratum,
> arundine verberatum,
> facie sputis illita.

Then, once more, as if it were a son of Francis speaking, the personal cry breaks out before the end :

> in hac tua passione
> me agnosce, pastor bone.
>
> .   .   .   .   .   .
>
> morte tibi iam vicinâ
> tuum caput hinc inclina,
> in meis pausa brachiis.

The vast body of poetry, which drew its inspiration from the Passion, is not of this high order. It was essentially popular in its appeal, and much of it was written, not in Latin, but in the vulgar tongue, in Dutch, in French, or in German. The commonest form was one which followed the canonical hours and fitted one scene of the Passion to each hour from Matins to Compline.[1] In a Latin example of these *Horae canonicae Salvatoris*,[2] at Matins, Jesus is taken by the Jews; at Prime brought before Pilate; at Tierce is crowned with thorns and carries His Cross; at Sext He is crucified and drinks the gall; at None He dies, and His side is pierced by the soldier; at Vespers He is taken down from the Cross, and at Compline He is buried. The poem ends with a prayer :

> has horas canonicas cum devotione
> tibi Iesu recolo pìa ratione,
> ut sicut tu passus es poenas in agone,
> sic labore consonans consors sim coronae.

---

[1] See, for examples, Mone, i. 108, 126.   [2] ib., i. 106.

Here are some verses of a second Franciscan *Stabat Mater*, where the inspiration is small, the poetry little above the level of rhetoric, and the feeling conventional :

plange Sion filia,
leva supercilia,
  vide pium Ihesum
per pectus per ilia,
per membra gracilia
  vulneratur, laesum
  graviterque caesum.

.   .   .   .
dolet maternaliter,
dolet visceraliter,
membra prolis taliter
  aspicit afflicta
  et flagellis icta.[1]

To the same tradition belongs an *Oratio de compassione beatae Virginis*,[2] which is an imitation of Bonaventura's *Recordare sanctae crucis.* It is a long litany invoking, by the memory of her passion and the passion of her Son, the spiritual aid of the Virgin. It is the same catalogue of sufferings as in the *Meditationes vitae Christi* :

recordare quod ut vermis
ligni tener et inermis
  in ligno erigitur ;
recordare quod invictus
victor tamquam maledictus
  sic pendere cernitur.

recordare, quia poris
carnis ruptis vi doloris
  cruor largus funditur ;
recordare, quanto zelo
cruor illo tuo velo
  roseus excipitur.

Another hymn is closely modelled on the description in the *Meditationes* of the scene when Christ is taken down from the Cross. The Virgin cries :

sustinete quod paululum
  dolorem meum plangam,
et quod meum dulcissimum
  deoscular et tangam.

mihi meum carissimum
  subtrahere nolite ;
si sepeliri debeat
  me secum sepelite !

accessit sic examinis,
  se super corpus iecit,.
et sacrum vultum lacrimis
  ubertim madefecit.[3]

It would seem that the true ring of passion left by degrees the Order of the Brothers Minor, as they forsook, under the stress of an inevitable evolution, the first gospel of Francis, 'the poor little one of Christ'. They became wealthy, they

[1] Mone, i. 104.
[2] ib., ii. 136 ; cf. ii. 135.
[3] ib., ii. 144 ; cf. *Medit.*, lxxxii, 'Rogat Ioseph Dominam, ut permittat eum volvi linteaminibus et sepeliri. Ipsa contendebat, dicens ; Nolite, amici mei, tam cito filium meum accipere, vel me cum ipso sepelite.'

became learned, they filled the universities, they became the confessors of kings and of princes. Although they still produced men and women after the pattern of their founder, their work had been done in the first generation which followed his death. They had come to the aid of the Church in her crisis, and they gave a new emotional outlook to the world, which profoundly affected the national literatures of Europe.

§ 5. *The Dies Irae.*

Thomas of Celano, a Brother Minor, and the biographer of S. Francis, is the reputed author of the *Dies Irae*,[1] the most majestic of medieval sequences. Perfect in form, and exhibiting complete mastery of the two-syllabled rime, it is the most sublime and poignant expression of the terror of the day, foretold by Jewish prophet or pagan Sybil, when the heavens and earth were to pass away, and Christ would appear in His glory to judge the living and the dead. This tremendous scene, pictured in stone above the doorway of so many churches, or, in gorgeous colours in the western window, where the rays of the setting sun gave it an unearthly glamour, profoundly impressed the imagination of generations of Christian people.[2] The first Jewish Christians brought with them the conception of the day of the Lord as pictured in the prophets, and invested with mystery and wonder in the pre-Christian Apocalyptic literature. With these materials to work on, and the addition of elements from Hellenistic-Oriental sources, the Church built up the great drama of the graves opening at the sound of the trumpet, the resurrection of the body, and the appearance of all men in the flesh before the Judge. So, in the art of the thirteenth century, Jesus is represented as the central figure of the great pageant. He is seated on His throne in the clouds of heaven, and His hands are raised,

---

[1] Bartholomew of Pisa, *Liber Conformitatum*, fructus xi, pars ii. (*Anal. Francisc.* iv. 530), says, 'locum Celani: de quo fuit frater Thomas, qui mandato apostolico scripsit sermone polito legendam primam beati Francisci, et prosam de mortuis, quae dicitur in missa, scilicet "Dies illa, dies irae", &c., dicitur fecisse'; for the little that is known of the life of Thomas see *The Lives of S. Francis of Assisi by Brother Thomas of Celano*, Introd., by A. G. F. Howell.

[2] e.g. the west window at Fairford, Gloucestershire; doorways at Chartres, Rouen (Cathedral and S. Maclou), Laon, Paris (Notre-Dame), Amiens, Reims, etc.; see on the whole subject of the last judgement in art Mâle, *L'art religieux du xiii*[e] *siècle*, pp. 413 sqq.; for a medieval summary of the various stages of the Judgement see Honorius 'Augustodunensis', *Elucidarium*, Migne, clxxii, col. 1158 sqq.

and His feet and side unclothed, so that the marks of His passion may be seen by all. 'Behold He cometh with the clouds ; and every eye shall see Him, and they which pierced Him ; and all the tribes of the earth shall mourn over Him.' On the right is the Virgin, on the left the Apostle John, or sometimes, John the Baptist; on each side stand the angels who bear the instruments of the Passion, the cross, the spear, the pillar of scourging, the reed, and the sponge. Below, in a crowded scene, the bodies of the dead are rising from the graves. They struggle with the sleep of death, like sleepers awaking from an earthly slumber. Above them, and beneath the figure of Jesus, the judgement is shown in process of execution. In the centre stands Michael, a mighty winged figure, serene and strong, holding in his hand the balances in which he weighs the souls of men.[1] On his left hand is the miserable array of the wicked who are driven by grinning fiends towards the open jaws of Leviathan which are ready to devour them. Bishops and kings, monks and nuns are among this unhappy crew, cut off for ever from the hope of salvation. On the right are the blessed, a happy smiling company, clad in white robes, with angels to make them welcome to the new Jerusalem, where Abraham receives them, literally, in his bosom.[2] In the early days of the Church, the whole expectation of the Christian community was fixed on the day of Christ's appearing, and they looked with hope and longing towards the time when the Lord would come and 'fashion anew the body of their humiliation, that it might be conformed to the body of His glory'.[3] This was the Christian hope, the earnest expectation of deliverance which was the joy and comfort of the early Church. But, as the years passed by and the Parousia delayed, this cheerful hope was changed to apprehension and fear. The Church was now established in the world; she was no longer a little group of communities, but a great organization, in which the sinners too obviously outnumbered the saints. The Church had, too, the task of ruling and instructing the barbarian peoples who had entered into the inheritance of Rome. Before their eyes she held the terror of judgement and the fear of eternal

[1] Cf. Johannes de Garlandia, *De triumphis ecclesiae*, ed. Wright, p. 9:
  caeli praepositus Michael animas legit, illas
  mittendas orco separat hasque polo.
[2] More properly, however, Abraham's bosom should represent the intermediate state of *refrigerium*, to which the righteous depart after death; cf. Dieterich, *Nekyia*, p. 96, note 5, Leipzig 1893. This was the view of Tertullian, *Adv. Marcion.* iv. 24, and *De idol.* xiii.
[3] Philip. iii. 21.

torment. No other message could hope to influence their passions and the unreflecting violence of their nature. In church and cathedral they saw portrayed the scene of judgement, the rewards of the righteous and the punishment of sinners. But this terror was not merely a tale to frighten unruly children. The most thoughtful and powerful minds among churchmen, and especially among those who were brought into contact with ecclesiastical politics, saw in the evil condition of the world the infallible signs of an approaching end. Speaking of the intolerable anarchy and wickedness of his own time, Otto of Freising declared that the world could not last long were it not sustained by the merits of saintly men, and he professed himself to be weary of life, 'feeling within himself the answer of death'.[1] This was the dread which drove men and women to the religious life and filled the.monasteries and convents, which appeared to be the only sure havens of refuge against God's wrath.[2] In the twelfth century, the problem of the coming of Antichrist and the impending judgement appeared a very practical one to churchmen like Otto of Freising and Gerhoh of Reichersperg.[3] Joachim of Flora, the Calabrian prophet, saw in the existing world merely an 'upper hell',[4] and looked forward to the end of all things after the establishment of the kingdom of the Holy Spirit. His teachings were eagerly taken up in the thirteenth century by a large group of Franciscans who saw in Joachim the prophet of Francis, and saw in Francis himself the angel of the Apocalypse ascending 'from the sunrising and having the seal of the living God'.[5] Francis was thus the precursor of the end.

So, for the medieval Christian, the Day of Judgement was almost wholly a day of terror. We have seen[6] how the soul of a Peter Damiani shrank before the anticipation of divine justice. This same sense of terror is expressed in the grand and gloomy music of the *Responsorium* which is sung at the Absolution after the Catholic Mass for the Dead:

> libera me, domine, de morte aeterna in die illa tremenda :
> quando caeli movendi sunt et terra :
> dies illa, dies irae, calamitatis et miseriae, dies magna et amara
> valde,[7]

[1] *Chronicon*, vii. 34.   [2] Cf. ib. 35.
[3] Cf. Otto, *Chronicon*, viii; Gerhoh, *De investigatione Antichristi* (*Libelli de Lite*, &c., ii. *M. G. H.*).
[4] 'Infernus superior est iste mundus praesens'; see Rousselot, *Histoire de l'évangile éternel*, Paris 1861, p. 87.
[5] i.e. the Stigmata; Rev. vii. 2.
[6] *Supra*, p. 252.
[7] Cf. Zephaniah i. 14–16.

quando caeli movendi sunt et terra.
tremens factus sum ego et timeo: dum discussio venerit atque
    ventura ira,
quando caeli movendi sunt et terra.
contremunt angeli et archangeli; impii autem ubi parebunt,
quando caeli movendi sunt et terra?
vix iustus salvabitur; et ego, miser, ubi parebo,
quando caeli movendi sunt et terra?
quid ergo miserrimus, quid dicam, vel quid faciam,
dum nihil boni perferam ante tantum iudicem,
quando caeli movendi sunt et terra?
vox de caelis: o vos mortui, qui iacetis in sepulchris,
surgite et occurrite ad iudicium salvatoris,
quando caeli movendi sunt et terra!
creator omnium rerum, deus qui me de limo terrae
formasti et mirabiliter proprio sanguine redemisti,
corpusque meum licet modo putrescat, de sepulchro
facies in die iudicii resuscitari,
quando caeli movendi sunt et terra.
libera me, domine, de morte aeterna, in die illa tremenda,
quando caeli movendi sunt et terra,
dum veneris iudicare saeculum per ignem.[1]

The recurring refrain in this noble prose adds to the sense
of fear and apprehension. The *Offertorium* sung at the Mass
begins:

'O Lord Jesus Christ, King of glory, deliver the souls of all the
faithful dead from the pains of hell, and from the deep pit; deliver
them from the mouth of the lion, lest hell (*tartarus*) swallow them up,
lest they fall into the darkness; but let S. Michael, the standard bearer,
bring them into the eternal light.'

The day of doom was foretold not only by the prophets, but
even, it was held, by the Erythraean Sibyl, whom S. Augustine,
in the *City of God*, had quoted as a witness to the last Judgement.[2] The verses began:

        iudicii signum: tellus sudore madescet,
        e coelo rex adveniet per saecla futurus,
        scilicet ut carnem praesens ut iudicet orbem.

---

[1] There are several versions of this
Responsory. The text as actually used in
the Mass for the Dead is abbreviated.

[2] Mâle, *L'art religieux du xiiie siècle*,
p. 392; Aug., *De civit. Dei*, xviii. 23; cf.

Bousset, *Antichrist Legend*, p. 233. The
verses of the Sibyl were sometimes sung at
Christmas; see text in *Anal. Hymn.* iii,
p. 15 sq.

So in the *Dies Irae*, the supreme expression of hope and fear in the face of the judgement, the Sibyl and David are the witnesses quoted in the opening verse :

> dies irae, dies illa,
> solvet saeclum in favilla,
> teste David cum Sibylla.

The rest of the poem shows unmistakably the influence of the great *Responsory* quoted above, and Thomas of Celano may also have been influenced by earlier hymns and poems on the same subject.

During his sojourn in Germany as *custos* and vicar to Caesarius of Spires (1221–3), he may have become acquainted with the long poem composed by Radewin, the continuator of Otto of Freising, on the favourite subject of Theophilus. It is not impossible that the line,

> quem nunc sanctorum mihi deprecer esse patronum ?

may have been in his mind when he composed his Sequence, and the following lines from the same poem bear a striking likeness to certain phrases of the *Dies Irae*:

> ante dei potero consistere quomodo vultum,
> cum nihil occultum, cum nil remanebit inultum ?
> quid faciam, iudex cum venerit ille timendus,
> ad cuius nutum tremit orbs discutiendus ?
> quis tunc (me miserum !) pro me miserendo loquetur,
> cum quivis proprii facti ratione tenetur ? [1]

But another and earlier poem, of the ninth century, may also have been known to the poet of the *Dies Irae*:

> cum ab igne rota mundi
> tota coeperit ardere,
> simul flamma concremare
> coelum ut liber plicare,
> sidera tota cadere,
> finem saeculi venire.

> dies irae, dies illa,
> dies nebulae et turbinis,
> dies tubae et clangoris,
> dies nebulosa valde,
> quando tenebrarum pondus
> cadet super peccatores.

---

[1] Text in Meyer, *Rythmik*, i. 109; cf. also Hrothswitha, *Theophilus* (ed. Winter- feld), p. 67 ; cf. 1 Peter iv. 18.

quid acturi erunt pravi,
quando ipsi tremunt sancti
ante tantam maiestatem
Iesu Christi, filii dei ?
et si iustus vix evadit,
impius ubi parebit ? [1]

The full text of the *Dies Irae* is as follows : [2]

dies irae, dies illa,
solvet saeclum in favilla,
teste David cum Sibylla.

quantus tremor est futurus,
quando iudex est venturus,
cuncta stricte discussurus !

tuba mirum sparget sonum
per sepulchra regionum,
coget omnes ante thronum.

mors stupebit et natura,
cum resurget creatura
iudicanti responsura.

liber scriptus proferetur,[3]
in quo totum continetur,
unde mundus iudicetur.

iudex ergo cum censebit,
quidquid latet, apparebit :
nil inultum remanebit.

quid sum miser tunc dicturus,
quem patronum rogaturus,
dum vix iustus sit securus?

rex tremendae maiestatis,
qui salvandos salvas gratis,
salva me, fons pietatis !

recordare, Iesu pie,
quod sum causa tuae viae ;
ne me perdas illa die.

quaerens me sedisti lassus ;
redemisti, crucem passus ;
tantus labor non sit cassus.

iuste iudex ultionis,
donum fac remissionis
ante diem rationis.

ingemisco tanquam reus,
culpa rubet vultus meus :
supplicanti parce, deus.

qui Mariam absolvisti
et latronem exaudisti,
mihi quoque spem dedisti ;

preces meae non sunt dignae,
sed tu, bonus, fac benigne,
ne perenni cremer igne.

inter oves locum praesta
et ab haedis me sequestra
statuens in parte dextra ;

confutatis maledictis,
flammis acribus addictis,
voca me cum benedictis.

oro supplex et acclinis,
cor contritum quasi cinis :
gere causam mei finis.

---

[1] *Anal. Hymn.* xxiii, p. 54, where two versions are given; cf. also text in *M.G.H., Poet. Kar.*, iv. ii, p. 521, where it is stated that this rhythm is found in codices of the ninth and tenth centuries.

[2] *Anal. Hymn.* liv, p. 269 sq.

[3] For the book of judgement cf. Malachi iii. 16, Apoc. xx. 12 ; this Jewish idea, described in the *Testament of Abraham*, has many heathen parallels ; see Dieterich, *Nekyia*, p. 126 sq.

This is the original text; as it stands, the poem is not a sequence, but a *pia meditatio*[1] on death and judgement. When it came to be used liturgically (and it was already in such use in the lifetime of Bartholomew of Pisa; d. 1401), two strophes were added, which had the aim of adapting it, in a somewhat clumsy manner, for its new purpose:

> lacrimosa dies illa,
> qua resurget ex favilla
> iudicandus homo reus ;
> huic ergo parce, deus.[2]

> pie Iesu domine,
> dona eis requiem.

A later addition, likewise, are the four introductory strophes of the so-called ' Mantuan' text, which the Bürgermeister Charisius of Stralsund copied in 1676 from a marble tablet in the Franciscan church at Mantua, and Chytraeus had found there, earlier, in 1531.[3]

1. quaeso, anima fidelis,
   ah, quid respondere velis
   Christo venturo de caelis,

2. cum a te poscet rationem
   ob boni omissionem
   et mali commissionem.

3. dies illa, dies irae,
   quam conemur praevenire
   obviamque deo ire.

4. seria contritione,
   gratiae apprehensione,
   vitae emendatione.

The poor quality of all these lines is enough to stamp them as additions to the original text, apart from the fact that they rudely disturb the personal meditation.

A large literature has grown up round this majestic composition, and countless attempts have been made to translate it into many languages.[4] It is used by Goethe in a wonderful

---

[1] Cf. Dreves, *Das Dies Irae, Stimmen aus Maria Laach*, xlii (1892), p. 523. For the theory that the *Dies Irae* was a *Trope* to the *Libera* before it was used as a sequence see Blume, *Dies Irae, Tropus zum Libera, dann Sequenz*, in *Cäzilien-Vereinsorgan*, 1914, No. 3, p. 55 sqq. ; *Anal. Hymn.* liv, p. 274 sq.

[2] This strophe was already in existence, in the following form, in the twelfth century (Mone, i. 408 ; *Anal. Hymn.* xlix, p. 385 sq. ; ib. liv, p. 274) :

' lacrimosa dies illa,
   qua resurget de favilla
   iudicandus homo reus ;
   tu peccatis parce deus.'

[3] *Anal. Hymn.* liv, p. 273.

[4] Dr. Irons's version is well known ; a fine seventeenth-century translation begins,

' Day of wrath, that dreadful day,
   Shall the world in ashes lay,
   David and the Sibyls say.'

There is another by the Earl of Ros-

scene in *Faust*; Sir Walter Scott made a splendid paraphrase of
its opening verses for the *Lay of the Last Minstrel*, and it is
retained by the Church as the sequence in the Mass for the
Dead. The *Dies Irae* shows the finest restraint, and a close
if not always perfect observance of the more rigid rules of
rhythmical composition. The terror of judgement is there, but
it is not the wild terror of Peter Damiani, which expresses itself
in long and overladen detail. The *Dies Irae* has the simplicity
of supreme art; the formal effect is achieved by the admirable
handling of the triple rhyme and it is heightened by the note of
personal passion which comes into the sequence before the end,
making the characteristic appeal to the Franciscan Saviour.

> recordare, Iesu pie,
> quod sum causa tuae viae:
> ne me perdas illa die.
>
> quaerens me sedisti lassus:
> redemisti crucem passus:
> tantus labor non sit cassus.

The appeal, however, in the later Middle Ages was not often
directly to the Judge. On that Day, Jesus was to appear as
the strict executor of justice and vengeance, and only an all-
powerful mediator could incline him to mercy. This mediator
was the Virgin Mary, who had earned the title of *Mater Misericordiae*, Mother of Mercy, because of her many miraculous
interventions in favour of those who called upon her name in
trouble or professed a particular devotion to her service. It
was firmly held that her power of intercession would be exercised
on behalf of men before the Judgement seat of her Son, who
could refuse no request when it was urged by his Mother. This
notion was eagerly propagated by the Franciscans, who, like the
rest of the religious orders, were ardent devotees of the Blessed
Virgin. In the thirteenth century *Liber Exemplorum*,[1] a book
of stories for the use of Franciscan preachers, it is related how

common, one by Worsley, to name only
a few, and a paraphrase by Crashaw,
which begins:
'Hear'st thou, my soul, what serious things
  Both the Psalm and Sybil sings
  Of a sure Judge, from Whose sharp ray
  The World in flames shall fly away.'
On the subject of translations see Julian,
p. 297 sqq.; and Daniel, ii. 105 sqq. A

German version begins,
  'Tag des Zorns, du Tag der Fülle,
  Kehrst die Welt in Staubgerülle—
  So zeugt David und Sibylle.'
[1] Ed. by A. G. Little, *British Society
for Franciscan Studies*, 1908, p. 30; for
another story based on a similar idea see
Caesarius of Heisterbach, *Dialogus mira-
culorum* (ed. Strange, Cologne 1851), ii. 3.

some priests who were on a journey were overtaken by a sudden storm of thunder and lightning. In their terror they began to sing the *Ave Maris Stella*. The Blessed Virgin heard them and spread a veil over them, and under its protection they rested in safety until the tempest had passed. 'Therefore', the Franciscan homilist continues, 'it is not to be doubted that, when the tempest of death bursts over us, she will overshadow her servants with the robe of her mercy, that they be not stricken by her Son.'[1] In the *Dies Irae* there is no mention of Mary as the intercessor before the Judge, but another hymn on the last judgement, which probably belongs to the Franciscan tradition, is devoted entirely to the *Mater Misericordiae*:

in tremendo dei iudicio,
quando fiet stricta discussio,
tunc etiam supplica filio,
ut cum sanctis sit nobis portio,
          o Maria.

nos timemus diem iudicii,
quia male et nobis conscii,
sed tu, mater summi consilii,
para nobis locum refugii,
          o Maria.

dies illa, dies terribilis,
dies malis intolerabilis,
sed tu, mater, semper amabilis,
fac sit nobis iudex placabilis,
          o Maria.

cum iratus iudex adveniat,
singulorum causas discutiat
personamque nullam respiciat,
sed singulis iuste definiat,
          o Maria.

illa die tantus servabitur
rigor, quo vix iustus salvabitur,
nemo reus iustificabitur,
sed singulis ius suum dabitur,
          o Maria.

summi regis mater et filia,
cui nullus par est in gloria,
tua, virgo, dulcis clementia
sit tunc et nunc nobis propitia,
          o Maria.[2]

Only by recourse to a woman's pity could the medieval imagination find a hope of robbing the terrible day of judgement of part at least of that terror which pressed so heavily upon the soul. In the later Middle Ages, and even as early as Anselm, Mary takes her place above all the saints as the most powerful agent of human succour; no prayers would weary her, her mercy and her might were alike unbounded. She could rescue her servants from straits which appeared to be hopeless, as when she delivered Theophilus, who had bound himself to the devil, or when she saved an abbess from the consequences of fleshly sin.[3]

---

[1] On the *Mater Misericordiae* in later medieval art, who is represented as gathering her servants under the folds of her mantle, see Mâle, *L'art religieux de la fin du moyen âge*, p. 205 sqq.
[2] Mone, i. 400.
[3] *Liber Exemplorum*, pp. 29, 33; on Theophilus see *The Golden Legend*.

No wonder, therefore, that it was firmly believed that her suffrages would avail in the last and most important of human issues.

§ 6.   *Conclusion.*

We have now traced the course of Christian Latin poetry through the space of a thousand years, from its beginnings in the middle of the third century under the shadow of the declining culture of the ancient world to its culmination in those two centuries, the twelfth and the thirteenth, which mark at once the height of the Catholic civilization of the Middle Ages and the starting-point of the Renaissance. Just as the art of Nicola Pisano and of Giotto, the *Divina Commedia* and the poetry of Petrarch belong on the one hand to the Middle Ages and on the other to the earlier history of the great awakening which was the prelude to the modern world ; so the great religious and intellectual ferments of the twelfth and thirteenth centuries, with their accompanying manifestations in politics, in speculation, and in poetry, stand in a similar relation to the past and to the future.

Our account of Christian Latin poetry closes with the *Stabat Mater* and the *Dies Irae*, the two supreme productions of the poetical genius of the Franciscan movement and the last authentic voices of Catholic hymnody. By the fourteenth century the Latin language could no longer compete with the national languages of Europe. In the chosen home of the classical tradition, Dante, Petrarch, and Boccaccio begin the modern literature of Italy. In Germany, the vernacular poetry had already a long history behind it, from the *Heliand* and the *Krist* to the *Minnelieder* of the twelfth century and the *Nibelungenlied*. Wolfram of Eschenbach with his *Parzival*, and Gottfried of Strassburg with his *Tristan*, belong to the early thirteenth century. In England, since the first great period of Anglo-Saxon literature, the popular language had to struggle against the foreign language of the court. But the struggle was at last successful. Layamon's *Brut*, *Havelok the Dane*, and other romances appeared in the vernacular verse, along with folk-songs religious and profane, hymns to the Virgin and Christ, or lyrics of love and of nature. In the fourteenth century, Langland, Wiclif and Chaucer preside at the beginnings of the modern language of England.

In France, the development of vernacular literature is longer and more complicated, and it was France in the twelfth and thirteenth centuries that fed the imagination of all the romantic poets of Europe. The epic of Roland began the *Chansons de geste* as early as the eleventh century ; then followed the romantic cycle of the Arthurian legend, in which Chrétien de Troyes in the later twelfth century, and Robert de Boron in the early thirteenth, are the conspicuous names. Guillaume de Lorris and Jean de Meung, the authors of the *Roman de la Rose*, belong to the thirteenth century.

Hence, by the end of the thirteenth century and the beginning of the fourteenth, the day of Latin literature and especially of Latin poetry is over. In the monastic and cathedral schools, and in the Universities, the language of S. Thomas and of Duns Scotus was still read and spoken, and a long array of hymns and sequences, composed in the fourteenth and fifteenth centuries, bears witness to the obstinate strength of the old tradition which refused to accept the answer of death. As is often the case in periods of apparent decline, the number of poets seemed to grow rather than to diminish,[1] but the sense of form was departing, and there was a tendency to sink back again into that system of merely numbering syllables from which the rhythmical principle had slowly emerged.

Poetry was employed for the adornment of any and every subject, and it is not surprising that with the multiplication of poems, the quality began to fall. Sermons in verse [2] were not unknown at any rate in England, during the fourteenth and fifteenth centuries. The large collection of rimed Offices, or *Historiae* in *Analecta Hymnica*,[3] illustrates the success of what might have seemed likely to prove an unpromising development. The germ of the idea was provided, it appears, by fragments of hymns which were already incorporated into the office as responses ;[4] and, at first, the intrusion of poetical pieces took place on a modest scale. 'The further development of the versified Offices went on parallel to that of the sequences. Beginning with a simple combination of portions in prose and poetry respectively, the whole Office [5] soon came to be clothed

---

[1] Dreves, *Die Kirche der Lateiner in ihren Liedern*, p. 111.
[2] G. R. Owst, *Preaching in Medieval England*, pp. 273 sqq., Cambridge 1926.
[3] vols. v, xiii, xvii, xxiv–xxvi, xxviii, xlv.

[4] Cf. Wagner, *History of Plain-Chant*, p. 242 ; on this semi-liturgical poetry, see Wilmart, *Rev. Bénéd.*, li (1939), p. 61 sq.
[5] Excluding, of course, the Psalms and Lessons.

in metrical forms, which at first appear in great variety, while no value is set on uniformity of structure.' Finally, it was seen that the whole *Historia*, as it was called, 'ought to carry out the same metrical or rhythmical type from beginning to end, and by means of rime to unite the different parts of a strophe.'[1] The Offices of S. Francis and S. Anthony, ascribed to Julian of Speyer (d. *circ.* 1278), mark the final perfection, if we may so call it, of this kind of composition,[2] which became increasingly popular in the later Middle Ages. Rimed 'Psalters' were another late development of religious verse—collections of spiritual songs, often in honour of the Virgin, and consisting of one hundred and fifty strophes, a number equal to that of the Psalms. Originally, each strophe contained some reference to its corresponding Psalm, but later poets abandoned all but the numerical relation to the Psalter.[3]

Versified inscriptions and epitaphs are innumerable throughout the whole Middle Ages. They are, for the most part, the work of mean poets, and the later examples show a fondness for leonine rimes.

> quamvis peccatrix, sum domna vocata Beatrix
> in tumulo missa iaceo quae comitissa,

so runs, in beautiful letters, the inscription on a tomb in the cloister of the Campo Santo at Pisa. The Rolls of the Dead (*rotuli*),[4] which monasteries and churches sent round to announce to other religious communities the death of a bishop or an abbot, were inscribed by each recipient in turn with the best verses which the monastic or clerical poet could produce for the occasion. They were often in leonines, and Baudry, Abbot of Bourgueil, as we have seen,[5] once blamed the authors of such verses for their tediousness.

Technical and scientific subjects were often treated in verse. Philosophical poems and treatises on the art of poetry have already been mentioned. There were versified school-books,

---

[1] Wagner, *History of Plain-Chant*, p. 269. Dreves (*Anal. Hymn.* v, p. 6) explains the term *Historia* from the fact that the Responsories, and often the antiphons in these offices, dealt with the history of a saint or a festival.

[2] Archbishop Pecham's office, *De sanctissima Trinitate* (*Anal. Hymn.* v, p. 9 sqq.; l, p. 593 sqq.), is also a remarkable composition; on the question of authorship see *Anal. Hymn.* xxiii, p. 5 sq.

[3] *Anal. Hymn.* xxxv, for examples, with Introduction.

[4] See L. Delisle, *Rouleaux des Morts*, Paris 1866; also Rock, *The Church of our Fathers*, ii. 308 sqq. (ed. Hart and Frere, London 1905).

[5] p. 280, note 4, above.

and poems on grammar, astronomy, and music.[1] Among medical poems, two of the most notable are Peter of Eboli's verses on the baths of Pozzuoli,[2] and the popular *Regimen Sanitatis Salernitanum*,[3] which was translated into English in the seventeenth century.

The *Physiologus* was put into verse in the eleventh century,[4] and Aesop's *Fables* and other beast-stories tempted many poets.[5] Bible stories, legends of saints, miracles of the Virgin,[6] accounts of supernatural visions provided inexhaustible material for the medieval versifier.

It is not possible to give names to many of the poets of the decline, but there are a few poets of some distinction who followed the old tradition of liturgical or lyrical verse.   Konrad of Haimburg (d. 1360), Prior of Gaming, is a German Carthusian much admired in his own day for hymns to the Virgin and the saints.[7] Walter Wiburn is an English Franciscan of the fourteenth century, who praised the Virgin in verses of formal correctness.[8]

> ave, virgo mater Christi,
> quae pudore meruisti
>   dici phoenix virginum:
> ave, virgo, cuius fructus
> nobis dedit finem luctus
> et lamenti terminum.

John of Jenstein, Archbishop of Prague (d. 1400),[9] likewise sang the praises of Mary.   In the fifteenth century, John Hus (d. 1415) comes into the list of Christian poets, with Thomas à Kempis (d. 1471), and John Gerson, the great Chancellor of Paris University (d. 1429).   John Mauburn (Mombaer), Abbot of Livry (d. 1503), closes the list with his *Carmen pro Fescenninis ad praesepii visitationem canendum*,[10] which contains some charming lines:

[1] Gröber, *Grundriss der romanischen Philologie*, ii, i. 383 sqq.

[2] C. Capaccio, *De balneis liber*, in J. Graevius, *Thesaurus Antiquitatum*, ix, iv. Lugd. Bat. 1704-25; the authorship of the poem was unknown until discovered by Huillard-Bréholles.

[3] *The School of Salernum* (Latin and English text), ed. Packard, Oxford 1922. The above-mentioned volume of Graevius also contains the Latin text.

[4] Migne, clxxi, col. 1217 sqq. ; ascribed to Hildebert of Tours, it appears to be the work of an Italian named Tedbald.

[5] Gröber, *Grundriss der romanischen Philologie*, ii, i. 409 sqq.

[6] Mussafia, *Studien zu den mittelalterlichen Marienlegenden, Wiener Sitzungsber.*, 1886, pp. 917 sqq. ; 1888, pp. 5 sqq. ; 1889, iii ; 1891, viii ; 1898, viii.

[7] *Anal. Hymn.* iii, pp. 1–14; pp. 21–102.

[8] ib., l, p. 631 sqq.

[9] ib., xlviii, pp. 421 sqq.

[10] ib., xlviii, pp. 515 sqq.

> heu, quid iaces stabulo,
>   omnium creator,
> vagiens cunabulo,
>   mundi reparator?
> si rex, ubi purpura
> vel clientum murmura,
>   ubi aula regis? —
> hic omnis penuria,
> paupertatis curia,
>   forma novae legis.

Here the medieval rhythmical verse has its end. The humanists of the Renaissance went back to the classical models, and began a fruitless attempt to bring life and beauty back into the old measures. The liturgical verse of the Middle Ages now appeared barbarous and despicable in the eyes of laymen and of churchmen alike. The sequences were abolished with few exceptions, and the hymns which remained in the Breviary were tolerated only on account of their venerable antiquity and after they had suffered a process of ignorant mutilation.[1]

The Latin poetry of the Middle Ages lay under a cloud of misunderstanding and unintelligent depreciation until the revival of historical studies in the nineteenth century. In the eighteenth century Polycarp Leyser [2] had, indeed, ventured to raise a voice in its favour, but even the French Benedictines did not care to defend it.

The erudition of Mabillon and of Muratori presided at the beginnings of the immense task of making available the sources from which the history of the Middle Ages was to be rewritten; but an epoch was marked when Stein, in the years after Waterloo, successfully launched the *Monumenta Germaniae Historica.*[3] At the same time the Romantic movement was investing the Middle Ages with a mysterious glamour, and it became the duty of the historian to 'divorce the study of the past from the passions of the present and to relate what actually occurred—*wie es eigentlich geworden ist*'.[4] The foundation of all historical progress was the study of original sources,

---

[1] The 'revision' of the hymns of the Breviary was carried out under Urban VIII (1623–44) by a commission of Jesuits, who in the words of the learned hymnologist, Canon Ulysse Chevalier, 'spoiled the work of Christian antiquity, under the pretext of restoring the hymns in accordance with the laws of metre and elegant language'.

[2] *Historia poetarum et poematum medii aevi*, Halle 1741.

[3] G. P. Gooch, *History and Historians in the nineteenth century*, London 1913, p. 65.

[4] ib., p. 101.

and in Germany, France, and England the Latin historians and poets of the Middle Ages appeared in editions of varying merit. In England, Thomas Wright, who with Brewer and others edited English and other poets in the *Rolls Series*, was an antiquarian of great zeal and productiveness.   If his conclusions were often unsound, he was a pioneer whose work was ably continued in France by men like Hauréau and Paul Meyer, to whom we still owe so much of our knowledge of the eleventh and twelfth centuries.   In Germany, Dümmler, Traube, von Winterfeld, and Strecker made an incomparable collection of the poetry of the Carolingian age, while for the earlier period the Vienna *Corpus Scriptorum Ecclesiasticorum Latinorum* has provided and is still providing texts of the Christian poets from Commodian onwards.   Wilhelm Meyer of Speyer has conducted patient research into the origins and principles of rhythmical verse, a sphere in which many have been ready to offer criticism, but few to assist.

The medieval poets, in the great collections which have been mentioned, were edited mainly for the service of the historian. But at the same time the first serious attempts were made to explore the origins and development of the Catholic liturgy. Many workers, of differing degrees of competence, turned to the hymns and sequences of the Latin Church. Daniel's *Thesaurus*, based on printed sources, stimulated Mone to turn to the manuscripts.   Neale and Trench did much to introduce to English readers the unfamiliar strains of a poetry which issued from what had been vaguely known as the 'dark ages'.   In France, Léon Gautier began an ambitious study of the liturgical verse of the Church, which he did not live to complete; but he made it impossible henceforth to ignore the great achievement of the Victorine sequences in the twelfth century.   In the same country, Ulysse Chevalier compiled his vast, if undigested, *Repertorium* of hymns, by the side of which must be placed the modest and orderly collections of Mearns in England.   But it is from Germany that the most systematic attempts have come to collect the sources of medieval hymnology, and these have culminated in the fifty-five volumes of *Analecta Hymnica*, in which the Jesuits Guido Maria Dreves and Clemens Blume, aided by Henry Marriott Bannister, have gathered together an immense array of texts, of all degrees of importance and interest, out of which the student must patiently select what is able to serve his purpose.

ADDITIONAL NOTES

P. 25. The piece, *Gaude, Maria Virgo!*, is an antiphon for Matins of the Assumption in the *Liber responsalis* of Gregory the Great (Migne, lxxviii, col. 799). In the early missals and sacramentaries there are traces of rimed prose, borrowed from sermons. It appears only in the *contestationes* (to use the Gallican equivalent of the Roman *praefationes*) of the Hispano-Gallican group; for it is foreign to books of Roman origin, like the Gregorian Sacramentary and the so-called Leonine Sacramentary, while in the Gelasian Sacramentary the rimed passages are due to the intrusion of Gallican elements. A feature of the Spanish and Gallican *Prefaces* is that they 'go on by slow meander to reach and develop' their theme (E. Bishop, *Liturgica Historica*, p. 5), and the rimed and rhythmic periods of the ecclesiastical orators afforded attractive material. On Spanish rimed prose see K. Polheim, *Die lateinische Reimprosa*, pp. 293 sqq.

P. 38, note 1. Amalar of Metz; Dom Morin has identified him with Amalar of Trèves, but Hauck and others have refused to admit this identity. For a list of Morin's writings on the subject see his *Études, textes, découvertes*, i, p. 62 sq., Paris 1913.

P. 83. Bardenhewer, iv. 642, has suggested that these two hymns may not be the work of Orientius.

P. 106, note 2. The *Te Deum*. It is very probable that Nicetas of Remesiana composed this famous hymn; see G. Morin, *Nouvelles recherches sur l'auteur du Te Deum*, Rev. Bénéd. xi (1894), pp. 49 sqq., and other articles in same periodical (list in Morin, *Études, textes, découvertes*, i, p. 16); A. E. Burn, *The Hymn 'Te Deum' and its Author*, London 1926. On the other side, P. Cagin, *Te Deum ou Illatio ?*, Paris 1906.

P. 122. For Gregory I's letters now refer to the edition by Ewald-Hartmann, *M. G. H. Epist.* I, i, p. 6; ii, p. 303; i, p. 354-7.

P. 133. Hisperica Famina; on the suggestion that we are not to regard this as a composition in rimed prose, but as an attempt at verse obscurely modelled on the hexameter, see K. Polheim, *Die lateinische Reimprosa*, p. 286, and the literature there quoted.

P. 138. sancte sator, &c. This poetical prayer is from the so-called *Book of Cerne*; see *The Book of Cerne*, ed. A. B. Kuypers, Cambridge 1902, p. 131 sq.

P. 293. Walter of Châtillon; a full account of his lyrical poetry is given in Raby, *Secular Latin Poetry*, ii, pp. 190 sqq., with many quotations. The numerous poems belonging to his school are dealt with as well.

P. 426. On *oci, oci*, the nightingale's song; cf. the poem cited by L. Delisle, *Note sur les mss. du Fonds Libri conservés à la Laurentienne, Notices et extraits des mss.,* xxxii, i, p. 68,

P. 426. On *oci, oci*, the nightingale's song; cf. the poem cited by L. Delisle, *Note sur les mss. du Fonds Libri conservés à la Laurentienne, Notices et extraits des mss.,* xxxii, i, p. 68,

> 'frondea tecta petens, le rosinol en cel este tens
> concinit o ci o ci gravitate loci.'

See also the poem by Maistre Willaumes li Viniers in K. Bartsch, *Altfranzösische Romanzen und Pastourellen*, Leipzig 1870, p. 83.

P. 453. Metrical offices are common, but a metrical mass is a rare curiosity. One is contained in the Reichenau palimpsest, a collection of Gallican masses about the middle of the seventh century (see A. Wilmart, *L'âge et l'ordre des messes de Mone*, *Revue Bénéd.* 1911, pp. 377 sqq.; texts in F. J. Mone, *Lateinische und griechische Messen aus dem zweiten bis sechsten Jahrhundert*, Frankfurt-am-Main 1850 : reproduced in Migne, cxxxviii, col. 863 sqq., and in J. M. Neale, *Missale Richer oviense* (G. H. Forbes, *The Ancient Liturgies of the Gallican Church*, Burntisland 1855).

H. Brewer, *Zeitschr. f. kathol. Theologie*, xliii (1919), pp. 693 sqq., tries to show that Fortunatus was the author of these hexameters. For some barbarous rhythmical 'hexameters' of somewhat earlier date, which Dom Wilmart describes as an 'invitatory formula' to a versified mass, see his article, *Benedictiones Bobienses*, *Bulletin d'ancienne littérature et d'archéologie chrétiennes*, iv (1914), pp. 179 sqq.

BIBLIOGRAPHY

I. LIST OF PRINCIPAL COLLECTIONS OF SOURCES

Analecta Hymnica Medii Aevi, ed. Dreves, G. M., Blume, C., and Bannister, H. M., Leipzig, 1886–1922, 55 vols.
Anthologia Latina, ed. Buecheler, F., and Riese, A., 2nd edit., Leipzig 1894–7, 2 vols. (supplement, ed. Ihm, M., Leipzig 1895).
Corpus Scriptorum Ecclesiasticorum Latinorum, Vienna 1866 et sqq.
Ein Jahrtausend lateinischer Hymnendichtung, ed. Dreves, G. M., and Blume, C., Leipzig 1909, 2 vols.
Lateinische Hymnen des Mittelalters, ed. Mone, F. J., Freiburg i. B. 1853–5, 3 vols.
Lateinische Sequenzen des Mittelalters, ed. Kehrein, J., Mainz 1873.
Monumenta Germaniae Historica [Scriptores, Hanover and Berlin 1826 et sqq.; Auctores Antiquissimi, 1877 et sqq.; Poetae Latini Aevi Carolini, 1881–1923, 4 vols.].
Patrologia Latina, ed. Migne, J.-P., Paris 1844 et sqq.
Poésies populaires latines antérieures au XIIme siècle, ed. Méril, É. du, Paris 1843.
Poésies populaires latines du moyen âge, ed. Méril, É. du, Paris 1847.
Poésies inédites du moyen âge, ed. Méril, É. du, Paris 1854.
Poetae Latini Minores, ed. Baehrens, E.; post Aemilium Baehrens iterum recensuit F. Vollmer, W. Morel, Leipzig 1910–35.
Rerum Britannicarum medii aevi Scriptores (Chronicles and Memorials of Great Britain and Ireland during the Middle Ages), London 1858 et sqq.
Sacred Latin Poetry, ed. Trench, R. C., 3rd edit., London 1874.
Sequentiae ex Missalibus, ed. Neale, J. M., London 1852.
Thesaurus Hymnologicus, ed. Daniel, H. A., Halle 1855–6, 5 vols.

II. GENERAL WORKS OF LITERARY HISTORY, BIBLIOGRAPHY, ETC.

Ampère, J. J., Histoire littéraire de la France, Paris 1839, 3 vols.
Bardenhewer, O., Geschichte der altkirchlichen Literatur, Freiburg i. B. 1894–1932, 5 vols.
Bäumer, S., art. Hymne, in Wetzer and Welte's Kirchenlexikon.
Bigg, C., Wayside Sketches in Ecclesiastical History, London 1906.
Blume, C., art. Hymnody in Catholic Encyclopaedia.
Boissier, G., La fin du paganisme, 7th edit., Paris 1913, 2 vols.
Brittain, F., The Medieval Latin and Romance Lyric to A.D. 1300, Cambridge 1953.
——, Latin in Church: Episodes in the History of its Pronunciation, Cambridge, 1934.
Cabrol, F., Dictionnaire d'archéologie chrétienne et de liturgie, Paris 1901, in progress.
Cambridge History of English Literature, I, Cambridge 1907.
Cambridge Medieval History, Cambridge 1911–36.
Chevalier, C. U. J., Repertorium Hymnologicum, Louvain and Brussels 1892–1920, 6 vols.
——, Poésie liturgique du moyen âge, Rhythme et histoire: Hymnaires italiens, Paris and Lyons 1893 (Bibl. Liturg. I).
——, Poésie liturgique traditionnelle de l'Église catholique en Occident, Tournai 1894 (Bibl. Liturg. II).

Courcelle, P., Les lettres grecques en occident de Macrobe à Cassiodore, Paris 1948.
Curtius, E. R., Europäische Literatur und lateinisches Mittelalter, Bern, 1948.
Dreves, G. M., Die Kirche der Lateiner in ihren Liedern, Kempten and Munich 1908.
Duckett, E. S., Latin Writers of the Fifth Century, New York 1930.
——, The Gateway to the Middle Ages, New York 1938.
Ebert, A., Allgemeine Geschichte der Literatur des Mittelalters im Abendlande bis zum Beginne des XI. Jahrhunderts, Leipzig, 2nd edit., vols. I and II, 1889; vol. III, 1887. (French trans., Paris 1883–9, 3 vols.)
Ghellinck, J. de, Littérature latine au moyen âge, Paris 1939, 2 vols.
Gröber, G., Grundriss der romanischen Philologie, Strassburg 1888–1902 [vol. II, part i, 1893, Übersicht über die lat. Lit. von dem vi. Jahrh. bis 1350].
Harnack, A., Geschichte der altchristlichen Literatur bis Eusebius, Leipzig 1893–1904, 3 vols.
Hauréau, B., Notices et extraits de quelques mss. latins de la Bibliothèque nationale, Paris 1890–3, 6 vols.
——, Singularités historiques et littéraires, Paris 1894.
Hélin, M., A History of Medieval Latin Literature, New York, 1949.
Histoire littéraire de la France par les religieux bénédictins de la congrégation de S. Maur, Paris 1733 et seqq.
Hörle, G. H., Frühmittelalterliche Mönchs- und Klerikerbildung in Italien, Freiburg i. B. 1914.
Jordan, H., Geschichte der altchristlichen Literatur, Leipzig 1911.
Julian, J., A Dictionary of Hymnology, 2nd edit., London 1907.
Ker, W. P., The Dark Ages, London 1904.
Labriolle, P. de, Histoire de la littérature latine chrétienne, 3rd edit., Paris 1947.
Leyser, P., Historia poetarum et poematum medii aevi, Halle 1721.
Manitius, M., Geschichte der christlich-lateinischen Poesie bis zur Mitte des VIII. Jahrhunderts, Stuttgart 1891.
——, Geschichte der lateinischen Literatur des Mittelalters, Munich 1911–31, 3 vols.
——, Beiträge zur Geschichte früh-christlicher Dichter im Mittelalter, Wiener Sitzungsber. cxvii, xii (1889); cxxi, vii (1890).
——, Zu späten lateinischen Dichtern, Rhein. Mus. xliv (1889), pp. 540 sqq.; xlv (1890), pp. 153, 316, 485 sqq.
Messenger, R. E., Ethical Teachings in the Latin Hymns of Medieval England, New York 1930.
Monceaux, P., Histoire littéraire de l'Afrique chrétienne depuis les origines jusqu'à l'invasion arabe, Paris 1901 et seqq., 7 vols.
Norden, E., Die lateinische Literatur im Übergang vom Altertum zum Mittelalter (Die Kultur der Gegenwart, I, viii), Leipzig 1912.
Sandys, J. E., A History of Classical Scholarship, I, 3rd edit., Cambridge 1920.
Schanz, M., Geschichte der römischen Literatur, Leipzig, 3rd edit., vol. iii, 1922; 2nd edit., vol. iv, i, 1914; vol. iv, ii, 1920.
Singer, S., Die religiöse Lyrik des Mittelalters, Bern 1933.
Taylor, H. O., The Medieval Mind, 2nd edit., London 1914, 2 vols.
Teuffel, W. S., and Schwabe, L., History of Latin Literature, London 1892, 2 vols. (6th edit. of vol. iii in German, ed. Kroll and Skutsch, Leipzig 1913).
Wagner, P., Introduction to the Gregorian Melodies (History of Plain Chant), Plainsong and Medieval Music Society, 1907.
Wattenbach, W., Deutschlands Geschichtsquellen im Mittelalter bis zur Mitte des XIII. Jahrhunderts, 6th edit., Berlin 1893–4, 2 vols.; vol. i, 7th edit. (ed. Dümmler, E.), Stuttgart and Berlin 1904.
Weyman, C., Miscellanea zu lateinischen Dichtern, Compte rendu du IVe Congrès international des catholiques, Freiburg i. d. Schw. 1897.
——, Beiträge zur Geschichte der christlich-lateinischen Poesie, Munich 1926 (some of the articles contained in this volume are noted separately below).

III. MONOGRAPHS, ETC.

I. THE BEGINNINGS OF CHRISTIAN-LATIN POETRY

§ 1. *Christianity and Hellenistic-Roman Civilization* (p. 1).

No attempt can, or need, be made here to give an extensive list of books on the subjects which are summarily treated in this section. The following may be useful:—

1. *General.*

Anrich, G., Das antike Mysterienwesen in seinem Einfluss auf das Christentum, Göttingen 1894.

Bousset, W., Kyrios Christos, 2nd edit., Göttingen, 1921.

Cochrane, C. N., Christianity and Classical Culture, Oxford 1940.

Cumont, F., The Oriental Religions in Roman Paganism, Chicago 1911.

Dieterich, A., Eine Mithrasliturgie, 2nd edit., Leipzig 1910 (and other works).

Duchesne, L., Les Origines du culte chrétien, 5th edit., Paris 1920 (English trans., 3rd edit., London 1910).

——, Histoire ancienne de l'Église, Paris 1907–10, 3 vols.

——, L'Église au VIᵉ siècle, Paris 1925.

Geffcken, J., Der Ausgang des griechisch-römischen Heidentums, Heidelberg 1920.

Harnack, A., History of Dogma, London 1894–9, 7 vols.

——, Mission and Expansion of Christianity, London 1908, 2 vols. (German, 4th edit., 1924, 2 vols.).

Hatch, E., The Influence of Greek Ideas and Usages upon the Christian Church (Hibbert Lectures 1888).

Heitmüller, D., Zum Problem Paulus und Jesus, Zeitschr. f. die N.-T. Wissenschaft, xiii (1912), pp. 320 sqq.

Kaerst, J., Das Wesen des Hellenismus, Leipzig 1909 (vol. ii of his Geschichte des hellenistischen Zeitalters).

Lietzmann, H., History of the Early Church, London 1949–50, 3 vols.

Norden, E., Agnostos Theos, Leipzig 1913.

Rand, E. K., The Building of Eternal Rome, Harvard 1943.

Reitzenstein, R., Die hellenistischen Mysterienreligionen, 3rd edit., Leipzig 1927 (and other works).

Wendland, P., Die hellenistisch-römische Kultur in ihren Beziehungen zu Judentum und Christentum, 2nd edit., Tübingen 1912.

2. *The schools and the Christian attitude to learning* (p. 4).

Labriolle, P. de, Culture classique et Christianisme, Bulletin d'ancienne littérature et d'archéologie chrétiennes, iv (1914), pp. 262 sqq.

Laistner, M. L. W., Christianity and Pagan Culture, New York and London, 1951.

Rauschen, G., Das griechisch-römische Schulwesen zur Zeit des ausgehenden Heidentums, Bonn 1901.

Roger, M., L'enseignement des lettres classiques d'Ausone à Alcuin, Paris 1905.

In addition, the reader may consult the following references to general works, some of which have been already mentioned:—

Boissier, G., La Fin du Paganisme, i, 199 sqq.

Eicken, H. von, Geschichte und System der mittelalterlichen Weltanschauung, Stuttgart 1887, pp. 672 sqq.

Graf, A., Roma nella memoria del medio evo, Turin 1883, ii, 153 sqq.

Hatch, E., The Influence of Greek Ideas and Usages upon the Christian Church, pp. 86 sqq.

Labriolle, P. de, Histoire de la littérature latine chrétienne, pp. 12 sqq.

Marrou, H.-I., S. Augustin et la fin de la culture antique, Paris 1938.

Rand, E. K., Founders of the Middle Ages, Harvard 1928.

Sandys, J. E., History of Classical Scholarship, i, 617 sqq.

Seeck, O., Geschichte des Untergangs der antiken Welt, Berlin 1895–1909, iv, 168 sqq.

3. *Vulgar Latin, &c.* (p. 9).

Felder, J., Die lateinische Kirchensprache nach ihrer geschichtlichen Entwicklung, Feldkirch 1905.

Koffmane, G., Geschichte des Kirchenlateins, Breslau 1879–81.

Kroll, W., Das afrikanische Latein, Rhein. Mus., lii (1897), pp. 569 sqq.

Monceaux, P., Le Latin vulgaire, Revue des Deux Mondes, July 15, 1891, pp. 429 sqq.

Rönsch, H., Itala und Vulgata, Marburg 2nd edit., 1875.

Sittl, K., Zu Beurteilung des sogenannten Mittellateins, Archiv f. lat. Lex. ii (1885), pp. 550 sqq.

Traube, L., Einleitung in die lateinische Philologie des Mittelalters, Munich 1911.

Stolz, F., and Schmalz, J. H., Lateinische Grammatik, 5th edit., ed. Leumann, M., and Hofmann, J. B., Munich, 1926–8.

Strecker, K., Einführung in das Mittellatein, 2nd edit., Berlin, 1929.

§ 2. *The Earliest Christian-Latin Poetry; from Commodian to Damasus* (p. 11). *Commodian.*

Alès, A. d', Commodien et son temps, Recherches de science religieuse, ii (Paris 1911), pp. 479 sqq.; 599 sqq.

Bardy, G., La notice de Gennadius sur Commodien, Recherches de science réligieuse, xiv (1924), pp. 444 sqq.

Boissier, G., Commodien, Paris 1886, bibl. de l'école des hautes études, lxxiii, pp. 37 sqq.

Brakman, C., Commodianea, Mnemosyne, lv (1927), pp. 121 sqq.

Brewer, H., Die Abfassungszeit der Dichtungen des Commodianus von Gaza, Zeitschr. f. kath. Theol. xxiii (1899), pp. 759 sqq.

——, Kommodian von Gaza, ein Arelatensischer Laiendichter aus der Mitte des fünften Jahrhunderts, Forschungen zur christlichen Literatur und Dogmengeschichte, vi, Mainz 1907 *(summarized in* J.T.S. ix (1907), pp. 143 sqq.).

——, Die Frage um das Zeitalter Kommodians, Forschungen zur christlichen Literatur und Dogmengeschichte, X, v, Mainz 1910.

Colombo, S., Una silloga Commodianea, Didaskaleion, i (1923), pp. 108 sqq.

Dombart, B., Commodian-Studien, Wiener Sitzungsber., xcvi (1880), pp. 447 sqq.; cvii (1884), pp. 731 sqq.

——, Über die Bedeutung Commodians für die Textkritik der *Testimonia* Cyprians, Zeitschr. f. wissenschaftl. Theologie, xxii (1879), p. 374.

Durel, J., Les Instructions de Commodien, Paris 1912.

Gasparetti, L., Quaestiones commodianeae, Didaskaleion, iv (1926), pp. 1 sqq.

Groot, A. W. de, Le rhythme de Commodien, Neophilologus, viii (1923), pp. 304 sqq.

Heer, M., Zur Frage nach der Heimat des Dichters Kommodianus, Römische Quartalschrift, xix (1905), pp. 64 sqq.

Katwijk, A. F. van, Lexicon Commodianeum, Amsterdam 1934.

Manitius, M., Zu Commodian, Rhein. Mus. xlvi (1891), pp. 150 sqq.

Martin, J., Studien und Beiträge zur Erklärung und Zeitbestimmung Commodians, Texte und Untersuchungen zur Geschichte der altchristlichen Literatur, xxxix, iv, Leipzig 1913.

——, Commodianea, textkritische Beiträge, Wiener Sitzungsber., clxxxi, vi (1917).

Ramundo, G. S., Quando visse Commodiano ? Archivio della R. società romana di storia patria, xxiv (1901), pp. 373 sqq.; xxv (1902), pp. 137 sqq.

——, Commodiano e la reazione pagana di Giuliano l'apostata, Scritti vari di filologia, Rome 1901, pp. 215 sqq.

Schils, L., Commodien poète rhythmique ? Neophilologus, xv (1929–30), pp. 51 sqq.

Vernier, A., La versification latine populaire en Afrique. Commodien et Verecundus. Revue de philologie, xv (1891), pp. 14 sqq.

Vroom, H. B., De Commodiani metris et syntaxi, Utrecht 1917.

Zeller, F. X., Die Zeit Kommodians, Theologische Quartalschrift, xci (1909), pp. 161 sqq.; pp. 352 sqq.

Lactantius, De Phoenice.

Baehrens, E., Zu des Lactantius' Phoenix, Rhein. Mus., xxix (1874), pp. 200 sqq.; xxx (1875), p. 308.
Birt, T., Ueber die Vocalverbindung *eu* im Lateinischen, Rhein. Mus., xxxiv (1879), pp. 1 sqq. [see pp. 8 sqq.].
Brandt, S., Zum Phönix des Lactantius, Rhein. Mus., xlvii (1892), pp. 390 sqq.
Dechent, H., Über die Echtheit des Phönix von Laktantius, Rhein. Mus., xxxv (1880) pp. 39 sqq.
Goetz, G., Zur lateinischen Anthologie, Rhein. Mus., xxx (1875), p. 477.
Hubaux, J., and Leroy, M., Le mythe du Phénix, Paris 1939.
Löbe, V. J., In scriptorem carminis de Phoenice quod L. Caelii Firmiani Lactantii esse creditur observationes, Brunswick 1891.
Pichon, R., Étude sur Lactance, Paris 1901.
Riese, A., Über den Phönix des Laktantius etc., Rhein. Mus., xxxi (1876), pp. 446 sqq.; lv (1900), pp. 316 sqq.
Ritschl, F., Zur lateinischen Anthologie, Rhein. Mus., xxviii (1873), pp. 189 sqq.
Schuster, M., Zur Echtheitsfrage und Abfassungszeit von Lactantius' Dichtung De ave Phoenice, Wiener Studien, liv (1936), pp. 118 sqq.
Weyman, C., Zum Phönix des Lactantius, Rhein. Mus., xlvii (1892), p. 640.

De Sodoma and de Jona.

Müller, L., Zu Tertullians Gedichten *de Sodoma* und *de Jona*, Rhein. Mus., xxii (1866), pp. 329 sqq.; pp. 464 sqq.; xxvii (1872), pp. 486 sqq. (Zu dem Gedichte *de Sodoma*).

Proba.

Aschbach, J., Die Anicier und die römische Dichterin Proba, Wiener Sitzungsber. lxiv (1870), pp. 369 sqq.

Juvencus.

Hatfield, J. T., A Study of Juvencus, Bonn 1890.
Petschenig, M., Zur Latinität des Juvencus. Archiv f. lat. Lex., vi (1889), pp. 267 sqq.
Widmann, H., De Gaio Vettio Aquilino Iuvenco carminis evangelici poeta et Vergilii imitatore, Breslau 1905.

Damasus.

Ihm, M., Die Epigramme des Damasus, Rhein. Mus., l (1895), pp. 191 sqq.
——, Ein verschollenes Gedicht des Damasus? Rhein. Mus., lii (1897), p. 212.
Rossi, G. B. di, I carmi di s. Damaso, Bullettino di archeol. crist., ser. 4, anno 3 (1884–5), pp. 7 sqq.
Weyman, C., De carminibus Damasianis et Pseudodamasianis observationes, Rev. d'hist. et de litt. relig., i (1896), pp. 58 sqq.
——, Ein verschollenes Gedicht des Damasus? Hist. Jahrb., xix (1898), pp. 89 sqq.
——, Notes de littérature chrétienne, diffusion des poésies damasiennes, Rev. d'hist. et de litt. relig., iii (1898), p. 564.
——, Vier Epigramme des heiligen Papstes Damasus I, Munich 1905.
Wittig, J., Papst Damasus I, Römische Quartalschrift, Supplementheft xiv (1902).

§ 3. *Augustine's Psalm and the Origins of Latin Rhythmical and Rimed Poetry* (p. 20).

Augustine's Psalm.

Daux, C., Le chant abécédaire de saint Augustin contre les Donatistes, Arras 1905.
Engelbrecht, A., Der hl. Augustinus als Volksdichter, Zeitschr. f. d. österreich Gymnas., lix (1908), pp. 580 sqq.
Ermini, F., Étude sur le psaume abécédaire *contra partem Donati*, Miscellanea Agostiniana, ii, Rome (1931), pp. 341 sqq.
Lambot, C., Texte complété et amendé du 'Psalmus contra partem Donati' de S. Augustin, Revue Bénéd., xlvii (1935), pp. 312 sqq.

Lambot, C., Un psaume abécédaire inédit de Fulgence de Ruspe contre les Vandales ariens, Revue Bénéd., xlviii (1936), pp. 221 sqq.

Vroom, H., Le psaume abécédaire de Saint Augustin et la poèsie latine rythmique, Paris 1934.

Rhythm and Rime.

Barry, Sister Inviolata, Augustine the Orator, Washington 1924.

Brandes, W., Die Epistel des Auspicius und die Anfänge der lateinischen Rhythmik, Rhein. Ms., lxiv (1909), pp. 57 sqq. [answered by Wm. Meyer, Gött. Nachr., 1909, pp. 373 sqq.; see below, p. 470, under *Auspicius of Toul*].

Cornu, J., Beiträge zur lateinischen Metrik, Wiener Sitzungsber., clix, iii (1871).

Dechevrens, A., Du rhythme dans l'hymnographie latine, Paris 1895.

Dreves, G. M., [criticism of Meyer's Theory], Gött. gelehrt. Anzeig. 1886, pp. 285 sqq.

Eskuche, G., Die Elisionen in den zwei letzten Füssen des lateinischen Hexameters von Ennius bis Walahfridus Strabo, Rhein. Mus., xlv (1890), pp. 236 and 385 sqq.

Grimm, W. C., Zur Geschichte des Reims, Kleinere Schriften, Gütersloh 1887, iv, pp. 125 sqq.

Havet, L., and Duvau, L., Métrique grecque et latine, Paris 1896.

Hoppe, H., Syntax und Stil des Tertullian, Leipzig 1903.

Huemer, J., Untersuchungen über den iambischen Dimeter bei den christlich-lateinischen Hymnendichtern der vorcarolingischen Zeit, Vienna 1876.

——, Untersuchungen über die ältesten lateinisch-christlichen Rhythmen, Vienna 1879.

Lejay, P., Virgile et les rhythmes latines, Revue de philologie, xix (1895), pp. 45 sqq.

Manitius, M., Ueber Hexameterausgänge in der lateinischen Poesie, Rhein. Mus., xlvi (1891), pp. 622 sqq.

Meyer, Wm., aus Speyer, Gesammelte Abhandlungen zur mittellateinischen Rythmik, Berlin 1905–36, 3 vols.

——, Die rythmischen Jamben des Auspicius, Gött. Nachr., 1906, pp. 192 sqq. (criticized by P. Maas, Byz. Zeitschr., xviii (1908), pp. 239 sqq.).

——, Lateinische Rythmik und byzantinische Strophik, Gött. Nachr., 1908, pp. 194 sqq. (*answers Maas*).

——, Ein Merowinger Rythmus über Fortunat und altdeutsche Rythmik in lateinischen Versen, Gött. Nachr., 1908, pp. 31 sqq.

Norden, E., Die antike Kunstprosa, Leipzig 1909 2nd edit., 2 vols.

Polheim, K., Die lateinische Reimprosa, Leipzig 1925.

Sedgwick, W. B., The Origin of Rhyme, Revue Bénéd., xxxvi (1924), pp. 330 sqq.

Strecker, K., Leoninische Hexameter und Pentameter im IX. Jahrh., Neues Archiv, xliv (1922), pp. 213 sqq.

Wattenbach, W., Die Anfänge lateinischer profaner Rhythmen des Mittelalters, Zeitschr. f. deutsch. Alt., iii (1872), pp. 469 sqq.

Winterfeld, P. von, Zur Geschichte der rhythmischen Dichtung, Neues Archiv, xxv (1900), pp. 381 sqq.

Wölfflin, E., Der Reim in Lateinischen, Archiv f. lat. Lex., i (1884), pp. 350 sqq.; pp. 576 sqq.

§ 4. *The Use of Hymns in the Latin Church; Ambrose*, A.D. 340–97 (p. 28).

(i) *The use of Hymns.*

Batiffol, P., Histoire du bréviaire romain, Paris 1911.

Bäumer, S., Geschichte des Breviers, Freiburg i. B., 1895 (*French Trans.*, Histoire du bréviaire, Paris 1905, 2 vols.).

Blume, C., Der Cursus S. Benedicti Nursini und die liturgischen Hymnen des 6.–9. Jahrhunderts, Leipzig 1908.

Kroll, J., Die christliche Hymnodie bis zu Klemens von Alexandrien, Königsberg, 1921.

Mearns, J., Early Latin Hymnaries, Cambridge 1913.

——, The Canticles of the Church in Early and Medieval Times, Cambridge 1914.

Messenger, R. E., Whence the Ninth-Century Hymnal ? Trs. Amer. Philol. Assoc. lxix (1938), pp. 446 sqq.
Walpole, A. S., and Mason, A. J., ed., Early Latin Hymns, Cambridge 1922.
Wilmart, A., Le psautier de la reine n° 11, sa provenance et sa date, Revue Bénéd. xxviii (1911), pp. 341 sqq.

(ii) *Ambrose.*

Biraghi, L., Inni sinceri e carmi di s. Ambrogio, Milan 1862.
Dreves, G. M., Aurelius Ambrosius, der Vater des Kirchengesanges, Freiburg i. B., 1893.
Dudden, F. Homes, The Life and Times of St. Ambrose, Oxford, 1935, 2 vols.
Labriolle, P. de, S. Ambroise, Paris 1908.
Steier, A., Untersuchungen über die Echtheit der Hymnen des Ambrosius, Leipzig 1903.
Walpole, A. S., Notes on Text of Hymns of S. Ambrose, J.T.S., ix (1908), pp. 428 sqq.
Weyman, C., Die Tituli des hl. Ambrosius zu den Gemälden der Mailänder Basilika, Zeitschr. f. d. österreich. Gymnas. xlix (1898), 699 sqq.

§ 5. *Hilary of Poitiers: circa* A.D. 310–66 (p. 41).

Engelbrecht, A., Zur Sprache des Hilarius Pictaviensis und seiner Zeitgenossen, Wiener Studien, xxix (1917), pp. 135 sqq.
Feder, A., Epilegomena zu Hilarius Pictaviensis, Wiener Studien, xli (1919), i, 51 sqq.; ii, 167 sqq.
Gamurrini, I. F., S. Hilarii Tractatus de mysteriis et Hymni et S. Silviae Peregrinatio, Rome 1887.
Mason, A. J., The First Latin Christian Poet, J.T.S., v (1904), pp. 413 sqq.
Meyer, W., Die drei Arezzaner Hymnen des Hilarius von Poitiers und Etwas über Rythmus, Gött. Nachr., 1909, pp. 373 sqq.
Walpole, A. S., Hymns attributed to Hilary of Poitiers, J.T.S., vi (1905), pp. 599 sqq.
Wilmart, A., Le *de mysteriis* de S. Hilaire au Mont-Cassin, Revue Bénéd. (xxvii), 1910, pp. 12 sqq.

II. PRUDENTIUS, A.D. 348–405 *(circ.)*.

§ 1. *The Cathemerinon* (p. 44).

Allard, P., Le Symbolisme chrétien au IVe siècle d'après les poèmes de Prudence, Revue de l'art chrétien, xxxv (1885), pp. 1 sqq.; pp. 139 sqq.
Bergman, J., De codicum Prudentianorum generibus et virtute, Wiener Sitzungsber., clvii, v (1908).
——, Aurelius Prudentius Clemens, der grösste christliche Dichter des Altertums, i, Dorpat 1921.
Brakman, C., Prudentiana, Mnemosyne, xlix (1921), pp. 106 sqq.
Brockhaus, C., Aurelius Prudentius Clemens in seiner Bedeutung für die Kirche seiner Zeit, Leipzig 1872.
Burnam, J. M., Commentaire anonyme sur Prudence d'après le MS. 413 de Valenciennes, Paris 1910.
Chavanne, P., Le patriotisme de Prudence, Revue d'hist. et de litt. relig., vi (1899), pp. 332 sq.; pp. 385 sqq.
Deferrari, R. J., and Campbell, J. M., Concordance of Prudentius, Med. Acad. of America, 1932.
Lease, E. B., A Syntactic, Stylistic, and Metrical Study of Prudentius, Baltimore 1895.
Maigret, F., Le poète chrétien Prudence, Paris 1903.
Meyer, G., Prudentiana, Philologus, lxxxvii (1932), pp. 249 sqq.; 332 sqq.
Puech, A., Prudence, étude sur la poésie latine chrétienne au IVe siècle, Paris 1888.
Schmitz, M., Die Gedichte des Prudentius und ihre Entstehungszeit, Aachen 1889.
Sixt, G., Die lyrischen Gedichte des Aurelius Prudentius Clemens, Stuttgart 1889.

Stettiner, R., Die illustrierte Prudentiushandschriften, Berlin 1895, 1905, in progress.

Weyman, C., Prudentius und Sulpicius Severus, Hist. Jahrb., xv (1894), pp. 370 sqq.

——, *Reviews of* Rösler, A., Der katholische Dichter Aurelius Prudentius Clemens, Freiburg i. B., 1886; *and of* Puech, A., Prudence, Paris 1888; Hist Jahrb., x (1889), pp. 116 sqq.

——, *Review of* Sixt, S., Die lyrischen Gedichte des Aurelius Prudentius Clemens, Stuttgart 1889; Hist. Jahrb., xi (1890), pp. 406 sqq.

Winstedt, E. O., The Double Recension in the Poems of Prudentius, Classical Review, 1903, pp. 203 sqq.

——, The Spelling of the Sixth-Century MS. of Prudentius, Classical Review, 1904, pp. 45 sqq.

——, Notes on the MSS. of Prudentius; reprint from Journal of Philology, xxix.

Woodruff, H., The Illustrated Manuscripts of Prudentius, Harvard 1930.

§ 2. *The Peristephanon and the Cult of the Martyrs* (p. 50).

Allard, P., L'hagiographie au IVe siècle . . . d'après les poèmes de Prudence, Revue des quest. hist., xxxvii (1885), pp. 353 sqq.

——, Prudence historien, ib., xxxv (1884), pp. 345 sqq.

——, Rome au IVe siècle d'après les poèmes de Prudence, ib., xxxvi (1884), pp. 5 sqq.

Corssen, P., Begriff und Wesen des Märtyrers in der alten Kirche, Neue Jahrb. f. d. klass. Alt., 1915, pp. 481 sqq.

Delehaye, H., Les origines du culte des martyrs, Brussels 1912.

——, Les passions des martyrs et les genres littéraires, Brussels 1921.

Holl, K., Die Vorstellung vom Märtyrer und Märtyrerakte in ihrer geschichtlichen Entwicklung, Neue Jahrb. f. d. klass. Alt., 1914, pp. 521 sqq.

Le Blant, E., Mémoire sur les martyrs chrétiens et les supplices destructeurs du corps, Mémoires de l'Académie des inscriptions, xxviii, ii (1876), pp. 75 sqq.

Lucius, E., Die Anfänge des Heiligenkults, Tübingen 1904.

§ 3. *The Apotheosis, Hamartigenia, Psychomachia, Contra Symmachum, and Dittochaeon* (p. 58).

Apotheosis.

Merkle, S., Prudentius und Priscillian, Theologische Quartalschrift, lxxvi (1894), pp. 77 sqq.

Hamartigenia.

Goldner, J., Der Sündenquell, Freysing 1851.

Psychomachia.

Bloomfield, M. W., A Source of Prudentius' *Psychomachia*, Speculum, xviii (1943), pp. 87 sqq.

Hench, A. L., Sources of Prudentius 'Psychomachia', Class. Philology, xix (1924), pp. 78 sqq.

Hoefer, O., De Prudentii poetae Psychomachia et carminum chronologia, Marburg 1900.

Melardi, A., La Psychomachia di Prudenzio, Pistoia 1900.

Tolkiehn, J., *Review of* Aurelii Prudentii Clementis Psychomachia, ed. J. Bergman, Upsala 1897. Wochenschrift für klassische Philologie, Aug. 16, 1899, pp. 926 sq.

Contra Symmachum.

Both, V., Des christlichen Dichters Prudentius Schrift gegen Symmachus, Rastatt, 1882.

Dabas, J. C., Sur une question soulevée par le poème de Prudence contre Symmachus, Paris 1866.

Dittochaeon.

Baumstark, A., Das Dittochaeon des Prudentius, Byzant. Zeitschr., xx (1911), pp. 179 sqq.

Kirsch, J. P., Le 'Dittochaeum' de Prudence et les monuments de l'antiquité chrétienne, Atti del secondo congresso internazionale di archeologia cristiana, Rome 1902, pp. 179 sqq.
Merkle, S., Prudentius' Dittochaeum, Festschrift zum 100jährigen Jubiläum des deutschen Campo Santo in Rom, Freiburg i. B., 1897, pp. 33 sqq.

III. THE CHRISTIAN POETS OF GAUL AND AFRICA IN THE FOURTH, FIFTH, AND SIXTH CENTURIES

§ 1. *Ausonius and the end of the old order* (p. 72).

Baehrens, E., Zu Ausonius, Rhein. Mus., xxix (1874), p. 509.
Brandes, W., Beiträge zu Ausonius, Wolfenbüttel 1895.
Jullian, C., Ausone et son temps, Revue historique, xlvii (1891), pp. 241 sqq.; xlviii (1892), pp. 1 sqq.
Kaufmann, G., Rhetorenschulen und Klosterschulen der heidnischen und christlichen Kultur in Gallien während des 5. und 6. Jahrhunderts, Hist. Taschenbuch (ed. Räumer), iv. Folge, x. Jahrg., Leipzig 1869.
Villani, L., Quelques observations sur les chants chrétiens d'Ausone, Revue des études anciennes, viii (1906), pp. 325 sqq.

§ 2. *Poets of the fifth century* (p. 75).
General.
Leyay, P., *Review of* C.S.E.L. xvi (*Poetae Christiani Latini Minores* I), Revue critique, xxv (1888), pp. 286 sqq

Cyprian's Heptateuchos.
Gamber, S., Le livre de la Genèse dans la poésie latine au Ve siècle, Paris 1889.
Mayor, J. E. B., The Latin Heptateuch, London 1889.
Müller, L., Zu Ennius und den christlichen Dichtern, Rhein. Mus. xxi (1866), pp. 123 sqq.
Stutzenberger, Der Heptateuch des gallischen Dichters Cyprianus, Zweibrücken 1903.

Claudius Marius Victor.
Ferrari, O., Un poeta cristiano del v. secolo, Claudio Mario Vittore, Pavia 1912.
Gamber, S., Un rhéteur chrétien au Ve siècle, Claudius Marius Victor, Marseilles 1884.
Krappe, A. H., A Persian Myth in the *Alethia* of Claudius Marius Victor, Speculum (xvii), 1942, pp. 255 sqq.

Avitus.
Goelzer, H., Le latin de saint Avit, Paris 1909.
Müller, L., Zu Hieronymus, Porfirius und Alcimus Avitus, Rhein. Mus., xxi (1866), pp. 263 sqq.
Weyman, C., Martialis und Alcimus Avitus, Rhein. Mus., xlii (1887), p. 637.

Sidonius Apollinaris.
Allard, P., S. Sidoine Apollinaire, Paris 1910.
Anderson, W. B., A Virgilian Reminiscence in Apollinaris Sidonius, Classical Review xli (1947), p. 124 sq.
Büdinger, M., Apollinaris Sidonius als Politiker, Wiener Sitzungsber., xcvii (1881), pp. 915 sqq.
Dalton, O. M., Letters of Sidonius Apollinaris, Oxford 1915, 2 vols.
Engelbrecht, A., Beiträge zum lateinischen Lexikon aus Sidonius, Wiener Studien, xx (1898), pp. 293 sqq.
——, Untersuchungen über die Sprache des Claudianus Mamertus, Wiener Sitzungsber., cx (1886), pp. 423 sqq. [comparisons with Sidonius].
Grupe, E., Zur Sprache des Apollinaris Sidonius, Zabern 1892.
Kaufmann, G., Die Werke des C. Sollius Apollinaris Sidonius als eine Quelle für die Geschichte seiner Zeit, Göttingen 1864.

Kretschmann, H., De latinitate C. Solli Apollin. Sidoni, Progr. d. städt. Gymn. zu Memel, i, 1870; ii, 1872.

Mommsen, T., Apollinaris Sidonius und seine Zeit, Reden und Aufsätze, Berlin 1905, pp. 132 sqq.

Stevens, C. E., Apollinaris Sidonius and his Age, Oxford 1933.

Paulinus of Périgueux.

Drevon, J. M., De Paulini Petricorii vita et scriptis, Toulouse 1889.

Huber, A., Die poetische Bearbeitung der Vita S. Martini des Sulpicius Severus durch Paulinus von Périgueux, Kempten 1901.

Auspicius of Toul; see above under Rhythm and Rime.

W. Meyer, in Gött. Nachr., 1906, pp. 192 sqq.; 1908, pp. 194 sqq.; 1909, pp. 373 sqq.; also Brandes, Rhein. Mus., lxiv (1899), pp. 57 sqq.; Maas, P. Byz. Zeitschr., xviii (1910), pp. 239 sqq.

Paulinus of Pella.

Brandes, W., Accipiter, 'Jagdfalke' (Paulinus Eucharisticos, Verse 145). Archiv f. lat. Lex., iv (1887), p. 141.

Devogel, L., Étude sur la latinité et le style de Paulin de Pella, Brussels 1898.

Funaioli, G., De Paulini Pellaei carminis 'Eucharisticos' fontibus, Le Musée belge, 1905, pp. 159 sqq.

Rocafort, J., Un type gallo-romain, Paulin de Pella, Paris 1896.

Orientius.

Bellanger, L., Le poème d'Orientius, étude philologique et littéraire, Paris 1903.

Hitchcock, F. R. M., Notes on the *Commonitorium* of Orientius, Classical Review, 1914, pp. 41 sq.

Manitius, M., Zu Orientius, Rhein. Mus., xlix (1894), pp. 172 sqq.

Purser, L. C., M. Bellanger's Orientius, Hermathena, 1904, pp. 36 sqq.

Prosper.

Couture, L., S. Prosper d'Aquitaine, Bulletin de litt. ecclés., 1900, pp. 269 sqq.; 1901, pp. 33 sqq.

Holder-Egger, O., Die Chronik Prospers von Aquitaine, Neues Archiv, i (1876), pp. 13 sqq.

Valentin, L., S. Prosper d'Aquitaine, Toulouse 1900.

§ 3. *Venantius Fortunatus*, 540–600 (p. 86).

Blomgren, S., Studia Fortunatiana, Uppsala 1933.

Đagianti, F., Studio sintattico delle 'opera poetica' di Venanzio Fortunato, Veroli 1921.

Delehaye, H., Une inscription de Fortunat sur S. Martin, i, 5, Extrait des Mélanges de Borman, Liège 1919.

Dill, S., Roman Society in Gaul in the Merovingian Age, London 1926.

Dostal, J., Über Identität und Zeit von Personen bei Venantius Fortunatus, Vienna 1901.

Dreves, G. M., Hymnologische Studien zu Fortunatus und Raban, Munich 1908 [see *Review by* K. Strecker, Anzeiger f. deutsch. Alt., xxxiii, pp. 43 sqq.].

Elss, H., Untersuchungen über den Stil und die Sprache des Venantius Fortunatus, Heidelberg 1907.

Köbner, R., Venantius Fortunatus, seine Persönlichkeit und seine Stellung in der geistigen Kultur des Merowinger-Reiches, Leipzig 1915.

Leo, F., Venantius Fortunatus, Deutsche Rundschau, 1882, pp. 414 sqq.

Nisard, C., Le poète Fortunat, Paris 1890 [also Des poésies de Ste. Radegonde attribuées jusqu'ici à Fortunat, Revue historique, xxxvii (1888), pp. 49 sqq.].

Meneghetti, A., La latinità di Venanzio Fortunato, Turin 1917.

Meyer, W., Der Gelegenheitsdichter Venantius Fortunatus, Berlin 1901.

——, Über Handschriften der Gedichte Fortunat's, Gött. Nachr., 1908, pp. 82 sqq.

Tardi, D., Fortunat, Paris 1927.

§ 4. *Christian Poetry in Africa* (p. 95).

Carmen ad Flavium Felicem.

Miltner-Zueunic, H., De carmine ad Flavium Felicem misso, quod inscribitur De resurrectione mortuorum, Wiener Studien, xlviii (1930), pp. 82 sqq.
Waszink, J. H., Carmen ad Flavium Felicem de resurrectione mortuorum et de iudicio Domini; proleg., etc., Bonn 1937.
Dracontius.
Barwinski, B., De Dracontio Catulli imitatore, Rhein. Mus., xliii (1888), pp. 310 sqq.
Bücheler, F., Zu Dracontius, Rhein. Mus., xxix (1874), pp. 362 sq. (see also Rhein. Mus., xxviii (1873), pp. 348 sqq.).
Ihm, M., Damasus und Dracontius, Rhein. Mus., liii (1898), pp. 165 sqq.
Manitius, M., Zu Dracontius' carmina minora, Rhein. Mus., xlvi (1891), pp. 493 sqq.
Meyer, W., Die Berliner Centones der Laudes Dei des Dracontius, Berlin. Sitzungsber. 1890, pp. 257 sqq.
Ribbeck, O., Kritische Beiträge zu Dracontius, Rhein. Mus., xxviii (1873), pp. 461 sqq.
Schmidt, M., Zu Dracontius, Rhein. Mus., xxix (1874), pp. 202 sqq.
Teuffel, W., Zu Dracontius, Rhein. Mus., xxx (1875), p. 320.

IV. THE CHRISTIAN POETS OF ITALY IN THE FOURTH, FIFTH, AND SIXTH CENTURIES

§ 1. *Paulinus of Nola*, A.D. 355*circ.*–431 (p. 101).

Baudrillart, A., S. Paulin, évêque de Nole, Paris 1905.
Fabre, P., Essai sur la chronologie de l'œuvre de Saint Paulin de Nole, Paris 1948.
——, Saint Paulin de Nole et l'amitié chrétienne, Paris 1949.
Favez, C., Note sur la composition du carmen 31 de Paulin de Nole, Revue des études latins, xiii (1935), pp. 266 sqq.
Hartel, W. von, Zu den Gedichten des hl. Paulinus von Nola, Wiener Sitzungsber., cxxxii, vii (1895).
Kraus, L., Die poetische Sprache des Paulinus Nolanus, Augsburg 1918.
Labriolle, P. de, La correspondance d'Ausone et de Paulin de Nole, Paris 1910.
Lagrange, F., Histoire de S. Paulin de Nole, Paris 1882, 2 vols.
Reinelt, P., Studien über die Briefe des heiligen Paulinus von Nola, Breslau 1904.
Weyman, C., Salvianus und Paulinus von Nola, Hist. Jahrb., xv (1894), pp. 373 sq.
Wiman, G., Till Paulinus Nolanus' carmina, Eranos, xxxii (1934), pp. 98 sqq.

§ 2. *Severus Sanctus Endelechius, Honorius Scholasticus, and Sedulius* (p. 107).

Sedulius.
Boissier, G., Sedulius, Journal des savants, 1881, pp. 553 sqq.
——, Le *carmen paschale* et l'*opus paschale* de Sedulius, Revue de philologie, vi (1882), pp. 28 sqq.
Huemer, J., De Sedulii poetae vita et scriptis commentatio, Vienna 1878.
Leimbach, C. L., Über den christlichen Dichter C. Sedulius und dessen *carmen paschale*, Goslar 1879.
McDonald, A. D., The Iconographic Tradition of Sedulius, Speculum, viii (1933), pp. 150 sqq.

§ 3. *The Sixth Century; Boethius, Ennodius, Arator* (p. 111).

Cassiodorus
Vyer, A. van der, Cassiodore et son œuvre, Speculum, vi (1931), pp. 244 sqq.
Jones, L. W., The Influence of Cassiodorus on Medieval Culture, Speculum, xx (1945), pp. 433 sqq.; xxii (1947), pp. 254 sqq.
Boethius.
Barrett, H. M., Boethius, Cambridge 1940.
Boissier, G., Le christianisme de Boëce, Journal des savants, 1889, p. 449.

Engelbrecht, A., Die *Consolatio philosophiae* des Boethius, Wiener Sitzungsber., cxliv, iii (1901).
Fortescue, A., Boethi de consolatione philosophiae libri quinque (Introd. by G. D. Smith; pp. xxv sqq., de religione Boethi), London 1925 (with good bibliography).
Hildebrand, A., Boëthius und seine Stellung zum Christentume, Regensburg 1885.
Klingner, F., De Boethii consolatione philosophiae; in Kiessling, A., and Wilamowitz-Moellendorff, Philologische Untersuchungen, xxvii, Berlin 1921 (reviewed by E. K. Rand, American Journal of Philology, xliv (1923), pp. 83 sq.).
Patch, H. R., The Tradition of Boethius, Oxford 1935.
Rand, E. K., On the Composition of Boëthius' Consolatio philosophiae, Harvard Studies in Classical Philology (1904), xv.
Stewart, H. F., Boëthius, an Essay, Edinburgh 1891.
Stone, L. W., Old French Translations of the *De Consolatione Philosophiae* of Boethius, Medium Aevum, vi (1937), pp. 21 sqq.
    Ennodius.
Dubois, A., La latinité d'Ennodius, Paris 1903.
Magani, F., Ennodio, Pavia 1886.
Vogel, F., Ennodiana, Archiv f. lat. Lex., i (1884), pp. 267 sqq.
    Arator.
Leimbach, C. L., Über den Dichter Arator, Theologische Studien und Kritiken, xlvi (1873), pp. 225 sqq.
McKinlay, A. P., Arator: the Codices, Med. Acad. of America, 1942.
——, *Membra Disiecta* of Manuscripts of Arator, Speculum, xv (1940), pp. 95 sqq.
Perugi, G. L., Aratore, Venice 1909.
Schrödinger, J., Das Epos des Arator, *De actibus apostolorum*, in seinem Verhältnis zu Vergil, Weiden 1911.

V. THE TRANSITION TO THE MEDIEVAL WORLD

§ 1. *The Age of Gregory the Great* (p. 121).

[For a general bibliography see Camb. Med. Hist. ii, pp. 743 sqq. On Gregory of Tours:
    Bonnet, M., Le Latin de Grégoire de Tours, Paris 1890.
    Manitius, M., Zur Frankengeschichte Gregors von Tours, Neues Archiv, xxi (1896), pp. 549 sqq.]
    Gregory the Great as Hymn-writer.
Blume, G., Gregor der Grosse als Hymnendichter, Stimmen aux Maria-Laach, lxxiv, iii (1908), pp. 269 sqq.
Dreves, G. M., Haben wir Gregor den Grossen als Hymnendichter anzusehen ?, Theologische Quartalschrift, xxi (1907), pp. 548 sqq.; xxiii (1909), pp. 436 sq. (see also Dreves's *Review* of Manitius, *Christl. Lat. Poesie*, in Zeitschr. f. kath. Theol., xvi (1892), pp. 313 sqq. (p. 316)).

§ 2. *Spanish Poets and the Mozarabic Hymnary* (p. 125).
General.

Gams, P. B., Die Kirchengeschichte von Spanien, Regensburg, 1862–74, 2 vols.
Hodgkin, T., Visigothic Spain, E.H.R., ii (1887), pp. 209 sqq.
Magnin, E., L'Église wisigothique au VIIe siècle, Paris 1912.
Menéndez y Pelayo, M., Historia de la poesía castellana en la edad media, Madrid 1911–13, i.
Messenger, R. E., The Mozarabic Hymnal, Trs. of American Philol. Assoc., lxxv (1944), pp. 103 sqq.
——, Mozarabic Hymns in Relation to Contemporary Culture in Spain, Traditio, iv (1946), pp. 149 sqq.
Raby, F. J. E., On the Date and Provenance of some early Latin Hymns, Medium Aevum, xvi (1947), pp. 1 sqq.

Merobaudes.
Baehrens, E., Zur lateinischen Anthologie, Rhein. Mus., xxxi (1876), p. 104.
Bickel, E., De Merobaude imitatore Senecae, Rhein. Mus., lx (1905), p. 317.
Sisebut.
Riese, A., Zur lateinischen Anthologie, Rhein. Mus., xxx (1875), pp. 133 sqq. (cf. ib. p. 320).
Isidore of Seville.
Beeson, C. H., Isidore's *Institutionum disciplinae* and Pliny the Younger, Classical Philology, viii (1913), pp. 93 sqq.
——, Isidorstudien, Munich 1913.
Weyman, C., Zu den Versen Isidors von Seville über seine Bibliothek, Hist. Jahrb., xxxii (1911), pp. 66 sqq.
Braulio of Saragossa.
Lynel, C. H., Saint Braulio, Bishop of Saragossa (631–651), Washington, D.C., 1938.
Galindo, P., San Braulio obispo de Zaragoza (631–651), Madrid, 1950.
Eugenius III of Toledo.
Reinwald, K., Die Ausgabe des ersten Buches der *Laudes Dei* und der *Satisfactio* des Dracontius durch Eugenius von Toledo, Speyer 1913.
Vollmer, F., Die Gedichtsammlung des Eugenius von Toledo, Neues Archiv, xxvi (1901), pp. 394 sqq.
Mozarabic liturgy.
Bishop, W. C., The Mozarabic and Ambrosian Rites, Alcuin Club Tracts, xv, London 1924.
Gilson, J. P., The Mozarabic Psalter, Henry Bradshaw Society, London 1905.

§ 3. *Irish Poets* (p. 131).
The Irish Church.
Bellesheim, A., Geschichte der katholischen Kirche in Irland, Mainz 1890–1, 3 vols.
Bury, J. B., Life of S. Patrick, London 1905.
Gougaud, L., Christianity in Celtic Lands, London, 1922.
——, L'œuvre des Scotti dans l'Europe continentale, Revue d'hist. ecclés., ix (1908), pp. 21 sqq.; pp. 255 sqq.
Kuypers, A. B., The Book of Cerne, Cambridge 1902 (contains text of some Celtic hymns).
Meyer, W., Poetische Nachlese aus dem sogenannten Book of Cerne in Cambridge und aus dem Londoner Codex Regius 2. A. xx, Gött. Nachr., 1917, pp. 597 sqq.
Warren, F. E., The Liturgy and Ritual of the Celtic Church, Oxford 1881.
Zimmer, H., Über die Bedeutung des irischen Elements für die mittelalterliche Kultur, Preuss. Jahrb., lix (1887), pp. 28 sqq.
——, Über direkte Handelsverbindungen Westgalliens mit Irland im Altertum und frühen Mittelalter, Berlin. Sitzungsber. 1909, pp. 543 sqq.
Gildas.
Stevens, C. E., Gildas Sapiens, E.H.R. 1941, pp. 353 sqq.
Meyer, W., Gildae Oratio rythmica, Gött. Nachr. 1912, pp. 48 sqq.
Columba.
Cuissard, C., La prose de S. Columba, Revue celtique, v (1881–3), pp. 205 sqq.
Hisperica Famina.
Geyer, P., Die Hisperica Famina, Archiv f. lat. Lex., ii (1885), pp. 255 sqq.
Goetz, G., Über Dunkel- und Geheimsprache im späten und mittelalterlichen Latein, Leipzig. Sitzungsber. 1896, pp. 62 sqq.
Jenkinson, F. J. H., The Hisperica Famina, Cambridge 1908.
Zimmer, H., Nennius Vindicatus, Berlin 1893.
——, Neue Fragmente von Hisperica Famina, Gött. Nachr. 1895, pp. 117 sqq.
Columbanus.
Domenici, G., S. Columbano, La Civiltà cattolica, Rome 1923.

Gundlach, W., Über die Columban-Briefe, Neues Archiv, xiii (1888), pp. 499 sqq. (especially pp. 514 sqq.).
Laur, J. J., Der heilige Kolumban, Freiburg i. B. 1919.
Martin, E., S. Columban, Paris 1905.
Metlage, G., The Life and Writings of S. Columban, Philadelphia 1914.
Pellizzari, A., S. Colombano e le lettere, Scuol. catt., 15 July 1923, pp. 524 sqq.
Roussel, J., S. Columban, Paris 1941–2, 2 vols.

§ 4. *Anglo-Saxon Poets* (p. 140).

General.

Crawford, S. J., Anglo-Saxon Influence in Western Christendom (600–800), Oxford 1933.
Duckett, E. S., Anglo-Saxon Saints and Scholars, New York 1947.
Ogilvy, J. D. A., Books known to Anglo-Latin Writers from Aldhelm to Alcuin, Med. Acad. of America, 1936.
Martin-Clarke, D. E., Culture in Early Anglo-Saxon England, Oxford 1947.
Stephens, W. R. W., and Hunt, W., History of the English Church, i (597–1066), London 1899.
Wright, T., Biographia Britannica Literaria (Anglo-Saxon Period), London 1842.

Aldhelm.

Browne, G. F., S. Aldhelm, London 1903.
Manitius, M., Zu Aldhelm und Beda, Wiener Sitzungsber., cxiii (1886), pp. 532 sqq.
Müller, L., Zu Aldhelmus, Rhein. Mus., xxii (1867), pp. 150 sq.
Pitman, J. H., The Riddles of Aldhelm, New Haven 1925.
Strecker, K., Aldhelms Gedichte in Tegernsee, Archiv f. d. Stud. der neueren Sprachen und Literaturen, cxliii (1922), pp. 177 sqq.
Zupitza, J., Eine Conjectur zu Aldhelm, Romanische Forschungen, iii (1887), p. 280.

Aethelwald.

Bradley, H., On Some Poems ascribed to Aldhelm, E.H.R., xv (1900), pp. 291 sq.
Bright, W., Chapters of Early English Church History (2nd edit.), p. 353, Oxford 1888.

Tatwine and Eusebius.

Bücheler, F., Coniectanea, Rhein. Mus., xxxvi (1881), pp. 340 sqq.

Bede.

Browne, G. F., The Venerable Bede, London 1919.
Lehmann, P., Die Erstveröffentlichung von Bedes Psalmengedichten, Zeitschr. für Kirchengeschichte, xxxiv (1908), pp. 89 sqq. Cf. Lehmann, Wert und Echtheit einer Beda abgesprochenen Schrift, Abh. d. Bayer. Akad., 1919, iv, p. 1.
Meyer, W., Bedae Oratio ad Deum, Gött. Nachr., 1912, pp. 228 sqq.
Plummer, C., Historia ecclesiastica gentis Anglorum (*Introd.*), Oxford 1896, 2 vols.
Whitbread, L., A Study of Bede's *Versus de die iudicii* Philological Quarterly, xxiii (1944), pp. 193 sqq.
Zimmer, H., Zur Orthographie des Namens Beda, Neues Archiv, xvi (1891), pp. 599 sqq.

Boniface and Lul.

Browne, G. F., Boniface of Crediton, London 1910.
Hahn, H., Bonifaz und Lul, Leipzig 1883.
James, M. R., S. Boniface's Poem to Nithardus, E.H.R., xxix (1914), p. 94.
Koch, H., Stellung des hl. Bonifaz zu Bildung und Wissenschaft, Pastoralbl. f. d. Diözese Ermland, 1905.
Laux, J. J., Der heilige Bonifatius, Freiburg i. B. 1922.
Müller, L., Zu den Räthseln des hl. Bonifacius, Rhein. Mus., xxii (1866), pp. 151 sq.
Tangl, M., Bonifatiusfragen, Abh. d. Berlin. Akad. 1919 (ii).
Traube, L., Die älteste Handschrift der Aenigmata Bonifatii, Neues Archiv, xxvii (1902), pp. 211 sqq.

Wulfstan.

Blume, C., Wolstan von Winchester und Vital von Saint-Evroult, Dichter der drei Lobgesänge auf die heiligen Aethelwold, Birin und Swithun, Wiener Sitzungsber., 1903, cxlvi, iii.

VI. THE CAROLINGIAN RENAISSANCE

§ 1. *Charles the Great and the revival of classical studies* (p. 154).

Abel, S., and Simson, B., Jahrbücher des fränkischen Reichs unter Karl dem Grossen, Leipzig, 2nd edit., vol. i, 1888; vol. ii, 1888.

Dümmler, E., Die handschriftliche Überlieferung der lateinischen Dichtungen aus der Zeit der Karolinger, Neues Archiv, iv (1879), pp. 89 sqq.; 241 sqq.; 511 sqq.

——, Nasos (Modoins) Gedichte an Karl den Grossen, Neues Archiv, xi (1886), pp. 77 sqq.

Ebert, A., Kleine Beiträge zur Geschichte der karolingischen Literatur, Verhandl. d. kgl. Sächs. Gesell. d. Wiss. zu Leipzig, xxx (1878), pp. 95 sqq.

Hodgkin, T., Charles the Great, London 1908.

Laistner, M. L. W., Thought and Letters in W. Europe, A.D. 500–900, London 1931.

Manitius, M., Karolus magnus und Leo Papa, Neues Archiv, viii (1883), pp. 11 sqq.

——, Zu karolingischen Gedichten, Neues Archiv, xi (1886), pp. 553 sqq.

——, Zur karolingischen Literatur, Neues Archiv, xi (1911), pp. 41 sqq.

——, Zur karolingischen Poesie, Neues Archiv, xvi (1891), pp. 175 sqq.

Monod, G., Études critiques sur les sources de l'histoire carolingienne, Paris 1898.

Mullinger, J. B., The Schools of Charles the Great, London 1877.

Renan, E., Les études classiques au moyen âge pendant la période carolingienne, Mélanges religieux et historiques, pp. 257 sqq., Paris 1904.

Simson, B., Über das Gedicht von der Zusammenkunft Karls des Grossen und Papst Leos III, Forsch. zur deutsch. Gesch., xii (1872), pp. 567 sqq.

Strecker, K., Studien zu karolingischen Dichtern, Neues Archiv, xliii (1921), pp. 479 sqq.; xliv (1922), pp. 209 sqq.; xlv (1923), pp. 14 sqq.

——, Zu den karolingischen Rhythmen, Neues Archiv, xxxiv (1909), pp. 599 sqq.

Tardi, D., Fortunat et Angilbert, Arch. lat. med. aevi, ii (1925), pp. 30 sqq.

Traube, L., Karolingische Dichtungen, Berlin 1888 (in Schriften zur germanischen Philologie, ed. M. Rödiger, i).

§ 2. *Alcuin (circ. 735–804); Paul the Deacon (730 circ.–99); Paulinus of Aquileia (d. 802)* (p. 159).

Alcuin.

Ditscheid, H., Alkuins Leben und Bedeutung f. d. religiösen Unterricht, Coblenz 1902.

Duckett, E. S., Alcuin, Friend of Charlemagne, New York 1951.

Dümmler, E., Alchvinstudien, Berlin. Sitzungsber. 1891, pp. 49 sqq.

——, Zur Lebensgeschichte Alchvins, Neues Archiv, xviii (1893), pp. 53 sqq.

Gaskoin, C. J. B., Alcuin, his Life and his Work, Cambridge 1904.

Kleinclausz, A., Alcuin, Paris 1948.

Monnier, F., Alcuin et Charlemagne, Paris 1864.

Sickel, T., Alcuinstudien, I, Wiener Sitzungsber. lxxix (1875), pp. 461 sqq.

Strecker, K., Drei Rhythmen Alkuins, Neues Archiv, xliii (1921), pp. 387 sqq.

Werner, K., Alcuin und sein Jahrhundert, Vienna 1881.

West, A. F., Alcuin, London 1893.

Wilmot-Buxton, E. M., Alcuin, New York 1922.

Winterfeld, P. von, Wie sah der *Codex Blandinius vetustissimus* des Horaz aus ? Rhein. Mus., lx (1905), pp. 31 sqq.

Paul the Deacon.

Amelli, A. M., Paolo Diacono, Carlo Magno e Paolino d'Aquileja in un epigrammo inedito estratto da un codice di Montecassino, Montecassino 1899.

476　　　　　　　　　　　　BIBLIOGRAPHY

Dahn, F., Paulus Diaconus, Leipzig 1876.
Dümmler, E., Zu den Gedichten des Paulus Diaconus, Neues Archiv, xv (1890),
　　pp. 199 sqq.; xvii (1892), pp. 397 sqq.
Maselli, A., Di alcune poesie dubbiamente attribute a Paolo Diacono, Montecassino 1905.
　　Paulinus of Aquileia.
Giannoni, Paulinus II, Patriarch von Aquileja, Vienna 1896.
Maurice, E., Di alcune carmi sacri di Paolino d'Aquileia, Scritti vari di filologia,
　　Rome 1901, pp. 169 sqq.
Paschini, P., San Paolino patriarcha e la chiesa aquileiese alla fine del secolo viii,
　　Udine 1906.
Strecker, K., Der Lazarusrhythmus des Paulinus von Aquileia, Neues Archiv, xlvii,
　　(1927), pp. 143 sqq.
Wilmart, A., L'hymne de Paulin sur Lazare dans un ms. d'Autun, Revue Bénéd., xxxiv
　　(1922), pp. 27 sqq.

§ 3. *Theodulf of Orleans, circ. 760–circ. 821* (p. 171).

Collins, S. T., Sur quelques vers de Théodulfe, Revue Bénéd., lx (1950), pp. 214 sqq.
Cuissard, C., Théodulfe, évêque d'Orléans, Orléans 1892.
Liersch, K., Die Gedichte Theodulfs, Bischofs von Orleans, Halle 1880.
Monod, G., Les mœurs judiciaires au VIIIe siècle d'après la *Paraenesis ad iudices* de
　　Théodulf, Revue historique, xxxv (1887), pp. 1 sqq.
Port, C., L'hymne *Gloria, laus*, Angers 1879.
Rzehulka, E., Theodulf, Bischof von Orleans, Breslau 1875.

§ 4. *Characteristics of the Literary Movement after Charles the Great* (p. 177).
Ermoldus Nigellus.

Henkel, O., Über den historischen Wert der Gedichte des Ermoldus Nigellus, Progr.
　　von Eilenburg 1876.

§ 5. *Raban Maur (776–856); Walafrid Strabo (circ. 809–49)* (p. 179).

Raban Maur (p. 179). [See also under Fortunatus, p. 470 above.]
Dümmler, E., Hrabanstudien, Berlin. Sitzungsber., 1898, pp. 34 sqq.
Hablitzel, J. B., Hrabanus Maurus, Biblische Studien, xi. 3, Freiburg 1906.
Lehmann, P., Fuldaer Studien, Abh. d. Kgl. Bayer. Akad., 1923, iii.
Schmidt, J., Rabanus Maurus, Katholik, lxxxvi, pp. 241 sqq.
Wilmart, A., L'hymne et la séquence du Saint-Esprit, La vie et les arts liturgiques,
　　July 1924, pp. 395 sqq.
Walafrid Strabo (p. 183).
Collins, S. T., Sur quelques vers de Walafrid Strabon, Rev. Bénéd., lviii (1948),
　　pp. 145 sqq.
Dümmler, E., Zu Walahfrid Strabo's *De imagine Tetrici*, Neues Archiv, xviii (1893),
　　pp. 664 sq.
Eigl, P., Walahfrid Strabo, Studien und Mitteilungen aus dem Kirchengesch. Seminar
　　d. theol. Fakultät, Vienna 1908.
Jundt, A., Walafrid Strabon, Cahors 1907.
Madeja, E., Aus Walahfrid Strabos Lehrjahren, Studien und Mitteilungen zur
　　Geschichte des Benediktinerordens, xl (1919–20), pp. 251 sqq.
Schlosser, J., Beiträge zur Kunstgeschichte aus den Schriftquellen des frühen Mittel-
　　alters, iii, Die Reiterstatue des Theodorich in Aachen, Wiener Sitzungsber.,
　　cxxiii, ii (1891), pp. 164 sqq.

§ 6. *Gottschalk of Fulda (circ. 805–69)* (p. 189).

Dinkler, E., and Wissmann, E., Gottschalk der Sachse, Stuttgart 1936.
Fickermann, N., Wiedererkannte Dichtungen Gottschalks, Revue Bénéd., xliv (1932),
　　pp. 314 sqq.

Freystedt, A., Studien zu Gottschalks Leben und Lehre, Zeitschr. f. Kirchengeschichte, xviii (1897), pp. 161 sqq., 529 sqq.
Morin, G., Gottschalk retrouvé, Revue Bénéd., xliii (1931), pp. 303 sqq.
Osternacher, J., Die Überlieferung der *Ecloga Theoduli*, Neues Archiv, xl (1915), pp. 331 sqq.
Perugi, G. L., Gottschalc, Rome 1911.
Strecker, K., Ist Gottschalk der Dichter der *Ecloga Theoduli* ?, Neues Archiv, xlv (1923), pp. 18 sqq.

§ 7. *Sedulius Scotus, Florus of Lyons, and others* (p. 193).

John Scotus Erigena.

Bett, H., Johannes Scotus Erigena, Cambridge 1925.
Rand, E. K., Johannes Scotus, Leipzig 1907.

Sedulius Scotus.

Hellmann, S., Sedulius Scottus, Munich 1906.
Pirenne, H., Sédulius de Liège, Mémoires couronnés et autres mémoires publiés par l'Académie royale de Belgique, xxxiii, Sept. 1882.
Traube, L., Sedulius Scottus, Abh. d. Bayer. Akad., xix (1891), pp. 338 sqq.

Florus of Lyons.

Streber, H., art. Florus, Wetzer–Welte, Kirchenlexikon.

Heiric of Auxerre.

Traube, L., Computus Helperici, Neues Archiv, xviii (1893), pp. 73 sqq.

Hincmar of Reims.

Freystedt, A., art. Hinkmar von Reims, Hauck's Realencykl.
Schrörs, H., Hinkmar, Erzbischof von Reims, Freiburg i. B. 1884.

VII. GERMAN RELIGIOUS POETRY IN THE TENTH AND ELEVENTH CENTURIES

§ 1. *The Tenth Century* (p. 202).

Gerbert of Aurillac.

Allen, R., Gerbert, Pope Silvester II, E.H.R. vii (1892), pp. 625 sqq.
Beer, R., Die Handschriften des Klosters Santa Maria de Ripoll, Wiener Sitzungsber., clv, iii, pp. 46 sqq. (1908).
Büdinger, M., Über Gerberts wissenschaftliche und politische Stellung, Kassel 1851.
Picavet, F. J., Gerbert: un pape philosophe, Paris 1897.

The School of S. Gall.

Schubiger, A., Die Sängerschule St. Gallens, Einsiedeln 1858.
Singer, S., Die Dichterschule von St. Gallen, Leipzig 1922.
Winterfeld, P. von, Die Dichterschule St. Gallens und der Reichenau unter den Karolingern und Ottonen, Neue Jahrb. f. d. klass. Alt., 1900, pp. 341 sqq.

Widukind.

Köpke, R., Widukind von Korvei, Berlin 1867.
Krause, K. E. H., Zu Widukind, I, 12, Neues Archiv, xvi (1891), pp. 610 sqq.

Ratpert.

Ratperti Casus Sancti Galli, ed. M. von Knonau, Mitteilungen zur vaterländ. Gesch., xiii, St. Gallen 1872.

Ekkehart I.

Heinzel, R., Über die Walthersage, Wiener Sitzungsber., cxvii, ii (1889).
Strecker, K., Probleme in der Walthariusforschung, Neue Jahrb. f. d. klass. Alt., 1899, pp. 573 sqq.; 629 sqq.
——, Waltharius, 263 f., Zeitschr. f. deutsch. Alt., xlii (1899), pp. 267 sqq.

Ecbasis captivi.

Erdmann, C., Konrad II und Heinrich III in der *Ecbasis captivi*, Deutsches Archiv, iv (1941), pp. 382 sqq.

Strecker, K., Ecbasisfragen, Hist. Vierteljahrschrift, xxix (1934), pp. 491 sqq.

Voigt, E., Untersuchungen über d. Ursprung d. *Ecbasis captivi*, Progr. von Berlin, 1874.

——, *Ecbasis captivi*, das älteste Tierepos des Mittelalters, Quellen und Forschungen zur Sprach- und Culturgeschichte der germanischen Völker, viii, Strassburg 1875.

Zarncke, F., Beiträge zur *Ecbasis captivi*, Leipzig. Sitzungsber., xlii (1890), pp. 109 sqq.

Hrotswitha.

Euringer, S., Drei Beiträge zur Roswitha-Forschung, Hist. Jahrbuch, liv (1934), pp. 75 sqq.

Frencken, G., Eine neue Hrotsvithhandschrift, Neues Archiv, xliv (1922), pp. 101 sqq.

Hudson, W. H., Hrotsvitha of Gandersheim, E.H.R., iii (1888), pp. 431 sqq.

Jarcho, B. J., Stilquellen der Hrotsvitha, Zeitschr. f. deutsch. Alt., lxii (1925), p. 326.

Schneiderhan, J., Roswitha von Gandersheim, Paderborn 1912.

Strecker, K., Hrotsvits Maria und Pseudo-Matthäus, Dortmund 1902.

——, *Review of* P. von Winterfeld's *Hrotswithae opera*, Anzeiger f. deutsch. Alt., xxix, (1904) pp. 34 sqq.

——, Hrotsvit von Gandersheim, Neue Jahrb. f. d. klass. Alt., 1903, pp. 569 sqq., pp. 629 sqq.

——, Textkritisches zu Hrotsvit, Beilage zum Programm des Gymn. zu Dortmund, Ostern 1906.

Winterfeld, P. von, Hrotsvits literarische Stellung, Archiv f. d. Studium der neueren Sprachen und Literaturen, cxiv (1905), pp. 293 sqq.

Zeydel, E. H., The Knowledge of Hrotsvitha's Works prior to 1500, Modern Language Review, lix (1944), pp. 382 sqq.

——, Were Hrotsvitha's Dramas performed during her Life-time? Speculum, xx (1945), pp. 443 sqq.

——, Ekkehard's Influence upon Hrotsvitha, Mod. Lang. Quarterly, vi (1943), pp. 333 sqq.

——, The Authenticity of Hrotsvitha's Works, Modern Language Notes, lxi (1946), pp. 50 sqq.

——, 'Ego clamor validus', Modern Language Notes, lxi (1946), pp. 281 sqq.

Froumond.

Kempf, J., Froumond von Tegernsee, Munich 1900.

Schepss, G., Zu Froumonds Briefcodex und zu *Ruodlieb*, Zeitschr. f. deutsche Philologie, xv (1883), pp. 419 sqq.

Seiler, F., Froumonds Briefcodex und die Gedichte desselben, Zeitschr. f. deutsche Philologie, xiv (1882), pp. 385 sqq.

Ruodlieb.

Laistner, L., *Review of* Ruodlieb, ed. Seiler, F., Halle 1882, Anzeiger f. deutsch. Alt., ix, pp. 70 sqq.

——, Die Lücken im *Ruodlieb*, Zeitschr. f. deutsch. Alt., xxix (1885), pp. 1 sqq.

Seiler, F., Die Anordnung der Ruodliebfragmente und der alte Ruodliebus, Zeitschr. f. deutsch. Alt., xxvii (1883), pp. 332 sqq.•

Strecker, K., Die deutsche Heimat des *Ruodlieb*, Neue Jahrb. f. d. klass. Alt., 1921, pp. 289 sqq.

Walter of Speier.

Harster, W., Walther von Speier, ein Dichter des X. Jahrhunderts, Speier 1877.

Schönbach, A., Review of the above and of *Harster's edition* of Vita et passio S. Christophori, Speier 1878, Anzeiger f. deutsch. Alt., vi, pp. 155 sqq.

Ekkehart IV.
Dümmler, E., Ekkehart IV von St. Gallen, Zeitschr. f. deutsch. Alt., ii (1871), pp. 1 sqq.

§§ 2 *and* 3. *The Origins of the Sequence and Tropes* (p. 210).
Bartsch, K., Die lateinischen Sequenzen des Mittelalters, Rostock 1868.
Clark, J. M., The Abbey of S. Gall, Cambridge 1926.
Frere, W. H., The Winchester Troper, Henry Bradshaw Society, London 1894.
Gautier, L., Histoire de la poésie liturgique au moyen âge, 1. Les tropes, Paris 1886.
Handschin, J., The Two Winchester Tropers, J.T.S. (1936), pp. 34 sqq.; 156 sqq.
Hughes, A. (after Bannister, H. M.), Anglo-French Sequelae, Plainsong and Mediaeval Music Society, 1934.
Neale, J. M., Sequentiae ex missalibus (de sequentiis dissertatio brevis), London 1852.
——, Epistola critica de sequentiis, in Daniel, Thesaurus Hymnologicus, v. 1 sqq.
Spanke, H., Über das Fortleben der Sequenzform in den romanischen Sprachen, Zeitschr. f. roman. Philol., li (1931), pp. 309 sqq.
——, Rhythmen- und Sequenzenstudien, Studi Medievali, iv (1931), pp. 306 sqq.
——, Fortschritte in der Geschichte mittelalterlicher Musik, Hist. Vierteljahrsschrift, xxvii (1932), pp. 374 sqq.
——, Aus der Vorgeschichte und Frühgeschichte der Sequenz, Zeitschr. f. deutsch. Alt., lxxi (1934), pp. 11 sqq.
Steinen, W. von den, Die Anfänge der Sequenzendichtung, Zeitschr. f. schweizerische Kirchengeschichte (1946), pp. 190 sqq.; 241 sqq.; (1947), pp. 19 sqq.; 122 sqq.
——, Notker der Dichter und seine geistige Welt, Bern 1948. 2 vols.
Wellesz, E., Eastern Elements in Western Chant, Monumenta Musicae Byzantinae, i, Oxford 1947.
——, A History of Byzantine Music and Hymnography, Oxford 1949.
Werner, J., Notkers Sequenzen, Beiträge zur Geschichte der lateinischen Sequenzendichtung, Aarau 1901.
Wilmanns, W., Welche Sequenzen hat Notker verfasst? Zeitschr. f. deutsch. Alt., iii (1872), pp. 267 sqq.

Notker Balbulus.
Schwalm, J., and Winterfeld, P. von, Zu Notker dem Stammler, Neues Archiv, xxvii (1902), pp. 740 sqq.
Strecker, K., Notkers *Vita S. Galli*, Neues Archiv, xxxviii (1913), pp. 59 sqq.
Winterfeld, P. von, Paulus Diaconus oder Notker der Stammler, Neues Archiv, xxix (1904), pp. 468 sqq.
——, Nochmals Notkers *Vita S. Galli*, Neues Archiv, xxviii (1903), pp. 63 sqq.
——, Welche Sequenzen hat Notker verfasst? Zeitschr. f. deutsch. Alt., xlvii (1904), pp. 321 sqq.
Wolf, F., Über die Lais, Sequenzen und Leiche, Heidelberg 1841.

The Liturgical Drama.
See the complete bibliography in Kretzmann, P. E., The Liturgical Element in the Earliest Forms of the Medieval Drama, Minneapolis 1916; and Young, K., Drama of the Medieval Church, Oxford 1933, 2 vols.

On the Easter Plays.
Grieshaber, F. K., Über die Ostersequenz *Victimae paschali* und deren Beziehung zu den religiösen Schauspielen des Mittelalters, Carlsruhe 1844.
Lange, C., Die lateinischen Osterfeiern, Munich 1887.
Milchsack, G., Die lateinischen Osterfeiern, Wolfenbüttel 1880.
Wirth, L., Die Oster- und Passionsspiele bis zum xvi. Jahrhundert, Halle 1889.
Young, K., Some Texts of Liturgical Plays, Publications of the Modern Language Association of America, xxiv (1909), pp. 294 sqq.
——, The Origin of the Easter Play, ibid., xxix (1914), pp. 1 sqq.

Wipo.

Köhler, F., Beiträge zur Textkritik Wipos, Neues Archiv, xxiii (1898). pp. 212 sqq.

Arnulf.

Voigt, E., Beiträge zur Textkritik und Quellenkunde von Arnulfs *Delicie cleri*, Romanische Forschungen, ii (1886), pp. 383 sqq.

——, Nachträge zu den *Delicie cleri*, Romanische Forschungen, iii (1887), pp. 461 sqq.

§ 4. *Other Eleventh-Century Sequences and Religious Verse* (p. 223).

General.

Breul, K., The Cambridge Songs, a Goliard's Song-book of the Eleventh Century. Cambridge 1915.

Strecker, K., Carmina Cantabrigiensia, M.G.H. 1926.

Gottschalk of Limburg.

Dreves, G. M., Gottschalk, Mönch von Limburg an der Hardt und Propst von Aachen, Leipzig 1897.

Winterfeld, P. von, Zur Gottschalkfrage, Neues Archiv, xxvii (1902), pp. 509 sqq.

Hermann the Lame.

May, J., Zu Hermannus Contractus, Neues Archiv, xii (1887), pp. 226 sqq.

Valois, J. de, En marge d'une antienne — Le 'Salve Regina', Paris 1912.

VIII. ITALIAN RELIGIOUS POETRY OF THE NINTH, TENTH, AND ELEVENTH CENTURIES

§ 1. *The Ninth and Tenth Centuries* (p. 230).

Dresdner, A., Kultur und Sittengeschichte der italienischen Geistlichkeit im X. und XI. Jahrhundert, Breslau 1890.

Dümmler, E., Anselm der Peripatetiker, Halle 1872.

Giesbrecht, W. von, De literarum studiis apud Italos primis medii aevi saeculis, Berlin 1845 (all references in the present volume are to the Italian translation by Pascal, C., L'istruzione in Italia nei primi secoli del medio evo, Florence 1895).

Novati, F., L'influsso del pensiero latino sopra la civiltà italiana del medio evo, Milan 1897.

——, Les rapports de l'Italie et de la France au XIe siècle, Comptes rendus des séances de l'année 1910, Académie des Inscriptions et Belles-Lettres, pp. 169 sqq.

Peebles, B. M., 'O Roma nobilis', American Benedictine Review, i (1950), pp. 67 sqq.

Ronca, E., Cultura medievale e poesia latina nei secoli xi e xii, Rome 1891, 2 vols.

Traube, L., Das Modeneser Lied, *O tu qui servas armis ista moenia*, Neues Archiv, xxvii (1902), pp. 233 sqq.

——, O Roma nobilis, Abhandl. d. Bayer. Akad., xix (1891), pp. 299 sqq.

Wilmart, A., Jean l'homme de Dieu, auteur d'un traité attribué à S. Bernard, Ligugé (Vienne) (extrait de la *Revue Mabillon*, janvier–mars 1925); see especially pp. 26–7.

§ 2. *Poets of Monte Cassino in the Eleventh Century: Guaiferius and Alphanus,*
d. 1085 (p. 236).

General.

Cassinensia: miscellanea di studi cassinensi, Monte Cassino 1929, 2 vols. (for Leo IX, Alberic, Alphanus).

Lowe, E. A., The Beneventan Script, Oxford 1914 (pp. 1–21).

Ozanam, A. F., Documents inédits pour servir à l'histoire littéraire de l'Italie, Paris 1850 (see also Renan, E., L'histoire littéraire de l'Italie, Mélanges religieux et historiques, pp. 319 sqq.).

Tosti, L., Storia della badia di Monte Cassino, Naples 1842–3, 3 vols.

Ughelli, F., Italia Sacra, vol. vii, Rome 1659; 2nd ed., Coleti, N., vol. x, Venice 1722.

Guaiferius.

Mirra, A., Guaiferio monaco poeta a Montecassino nel secolo XI, Bull. . . . Archivio Murator., xlvii (1932), pp. 199 sqq.

Alphanus.

Albers, B., Verse des Erzbischofs Alfanus von Salerno für Monte Cassino, Neues Archiv, xxxviii (1913), pp. 667 sqq.

Baeumker, C., Die Übersetzung des Alfanus von Nemesius' Περὶ φύσεως ἀνθρώπου, Wochenschrift für klassische Philologie, xiii (1896), pp. 1095 sqq.

Creutz, R., Erzbischof Alfanus I, ein frühsalernitanischer Arzt, Studien und Mitteilungen zur Geschichte des Benediktinerordens, xlvii (1929), pp. 414 sqq.

Dümmler, E., Lateinische Gedichte des neunten bis elften Jahrhunderts, Neues Archiv, x (1885), pp. 333 sqq. (see pp. 356 sqq.).

Falco, G., Sull' autenticità delle opere di Alfano, arcivescovo di Salerno, Bullettino dell' Istituto storico italiano, no. xxxii (Rome 1912), pp. 1 sqq.

——, Un vescovo poeta del secolo xi, Alfano di Salerno, Archivio della R. Società romana di storia patria, xxxv (1912), pp. 439 sqq.

Schipa, M., Alfano I, arcivescovo di Salerno, studio storico-letterario, Salerno 1880.

——, Versi di Alfano, Archivio storico per le province napoletane pubblicato a cura della Società di storia patria, xii, pp. 767 sqq. (Naples 1887).

§ 3. *Peter Damiani*, 1007–72. *The Poetry of Asceticism* (p. 250).

Biron, R., S. Pierre Damien, Paris 1908.

Blum, O. J., St. Peter Damian. His Teaching on the Spiritual Life, Washington 1947.

Endres, J. A., Petrus Damiani und die weltliche Wissenschaft, Münster 1910.

Wilmart, A., Le recueil des poèmes et des prières de S. Pierre Damien, Revue Bénéd., xli (1929), pp. 342 sqq.

——, Les prières de S. Pierre Damien pour l'Adoration de la Croix, Recherches de science religieuse, ix (1929), pp. 513 sqq.

IX. FRENCH POETS OF THE CATHEDRAL SCHOOLS; ELEVENTH CENTURY

§ 1. *The Cathedral Schools; Fulbert of Chartres* (circ. 975–1028) *and Berengar of Tours* (999–1088) (p. 257).

Baehrens, E., Fulbert von Chartres in der lateinischen Anthologie, Rhein. Mus., xxxii (1877), p. 225.

Clerval, A., Les écoles de Chartres au moyen âge, Chartres 1895.

Johnstone, H., Fulbert, Bishop of Chartres, Church Quarterly Review, April, 1926, pp. 45 sqq.

Maître, L., Les écoles épiscopales et monastiques en Occident avant les universités (768–1180), 2nd edit., Paris 1924.

Paré, G., Brunet, A., Tremblay, P., La renaissance du XIIᵉ siècle: les écoles et l'enseignement, Ottawa 1933.

Pfister, C., De Fulberti Carnotensis vita et operibus, Paris 1885.

——, Études sur le règne de Robert le Pieux, Paris 1885.

Rashdall, H., The Universities of Europe in the Middle Ages, Oxford 2nd ed., Powicke, F. M., and Emden, A. B., 1936, vol. i.

Warren, F. M., A Plea for the Study of Medieval Latin, Modern Language Association of America, xxiv (1909), Proceedings for 1908, pp. xlviii sqq. (p. lxxi on Fulbert's Ode to the nightingale).

§ 2. *Hildebert of Lavardin*, 1056–1133 (p. 265).

Böhmer, H., art. Hildebert, Hauck's Realencykl.

Dieudonné, A., Hildebert de Lavardin, Paris 1898 (republished from Rev. hist. archéol. Maine (1896–7), xl, pp. 225 sqq.; xli, pp. 179 sqq.; xlii, pp. 5 sqq., 165 sqq. 236 sqq.).

Hammond, M., Notes on Some Poems of Hildebert in a Harvard MS. (MS. Riant 36), Speculum, vii (1932), pp. 530 sqq.

Hauréau, B., Notice sur les Mélanges poétiques d'Hildebert de Lavardin, Notices et extraits des mss., xxviii, ii, pp. 289 sqq.

——, Notice sur les sermons attribués à Hildebert de Lavardin, Notices et extraits des mss., xxxii, ii, pp. 106 sqq.

Schramm, P. E., Kaiser, Rom und Renovatio, Leipzig 1929 (pp. 296 sqq., on Hildebert).

Wilmart, A., Le *Tractatus Theologicus* attribué à Hildebert, Revue Bénéd., xlv (1933), pp. 163 sqq.

——, Les épigrammes liées d'Hugues Primat et d'Hildebert, Revue Bénéd., xlvii (1935), pp. 175 sqq.

——, Le florilège de Saint-Gatien, contribution à l'étude des poèmes d'Hildebert et de Marbode, Revue Bénéd., xlviii (1936), pp. 3 sqq.; 147 sqq.; 235 sqq.

——, L'élégie d'Hildebert pour Muriel, Revue Bénéd., xlix (1937), pp. 376 sqq.

——, L'Épitaphe d'Orieldis, Revue Bénéd., xlix (1937), pp. 381 sqq.

§ 3. *Marbod of Rennes*, 1035 *circa*–1123 (p. 273).

Ernault, E., Marbod, évêque de Rennes, Mémoires de la Société archéologique d'Ille-et-Vilaine, 1890.

Ferry, C., De Marbodi Rhedonensis vita et carminibus, Nîmes 1877.

Mann, M. F., Eine altfranzösische Prosaversion des Lapidarius Marbod's, Romanische Forschungen, ii (1886), pp. 363 sqq.

Nunemaker, J. H., A Comparison of the *Lapidary* of Marbode with a Spanish Fifteenth-Century Adaptation, Speculum, xiii (1938), pp. 62 sqq.

Pannier, L., Les lapidaires français du moyen âge, Paris 1882.

Studer, P., and Evans, J., Anglo-Norman Lapidaries, Paris 1925.

Wilmart, A., Un nouveau poème de Marbode. Hildebert et Rivallon, Revue Bénéd., li (1939), pp. 169 sqq.

§ 4. *Baudry of Bourgueil*, 1046–1130, *and Geoffrey of Vendôme*, 1070–1132 (p. 277).

Baudry.

Delisle, L., Notes sur les poésies de Baudri, abbé de Bourgueil, Romania, i (1872), pp. 23 sqq.

Lauer, P., Le poème de Baudri de Bourgueil adressé à Adèle, fille de Guillaume le Conquérant, et la date de la tapisserie de Bayeux, Mélanges d'histoire offerts à Charles Bémont, Paris 1913.

Pasquier, H., Un poète chrétien à la fin du XIe siècle, Baudri, abbé de Bourgueil, archevêque de Dol, Paris and Angers 1878.

Schumann, O., Baudri von Bourgueil als Dichter, Studien zur lateinischen Dichtung des Mittelalters, Ehrengabe für Karl Strecker, Dresden (1931), pp. 158 sqq.

Godfrey of Reims.

Williams, J. R., Godfrey of Reims, a Humanist of the Eleventh Century, Speculum, xxii (1927), pp. 29 sqq.

Geoffrey of Vendôme.

Compain, L., Étude sur Geoffroi de Vendôme, Paris 1891.

Wilmart, A., La collection chronologique des écrits de Geoffroi, abbé de Vendôme, Revue Bénéd., xliii (1931), pp. 239 sqq.

X. THE TWELFTH CENTURY

§ 1. *General Survey of Twelfth-century Latin Verse* (p. 288).

General.

Ghellinck, J. de, Le mouvement théologique du xiie siècle, 2nd edit., Bruges 1948.

Ghellinck, J. de, L'Essor de la littérature latine au XIIᵉ siècle, Paris 1946, 2 vols.
Gilson, É., La Philosophie au Moyen Âge, 3rd edit., Paris 1947.
Haskins, C. H., Studies in the History of Mediaeval Science, Harvard 1924.
——, The Renaissance of the Twelfth Century, Harvard 1927.
Poole, R. L., Illustrations of the History of Medieval Thought and Learning, 2nd edit., London 1920.
Reuter, H., Geschichte der religiösen Aufklärung im Mittelalter, Berlin 1875, 2 vols.

Guibert of Nogent.

Monod, B., Le moine Guibert et son temps, Paris 1905.

Walter of Châtillon.

For bibliography see F. J. E. Raby, History of Secular Latin Poetry in the Middle Ages, Oxford 1934, 2 vols.; *in addition*, Wilmart, A., Poèmes de Gautier de Châtillon dans un ms. de Charleville, Revue Bénéd., xlix (1937), pp. 121 sqq.; 322 sqq.

Peter of Eboli.

Block, P., Zur Kritik des Petrus de Ebulo, Prenzlau 1883.
Hagen, F. H., Bemerkungen zu Petrus de Ebulo's Gedicht *De bello Siculo*, Forschungen zur deutschen Geschichte, xv (1875), pp. 605 sqq.
Huillard-Bréholles, J. L. A., Notice sur le véritable auteur du poème *De balneis Puteolanis*, Paris 1852.
Marignan, A., Études sur l'histoire de l'art italien du xiᵉ–xiiiᵉ siècle (le poème de Pietro d'Eboli sur la conquête de la Sicile par l'empereur Henri VI), 1911 [Zur Kunstgeschichte des Auslandes, Heft lxxxviii, Strassburg].
Percopo, E., I bagni di Pozzuoli, poemetto napoletano del secolo xiv, Archivio storico per le provincie napoletane, xi (1886), pp. 597 sqq.
Sackur, E., Handschriftliches aus Frankreich, Neues Archiv, xv (1890), pp. 387 sqq.
Schwalm, J., Reise nach Oberitalien und Burgund im Herbst, 1901 (iii, iv, Zu Petrus de Ebulo), Neues Archiv, xxviii (1903), pp. 497 sqq.
Winkelmann, E., Des Magisters Petrus de Ebulo *Liber ad honorem Augusti*, Leipzig 1874 (with text).

Herrat of Hohenburg.

Dreves, G. M., Herrad von Landsperg, Zeitschr. f. kath. Theologie, xxiii (1899), pp. 632 sqq.
Engelhardt, C. M., Herrad von Landsperg und ihr Werk: *Hortus deliciarum*, Stuttgart and Tübingen 1818.

Secular Lyrics.
See *Bibliography in* Raby, Secular Latin Poetry.

§ 2. *French Poets: Philosophers and Men of Letters* (p. 296).

Bernard Silvestris.

Schedler, M., Die Philosophie des Macrobius und ihr Einfluss auf die Wissenschaft des christlichen Mittelalters, Münster 1916.

Alan of Lille.

Baumgartner, M., Die Philosophie des Alanus de Insulis im Zusammenhange mit den Anschauungen des xii. Jahrhunderts, Münster 1896.
Bäumker, C., Handschriftliches zu den Werken des Alanus, Fulda 1894.
Bossard, E., Alani de Insulis *Anticlaudianus*, Angers 1885.
D'Aussy, Le Grand, Sur un poème intitulé *Anti-Claudien*, Notices et extraits des mss., v, pp. 546 sqq.
Hutchings, C. M., L'*Anticlaudianus* d'Alain de Lille, étude de chronologie, Romania, l (1924), pp. 1 sqq.
Large, G. R., de, Alain de Lille, poète du XIIᵉ siècle, Paris, 1951.
Leist, O., Der *Anticlaudianus*, ein lateinisches Gedicht des xii. Jahrhunderts, und sein

Verfasser Alanus ab Insulis, Beilage zum Programm des Gymnasiums zu See-hausen i. d. Altm. 1878–82.

Peter of Riga.

Beichner, P. E., The *cursor mundi* and Petrus Riga, Speculum, xxiv (1949), pp. 239 sqq.

Dümmler, E., Zu Petrus von Riga, Neues Archiv, xx (1895), pp. 231 sqq.

Fierville, C., Notice et extraits des mss. de la bibliothèque de Saint-Omer, Notices et extraits des mss., xxxi, i, pp. 49 sqq. [pp. 60 sqq.].

Hauréau, B., Un poème inédit de Pierre de Riga, Bibl. de l'École des Chartes, xliv (1883), pp. 1 sqq.

——, Le *Mathematicus* de Bernard Silvestris et la *Passio sanctae Agnetis* de Pierre de Riga, Paris 1895.

Matthew of Vendôme.

Faral, E., Les arts poétiques du xiie et du xiiie siècle, Paris 1924.

——, Le fabliau latin au moyen âge, Romania, l (1924), pp. 321 sqq. (pp. 348 sqq.).

Hauréau, B., *Review of* Matthaei Vindocinensis Ars Versificatoria, ed. L. Bourgain, 1879, Journal des Savants, 1883, p. 207 sq.

Guido of Bazoches.

Lippert, W., Zu Guido von Bazoches und Alberich von Troisfontaines, Neues Archiv, xvi (1891), pp. 408 sqq.

Wattenbach, W., Die Briefe des Canonicus Guido von Bazoches, Cantors zum Châlons im zwölften Jahrhundert, Berlin. Sitzungsber. 1890, pp. 161 sqq.

——, Aus den Briefen des Guido von Bazoches, Neues Archiv, xvi (1891), pp. 69 sqq.

——, Die Apologie des Guido von Bazoches, Berlin. Sitzungsber. 1893, pp. 395 sqq.

§ 3. *Poets of Cluny: Odo, 879–943; Peter the Venerable, d. 1156; and Bernard of of Morlas* (p. 310).

General.

Sackur, E., Die Cluniacenser, Halle 1892–4, 2 vols.

Smith, L. M., The Early History of Cluny, Oxford 1920.

Wilmart, A., Le convent et la bibliothèque de Cluny vers le milieu du onzième siècle, Revue Mabillon, 1921, pp. 89 sqq.

Odo.

Bourg, Dom du, S. Odon, Paris 1905.

Hessel, A., Odo von Cluni und das französische Kulturproblem im früheren Mittel-alter, Hist. Zeitschr., cxxviii (1923), pp. 1 sqq.

Manitius, M., *Review of* Odonis abbatis Cluniacenis Occupatio, ed. Swoboda, A., Leipzig 1900, Zeitschr. f. d. österreich. Gymnas., lii (1901), pp. 226 sqq.

Weyman, C., *Review of the same*, Literarisches Centralblatt für Deutschland, lii (1901), p. 1063.

Peter the Venerable.

Wilmart, A., Le poème apologétique de Pierre le Vénérable et les poèmes connexes, Revue Bénéd., li (1939), pp. 53 sqq.

Odilo.

Morin, G., Un hymne inédit de S. Odilon, Rev. Bénéd., xxxviii (1926), pp. 56 sqq.

Sackur, E., Handschriftliches aus Frankreich, Neues Archiv, xv (1890), pp. 105 sqq. (especially pp. 117 sqq., Zu *Iotsaldi Vita Odilonis* und Verse auf Odilo).

Bernard of Morlas.

D'Evelyn, C., A Lost MS. of the *De contemptu mundi* (B.M. Harl. 4092), Speculum vi (1931), pp. 132 sq.

Jackson, S. M., The Source of 'Jerusalem the Golden', Chicago 1910.

Morin, G., L'auteur du *Mariale* et l'hymne *Omni die*, Revue des quest. hist., xl (1886), pp. 603 sqq. [cf. also Bulletin critique, xi (1890), p. 297].

Petry, R. C., Medieval Eschatology in Bernard of Morval's *De contemptu mundi*, Speculum, xxiv (1949), pp. 207 sqq.
Wilmart, A., Grands poèmes inédits de Bernard le clunisien, Revue Bénéd., xlv (1933), pp. 249 sqq.

§ 4. *The Hymns of Peter Abélard*, 1079–1142 (p. 319).

Dreves, G. M., Petri Abaelardi Hymnarius Paraclitensis, Paris 1891.
Hauréau, B., Le poème adressé par Abélard à son fils Astralabe, Notices et extraits des mss., xxxiv, ii, pp. 153 sqq.
Meyer, W., Petri Abaelardi Planctus, i, ii, iv, v, vi, Romanische Forschungen, v (1890), pp. 419 sqq.
Rémusat, C. de, Abélard, Paris 1845, 2 vols.

§ 5. *S. Bernard of Clairvaux and the Poetry of the Name of Jesus* (p. 326).

Gilson, E., La Théologie mystique de S. Bernard, Paris 1934 (Eng. trs. 1940).
Hauréau, B., Sur les poèmes latins attribués à S. Bernard, Journal des Savants, 1882, pp. 106 sqq., 166 sqq., 280 sqq., 400 sqq.
——, Des poèmes latins attribués à S. Bernard, Paris 1890 (*separate publication, revised, of the above*).
Morison, J. C., S. Bernard, London 1901.
Raby, F. J. E., The Poem 'Dulcis Iesu Memoria', Hymn Society Bulletin, xxxiii (1945), pp. 1 sqq.
Thomson, S. H., The *Dulcis Jesu Memoria* in Anglo-Norman and Middle French, Medium Aevum, xi (1942), pp. 68 sqq.
Vacandard, E., Les poèmes latins attribués à S. Bernard, Revue des quest. hist., xlix (1891), pp. 218 sqq.
——, Vie de S. Bernard, Paris 1910, 2 vols.
Vaux, R., 'Jesu dulcis memoria', Church Quarterly Review, cviii (1929), pp. 120 sqq.
Wilmart, Le 'Jubilus' dit de S. Bernard, étude avec textes, Rome 1944.

§ 6. *English Poets under the Norman and Angevin Kings, Eleventh and Twelfth Centuries* (p. 332).

General.

Stephens, W. R. W., The English Church from the Norman Conquest to the Accession of Edward I, London 1901.
Stubbs, W., Literature and Learning at the Court of Henry II, Oxford 1886.

Reginald of Canterbury.

Hunt, W., art. Reginald of Canterbury, *D.N.B.*
Lind, R. L., Reginald of Canterbury and the Rhyming Hexameter, Neophilologus, xxv (1940), pp. 273 sqq.
Liebermann, M., Reginald von Canterbury, Neues Archiv, xiii (1888), pp. 519 sqq.

John of Salisbury.

Schaarschmidt, C., Johannes Saresberiensis, Leipzig 1862.
Webb, C. C. J., John of Salisbury, 1932.

Giraldus Cambrensis.

Luard, H. R., art. Giraldus Cambrensis, *D.N.B.*

Serlo of Wilton.

Hauréau, B., Notice sur un MS. de la reine Christine à la bibliothèque du Vatican, Notices et extraits des mss., xxix, ii, pp. 231 sqq.
——, Notices et extraits de quelques mss., i, p. 303 sqq.
Meyer, P., Troisième rapport sur une mission littéraire en Angleterre et en Écosse, Archives des missions scientifiques et littéraires, 2e série, v (1868), pp. 139 sqq.

Geoffrey de Vinsauf.

Langlois, Ch. V., Formulaires des lettres du xiie, du xiiie et du xive siècle, Notices et extraits des mss., xxxv, ii, pp. 427 sqq.

Veni, sancte spiritus.

Wilmart, A., L'hymne et la séquence du Saint-Esprit, La vie et les arts liturgiques, July 1924, pp. 395 sqq. (cf. Lehmann, P., Mittellateinische Verse in *Distinctiones monasticae et morales* vom Anfang des XIII. Jahrhunderts, Abh. d. Bayer. Akad., (1922) ii, p. 19).

Osbert of Clare.

Bishop, E., Liturgica Historica, Oxford 1918, pp. 242 sqq.

Bloch, M., La vie de s. Édouard le Confesseur par Osbert de Clare, Analecta Bollandiana, xli (1923), pp. 1 sqq.

Haskins, C. H., Henry II as a Patron of Literature, Essays in Medieval History presented to T. F. Tout, Manchester 1925, pp. 71 sqq. [*see p.* 74].

Robinson, J. A., Westminster in· the Twelfth Century: Osbert of Clare, Church Quarterly Review, lxviii (1909), pp. 336 sqq.

Wilmart, A., Les compositions d'Osbert de Clare en honneur de Sainte Anne, Annales de Bretagne, xxxvii (1926), pp. 1 sqq.

XI. ADAM OF S. VICTOR AND THE REGULAR SEQUENCE (p. 345).

§ 2. *Adam and the School of S. Victor* (p. 348).

Dreves, G. M., Adam von St. Victor, Studie zur Literaturgeschichte des Mittelalters, Stimmen aus Maria-Laach, xxix (1885), pp. 278 sqq., pp. 416 sqq.

Gautier, L., Œuvres poétiques d'Adam de S. Victor, précédées d'un essai sur sa vie et ses ouvrages, Paris 1858–9, 2 vols.; 3rd edit., 1 vol., 1894.

Legrain, M., Proses d'Adam de S. Victor, Bruges 1899.

Misset, E., Essai philologique et littéraire sur les œuvres poétiques d'Adam de S. Victor, Paris 1881.

——, and Aubry, P., Adam de S. Victor: les Proses, Texte et musique; précédées d'une étude critique, Paris 1900.

Wellner, F., Adam a Sancto Victore, Sämtliche Sequenzen, Vienna 1937.

Wrangham, D. S., The Liturgical Poetry of Adam of S. Victor, with trans., London 1881, 3 vols.

§ 3. *The Victorine Sequences and Medieval Symbolism* (p. 355).

Durandus, W., Rationale divinorum officiorum, Lyons 1584.

Mâle, E., L'art religieux du xiie siècle en France, Paris 1922.

——, L'art religieux du xiiie siècle en France, Paris 1910 (English trans., London 1913).

Schlesinger, M., Geschichte des Symbols, Berlin 1912.

§ 4. *Adam of S. Victor and the Symbolism of the Virgin Mary* (p. 363).

Fleury, Rohaut de, La sainte Vierge, Paris 1878.

Hirn, H., The Sacred Shrine, London 1912 (with bibliography).

Jameson, A. B., Legends of the Madonna, London 1903.

XII. THE THIRTEENTH CENTURY

§ 1. *English Poets in the Thirteenth Century: Alexander Neckham, John Garland, John of Hoveden* (p. 376).

Alexander Neckham.

Ellis, R., Notes of a Fortnight's Research in the Bibliothèque Nationale of Paris, Journal of Philology, xv (1886), pp. 241 sqq.

Ellis, R., A Contribution to the History of the Transmission of Classical Literature in the Middle Age, from Oxford MSS., American Journal of Philology, x (1889), p. 159.

Esposito, M., On Some Unpublished Poems attributed to Alexander Neckham, E.H.R., xxx (1915), pp. 450 sqq.

Hauréau, B., art. Alexander Neckham, Nouvelle biographie universelle.

——, Mémoires sur deux écrits intitulés *De motu cordis*, Mémoires de l'Académie des Inscriptions, xxviii, ii, pp. 317 sqq.

Hervieux, L., Les fabulistes latins, Paris 1893–9, 5 vols.

Hunt, W., art. Alexander Neckham, *D.N.B.*

Meyer, P., Notice sur les *Corrogationes Promethei* d'Alexandre Neckham, Notices et extraits des mss., xxxv, ii, pp. 641 sqq.

Mortet, V., Hugue de Fouillou, Pierre le Chantre, Alexandre Neckam, et les critiques dirigées au xiime siècle contre le luxe des constructions, Mélanges d'histoire offerts à M. Charles Bémont, Paris 1913, pp. 105 sqq.

Thorndike, L., History of Magic and Experimental Science, New York 1923, ii, cap. 43.

John Garland.

Habel, E., Johannes de Garlandia, ein Schulmann des xiii. Jahrhunderts, Mitteilungen der Gesellschaft für deutsche Erziehungs- und Schulgeschichte, 1909, pp. 1 sqq.; 119 sqq.

——, Die *Exempla honestae vitae* des Johannes de Garlandia, Romanische Forschungen, xxix (1911), pp. 131 sqq.

Hauréau, B., Les œuvres de Jean de Garlande, Notices et extraits des mss., xxvii, ii, pp. 1 sqq.

Kingsford, C. L., art. John Garland, *D.N.B.*

Wilson, E. F., The *Stella Maris* of John of Garland, Cambridge, Mass. 1946.

Zarncke, F., Zwei mittelalterliche Abhandlungen über den Bau rhythmischer Verse, Leipzig. Sitzungsber., xxiii (1871), pp. 34 sqq.

John of Howden.

D'Evelyn, C., Meditations on the Life and Passion of Christ: a Note on its Literary Relationships, Essays and Studies in Honor of Carleton Brown, New York 1940, pp. 79 sqq.

Kingsford, C. L., art. John Hoveden, *D.N.B.*

Raby, F. J. E., John of Hoveden, Laudate, xii (1935), pp. 87 sqq.

——, A Middle English Paraphrase of John of Hoveden's 'Philomena' and the Text of his 'Viola', Mod. Lang. Review, xxx (1935), pp. 339 sqq.

Stone, L. W., Jean de Howden, poète anglo-normand du XIIIe siècle, Romania, lxix (1946–7), pp. 496 sqq.

§ 2. *Philip the Chancellor* (p. 395).

Callus, D. A., Philip the Chancellor and the *De Anima* ascribed to Robert Grosseteste, Mediaeval and Renaissance Studies, i (1941), pp. 105 sqq.

Hauréau, B., Quelques lettres d'Honorius III, extraits des mss. de la Bibliothèque nationale, Notices et extraits des mss., xxi, ii, pp. 162 sqq.

Meyer, P., Henri d'Ardeli et le chancelier Philippe, Romania, i (1872), pp. 190 sqq.

——, Rapport sur une mission littéraire en Angleterre, Archives des missions scientifiques et littéraires, 2me série, iii (1866), pp. 253 sqq. (on MS. Egerton 274, Brit. Mus.).

Roth, F. W. E., Mittheilungen aus lateinischen Handschriften zu Darmstadt, Mainz, Coblenz, etc., Romanische Forschungen, vi (1891), pp. 444 sqq.

§ 3. *Thomas Aquinas (c. 1225–74) and the Poetry of the Eucharist* (p. 402).

Aquinas, S. Thomas, Summa Theologiae (Opera, Rome 1882 et sqq.).

——, The Venerable Sacrament of the Altar, trans. J. M. Neale, London 1871.

Blume, C., Thomas von Aquin und das Fronleichnamsoffizium, insbesondere der Hymnus *Verbum Supernum*, Theologie und Glaube, iii (1911), pp. 358 sqq.

Cormier, H., Étude sur S. Thomas d'Aquin et l'office du très saint Sacrement, Lille 1886.

Endres, J. A., Studien zur Biographie des hl. Thomas von Aquin, Hist. Jahrb., xxix (1908), pp. 537 sqq., pp. 774 sqq.

——, Thomas von Aquin, Mainz 1910.

Gaselee, S., An Emendation in *Sacris solemniis*, Medium Aevum, x (1941), p. 101.

Grabmann, M., Thomas von Aquin, Kempten and Munich 1917 (see Bibliography, pp. 165 sqq.).

——, Die echten Schriften des hl. Thomas von Aquin, 2nd edit., Münster 1949.

Mandonnet, P., Des écrits authentiques de S. Thomas d'Aquin, Fribourg 1910.

—— and Destrez, J., Bibliographie Thomiste, Kain 1921.

Morin, G., L'office cistercien pour la Fête-Dieu comparé avec celui de S. Thomas d'Aquin, Rev. Bénéd. xxvii (1910), pp. 236 sqq.

Raby, F. J. E., The Date and Authorship of the Poem *Adoro te devote*, Speculum, xx (1945), pp. 236 sqq.

Rotta, P., S. Tommaso e il pensiero classico, S. Tommaso d'Aquino, pubblicazione commemorativa del sesto centenario della canonizzazione, Milan 1923, pp. 51 sqq.

Wilmart, A., La tradition littéraire et textuelle de l'*Adoro te devote*, Recherches de Théologie ancienne et médiévale, i (1929), pp. 21 sqq.; 149 sqq.

XIII. THE FRANCISCAN POETS

§ 1. *Franciscan Christianity* (p. 415).

Cuthbert, Fr., Life of St. Francis of Assisi, 2nd ed., London, 1921.

——, The Romanticism of St. Francis, 2nd ed., London, 1924.

Döllinger, I. von, Beiträge zur Sektengeschichte des Mittelalters, Munich 1890, 2 vols.

Fournier, P., Études sur Joachim de Flore et ses doctrines, Paris 1909.

Gebhart, E., L'Italie mystique, Paris 1911.

Grundmann, H., Religiöse Bewegungen im Mittelalter, Hist. Studien, 267, Berlin, 1935.

——, Studien über Joachim von Floris, Beiträge zur Kulturgesch. des Mittelalters, xxxii, Leipzig–Berlin, 1927.

Holzapfel, H., Handbuch der Geschichte des Franziskanerordens, Freiburg i. B., 1909.

Ozanam, A.-F., Les poètes franciscains en Italie, Paris 1872.

Thode, H., Franz von Assisi und die Anfänge der Kunst der Renaissance in Italien, 2nd ed., Berlin 1904 (French trans., Paris 1909, 2 vols.).

Tocco, F., L'eresia nel medio evo, Florence 1884.

Vismara, F., S. Francesco d'Assisi e la poesia del suo tempo, Milan 1901.

§ 2. *The Poetry of the Passion; Bonaventura* (1221–74) *and Pecham* (d. 1292), (p. 421).

Bonaventura.

Deanesly, M., The Gospel Harmony of John de Caulibus or S. Bonaventura, Collectanea Franciscana, ii, pp. 10 sqq., Brit. Soc. of Franciscan Studies, x, Manchester 1922.

Ehrle, P., Der heilige Bonaventura und seine drei Lebensaufgaben, Festnummer zur Siebenhundertjahrfeier der Geburt des hl. Bonaventura, Franziskanische Studien, Jahrg. viii, Heft 2, 3, Münster 1921.

Fanna, F. da, Ratio novae collectionis operum omnium S. Bonaventurae, Turin 1874.

Gilson, E., S. Bonaventure et l'iconographie de la Passion, Revue d'histoire francis-caine, i (1924), pp. 405 sqq.

——, La philosophie de S. Bonaventure, Paris 1924.

Mâle, E., L'art religieux de la fin du moyen âge en France, Paris 1909.

Meditationes vitae Christi, Bonaventurae opera omnia, xii, pp. 509 sqq., Paris 1868.

Pecham.

Glauning, O., Two Nightingale Poems by John Lydgate, E.E.T.S., extra series, lxxx, 1900.

Kingsford, C. L., art. Pecham in *D.N.B.*

Knowles, M. D., Some aspects of the career of John Pecham, E.H.R., lvii (1942), pp. 1 sqq.; 179 sqq.

Little, A. G., Tocco, F., Fratris Johannis Pecham Tractatus tres de paupertate, Brit. Soc. of Franciscan Studies, ii, Aberdeen 1909.

Köhler, R., *Oci, oci* als Nachtigallengesang, Zeitschr. f. roman. Philologie, viii (1884), pp. 120 sqq.

Martin, C. T., Registrum epistolarum fratris Johannis Peckham, Rolls Series, London 1882–5, 3 vols.

Raby, F. J. E., *Philomena, praevia temporis amoeni*, in Mélanges Joseph de Ghellinck, S. J., Gembloux, 1951, vol. ii, pp. 435 sqq.

Uhland, L., Schriften zur Geschichte der Dichtung und Sage, iv, Stuttgart 1866.

§ 3. *The 'Laude' of Jacopone da Todi* (1230 *circ.*–1306) (p. 429).

Ancona, A. d', Origini del teatro italiano, 2nd edit., Turin 1891.

——, Jacopone da Todi, il giullare di Dio del secolo xiii, Todi 1914.

Brugnoli, B., Le satire di Jacopone da Todi, Florence 1914.

Felder, H., Geschichte der wissenschaftlichen Studien im Franziskanerorden, Freiburg i. B. 1904.

Furnivall, F. J., Hymns to the Virgin and Christ, E.E.T.S., 1867.

Macdonell, A., Sons of Francis, London 1902.

Pacheu, J., Jacopone de Todi, Paris 1914.

Tobler, A., Vita del beato Jacopone da Todi, Zeitschr. f. roman. Philologie, ii (1878), pp. 25 sqq.; iii (1879), pp. 192 sqq.

Underhill, E., Jacopone da Todi, London 1919.

Wadding, L., Annales minorum, v, vi, Rome 1738.

§ 4. *The Donna del Paradiso and the Stabat Mater* (p. 436).

Ermini, F., Lo *Stabat Mater* e i pianti della Vergine nella poesia lirica del medio evo, Città di Castello 1916.

Felder, H., La Madone dans la poésie de Fra Jacopone, Études franciscaines, March 1904.

Gregorovius, F., Latian Summers, London 1903.

Henry, H. T., The Two *Stabats*, American Catholic Quarterly Review, Jan. 1903, pp. 68 sqq.; April 1903, pp. 291 sqq.

§ 5. *The Dies Irae* (p. 443).

Blume, C., *Dies Irae*, Tropus zum *Libera*, dann Sequenz, Cäzilien-Vereinsorgan, 1914, No. iii, pp. 55 sqq.

Dreves, G. M., *Dies Irae*, Stimmen aus Maria-Laach, xlii (1892), pp. 512 sqq.

Ermini, F., Il *Dies Irae* e l'innologia ascetica nel secolo decimo-terzo, Rome 1903.

——, Il poeta del *Dies Irae*, atti dell' Accademia degli Arcadi, vii–viii (1931), pp. 213 sqq.

Howell, A. G. F., The Lives of S. Francis of Assisi by Brother Thomas of Celano, London 1908 (Introd.).

Leclercq, H., *Dies Irae*, in Cabrol, *Dict. d'archéologie chrétienne et de liturgie*

Perdrizet, P., La Vierge de miséricorde, Paris 1908.

Strecker, K., *Dies Irae*, Zeitschr. f. deutsch. Alt., li (1908), pp. 227 sqq.

INDEX

INDEX